SERVICES MARKETING

Integrating Customer Focus Across the Firm

Third Edition

Valarie A. Zeithaml
University of North Carolina

Mary Jo Bitner
Arizona State University

Boston   Burr Ridge, IL   Dubuque, IA   Madison, WI   New York   San Francisco   St. Louis
Bangkok   Bogotá   Caracas   Kuala Lumpur   Lisbon   London   Madrid   Mexico City
Milan   Montreal   New Delhi   Santiago   Seoul   Singapore   Sydney   Taipei   Toronto

McGraw-Hill Higher Education

A Division of The **McGraw-Hill** *Companies*

SERVICES MARKETING: INTEGRATING CUSTOMER FOCUS ACROSS THE FIRM
Published by McGraw-Hill/Irwin, a business unit of The McGraw-Hill Companies, Inc., 1221 Avenue of the Americas, New York, NY, 10020. Copyright © 2003, 2000, 1996 by The McGraw-Hill Companies, Inc. All rights reserved. No part of this publication may be reproduced or distributed in any form or by any means, or stored in a database or retrieval system, without the prior written consent of The McGraw-Hill Companies, Inc.., including, but not limited to, in any network or other electronic storage or transmission, or broadcast for distance learning.
Some ancillaires, including electronic and print components, may not be available to customers outside the United States.

This book is printed on acid-free paper.

domestic   1 2 3 4 5 6 7 8 9 0 CCW/CCW 0 9 8 7 6 5 4 3 2
international   1 2 3 4 5 6 7 8 9 0 CCW/CCW 0 9 8 7 6 5 4 3 2

ISBN 0-07-247142-5

Publisher: *John E. Biernat*
Executive editor: *Gary L. Bauer*
Developmental editor: *Scott Becker*
Marketing manager: *Kim Kanakes*
Producer, media technology: *Todd Labak*
Project manager: *Destiny Rynne*
Senior production supervisor: *Michael R. McCormick*
Coordinator freelance design: *Artemio Ortiz, Jr.*
Photo research coordinator: *Jeremy Cheshareck*
Photo researcher: *Jennifer Blankenship*
Supplemt producer: *Betty Hadala*
Cover design: *Trudi Gershenov*
Typeface: *10.5/12 New Times Roman*
Compositor: *ElectraGraphics, Inc.*
Printer: *Courier/Westford*

Library of Congress Cataloging-in-Publication Data

Zeithaml, Valarie A.
    Services marketing: integrating customer focus across the firm / Valarie A. Zeithaml,
Mary Jo Bitner.—3rd ed.
        p. cm.
    Includes index.
        ISBN 0-07-247142-5 (alk. paper)—ISBN 0-07-119914-4 (international ed.: alk. paper)
        1. Service industries—Marketing. 2. Customer services. 3. Marketing. I. Bitner, Mary
Jo. II. Title.
    HD9980.5 .Z45 2003
    658.8—dc21   20020255 44

INTERNATIONAL EDITION ISBN 0-07-119914-4
Copyright © 2003. Exclusive rights by The McGraw-Hill Companies, Inc. for manufacture and export.
This book cannot be re-exported from the country to which it is sold by McGraw-Hill.
The International Edition is not available in North America.

www.mhhe.com

ABOUT THE AUTHORS

Valarie A. Zeithaml
University of North Carolina—Chapel Hill

VALARIE A. ZEITHAML is the Roy and Alice H. Richards Bicentennial Professor and Area Chair of Marketing at the Kenan-Flagler Business School of the University of North Carolina, Chapel Hill. She obtained a master of business administration and doctorate from the University of Maryland. She is the author of more than 60 articles, 10 monographs, and four books including the best-selling business books *Delivering Quality Service: Balancing Customer Perceptions and Expectations* and *Driving Customer Equity*. Previously the owner of her own consulting firm specializing in strategy, measurement, and implementation of services marketing and service quality, Dr. Zeithaml has researched customer expectations in more than 40 industries including information technology, insurance, engineering, and finance. She has won numerous research awards including the Ferber Award from the *Journal of Consumer Research*, the Maynard Award from the *Journal of Marketing*, the Jagdish Sheth Award from the *Journal of the Academy of Marketing Science*, and the O'Dell Award from the *Journal of Marketing Research*. Dr. Zeithaml has consulted with many product and service companies including IBM, General Electric, John Hancock Financial Services, Aetna, Bank of America, U.S. West, Pacific Bell, and Procter & Gamble.

Mary Jo Bitner
Arizona State University

MARY JO BITNER is the AT&T professor of services marketing and management at Arizona State University and research director for ASU's Center for Services Leadership. She is also faculty coordinator for the ASUMBA Services Marketing and Management Concentration, a unique full-year focus within the college's nationally ranked MBA program. Dr. Bitner has published more than 50 articles and has received a number of awards for her research in leading journals including the *Journal of Marketing, Journal of Retailing, Journal of the Academy of Marketing Science, Journal of Business Research,* and the *International Journal of Service Industry Management*. She served as Special Issue Editor for two volumes of the *Journal of Retailing* devoted to services marketing research. Dr. Bitner has consulted and presented seminars and workshops for numerous businesses and cross-industry groups in services, information technology, and manufacturing including AT&T, Yellow Freight System, Advance PCS, IBM Global Services, Information Technology Services Marketing Association, Ford Motor Company, and Johnson & Johnson. She obtained her master of business administration and Ph.D. degrees from the University of Washington in Seattle.

PREFACE

This is a text for students and businesspeople who recognize the vital role that services play in the economy and its future. The advanced economies of the world are now dominated by services, and virtually all companies view service as critical to retaining their customers today and in the future. Even manufacturing companies that, in the past, have depended on their physical products for their livelihood now recognize that service provides one of their few sustainable competitive advantages.

We wrote this book in recognition of the ever-growing importance of services and the unique challenges faced by managers of services.

WHY A SERVICES MARKETING TEXT?

Since the beginning of our academic careers in marketing, we have devoted our research and teaching efforts to the topic of services marketing. We strongly believe that services marketing is different from goods marketing in significant ways and that it requires different strategies and tactics that traditional marketing texts do not fully reflect. This text is unique in both content and structure, and we hope that you will learn from it as we have in writing it.

Content Overview

The foundation of the text is the recognition that services present special challenges that must be identified and addressed. Problems commonly encountered in service organizations not faced by goods businesses—the inability to inventory, difficulty in synchronizing demand and supply, and challenges in controlling the performance quality of human interactions—need to be articulated and tackled by managers. Many of the strategies include information that is new to marketing. We wrote the text to help students and managers understand and address these special problems of services marketing.

The attraction, retention, and building of strong customer relationships through quality service (and services) are at the heart of the book's content. The topics covered are equally applicable to organizations whose core product is service (such as banks, transportation companies, hotels, hospitals, educational institutions, professional services, telecommunication) and to organizations that depend on service excellence for competitive advantage (high-technology manufacturers, automotive and industrial products, and so on).

Rarely do we repeat material from marketing principles or marketing strategy texts, although in some chapters we include a concise overview of principles from basic marketing texts. Instead, we adjust, when necessary, standard content on topics such as distribution, pricing, and promotion to account for service differences of intangibility, heterogeneity, inseparability, and perishability.

The book's content focuses on knowledge needed to implement quality service and service strategies for competitive advantage across industries. Included are frameworks for customer-focused management, and strategies for how to increase customer satisfaction and retention through service strategies. In addition to standard marketing topics (such as market segmentation), this text introduces students to entirely new topics that include management and measurement of service quality, service recovery, the linking of customer measurement to performance measurement, service mapping, and cross-functional treatment of issues through integration of marketing with disciplines such as operations and human resources. Each of these topics represents pivotal content for tomorrow's businesses as they structure around process rather than task, engage in one-to-one marketing, mass customize their offerings, and attempt to build strong relationships with their customers.

Distinguishing Content Features

The distinguishing features of our text and the new features in this edition include the following:

1. Greater emphasis on the topic of service quality than existing marketing and service marketing texts.

2. Increased focus on customer expectations and perceptions and what they imply for marketers.

3. Increased coverage of business-to-business application.

4. Increased technology and Internet coverage.

5. A chapter on service recovery that includes a conceptual framework for understanding the topic.

6. A chapter on the financial and economic impact of service quality.

7. A chapter on customer-defined service standards.

8. Cross-functional treatment of issues through integration of marketing with other disciplines such as operations and human resources.

9. Consumer-based pricing and value pricing strategies.

10. A chapter on integrated services marketing communications.

11. Description of a set of tools that must be added to basic marketing techniques when dealing with services rather than goods.

12. Introduction of three service Ps to the traditional marketing mix and increased focus on customer relationships and relationship marketing strategies.

13. An entire chapter that recognizes human resource challenges and human resource strategies for delivering customer-focused services.

14. Coverage of new service development processes and a detailed and complete introduction to service blueprinting—a tool for describing, designing, and positioning services.

15. Coverage of the customer's role in service delivery and strategies for making customers productive partners in service creation.

16. A chapter on the role of physical evidence, particularly the physical environment or "servicescape."

17. Global features in each chapter.

18. Fully updated technology spotlights in each chapter.

19. Exercises in each chapter.

20. Updated or new examples throughout the text.

Conceptual and Research Foundations

We synthesized research and conceptual material from many talented academics and practitioners to create this text. We relied on pioneering work of researchers and businesspeople from diverse disciplines such as marketing, human resources, operations, and management. Because the field of services marketing is international in its roots, we also drew from work originating around the globe. We have continued this strong conceptual grounding in the third edition by integrating new research into every chapter. The framework of the book is managerially focused, with every chapter presenting company examples and strategies for addressing issues in the chapter.

Conceptual Frameworks in Chapters

We developed integrating frameworks in most chapters. For example, we created new frameworks for understanding service recovery strategies, service pricing, integrated marketing communications, customer relationships, customer roles, and internal marketing.

Unique Structure

The text features a structure completely different from the standard 4P (marketing mix) structure of introductory marketing texts. Beginning with Chapter 2, it is organized into parts around the gaps model of service quality. For example, Chapters 2, 3, and 4 each deal with an aspect of the customer gap—customer behavior, expectations, and perceptions, respectively—to form the focus for services marketing strategies. The managerial content in the rest of the chapters is framed by the gaps model using part openers that build the model gap by gap. Each part of the book includes multiple chapters with strategies for understanding and closing these critical gaps. The final chapter sums up the text using the fully integrated gaps model.

Fully Integrated Text

In the 1980s and early 1990s, the field of services marketing was so new that insufficient material had been written on the topic to create a traditional text. For that reason, the books used as texts contained cases and readings that had to be interpreted by educators for their students. These early services marketing books were therefore different from standard texts—where the major function is to synthesize and conceptualize the material—and placed a burden on the professor to blend the components. This book contains integrated text materials, thereby removing from professors and students the tremendous burden of synthesis and compilation.

WHAT COURSES AND STUDENTS CAN USE THE TEXT?

In our years of experience teaching services marketing, we have found that a broad cross section of students is drawn to learning about services marketing. Students with career interests in services industries as well as goods industries with high service components (such as industrial products, high-tech products, and durable products) want and need to understand these topics. Students who wish to become consultants and entrepreneurs want to learn the strategic view of marketing, which involves not just physical goods but also the myriad services that envelop these goods. Virtually all students—even those who will work for packaged goods firms—will face employers needing to understand the basics of services marketing and management.

Although services marketing courses are usually designated as marketing electives, a large number of enrollees in our classes have been finance students seeking to broaden their knowledge and career opportunities in financial services. Business students with human resource, information technology, accounting, and operations majors also enroll, as do nonbusiness students from such diverse disciplines as health administration, recreation and parks, public and nonprofit administration, law, and library science.

Students need only a basic marketing course as a prerequisite for a services marketing course and this text. The primary target audience for the text is services marketing classes at the undergraduate (junior or senior elective courses), graduate (both masters and doctoral courses), and executive student levels. Secondary target audiences are (1) service management classes at both the undergraduate and graduate levels and (2) marketing management classes at the graduate level where a professor wishes to provide more comprehensive teaching of services than is possible with a standard marketing management text. A subset of chapters would also provide a more concise text for use in a quarter-length or mini-semester course. A further reduced set of chapters may be used to supplement undergraduate and graduate basic marketing courses to enhance the treatment of services.

WHAT CAN WE PROVIDE EDUCATORS TO TEACH SERVICES MARKETING?

As a team, we have accumulated more than 30 years of experience teaching the subject of services marketing. We set out to create a text that represents the approaches we have found most effective. We incorporated all that we have learned in our many years of teaching services marketing—teaching materials, student exercises, case analyses, research, and PowerPoint slides on a CD-ROM.

HOW MANY PARTS AND CHAPTERS ARE INCLUDED, AND WHAT DO THEY COVER?

The text material includes 18 chapters divided into six parts. After an introduction in Chapter 1, Part 1 discusses the focus on the customer. Part 2 focuses on listening to customer requirements, including chapters covering marketing research for services, building customer relationships, and service recovery. Part 3 involves aligning service strategy through design and standards and includes chapters on service development and design, customer-defined service standards, and physical evidence and the servicescape. Part 4 concerns the delivery and performance of service and has chapters on employees' and customers' roles in service delivery, conveying service through intermediaries and electronic channels, and managing demand and capacity. Part 5 focuses on managing services promises and includes chapters on integrated services marketing communications and pricing of services. Finally, Part 6 examines the overall picture of services marketing and the text, including two chapters—one on the financial and economic effect of service quality and the other on the integrated gaps model of service quality.

THE SUPPLEMENTARY MATERIALS

Instructor's Manual

The *Instructor's Manual* includes sample syllabi, suggestions for in-class exercises and projects, and answers to end-of-chapter discussion questions and exercises. The *Instructor's Manual* uses the "active learning" educational paradigm, which involves students in constructing their own learning experiences and exposes them to the collegial patterns present in work situations. Active learning offers an educational underpinning for the pivotal workforce skills required in business, among them oral and written communication skills, listening skills, and critical thinking and problem solving.

PowerPoint CD-ROM

We offer a CD-ROM that contains figures and tables from the text that are useful for instructors in class. The full-color PowerPoint slides contained on the CD-ROM were created to present a coordinated look for course presentation.

ACKNOWLEDGMENTS

We owe a great deal to the pioneering service researchers and scholars who developed the field of services marketing. They include John Bateson, Leonard Berry, Bernard Booms, Dave Bowen, Steve Brown, Larry Crosby, John Czepiel, Ray Fisk, William George, Christian Gronroos, Steve Grove, Evert Gummesson, Chuck Lamb, Christopher Lovelock, Parsu Parasuraman, Ben Schneider, Lynn Shostack, and Carol Surprenant. We also owe gratitude to the second generation of service researchers who broadened and enriched the services marketing field. When we attempted to compile a list of those researchers, we realized that it was too extensive to include here. The length of that list is testament to the influence of the early pioneers and to the importance that services marketing has achieved both in academia and practice.

We sincerely thank Dwayne Gremler, who drew on his extensive experience teaching services marketing to work with us to creating the *Instructor's Manual* for the text.

We remain indebted to Parsu Parasuraman and Len Berry, who have been research partners of Dr. Zeithaml's since 1982. The gaps model around which the text is structured was developed in collaboration with them, as was the model of customer expectations used in Chapter 3. Much of the research and measurement content in this text was shaped by what the team found in a 15-year program of research on service quality.

Dr. Zeithaml also expresses special thanks to her colleagues at the University of North Carolina. Gary Armstrong has been a particular mentor and "adult" in all matters relating to textbook writing, marketing education, and academic life. Bill Perreault shared his extensive experience in textbook writing and research, as well as provided support and creative ideas about marketing education. Charlotte Mason and Rebecca Ratner were intellectual catalysts and friends, as were C. L. Kendall and Paul Bloom.

Dr. Bitner expresses special thanks to Steve Brown, Michael Mokwa, and the Center for Services Leadership and the Department of Marketing at Arizona State. Their support and encouragement were invaluable in bringing this project to reality. She also thanks Bernard Booms and Mike Hutt for their valued advice, mentorship, and support throughout the process. She acknowledges and thanks Amy Ostrom for her support and invaluable assistance in sharing examples, new research, and creative teaching innovations. Dr. Bitner also acknowledges and is grateful to the fine group of Arizona State services doctoral graduates she has worked with who have shaped her thinking and supported the text: Lois Mohr, Bill Faranda, Amy Rodie, Kevin Gwinner, Matt Meuter, Steve Tax, Dwayne Gremler, Lance Bettencourt, and Susan Cadwalladee.

Dr. Bitner acknowledges the many ideas and examples provided by the member companies of the Center for Services Leadership: AdvancePCS, Allegiance Healthcare, Annenberg Center for Health Services, AT&T, AT&T Wireless, Avaya, Avnet, Bank One, B-D Healthcare Consulting & Services, Blue Cross and Blue Shield, Boston Scientific, Cardinal Health, Inc., Charles Schwab & Co., Compaq, The Co-Operators, Elrick and Lavidge, Inc., Environmental Industries, Ford Motor Company, Harley-Davidson Motor Company, Harrah's Entertainment, Hewlett-Packard Company, Honeywell, IBM Global Services, IBM North America, The INSIGHT Group, Intel, LensCrafters, Inc., Marriott International, Inc., Marsh, Mayo Clinic, McKesson, McKinsey & Company, Neoforma, neoIT, PDVSA-CIED, PETSMAR, ProNet Solutions, Siemens Medical Solutions, State Farm Insurance, Symmetrics Marketing, R. R. Donnelley & Sons, Xerox Corporation, and Yellow Corporation. Their insights provided the grounding for many strategies and examples included in the book.

We would like to acknowledge the suggestions and improvements made by Clare Comm, University of Massachusetts, Lowell; Susan M. Keaveney, University of Colorado, Denver; Alex P. Sharland, Hofstra University; and Raymond Phelps, Milsaps College.

Finally, we would like to acknowledge the professional efforts of the McGraw-Hill/Irwin staff. Our sincere thanks to Gary Bauer, Scott Becker, Destiny Rynne, Betty Hadala, Kimberly Kanakes, Artemio Ortiz, Michael McCormick, Kathy Shive, and Virginia Scoville.

Valarie A. Zeithaml

Mary Jo Bitner

BRIEF CONTENTS

CONTENTS

LIST OF BOXES

Chapter 1

INTRODUCTION TO SERVICES

This chapter's objectives are to

1. Explain what services are and identify trends in the service sector.

2. Explain the need for special services marketing concepts and practices and why the need has developed and accelerated over the last several decades.

3. Explore the profound impact of technology on service.

4. Outline the basic differences between goods and services (intangibility, heterogeneity, simultaneous production and consumption, perishability) and the resulting challenges for service businesses.

5. Introduce the expanded marketing mix for services, the philosophy of customer focus, and the gaps model of service quality as powerful frameworks and themes that form the foundation for the rest of the text.

"Services are going to move in this decade to being the front edge of the industry."

Louis V. Gerstner, 2001[1]

This quote from IBM's then CEO, Louis V. Gerstner, illustrates the changes sweeping across industry today. Many businesses that were once viewed as manufacturing giants are shifting their focus to services. IBM has led the pack in its industry. Mr. Gerstner predicts that in the IT industry over the next decade services will lead the market instead of hardware and software to the extent that "hardware and software will be sold inside a services wrapper."

In a company brochure IBM states that it is the largest *service* business in the world. Services led IBM's growth strategy in the mid-1990s and will continue to do so into the first decade of the 21st century. Through its Global Services division, IBM offers product support services, professional consulting services, and network computing services around the globe. Many businesses have outsourced entire service functions to IBM, counting on the company to provide the services better than anyone else.

The services strategy has been very successful for IBM. In the first quarter of 2001, services and parts became the majority of IBM's sales for the first time. Through difficult times in 2000–2001 that saw its peers suffering major downturns in sales, growth, and stock price, IBM has posted rising sales and increased market share in services (where it is ranked first) and also in semiconductors, supercomputers, laptops, and database software. In 2000, IBM Global Services had $33.1 billion in sales.

No one in IBM would suggest that these positive results have been easily achieved. Switching from a manufacturing to a service and customer focus is indeed a challenge. It requires a change in management mind-set, change in culture, changes in the ways people work and are rewarded, and new ways of implementing customer solutions. At IBM this change has evolved over at least a decade. It is suggested that Lou Gerstner's legacy at IBM may well be the definitive switch that the company has made from hardware to services. It is indicative that Samuel Palmisano, Gerstner's successor in 2002, has deep roots in IBM's service business.

Many companies (such as Hewlett Packard, Sun Microsystems, and Cisco) have viewed IBM's success and are attempting to make the same transition to services. It is not as easy as it looks. In moving into services companies discover what service businesses like hospitality, consulting, health care, financial services, and telecommunications have known for years: services marketing and management are different—not totally unique, but different. Selling and delivering a box are not the same as selling and delivering a service that solves a customer's problem.

Service businesses, and manufacturers like IBM that are shifting to become service businesses, face a number of often challenging questions such as these: What really are the differences in marketing a service versus a product? Simply defining the product can sometimes be difficult. For example, what exactly are the components of the services IBM offers? What is the bundle of benefits from the customer's point of view? How can these services be described to customers? How do IBM's services differ from those offered by its competitors? What roles do the sales, service, and delivery people play in building and maintaining customer relationships? How are these roles different from their roles in selling hardware? What is the demand for these types of services? What happens when there isn't enough business? What happens when demand exceeds supply? How can the firm be sure it is delivering quality service consistently to ensure repeat business? How should a service solution be priced when it is very complex and customized to fit an individual customer? All service industries face these issues at some level, and those like IBM that move from manufacturing to a service focus face the challenges even more vividly.

As the opening vignette suggests, services are not limited to service industries, services can be very profitable, and services are challenging to manage and market. Services represent a huge and growing percentage of the world economy; yet particularly in the United States, customer perceptions of service are not good.[2] In fact, the University of Michigan's American Customer Satisfaction Index has shown a steady decline in customer satisfaction with services.[3] Given the economic growth in services, their profit and competitive advantage potential, and the overall decline in customer satisfaction with services, it seems that the potential and opportunities for companies who can excel in services marketing, management, and delivery have never been greater.

This text will give you a lens with which to approach the marketing and management of services, along with marketing and management tools unique for service contexts. What you learn can be applied in a company like IBM with a traditional manufacturing history or in pure service businesses. You will learn tools, strategies, and approaches for developing and delivering profitable services that can provide competitive advantage to firms. At the base of services marketing and management you will find a strong customer focus that extends across all functions of the firm—thus the subtitle of this book, "integrating customer focus across the firm." Many of the ideas and strategies you have learned and will learn in other business courses certainly apply (either totally or to some extent) to service businesses and to the management of services within manufacturing and high-technology industries. What we will focus on in this book, therefore, are those aspects that are different, and the special tools and strategies you will need to be an effective manager and marketer of services.

WHAT ARE SERVICES?

Put in the most simple terms, *services are deeds, processes, and performances.* Our opening vignette illustrates what is meant by this definition. The services offered by IBM are not tangible things that can be touched, seen, and felt, but rather are intangible deeds and performances. To be concrete, IBM offers repair and maintenance service for its equipment, consulting services for IT and e-commerce applications, training services, Web design and hosting, and other services. These services may include a final, tangible report, a website, or, in the case of training, tangible instructional materials. But for the most part, the entire service is represented to the client through problem analysis activities, meetings with the client, follow-up calls, and reporting—a series of deeds, processes, and performances. Similarly, the core offerings of hospitals, hotels, banks, and utilities comprise primarily deeds and actions performed for customers.

While we will rely on the simple, broad definition of *services,* you should be aware that over time *services* and the *service sector of the economy* have been defined in subtly different ways. The variety of definitions can often explain the confusion or disagreements people have when discussing services and when describing industries that comprise the service sector of the economy. Compatible with our simple, broad definition is one that defines services to "include all economic activities whose output is not a physical product or construction, is generally consumed at the time it is produced, and provides added value in forms (such as convenience, amusement, timeliness, comfort, or health) that are essentially intangible concerns of its first purchaser."[4] This definition has been used also to delineate the service sector of the economy, as illustrated in Table 1.1.

Services versus Customer Service

As we begin our discussion of services marketing and management, it is important to draw the distinction between *services* and *customer service.* **Services,** as we have broadly defined, encompass a wide range of industries. All of the following companies are considered service companies: AT&T (telecommunications), Marriott International (hotels), American Airlines (transportation), Bank One (financial services). However, services can be offered to the marketplace by manufacturers and technology companies as well. IBM and Compaq (traditionally considered manufacturers) offer information technology (IT) consulting services to the marketplace, competing with

TABLE 1.1
Industries Classified within the Service Sector*

Transportation and public utilities	Other services
Transportation	Hotels and other lodging places
Railroad transportation	Personal services
Local and interurban transit	Business services
Trucking and warehousing	Auto repair, services, and parking
Water transportation	Miscellaneous repair services
Air transportation	Motion pictures
Pipelines, except natural gas	Amusement and recreation services
Transportation services	Health services
Communication	Legal services
Telephone and telegraph	Management consulting services
Radio and television broadcasting	Educational services
Electric, gas, and sanitary services	Social services
Wholesale trade	Membership organizations
Retail trade	Miscellaneous services
Finance, insurance, and real estate	Private household services
Depository institutions	Federal government
Nondepository institutions	State and local government
Security and commodity brokers	E-commerce
Insurance agents and brokers	Internet-based services
Real estate	
Holding and investment companies	

*Using the broad definition of service industries, this list was adapted from *Survey of Current Business,* 1998.

firms like EDS and Accenture, traditional service industry firms. All of the companies just mentioned are marketing and delivering services to customers.

Customer service is also provided by all types of companies—including manufacturers, IT companies, and service companies. *Customer service is the service provided in support of a company's core products.* Customer service most often includes answering questions, taking orders, dealing with billing issues, handling complaints, and perhaps scheduling maintenance or repairs. Customer service can occur on site (as when a retail employee helps a customer find a desired item or answers a question), or it can occur over the phone or via the Internet. Many companies operate customer service call centers, often staffed around the clock. Typically there is no charge for customer service. Quality customer service is essential to building customer relationships. It should not, however, be confused with the services provided for sale by a company.

To illustrate: Federal Express markets and delivers services, but it also provides a high level of customer service. Its services include overnight package delivery and also logistical services including inventory management, warehousing, and distribution using state-of-the-art technology. These services are offered worldwide, currently in more than 200 countries. FedEx's high levels of customer loyalty depend on the quality of these core services, as well as the customer service the company provides to back up its offerings. A well-trained and empowered telephone staff as well as high-tech tracking online systems accessible to its customers ensure that FedEx's customer service is superb.[5]

As we progress through the text, you will see many examples of services offered for sale as well as customer service in support of product and service offerings.

Tangibility Spectrum

The broad definition of services implies that intangibility is a key determinant of whether an offering is a service. While this is true, it is also true that very few products are purely intangible or totally tangible. Instead, services tend to be *more intangible* than manufactured products, and manufactured products tend to be *more tangible* than services. For example, the fast-food industry, while classified as a service, also has many tangible components such as the food, the packaging, and so on. Automobiles, while classified within the manufacturing sector, also supply many intangibles, such as transportation. The tangibility spectrum shown in Figure 1.1 captures this idea. Throughout this text, when we refer to services we will be assuming the broad definition of services and acknowledging that there are very few "pure services" or "pure goods." The issues and approaches we discuss are directed toward those offerings that lie on the right side, the intangible side, of the spectrum shown in Figure 1.1.

As suggested earlier, intangibles are *not* produced only in the service sector of the economy. Manufacturers such as Boeing Airplane Company and Ford Motor Company also produce products on the right end of the spectrum, both for sale to external consumers and to support internal production processes. For example, Boeing has provided consulting services and demand forecasting services for its airline customers. And within Boeing large departments (such as data processing and legal services) provide internal services to the organization.

Trends in the Service Sector

Although we often hear and read that many modern economies are dominated by services, the United States and other countries did not become service economies overnight. As early as 1929, 55 percent of the working population was employed in the service sector in the United States, and approximately 54 percent of the gross national product was generated by services in 1948. The data in Figures 1.2 and 1.3 show that the trend toward services has continued, until in 1999 services represented 78 percent of the gross domestic product (GDP) and 80 percent of employment. Note also that these data do not include internal services provided within a manufacturing company (such as IBM or Boeing) or services that these manufacturers sell externally. The

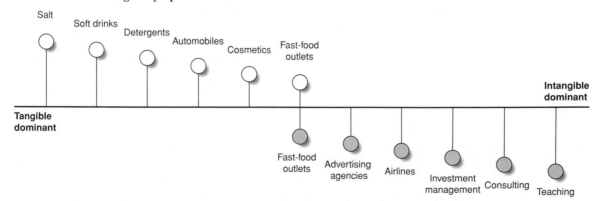

FIGURE 1.1 **Tangibility Spectrum**

Source: G. Lynn Shostack, "Breaking Free from Product Marketing," *Journal of Marketing* 41 (April 1977), pp. 73–80. Reprinted with permission of the American Marketing Association.

FIGURE 1.2
Percentage of U.S. Labor Force by Industry

Source: *Survey of Current Business,* February 2001, Table B.8, July 1988, Table 6.6B, and July 1992, Table 6.4C; E. Ginzberg and G. J. Vojta, "The Service Sector of the U.S. Economy," *Scientific American* 244, no. 3 (1981), pp. 31–39.

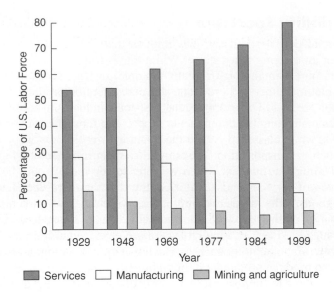

FIGURE 1.3
Percentage of U.S. Gross Domestic Product by Industry

Source: *Survey of Current Business,* February 2001, Table B.3, and August 1996, Table 11; E. Ginzberg and G. J. Vojta, "The Service Sector of the U.S. Economy," *Scientific American* 244, no. 3 (1981), pp. 31–39.

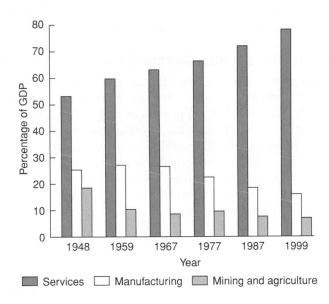

number of employees and value of the services they produce would be classified as manufacturing sector data.

WHY SERVICES MARKETING?

Why is it important to learn about services marketing, service quality, and service management? What are the differences in services versus manufactured-goods marketing that have led to the demand for books and courses on services? Many forces have led to the growth of services marketing, and many industries, companies, and individuals have defined the scope of the concepts, frameworks, and strategies that define the field. It is important to note that the field of services marketing and management has evolved as a result of these combined forces and that the roots and scope of the field are global, as described in our Global Feature.

A Service-Based Economy

First, services marketing concepts and strategies have developed in response to the tremendous growth of service industries, resulting in their increased importance to the U.S. and world economies. As was noted, in 1999 the service sector represented 80 percent of total employment and at least 78 percent of the gross domestic product of the United States. Almost all of the absolute growth in numbers of jobs and the fastest growth rates in job formation are in service industries.

Another indicator of the economic importance of services is that trade in services is growing worldwide. In fact, while the U.S. balance of trade in goods remains in the red, in 2000 there was an $81 billion trade *surplus* in services.[6] World-class providers of services such as American Express, McDonald's, and Marriott Hotels, together with many small service companies, are exporting information, knowledge, creativity, and technology that the world badly needs.

There is a growing market for services and increasing dominance of services in economies worldwide, not just in the United States. The tremendous growth and economic contributions of the service sector have drawn increasing attention to the issues and problems of service sector industries worldwide.

Service as a Business Imperative in Manufacturing and IT

Early in the development of the field of services marketing and management, most of the interest and impetus came from service industries such as banking and health care. As these traditional service industries continue to evolve and become more competitive, the need for effective services management and marketing strategies is still there. Now, however, manufacturing and technology industries such as automobiles, computers, and software are also recognizing the need to provide quality service in order to compete worldwide. These companies are realizing that a large percentage of their revenues and profits is coming from services, as illustrated in our opening vignette about IBM.

"From General Electric to Wang, from Xerox to Hewlett-Packard, companies that a few years ago got almost all of their profits from selling widgets are rapidly transforming themselves into service providers."[7] At General Electric (GE), then chief executive officer (CEO) Jack Welch launched what has been termed the "third revolution" at GE in an effort to boost growth to double digits. A major thrust of the third revolution is a push to move GE ever deeper into services. This includes everything from aftermarket services for products GE produces such as medical imaging equipment and jet engines to financial services (GE Capital), broadcasting, management consulting, and other services as far afield as health care and utilities. In 2000, GE was generating approximately 75 percent of its revenues from services.[8]

In most industries providing quality service is no longer simply an option. The quick pace of developing technologies and increasing competition make it difficult to gain strategic competitive advantage through physical products alone. Plus, customers are more demanding. They not only expect excellent, high-quality goods; they also expect high levels of service along with them. As manufacturers and IT companies such as GE and IBM become more and more service-focused, the need for special concepts and approaches for managing and marketing services becomes even more apparent. Figure 1.4 illustrates IBM's shift in focus from hardware to service and people.

Since the late 1970s services marketing and management researchers and their partners in industry have focused on issues such as customer satisfaction, service quality, customer relationships, service process management, service encounters, cross-functional integration, and competing through service in manufacturing. While many of these topics are currently top of mind for senior executives around the world, in the 1980s and well into the 1990s they were obscure topics for many companies. It is hard to imagine that 15 or 20 years ago relatively few companies were even measuring customer satisfaction, let alone developing customer loyalty programs or focusing on service quality.

The roots for the development of many of the services concepts and ideas that you will learn about in this book were spawned in those early years through the dedicated work of international researchers. Two thought leaders from Scandinavia, Evert Gummesson (Stockholm University) and Christian Gronroos (Swedish School of Economics Finland), were very early pioneers in the field. They are credited with bringing to the forefront concepts such as internal marketing, relationship marketing, interactive marketing, and the idea that marketing is everybody's business. Both are active in continuing to build the field today. They, together with their colleagues, are linked closely with Bo Edvardsson (Karlstad University, Sweden) in forming what is known at the "Nordic School" of services, a school of thought that is grounded firmly in relationships and marketing as a customer-focused process.

Other early pioneers include French researchers Eric Langeard and Pierre Eigler of the Institut d' Administration des Entreprises (IAE) in Aix-Marseille, credited with developing the notion of services as "servuction" and other basic concepts that have inspired the field. Building from his training at Harvard, John Bateson (London Business School and Gemini Consulting) was also a very early and prolific contributor to the development of services ideas.

These British, French, and Scandinavian researchers joined with many in the United States to form the underpinnings of what has become a burgeoning worldwide community. The United States academic pioneers in this field include Len Berry (Texas A&M), A. Parasuraman (University of Miami), Valarie Zeithaml (University of North Carolina), David Bowen (Thunderbird School of International Management), Benjamin Schneider (University of Maryland), Roland Rust (University of Maryland), Christopher Lovelock (Lovelock Associates), Stephen Brown (Arizona State University), Mary Jo Bitner (Arizona State University), Jim Fitzsimmons (University of Texas, Austin), and Raymond Fisk (University of New Orleans). The field reflects the cross-disciplinary nature of services research as many of these individuals are not marketing scholars, but rather have their training in human resources, operations, and management disciplines.

Institutions such as the American Marketing Association and Marketing Science Institute in the United States, together with services research centers at a number of universities, have provided support and impetus for the development of key ideas. In the United States, the Center for Services Leadership (formerly Center for Services Marketing & Management) at Arizona State University and the Center for E-Service at the University of Maryland have provided leadership and links to the international community of scholars and companies focused on services. In fact, there now exists an International Academy of Services Research and Education with members from around the world. This academy—organized by the Service Research Center at Karlstad University, the Center for Services Leadership at Arizona State University, and Warwick Business School, University of Warwick—includes these members:

Karlstad University, Sweden

Arizona State University, USA

Warwick University, UK

Texas A&M University, USA

University of Aukland, New Zealand

Institut d'Administration des Enterprises (IAE), France

Stockholm University, Sweden

Maastricht University, The Netherlands

Tama University, Japan

Manchester School of Management, UK

University of Munich, Germany

Cranfield University, UK

University of Maryland, USA

Katholische Universitat Eichstatt, Germany

University of Ghent, Belgium

ITESM, Monterrey, Mexico

University of Westminster, UK

University of Victoria, Canada

Indian Institute of Management, India

Today academic services research is conducted across the world, and the practice of services marketing touches every continent. The field continues to build knowledge related to services and customer focus, knowledge that is in demand in today's business environment. It is truly a global field that was ahead of its time.

Sources: For more information and background on the development of the field of services marketing and management, see L. L. Berry and A. Parasuraman, "Building a New Academic Field—The Case of Services Marketing," *Journal of Retailing* 69 (Spring 1993), pp. 13–60; R. P. Fisk, S. W. Brown, and M. J. Bitner, "Tracking the Evolution of the Services Marketing Literature," *Journal of Retailing* 69 (Spring 1993), pp. 61–103; R. P. Fisk, S. J. Grove, and J. John (eds.), *Services Marketing Self-Portraits: Introspections, Reflections, and Glimpses from the Experts* (Chicago: American Marketing Association, 2000); Service Research Center, Karlstad University (www.ctf.kau.se); and Center for Services Leadership, Arizona State University (www.cob.asu.edu/csl).

FIGURE 1.4
Services are driving IBM's growth into the 21st century

Source: Reprinted with permission of IBM Global Services. (IBM)

Deregulated Industries and Professional Service Needs

Specific demand for services marketing concepts has come from the deregulated industries and professional services as both of these groups have gone through rapid changes in the ways they do business. In the past several decades many very large service industries, including airlines, banking, telecommunications, and trucking, have been deregulated by the U.S. government. Similar deregulatory moves have taken place in many other countries as well. As a result, marketing decisions that used to be tightly controlled by the government are now partially, and in some cases totally, within the control of individual firms.[9] For example, until 1978 all airline fares, routes, and commissions paid to travel agents were determined and monitored by the government. Now individual airlines are free to set their own pricing structures and determine which routes they will fly. Needless to say, deregulation created turmoil in the airline industry, accelerating the need for more sophisticated, customer-based, and competition-sensitive marketing. In the late 1990s and into the turn of the century, the electric utility industry in the United States has been experiencing many of these same changes. Market forces, regulatory and political forces, and technological forces are combining to change the face of competition and marketing in that industry.[10]

Providers of professional services (such as dentists, lawyers, accountants, engineers, and architects) have also demanded new concepts and approaches for their businesses as these industries have become increasingly competitive and as professional standards have been modified to allow at least limited advertising. Whereas traditionally the professions avoided even using the word *marketing,* they are now seeking better ways to understand and segment their customers, to ensure the delivery of quality services, and to strengthen their positions amidst a growing number of competitors.

Services Marketing Is Different

As the forces described coincided and evolved, those involved realized that there was something different about marketing services and managing services. (There were issues and problems they hadn't faced in manufacturing and packaged goods companies.) These differences and challenges were captured in a series of interviews by management consultant Gary Knisely in 1979 (see Exhibit 1.1).[11] For example, when a firm's core offering is a deed performed by an employee (such as engineering consulting), how can the firm ensure consistent product quality to the marketplace? As service businesses began to turn to marketing and decided to hire marketing people, they naturally recruited from the best marketers in the world—Procter & Gamble, General Foods, Kodak. People who moved from marketing in packaged goods industries to marketing in health care, banking, and other service industries found their skills and experiences were not directly transferable. They faced issues and dilemmas in marketing services that their experiences in packaged goods and manufacturing had not prepared them for. These people realized the need for new concepts and approaches for marketing and managing service businesses.

As noted earlier in our Global Feature, service marketers responded to these forces and began to work across disciplines and with academics and business practitioners from around the world to develop and document marketing practices for service industries. As the field evolved, it expanded to address the concerns and needs of *any* business where service is an integral part of the offering. Frameworks, concepts, and strategies developed to address the fact that "services marketing is different." As the field continues to evolve into the 21st century, new trends are developing that will shape the field and continue the need for services marketing concepts and tools.

Service Equals Profits

Through the 1980s and early 1990s many firms jumped on the service bandwagon, investing in service initiatives and promoting service quality as ways to differentiate themselves and create competitive advantage. Many of these investments were made based on faith and intuition by managers who believed in serving customers well and who believed in their hearts that quality service made good business sense. Indeed, a dedication to quality service has been the foundation for success for many firms, across industries. In his book *Discovering the Soul of Service,* Leonard Berry

1.1 IS THE MARKETING OF SERVICES DIFFERENT? A HISTORICAL PERSPECTIVE

In 1979 Gary Knisely, a principal of the consulting firm Johnson Smith & Knisely, asked the above question to practicing services marketers. Specifically, Knisely interviewed several high-ranking marketing executives who had all gone to work in the consumer service industry after extensive experience in the consumer packaged goods industry (known for its marketing prowess).

These executives found differences, all right. Their discoveries came from attempts to apply (with mixed success, it turned out) consumer goods marketing practices directly to services. James L. Schorr of Holiday Inns Inc., formerly with Procter & Gamble, found that he could not overlay a consumer goods firm's marketing system onto a service firm. He, and the other executives interviewed, expressed certain recurring themes. First, more variables exist in the marketing mix for services than for consumer goods. Schorr claimed that in a service business, marketing and operations are more closely linked than in a manufacturing business; thus the service production process is part of the marketing process. Second, customer interface is a major difference between goods marketing and services marketing. Executives from packaged goods companies never had to think in terms of a direct dialogue with their customers. For Schorr, the marketing of hotel rooms boiled down to a "people-on-people" sale. Robert L. Catlin, in relating his experience in the airline industry, stated, "Your people are as much of your product in the consumer's mind as any other attribute of the service." People buy products because they believe they work. But with services, people deal with people they like and they tend to buy services because they believe they will like them. This makes the customer–employee interface a critical component of marketing.

The executives also commented on how the marketing mix variables common to both goods and services have vastly different implications for marketing strategy in the two industries. In the distribution and selling of services, the firm cannot rely on well-stocked shelves past which the consumer can push a cart and make selections. Consumers' exposure to the full range of need-fulfilling service products may be limited by the salesperson's "mental inventory" of services and how he or she prioritizes them. We can say that the service product manager is competing for the "mental shelf space" of the firm's sales personnel. For Rodney Woods, group marketing officer at United States Trust Co., pricing was the most critical factor in the marketing of services versus products. For Woods, determining the costs associated with service production and delivery proved very difficult, much more of a challenge than he had faced in his earlier career working with such large packaged goods companies as Pillsbury, Procter & Gamble, and Bristol-Myers. Also, the benefits of using price as a promotional weapon were not as apparent. Promotional price cuts tended to erode hard fought positioning and image.

While scholars debated early on the issue of whether marketing management differs for goods versus services, for top managers with experience in both areas the differences were pronounced in 1979. They still are today. The differences these early service marketers noted were the impetus for many of the ideas, concepts, and strategies practiced today.

Source: This discussion is based on interviews conducted by Gary Knisely that appeared in *Advertising Age* on January 15, 1979; February 19, 1979; March 19, 1979; and May 14, 1979.

describes in detail 14 such companies.[12] The companies featured in his book had been in business an average of 31 years in 1999 when the book was written. These companies had been profitable in all but 5 of their combined 407 years of existence. Dr. Berry discovered through his research that these successful businesses share devotion to nine common service themes, among them values-driven leadership, commitment to investments in employee success, and trust-based relationships with customers and other partners at the foundation of the organization. Earlier we described the highly successful service strategies of manufacturers like IBM and GE, noting that service can be profitable for manufacturers as well as traditional service businesses such as those represented in Dr. Berry's book.

Since the mid-1990s firms have begun to demand hard evidence of the bottom-line effectiveness of service strategies. And researchers are building a convincing case that

- Customer expectations are higher because of the excellent service they receive from some companies. Thus they expect the same from all and are frequently disappointed.

- Organizations have cut costs to the extent that they are too lean and too understaffed to provide quality service.

- The intensely competitive job market results in less-skilled people working in front-line service jobs; talented workers soon get promoted or leave for better opportunities.

- Many companies give lip service to customer focus and service quality, but they fail to provide the training, compensation, and support needed to actually deliver quality service.

- Delivering consistent, high-quality service is not easy, yet many companies promise it.

These theories as to the causes of declining customer satisfaction can be debated. But for managers, students, and teachers of services marketing and management, the message is clear: there is plenty of work to be done. Services can be profitable, customers demand services, and yet overall quality perceptions and customer satisfaction are declining. In this text we will provide many examples of best practices—companies that understand how to get it right and are succeeding with service. We will also delineate many tools, concepts, and strategies that can help to reverse this trend.

SERVICE AND TECHNOLOGY

The preceding sections examined the roots of services marketing and the reasons why the field exists. Clearly the field and the related business tools and strategies are built upon challenges and issues that service providers and service businesses have faced over the last several decades. Another major trend—technology, specifically information technology—is currently shaping the field and influencing the practice of services marketing. Technology is dramatically changing the nature of services, resulting in tremendous potential for new service offerings not imaginable even a decade ago. Technology is profoundly changing how services are delivered, enabling both customers and employees to get and provide better, more efficient, customized services. Technology facilitates the global reach of services that historically were tied to their home locations. In fact, some would argue that the Internet, the king of current technologies, is "one big service" vehicle.

Given the many potential positives, it is important to recognize there are paradoxes and a dark side to the infusion of technology into every aspect of service as well. Customers don't always welcome technology, and it threatens their privacy in many ways. Employees resist change and often don't see the value in technology. There is a loss of human contact and personal interaction. And there are tremendous investment costs in technology for firms, often with uncertain payback.

In this section we explore these trends in technology to set the stage for topics that will be discussed throughout this text. In each chapter you will find a Technology Spotlight box that highlights the influence of technology on issues related to the particular chapter. We will also raise technology and service issues as appropriate throughout the general discussion in the text and have included several cases that explore the opportunities and challenges of services and technology. Together with globalization, the influence of technology on service is the most profound trend affecting the field today.

service strategies, implemented appropriately, can be very profitable. Work sponsored by the Marketing Science Institute suggests that corporate strategies focused on customer satisfaction, revenue generation, and service quality may actually be more profitable than strategies focused on cost cutting or strategies that attempt to do both simultaneously.[13] Research out of the Harvard Business School builds a case for the "service–profit chain," linking internal service and employee satisfaction to customer value and ultimately to profits.[14] And considerable research shows linkages from customer satisfaction (often driven by service outcomes) to profits.[15] From the University of Michigan American Customer Satisfaction Index (ACSI) we even see data suggesting customer satisfaction is directly linked to shareholder value. Firms in the top 50 percent of the ACSI rankings show significantly higher shareholder value than firms in the bottom 50 percent.[16]

An important key to these successes is that the right strategies are chosen and that these strategies are implemented appropriately and well. Much of what you learn from this text will guide you in making such correct choices and in providing superior implementation. Throughout the text we will point out the profit implications and trade-offs to be made with service strategies. In Chapter 17 we will come back to this issue, providing integrated coverage of the financial and profit impact of service.

But "Service Stinks"

Despite the importance of service and the bottom-line profit potential for service, consumers perceive that overall the quality of service is declining.[17] We see the cover of *Business Week* magazine blatantly condemning service in its cover story, "Why Service Stinks."[18] And although there are exceptions in every industry, the American Customer Satisfaction Index (ACSI) shows an overall decline, particularly in service industries.[19]

This condemnation of service is troubling when we know that at some level service has never been better. For example, think of just one industry—health care. The ability to prevent and treat diseases has never been greater, resulting in an ever-increasing life expectancy in the United States and in most industrialized countries. Or take the communications industries—communicating quickly, effectively, and cheaply with people all over the world has never been easier. Access to vast quantities of information, entertainment, and music is unbelievable compared to what we had just 10 years ago. So clearly, in some ways and in many industries services are better than ever.

Yet there is hard evidence that consumers perceive lower quality of service overall and are less satisfied. There are many theories as to why this decline in customer satisfaction with services has occurred, but it is difficult to point precisely to the reason. Plausible theories include these:

- With more companies offering tiered service based on the calculated profitability of different market segments, many customers are in fact getting less service than they have in the past.

- Increasing use by companies of self-service and technology-based service is perceived as less service because no human interaction or human personalization is provided.

- Technology-based services (automated voice systems, Internet-based services, technology kiosks) are hard to implement, and there are many failures and poorly designed systems in place.

Potential for New Service Offerings

If we look back just 10 to 15 years, we see how technology has been the basic force behind service innovations we now take for granted. Automated voice mail, interactive voice response systems, fax machines, ATMs, and other common services were possible only because of new technologies. Just think how dramatically different your world would be without these basic technology services.

More recently, we have seen the explosion of the Internet, resulting in a host of new services. Internet-based companies like amazon.com and eBay offer services previously unheard of. And established companies find that the Internet provides a way to offer new services as well.[20] For example, Dow Jones, publisher of *The Wall Street Journal,* offers an interactive edition allowing customers to organize the newspaper's content to suit their individual preferences and needs. MeritaNordbanken in Scandinavia found it could be successful in introducing an Internet-based bill-paying service for its customers, helping them efficiently accomplish a necessary task that most disliked.

As we look forward, many new technology services are on the horizon. For example, some project that the "connected car" will allow people to access all kinds of existing and new services while on the road. Already many cars are equipped with map and routing software that direct drivers to specific locations. In the future, in-car systems may provide recommendations for shopping by informing drivers when they are within a certain number of miles of their preferred retailer. On a road trip, the system may provide weather forecasts and warnings, and when it is time to stop for the night, the car's system could book a room at a nearby hotel, recommend a restaurant, and make dinner reservations.[21]

The mobile Internet is also likely to result in new service offerings. Small screens and clumsy controls mean that cell phone Internet access is less desirable than other points of access. However, accessing the Web via cell phones is certainly a possibility today, and in fact it is a reality in many European countries and in Japan, where cell phone usage is greater than in the United States. In Finland, for example, consumers can charge vending machine and gasoline purchases through their cell phones. And in Europe and Japan marketers are experimenting with some success in delivering advertising messages via cell phones.[22]

The spread of mobile Internet services is likely to be constrained by the rate of mobile phone subscriptions and the awkwardness of the small screen technology:

Rate of Mobile Phone Subscriptions per 100 Inhabitants in Selected Countries as of 1999[23]	
Finland	65
Sweden	58
Japan	45
United Kingdom	40
United States	38
Germany	29
Canada	23

New Ways to Deliver Service

In addition to providing opportunities for new service offerings, technology is providing vehicles for delivering existing services in more accessible, convenient, productive ways. Technology facilitates basic customer service functions (bill paying, questions,

Technology Spotlight
The Changing Face of Customer Service

Excellent customer service—the daily, ongoing support of a company's offerings—is critical in creating brand identity and ultimate success. It includes answering questions, taking orders, dealing with billing issues, handling complaints, scheduling appointments, and similar activities. These essential functions can make or break an organization's relationships with its customers. The quality of customer care can significantly impact brand identity for service, manufacturing, and consumer products companies. Because of its importance in creating impressions and sustaining customer relationships, customer service has sometimes been called the "front door" of the organization or its "face."

So how has the "face" of customer service changed with the influx of technology? Long ago all customer service was provided face-to-face through direct personal interaction between employees and customers. To get service you had to visit stores or service providers in person. The telephone changed this, allowing customers to call companies and speak directly with employees, typically Monday–Friday, 8 A.M.–5 P.M. Customer service became less personal, but without a doubt more efficient, through use of the telephone. With the evolution of computer technology, customer service representatives (CSRs) became even more efficient. Through computer information systems and customer data files, CSRs are able to call up customer

records at their workstations to answer questions on the spot.

Over time, because communication and computer technologies allowed it, large organizations began to centralize their customer service functions, consolidating into a few large call centers that could be located anywhere in the country or the world. For example, a large percentage of IBM's customer service calls in North America are handled out of its sales and service center in Toronto, Canada, and calls can be handled 24 hours per day. But still, in these types of call centers, customer service is for the most part an interpersonal event with customers talking directly, one-on-one with an employee.

The advent and rapid proliferation of the efficient, but much maligned, automated voice response systems have changed personal customer service in many organizations into menu-driven, automated exchanges. In almost every industry and any business context consumers encounter these types of systems, and many are quite frustrating—for example, when a system has a long, confusing set of menu options or when no menu option seems to fit the purpose of the call. Similarly, consumers become angered when they cannot get out of the automated system easily, or when there is no option to speak to a live person.

Some companies have overcome these obstacles, however, and have well-designed automated telephone

checking account records, tracking orders), transactions (both retail and business-to-business), and learning or information seeking. Our Technology Spotlight traces how technology has changed customer service forever. We have moved from face-to-face service to telephone-based service to widespread use of interactive voice response systems to Internet-based customer service and now to wireless service. Interestingly, many companies are coming full circle and now offer human contact as the ultimate form of customer service!

Technology also facilitates transactions by offering a direct vehicle for making purchases. In the financial services field Charles Schwab transformed itself from a traditional broker to an online financial services company that currently conducts more than 70 percent of its customer transactions online. GEPolymerland is General Electric's successful business-to-business online resins marketplace. Over 25 percent of GE's resin sales are handled through the site, and 95 percent of those online orders go directly into the information management system without human intervention.[24] Technology giant Cisco Systems offers virtually all of its customer service and ordering functions to its business customers via technology. Over 90 percent of its transactions

systems that work well for customers. Charles Schwab provides a notable example. Schwab completes more than 75 percent of its 82 million annual calls through speech and touch-tone automated response systems. Its automated voice response system has been designed to give quick answers with a minimum of navigation beyond the first menu. This is accomplished through a form of natural-language speech recognition technology that allows customers to easily interact through the telephone in ways that are much like talking to a real person. Further, a human contact is always easy to get to if needed. Customer satisfaction at Schwab is rated among the highest in any industry. One of the keys may be that at Charles Schwab, the vice president of retail voice technology occupies a senior management position, showing the importance placed on this function. In general, satisfaction levels for automated speech recognition systems are higher than satisfaction with touch-tone systems and in some cases are higher than for live agents.

Beyond automated telecom systems, explosion of the Internet is also dramatically changing customer service for many companies. Service can now be provided on the Internet via e-mail, website robots, FAQs, and online chat. In these cases there is no direct human interaction, and customers actually perform their own service. An example is Ford Motor Company's technology that allows dealership customers to set their own service

appointments, send messages regarding their specific repair needs, and monitor the status of their vehicles, all online.

With the relentless proliferation of technology solutions, firms are finding that expectations for customer service have changed. Customers are demanding choices in how they get customer service, whether it be over the phone, automated voice systems, via fax or e-mail, or through Internet self-service. However, while customers often enjoy technology-based service and even demand it in many cases, they dislike it when it doesn't work reliably (a common problem), when it doesn't seem to have any advantages over the interpersonal service alternatives, and when there are no systems in place to recover from failures. Interestingly, when things don't work as they are supposed to on an Internet site or through an automated response system, customers are quick to look for more traditional interpersonal (in person or via telephone) options, coming full circle to where we started!

Sources: J. A. Nickell, "To Voice Mail Hell and Back," *Business 2.0,* July 10, 2001, pp. 49–53; D. Ward, "The Web's Killer App: A Human Being," *Revolution,* March 2000, pp. 82–88; M. L. Meuter, A. L. Ostrom, R. I. Roundtree, and M. J. Bitner, "Self-Service Technologies: Understanding Customer Satisfaction with Technology-Based Service Encounters," *Journal of Marketing* 64 (July 2000), pp. 50–64.

with customers are completed online. Williams-Sonoma, the successful high-end retailer of kitchen and home products, has been very successful with its introduction of an online bridal registry service that allows couples to register and select and try out products. Friends and relatives can then also preview and order gifts for the couple online.

Finally, technology, specifically the Internet, provides an easy way for customers to learn and research. Access to information has never been easier. For example, over 20,000 websites currently offer health-related information. Many provide answers to specific disease, drug, and treatment questions. In a study of online health care information usage, the Pew organization found that among Americans with Internet access, 55 percent had looked for health or medical information on the Web.[25]

Enabling Both Customers and Employees

Technology enables both customers and employees to be more effective in getting and providing service.[26] Through self-service technologies customers can serve themselves more effectively. For example, via online banking customers can access their accounts, check balances, apply for loans, shift money among accounts, and take care of just about any banking need they might have—all without the assistance of the bank's employees. Wells Fargo, the first bank to offer online services in the United States, finds that its online customers are its most satisfied customers. Self-service technologies are proliferating across industries.

For employees, technology can provide tremendous support in making them more effective and efficient in delivering service. Customer relationship management and sales support software are broad categories of technology that can aid front-line employees in providing better service. By having immediate access to information about their product and service offerings as well as about particular customers, employees are better able to serve them. This type of information allows employees to customize services to fit the customer's needs. They can also be much more efficient and timely than in the old days when most customer and product information was in paper files or in the heads of sales and customer service representatives.

Extending the Global Reach of Services

Technology infusion results in the potential for reaching out to customers around the globe in ways not possible before. The Internet itself knows no boundaries, and therefore information, customer service, and transactions can move across countries and across continents, reaching any customer who has access to the Web. Technology also allows employees of international companies to stay in touch easily—to share information, to ask questions, to serve on virtual teams together. All of this facilitates the global reach as well as the effectiveness of service businesses.

The Internet *Is* a Service

An interesting way to look at the influence of technology is to realize that the Internet is just "one big service." All businesses and organizations that operate on the Internet are essentially providing services—whether they are giving information, performing basic customer service functions, or facilitating transactions. Thus all of the tools, concepts, and strategies you learn in studying services marketing and management have direct application in an Internet or e-business world. Although technology and the Internet are profoundly changing how we do business and what offerings are possible, it is clear the customers still want basic service. They want what they have always wanted: dependable outcomes, easy access, responsive systems, flexibility, apologies, and compensation when things go wrong. But now they expect these same outcomes from technology-based businesses and from e-commerce solutions.[27] With hindsight it is obvious that many dot-com start-ups suffered and even failed due to lack of basic customer knowledge and failure of implementation, logistics, and service follow-up.[28]

The Paradoxes and Dark Side of Technology and Service

Although there is clearly great potential for technology to support brand new service concepts, provide new ways of delivering service, and enable customers and employees in achieving better-quality services, there are potential negative outcomes as well. Mick and Fournier, well-regarded consumer researchers, have pointed out the many paradoxes of technology products and services for consumers. For example, technology can assimilate people while isolating them; it can provide a sense of control and at the same time feelings of ineptitude.[29] These types of paradoxes listed in Table 1.2, as well as the negatives associated with technology, will be explored throughout the text.

TABLE 1.2   **Eight Central Paradoxes of Technological Products**

Paradox	Description
Control/chaos	Technology can facilitate regulation or order, and technology can lead to upheaval or disorder.
Freedom/enslavement	Technology can facilitate independence or fewer restrictions, and technology can lead to dependence or more restrictions.
New/obsolete	New technologies provide the user with the most recently developed benefits of scientific knowledge, and new technologies are already or soon to be outmoded as they reach the marketplace.
Competence/incompetence	Technology can facilitate feelings of intelligence or efficacy, and technology can lead to feelings of ignorance or ineptitude.
Efficiency/inefficiency	Technology can facilitate less effort or time spent in certain activities, and technology can lead to more effort or time in certain activities.
Fulfills/creates needs	Technology can facilitate the fulfillment of needs or desires, and technology can lead to the development or awareness of needs or desires previously unrealized.
Assimilation/isolation	Technology can facilitate human togetherness, and technology can lead to human separation.
Engaging/disengaging	Technology can facilitate involvement, flow, or activity, and technology can lead to disconnection, disruption, or passivity.

Source: D. G. Mick and S. Fournier, "Paradoxes of Technology: Consumer Cognizance, Emotions, and Coping Strategies," *Journal of Consumer Research* 25 (September 1998), pp. 123–47.

Customer concerns about privacy and confidentiality raise major issues for firms as they seek to learn about and interact directly with customers through the Internet. These types of concerns are what have stymied and precluded many efforts to advance technology applications in the health care industry, for example. Nor are all customers equally interested in using technology as a means of interacting with companies. Research exploring "customer technology readiness" suggests that some customers are simply not interested or ready to use technology.[30]

Employees can also be reluctant to accept and integrate technology into their work lives—especially when they perceive, rightly or wrongly, that the technology will substitute for human labor and perhaps eliminate their jobs. Even when this is not the case, employees are often reluctant to embrace technology simply because they don't want to change or don't see the value in learning the new technology.

With technology infusion there is a loss of human contact, which many believe is detrimental purely from a quality of life and human relationships perspective. Frequently we hear of parents lamenting that their children spend hours in front of computer screens, interacting with games, seeking information, and relating to their friends only through instant messaging without any face-to-face human contact. And in organizations we become more and more reliant on communicating through technology—even communicating via e-mail with the person in the office next to us!

Finally, the payback in technology investments is often uncertain. It may take a long time for an investment to result in productivity or customer satisfaction gains. Sometimes it never happens. For example, McKinsey & Company reports that a firm projected a $40 million savings from moving its billing and service calls to the Web. Instead it suffered a $16 billion loss as a result of lower usage by customers than projected, unanticipated follow-up calls and e-mails to the call center from those who had used the Web application initially, and loss of revenue from lack of cross-selling opportunities.[31]

DIFFERENCES IN GOODS VERSUS SERVICES MARKETING

There is general agreement that inherent differences between goods and services exist and that they result in unique, or at least different, management challenges for service businesses and for manufacturers that sell services as a core offering.[32] These differences and associated marketing implications are shown in Table 1.3. The remaining chapters in the book address these challenges and specific strategies for overcoming them.

Intangibility

The most basic, and universally cited, difference between goods and services is **intangibility.** Because services are performances or actions rather than objects, they cannot be seen, felt, tasted, or touched in the same manner that we can sense tangible goods. For example, health care services are actions (such as surgery, diagnosis, examination, and treatment) performed by providers and directed toward patients and their families. These services cannot actually be seen or touched by the patient, although the patient may be able to see and touch certain tangible components of the service (like the equipment or hospital room). In fact, many services such as health care are difficult for the consumer to grasp even mentally. Even after a diagnosis or surgery has been completed the patient may not fully comprehend the service performed.

TABLE 1.3 **Services Are Different**

Goods	Services	Resulting Implications
Tangible	Intangible	Services cannot be inventoried.
		Services cannot be patented.
		Services cannot be readily displayed or communicated.
		Pricing is difficult.
Standardized	Heterogeneous	Service delivery and customer satisfaction depend on employee actions.
		Service quality depends on many uncontrollable factors.
		There is no sure knowledge that the service delivered matches what was planned and promoted.
Production separate from consumption	Simultaneous production and consumption	Customers participate in and affect the transaction.
		Customers affect each other.
		Employees affect the service outcome.
		Decentralization may be essential.
		Mass production is difficult.
Nonperishable	Perishable	It is difficult to synchronize supply and demand with services.
		Services cannot be returned or resold.

Source: Reprinted by permission from the American Marketing Association, *Journal of Marketing* 49 (Fall 1985), A. Parasuraman, V. A. Zeithaml, and L. L. Berry, "A Conceptual Model of Service Quality and Its Implications for Future Research," pp. 41–50.

Resulting Marketing Implications   Intangibility presents several marketing challenges. Services cannot be inventoried, and therefore fluctuations in demand are often difficult to manage. For example, there is tremendous demand for resort accommodations in Phoenix in February, but little demand in July. Yet resort owners have the same number of rooms to sell year-round. Services cannot be easily patented, and new service concepts can therefore easily be copied by competitors. Services cannot be readily displayed or easily communicated to customers, so quality may be difficult for consumers to assess. Decisions about what to include in advertising and other promotional materials are challenging, as is pricing. The actual costs of a "unit of service" are hard to determine, and the price–quality relationship is complex.

Heterogeneity

Because services are performances, frequently produced by humans, no two services will be precisely alike. The employees delivering the service frequently *are* the service in the customer's eyes, and people may differ in their performance from day to day or even hour to hour. **Heterogeneity** also results because no two customers are precisely alike; each will have unique demands or experience the service in a unique way. Thus the heterogeneity connected with services is largely the result of human interaction (between and among employees and customers) and all of the vagaries that accompany it. For example, a tax accountant may provide a different service experience to two different customers on the same day depending on their individual needs and personalities and on whether the accountant is interviewing them when he or she is fresh in the morning or tired at the end of a long day of meetings.

Resulting Marketing Implications   Because services are heterogeneous across time, organizations, and people, ensuring consistent service quality is challenging. Quality actually depends on many factors that cannot be fully controlled by the service supplier, such as the ability of the consumer to articulate his or her needs, the ability and willingness of personnel to satisfy those needs, the presence (or absence) of other customers, and the level of demand for the service. Because of these complicating factors, the service manager cannot always know for sure that the service is being delivered in a manner consistent with what was originally planned and promoted. Sometimes services may be provided by a third party, further increasing the potential heterogeneity of the offering. For example, a consulting organization may choose to subcontract certain elements of its total offering. From the customer's perspective, these subcontractors still represent the consulting organization, even though their actions cannot be totally predicted or controlled by the contractor.

Simultaneous Production and Consumption

Whereas most goods are produced first, then sold and consumed, most services are sold first and then produced and consumed simultaneously. For example, an automobile can be manufactured in Detroit, shipped to San Francisco, sold two months later, and consumed over a period of years. But restaurant services cannot be provided until they have been sold, and the dining experience is essentially produced and consumed at the same time. Frequently this also means that the customer is present while the service is being produced and thus views and may even take part in the production process. This also means that frequently customers will interact with each other during the service production process and thus may affect each others' experiences. For example, strangers seated next to each other in an airplane may well affect the nature of the service experience for each other. That passengers understand this fact is clearly apparent in the way business travelers will often go to great lengths to be sure they are not seated next to families with small children. Another outcome of **simultaneous production and consumption** is that service producers find themselves playing a role as part of the product itself and as an essential ingredient in the service experience for the consumer.

Resulting Marketing Implications   Because services often are produced and consumed at the same time, mass production is difficult if not impossible. The quality of service and customer satisfaction will be highly dependent on what happens in "real time," including actions of employees and the interactions between employees and customers. Similarly, it is not usually possible to gain significant economies of scale through centralization. Usually operations need to be relatively decentralized so that the service can be delivered directly to the consumer in convenient locations. Also because of simultaneous production and consumption, the customer is involved in and observes the production process and thus may affect (positively or negatively) the outcome of the service transaction. In a related vein, "problem customers" (those who disrupt the service process) can cause problems for themselves or others in the service setting, resulting in lowered customer satisfaction. For example, in a restaurant setting, an overdemanding and intoxicated patron will command extra attention from the service provider and negatively impact the experiences of other customers.

Perishability

Perishability refers to the fact that services cannot be saved, stored, resold, or returned. A seat on an airplane or in a restaurant, an hour of a lawyer's time, or telephone line capacity not used cannot be reclaimed and used or resold at a later time. This is in contrast to goods that can be stored in inventory or resold another day, or even returned if the consumer is unhappy. Wouldn't it be nice if a bad haircut could be returned or resold to another consumer? Perishability makes this an unlikely possibility for most services.

Resulting Marketing Implications   A primary issue that marketers face in relation to service perishability is the inability to inventory. Demand forecasting and creative planning for capacity utilization are therefore important and challenging decision areas. The fact that services cannot typically be returned or resold also implies a need for strong recovery strategies when things do go wrong. For example, while a bad haircut cannot be returned, the hairdresser can and should have strategies for recovering the customer's goodwill if and when such a problem occurs.

Challenges and Questions for Service Marketers

Because of these basic differences between goods and services, marketers of services face some very real and distinctive challenges. The challenges revolve around understanding customer needs and expectations for service, making the service offering tangible, dealing with myriad people and delivery issues, and keeping promises made to customers. Answers to questions such as the ones listed here still elude managers of services:

How can service quality be defined and improved when the product is intangible and nonstandardized?

How can new services be designed and tested effectively when the service is essentially an intangible process?

How can the firm be certain it is communicating a consistent and relevant image when so many elements of the marketing mix communicate to customers and some of these elements are the service providers themselves?

How does the firm accommodate fluctuating demand when capacity is fixed and the service itself is perishable?

How can the firm best motivate and select service employees who, because the service is delivered in real time, become a critical part of the product itself?

How should prices be set when it is difficult to determine actual costs of production and price may be inextricably intertwined with perceptions of quality?

How should the firm be organized so that good strategic and tactical decisions are made when a decision in any of the functional areas of marketing, operations, and human resources may have significant impact on the other two areas?

How can the balance between standardization and personalization be determined to maximize both the efficiency of the organization and the satisfaction of its customers?

How can the organization protect new service concepts from competitors when service processes cannot be patented?

How does the firm communicate quality and value to consumers when the offering is intangible and cannot be readily tried or displayed?

How can the organization ensure the delivery of consistent quality service when both the organization's employees and the customers themselves can affect the service outcome?

SERVICES MARKETING MIX

The preceding questions are some of the many raised by managers and marketers of services that will be addressed throughout the text through a variety of unique and adapted tools and strategies. Sometimes these tools are adaptations of traditional marketing tools, as with the services marketing mix presented here. Other times they are radically new, as in the case of service mapping presented in Chapter 8.

Traditional Marketing Mix

One of the most basic concepts in marketing is the **marketing mix,** defined as the elements an organization controls that can be used to satisfy or communicate with customers. The traditional marketing mix is composed of the four P's: *product, price, place* (distribution), and *promotion.*[33] These elements appear as core decision variables in any marketing text or marketing plan. The notion of a mix implies that all of the variables are interrelated and depend on each other to some extent. Further, the marketing mix philosophy implies that there is an optimal mix of the four factors for a given market segment at a given point in time.

Key strategy decision areas for each of the four P's are captured in the first four columns in Table 1.4. Careful management of product, place, promotion, and price will clearly also be essential to the successful marketing of services. However, the strategies for the four P's require some modifications when applied to services. For example, traditionally promotion is thought of as involving decisions related to sales,

TABLE 1.4
Expanded Marketing Mix for Services

Product	Place	Promotion	Price
Physical good features	Channel type	Promotion blend	Flexibility
Quality level	Exposure	Salespeople	Price level
Accessories	Intermediaries	Number	Terms
Packaging	Outlet locations	Selection	Differentiation
Warranties	Transportation	Training	Discounts
Product lines	Storage	Incentives	Allowances
Branding	Managing channels	Advertising	
		Targets	
		Media types	
		Types of ads	
		Copy thrust	
		Sales promotion	
		Publicity	

People	Physical Evidence	Process
Employees	Facility design	Flow of activities
Recruiting	Equipment	Standardized
Training	Signage	Customized
Motivation	Employee dress	Number of steps
Rewards	Other tangibles	Simple
Teamwork	Reports	Complex
Customers	Business cards	Customer involvement
Education	Statements	
Training	Guarantees	

advertising, sales promotions, and publicity. In services these factors are also important, but because services are produced and consumed simultaneously, service delivery people (such as clerks, ticket takers, nurses, and phone personnel) are involved in real-time promotion of the service even if their jobs are typically defined in terms of the operational function they perform. Pricing also becomes very complex in services where unit costs needed to calculate prices may be difficult to determine, and where the customer frequently uses price as a cue to quality.

Expanded Mix for Services

Because services are usually produced and consumed simultaneously, customers are often present in the firm's factory, interact directly with the firm's personnel, and are actually part of the service production process. Also, because services are intangible customers will often be looking for any tangible cue to help them understand the nature of the service experience. These facts have led services marketers to conclude that they can use additional variables to communicate with and satisfy their customers. For example, in the hotel industry the design and decor of the hotel as well as the appearance and attitudes of its employees will influence customer perceptions and experiences.

Acknowledgment of the importance of these additional communication variables has led services marketers to adopt the concept of an expanded marketing mix for services shown in the three remaining columns in Table 1.4.[34] In addition to the traditional four P's, the services marketing mix includes *people, physical evidence,* and *process.*

People All human actors who play a part in service delivery and thus influence the buyer's perceptions: namely, the firm's personnel, the customer, and other customers in the service environment.

All of the human actors participating in the delivery of a service provide cues to the customer regarding the nature of the service itself. How these people are dressed, their personal appearance, and their attitudes and behaviors all influence the customer's perceptions of the service. The service provider or contact person can be very important. In fact, for some services, such as consulting, counseling, teaching, and other professional relationship-based services, the provider *is* the service. In other cases the contact person may play what appears to be a relatively small part in service delivery—for instance, a telephone installer, an airline baggage handler, or an equipment delivery dispatcher. Yet research suggests that even these providers may be the focal point of service encounters that can prove critical for the organization.

In many service situations, customers themselves can also influence service delivery, thus affecting service quality and their own satisfaction. For example, a client of a consulting company can influence the quality of service received by providing needed and timely information and by implementing recommendations provided by the consultant. Similarly, health care patients greatly affect the quality of service they receive when they either comply or don't comply with health regimens prescribed by the provider.

Customers not only influence their own service outcomes, but they can influence other customers as well. In a theater, at a ballgame, or in a classroom, customers can influence the quality of service received by others—either enhancing or detracting from other customers' experiences.

> **Physical evidence**   The environment in which the service is delivered and where the firm and customer interact, and any tangible components that facilitate performance or communication of the service.

The physical evidence of service includes all of the tangible representations of the service such as brochures, letterhead, business cards, report formats, signage, and equipment. In some cases it includes the physical facility where the service is offered—the "servicescape"—for example, the retail bank branch facility. In other cases, such as telecommunication services, the physical facility may be irrelevant. In this case other tangibles such as billing statements and appearance of the repair truck may be important indicators of quality. Especially when consumers have little on which to judge the actual quality of service they will rely on these cues, just as they rely on the cues provided by the people and the service process. Physical evidence cues provide excellent opportunities for the firm to send consistent and strong messages regarding the organization's purpose, the intended market segments, and the nature of the service.

> **Process**   The actual procedures, mechanisms, and flow of activities by which the service is delivered—the service delivery and operating systems.

The actual delivery steps the customer experiences, or the operational flow of the service, also give customers evidence on which to judge the service. Some services are very complex, requiring the customer to follow a complicated and extensive series of actions to complete the process. Highly bureaucratized services frequently follow this pattern, and the logic of the steps involved often escapes the customer. Another distinguishing characteristic of the process that can provide evidence to the customer is whether the service follows a production-line/standardized approach or whether the process is an empowered/customized one. None of these characteristics of the service is inherently better or worse than another. Rather, the point is that these process characteristics are another form of evidence used by the consumer to judge service. For example, two successful airline companies, Southwest and Singapore Airlines, follow extremely different process models. Southwest is a no-frills (no food, no assigned

1.2 SOUTHWEST AIRLINES: ALIGNING PEOPLE, PROCESSES, AND PHYSICAL EVIDENCE

Southwest Airlines occupies a solid position in the minds of U.S. air travelers as a reliable, convenient, fun, low-fare, no-frills airline. Translated, this position means high value—a position reinforced by all elements of Southwest's services marketing mix. It has maintained this position consistently over 30 years while making money every year; no other U.S. airline comes close to this record. As further evidence of the airline's financial stability, Southwest was the only airline to remain profitable in the months immediately following the September 11, 2001, tragedies in the United States that sent many airlines to near bankruptcy.

Success has come for a number of reasons. One is the airline's low cost structure. It flies only one type of plane (Boeing 737s), which lowers costs because of the fuel efficiency of the aircraft itself combined with the ability to standardize maintenance and operational procedures. The airline also keeps its costs down by not serving meals, having no preassigned seats, and keeping employee turnover very low. Southwest Airlines' Herb Kelleher (president of Southwest from its inception until 2001, and currently serving as chairman) is famous for his belief that employees come first, not customers. The Dallas-based carrier has managed to be the low-cost provider and a preferred employer while enjoying high levels of customer satisfaction and strong customer loyalty. Southwest Airlines has the best customer service record in the airline industry and has won the industry's "Triple Crown" for best baggage handling, on-time performance, and best customer complaint statistics many years in a row. This is a feat accomplished by no other airline. Southwest is also the number one airline in volume of tickets sold over the Internet.

Observing Southwest Airlines' success, it is clear that all of its marketing mix is aligned around its highly successful market position. The three new marketing mix elements all strongly reinforce the value image of the airline:

- **People** Southwest uses its people and its customers very effectively to communicate its position. Employees are unionized, yet they are trained to have fun, allowed to define what "fun" means, and given authority to do what it takes to make flights lighthearted and enjoyable. People are hired at Southwest for their attitudes; technical skills can be and are trained. And they are the most productive workforce in the U.S. airline industry. Cus-

tomers also are included in the atmosphere of fun, and many get into the act by joking with the crew and each other and by flooding the airline with letters expressing their satisfaction.

- **Process** The service delivery process at Southwest also reinforces its position. There are no assigned seats on the aircraft, so passengers line up and are "herded" by number onto the plane, where they jockey for seats. The airline does not transfer baggage to connecting flights on other airlines. Food is not served in flight. In all, the process is very efficient, standardized, and low-cost, allowing for quick turnaround and low fares. Customers are very much part of the service process, taking on their roles willingly.

- **Physical evidence** All of the tangibles associated with Southwest further reinforce the market position. Southwest's aircraft are orange and mustard brown, which accentuates their uniqueness and low-cost orientation. Employees dress casually, wearing shorts in the summer to reinforce the "fun" and further emphasize the airline's commitment to its employees' comfort. The reusable plastic boarding passes are another form of physical evidence that signals low cost and no frills to customers. No in-flight meal service confirms the low-price image through the absence of tangibles—no food. Because many people joke about airline food, its absence for many is not viewed as a value detractor. Southwest's simple, easy-to-use website is yet another form of consistent, tangible evidence that supports the airline's strong positioning and reinforces its image.

The consistent positioning using the services marketing mix reinforces the unique image in the customer's mind, giving Southwest Airlines its high-value position, which has resulted in a huge and committed following of satisfied customers and consistently increasing profits.

Source: K. Freiberg and J. Freiberg, *Nuts! Southwest Airlines' Crazy Recipe for Business and Personal Success* (Austin, TX: Bard Press, Inc., 1996); and K. Labich, "Is Herb Kelleher America's Best CEO?" *Fortune,* May 2, 1994; H. Kelleher and K. Brooker, "The Chairman of the Board Looks Back," *Fortune,* May 28, 2001, pp. 62–76.

seats), no exceptions, low-priced airline that offers frequent, relatively short domestic flights. All of the evidence it provides is consistent with its vision and market position, as illustrated in Exhibit 1.2. Singapore Airlines, on the other hand, focuses on the business traveler and is concerned with meeting individual traveler needs. Thus its process is highly customized to the individual, and employees are empowered to provide nonstandard service when needed. Both airlines have been very successful.

The three new marketing mix elements (people, physical evidence, and process) are included in the marketing mix as separate elements because they are within the control of the firm and any or all of them may influence the customer's initial decision to purchase a service, as well as the customer's level of satisfaction and repurchase decisions. The traditional elements as well as the new marketing mix elements will be explored in depth in future chapters.

STAYING FOCUSED ON THE CUSTOMER

A critical theme running throughout the text is *customer focus*. In fact, the subtitle of the book is "integrating customer focus across the firm." From the firm's point of view, this means that all strategies are developed with an eye on the customer, and all implementations are carried out with an understanding of their impact on the customer. From a practical perspective this means that decisions regarding new services and communication plans will integrate the customer's point of view; operations and human resource decisions will be considered in terms of their impact on customers. All of the tools, strategies, and frameworks included in this text have customers at their foundation. The services marketing mix just described is clearly an important tool that addresses the uniqueness of services, keeping the customer at the center.

We also view customers as assets to be valued, developed, and retained. The strategies and tools in the text thus focus on customer relationship building and loyalty as opposed to a more transactional focus where customers are viewed as one-time revenue producers. This text views customer relationship management not as a software program, but as an entire architecture or business philosophy. Every chapter in the text can be viewed as a component needed to build a complete customer relationship management approach.

THE GAPS MODEL OF SERVICE QUALITY

Service excellence is another key theme running through the text. The gaps model of service quality brings customer focus and service excellence together in a structured, practical way.[35] The model focuses on strategies and processes that firms can employ to drive service excellence while maintaining a focus on customers. The gaps model will be used to frame this entire text and is the organizational structure for the rest of the chapters. It is a model that can drive strategy as well as implementation decisions. The model and its components are overviewed in the part opener that follows this chapter. Subsequent part openers focus on specific aspects of the gaps model that are covered in the chapters in that section. The full model is drawn together and summarized in the concluding chapter of the text.

Summary

This chapter has set the stage for further learning about services marketing by presenting information about changes in the world economy and business practice that have driven the focus on service: the fact that services dominate the modern economies of the world; the focus on service as a competitive business imperative; specific needs of the deregulated and professional service industries; the role of new service concepts growing from technological advances; and the realization that services marketing is different. A broad definition of services as deeds, processes, and performances was presented, and distinctions between service and customer service were drawn.

Building on this fundamental understanding of the service economy, the chapter went on to present the key differences between goods and services that underlie the need for distinct strategies and concepts for managing service businesses. These basic differences are that services are intangible, heterogeneous, produced and consumed simultaneously, and perishable. Because of these basic differences, service managers face a number of challenges in marketing, including the complex problem of how to deliver quality services consistently.

The chapter ended by describing three themes that provide the foundation for future chapters: the expanded marketing mix for services; customer focus as a unifying theme; and the gaps model of service quality, the framework for organizing the rest of the chapters in the book. The remainder of the text focuses on exploring the unique challenges faced by organizations that sell and deliver services and on developing solutions for dealing with these challenges that will help you become an effective services champion and manager.

Discussion Questions

1. What distinguishes service offerings from customer service? Provide specific examples.
2. How is technology changing the nature of service?
3. What are the basic differences in marketing goods versus services? What are the implications of these differences for IBM Global Service or for Southwest Airlines?
4. One of the underlying frameworks for the text is the services marketing mix. Discuss why each of the three new mix elements (process, people, and physical evidence) is included. How might each of these communicate with or help to satisfy an organization's customers?
5. Think of a service job you have had or currently have. How effective, in your opinion, was or is the organization in managing the elements of the services marketing mix?
6. Again, think of a service job you have had or currently have. How did or does the organization handle relevant problems listed in Table 1.3?
7. How can quality service be used in a manufacturing context for competitive advantage? Think of your answer to this question in the context of automobiles or computers or some other manufactured product you have actually purchased.

Exercises

1. Roughly calculate your budget for an average month. What percentage of your budget goes for services versus goods? Do the services you purchase have value? In what sense? If you had to cut back on your expenses what would you cut out?
2. Visit two local retail service providers that you believe are positioned very differently (such as Kmart and Nordstrom, or Burger King and a fine restaurant). From your own observations, compare their strategies on the elements of the services marketing mix.

3. Try a service you have never tried before on the Internet. Analyze the benefits of this service. Was enough information provided to make the service easy to use? How would you compare this service to other methods of obtaining the same benefits?

Notes

1. "IBM: Back to Double-Digit Growth?" *Business Week,* June 1, 1998, pp. 116–22; D. Kirkpatrick, "IBM, from Big Blue Dinosaur to E-Business Animal," *Fortune,* April 26, 1999, pp. 116–26; W. M. Bulkeley, "These Days, Big Blue Is About Big Services Not Just Big Boxes," *The Wall Street Journal,* June 11, 2001, p. A1; and Spencer E. Ante and Ira Sager, "IBM's New Boss," *Business Week,* February 11, 2002, pp. 66–72.
2. D. Brady, "Why Service Stinks," *Business Week,* October 23, 2000, pp. 118–28.
3. P. Barta and A. M. Chaker, "Consumers Voice Rising Dissatisfaction with Companies," *The Wall Street Journal,* May 21, 2001, p. A2.
4. J. B. Quinn, J. J. Baruch, and P. C. Paquette, "Technology in Services," *Scientific American* 257, no. 6 (December 1987), pp. 50–58.
5. J. E. Garten, "Why the Global Economy Is Here to Stay," *Business Week,* March 23, 1998, p. 21.
6. C. L. Bach, "U.S. International Transactions, Fourth Quarter and Year 2000," *Survey of Current Business,* April 2001, pp. 21–68.
7. C. H. Deutsch, "Services Becoming the Goods in Industry," *The New York Times,* January 7, 1997, p. C1.
8. T. Smart, "Jack Welch's Encore," *Business Week,* October 28, 1996, pp. 155–60; and GE company data, 2000.
9. R. H. K. Vietor, *Contrived Competition* (Cambridge, MA: Harvard University Press, 1994).
10. M. Weiner, N. Nohria, A. Hickman, and H. Smith, "Value Networks—The Future of the U.S. Electric Utility Industry," *Sloan Management Review,* Summer 1997, pp. 21–34.
11. This discussion is based on interviews conducted by Gary Knisely that appeared in *Advertising Age* on January 15, 1979; February 19, 1979; March 19, 1979; and May 14, 1979.
12. L. Berry, *Discovering the Soul of Service* (New York: The Free Press, 1999).
13. R. T. Rust, C. Moorman, and P. R. Dickson, "Getting Returns from Service Quality: Is the Conventional Wisdom Wrong?" (Boston: Marketing Science Institute, Working Paper, Report 00-120, 2000).
14. J. L. Heskett, T. O. Jones, G. W. Loveman, W. E. Sasser, Jr., and L. A. Schlesinger, "Putting the Service–Profit Chain to Work," *Harvard Business Review,* March–April 1994, pp. 164–74.
15. E. W. Anderson and V. Mittal, "Strengthening the Satisfaction–Profit Chain," *Journal of Service Research,* vol. 3, no. 2, November 2000, pp. 107–20.
16. B. Fryer, "High Tech the Old Fashioned Way," *Harvard Business Review,* March 2001, pp. 119–25.
17. C. Fishman, "But Wait, You Promised . . . ," *Fast Company,* April 2001, pp. 116–27.
18. D. Brady, "Why Service Stinks," *Business Week,* October 23, 2000, pp. 116–28.
19. P. Barta and A. M. Chaker, "Consumers Voice Rising Dissatisfaction with Companies," *The Wall Street Journal,* May 21, 2001, p. A2.
20. L. P. Willcocks and R. Plant, "Getting from Bricks to Clicks," *Sloan Management Review,* Spring 2001, pp. 50–59.

21. "Revolution Digital Tomorrow Report: Technologies That Will Change Marketing," *Revolution,* February 2001, pp. 51–65.

22. Ibid.

23. Source of data: Organization for Economic Cooperation and Development.

24. A. Frangos, "Just One Word: Plastics," *The Wall Street Journal, E-Commerce Report,* May 21, 2001, p. R20.

25. "The Online Health Care Revolution: How the Web Helps Americans Take Better Care of Themselves," Washington, DC: *The Pew Internet & American Life Project,* http://www.pewinternet.org., 2000.

26. M. J. Bitner, S. W. Brown, and M. L. Meuter, "Technology Infusion in Service Encounters," *Journal of the Academy of Marketing Science,* vol. 28, no. 1 (2000), pp. 138–49.

27. M. J. Bitner, "Self-Service Technologies: What Do Customers Expect?" *Marketing Management,* Spring 2001, pp. 10–11.

28. R. Hallowell, "Service in E-Commerce: Findings from Exploratory Research," Harvard Business School, Module Note, N9-800-418, May 31, 2000.

29. D. G. Mick and S. Fournier, "Paradoxes of Technology: Consumer Cognizance, Emotions, and Coping Strategies," *Journal of Consumer Research* 25 (September 1998), pp. 123–47.

30. A. Parasuraman and C. L. Colby, *Techno-Ready Marketing: How and Why Your Customers Adopt Technology* (New York: The Free Press, 2001).

31. "Customer Care in a New World," McKinsey & Company, 2001.

32. Discussion of these issues is found in many services marketing publications. The discussion here is based on V. A. Zeithaml, A. Parasuraman, and L. L. Berry, "Problems and Strategies in Services Marketing," *Journal of Marketing* 49 (Spring 1985), pp. 33–46; and S. W. Brown and M. J. Bitner, "Services Marketing," *AMA Management Handbook,* 3rd ed. (New York: AMACOM Books, 1994), pp. 15-5 15-15.

33. E. J. McCarthy and W. D. Perrault, Jr., *Basic Marketing, A Global Managerial Approach* (Burr Ridge, IL: Richard D. Irwin, 1993).

34. B. H. Booms and M. J. Bitner, "Marketing Strategies and Organizational Structures for Service Firms," in *Marketing of Services,* ed. J. H. Donnelly and W. R. George (Chicago: American Marketing Association, 1981), pp. 47–51.

35. A. Parasuraman, V. A. Zeithaml, and L. L. Berry, "A Conceptual Model of Service Quality and Its Implications for Future Research," *Journal of Marketing* 49 (Fall 1985), pp. 41–50.

Part

1

Focus
on the Customer

This textbook is structured around a conceptual model that positions the key concepts, strategies, and decisions in services marketing. We develop the model, called the *gaps model of service quality,* in these special divider sections as we go through the book. We present the framework briefly here to give you an overall familiarity with its components. The model itself is used to guide the structure of the rest of this book, with sections of the book tied to each of the gaps described herein and illustrated in the accompanying figure.

Gaps Model of Service Quality

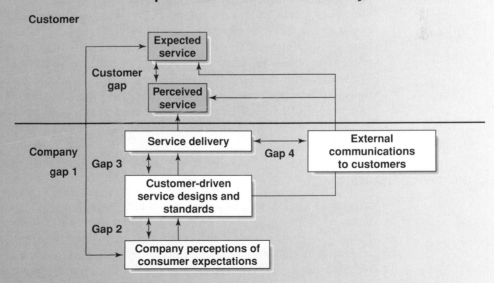

THE CUSTOMER GAP

The central focus of the gaps model is the *customer gap,* the difference between customer expectations and perceptions. Expectations are the reference points customers have coming in to a service experience; perceptions reflect the service as actually received. The idea is that firms will want to close this gap—between what is expected and what is received—to satisfy their customers and build long-term relationships with them. To close this all-important customer gap, the model suggests that four other gaps—the *provider gaps*—need to be closed.

THE PROVIDER GAPS

The provider gaps are the underlying causes behind the customer gap:

Gap 1—Not knowing what customers expect.

Gap 2—Not selecting the right service designs and standards.

Gap 3—Not delivering to service standards.

Gap 4—Not matching performance to promises.

A primary cause in many firms for not meeting customers' expectations is that the firm lacks accurate understanding of exactly what those expectations are. A gap exists (gap 1) between company perceptions of customer expectations and what customers actually expect. In the first major section of this text we explore why this gap occurs and develop strategies for closing it.

Even if a firm does clearly understand its customers' expectations, there still may be problems if that understanding is not translated into customer-driven service designs and standards (gap 2). The second major section of this text focuses on reasons for gap 2 and strategies for designing services and developing standards to meet customer expectations.

Once service designs and standards are in place, it would seem the firm is well on its way to delivering high-quality services. This is true, but still not enough. There must be systems, processes, and people in place to ensure that service delivery actually matches (or is even better than) the designs and standards in place (gap 3). The third major section of the text focuses on how and why gap 3 can occur and specific process, people, and infrastructure strategies for closing this gap.

Finally, with everything in place to effectively meet or exceed customer expectations, the firm must ensure that what is promised to customers matches what is delivered (gap 4). In the last major section of the text we focus on strategies for communicating effectively with customers and for ensuring that promises, once made, can and will be kept.

CLOSING THE CUSTOMER GAP

In a broad sense, the gaps model says that a service marketer must first close the customer gap, shown in the accompanying figure, between customer perceptions and expectations. To do so, the provider must close the four provider gaps, or discrepancies within the organization that inhibit delivery of quality service. These are explained as we go through the book. The gaps model focuses on strategies and processes that firms can employ to drive service excellence. It is used to frame the entire text and as an organizing structure for the rest of the chapters. Each section divider focuses on specific aspects of the gaps model that are covered in the chapters that follow it. The full model is drawn together and summarized in the concluding chapter of the text.

The following figure shows a pair of boxes that correspond to two concepts—*customer expectations* and *customer perceptions*—that play a major role in services marketing. Customer perceptions are subjective assessments of actual service experiences. Customer expectations are the standards or reference points for performance against which service experiences are compared and are often formulated in terms of what a customer believes should or will happen. For example, when you visit an expensive restaurant, you expect a certain level of service, one that is considerably different from the level you would expect in a fast-food restaurant.

The Customer Gap

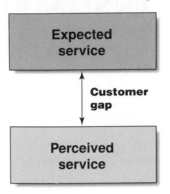

The sources of customer expectations consist of marketer-controlled factors (such as pricing, advertising, and sales promises) as well as factors that the marketer has limited ability to affect (innate personal needs, word-of-mouth communications, and competitive offerings). In a perfect world, expectations and perceptions would be identical: customers would perceive that they receive what they thought they would and should. In practice these concepts are often, even usually, separated by some distance. Broadly, it is the goal of services marketing to bridge this distance, and we devote virtually the entire text to describing strategies and practices designed to close this customer gap.

Considerable evidence exists that consumer evaluation processes differ for goods and services and that these differences affect the way service providers market their organizations. Unfortunately, much of what is known and written about consumer evaluation processes pertains specifically to goods. The assumption appears to be that services, if not identical to goods, are at least similar enough in the consumer's mind that they are chosen and evaluated in the same manner. In Part 1, we show that the unique characteristics of services discussed in Chapter 1—intangibility, heterogeneity, inseparability of production and consumption, and perishability—necessitate different consumer evaluation processes from those used to assess goods.

Because customer satisfaction and customer focus are so critical to competitiveness of firms, any company interested in delivering quality service must begin with a clear understanding of its customers. For this reason we devote the first part of this text to describing the relevant customer concepts so that the focus of everything can relate back to them. We detail what is known about customer behavior in Chapter 2, customer expectations in Chapter 3, and customer perceptions in Chapter 4. Knowing what customers want and how they assess what they receive is the best way to design effective services.

Chapter 2

CONSUMER BEHAVIOR IN SERVICES

This chapter's objectives are to

1. Overview the generic differences in consumer behavior between services and goods.

2. Introduce the aspects of consumer behavior that a marketer must understand in five categories of consumer behavior:
   - Need recognition.
   - Information search.
   - Evaluation of service alternatives.
   - Service purchase and consumption.
   - Postpurchase evaluation.

3. Understand the roles of culture and group consumer behavior in services.

Consumer Problem: Time Deficiency
The Solution: Services

Today's dual-career couples, single-parent families, and two-job families are realizing a burning consumer need: more time. Individuals in these and other nontraditional family configurations are overstressed with their work and home obligations and find dealing with many of life's everyday tasks overwhelming. In a recent study, 50 percent of dual-income primary shoppers with children and 35 percent of their single-income counterparts contend that shopping and service tasks contribute to life's stresses. For many customers all types of shopping have become "drudgery or worse."[1]

The antidote to time deficiency? New services and service features of retailers that recover time for consumers. Innovative new services—pet sitting, plant watering, mail packaging, wedding advising, baby-proofing, executive organizing, personal shopping, even health form preparing—are emerging to deal with tasks that used to be performed by the household but now can be purchased by the time-buying consumer.[2] Conventional services such as retailing and banking are also adding peripheral services to make shopping easier, increasing their hours to suit customer schedules, reducing transaction time, accessing sales and service personnel more easily, improving delivery, and providing merchandise or services at home or work.[3]

And there is an increasingly popular parallel phenomenon in business today called *outsourcing*, which means purchasing whole service functions (such as billing, secretarial services, maintenance, inventory, computer operations, and marketing) from other firms rather than executing them in-house. The motivation in corporations, however, is not so much saving time as it is saving money. Companies that are becoming leaner through corporate restructuring have discovered that in many cases purchasing services outright from another company can be far more economical than the payroll and capital costs of performing them inside.

The primary objective of service producers and marketers is identical to that of all marketers: to develop and provide offerings that satisfy consumer needs and expectations, thereby ensuring their own economic survival. In other words, service marketers need to be able to close the customer gap between expectations and perceptions. To achieve this objective, service providers need to understand how consumers choose and evaluate their service offerings. Unfortunately, most of what is known about consumer evaluation processes pertains specifically to goods. The assumption appears to be that services, if not identical to goods, are at least similar enough in the consumer's mind that they are chosen and evaluated in the same manner.

This chapter challenges that assumption and shows that services' unique characteristics require different consumer evaluation processes from those used in assessing

FIGURE 2.1

Service tasks contribute to consumers' time deficiency

Source: Ryan McVay/ Getty Images

goods. Recognizing these differences and thoroughly understanding consumer evaluation processes are critical for the customer focus on which effective services marketing is based. Because the premise of this text is that the customer is the heart of effective services marketing, we begin with the customer and maintain this focus throughout the text.

Consumers have a more difficult time evaluating and choosing services than goods, partly because services are intangible and nonstandardized and partly because consumption is so closely intertwined with production. These characteristics lead to differences in consumer evaluation processes for goods and services in all stages of the buying process. The chapter is organized into five categories of customer behavior that correspond roughly to stages in the buying process: (1) need recognition, (2) information search, (3) evaluation of alternatives, (4) purchase and consumption, and (5) postpurchase evaluation. Lack of understanding of the way customers assess and choose services in these five fundamental stages leads to a customer gap that must be closed by service marketers.

SERVICES: SEARCH VERSUS EXPERIENCE VERSUS CREDENCE PROPERTIES?

One framework for isolating differences in evaluation processes between goods and services is a classification of properties of offerings proposed by economists.[4] Economists first distinguished between two categories of properties of consumer products: **search qualities,** attributes that a consumer can determine before purchasing a product; and **experience qualities,** attributes that can be discerned only after purchase or during consumption. Search qualities include color, style, price, fit, feel, hardness, and smell; experience qualities include taste and wearability. Goods such as automobiles, clothing, furniture, and jewelry are high in search qualities because their attributes can be almost completely determined and evaluated before purchase. Goods and services such as vacations and restaurant meals are high in experience qualities because their attributes cannot be known or assessed until they have been purchased and are being consumed. A third category, **credence qualities,** includes characteristics that the consumer may find impossible to evaluate even after purchase and consumption.[5] Examples of offerings high in credence qualities are appendix operations and brake relinings on automobiles. Few consumers possess medical or mechanical skills sufficient to evaluate whether these services are necessary or are performed properly, even after they have been prescribed and produced by the seller.

Figure 2.2 arrays goods and services high in search, experience, or credence qualities along a continuum of evaluation ranging from easy to evaluate to difficult to evaluate. Goods high in search qualities are the easiest to evaluate (left end of the continuum). Goods and services high in experience qualities are more difficult to evaluate because they must be purchased and consumed before assessment is possible (center of continuum). Goods and services high in credence qualities are the most difficult to evaluate because the consumer may be unaware of or may lack sufficient knowledge to appraise whether the offerings satisfy given wants or needs even after consumption (right end of the continuum). The major premise of this chapter is that most goods fall to the left of the continuum, whereas most services fall to the right due to three of the distinguishing characteristics described in Chapter 1—intangibility, heterogeneity, and inseparability of production and consumption. These characteristics make services more difficult to evaluate than goods. Difficulty in evaluation, in turn, forces consumers to rely on different cues and processes when evaluating services.

FIGURE 2.2
**Continuum of
Evaluation for
Different Types of
Products**

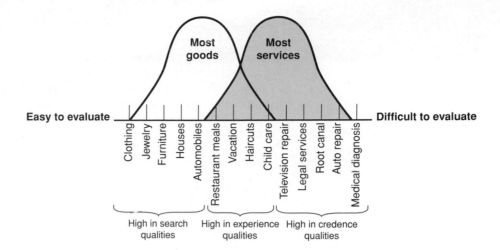

Easy to evaluate ———————————————————— Difficult to evaluate

Clothing
Jewelry
Furniture
Houses
Automobiles
Restaurant meals
Vacation
Haircuts
Child care
Television repair
Legal services
Root canal
Auto repair
Medical diagnosis

High in search
qualities

High in experience
qualities

High in credence
qualities

Most
goods

Most
services

Because experience and credence qualities dominate in services, consumers employ different evaluation processes than those they use with goods, where search qualities dominate. They are also likely to experience the steps in the decision-making process in different orders and at different times from the steps in the classic goods-driven decision-making process (see Exhibit 2.1). Specific areas where characteristics of services may lead to divergent evaluation processes and altered consumer behavior are information search, evaluative criteria, size and composition of the evoked set of alternatives, perceived risk, adoption of innovations, brand loyalty, assessment of value, and attribution of dissatisfaction. Specific topics that need to be understood for services that are not issues in physical goods include services as drama, emotions and mood, role playing, and customer compatibility. Each of these areas is described and discussed in this chapter.

SERVICES: CATEGORIES IN THE DECISION-MAKING PROCESS AND FRAMEWORK OF THE CHAPTER

Using an adaptation of the basic consumer decision-making process shown in Exhibit 2.1, we have organized this chapter into five decision-making categories: (1) need recognition, (2) information search, (3) evaluation of alternatives, (4) purchase and consumption, and (5) postpurchase evaluation (Figure 2.3). In purchase of services, these categories do not occur in a linear sequence as they most often do in the purchase of goods. As you will see in this chapter, one of the major differences between

FIGURE 2.3 **Stages in Consumer Decision Making and Evaluation of Services**

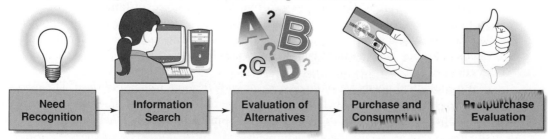

| Need
Recognition | Information
Search | Evaluation of
Alternatives | Purchase and
Consumption | Postpurchase
Evaluation |

2.1 REVIEW OF SELECTED BASIC MARKETING PRINCIPLES: CONSUMER BEHAVIOR

If you have taken a basic marketing course, you learned certain core material about consumer behavior. In writing this text we set out to extend the basic marketing information you currently possess and convey to you (1) completely new material not contained in basic marketing courses and (2) ways to adjust familiar marketing principles to make them effective in services marketing.

In many of the chapters that are not completely new material (such as this chapter), we will offer you an "Exhibit" such as this one that provides a concise overview of marketing basics you should already possess to fully understand the chapter. For most of you, this overview will jog your memory and position the chapter material in the context of what you already know. For others, this overview may alert you to information you missed in your basic course or that is wholly new because you have not taken a previous marketing course. For those in the latter category, we provide references in many of the exhibits that can be examined to bring you to the same level as those who have taken a marketing course previously.

Now to get back to marketing basics about consumer behavior. Among these basics are the following:

Marketing Basic 2-1
Consumers make decisions and process information about products and services in different ways. Sometimes they go through an effortful, systematic, step-by-step process. They experience a need, consider alternatives to fill that need,

evaluate each alternative, and then select one of the considered alternatives. Often they use this form of processing when making expensive purchases such as cars and education. Other times they use a more mindless, less effortful style of decision making. They may purchase a meal at Burger King simply because they are passing by, and they may choose a particular form of car insurance just because they know its brand name. A basic marketing text or consumer behavior text can provide greater detail on these different approaches to processing.

For this chapter we will use an adapted version of the traditional decision-making process to structure a discussion of consumer behavior in services. Although we recognize that not all service decisions are made this way, we find it the best way to organize our discussion of consumer behavior. The steps in the traditional process include

1. *Need recognition* The customer has a need to fulfill or a problem to solve.

2. *Information search* The customer seeks out information to help satisfy the need.

3. *Evaluation of alternatives* The customer selects a subset of the alternatives and evaluates them.

4. *Purchase* The customer chooses a particular brand and then buys it.

5. *Purchase outcome* The customer evaluates the choice made and decides whether it lives up to expectations.

goods and services is that a greater portion of the evaluation of services succeeds purchase and consumption than is the case with goods. Therefore, while our categorization here follows the sequence consumers use with goods, we will show how these stages in services depart from evaluation of goods.

Need Recognition

The process of buying a service begins with the recognition that a need or want exists. Although there are many different ways to characterize needs, the most widely known is Maslow's hierarchy, which specifies five need categories arranged in a sequence from basic lower-level needs to higher-level needs. Five needs are identified: physiological, safety and security, social, ego, and self-actualization. Services can fill all these needs, and they become increasingly important for social, ego, and self-actualization needs.

Physiological needs are *biological needs such as food, water, and sleep.* The recognition of these basic needs is fairly straightforward. Recall the last time you were on vacation, perhaps sightseeing in a new place. At some point around lunchtime, you recognized that you were thirsty and hungry and needed to stop and have lunch. Restaurants, coffee shops, bistros, and other service establishments that provided food and water likely became more noticeable. If you were sightseeing in Tokyo, you would notice that virtually every other street contains a large vending machine with ice cold drinks to quench the thirst of citizens and visitors that are suffering from the intense heat. If you have ever backpacked in Europe, you probably identified the need for sleep the same way you realized your hunger or thirst, reaching a point of exhaustion at the end of a day.

Safety and security needs include *shelter, protection, and security.* Immediately following the terrorist attacks on New York, consumers began to recognize their vulnerability and sought ways to increase their safety and security. Instead of purchasing vacations and making business trips, consumers switched service purchases to bus tickets, movie rentals, insurance, and other services to satisfy their needs for safety and security.

Social needs are for *affection, friendship, and acceptance.* Social needs are critical to all cultures but are particularly important in the East. In countries like Japan and China, consumers place a great deal of value on social and belonging needs.[6] They spend more time with their families and work colleagues than Westerners and therefore consume more services that can be shared. The Japanese spend more annually per capita in restaurants, for example, than any other country—$1,670 per year compared to $936 in the United States, $767 in Britain, and a mere $466 in France.[7] Consumers in all cultures use many types of services to address social needs, including health and dance clubs, dating services, and vacations (like Club Med), where socializing among strangers is encouraged.

Ego needs are for *prestige, success, accomplishment, and self-esteem.* Food, safety, and belonging are not enough for many consumers, especially those from Western cultures. Individuals also seek to look good to others and to feel good about themselves because of what they have accomplished. Needs to improve oneself and achieve success are responsible for the growth of education, training, and other services that increase the skills and prestige of consumers.

Self-actualization involves *self-fulfillment and enriching experiences.* Consumers desire to live up to their full potential and enjoy themselves. Some consumers purchase experiences such as skydiving, jungle safaris, and bungee jumping for the pure thrill of the experience, a need quite different from the others in Maslow's hierarchy. Others self-actualize through taking oil-painting or poetry-writing classes, thereby expressing feelings and meanings that are unrelated to the basic needs of day-to-day living.

The hierarchical nature of Maslow's need categorization has been disputed, and evidence exists that people with unfilled basic needs can be motivated to self-actualize. We are not concerned with the hierarchical nature in this section; we use it only as a way to discuss different drives that lead customers to the next stages of consumer behavior in services.

Information Search

Use of Personal Sources

Consumers obtain information about products and services from personal sources (like friends or experts) and from nonpersonal sources (such as mass or selective media). When purchasing goods, consumers make generous use of both personal and nonpersonal sources because both effectively convey information about search qualities.

When purchasing services, on the other hand, consumers seek and rely to a greater extent on personal sources for several reasons. First, mass and selective media can

FIGURE 2.4

Consumers seek and rely on personal sources in purchasing experience goods and services.

Source: Mark Lewis/Getty Images

convey information about search qualities but can communicate little about experience qualities. By asking friends or experts about services, however, the consumer can obtain information vicariously about experience qualities. Second, nonpersonal sources of information may not be available because (*a*) many service providers are local, independent merchants with neither the experience nor the funds for advertising; (*b*) cooperative advertising (advertising funded jointly by the retailer and the manufacturer) is used infrequently with services because most local providers are both producer and retailer of the service; and (*c*) professional associations banned advertising for so many years that both professionals and consumers tend to resist its use even though it is now permitted. Third, because consumers can discover few attributes before purchase of a service, they may feel greater risk in selecting a little-known alternative.

Personal influence becomes pivotal as product complexity increases and when objective standards by which to evaluate a product decrease (that is, when experience qualities are high).[8] Most managers in service industries recognize the strong influence of word of mouth in services (Figure 2.4).

Next, consumers may find postpurchase information seeking more essential with services than with goods because services possess experience qualities that cannot be adequately assessed before purchase. One model of audience response to communication[9] describes the situation that occurs frequently when consumers select services:

1. The consumer selects from among virtually indistinguishable alternatives.

2. Through experience the consumer develops an attitude toward the service.

3. After the development of an attitude, the consumer learns more about the service by paying attention to messages supporting his or her choice.

In contrast to the conventional view of audience response to communication, where consumers seek information and evaluate products before purchase, with services most evaluation follows purchase.

Perceived Risk

Although some degree of perceived risk probably accompanies all purchase transactions, more risk would appear to be involved in the purchase of services than in the purchase of goods because services are intangible, nonstandardized, and usually sold without guarantees or warranties.

First, the intangible nature of services and their high level of experience qualities imply that services generally must be selected on the basis of less prepurchase information than is the case for products. Second, because services are nonstandardized, there will always be uncertainty about the outcome and consequences each time a service is purchased. Third, service purchases may involve more perceived risk than product purchases because, with few exceptions, services are not accompanied by warranties or guarantees. The dissatisfied service purchaser can rarely "return" a service; he or she has already consumed it by the time he or she realizes his or her dissatisfaction. Finally, many services (like medical diagnosis or pest control) are so technical or specialized that consumers possess neither the knowledge nor the experience to evaluate whether they are satisfied, even after they have consumed the service.

The increase in perceived risk involved in purchasing services suggests the use of strategies to reduce risk. Where appropriate, guarantees of satisfaction may be offered. To the extent possible, service providers should emphasize employee training and other procedures to standardize their offerings so that consumers learn to expect a given level of quality and satisfaction.

Evaluation of Service Alternatives

Evoked Set

The evoked set of alternatives—that group of products a consumer considers acceptable options in a given product category—is likely to be smaller with services than with goods. One reason involves differences in retailing between goods and services. To purchase goods, consumers generally shop in retail stores that display competing products in close proximity, clearly demonstrating the possible alternatives. To purchase services, on the other hand, the consumer visits an establishment (such as a bank, a dry cleaner, or a hair salon) that almost always offers only a single "brand" for sale. A second reason for the smaller evoked set is that consumers are unlikely to find more than one or two businesses providing the same services in a given geographic area, whereas they may find numerous retail stores carrying the identical manufacturer's product. A third reason for a smaller evoked set is the difficulty of obtaining adequate prepurchase information about services.

Faced with the task of collecting and evaluating experience qualities, consumers may simply select the first acceptable alternative rather than searching many alternatives. In consumer behavior terms, the consumer's evoked set of alternatives is smaller with services than with goods. The Internet has the potential to widen the set of alternatives.

For nonprofessional services, consumers' decisions often entail the choice between performing the services for themselves or hiring someone to perform them. Working people may choose between cleaning their own homes or hiring housekeepers, between altering their families' clothes or taking them to a tailor, even between staying home to take care of their children or engaging a day care center to provide child care. Consumers may consider themselves as sources of supply for many services, including lawn care, tax preparation, and preparing meals. This means that the customer's evoked set frequently includes self-provision of the service.

Nonprofessional service providers must recognize that they often replace or compete with the consumer, which may imply more exacting standards from the consumer and may require more individualized, personal attention from the service provider. Consumers know what they expect from providers of housecleaning or lawn care or day care because they know what they are accustomed to providing for themselves. The alert service marketer will be certain to research consumers' expectations and demands in such situations.

Technology is also a viable alternative for many services, as the Technology Spotlight demonstrates.

Technology Spotlight

Self-Service Technologies: How Much Do Customers Like Providing Their Own Services?

One of the major recent changes in consumer behavior is the growing tendency for consumers to interact with technology to create services instead of interacting with a live service firm employee. *Self-service technologies (SSTs)* are technological interfaces that allow customers to produce services independent of direct service employee involvement. Examples of SSTs that you are probably very familiar with are automated teller machines, pay-at-the-pump terminals at gas stations, and automated hotel checkout and check-in. All forms of services over the Internet are also SSTs, many of which are very innovative. In some states, for example, users can file for divorce or evict a tenant using an automated kiosk rather than go through the traditional court system. Electronic self-ordering is being developed at fast-food chains, and self-scanning at grocery stores is already available through companies such as Harris Teeter.

The accompanying figure shows a comprehensive set of categories and examples of SSTs in use today. The columns of the matrix represent the types of technologies that companies are using to interface with customers in self-service encounters, and the rows show purposes of the technologies from the customer perspective. As you can see, customers use the technologies to provide customer service (deal with questions about accounts, bill paying, and delivery tracking), to conduct transactions (order, buy, and exchange resources with companies without direct interaction), and to provide self-help (learn, receive information, train themselves, and provide their own services).

A recent study asked customers across a wide range of industries and applications what they think of SSTs and found that they have very strong feelings about them. They both love and hate them depending on a few key conditions. Customers love them when:

- *SSTs bail them out of difficult situations.* A single parent with a sleeping child in the car needs to get gas and money for work the following morning. Using a pay-at-the-pump gas station and drive-up ATM allows the parent to accomplish these tasks without leaving the sleeping child.

- *SSTs are better than the interpersonal alternative.* SSTs have the potential to save customers time, money, and psychological costs. The Internet, in particular, allows customers to shop at any time and complete transactions more quickly than they could in person. Internet loans and mortgages also allow customers to avoid the anxiety of meeting a banker in person and feeling judged.

- *SSTs work.* When SSTs work as they are supposed to, customers are impressed. Many of you have had the experience of using one-click ordering at amazon.com. When these transactions work smoothly, as they usually do after the proper setup, the transactions are satisfying.

On the other hand, customers hate SSTs when the following problems occur:

- *They fail.* The researchers found that 60 percent of the negative stories they heard stemmed from failures of SSTs. Broken machines, failed PIN numbers, websites that were down, and items not shipped as promised all frustrate consumers.

- *They are poorly designed.* Poorly designed technologies that are difficult to use or understand create hassles for customers, making them feel it is not worth using them. Websites that are difficult to maneuver are particularly troublesome. If customers cannot

Service Purchase and Consumption

Emotion and Mood

Emotion and mood are feeling states that influence people's (and therefore customers') perceptions and evaluations of their experiences. Moods are distinguished from emotions in that *moods* are transient feeling states that occur at specific times and in specific situations, whereas *emotions* are more intense, stable, and pervasive.[10]

Because services are experiences, moods and emotions are critical factors that

reach information they need within a few clicks (some say two clicks are all that customers will tolerate), then customers shun the website.

- *The customer messes up.* Customers dislike using technologies they feel they cannot perform adequately. Even though they feel partial responsibility, they will avoid using them in the future. A common frustration today is having various user names and passwords for different websites. When confronted with a screen requiring this information—and not recalling it accurately—many customers will give up and go elsewhere.

- *There is no service recovery.* When the process or technology fails, SSTs rarely provide ways to recover on the spot. In these cases customers must then call or

visit the company, precisely what they were trying to avoid by using the self-service technology.

It is increasingly evident that these technological innovations will be a critical component of customer–firm interactions. If these SSTs are to succeed, the researchers contend, they must become more reliable, be better than the interpersonal alternatives, and have recovery systems in place when they fail.

Sources: M. L. Meuter, A. L. Ostom, R. I. Roundtree, and M. J. Bitner, "Self-Service Technologies: Understanding Customer Satisfaction with Technology-Based Service Encounters," *Journal of Marketing* 64 (July 2000), pp. 50–64; M. J. Bitner, "Self-Service Technologies: What Do Customers Expect?" *Marketing Management,* Spring 2001, pp. 10–11.

Interface ↘ Purpose	Categories and Examples of SSTs in Use			
	Telephone/Interactive Voice Response	**Online/Internet**	**Interactive Kiosks**	**Video/CD**
Customer Service	• Telephone banking • Flight information • Order status	• Package tracking • Account information	• ATMs • Hotel checkout	
Transactions	• Telephone banking • Prescription refills	• Retail purchasing • Financial transactions	• Pay at the pump • Hotel checkout • Car rental	
Self-Help	• Information telephone lines	• Internet information search • Distance learning	• Blood pressure machines • Tourist information	• Tax preparation software • Television/CD-based training

shape the perceived effectiveness of service encounters. If a service customer is in a bad mood when she enters a service establishment, service provision will likely be interpreted more negatively than if she were in a buoyant, positive mood. Similarly, if a service provider is irritable or sullen, his interaction with customers will likely be colored by that mood. Furthermore, when another customer in a service establishment is cranky or frustrated, whether from problems with the service or from existing emotions unrelated to the service, his or her mood affects the provision of service for all customers who sense the negative mood. In sum, any service characterized by human interaction is strongly dependent on the moods and emotions of the service provider, the service customer, and other customers receiving the service at the same time.

In what specific ways can mood affect the behavior of service customers? First, positive moods can make customers more obliging and willing to participate in behaviors that help service encounters succeed.[11] A customer in a good emotional state is probably more willing to follow an exercise regimen prescribed by a physical therapist, bus his or her own dishes at a fast-food restaurant, and overlook delays in service. A customer in a negative mood may be less likely to engage in behaviors essential to the effectiveness of the service but that seem difficult or overwhelming: abstaining from chocolates when on a diet program with Weight Watchers, taking frequent aerobic classes from a health club, or completing homework assigned in a class.

A second way that moods and emotions influence service customers is to bias the way they judge service encounters and providers. Mood and emotions enhance and amplify experiences, making them either more positive or more negative than they might seem in the absence of the moods and emotions.[12] After losing a big account, a saleswoman catching an airline flight will be more incensed with delays and crowding than she might be on a day when business went well. Conversely, the positive mood of a services customer at a dance or restaurant will heighten the experience, leading to positive evaluations of the service establishment. The direction of the bias in evaluation is consistent with the polarity (positive or negative) of the mood or emotion.

FIGURE 2.5

Positive moods of customers in a dance club heighten their service experiences

Source: Mark Richards/Photo Edit

Finally, moods and emotions affect the way information about service is absorbed and retrieved. As memories about a service are encoded by a consumer, the feelings associated with the encounter become an inseparable part of the memory. If travelers fall in love during a vacation in the Bahamas, they may hold favorable assessments of the destination due more to their emotional state than to the destination itself. Conversely, if a customer first realizes his level of fitness is poor when on a guest pass in a health club, the negative feelings may be encoded and retrieved every time he thinks of the health club or, for that matter, any health club.

Service marketers need to be aware of the moods and emotions of customers and of service employees and should attempt to influence those moods and emotions in positive ways. They need to cultivate positive moods and emotions such as joy, delight, and contentment and discourage negative emotions such as distress, frustration, anger, and disgust.

Service Provision as Drama

The metaphor of a theater is a useful framework for describing and analyzing service performances. Both the theater and service organizations aim to create and maintain a desirable impression before an audience and recognize that the way to accomplish this is by carefully managing the actors and the physical setting of their behavior.[13] The service marketer must play many drama-related roles—including director, choreographer, and writer—to be sure the performances of the actors are pleasing to the audience. The Walt Disney Company explicitly considers its service provision a "performance," even using show business terms such as "cast member," "onstage," and "show" to describe the operations at Disneyland and Walt Disney World.[14]

The skill of the service **actors** in performing their routines, the way they appear, and their commitment to the "show" are all essential to service delivery. Although service actors are present in most service performances, their importance increases in three conditions. First, service actors are critical when the degree of direct personal contact is high. Consider the difference between a visit to Denny's and a trip to a Japanese restaurant like Benihana. In many cases customers go to Japanese steakhouses as much for the show as for the food, and they eagerly anticipate the performance of the real-time chef who twirls knives, jokes with the guests, and even flips shrimp into his hat or onto guests' plates. (It is interesting to note that in Japan the chef is not the focus of attention in this type of restaurant and prepares the food with quiet dignity.) The second condition where service actors' skills are critical is when the services involve repeat contact. Nurses in hospitals, favorite waiters or tennis pros in resorts, or captains on cruises are essential characters in service theater, and their individual performances can make or break the success of the services. The third condition in which contact personnel are critical is when they have discretion in determining the nature of the service and how it is delivered. When you consider the quality of the education you are receiving in college, you are certain to focus most of your evaluation on your professors' delivery of classes. In education, as in other services such as medical and legal services, the professional is the key actor in the performance.[15]

FIGURE 2.6
The delivery of service can be conceived as drama

Source: © Dean Conger/CORBIS

Ray Fisk and Steve Grove, two experts in the area of service dramaturgy, point out that service actors' performances can be characterized as sincere or cynical.[16] A sincere performance occurs when an actor becomes one with the role that she is playing, whereas a cynical performance occurs when an actor views a performance only as a means to an end, such as getting paid for doing the job. When a service employee takes the time to listen and help, the performance is sincere and often noteworthy. Unfortunately, all too many examples of cynical performances exist where front line "actors" seem to care little about the "audience" of customers. As Grove and Fisk point out, a single employee can ruin the service experience by ridiculing other cast members' efforts, failing to perform his role correctly, or projecting the wrong image. To create the right impression, three characteristics are necessary: loyalty, discipline, and circumspection.[17]

The **physical setting** of the service can be likened to the staging of a theatrical production including scenery, props, and other physical cues to create desired impressions. Among a setting's features that may influence the character of a service are the colors or brightness of the service's surroundings; the volume and pitch of sounds in the setting; the smells, movement, freshness, and temperature of the air; the use of space; the style and comfort of the furnishings; and the setting's design and cleanliness.[18] As an example, the service provided by a cruise ship features its layout (broad and open), decor and comfort (large, cushioned deck chairs), furnishings (lots of polished wood and brass), and cleanliness ("ship shape"). The setting increases in importance when the environment distinguishes the service. Consider how critical the setting is for a downtown law firm, which must appear professional, capable, even imposing.[19] In essence, the delivery of service can be conceived as drama, where service personnel are the actors, service customers are the audience, physical evidence of the service is the setting, and the process of service assembly is the performance.[20]

The drama metaphor offers a useful way to improve service performances. Selection of personnel can be viewed as auditioning the actors. An actor's personal appearance, manner, facial expression, gestures, personality, and demographic profile can be determined in large part in the interview or audition. Southwest Airlines is well known for auditioning personnel in teams, watching how potential employees interact with each other and whether their personalities are sociable. Training of personnel can become rehearsing. Clearly defining the role can be seen as scripting the performance. Creation of the service environment involves setting the stage. Finally, deciding which aspects of the service should be performed in the presence of the customer (onstage) and which should be performed in the back room (backstage) helps define the performances the customer experiences.

Service Roles and Scripts

Roles are combinations of social cues that guide and direct behavior in a given setting.[21] Just as there are roles in dramatic performances, there are roles in service delivery. For example, the role of a hostess in a restaurant is to acknowledge and greet customers, find out how many people are in their group, and then lead them to a table where they will eat. The success of any service performance depends in part on how well the role is performed by the service actor and how well the team of players—the "role set" of both service employees and customers—acts out their roles.[22] Service employees need to perform their roles according to the expectations of the customer; if they do not, the customer may be frustrated and disappointed. As we discussed earlier in this chapter, the customer's role must also be performed well. If customers are informed and educated about their roles, and if they cooperate with the provider in following the script, successful service provision is likely.

One factor that influences the effectiveness of role performance is the **script**—the logical sequence of events expected by the customer, involving her as either a participant or an observer.[23] Service scripts consist of sequences of actions associated with actors and objects that, through repeated involvement, define what the customer expects.[24] Receiving a dental checkup is a service experience for which a well-defined script exists. For a checkup the consumer expects the following sequence: enter the reception area, greet a receptionist, sit in a waiting room, follow the dental hygienist to a separate room, recline in a chair while his teeth are cleaned by the hygienist, be examined by the dentist, then pay for the services. When the service conforms to this script, there is a feeling of confirmed expectations and satisfaction. Deviations from the service script lead to confusion and dissatisfaction. Suppose, upon moving to a new town, you went to a dentist who had no receptionist and no waiting area, only a doorbell in a cubicle. Suppose, upon answering the doorbell, an employee in shorts took you to a large room where all patients were in a dental chairs facing each other. These actions and objects are certainly not in the traditional service script for dentistry and might create considerable uncertainty and doubt in patients.

Some services are more scripted than others. We would expect very expensive, customized services like spa vacations to be less scripted than mass-produced services such as fast food ("Have a nice day!") and airline travel.

The Compatibility of Service Customers

We have just discussed the roles of employees and customers receiving service. We now want to focus on the role of *other customers* receiving service at the same time. Consider how central the mere presence of other customers is in churches, restaurants, dances, bars, clubs, and spectator sports: If no one else shows up, customers will not get to socialize with others, one of the primary expectations in these types of services. However, if customers become so dense that crowding occurs, customers may also be dissatisfied.[25] The way other customers behave with many services such as airlines, education, clubs, and social organizations also exerts a major influence on a customer's experience.[26] In general, the presence, behavior, and similarity of other customers receiving services has a strong impact on the satisfaction and dissatisfaction of any given customer.[27]

Customers can be incompatible for many reasons—differences in beliefs, values, experiences, abilities to pay, appearance, age, and health, to name just a few. The service marketer must anticipate, acknowledge, and deal with heterogeneous consumers who have the potential to be incompatible. The service marketer can also bring homogeneous customers together and solidify relationships between them, which increases the cost to the customer of switching service providers.[28] Customer compatibility is a factor that influences customer satisfaction, particularly in high-contact services.

Postpurchase Evaluation

Attribution of Dissatisfaction

When consumers are disappointed with purchases—because the products did not fulfill the intended needs, did not perform satisfactorily, or were not worth their price—they may attribute their dissatisfaction to a number of different sources, among them the producers, the retailers, or themselves. Because consumers participate to a greater extent in the definition and production of services, they may feel more responsible for their dissatisfaction when they purchase services than when they purchase goods. As an example, consider a consumer purchasing a haircut; receiving the cut she desires depends in part on her clear specifications of her needs to the stylist. If disappointed, she may blame either the stylist (for lack of skill) or herself (for choosing the wrong stylist or for not communicating her own needs clearly).

The quality of many services depends on the information the customer brings to the service encounter: A doctor's accurate diagnosis requires a conscientious case history and a clear articulation of symptoms; a dry cleaner's success in removing a spot depends on the consumer's knowledge of its cause; and a tax preparer's satisfactory performance relies on the receipts saved by the consumer. Failure to obtain satisfaction with any of these services may not be blamed completely on the retailer or producer, because the consumer must adequately perform his or her part in the production process also.

With products, on the other hand, a consumer's main form of participation is the act of purchase. The consumer may attribute failure to receive satisfaction to her own decision-making error, but she holds the producer responsible for product performance. Goods usually carry warranties or guarantees with purchase, emphasizing that the producer believes that if something goes wrong, it is not the fault of the consumer. With services, consumers attribute some of their dissatisfaction to their own inability to specify or perform their part of the service. They also may complain less frequently about services than about goods because of their belief that they themselves are partly responsible for their dissatisfaction.

Innovation Diffusion

The rate of diffusion of an innovation depends on consumers' perceptions of the innovation with regard to five characteristics: relative advantage, compatibility, communicability, divisibility, and complexity.[29] An offering that has a relative advantage over existing or competing products; that is compatible with existing norms, values, and behaviors; that is communicable; and that is divisible (can be tried or tested on a limited basis) diffuses more quickly than others. An offering that is complex (difficult to understand or use) diffuses more slowly than others.

Considered as a group, services are less communicable, less divisible, more complex, and probably less compatible than goods. They are less communicable because they are intangible (their features cannot be displayed, illustrated, or compared) and because they are often unique to each buyer (as in a medical diagnosis or dental care). Services are less divisible because they are usually impossible to sample or test on a limited basis. (How does one "sample" a medical diagnosis? A lawyer's services in settling a divorce? A haircut?) Services are frequently more complex than goods because they are composed of a bundle of different attributes, not all of which will be offered to every buyer on each purchase.

Finally, services may be incompatible with existing values and behaviors, especially if consumers are accustomed to providing the service for themselves. As an illustration, consider a novel day care center that cooks breakfast for children so that parents can arrive at work early. Mothers accustomed to performing this service for their children may resist adopting the innovation because it requires a change in habit, in behavior, even in values. Consumers adopt innovations in services more slowly than they adopt innovations in goods.

Marketers may need to concentrate on incentives to trial when introducing new services. The awareness–interest–evaluation stages of the adoption process may best be bypassed in some service situations because of the difficulty and inefficiency of communicating information about intangibles. Offering free visits, dollars-off coupons, and samples may be appropriate strategies to speed diffusion of innovations in services.

Brand Loyalty

The degree to which consumers are committed to particular brands of goods or services depends on a number of factors: the cost of changing brands (switching cost), the availability of substitutes, the perceived risk associated with the purchase, and the degree to which they have obtained satisfaction in the past. Because it may be more costly to change brands of services, because awareness of substitutes is limited, and because higher risks may accompany services, consumers are more likely to remain customers of particular companies with services than with goods.

Greater search costs and monetary costs may be involved in changing brands of services than in changing brands of goods. Because of the difficulty of obtaining information about services, consumers may be unaware of alternatives or substitutes for their brands, or they may be uncertain about the ability of alternatives to increase satisfaction over present brands. Monetary fees may accompany brand switching in many services: physicians often require complete physicals on the initial visit; dentists sometimes demand new X rays; and health clubs frequently charge "membership fees" at the outset to obtain long-term commitments from customers.

If consumers perceive greater risks with services, as is hypothesized here, they probably depend on brand loyalty to a greater extent than when they purchase products. Brand loyalty, described as a means of economizing decision effort by substituting habit for repeated, deliberate decision, functions as a device for reducing the risks of consumer decisions.

A final reason consumers may be more brand loyal with services is the recognition of the need for repeated patronage in order to obtain optimum satisfaction from the seller. Becoming a "regular customer" allows the seller to gain knowledge of the customer's tastes and preferences, ensures better treatment, and encourages more interest in the consumer's satisfaction. Thus a consumer may exhibit brand loyalty to cultivate a satisfying relationship with the seller.

Brand loyalty has two sides. The fact that a service provider's own customers are brand loyal is not a problem. The fact that the customers of the provider's competition are difficult to capture, however, creates special challenges. The marketer may need to direct communications and strategy to the customers of competitors, emphasizing attributes and strengths that he or she possesses and the competitor lacks. Marketers can also facilitate switching from competitors' services by reducing switching costs. For example, AT&T promised MCI customers that it would handle the transfer from MCI to AT&T and also guaranteed it would pay to allow the customer to switch back if necessary, making it virtually costless for customers to switch long-distance carriers.

THE ROLE OF CULTURE IN SERVICES

Culture is learned, shared, and transmitted from one generation to the next, and is multidimensional. Culture is important in services marketing because of its effects on the ways customers evaluate and use services. It also influences how companies and their service employees interact with customers. Culture is important when we consider international services marketing—taking the services from one country and offering them in others—but it is also critical within countries. More and more, individual countries are becoming multicultural, making the need to understand how this factor affects evaluation, purchase, and use of services critical. Because culture is important in every stage of the decision-making process for services—and is likely to become more so in the future—we show it as surrounding the chapter's framework (see Figure 2.7).

FIGURE 2.7 **Culture Pervades all Categories of the Consumer Decision-Making Process in Services**

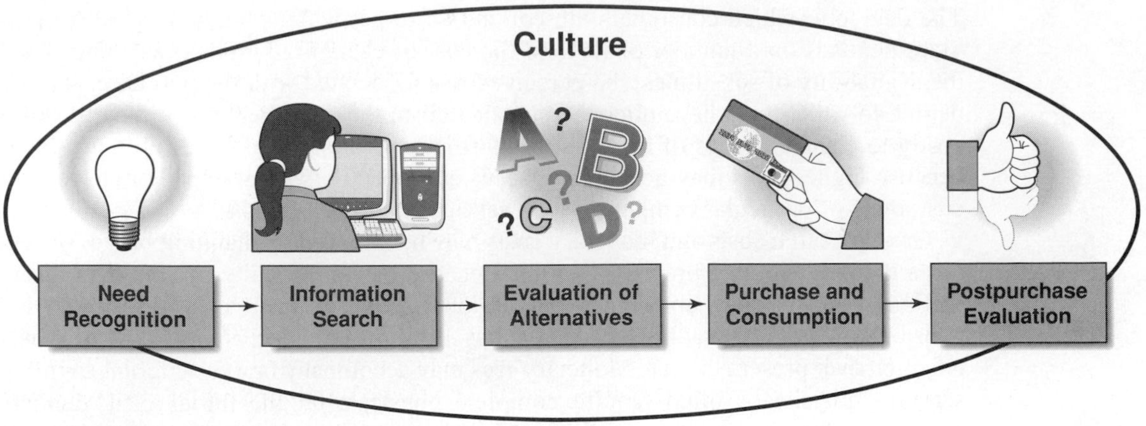

Unfortunately, human nature dictates that we tend to view other cultures through the often cluttered lens of our own.[30] One expert on culture, Edward T. Hall, observed that in the United States people tend to view foreigners as "underdeveloped Americans."[31] Another, Geert Hofstede, sums up the message of one of his books as follows:

> Everybody looks at the world from behind the windows of a cultural home, and everybody prefers to act as if people from other countries have something special about them (a national character) but home is normal. Unfortunately, there is no normal position in cultural matters.[32]

Definitions of the elements of culture vary, but a simple list of the major areas would include (1) language (both verbal and nonverbal), (2) values and attitudes, (3) manners and customs, (4) material culture, (5) aesthetics, and (6) education and social institutions.[33] These **cultural universals** are manifestations of the way of life of any group of people. Services marketers must be particularly sensitive to culture because of customer contact and interaction with employees. Language is discussed in a later chapter, but the other elements of culture as they affect consumer behavior are covered next.

Values and Attitudes Differ across Cultures

Values and attitudes help to determine what members of a culture think is right, important, and/or desirable. Because behaviors, including consumer behaviors, flow from values and attitudes, services marketers who want their services adopted across cultures must understand these differences.

Although American brands often have an "exotic" appeal to other cultures, U.S. firms should not count on this as a long-term strategy. In the late 1990s Wal-Mart found that the cachet of U.S. brands was falling in Mexico. The Mexican news media alerted consumers to shoddy foreign goods, and some Wal-Mart customers turned to a spirit of nationalism. The retailer responded with an "Hecho en Mexico" program similar to the "Made in the U.S.A." program that was successful in the United States. In some situations it is more than a case of nationalism: brand attitudes are negatively influenced by specific prejudices toward "dominating" cultures. The Korean ban on Japanese movies and the French phobia about EuroDisney are good examples of the latter.

Manners and Customs

Manners and customs represent a culture's views of appropriate ways of behaving. It is important to monitor differences in manners and customs because they can have a direct effect on the service encounter. Central and Eastern Europeans are perplexed by Western expectations that unhappy workers put on a "happy face" when dealing with customers. As an example, McDonald's requires Polish employees to smile whenever they interact with customers. Such a requirement strikes many employees as artificial and insincere. The fast-food giant has learned to encourage managers in Poland to probe employee problems and to assign troubled workers to the kitchen rather to the food counter.[34]

Habits are similar to customs, and these tend to vary by culture. Japanese take very few vacations, and when they do they like to spend 7 to 10 days. Their vacations are unusually crammed with activities—Rome, Geneva, Paris, and London in 10 days is representative.[35] The travel industry has been responsive to the special preferences of these big-spending Japanese tourists. The Four Seasons Hotel chain provides special pillows, kimonos, slippers, and teas for Japanese guests. Virgin Atlantic Airways and other long-haul carriers have interactive screens available for each passenger, allowing viewing of Japanese (or American, French, and so on) movies, TV, and even gambling if regulators approve. Differences across cultures influence how consumers evaluate service, as is explained in the Global Feature.

Material Culture

Material culture consists of the tangible products of culture, or as comedian George Carlin puts it, "the stuff we own." What people own and how they use and display material possessions vary around the world. Cars, houses, clothes, and furniture are examples of material culture.

The majority of Mexicans do not own cars, limiting retailers' geographic reach. Further, most Mexicans own small refrigerators and have limited incomes that restrict the amount of groceries they can purchase at one time. Instead of the once-per-week shopping trip typical in the United States, Mexicans make frequent smaller trips. Promotional programs in Mexico are also constrained by the availability of media. Ownership of televisions and radios affects the ability of services marketers to reach target audiences.

Zoos as entertainment represent an interesting reflection of culture's influence. Any American visiting the Tokyo Zoo is impressed by two things: the fine collection of animals and the small cages in which the animals are kept. To the Japanese who live in one of the most crowded countries in the world and own relatively small houses, the small cages seem appropriate, whereas to the American eye the small cages may look like mistreatment.

Sometimes the most mundane financial services require special attention in foreign markets. Bank branches in Spain, compared with branches in many other European countries, have traditionally been unusually small and numerous. Spaniards like to use and therefore be close to their cash. They seem to have an aversion to checks and credit cards because, according to some, both instruments create transaction records that can be tracked by tax authorities. Thus walking-distance convenience is a key attribute of banking services in Spain. Meanwhile, in Mexico with interest rates of more than 30 percent and credit purchases representing few sales, customers also need access to cash. One reason for Kmart's greater success in Mexico compared with Wal-Mart's is its decision to place a bank branch inside the store to facilitate customers' cash access.[36]

As we emphasize in this chapter, the way service experiences differ across cultures influences how consumers evaluate service. Until recently, service differences across cultures were observed anecdotally rather than systematically, and we had few guidelines or criteria on which to evaluate these differences. One notable exception is a current study that examined differences in the service experience across two cultures, the United States and Japan, and provided both vivid examples and solid evidence of cultural subtleties that affect service encounters. The examples came from interviews with Japanese students studying at an American university and are categorized by dimensions of service behavior. Following these examples, which come directly from the study, we summarize a few of the interesting research findings.

- *Authenticity.* In Japan, "every clerk has the same type of smile . . . the smile is not natural," and "everything is done according to the manual." In the United States, clerks "act independently," and "there is more variation in treatment." This is very refreshing.

- *Caring.* Caring or concern is the most important dimension in Japan. The "customer is God." In the United States, sales clerks are always answering, "I don't know," and "they don't seem to care."

- *Control.* Control seems very important to Americans. In Japan, on the other hand, customers are "kind of timid or nervous. They tend to give the controlling interest to the clerk." Control is not important in Japan.

- *Courtesy.* In Japan, "if we find something bad about the service like, for example, they didn't apologize for spilling water, we never go back there again." Courtesy is very important in Japan.

- *Formality.* In Japan, formal treatment is a requirement for all service. Treatment in the United States is much more informal.

- *Friendliness.* "In the U.S. I feel like I'm supposed to treat serving people as equals. In Japan, that is not so." In Japan, friendliness can be disrespectful and formality is usually preferred. In the United States, friendliness is expected.

- *Personalization.* "In Japan, you are treated the same." The waiters "are almost faceless, too businesslike and whoever comes, they treat them like the same person." In the United States, service is much more personalized and names are used more frequently.

- *Promptness.* "In the U.S., the sales clerk and the customer expect to have a nice little chat . . . in Japan, many people would prefer a sales clerk who is quick but unfriendly."

After measuring and testing cultural dimensions across samples from the two countries, the author developed several compelling insights that are critical for understanding what service providers need to do to influence perceptions and evaluation of service encounters.

First, themes of friendliness, being personal, authenticity, and promptness dominate in the United States, whereas caring and concern are central in Japan. This difference can be explained by the cultural focus on individualism in the United States and the emphasis on empathy (being attentive, caring, and kind) in Japan. Civility, an important dimension in both countries, had different meanings: in the United States it meant paying attention and providing good service, whereas in Japan it meant being patient and fair. Authenticity is a relevant dimension in the United States but not in Japan, likely based on the Japanese focus on playing a role rather than expressing individual feelings.

It is evident from this study, and from others like it, that understanding culture is pivotal to being evaluated as an effective service provider. Providing the same service experience offered in the home country may not be successful when a service is extended to other cultural groups.

Source: Reprinted with permission of Elsevier Science Limited from K. F. Winsted, "The Service Experience in Two Cultures," *Journal of Retailing* 73, no. 3 (1997), pp. 337–60.

Terms of mortgages are another interesting area of cross-cultural differences in financial services. The typical mortgage in the United States is for 30 years. In Mexico, most people pay cash for houses because mortgages are virtually unavailable. And in Japan 100-year mortgages are quite common and often pass along with the house or flat to the next generation.

Aesthetics

Aesthetics refers to cultural ideas about beauty and good taste. These are reflected in music, art, drama, and dance, as well as the appreciation of color and form.

FIGURE 2.8
Ideas about aesthetics differ across cultures

Source: Ryan McVay/Getty Images

Perhaps Madonna and MTV sell well internationally, but even so the adage[37] "There's no accounting for taste" still rings quite true with most consumers around the world. A summer stroll through one of Madrid's important tourist attractions, Parque de Retiro, provides a simple but memorable lesson in how aesthetics vary across cultures. There are trash cans everywhere, but somehow the refuse doesn't make it into them. Spaniards litter. From the American perspective, the litter detracts from the otherwise beautiful park. German tourists, used to the clean organization of their own fastidiously tidy forests, react with disgust. As another example of differences in aesthetic preferences, consider the earth tones in the decor of Japanese restaurants around the world versus the glossy reds evident in their Chinese competitors' establishments.

Educational and Social Institutions

Both kinds of institutions are affected by, and are transmission agents of, culture. Education includes the process of transmitting skills and knowledge, and thus may take place in schools and in less formal training circumstances. The structure and functioning of each are heavily influenced by culture. Culture manifests itself most dramatically in the people-to-people contact of our social institutions. Notice if the student from Japan sitting next to you in class verbally disagrees with your instructor. Classroom interactions vary substantially around the world. Japanese students are used to listening to lectures, taking notes, and asking questions only after class, if then. In Japan the idea of grading class participation is nonsense. Alternatively, because Spaniards are used to huge undergraduate classes (hundreds rather than dozens), they tend to talk to their friends even when the instructor is talking.

Like education, health care delivery systems and doctor/patient interactions also reflect cultural differences. Americans ask questions and get second opinions about medical care in the United States, and innovative health care services are developed on the basis of extensive marketing research. Alternatively, the social hierarchy is heavily reflected in the Japanese health care system; instead of patients being most important, the doctors command deference. Thus the Japanese health care system, while delivering the best longevity statistics of any country, is relatively unresponsive to concerns of customers.

What Japan lacks in terms of customer orientation in health care innovation it more than makes up for in funeral services. The millennia of crowding have forced the mortuary industry in Japan to use cremation almost exclusively. There simply is no room for all the dead bodies. But according to *Business Week,* the ash-filled urns can get a real send-off, including ceremonies with synthesized music, pink and green laser lights, and dry-ice smoke.[38]

ORGANIZATION AND HOUSEHOLD CONSUMER BEHAVIOR

To a large extent, the consumer behavior topics we have addressed in this chapter are relevant whether the buying entity is an individual or a group. A **group** involves two or more individuals who have implicitly or explicitly defined relationships to one another such that their behavior is interdependent.[39] Groups—whether they are households, organizations, or other affiliated networks—experience needs, make purchasing decisions, and evaluate their purchases. However, some aspects of groups introduce other factors that we need to consider to fully understand consumer behavior in services.

Among the aspects that are different for group buying are collective decision making, mixed motives or goals, roles in the purchasing process, and group culture. When a family makes a service purchase decision, it has a collective style of decision making that often differs from what any of the individuals would use if making an independent choice. When a family chooses a vacation destination, for example, its style may involve one of the following: (1) one parent makes a unilateral decision that the family will go to Disneyland; (2) the family discusses possible destinations at the dinner table, taking each person's ideas and suggestions into account, and selects three locations that a parent will investigate further; (3) the parents provide a budget and a list of the destinations that can be visited within that budget, then allow the children to choose among them. Once a destination has been chosen, the mix of motives or goals of the group comes into play. The mother may want to sightsee, the father to rest, and the children to visit local theme parks. In this and other group purchasing decisions, the needs and goals of the various members must be balanced so that the service (in this case the vacation) delivers optimal satisfaction for as many members as possible. Group roles are also a key consideration. In a household, one individual often identifies a need and initiates the purchase, someone else may influence which service provider is selected, someone else may pay, and someone else may become the ultimate user of the service. For example, the father may decide that the family needs to visit the dentist, a teenager may recommend a dentist that her friend uses, the mother may pay the bills, and all the family members may go to the dentist to receive treatment. Finally, group culture affects purchase and consumption behaviors. Ethnic and cultural groups vary in their group cultures, with some being very patriarchal, others egalitarian, and still others autocratic.

Organizational consumers are a special category of group consumers. Organizations often rely on a small number of buyers within the company to fill their purchasing needs, many of whom specialize in purchasing rather than performing other functions in the company. These buyers are typically organized either formally or informally into **buying centers,** which include all people involved in the decision process:

- The *initiator* identifies the organizational need.

- The *gatekeeper* collects and controls information about the purchase.

- The *decider* determines what service to purchase.

- The *buyer* or *purchasing agent* physically acquires the service.

- The *user* consumes the service.

Among the characteristics of organizational buyers (compared to consumers) are geographic concentration, professionalism, price inelasticity, and desire for close customer–supplier relationships.[40] Organizational purchases tend to differ by **buy classes,** which include new task buys (large purchases that require careful consideration of needs and evaluation of alternatives), straight rebuys (simple reorders of past purchases), and modified rebuys (a mix of new task and straight rebuy features).[41]

Summary

Intangibility, heterogeneity, and inseparability of production and consumption give services high levels of experience and credence properties, which, in turn, make them more difficult to evaluate than tangible goods. We isolated and discussed five categories of consumer behavior that reflect the differences between goods and services: (1) need recognition, (2) information search, (3) evaluation of service alternatives, (4) service purchase and consumption, and (5) postpurchase evaluation. The meaning and impact of culture in consumer behavior in services was also described. Consumer behavior in services was discussed, accompanied by strategic implications for marketers. To be effective, service providers may need to alter their marketing mixes to recognize these different consumer behaviors and evaluation processes.

Discussion Questions

1. This chapter focused on aspects of consumer behavior that are different depending on whether goods or services are being purchased. What aspects of consumer behavior in the purchase of goods and services are similar?
2. Where does a college education fit on the continuum of evaluation for different types of products? Where does computer software fit? Consulting? Retailing? Fast food?
3. What are examples (other than those given in the chapter) of services that are high in credence properties?
4. For what types of services might consumers depend on mass communication (nonpersonal sources of information) in the purchase decision?
5. Which of the aspects discussed in the chapter describe your behavior when it comes to purchasing services?
6. For what types of services would consumers tend to engage in the most postpurchase evaluation? The least?
7. Name three high-technology services (other than ATMs) that consumers resisted in the early stages of introduction but then accepted and used.
8. What is the impact of a service guarantee on the perceived risk customers experience in purchasing services?
9. List five services for which customer compatibility is essential.
10. What are examples of services where brand switching is difficult for consumers?

Exercises

1. Choose a particular end-consumer services industry and one type of service provided in that industry (such as the financial services industry for mortgage loans or the legal services industry for wills). Talk to five customers who have purchased that service and determine to what extent what we have said in this chapter described their behavior in information search, evaluating alternatives, purchase and consumption, and postpurchase evaluation for that service.
2. Choose a particular business-to-business service industry and one type of service provided in that industry (such as the information services industry for computer maintenance services or the consulting industry for management consulting). Talk to five customers in that industry and determine to what extent what we have said in this chapter described their behavior in information search, evaluation of alternatives, purchase and consumption, and postpurchase evaluation for that service.

Notes

1. E. H. Fram, "Stressed-out Consumers Need Timesaving Innovations," *Marketing News,* March 2, 1992, p. 10.
2. L. L. Berry, "The Time-Buying Customer," *Journal of Retailing* 55, no. 4 (Winter 1979), pp. 58–69.
3. Fram, "Stressed-out Consumers."
4. P. Nelson, "Information and Consumer Behavior," *Journal of Political Economy* 78, no. 20 (1970), pp. 311–29.

5. M. R. Darby and E. Karni, "Free Competition and the Optimal Amount of Fraud," *Journal of Law and Economics* 16 (April 1973), pp. 67–86.

6. E. C. Nevis, "Cultural Assumptions and Productivity: The United States and China," *Sloan Management Review* 24, no. 3 (Spring 1983), pp. 17–29.

7. "USA Snapshots, A Look at Statistics That Shape Our Lives," *USA Today,* November 1, 1998, p. D-1.

8. T. S. Robertson, *Innovative Behavior and Communication* (New York: Holt, Rinehart & Winston, 1971).

9. N. L. Ray, "Marketing Communication and the Hierarchy of Effects," unpublished research paper 180, Stanford University, Stanford, CA. August 1973.

10. M. P. Gardner, "Mood States and Consumer Behavior: A Critical Review," *Journal of Consumer Research* 12 (December 1985), pp. 281–300.

11. Ibid., p. 288.

12. S. S. Tomkins, "Affect as Amplification: Some Modifications in Theory," in *Emotion: Theory, Research, and Experience,* ed. R. Plutchik and H. Kellerman (New York: Academic Press, 1980), pp. 141–64.

13. S. J. Grove and R. P. Fisk, "Service Theater: An Analytical Framework for Services Marketing," in Christopher Lovelock, *Services Marketing,* 4th ed. (Englewood Cliffs, NJ: Prentice Hall, 2001), pp. 83–92.

14. S. J. Grove, R. P. Fisk, and M. J. Bitner, "Dramatizing the Service Experience: A Managerial Approach," in *Advances in Services Marketing and Management,* ed. T. A. Swartz, D. E. Bowen, and S. W. Brown (Greenwich, CT: JAI Press), vol. 1 (1992), pp. 91–121.

15. Grove, Fisk, and Bitner, "Dramatizing the Service Experience."

16. Grove and Fisk, "Service Theater."

17. Ibid.

18. Grove, Fisk, and Bitner, "Dramatizing the Service Experience."

19. Ibid.

20. Ibid.

21. M. R. Solomon, C. Surprenant, J. A. Czepiel, and E. G. Gutman, "A Role Theory Perspective on Dyadic Interactions: The Service Encounter," *Journal of Marketing* 49 (Winter 1985), pp. 99–111.

22. Ibid.

23. R. F. Abelson, "Script Processing in Attitude Formation and Decision Making," in *Cognition and Social Behavior,* ed. J. S. Carroll and J. S. Payne (Hillsdale, NJ: Erlbaum, 1976).

24. R. A. Smith and M. J. Houston, "Script-Based Evaluations of Satisfaction with Services," in *Emerging Perspectives on Services Marketing,* ed. L. Berry, G. L. Shostack, and G. Upah (Chicago: American Marketing Association, 1982), pp. 59–62.

25. J. E. G. Bateson and M. K. M. Hui, "Crowding in the Service Environment," in *Creativity in Services Marketing: What's New, What Works, What's Developing,* ed. M. Venkatesan, D. M. Schmalensee, and C. Marshall (Chicago: American Marketing Association, 1986), pp. 85–88.

26. J. Baker, "The Role of the Environment in Marketing Services: The Consumer Perspective," in *The Services Challenge: Integrating for Competitive Advantage,* ed. J. A. Czepiel, C. A. Congram, and J. Shanahan (Chicago: American Marketing Association, 1987), pp. 79–84.

27. C. L. Martin and C. A. Pranter, "Compatibility Management: Customer-to-Customer Relationships in Service Environments," *Journal of Services Marketing* 3 (Summer 1989).

28. Ibid.
29. E. M. Rogers, *Diffusion of Innovations* (New York: Free Press, 1962).
30. R. B. Money, M. C. Gilly, and J. L. Graham, "Explorations of National Culture and Word-of-Mouth Referral Behavior in the Purchase of Industrial Services in the United States and Japan," *Journal of Marketing,* October 1998.
31. E. T. Hall, *Silent Language* (Garden City, NY: Anchor Press/Doubleday, 1959).
32. G. Hofstede, *Culture and Organizations, Software of the Mind* (New York: McGraw-Hill, 1991), p. 235.
33. M. R. Czinkota and I. A. Ronkainen, *International Marketing* (Hinsdale, IL: Dryden Press, 1988).
34. D. E. Murphy, "New East Europe Retailers Told to Put on a Happy Face," *Los Angeles Times,* November 26, 1994, pp. A1, A18.
35. "Japanese Put Tourism on a Higher Plane," *International Herald Tribune,* February 3, 1992, p. 8.
36. B. Ortega, "Wal-Mart Is Slowed by Problems of Price and Culture in Mexico," *The Wall Street Journal,* July 29, 1994, pp. A1, A4.
37. V. Terpstra and R. Sarathy, *International Marketing,* 6th ed. (Fort Worth, TX: Dryden Press, 1994).
38. K. L. Miller, "Rest in Peace . . . with Lasers, Smoke, and Synthesizer Music," *Business Week,* September 16, 1991, p. 48.
39. E. Arnould, L. Price, and G. Zinkhan, *Consumers* (New York: McGraw-Hill, 2002), p. 496.
40. Arnould, Price, and Zinkhan, *Consumers,* p. 503.
41. Arnould, Price, and Zinkhan, *Consumers,* pp. 505–6.

3

CUSTOMER EXPECTATIONS OF SERVICE

This chapter's objectives are to

1. Recognize that customers hold different types of expectations for service performance.

2. Discuss the sources of customer expectations of service, including those that are controllable and uncontrollable by marketers.

3. Acknowledge that the types and sources of expectations are similar for end consumers and business customers, for pure service and product-related service, for experienced customers and inexperienced customers.

4. Delineate the most important current issues surrounding customer expectations.

Undoubtedly, the greatest gap between customer expectations and service delivery exists when the Japanese meet Russians. In Japan the customer is supreme. At the morning opening of large department stores in Tokyo, sales personnel line up to welcome patrons and bow as they enter! When one of the authors—who could speak no Japanese—visited Tokyo recently, as many as eight salespeople willingly tried to help her find a calligraphy pen. Although the pen was a very low-priced item, several attendants rushed from counter to counter to find someone to translate, several others spread out to find pens that might serve as the perfect gift, and still others searched for maps to other stores where the perfect pen could be found.

Because of the wonderful treatment Japanese customers are used to in their home country, they often have service expectations that exceed service delivery even when shopping in "civilized" countries such as Great Britain: "Hideo Majima, 57, a Japanese tourist, looked puzzled and annoyed. He was standing in a London department store while two shop assistants conversed instead of serving him. He left without buying anything."[1] His annoyance is understandable when you realize the standard of service treatment in Japan.

FIGURE 3.1

Source: © Charles Gupton/
Stock Boston Inc./
PictureQuest

Given how our friend Majima-san felt about shopping in Britain, try to imagine his perceptions of this actual dining experience in many Russian restaurants. Remember that in Russia's economy, products are still so scarce that suppliers rule. Sellers decide who gets what, and the concept of customer service is virtually meaningless. In a real-life experience, a customer visiting the Izmailova Hotel had to excuse the waiters if they were too busy to serve customers—they were playing chess. "'Can't you see we're one move away from checkmate?' yelled waiter Oleg Shamov, surrounded by six other waiters in a restaurant back room. The match kept customers waiting for 40 minutes."[2] Free enterprise is apparently having strong effects in the former Soviet Union. Professor Peter Shikkirev at the Graduate School of International Business in Moscow assures us that some Russian restaurants are now providing service comparable to fine American restaurants. However, we doubt that even that level of customer service would delight Japanese customers.

Customer expectations are beliefs about service delivery that function as standards or reference points against which performance is judged. Because customers compare their perceptions of performance with these reference points when evaluating service quality, thorough knowledge about customer expectations is critical to services marketers. Knowing what the customer expects is the first and possibly most critical step in delivering quality service. Being wrong about what customers want can mean losing a customer's business when another company hits the target exactly. Being wrong can also mean expending money, time, and other resources on things that don't count to the customer. Being wrong can even mean not surviving in a fiercely competitive market.

Among the aspects of expectations that need to be explored and understood for successful services marketing are the following: What types of expectation standards do customers hold about services? What factors most influence the formation of these expectations? What role do these factors play in changing expectations? How can a service company meet or exceed customer expectations?

In this chapter we provide a framework for thinking about customer expectations.[3] The chapter is divided into four main sections: (1) the meaning and types of expected service, (2) factors that influence customer expectations of service, (3) a model of service expectations, and (4) current issues involving customer service expectations.

FIGURE 3.2
Possible Levels of Customer Expectations

Source: Ideas drawn from R. K. Teas, "Expectations, Performance Evaluation and Consumers' Perceptions of Quality," *Journal of Marketing* 57 (October 1993), pp. 18–34.

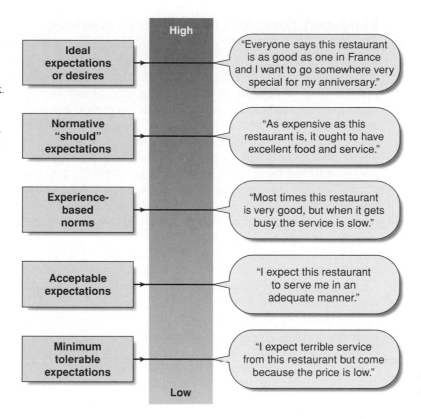

MEANING AND TYPES OF SERVICE EXPECTATIONS

To say that expectations are reference points against which service delivery is compared is only a beginning. The level of expectation can vary widely depending on the reference point the customer holds. Although most everyone has an intuitive sense of what expectations are, service marketers need a far more thorough and clear definition of expectations in order to comprehend, measure, and manage them.

Let's imagine that you are planning to go to a restaurant. Figure 3.2 shows a continuum along which different possible types of service expectations can be arrayed from low to high. On the left of the continuum are different types or levels of expectations, ranging from high (top) to low (bottom). At each point we give a name to the type of expectation and illustrate what it might mean in terms of a restaurant you are considering. Note how important the expectation you held will be to your eventual assessment of the restaurant's performance. Suppose you went into the restaurant for which you held the minimum tolerable expectation, paid very little money, and were served immediately with good food. Next suppose that you went to the restaurant for which you had the highest (ideal) expectations, paid a lot of money, and were served good (but not fantastic) food. Which restaurant experience would you judge to be best? The answer is likely to depend a great deal on the reference point that you brought to the experience.

Because the idea of customer expectations is so critical to evaluation of service, we start this chapter by talking about the levels of expectations.

Expected Service: Levels of Expectations

As we showed in Figure 3.2, customers hold different types of expectations about service. For purposes of our discussion in the rest of this chapter, we focus on two types. The highest can be termed *desired service:* the level of service the customer hopes to receive—the "wished for" level of performance. Desired service is a blend of what the customer believes "can be" and "should be."[4] For example, consumers who sign up for a computer dating service expect to find compatible, attractive, interesting people to date and perhaps even someone to marry. The expectation reflects the hopes and wishes of these consumers; without these hopes and wishes and the belief that they may be fulfilled, they would probably not purchase the dating service. In a similar way, you will engage the services of your college's placement office when you are ready to graduate. What are your expectations of the service? In all likelihood you want the office to find you a job—the right job in the right place for the right salary—because that is what you hope and wish for.

However, you probably also see that the economy may constrain the availability of ideal job openings in companies. And not all companies you may be interested in have a relationship with your placement office. In this situation and in general, customers hope to achieve their service desires but recognize that this is not always possible. We call the threshold level of acceptable service *adequate service*—the level of service the customer will accept.[5] In the economic slowdown following the World Trade Center disaster, many college graduates trained for high-skilled jobs accepted entry-level positions at fast-food restaurants or internships for no pay. Their hopes and desires were still high, but they recognized that they could not attain those desires in the market that existed at the time. Their standard of adequate service was much lower than their desired service. Some graduates accepted any job for which they could earn a salary, and others agreed to nonpaying, short-term positions as interns to gain experience. Adequate service represents the "minimum tolerable expectation,"[6] the bottom level of performance acceptable to the customer.

Figure 3.3 shows these two expectation standards as the upper and lower boundaries for customer expectations. This figure portrays the idea that customers assess service performance on the basis of two standard boundaries: what they desire and what they deem acceptable.

Among the intriguing questions about service expectations is whether customers hold the same or different expectation levels for service firms in the same industry. For example, are desired service expectations the same for all restaurants? Or just for all fast-food restaurants? Do the levels of adequate service expectations vary across restaurants? Consider the following quotation:

> Levels of expectation are why two organizations in the same business can offer far different levels of service and still keep customers happy. It is why McDonald's can extend excellent

FIGURE 3.3
Dual Customer Expectation Levels

Desired Service

Adequate Service

industrialized service with few employees per customer and why an expensive restaurant with many tuxedoed waiters may be unable to do as well from the customer's point of view.[7]

Customers typically hold similar desired expectations across categories of service, but these categories are not as broad as whole industries. Among subcategories of restaurants are expensive restaurants, ethnic restaurants, fast-food restaurants, and airport restaurants. A customer's desired service expectation for fast-food restaurants is quick, convenient, tasty food in a clean setting. The desired service expectation for an expensive restaurant, on the other hand, usually involves elegant surroundings, gracious employees, candlelight, and fine food. In essence, desired service expectations seem to be the same for service providers within industry categories or subcategories that are viewed as similar by customers.

The adequate service expectation level, on the other hand, may vary for different firms within a category or subcategory. Within fast-food restaurants, a customer may hold a higher expectation for McDonald's than for Burger King, having experienced consistent service at McDonald's over time and somewhat inconsistent service at Burger King. It is possible, therefore, that a customer can be more disappointed with service from McDonald's than from Burger King even though the actual level of service at McDonald's is higher than the level at Burger King. The Global Feature further discusses how culture influences expectations.

The Zone of Tolerance

As we discussed in earlier chapters of this textbook, services are heterogeneous in that performance may vary across providers, across employees from the same provider, and even with the same service employee. The extent to which customers recognize and are willing to accept this variation is called the *zone of tolerance* and is shown in Figure 3.4. If service drops below adequate service—the minimum level considered acceptable—customers will be frustrated and their satisfaction with the company will be undermined. If service performance is higher than the zone of tolerance at the top end—where performance exceeds desired service—customers will be very pleased and probably quite surprised as well. You might consider the zone of tolerance as the range or window in which customers do not particularly notice service performance. When it falls outside the range (either very low or very high), the service gets the customer's attention in either a positive or negative way. As an example, consider the service at a checkout line in a grocery store. Most customers hold a range of acceptable times for this service encounter—probably somewhere between 5 and 10 minutes. If service consumes that period of time, customers probably do not pay much attention to the wait. If a customer enters the line and finds sufficient checkout personnel to serve her in the first two or three minutes, she may notice the service and judge it as

FIGURE 3.4
The Zone of Tolerance

Chapter 2 discussed values and attitudes as critical dimensions of culture. To better understand how consumers behave across cultures, we can further subdivide the dimension of values and attitudes into five universal values across cultures. These universal values are well documented; they are based on a study using 72,215 employees working in 66 different national subsidiaries of IBM Corporation. The universal values, which collectively distinguish members of different cultures, include power distance, uncertainty avoidance, individualism–collectivism, masculinity–femininity, and Confucian dynamic or long-term orientation.[8] We explain how Hofstede, the author of this research, defined each of these subdimensions and then describe one of many ways they might affect consumer expectations in services.

- *Power distance* involves the way the less powerful members of institutions and organizations within a country expect and accept that power is distributed unequally. Part of power distance involves human inequality in areas such as prestige, wealth, power, and law. People from cultures high in power distance are comfortable with power hierarchy, discrimination, and tolerance of inequalities.

- *Uncertainty avoidance* is the extent to which the members of a culture feel threatened by uncertain or unknown situations. With high uncertainty avoidance, people like clear rules and explicit situations; with low uncertainty avoidance, people can accept uncertainty without discomfort and tolerate inexplicit rules.

- *Individualism* exists in societies where the ties between individuals are loose; everyone is expected to look after him- or herself and his or her immediate family. *Collectivism,* the opposite, exists in societies where people from birth onward are integrated into strong, cohesive groups that offer lifetime protection in exchange for loyalty. This subdimension can be summed up in three words: I versus we.

- *Masculinity* and *femininity* are the dominant sex role patterns in the vast majority of both traditional and modern societies. Masculine societies value assertiveness, performance,

excellent. On the other hand, if a customer has to wait in line for 15 minutes, he may begin to grumble and look at his watch. The longer the wait is below the zone of tolerance, the more frustrated he becomes.

Customers' service expectations are characterized by a range of levels (like those shown in Figure 3.3), bounded by desired and adequate service, rather than a single level. This tolerance zone, representing the difference between desired service and the level of service considered adequate, can expand and contract within a customer. An airline customer's zone of tolerance will narrow when she is running late and is concerned about making her plane. A minute seems much longer, and her adequate service level increases. On the other hand, a customer who arrives at the airport early may have a larger tolerance zone, making the wait in line far less noticeable than when he or she is pressed for time. This example shows that the marketer must understand not just the size and boundary levels for the zone of tolerance but also when and how the tolerance zone fluctuates with a given customer.

ambition, and independence, whereas feminine societies value nurturance, quality of life, service, and interdependence.

- The *Confucian dynamic* or *long-term versus short-term orientation dimension* refers to the way people look at the future. Long-term orientation emphasizes perseverance, ordering relationships by status, thrift, and a sense of shame. On the other hand, short-term orientation focuses on personal steadiness and stability, saving face, respect for tradition, and reciprocation of greetings, favors, and gifts.

The impact of culture on consumer expectations can be illuminated using these five sub-dimensions of values and attitudes. In a recent study, for example, researchers found the following:[9]

- Consumers low on power distance have high overall expectations of service and particularly expect responsive and reliable service.

- Individualistic consumers have high overall service quality expectations and expect empathy and assurance from the service provider.

- Consumers high on uncertainty avoidance and short-term–oriented consumers have high overall service quality expectations.

As the authors of the study point out, marketing efforts will perform better when matched with cultural characteristics. This and other typologies that help us understand the differences in values across cultures will be of immense importance as service marketers develop and market service offerings.

Source: Based on background research and a study conducted by N. Donthu and B. Yoo, *Journal of Service Research* 1, no. 2 (November 1998), pp. 178–86.

Different Customers Possess Different Zones of Tolerance   Another aspect of variability in the range of reasonable services is that different customers possess different tolerance zones. Some customers have narrow zones of tolerance, requiring a tighter range of service from providers, whereas other customers allow a greater range of service. For example, very busy customers would likely always be pressed for time, desire short wait times in general, and also hold a constrained range for the length of acceptable wait times. When it comes to meeting plumbers or repair personnel at their homes for appliance problems, customers who work outside the home have a more restricted window of acceptable time duration for that appointment than do customers who work in their homes or do not work at all.

An individual customer's zone of tolerance increases or decreases depending on a number of factors, including company-controlled factors such as price. When prices increase, customers tend to be less tolerant of poor service. In this case, the zone of tolerance decreases because the adequate service level shifts upward. Later in this

FIGURE 3.5
Zones of Tolerance for Different Service Dimensions

Source: Berry, Parasuraman, and Zeithaml (1993).

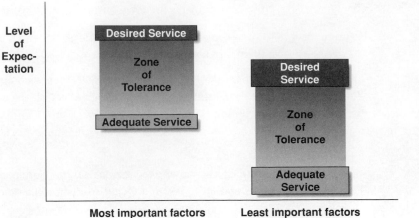

chapter we will describe many different factors, some company controlled and others customer controlled, that lead to the narrowing or widening of the tolerance zone.

Zones of Tolerance Vary for Service Dimensions Customers' tolerance zones also vary for different service attributes or dimensions. The more important the factor, the narrower the zone of tolerance is likely to be. In general, customers are likely to be less tolerant about unreliable service (broken promises or service errors) than other service deficiencies, which means that they have higher expectations for this factor. In addition to higher expectations for the most important service dimensions and attributes, customers are likely to be less willing to relax these expectations than those for less important factors, making the zone of tolerance for the most important service dimension smaller and the desired and adequate service levels higher.[10] Figure 3.5 portrays the likely difference in tolerance zones for the most important and the least important factors.[11]

The fluctuation in the individual customer's zone of tolerance is more a function of changes in the adequate service level, which moves readily up and down due to situational circumstances, than in the desired service level, which tends to move upward incrementally due to accumulated experiences. Desired service is relatively idiosyncratic and stable compared with adequate service, which moves up and down and in response to competition and other factors. Fluctuation in the zone of tolerance can be likened to an accordion's movement, but with most of the gyration coming from one side (the adequate service level) rather than the other (the desired service level).

In summary, we can express the boundaries of customer expectations of service with two different levels of expectations: desired service and adequate service. The desired service level is less subject to change than the adequate service level. A zone of tolerance separates these two levels. This zone of tolerance varies across customers and expands or contracts with the same customer.

FACTORS THAT INFLUENCE CUSTOMER EXPECTATIONS OF SERVICE

Because expectations play such a critical role in customer evaluation of services, marketers need and want to understand the factors that shape them. Marketers would also like to have control over these factors as well, but many of the forces that influence customer expectations are uncontrollable. In this section of the chapter we try to separate the many influences on customer expectations.

Sources of Desired Service Expectations

As shown in Figure 3.6, the two largest influences on desired service level are personal needs and philosophies about service. *Personal needs,* those states or conditions essential to the physical or psychological well-being of the customer, are pivotal factors that shape what we desire in service. Personal needs can fall into many categories, including physical, social, psychological, and functional. A fan who regularly goes to baseball games right from work, and is therefore thirsty and hungry, hopes and desires that the food and drink vendors will pass by his section frequently, whereas a fan who regularly has dinner elsewhere has a low or zero level of desired service from the vendors. A customer with high social and dependency needs may have relatively high expectations for a hotel's ancillary services, hoping, for example, that the hotel has a bar with live music and dancing. The effect of personal needs on desired service is illustrated by the different expectations held by two business insurance customers:

> I expect [an insurance] broker to do a great deal of my work because I don't have the staff . . . I expect the broker to know a great deal about my business and communicate that knowledge to the underwriter.

> My expectations are different . . . I do have a staff to do our certificates, etc., and use the broker minimally.[12]

Some customers are more demanding than others, having greater sensitivity to, and higher expectations of, service. *Enduring service intensifiers* are individual, stable factors that lead the customer to a heightened sensitivity to service. One of the most important of these factors can be called *derived service expectations,* which occur when customer expectations are driven by another person or group of people. A niece from a big family who is planning a 90th birthday party for a favorite aunt is representing the entire family in selecting a restaurant for a successful celebration. Her needs are driven in part by the derived expectations from the other family members. A parent choosing a vacation for the family, a spouse selecting a home-cleaning service,

FIGURE 3.6
Factors That Influence Desired Service

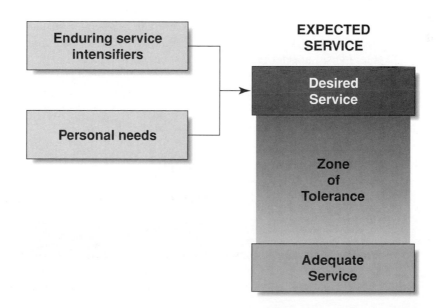

an employee choosing an office for the firm—all these customers' individual expectations are intensified because they represent and must answer to other parties who will receive the service. In the context of business-to-business service, customer expectations are driven by the expectations of their own customers. The head of an information technology department in an insurance company, who is the business customer of a large computer vendor, has expectations based on those of the insurance customers she serves: when the computer equipment is down, her customers complain. Her need to keep the system up and running is not just her own expectation but is derived from the pressure of customers.

Business-to-business customers may also derive their expectations from their managers and supervisors. Employees of a marketing research department may speed up project cycles (increase their expectations for speed of delivery) when pressured by their management to deliver the study results. Purchasing agents may increase demands for faster delivery at lower costs when company management is emphasizing cost reduction in the company.

Another enduring service intensifier is *personal service philosophy*—the customer's underlying generic attitude about the meaning of service and the proper conduct of service providers. If you have ever been a waitress or a waiter in a restaurant, you are likely to have standards for restaurant service that were shaped by your training and experience in that role. You might, for example, believe that waitresses should not keep customers waiting longer than 15 minutes to take their orders. Knowing the way a kitchen operates, you may be less tolerant of lukewarm food or errors in the order than others who have not held the role of waitperson. In general, customers who are themselves in service businesses or have worked for them in the past seem to have especially strong service philosophies.

To the extent that customers have personal philosophies about service provision, their expectations of service providers will be intensified. Personal service philosophies and derived service expectations elevate the level of desired service.

Sources of Adequate Service Expectations

A different set of determinants affects adequate service, the level of service the customer finds acceptable. In general, these influences are short-term and tend to fluctuate more than the factors that influence desired service. In this section we explain the five factors shown in Figure 3.7 that influence adequate service: (1) transitory service intensifiers, (2) perceived service alternatives, (3) customer self-perceived service role, (4) situational factors, and (5) predicted service.

FIGURE 3.7
Factors That Influence Adequate Service

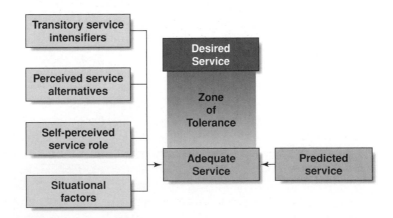

The first set of elements, *transitory service intensifiers,* consists of temporary, usually short-term, individual factors that make a customer more aware of the need for service. Personal emergency situations in which service is urgently needed (such as an accident and the need for automobile insurance or a breakdown in office equipment during a busy period) raise the level of adequate service expectation, particularly the level of responsiveness required and considered acceptable. A mail-order company that depends on 800-number phone lines for receiving all customer orders will tend to be more demanding of the telephone service during peak periods of the week, month, and year. Any system breakdown or lack of clarity on the lines will be tolerated less during these intense periods than at other times. The impact of transitory service intensifiers is evident in these two comments by two participants in a research study conducted by one of the authors:

> An automobile insurance customer: The nature of my problem influences my expectations, for example, a broken window versus a DWI accident requiring brain surgery.

> A business equipment repair customer: I had calibration problems with the X-ray equipment. They should have come out and fixed it in a matter of hours because of the urgency.[13]

Problems with the initial service can also lead to heightened expectations. Performing a service right the first time is very important because customers value service reliability above all other dimensions. If the service fails in the recovery phase, fixing it right the second time (that is, being reliable in service recovery) is even more critical than it was the first time. Automobile repair service provides a case in point. If a problem with your automobile's brakes sends you to a car repair provider, you expect the company to fix the brakes. If you experience further problems with the brakes after the repair (a situation that is not all that uncommon with car repair), your adequate service level will increase. In these and other situations where transitory service intensifiers are present, the level of adequate service will increase and the zone of tolerance will narrow.

Perceived service alternatives are other providers from whom the customer can obtain service. If customers have multiple service providers to choose from, or if they can provide the service for themselves (such as lawn care or personal grooming), their levels of adequate service are higher than those of customers who believe it is not possible to get better service elsewhere. An airline customer who lives in a small town with a tiny airport, for example, has a reduced set of options in airline travel. This customer will be more tolerant of the service performance of the carriers in the town because few alternatives exist. She will accept the scheduling and lower levels of service more than the customer in a big city who has myriad flights and airlines to choose from. The customer's perception that service alternatives exist raises the level of adequate service and narrows the zone of tolerance.

It is important that service marketers fully understand the complete set of options that customers view as perceived alternatives. In the small town–small airport example just discussed, the set of alternatives from the customer's point of view is likely to include more than just other airlines—limousine service to a nearby large city, rail service, or driving. In general, service marketers must discover the alternatives the customer views as comparable, rather than those in the company's competitive set. For example, many new technologies require that companies fully understand customer views of what entertainment options compete with each other (see the Technology Spotlight).

A third factor affecting the level of adequate service is the *customer's self-perceived service role.* We define this as customer perceptions of the degree to which customers

Technology Spotlight
Customer Expectations of Interactive TV

One of the most difficult tasks marketers face is understanding what customers expect from completely new services, and nowhere is this more evident than when those new services involve technology. Can you remember back to the first time you signed onto the Internet? If you were like most consumers, your frames of reference were the computer and the television. You expected Internet services to be as responsive and easy to use as traditional computers (which, of course, to some consumers are neither responsive nor easy to use!) with the video speed and quality of television. Unfortunately, the first Internet services—even market leaders such as America Online—were slow, confusing, and not visually appealing. In most cases, the promises made by the new companies did not match reality for several years, and as recently as 2001 America Online customers were still facing unresponsive networks as the systems upgraded to meet growing demand.

Sometimes the problem is that the new services themselves are not clearly defined or developed with particular customer needs in mind. A good case in point is interactive television, one of the newer service technologies being marketed. What exactly is interactive television, what can it actually do, and what do customers expect it to do? See if you know the answer. Which of the following best defines interactive television?

1. Interactive television is a video-on-demand service where customers can choose from hundreds of movie and program titles on their cable system, order them, and watch them whenever they want to.

2. Interactive television is a service where an icon will appear in the corner of the television screen that allows viewers to click the remote and pull up related information about the show being watched, similar shows, and ordering information for products.

3. Interactive television is a service that allows customers to interact with hosts of television shows, thereby participating in the audience.

4. All of the above.

5. 1 and 2 above.

If you stop and think about it, options 1, 2, and 3 could all be forms of interactive TV. Only 1 and 2 are currently offered, and not in the same areas of the country, not by the same cable companies, and not for very many service customers. Therefore, we do not yet have a good answer for what interactive television is. No wonder customer expectations for the service are not well defined!

Source: E. W. Desmond, "Interactive TV Has Arrived," *Fortune*, February 2, 1998, pp. 135–36; and M. Gunther, "Interactive TV: It's Baaack!" *Fortune*, July 20, 1998, pp. 136–37.

exert an influence on the level of service they receive. In other words, customers' expectations are partly shaped by how well they believe they are performing their own roles in service delivery.[14] One role of the customer is specifying the level of service expected. A customer who is very explicit with a waiter about how rare he wants his steak cooked in a restaurant will probably be more dissatisfied if the meat comes to the table overcooked than a customer who does not articulate the degree of doneness expected. The customer's active participation in the service also affects this factor. A customer who doesn't show up for many of her allergy shots will probably be more lenient on the allergist when she experiences symptoms than one who conscientiously shows up for every shot.

A final way the customer defines his or her role is in assuming the responsibility for complaining when service is poor. A dissatisfied customer who complains will be less tolerant than one who does not voice his or her concerns. An automobile insurance customer acknowledged his responsibility in service provision this way: "You can't blame it all on the insurance agent. You need to be responsible too and let the agent know what exactly you want." A truck-leasing customer recognized her role by stating, "There are a lot of variables that can influence how you get treated, including how you deal with them."[15]

Customers' zones of tolerance seem to expand when they sense they are not fulfilling their roles. When, on the other hand, customers believe they are doing their part in delivery, their expectations of adequate service are heightened and the zone of tolerance contracts. The comment of an automobile repair customer illustrates: "Service writers are not competent. I prepare my own itemized list of problems, take it to the service writer, and tell him or her, 'Fix these.' " This customer will expect more than one who did not prepare as well to receive the service.

Levels of adequate service are also influenced by *situational factors,* defined as service performance conditions that customers view as beyond the control of the service provider. For example, where personal emergencies such as serious automobile accidents would likely intensify customer service expectations of insurance companies (because they are transitory service intensifiers), catastrophes that affect a large number of people at one time (tornadoes or earthquakes) may lower service expectations because customers recognize that insurers are inundated with demands for their services. During the days following the World Trade Center disaster, telephone and Internet service was poor because so many people were trying to get in touch with friends and relatives. However, customers were forgiving because they understood the source of the problem. Customers who recognize that situational factors are not the fault of the service company may accept lower levels of adequate service given the context. In general, situational factors temporarily lower the level of adequate service, widening the zone of tolerance.

The final factor that influences adequate service is *predicted service* (Figure 3.8), the level of service customers believe they are likely to get. This type of service expectation can be viewed as predictions made by customers about what is likely to happen during an impending transaction or exchange. Predicted service performance implies some objective calculation of the probability of performance or estimate of anticipated service performance level. If customers predict good service, their levels of adequate service are likely to be higher than if they predict poor service. For example, full-time residents in a college town usually predict faster restaurant service during the summer months when students are not on campus. This will probably lead them to have higher standards for adequate service in restaurants during the summer than during school months. On the other hand, customers of telephone companies and utilities know that installation service from these firms will be difficult to obtain during the first few weeks of school when myriad students are setting up their apartments for the year. In this case, levels of adequate service decrease and zones of tolerance widen.

Predicted service is typically an estimate or calculation of the service a customer will receive in an individual transaction rather than in the overall relationship with a service provider. Whereas desired and adequate service expectations are global assessments comprising many individual service transactions, predicted service is almost always an estimate of what will happen in the next service encounter or transaction that the customer experiences. This is one of the reasons predicted service is viewed in this model as an influencer of adequate service.

Because predictions are about individual service encounters, they are likely to be more concrete and specific than the types of expectation levels customers hold for adequate service or desired service. For example, your predicted service expectations about the length of time you will spend in the waiting room the next time you visit your doctor will likely be expressed in terms of the number of minutes or hours you have spent in the waiting room this time.

Service Encounter Expectations versus Overall Service Expectations

In Chapter 4 we discuss the difference between overall service quality and service encounter quality, viewing the service encounter as a discrete event occurring over a definable period of time (such as a particular hotel stay or a particular check-in experience at the hotel). Customers hold expectations of the quality of each service encounter, just as they hold expectations about the overall service quality of a firm. When the expectations are about individual service encounters, they are likely to be more specific and concrete (such as the number of minutes one must wait for a front desk clerk) than the expectations about overall service quality (like speedy service).

Sources of Both Desired and Predicted Service Expectations

When consumers are interested in purchasing services, they are likely to seek or take in information from several different sources. For example, they may call a store, ask a friend, or deliberately track newspaper advertisements to find the needed service at the lowest price. They may also receive service information by watching television or hearing an unsolicited comment from a colleague about a service that was performed well. In addition to these active and passive types of external search for information, consumers may conduct an internal search by reviewing the information held in memory about the service. This section discusses one internal and three external factors that influence both desired service and predicted service expectations: (1) explicit service promises, (2) implicit service promises, (3) word-of-mouth communications, and (4) past experience.

Explicit service promises are personal and nonpersonal statements about the service made by the organization to customers. The statements are personal when they are communicated by salespeople or service or repair personnel; they are nonpersonal

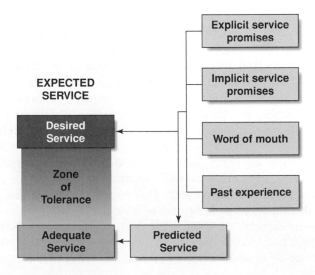

FIGURE 3.8
Factors That Influence Desired and Predicted Service

when they come from advertising, brochures, and other written publications. Explicit service promises are one of the few influences on expectations that are completely in the control of the service provider.

Promising exactly what will ultimately be delivered would seem a logical and appropriate way to manage customer expectations and ensure that reality fits the promises. However, companies and the personnel who represent them often deliberately overpromise to obtain business or inadvertently overpromise by stating their best estimates about delivery of a service in the future. In addition to overpromising, company representatives simply do not always know the appropriate promises to make because services are often customized and therefore not easily defined and repeated; the representative may not know when or in what final form the service will be delivered.

All types of explicit service promises have a direct effect on desired service expectation. If the sales visit portrays a banking service that is available 24 hours a day, the customer's desires for that service (as well as the service of competitors) will be shaped by this promise. A hotel customer describes the impact of explicit promises on expectations: "They get you real pumped up with the beautiful ad. When you go in you expect the bells and whistles to go off. Usually they don't." A business equipment repair customer states, "When you buy a piece of equipment you expect to get a competitive advantage from it. Service is promised with the sale of the equipment." A particularly dangerous promise that many companies today make to their business customers is to provide a "total solution" to their business needs. This promise is very difficult to deliver.

Explicit service promises influence the levels of both desired service and predicted service. They shape what customers desire in general as well as what they predict will happen in the next service encounter from a particular service provider or in a certain service encounter.

Implicit service promises are service-related cues other than explicit promises that lead to inferences about what the service should and will be like. These quality cues are dominated by price and the tangibles associated with the service. In general, the higher the price and the more impressive the tangibles, the more a customer will expect from the service. Consider a customer who shops for insurance, finding two firms charging radically different prices. She may infer that the firm with the higher price should and will provide higher-quality service and better coverage. Similarly, a customer who stays at a posh hotel is likely to desire and predict a higher standard of service than from a hotel with less impressive facilities.

The importance of *word-of-mouth communication* in shaping expectations of service is well documented.[16] These personal and sometimes nonpersonal statements made by parties other than the organization convey to customers what the service will be like and influence both predicted and desired service. As we discussed in Chapter 2, word-of-mouth communication carries particular weight as an information source because it is perceived as unbiased. Word of mouth tends to be very important in services that are difficult to evaluate before purchase and direct experience of them. Experts (including *Consumer Reports,* friends, and family) are also word-of-mouth sources that can affect the levels of desired and predicted service.

Past experience, the customer's previous exposure to service that is relevant to the focal service, is another force in shaping predictions and desires. The service relevant for prediction can be previous exposure to the focal firm's service. For example, you probably compare each stay in a particular hotel with all previous stays in that hotel. But past experience with the focal hotel is likely to be a very limited view of your past experience. You may also compare each stay with your experiences in other hotels and hotel chains. Customers also compare across industries: hospital patients, for example, compare hospital stays against the standard of hotel visits. Cable service customers tend to compare cable service with the standards set by telephone service, one reason cable service is often judged to be poor. In a general sense, past experience may incorporate previous experience with the focal brand, typical performance of a favorite brand, experience with the brand last purchased or the top-selling brand, and the average performance a customer believes represents a group of similar brands.[17]

A MODEL OF CUSTOMER SERVICE EXPECTATIONS

How might a manager of a service organization use the model we have developed in this chapter to create, improve, or market services? First, managers need to know the pertinent expectation sources and their relative importance for a customer population, a customer segment, and perhaps even a particular customer. They need to know, for instance, the relative weight of word of mouth, explicit service promises, and implicit service promises in shaping desired service and predicted service. Some of these sources are more stable and permanent in their influence (such as enduring service intensifiers and personal needs) than the others, which fluctuate considerably over time (like perceived service alternatives and situational factors).

The different sources vary in terms of their credibility as well as their potential to be influenced by the marketer. Exhibit 3.1 shows the breakdown of typically controllable and uncontrollable factors and suggests how services marketers can influence the factors. Chapter 15 will detail these and other strategies that services marketers can use to match delivery to promises and thereby manage expectations.

ISSUES INVOLVING CUSTOMER SERVICE EXPECTATIONS

The following issues represent current topics of particular interest to service marketers about customer expectations. In this section we discuss five of the most frequently asked questions about customer expectations:

1. What does a service marketer do if customer expectations are "unrealistic"?

2. Should a company try to delight the customer?

3. How does a company exceed customer service expectations?

4. Do customer service expectations continually escalate?

5. How does a service company stay ahead of competition in meeting customer expectations?

What Does a Services Marketer Do If Customer Expectations Are "Unrealistic"?

One inhibitor to learning about customer expectations is management's and employees' fear of asking. This apprehension often stems from the belief that customer expectations will be extravagant and unrealistic, and that by asking about them a company will set itself up for even loftier expectation levels (that is, "unrealistic" levels). Compelling evidence, shown in Exhibit 3.2, suggests that customers' main expectations of service are quite simple and basic: "simply put, customers expect service companies to do what

3.1 WAYS SERVICES MARKETERS CAN INFLUENCE FACTORS

Controllable Factors	Possible Influence Strategies
Explicit service promises	Make realistic and accurate promises that reflect the service actually delivered rather than an idealized version of the service.
	Ask contact people for feedback on the accuracy of promises made in advertising and personal selling.
	Avoid engaging in price or advertising wars with competitors because they take the focus off customers and escalate promises beyond the level at which they can be met.
	Formalize service promises through a service guarantee that focuses company employees on the promise and that provides feedback on the number of times promises are not fulfilled.
Implicit service promises	Ensure that service tangibles accurately reflect the type and level of service provided.
	Ensure that price premiums can be justified by higher levels of performance by the company on important customer attributes.

Less Controllable Factors	Possible Influence Strategies
Enduring service intensifiers	Use market research to determine sources of derived service expectations and their requirements. Focus advertising and marketing strategy on ways the service allows the focal customer to satisfy the requirements of the influencing customer.
	Use market research to profile personal service philosophies of customers and use this information in designing and delivering services.
Personal needs	Educate customers on ways the service addresses their needs.
Transitory service intensifiers	Increase service delivery during peak periods or in emergencies.
Perceived service alternatives	Be fully aware of competitive offerings and, where possible and appropriate, match them.
Self-perceived service role	Educate customers to understand their roles and perform them better.
Word-of-mouth communications	Simulate word of mouth in advertising by using testimonials and opinion leaders.
	Identify influencers and opinion leaders for the service and concentrate marketing efforts on them.
	Use incentives with existing customers to encourage them to say positive things about the service.
Past experience	Use marketing research to profile customers' previous experience with similar services.
Situational factors	Use service guarantees to assure customers about service recovery regardless of the situational factors that occur.
Predicted service	Tell customers when service provision is higher than what can normally be expected so that predictions of future service encounters will not be inflated.

they are supposed to do. They expect fundamentals, not fanciness; performance, not empty promises."[18] Customers want service to be delivered as promised. They want planes to take off on time, hotel rooms to be clean, food to be hot and service providers to show up when scheduled. Unfortunately, many service customers are disappointed and let down by companies' inability to meet these basic service expectations.

Type of Service	Type of Customer	Principal Expectations
Automobile repair	Consumers	Be competent. ("Fix it right the first time.")
		Explain things. ("Explain why I need the suggested repairs—provide an itemized list.")
		Be respectful. ("Don't treat me like a dumb female.")
Automobile insurance	Consumers	Keep me informed. ("I shouldn't have to learn about insurance law changes from the newspaper.")
		Be on my side. ("I don't want them to treat me like a criminal just because I have a claim.")
		Play fair. ("Don't drop me when something goes wrong.")
		Protect me from catastrophe. ("Make sure my estate is covered in the event of a major accident.")
		Provide prompt service. ("I want fast settlement of claims.")
Hotel	Consumers	Provide a clean room. ("Don't have a deep-pile carpet that can't be completely cleaned . . . you can literally see germs down there.")
		Provide a secure room. ("Good bolts and peephole on door.")
		Treat me like a guest. ("It is almost like they're looking you over to decide whether they're going to let you have a room.")
		Keep your promise. ("They said the room would be ready, but it wasn't at the promised time.")
Property and casualty insurance	Business customers	Fulfill obligations. ("Pay up.")
		Learn my business and work with me. ("I expect them to know me and my company.")
		Protect me from catastrophe. ("They should cover my risk exposure so there is no single big loss.")
		Provide prompt service. ("Fast claim service.")
Equipment repair	Business customers	Share my sense of urgency. ("Speed of response. One time I had to buy a second piece of equipment because of the huge downtime with the first piece.")
		Be competent. ("Sometimes you are quoting stuff from their instruction manuals to their own people and they don't even know what it means.")
		Be prepared. ("Have all the parts ready.")
Truck and tractor rental/leasing	Business customers	Keep the equipment running. ("Need to have equipment working all of the time—that is the key.")
		Be flexible. ("The leasing company should have the flexibility to rent us equipment when we need it.")
		Provide full service. ("Get rid of all the paperwork and headaches.")

Source: Reprinted from A. Parasuraman, L. L. Berry, and V. A. Zeithaml, "Understanding Customer Expectations of Service," *Sloan Management Review,* Spring 1991, pp. 33–46. Copyright 1991 by Sloan Management Review Association. All rights reserved.

Asking customers about their expectations does not so much raise the levels of the expectations themselves but rather heightens the belief that the company will do something with the information that surfaces. Arguably the worst thing a company can do is show a strong interest in understanding what customers expect and then never act on the information. At a minimum, a company should acknowledge to customers that it has received and heard their input and that it will expend effort trying to address their issues. The company may not be able to—and indeed does not always have to—deliver to expressed expectations. An alternative and appropriate response would be to let customers know the reasons desired service is not being provided at the present time and describe the efforts planned to address them. Another approach could be a campaign to educate customers about ways to use and improve the service they currently receive. Giving customers progress updates as service is improved to address their needs and desires is sensible because it allows the company to get credit for incremental efforts to improve service.

Some observers recommend deliberately underpromising the service to increase the likelihood of meeting or exceeding customer expectations.[19] While underpromising makes service expectations more realistic, thereby narrowing the gap between expectations and perceptions, it also may reduce the competitive appeal of the offer. Also, some research has indicated that underpromising may have the inadvertent effect of lowering customer *perceptions* of service, particularly in situations where customers have little experience with a service.[20] In these situations customer expectations may be self-fulfilling; that is, if the customer goes into the service experience expecting good service, he or she will focus on the aspects of service provision that are positive, but if she expects low service she may focus on the negative. Thus a salesperson who pitches a customer with a realistic promise may lose the sale to another who inflates the offering. In Chapter 15 we describe various techniques for controlling a firm's promises, but for now consider two options. First, if the salesperson knows that no competitor can meet an inflated sales promise in an industry, he or she could point that fact out to the customer, thereby refuting the promise made by competitive salespeople.

The second option is for the provider to follow a sale with a "reality check" about service delivery. One of the authors of this textbook bought a new house from a builder. Typical sales promises were made about the quality of the home, some less than accurate, in order to make the sale. Before closing on the house, the buyer and builder conducted a final check on the house. At the front door, the builder turned to the buyer and pointed out that each new home has between 3,000 and 5,000 individual elements and that in his experience the typical new home had 100 to 150 defects. Armed with this "reality check," the buyer thought the 32 defects found in the house seemed minor. Consider the buyer's response in the absence of that reality check.

Should a Company Try to Delight the Customer?

Some management consultants urge service companies to "delight" customers to gain a competitive edge. The *delight* that they refer to is a profoundly positive emotional state that results from having one's expectations exceeded to a surprising degree.[21] One author has described the type of service that results in delight as "positively outrageous service"—that which is unexpected, random, extraordinary, and disproportionately positive.[22]

A way that managers can conceive of delight is to consider product and service features in terms of concentric rings.[23] The innermost bull's-eye refers to attributes that are central to the basic function of the product or service, called *musts*. Their provision isn't particularly noticeable, but their absence would be. Around the musts is a ring called *satisfiers:* features that have the potential to further satisfaction beyond the basic function of the product. At the next and final outer level are *delights,* or product features that are unexpected and surprisingly enjoyable. These are things that consumers would not expect to find and are therefore highly surprised and sometimes excited when they receive them. For example, in your classes the musts consist of professors, rooms, syllabi, and class meetings. Satisfiers might include professors who are entertaining or friendly, interesting lectures, and good audiovisual aids. A delight might include a free textbook for students signing up for the course.

Delighting customers may seem like a good idea, but this level of service provision comes with extra effort and cost to the firm. Therefore, the benefits of providing delight must be weighed. Among the considerations are the staying power and competitive implications of delight.

Staying power involves the question of how long a company can expect an experience of delight to maintain the consumer's attention. If it is fleeting and the customer forgets it immediately, it may not be worth the cost. Alternatively, if the customer remembers the delight and adjusts her level of expectation upward accordingly, it will cost the company more just to satisfy, effectively raising the bar for the future. Recent research indicates that delighting customers does in fact raise expectations and make it more difficult for a company to satisfy customers in the future.[24]

The competitive implication of delight relates to its impact on expectations of other firms in the same industry. If a competitor in the same industry is unable to copy the delight strategy, it will be disadvantaged by the consumer's increased expectations. If you were offered that free textbook in one of your classes, you might then expect to receive one in each of your classes. Those classes not offering the free textbook might not have high enrollment levels compared to the delighting class. If a competitor can easily copy the delight strategy, however, neither firm benefits (although the consumer does!), and all firms may be hurt because their costs increase and profits erode. The implication is that if companies choose to delight, they should do so in areas that cannot be copied by other firms.

How Does a Company Exceed Customer Service Expectations?

Many companies today talk about exceeding customer expectations—delighting and surprising them by giving more than they expect. This philosophy raises the question, Should a service provider try simply to meet customer expectations or to exceed them?

First, it is essential to recognize that exceeding customer expectations of the basics is virtually impossible. Honoring promises—having the reserved room available, meeting deadlines, showing up for meetings, delivering the core service—is what the company is supposed to do. Companies are *supposed* to be accurate and dependable and provide the service they promised to provide.[25] As you examine the examples of basic expectations of customers in Exhibit 3.2, ask yourself if a provider doing any of these things would delight you. The conclusion you should reach is that it is very difficult to surprise or delight customers consistently by delivering reliable service.

How, then, does a company delight its customers and exceed their expectations? In virtually any service, developing a customer relationship is one approach for exceeding service expectations. The United States Automobile Association (USAA), a provider of insurance to military personnel and their dependents, illustrates how a large company that never interacts personally with its customers can surprise and delight them with its personalization of service and knowledge of the customer. Using a state-of-the-art imaging system, all USAA employees can access any customer's entire information file in seconds, giving them full knowledge of the customer's history and requirements and the status of the customer's recent interactions with the company. Expecting a lower level of personalization from an insurance company and from most any service interaction on the telephone, USAA's customers are surprised and impressed with the care and concern employees demonstrate.

Using a similar type of information technology, Ritz-Carlton Hotels, a winner of the Malcolm Baldrige Quality Award, provides highly personalized attention to its customers. The company trains each of its employees to note guest likes and dislikes and to record these into a computerized guest history profile. The company now has information on the preferences of more than 240,000 repeat Ritz-Carlton guests, resulting in more personalized service. The aim is not simply to meet expectations of guests but to provide them with a "memorable visit." The company uses the guest history information to exceed customers' expectations of the way they will be treated. When a repeat customer calls the hotel's central reservations number to book accommodations, the reservation agent can call up the individual's preference information. He or she then sends this information electronically to the particular hotel at which the reservation is made. The hotel puts the data in a daily guest recognition and preference report that is circulated to employees. Employees then greet the repeat guest personally at check-in and ensure that the guest's needs/preferences are anticipated and met.[26]

How well does this approach work? According to surveys conducted for Ritz-Carlton by an independent research firm, 92 to 97 percent of the company's guests leave satisfied.[27] A survey by Gallup Surveys found the Ritz-Carlton Hotel Company to be the first choice of its customers for the last two years, a 95 percent satisfaction rating, compared with a 57 percent satisfaction rating for the nearest competitor. And the Ritz-Carlton maintains a 10 percent performance gap over the next best competitor out of those hotels rated four or five stars by the *Mobil Travel Guide.*[28]

Do Customer Service Expectations Continually Escalate?

As we illustrated in the beginning of this chapter, customer service expectations are dynamic. In the credit card industry, as in many competitive service industries, battling companies seek to best each other and thereby raise the level of service above that of competing companies. Service expectations—in this case adequate service expectations—rise as quickly as service delivery or promises rise. In a highly competitive and rapidly changing industry, expectations can thus rise quickly. For this reason companies need to monitor adequate service expectations continually—the more turbulent the industry, the more frequent the monitoring needed.

Desired service expectations, on the other hand, are far more stable. Because they are driven by more enduring factors, such as personal needs and enduring service intensifiers, they tend to be high to begin with and remain high.

How Does a Service Company Stay Ahead of Competition in Meeting Customer Expectations?

All else being equal, a company's goal is to meet customer expectations better than its competitors. Given the fact that adequate service expectations change rapidly in a turbulent environment, how can a company ensure that it stays ahead of competition?

The adequate service level reflects the minimum performance level expected by customers after they consider a variety of personal and external factors (Figure 3.7), including the availability of service options from other providers. Companies whose service performance falls short of this level are clearly at a competitive disadvantage, with the disadvantage escalating as the gap widens. These companies' customers may well be "reluctant" customers, ready to take their business elsewhere the moment they perceive an alternative.

If they are to use service quality for competitive advantage, companies must perform above the adequate service level. This level, however, may signal only a temporary advantage. Customers' adequate service levels, which are less stable than desired service levels, will rise rapidly when competitors promise and deliver a higher level of service. If a company's level of service is barely above the adequate service level to begin with, a competitor can quickly erode that advantage. Companies currently performing in the region of competitive advantage must stay alert to the need for service increases to meet or beat competition.

To develop a true customer franchise—immutable customer loyalty—companies must consistently exceed not only the adequate service level but also reach the desired service level. Exceptional service can intensify customers' loyalty to a point where they are impervious to competitive options.

Summary

Using a conceptual framework of the nature and determinants of customer expectations of service, we showed in this chapter that customers hold different types of service expectations: (1) desired service, which reflects what customers want; (2) adequate service, what customers are willing to accept; and (3) predicted service, what customers believe they are likely to get.

Customer expectations are influenced by a variety of factors, some controllable and others uncontrollable by service marketers. The types and sources of expectations are the same for end consumers and business customers, for pure service and product-related service, and for experienced customers and inexperienced customers.

Discussion Questions

1. What is the difference between desired service and adequate service? Why would a services marketer need to understand both types of service expectations?

2. Consider a recent service purchase that you have made. Which of the factors influencing expectations were the most important in your decision? Why?

3. Why are desired service expectations more stable than adequate service expectations?

4. How do the technology changes discussed in the Technology Spotlight in this chapter influence customer expectations?

5. Describe several instances where a service company's explicit service promises were inflated and led you to be disappointed with the service outcome.

6. Consider a small business preparing to buy a computer system. Which of the influences on customer expectations do you believe will be pivotal? Which factors will have the most influence? Which factors will have the least importance in this decision?

7. What strategies can you add to Exhibit 3.1 for influencing the factors?

8. Do you believe any of your service expectations are unrealistic? Which ones? Should a service marketer try to address unrealistic customer expectations?

9. In your opinion, what service companies have effectively built customer franchises (immutable customer loyalty)?

10. Intuitively, it would seem that managers would want their customers to have wide tolerance zones for service. But if customers do have these wide zones of tolerance for service, is it more difficult for firms with superior service to earn cus-

tomer loyalty? Would superior service firms be better off to attempt to narrow customers' tolerance zones to reduce the competitive appeal of mediocre providers?

11. Should service marketers delight their customers?

Exercises

1. What factors do you think influenced your professor to adopt this text? In the case of text adoption, what do you think are the most important factors? After you have formulated your ideas, ask your professor in class to talk about the sources of his or her expectations.

2. Keep a service journal for a day and document your use of services. Ask yourself before each service encounter to indicate your predicted service of that encounter. After the encounter, note whether your expectations were met or exceeded. How does the answer to this question relate to your desire to do business with that service firm again?

3. List five incidents when a service company has exceeded your expectations. How did you react to the service? Did these incidents change the way you viewed subsequent interactions with the companies? In what way?

Notes

1. "Japanese Put Tourism on a Higher Plane," *International Herald Tribune,* February 3, 1992, p. 8.

2. J. Kelley, "Service without a Smile, Russians Find a Friendly Face Works Better," *USA Today,* January 22, 1992, p. 1.

3. The model on which this chapter is based is taken from V. A. Zeithaml, L. L. Berry, and A. Parasuraman, "The Nature and Determinants of Customer Expectations of Service," *Journal of the Academy of Marketing Science* 21, no. 1 (1993), pp. 1–12.

4. See sources such as C. Gronroos, *Strategic Management and Marketing in the Service Sector* (Helsingfors, Sweden: Swedish School of Economics and Business Administration, 1982); U. Lehtinen and J. R. Lehtinen, "Service Quality: A Study of Quality Dimensions," unpublished working paper, Helsinki, Finland OY, Service Management Institute, 1982; and S. W. Brown and T. A. Swartz, "A Dyadic Evaluation of the Professional Services Encounter," *Journal of Marketing* 53 (April 1989), pp. 92–98.

5. R. B. Woodruff, E. R. Cadotte, and R. L. Jenkins, "Expectations and Norms in Models of Consumer Satisfaction," *Journal of Marketing Research* 24 (August 1987), pp. 305–14.

6. J. A. Miller, "Studying Satisfaction, Modifying Models, Eliciting Expectations, Posing Problems, and Making Meaningful Measurements," in *Conceptualization and Measurement of Consumer Satisfaction and Dissatisfaction,* ed. H. K. Hunt (Bloomington, IN: Indiana University School of Business, 1977), pp. 72–91.

7. W. H. Davidow and B. Uttal, "Service Companies: Focus or Falter," *Harvard Business Review,* July–August 1989, pp. 77–85.

8. G. Hofstede, *Cultures and Organizations: Software of the Mind* (Berkshire, UK: McGraw-Hill, 1991).

9. N. Donthu and B. Yoo, "Cultural Influences on Service Quality Expectations," *Journal of Service Research* 1, no. 2 (November 1988), pp. 178–86.

10. A. Parasuraman, L. L. Berry, and V. A. Zeithaml, "Understanding Customer Expectations of Service," *Sloan Management Review* 32, no. 3 (Spring 1991), p. 42.

11. L. L. Berry, A. Parasuraman, and V. A. Zeithaml, "Ten Lessons for Improving Service Quality," *Marketing Science Institute,* Report No. 93-104 (May 1993).

12. Zeithaml, Berry, and Parasuraman, "Customer Expectations of Service," p. 7.

13. Ibid., p. 8.

14. D. Bowen, "Leadership Aspects and Reward Systems of Customer Satisfaction," speech given at CTM Customer Satisfaction Conference, Los Angeles, March 17, 1989.

15. Zeithaml, Berry, and Parasuraman, "Customer Expectations of Service," p. 8.

16. D. L. Davis, J. G. Guiltinan, and W. H. Jones, "Service Characteristics, Consumer Research and the Classification of Retail Services," *Journal of Retailing* 55 (Fall 1979), pp. 3–21; and W. R. George and L. L. Berry, "Guidelines for the Advertising of Services," *Business Horizons* 24 (May–June 1981), pp. 52–56.

17. E. R. Cadotte, R. B. Woodruff, and R. L. Jenkins, "Expectations and Norms in Models of Consumer Satisfaction," *Journal of Marketing Research* 14 (August 1987), pp. 353–64.

18. Parasuraman, Berry, and Zeithaml, "Understanding Customer Expectations," p. 40.

19. Davidow and Uttal, "Service Companies."

20. W. Boulding, A. Kalra, R. Staelin, and V. A. Zeithaml, "A Dynamic Process Model of Service Quality: From Expectations to Behavioral Intentions," *Journal of Marketing Research* 30 (February 1993), pp. 7–27.

21. R. T. Rust and R. L. Oliver, "Should We Delight the Customer," *Journal of the Academy of Marketing Science* 28 (Winter 2000), pp. 86–94.

22. T. S. Gross, *Positively Outrageous Service* (New York: Warner Books, 1994).

23. J. Clemmer, "The Three Rings of Perceived Value," *Canadian Manager* (Summer 1990), pp. 30–32.

24. Rust and Oliver, op cit.

25. Parasuraman, Berry, and Zeithaml, "Understanding Customer Expectations," p. 41.

26. "How the Ritz-Carlton Hotel Company Delivers 'Memorable' Service to Customers," *Executive Report on Customer Satisfaction* 6, no. 5 (March 15, 1993), pp. 1–4.

27. Ibid.

28. Ibid.

Chapter 4

CUSTOMER PERCEPTIONS OF SERVICE

This chapter's objectives are to

1. Provide you with definitions and understanding of customer satisfaction and service quality and of how these two types of customer perceptions are related.

2. Show that service encounters or the "moments of truth" are the essential foundation of customer perceptions.

3. Highlight strategies for managing customer perceptions of service.

At Coors Field, Great Service Is More than Winning Games

For the 3.4 million baseball fans who attended one of the Colorado Rockies' 81 home games, hits, runs, and errors—along with a helping or two of peanuts, popcorn, and Cracker Jacks—were probably the measure of a good day. But for the five groups that work together to provide customer service at every Rockies home game at Denver's Coors Field, a good day at the ballpark is measured as much by the number of lost Little Leaguers united with parents, valuables returned to their rightful owners, and special requests responded to, as it is by the box score of the game. The Rockies receive roughly 150 comment cards per game, which translates into about 12,450 for the season. Some of these comments are simple requests for seat repair or missing cup holders, but about 40 each game receive a personal response from a member of the stadium services department—about 3,320 each season.

What does great service look like at Coors Field? It looks like Brian S., who spent an hour and a half after a Rockies game walking the surrounding neighborhood with a six-year-old child who had become separated from his older brother and couldn't remember his address. The boys had walked the 12 blocks from home to the game. And great service looks like Kelly G., who pushed a fan the 14 blocks from the park to his home when the battery on his electric wheelchair went dead. Not to be outdone, Rockies' service team member Stacy S. drove a family of four

Dear Lands' End,

Recognizing that all good things must come to an end, I was still a little sad opening my very last Rugby Bear under the soft lights of my family Christmas tree. The bears had been a cherished annual gift from my family since my freshman year of college, So Kid Kodiak marked the end of an era for me.

I immediately fell in love with Kid's cute scowl, potbelly, and affinity for blueberry pies. But something was missing—one little thing that kept me from being totally happy at getting the final member of my team.

That one little thing? Big Daddy, from 1992. I don't know how, but somehow the bear for that year did not make it under the tree. I realized it too late and it appeared impossible to get him. Lands' End phone reps said it was too late and he couldn't be ordered anymore. So I dropped it and tried to be content that I had the other six bears. But still . . .

Imagine my surprise when I opened up one of my last presents from my boyfriend and found—BIG DADDY! I was absolutely stunned—how could he have gotten this if LE said it was not available anymore?

I don't have the complete details from him yet (and maybe it's best that way to keep some of the "magic" of Christmas), but apparently he spoke with someone in Customer Service who helped him track down the "owner" of the '26 Championship team with the use of an internal newsletter for the employees of Lands' End.

So, this is my little way of saying thanks to the mystery woman in Customer Service for helping beyond the call of duty, the mystery employee who contributed Big Daddy, and Lands' End for being the best company.

And if I may a huge public thank you for my boyfriend, Patrick. My Christmas present for him this year? A Lands' End travel golf bag, of course! (He loved it!)

Jennifer
Salisbury, NC

PS Are you sure I can't convince you to conjure up a few more teammates????

Source: K. Anderson and R. Zemke, *Tales of Knock Your Socks Off Service* (New York: AMACOM, 1998), pp. 156–57. Reprinted courtesy of Lands' End, Inc.

home to Ft. Collins, an hour and a half away, when they became separated from their car keys.

Taking care of customers sometimes extends beyond the members of the guest services team to the ballplayers themselves. During one game, a guest was hit by a foul ball off the bat of outfielder Dante Bichette. The next day Bichette visited the guest at her home—and ended up staying for dinner.

By the way, if you're ever at Coors Field and need a guest relations person, they're easy to find—they are, quite literally, the ones in the white hats.[1]

Great games, fun atmosphere, excellent service quality, lots of little extras, and the unexpected over-the-top kindness of service team members all add up to customer satisfaction for guests of the Colorado Rockies. The same is true for other landmark service companies such as Lands' End (see Exhibit 4.1), IBM Global Services, and Ritz Carlton Hotels. In all of these companies, the quality of the core product and exemplary customer service result in high customer satisfaction ratings.

So what is it that brings about customer satisfaction? How do customers evaluate service quality? How do they form their perceptions of service? Answers to these questions are the subjects of this chapter.

CUSTOMER PERCEPTIONS

How customers perceive services, how they assess whether they have experienced quality service, and whether they are satisfied are the subjects of this chapter. We will be focusing on the *perceived service* box in the gaps model. As we move through this chapter, keep in mind that perceptions are always considered relative to expectations. Because expectations are dynamic, evaluations may also shift over time—from person to person and from culture to culture. What is considered quality service or the things that satisfy customers today may be different tomorrow. Also keep in mind that the entire discussion of quality and satisfaction is based on *customers' perceptions of the service*—not some predetermined objective criteria of what service is or should be.

Customers perceive services in terms of the quality of the service and how satisfied they are overall with their experiences. These customer-oriented terms—*quality* and *satisfaction*—have been the focus of attention for executives and researchers alike over the last decade or more. Companies today recognize that they can compete more effectively by distinguishing themselves with respect to service quality and improved customer satisfaction.

Satisfaction versus Service Quality

Practitioners and writers in the popular press tend to use the terms *satisfaction* and *quality* interchangeably, but researchers have attempted to be more precise about the meanings and measurement of the two concepts, resulting in considerable debate.[2] Consensus is growing that the two concepts are fundamentally different in terms of their underlying causes and outcomes.[3] Although they have certain things in common, **satisfaction** is generally viewed as a broader concept, whereas **service quality assessment** focuses specifically on dimensions of service. Based on this view, **perceived service quality** is a component of customer satisfaction. Figure 4.1 graphically illustrates the distinctions between the two concepts.

FIGURE 4.1
Customer Perceptions of Quality and Customer Satisfaction

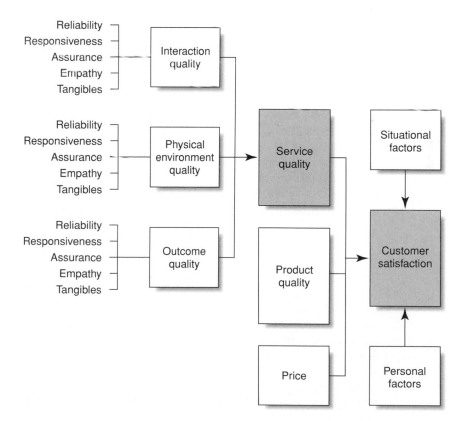

As shown in Figure 4.1, service quality is a focused evaluation that reflects the customer's perception of elements of service such as interaction quality, physical environment quality, and outcome quality.[4] These elements are in turn evaluated based on specific service quality dimensions: reliability, assurance, responsiveness, empathy, and tangibles.[5] Satisfaction, on the other hand, is more inclusive: It is influenced by perceptions of service quality, product quality, and price as well as situational factors and personal factors. For example, *service quality* of a health club is judged on attributes such as whether equipment is available and in working order when needed, how responsive the staff are to customer needs, how skilled the trainers are, and whether the facility is well-maintained. *Customer satisfaction* with the health club is a broader concept that will certainly be influenced by perceptions of service quality but that will also include perceptions of product quality (such as quality of products sold in the pro shop), price of membership,[6] personal factors such as the consumer's emotional state, and even uncontrollable situational factors such as weather conditions and experiences driving to and from the health club.[7]

CUSTOMER SATISFACTION

What Is Customer Satisfaction?

"Everyone knows what satisfaction is, until asked to give a definition. Then, it seems, nobody knows."[8] This quote from Richard L. Oliver, respected expert and long-time writer and researcher on the topic of customer satisfaction, expresses the challenge of defining this most basic of customer concepts. Building from previous definitions, Oliver offers his own formal definition:

> Satisfaction is the consumer's fulfillment response. It is a judgment that a product or service feature, or the product or service itself, provides a pleasurable level of consumption-related fulfillment.[9]

In less technical terms, we translate this definition to mean that *satisfaction* is the customers' evaluation of a product or service in terms of whether that product or service has met their needs and expectations. Failure to meet needs and expectations is assumed to result in *dissatisfaction* with the product or service.

In addition to a sense of *fulfillment* in the knowledge that one's needs have been met, satisfaction can also be related to other types of feelings, depending on the particular context or type of service.[10] For example, satisfaction can be viewed as *contentment*—more of a passive response that consumers may associate with services they don't think a lot about or services that they receive routinely over time. Satisfaction may also be associated with feelings of *pleasure* for services that make the consumer feel good or are associated with a sense of happiness. For those services that really surprise the consumer in a positive way, satisfaction may mean *delight*. And in some situations, where the removal of a negative leads to satisfaction, the consumer may associate a sense of *relief* with satisfaction.

It is also important to recognize that although we tend to measure consumer satisfaction at a particular point in time as if it were static, satisfaction is a dynamic, moving target that may evolve over time, influenced by a variety of factors.[11] Particularly when product usage or the service experience takes place over time, satisfaction may be highly variable depending on which point in the usage or experience cycle one is focusing on. Similarly, in the case of very new services or a service not previously experienced, customer expectations may be barely forming at the point of initial purchase; these expectations will solidify as the process unfolds and the consumer begins to form his or her perceptions. Through the service cycle the consumer may have a variety of different experiences—some good, some not good—and each will ultimately impact satisfaction.

What Determines Customer Satisfaction?

Customer satisfaction is influenced by specific product or service features and by perceptions of quality as suggested by Figure 4.1. Satisfaction is also influenced by customers' emotional responses, their attributions, and their perceptions of equity.

Product and Service Features   Customer satisfaction with a product or service is influenced significantly by the customer's evaluation of product or service features.[12] For a service such as a resort hotel, important features might include the pool area, access to golf facilities, restaurants, room comfort and privacy, helpfulness and courtesy of staff, room price, and so forth. In conducting satisfaction studies, most firms will determine through some means (often focus groups) what the important features and attributes are for their service and then measure perceptions of those features as well as overall service satisfaction. Research has shown that customers of services will make trade-offs among different service features (for example, price level versus quality versus friendliness of personnel versus level of customization), depending on the type of service being evaluated and the criticality of the service.[13]

Consumer Emotions   Customers' emotions can also affect their perceptions of satisfaction with products and services.[14] These emotions can be stable, preexisting emotions—for example, mood state or life satisfaction. Think of times when you are at a very happy stage in your life (such as when you are on vacation), and your good, happy mood and positive frame of mind have influenced how you feel about the services you experience. Alternatively, when you are in a bad mood, your negative feelings may carry over into how you respond to services, causing you to overreact or respond negatively to any little problem.

Specific emotions may also be induced by the consumption experience itself, influencing a consumer's satisfaction with the service. Research done in a river-rafting context showed that the river guides had a strong effect on their customers' emotional responses to the trip and that those feelings (both positive and negative) were linked to overall trip satisfaction.[15] Positive emotions such as happiness, pleasure, elation, and a sense of warm-heartedness enhanced customers' satisfaction with the rafting trip. In turn, negative emotions such as sadness, sorrow, regret, and anger led to diminished customer satisfaction. Overall, in the rafting context, positive emotions had a stronger effect than negative ones. (These positive emotions are apparent in the ad shown in Figure 4.2.) Similar effects of emotions on satisfaction were found in a Finnish study that looked at consumers' satisfaction with a government labor bureau service.[16] In that study, negative emotions including anger, depression, guilt, and humiliation had a strong effect on customers' dissatisfaction ratings.

Attributions for Service Success or Failure   Attributions—the perceived causes of events—influence perceptions of satisfaction as well.[17] When they have been surprised by an outcome (the service is either much better or much worse than expected), consumers tend to look for the reasons, and their assessments of the reasons can influence their satisfaction. For example, if a customer of a weight-loss organization fails to lose weight as hoped for, she will likely search for the causes—was it something she did, was the diet plan ineffective, or did circumstances simply not allow her to follow the diet regimen—before determining her level of satisfaction or dissatisfaction with the

FIGURE 4.2
River rafters
experience many
positive emotions,
increasing their
satisfaction with the
service.

Source: River Odysseys West,
www.rowinc.com

weight-loss company.[18] For many services customers take at least partial responsibility for how things turn out.

Even when they don't take responsibility for the outcome, customer satisfaction may be influenced by other kinds of attributions. For example, in research done in a travel agency context it was found that customers were less dissatisfied with a pricing error made by the agent if they felt the reason was outside the agent's control or if they felt it was a rare mistake, unlikely to occur again.[19]

Perceptions of Equity or Fairness   Customer satisfaction is also influenced by perceptions of equity and fairness.[20] Customers ask themselves: Have I been treated fairly compared with other customers? Did other customers get better treatment, better prices, or better quality service? Did I pay a fair price for the service? Was I treated well in exchange for what I paid and the effort I expended? Notions of fairness are central to customers' perceptions of satisfaction with products and services. The example of Sears Auto Centers division illustrates consumers' strong reactions to unfair treatment.[21] Over a decade ago the division was charged with defrauding customers in 44 states by performing unnecessary repairs. Sears employees had been rewarded based on the quantity of repairs sold, resulting in substantial unnecessary charges to customers. The $27 million Sears paid settling complaints and the additional loss of business all resulted from extreme dissatisfaction of its customers over the unfair treatment.

Other Consumers, Family Members, and Coworkers   In addition to product and service features and one's own individual feelings and beliefs, consumer satisfaction is often influenced by other people.[22] For example, satisfaction with a family vacation trip is a dynamic phenomenon, influenced by the reactions and expressions of individual family members over the duration of the vacation. Later, what family members express in terms of satisfaction or dissatisfaction with the trip will be influenced by stories that are retold among the family and selective memories of the events. Similarly, the satisfaction of the rafters in Figure 4.2 is certainly influenced by individual perceptions, but it is also influenced greatly by the experiences, behavior, and views of the other rafters. In a business setting, satisfaction with a new service or technology—

for example, a new customer relationship management software service—will be influenced by individuals' personal experiences with the software itself, but also by what others say about it in the company, how others use it and feel about it, and how widely it is adopted in the organization. In Chapter 12 we will come back to this topic as we look at strategies for involving and managing other consumers to maximize satisfaction in the service experience.

National Customer Satisfaction Indexes

Because of the importance of customer satisfaction to firms and overall quality of life, many countries how have a national index that measures and tracks customer satisfaction at a macro level.[23] Many public policymakers believe that these measures could and should be used as tools for evaluating the health of the nation's economy, along with traditional measures of productivity and price. Customer satisfaction indexes begin to get at the *quality* of economic output, whereas more traditional economic indicators tend to focus only on *quantity*. The first such measure was the Swedish Customer Satisfaction Barometer introduced in 1989.[24] Throughout the 1990s similar indexes were introduced in Germany (Deutsche Kundenbarometer, or DK, in 1992), the United States (American Customer Satisfaction Index, ACSI, in 1994), and Switzerland (Swiss Index of Customer Satisfaction, SWICS, in 1998).[25]

The American Customer Satisfaction Index (ACSI)[26]   The ACSI, developed by researchers at the National Quality Research Center at the University of Michigan, is a measure of quality of goods and services as experienced by consumers. The measure tracks customer perceptions across 200 firms representing all major economic sectors, including government agencies. Within each industry group, major industry segments are included, and within each industry the largest companies in that industry are selected to participate. For each company approximately 250 interviews are conducted with current customers. Each company receives an ACSI score computed from its customers' perceptions of quality, value, satisfaction, expectations, complaints, and future loyalty.[27]

The 2001 ACSI results by industry are shown in Table 4.1.[28] The table shows that, overall, consumers tend to be most satisfied with nondurables (like soft drinks, pet foods, and personal care products), a bit less satisfied with durables (such as cars, consumer electronics, and household appliances), and the least satisfied with services (like airlines, hospitals, energy utilities, and Internet portals). In the year 2000 e-commerce retailers and services were assessed for the first time. With the exception of Internet portals, which ranked near the bottom, other e-commerce categories (online retailers, auctions, and brokerage services) ranked in the middle ranges. The observation that services tend to rank lower in the ACSI rankings than do durable and nondurable products is a trend observed across six years of the ACSI's history. It is important to point out, however, that these are industry averages. In virtually every industry there are stronger performers in terms of customer satisfaction. For example, in the restaurant and fast-food category, the average score is 70; however, Papa John's International scored a 77. The overall rating for personal computers is 71, but Dell received a 78. For all federal tax filers the average score is a low 56; however, among electronic tax filers the IRS receives a score of 75.

We can only conjecture about the reasons for lower satisfaction with services in general. Perhaps it is because downsizing and right-sizing in service businesses has resulted in stressed and overworked front-line service providers who are unable to provide the level of service demanded. Perhaps it is due to the inherent heterogeneity of

TABLE 4.1
American Customer Satisfaction Index—Ratings by Industry

Source: ACSI website, www.bus.umich.edu/research.nqrc/.
NA Not available. NC No change.

Industry	Customer Satisfaction 2000/2001 Score	Change from Previous Year
Beverages, soft drinks	86	2.4
Personal care products	84	3.7
Pet foods	83	1.2
Beverages, beer	82	3.8
Household appliances	82	−3.5
Food processing	81	NC
Consumer electronics	81	−2.4
Automobiles, vans, light trucks	80	NC
Insurance, casualty, property	79	NC
Apparel, athletic shoes	79	NC
Parcel delivery, express mail	78	−3.7
Tobacco, cigarettes	78	2.6
Internet retailers	78	NA
Gasoline	75	−1.3
Insurance, life	75	−1.3
Supermarkets	73	−1.4
Department and discount stores	72	NC
Internet brokerage services	72	NA
Internet auctions	72	NA
Telecommunications	70	−2.8
Hotels	71	−1.4
Motion pictures	71	4.4
Personal computers	71	−4.1
Commercial banks	70	2.9
U.S. Postal Service	70	−2.8
Restaurants, fast-food, pizza, carryout	70	1.4
Energy utilities	69	−8.0
Publishing, newspapers	68	NC
Hospitals	68	−1.4
Internet portals	63	NA
Broadcasting, national news	62	−3.1
Airlines, scheduled	61	−3.2
Internal Revenue Service	56	−1

services discussed in Chapter 1; in other words, because services are difficult to standardize, and each customer has his or her own unique expectations, the result may be greater variability and potentially lower overall satisfaction. Perhaps it is due to low unemployment over the many years of the ACSI, resulting in difficulty finding qualified front-line service providers for consumer-service businesses. Perhaps it is due to rising customer expectations rather than any real or absolute decline in actual service. Whatever the reason, it is apparent that there is much room for improvement in customer satisfaction ratings across consumer-service industries.

Outcomes of Customer Satisfaction

Why all of this attention to customer satisfaction? As mentioned earlier, some public policymakers believe that customer satisfaction is an important indicator of national economic health. They believe that it is not enough to track economic efficiency and

FIGURE 4.3
ACSI and Annual Percentage Growth in S&P 500 Earnings

Source: C. Fornell, "Customer Satisfaction and Corporate Earnings," commentary appearing on ACSI website, May 1, 2001, www.bus.umich.edu/research/nqrc/Q1-01c.html.

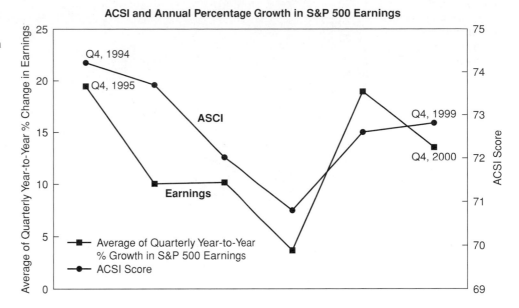

pricing statistics. Satisfaction, they believe, is just as important an indicator of quality of life. Further, many believe that customer satisfaction is correlated with other measures of economic health such as corporate earnings and stock value. Through the ACSI data, researchers at the University of Michigan have been able to document a clear correlational relationship between the ACSI average in a year and the S&P 500 earnings in the following year, suggesting strong relationships between customer satisfaction and important earnings outcomes. This relationship is depicted in Figure 4.3.[29]

Beyond these macroeconomic implications, however, individual firms have discovered that increasing levels of customer satisfaction can be linked to customer loyalty and profits.[30] As shown in Figure 4.4, there is an important relationship between customer satisfaction and customer loyalty. This relationship is particularly strong when customers are very satisfied. Thus firms that simply aim to satisfy customers may not be doing enough to engender loyalty—they must instead aim to more than satisfy or even delight their customers. Xerox Corporation was one of the first, if not the first, companies to pinpoint this relationship. In the 1980s Xerox discovered through its extensive customer research that customers giving Xerox a 5 (very satisfied) on a satisfaction scale were six times more likely to repurchase Xerox equipment than those giving the company a 4 (somewhat satisfied).[31] Many other companies have drawn this same conclusion.

At the opposite end of the satisfaction spectrum, researchers have also found that there is a strong link between dissatisfaction and disloyalty—or defection. Customer loyalty can fall off precipitously when customers reach a particular level of dissatisfaction or when they are dissatisfied with critically important service attributes.[32] We discuss these relationships and the implications for relationship and loyalty marketing in Chapter 6, but suffice it to say here that clear linkages have been drawn between customer satisfaction, loyalty, and firm profitability. Thus, many companies are spending more time and money understanding the underpinnings of customer satisfaction and ways that they can improve.

FIGURE 4.4

Relationship between Customer Satisfaction and Loyalty in Competitive Industries

Source: J. L. Heskett, W. E. Sasser, Jr., and L. A. Schlesinger, *The Service Profit Chain: How Leading Companies Link Profit and Growth to Loyalty, Satisfaction, and Value* (New York: The Free Press, 1997), p. 83. Copyright © 1997 by J. L. Heskett, W. E. Sasser, Jr., and L. A. Schlesinger. Reprinted with the permission of The Free Press, a Division of Simon & Schuster, Inc.

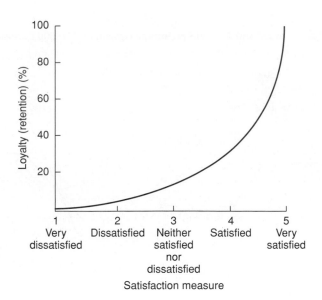

SERVICE QUALITY

We now turn to *service quality,* a critical element of customer perceptions. In the case of pure services, service quality will be the dominant element in customers' evaluations. In cases where customer service or services are offered in combination with a physical product, service quality may also be very critical in determining customer satisfaction. Figure 4.1 highlighted these relationships. We will focus here on the left side of Figure 4.1, examining the underlying factors that form perceptions of service quality. First we discuss *what* customers evaluate; then we look specifically at the five dimensions of service that customers rely on in forming their judgments.

Outcome, Interaction, and Physical Environment Quality

What is it that consumers evaluate when judging service quality? Over the years, services researchers have suggested that consumers judge the quality of services based on their perceptions of the technical outcome provided, the process by which that outcome was delivered, and the quality of the physical surroundings where the service is delivered. These elements of service quality are depicted in Figure 4.1 as outcome, interaction, and physical environment quality.[33] For example, in the case of a lawsuit, a legal services client will judge the quality of the technical outcome, or how the court case was resolved, and also the quality of the interaction. Interaction quality would include such things as the lawyer's timeliness in returning phone calls, his empathy for the client, and his courtesy and listening skills. Similarly, a restaurant customer will judge the service on her perceptions of the meal (technical outcome quality) and on how the meal was served and how the employees interacted with her (interaction quality). The decor and surroundings (physical environment quality) of the restaurant will also impact the customer's perceptions of overall service quality.

This depiction of service quality as outcome quality, interaction quality, and physical environment quality is most recently captured by Brady and Cronin in their empirical research published in the *Journal of Marketing.*[34] Other researchers have defined similar aspects of service in their examinations of service quality. Gronroos defined two types of quality—technical and functional—referring to the outcome of the service and the manner in which it is delivered.[35] Rust and Oliver later defined three aspects of service quality as service product, service delivery, and service environment.[36] And Bitner describes the "evidence of service" quality as consisting of the three new Ps for services: people, process, and physical evidence.[37] All of these researchers suggest that there are common aspects of service that a consumer will evaluate in forming his or her perceptions of quality.

In some cases, as with restaurant services, all three aspects of service are likely to be important to the overall assessment of quality. Other times, as in the case of a kiosk-based ticketing service, only technical outcome and physical environment quality are likely to come into play in the consumer's evaluation process. Because the technical outcome for many services is highly complex and sometimes ambiguous, the quality of the technical outcome is not always evident. For example, the technical quality of services offered by lawyers, doctors, engineers, college professors, accountants, and architects, among others—as well as many routine services such as termite inspection and automobile or computer repair—may be difficult to assess. In such cases consumers may rely on their assessments of interaction and physical environment quality as cues for technical quality.

Service Quality Dimensions

Research suggests that customers do not perceive quality in a unidimensional way, but rather judge quality based on multiple factors relevant to the context. For example, quality of automobiles is judged by such factors as reliability, serviceability, prestige, durability, functionality, and ease of use, whereas quality of food products might be assessed on other dimensions (flavor, freshness, aroma, and so on). Similarly, specific dimensions of service quality have been identified through the pioneering research of Parasuraman, Zeithaml, and Berry. Their research identified five specific dimensions of service quality that apply across a variety of service contexts.[38] The five dimensions defined here are shown in Figure 4.1 as criteria by which interaction, physical environment, and outcome quality may be judged. These five dimensions are discussed further in Chapter 5, along with the scale developed to measure them.

- *Reliability:* ability to perform the promised service dependably and accurately.

- *Responsiveness:* willingness to help customers and provide prompt service.

- *Assurance:* employees' knowledge and courtesy and their ability to inspire trust and confidence.

- *Empathy:* caring, individualized attention given to customers.

- *Tangibles:* appearance of physical facilities, equipment, personnel, and written materials.

These dimensions represent how consumers organize information about service quality in their minds. On the basis of exploratory and quantitative research, these five dimensions were found relevant for banking, insurance, appliance repair and maintenance, securities brokerage, long-distance telephone service, automobile repair service, and others. The dimensions are also applicable to retail and business services, and logic suggests they would be relevant for internal services as well. Sometimes customers will use all of the dimensions to determine service quality perceptions, at other times not. For example, in a remote encounter such as with an ATM, empathy is not likely to be a relevant dimension. And in a phone encounter such as scheduling a repair call, tangibles will not be relevant. Research suggests that cultural differences will also affect the relative importance placed on the five dimensions, as discussed in our Global Feature.

The development of the service quality dimensions of reliability, responsiveness, assurance, empathy, and tangibles was based on research conducted across multiple contexts within the United States. As a general rule, reliability comes through as the most important dimension of service quality in the United States, with responsiveness also being relatively important when compared to the remaining three dimensions. But what happens when we look across cultures? Are the service quality dimensions still important? Which ones are most important? Answers to these questions can be extremely valuable for companies delivering services across cultures or in multicultural environments.

Researchers have used Hofstede's well-established cultural dimensions to assess whether service quality importance would vary across different cultural orientations. For example, *power distance* refers to the extent to which status differences are expected and accepted within a culture. Research has suggested that most Asian countries are characterized by high power distance, whereas many Western countries score lower on power distance measures. Broadly speaking, *individualism* reflects a self-orientation that is characteristic of Western culture while its opposite, *collectivism,* is more typical of the East. Similar comparisons across cultures have been made for the other dimensions: *masculinity, uncertainty avoidance,* and *long-term orientation.* The question is whether these types of cultural differences may affect the importance consumers place on the service quality dimensions.

The figure shown here from research published by Furrer, Liu, and Sudharshan suggests that there will be strong differences in the importance of service quality dimensions across clusters of customers defined by different cultural dimensions. The cultural profile of the clusters is described as follows:

Followers: Large power distance, high collectivism, high masculinity, neutral uncertainty avoidance, and short-term orientation.

Balance seekers: Small power distance, high collectivism, neutral masculinity, high uncertainty avoidance, and medium-term orientation.

Self-confidents: Small power distance, high individualism, medium femininity, low uncertainty avoidance, and long-term orientation.

Sensory seekers: Large power distance, medium individualism, high masculinity, low uncertainty avoidance, and short-term orientation.

Functional analyzers: Small power distance, medium individualism, high femininity, high uncertainty avoidance, and long-term orientation.

From this figure it is clear that the service quality dimensions are important across cultures, but their relative importance varies depending on cultural value orientation. For example, small power distance cultures with high to medium individualism and long-term

We will expand on each of the five dimensions of service quality and provide illustrations of how customers judge each dimension. Table 4.2 gives examples of each for consumer services (car repair, airline, medical care, Internet brokerage), business-to-business service (architecture), and internal service (information processing within a company).

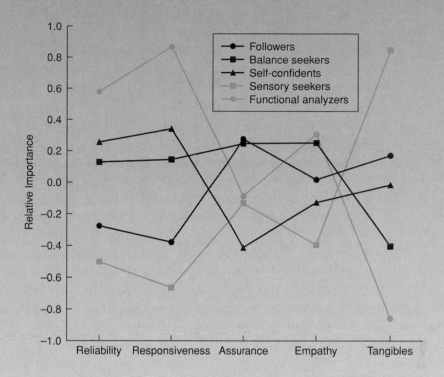

orientation (self-confidents and functional analyzers) rate reliability and responsiveness as most important. On the other hand, cultures with large power distance and high masculinity (followers and sensory seekers) rate these same dimensions as less important. The tangibles dimension shows the widest variation, with sensory seekers rating it most important and functional analyzers rating it least important.

The researchers in this study suggest a number of implications for companies serving multiple cultures. For example, if the target market has a follower cultural profile, service providers may want to emphasize training their employees to have professional knowledge and be trustworthy to gain the trust of these customers, combined with tangibles and empathy to convey service quality. On the other hand, to serve self-confidents, providers should emphasize equipping and empowering the employees so they are capable of providing reliable, responsive service.

Sources: G. Hofstede, *Cultures and Organizations: Software of the Mind* (New York, McGraw-Hill, 1991); O. Furrer, B. Shaw-Ching Liu, and D. Sudharshan, "The Relationships between Culture and Service Quality Perceptions," *Journal of Service Research*, vol. 2, no. 4 (May 2000), pp. 355–71.

Reliability: Delivering on Promises Of the five dimensions, reliability has been consistently shown to be the most important determinant of perceptions of service quality among U.S. customers.[39] **Reliability** is defined as the ability to perform the promised service dependably and accurately. In its broadest sense, reliability means that the company delivers on its promises—promises about delivery, service provision,

TABLE 4.2 **Examples of How Customers Judge the Five Dimensions of Service Quality**

	Reliability	Responsiveness	Assurance	Empathy	Tangibles
Car repair (consumer)	Problem fixed the first time and ready when promised	Accessible; no waiting; responds to requests	Knowledgeable mechanics	Acknowledges customer by name; remembers previous problems and preferences	Repair facility; waiting area; uniforms; equipment
Airline (consumer)	Flights to promised destinations depart and arrive on schedule	Prompt and speedy system for ticketing, in-flight baggage handling	Trusted name; good safety record; competent employees	Understanding of special individual needs; anticipates customer needs	Aircraft; ticketing counters; baggage area; uniforms
Medical care (consumer)	Appointments are kept on schedule; diagnoses prove accurate	Accessible; no waiting; willingness to listen	Knowledge, skills, credentials, reputation	Acknowledges patient as a person; remembers previous problems; good listening; patience	Waiting room; exam room; equipment; written materials
Architecture (business)	Delivers plans when promised and within budget	Returns phone calls; adapts to changes	Credentials; reputation; name in the community; knowledge and skills	Understands client's industry; acknowledges and adapts to specific client needs; gets to know the client	Office area; reports; plans themselves; billing statements; dress of employees
Information processing (internal)	Provides needed information when requested	Prompt response to requests; not "bureaucratic"; deals with problems promptly	Knowledgeable staff; well-trained; credentials	Knows internal customers as individuals; understands individual and departmental needs	Internal reports; office area; dress of employees
Internet brokerage (consumer and business)	Provides correct information and executes customer requests accurately	Quick website with easy access and no down time	Credible information sources on the site; brand recognition; credentials apparent on site	Ability to respond with human interaction as needed	Appearance of the website and collateral

problem resolution, and pricing. Customers want to do business with companies that keep their promises, particularly their promises about the service outcomes and core service attributes.

One company that effectively communicates and delivers on the reliability dimension is Federal Express (FedEx). The reliability message of FedEx—when it "absolutely, positively has to get there"—reflects the company's service positioning. In a later chapter we discuss specifically how FedEx has managed to ensure that it keeps this promise. But even when firms don't choose to position themselves explicitly on reliability as FedEx has, this dimension is extremely important to consumers. All firms need to be aware of customer expectations of reliability. Firms that do not provide the core service that customers think they are buying fail their customers in the most direct way.

Responsiveness: Being Willing to Help   **Responsiveness** is the willingness to help customers and to provide prompt service. This dimension emphasizes attentiveness and promptness in dealing with customer requests, questions, complaints, and problems. Responsiveness is communicated to customers by the length of time they have to wait for assistance, answers to questions, or attention to problems. Responsiveness also captures the notion of flexibility and ability to customize the service to customer needs.

To excel on the dimension of responsiveness, a company must be certain to view the process of service delivery and the handling of requests from the customer's point of view rather than from the company's point of view. Standards for speed and promptness that reflect the company's view of internal process requirements may be very different from the customer's requirements for speed and promptness. To truly distinguish themselves on responsiveness, companies need well-staffed customer service departments as well as responsive front-line people in all contact positions. Responsiveness perceptions diminish when customers wait to get through to a company by telephone, are put on hold, are put through to a phone mail system, or have trouble accessing the firm's website.

Assurance: Inspiring Trust and Confidence   **Assurance** is defined as employees' knowledge and courtesy and the ability of the firm and its employees to inspire trust and confidence. This dimension is likely to be particularly important for services that the customer perceives as involving high risk and/or about which they feel uncertain about their ability to evaluate outcomes—for example, banking, insurance, brokerage, medical, and legal service.

Trust and confidence may be embodied in the person who links the customer to the company, such as securities brokers, insurance agents, lawyers, or counselors. In such service contexts the company seeks to build trust and loyalty between key contact people and individual customers. The "personal banker" concept captures this idea: customers are assigned to a banker who will get to know them individually and who will coordinate all of their banking services.

In other situations, trust and confidence are embodied in the organization itself. Insurance companies such as Allstate ("You're in good hands with Allstate") and Prudential ("Own a piece of the rock") illustrate efforts to create trusting relationships between customers and the company as a whole. In the early stages of a relationship, the customer may use tangible evidence to assess the assurance dimension. Visible evidence of degrees, honors, and awards and special certifications may give a new customer confidence in a professional service provider.

Empathy: Treating Customers as Individuals **Empathy** is defined as the caring, individualized attention the firm provides its customers. The essence of empathy is conveying, through personalized or customized service, that customers are unique and special. Customers want to feel understood by and important to firms that provide service to them. Personnel at small service firms often know customers by name and build relationships that reflect their personal knowledge of customer requirements and preferences. When such a small firm competes with larger firms, the ability to be empathetic may give the small firm a clear advantage.

In business-to-business services, customers want supplier firms to understand their industries and issues. Many small computer consulting firms successfully compete with large vendors by positioning themselves as specialists in particular industries. Even though larger firms have superior resources, the small firms are perceived as more knowledgeable about customer's issues and needs and are able to offer more customized services.

Tangibles: Representing the Service Physically **Tangibles** are defined as the appearance of physical facilities, equipment, personnel, and communication materials. All of these provide physical representations or images of the service that customers, particularly new customers, will use to evaluate quality. Service industries that emphasize tangibles in their strategies include hospitality services where the customer visits the establishment to receive the service, such as restaurants and hotels, retail stores, and entertainment companies.

Although tangibles are often used by service companies to enhance their image, provide continuity, and signal quality to customers, most companies combine tangibles with another dimension to create a service quality strategy for the firm (for example, Jiffy Lube emphasizes both responsiveness and tangibles—providing fast, efficient service and a comfortable, clean waiting area). In contrast, firms that don't pay attention to the tangibles dimension of the service strategy can confuse and even destroy an otherwise good strategy.

E-Service Quality

The growth of e-tailing has led many companies to wonder how consumers evaluate service quality on the Web. Some commercial surveys, such as BizRate.com, have been used to capture customer perceptions of these sites. A more systematic study to understand how consumers judge e-service quality has recently been conducted.[40] In that study, *e-SQ* is defined as the extent to which a website facilitates efficient and effective shopping, purchasing, and delivery. In exploratory research involving focus groups of experienced and inexperienced users, consumers reported that they used 11 dimensions to evaluate e-SQ. These included access, ease of navigation, efficiency, flexibility, reliability, personalization, security/privacy, responsiveness, assurance/trust, site aesthetics, and price knowledge. Further study identified four core dimensions that consumers use to evaluate sites:

Efficiency: the ease and speed of accessing and using the site.

Fulfillment: the extent to which the site's promises about order delivery and item availability are fulfilled.

Reliability: the correct technical functioning of the site.

Privacy: the degree to which the site is safe and protects customer information.

The study also showed that when consumers have problems or questions with the sites, they use three additional dimensions to judge the e-service quality:

Responsiveness: handling of problems and returns through the site.

Compensation: the degree to which customers are compensated for problems.

Contact: the degree to which help can be accessed by telephone or online representatives.

In comparing the dimensions of traditional service quality and e-service quality, we can make several observations. First, the traditional dimensions can and should be considered for e-tailing and Internet-based services, as illustrated by the Internet brokerage example in Table 4.2. However, both similar and different dimensions emerge in the research on e-tailing. Reliability and responsiveness are shared dimensions, but new Internet-specific dimensions appear to be critical in that context. Efficiency and fulfillment are core dimensions in e-service quality, and both share some elements of the traditional reliability and responsiveness dimensions. The personal (that is, friendly, empathetic, and understanding) flavor of perceived service quality's empathy dimension is not required on the Internet except as it makes transactions more efficient or in nonroutine or problem situations. While not emerging as a dimension of e-service quality, tangibles are clearly relevant given that the entire service is delivered through technology, and the tangible, visual elements of the site will be critical to efficiency as well as to overall perceptions of the firm and the brand.

SERVICE ENCOUNTERS: THE FOUNDATIONS FOR SATISFACTION AND SERVICE QUALITY

We have just finished a discussion of customer satisfaction and service quality. Here we turn to what have been termed the foundations or building blocks for satisfaction and service quality—namely, service encounters or the "moment of truth." It is where promises are kept or broken and where the proverbial rubber meets the road—sometimes called "real-time marketing." It is from these service encounters that customers build their perceptions.

Service Encounters or "Moments of Truth"

From the customer's point of view, the most vivid impression of service occurs in the **service encounter** or **"moment of truth,"** when the customer interacts with the service

FIGURE 4.5
A Service Encounter Cascade for a Hotel Visit

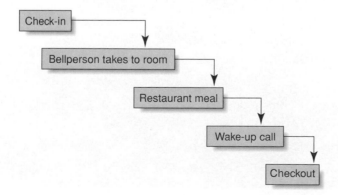

firm. For example, among the service encounters a hotel customer experiences are checking into the hotel, being taken to a room by a bellperson, eating a restaurant meal, requesting a wake-up call, and checking out. You could think of the linking of these moments of truth as a service encounter cascade (see Figure 4.5). It is in these encounters that customers receive a snapshot of the organization's service quality, and each encounter contributes to the customer's overall satisfaction and willingness to do business with the organization again. From the organization's point of view, each encounter thus presents an opportunity to prove its potential as a quality service provider and to increase customer loyalty, as suggested by the ad for Doubletree Hotels shown in Figure 4.6.

Some services have few service encounters, and others have many. The Disney Corporation estimates that each of its amusement park customers experiences about 74

FIGURE 4.6

Every service encounter is an opportunity to build satisfaction and quality.

Source: Reprinted with permission, Hilton Hospitality, Inc./Doubletree ® Hotels, Suites, Resorts, Clubs. Photographer: Chris Schrameck.

service encounters and that a negative experience in any one of them can lead to a negative overall evaluation. Mistakes or problems that occur in the early levels of the service cascade are particularly critical because a failure at one point results in greater risk for dissatisfaction at each ensuing level. Marriott Hotels learned this through their extensive customer research to determine what service elements contribute most to customer loyalty. They found that four of the top five factors came into play in the first 10 minutes of the guest's stay.[41]

The Importance of Encounters

Although early events in the encounter cascade are likely to be especially important, *any* encounter can potentially be critical in determining customer satisfaction and loyalty. If a customer is interacting with a firm for the first time, that initial encounter will create a first impression of the organization. In these first encounter situations, the customer frequently has no other basis for judging the organization, and the initial phone contact or face-to-face experience with a representative of the firm can take on excessive importance in the customer's perceptions of quality. A customer calling for repair service on a household appliance may well hang up and call a different company if he is treated rudely by a customer service representative, put on hold for a lengthy period, or told that two weeks is the soonest someone can be sent out to make the repair. Even if the technical quality of the firm's repair service is superior, the firm may not get the chance to demonstrate it if the initial telephone encounter drives the customer away.

Even when the customer has had multiple interactions with a firm, each individual encounter is important in creating a composite image of the firm in the customer's memory. Many positive experiences add up to a composite image of high quality, whereas many negative interactions will have the opposite effect. On the other hand, a combination of positive and negative interactions will leave the customer feeling unsure of the firm's quality, doubtful of its consistency in service delivery, and vulnerable to the appeals of competitors. For example, a large corporate customer of an institutional food provider that provides food service in all of its company dining rooms and cafeterias could have a series of positive encounters with the account manager or salesperson who handles the account. These experiences could be followed by positive encounters with the operations staff who actually set up the food service facilities. However, even with these positive encounters, later negative experiences with the staff who serve the food or the accounting department that administers the account and billing procedures can result in a mixture of overall quality impressions. This variation in experiences could result in the corporate customer wondering about the quality of the organization and unsure of what to expect in the future. Each encounter with different people and departments representing the food service provider adds to or detracts from the potential for a continuing relationship.

Logic suggests that not all encounters are equally important in building relationships. For every organization, certain encounters are probably key to customer satisfaction. For Marriott Hotels, as noted, it is the early encounters that are most important. In a hospital context, a study of patients revealed that encounters with nursing staff were more important in predicting satisfaction than were encounters with meal service or patient discharge personnel.[42] And research at GTE Laboratories documents that small business customers' relationships with GTE depend on specific installation, repair, and sales encounters.[43]

Aside from common key encounters, there are some momentous encounters that, like the proverbial "one bad apple," simply ruin the rest and drive the customer away

4.2 ONE CRITICAL ENCOUNTER DESTROYS 30-YEAR RELATIONSHIP

"If you have $1 in a bank or $1 million, I think they owe you the courtesy of stamping your parking ticket," said John Barrier. One day in 1989 Mr. Barrier paid a visit to his bank in Spokane, Washington. He was wearing his usual shabby clothes and pulled up in his pickup truck, parking in the lot next to the bank. After cashing a check, he went outside to drive away and was stopped by a parking attendant who told him there was a 60-cent fee, but that he could get his parking slip validated in the bank and park for free. No problem, Barrier thought, and he went back into the bank (where, by the way, he had been banking for 30 years). The teller looked him up and down and refused to stamp his slip, telling him that the bank validated parking only for people who have transactions with the bank and that cash-

ing a check wasn't a transaction. Mr. Barrier then asked to see the bank manager, who also looked him up and down, stood back, and "gave me one of those kinds of looks," also refusing to validate the parking bill. Mr. Barrier then said, "Fine. You don't need me, and I don't need you." He withdrew all his money and took it down the street to a competing bank, where the first check he deposited was for $1,000,000.

Source: "Shabby Millionaire Closes Account, Gives Bank Lesson about Snobbery." Reprinted with permission of United Press International from *The Arizona Republic* issue of February 21, 1989, p. A3.

no matter how many or what type of encounters have occurred in the past. These can occur in connection with very important events (such as the failure to deliver an essential piece of equipment before a critical deadline) or they may seem inconsequential, as in the story of the bank customer described in Exhibit 4.2. Similarly, momentous positive encounters can sometimes bind a customer to an organization for life.

Types of Service Encounters

A service encounter occurs every time a customer interacts with the service organization. There are three general types of service encounters: *remote encounters, phone encounters,* and *face-to-face encounters.*[44] A customer may experience any of these types of encounters, or a combination of all three, in his or her relations with a service firm.

First, encounters can occur without any direct human contact **(remote encounters),** such as when a customer interacts with a bank through the ATM system, with Ticketron through an automated ticketing machine, with a retailer through its Internet website, or with a mail-order service through automated dial-in ordering. Remote encounters also occur when the firm sends its billing statements or communicates other types of information to customers by mail. Although there is no direct human contact in these remote encounters, each represents an opportunity for the firm to reinforce or establish quality perceptions in the customer. In remote encounters the tangible evidence of the service and the quality of the technical processes and systems become the primary bases for judging quality.

More and more services are being delivered through technology, particularly with the advent of Internet applications. Retail purchases, airline ticketing, repair and maintenance troubleshooting, and package and shipment tracking are just a few examples of services available via the Internet. All of these types of service encounters can be considered remote encounters (see the Technology Spotlight).

In many organizations (such as insurance companies, utilities, and telecommunications), the most frequent type of encounter between an end customer and the firm occurs over the telephone **(phone encounters).** Almost all firms (whether goods man-

Technology Spotlight
Customers Love Amazon.com

Although its stock price suffered in 2000–2001 along with just about every Internet-based company, and the company had never reported a profit until early in 2002, customers have always loved Amazon.com. The 2000 American Customer Satisfaction Index reflected a rating of 84 for Amazon—one of the highest ratings of any company in any industry, and certainly way higher than the 73 average rating for e-commerce endeavors and the 60–70 point ratings for many other service businesses. Jeff Bezos, CEO of Amazon, whose name has become a household word worldwide, believes that his customers come first. With a continued focus on customers, relationships, value, and the brand itself, Bezos and others believe that sales will continue to grow ($2.8 billion in 2000) and profits will continue. According to Bezos, "Customers come first. If you focus on what customers want and build a relationship, they will allow you to make money."

Few would deny that Amazon is a master of technology and technology-based services for consumers. In fact, others like Toys R Us and Borders Books have sought a technology partnership with Amazon in order to benefit from the company's experience and success with customers. Amazon now provides the Internet retail services for both these companies.

Amazon has taken a historically interpersonally dominated transaction and successfully transformed it to a Web-based service experience. Let's take a closer look at what the company is doing and why customers love it so much. Since its inception in July 1995, Amazon has grown to the point where it offers more book titles than any bricks-and-mortar bookstore could ever hope to stock. So selection and availability of titles are one key to its popularity with customers. But that is just the beginning.

In addition to a wide selection, Amazon has invested significant effort to simulate the feel of a neighborhood bookstore, where a patron can mingle with other customers, discuss books, and get recommendations from bookstore employees. Amazon allows customers to find related books on virtually any topic by simply typing key words and initiating a search of its massive database. Its one-to-one marketing system allows the company to track what individual consumers buy and let them know of additional titles that might interest them. This is done while the customer is shopping as well as through periodic direct e-mail that identifies books specifically related to the customer's past purchase patterns and interests.

Customers use an electronic shopping cart and can easily browse, explore links to related titles, place books in their shopping cart, and purchase all of the books at once. Amazon's famous "one-click" ordering makes this very easy once the customer has set up an initial account with the company. An e-mail is sent when the book order is confirmed and again when it is shipped. Delivery can occur as soon as two days later. Amazon also holds contests for its customers, delivers online interviews with popular authors, and provides deep discounts on many titles. In addition, customers can easily find descriptions and reviews of books not only from published book reviews but also from other customers.

To maintain a personal touch with all customers, Amazon tracks past purchases and queries customers regarding their interests and likes. This customer profile allows the company to send e-mail messages notifying customers when a new book in a related category or by a favorite author becomes available. Clearly, the book-buying encounter with Amazon is a unique experience that integrates high technology with high-touch service. Customers' positive response to this strategy is reflected in high customer satisfaction scores, a loyal customer base, and growing sales. As Amazon refocuses its efforts onto books and away from some of the other retail ventures it has moved into, many observers are confident that the company can continue to profit and succeed. Its loyal customers certainly hope so.

Sources: S. Alsop, "I'm Betting on Amazon.com," *Fortune,* April 30, 2001, p. 48; M. Helft, "The Trials of Jeff Bezos," *The Industry Standard,* April 23, 2001, pp. 29–32; M. Prior, "Amazon to Operate Borders.com," *Dsn-Retailing-Today,* May 1, 2001, pp. 6, 34; ACSI results at www.bus.umich.edu/research/nqrc; Robert D. Hof, "How Amazon Cleared That Hurdle," *Business Week,* February 4, 2002, pp. 60–61.

ufacturers or service businesses) rely on phone encounters in the form of customer service, general inquiry, or order-taking functions. The judgment of quality in phone encounters is different from remote encounters because there is greater potential variability in the interaction.[45] Tone of voice, employee knowledge, and effectiveness/efficiency in handling customer issues become important criteria for judging quality in these encounters.

A third type of encounter is the one that occurs between an employee and a customer in direct contact **(face-to-face encounters).** At Disney theme parks, face-to-face encounters occur between customers and ticket-takers, maintenance personnel, actors in Disney character costumes, ride personnel, food and beverage servers, and others. For a company such as IBM, in a business-to-business setting direct encounters occur between the business customer and salespeople, delivery personnel, maintenance representatives, and professional consultants. Determining and understanding service quality issues in face-to-face contexts is the most complex of all. Both verbal and nonverbal behaviors are important determinants of quality, as are tangible cues such as employee dress and other symbols of service (equipment, informational brochures, physical setting). In face-to-face encounters the customer also plays a role in creating quality service for herself through her own behavior during the interaction.

Sources of Pleasure and Displeasure in Service Encounters

Because of the importance of service encounters in building quality perceptions and ultimately influencing customer satisfaction, researchers have extensively analyzed service encounters in many contexts to determine the sources of customers' favorable and unfavorable perceptions. The research uses the critical incident technique to get customers and employees to provide verbatim stories about satisfying and dissatisfying service encounters they have experienced.[46] With this technique, customers (either internal or external) are asked the following questions:

Think of a time when, as a customer, you had a particularly *satisfying* (or *dissatisfying*) interaction with _____.

When did the incident happen?

What specific circumstances led up to this situation?

Exactly what did the employee (or firm) say or do?

What resulted that made you feel the interaction was *satisfying* (or *dissatisfying*)?

What could or should have been done differently?

Sometimes contact employees are asked to put themselves in the shoes of a customer and answer the same questions: "Put yourself in the shoes of *customers* of your firm. In other words, try to see your firm through your customers' eyes. Now think of a recent time when a customer of your firm had a particularly *satisfying/unsatisfying* interaction with you or a fellow employee." The stories are then analyzed to determine common themes of satisfaction/dissatisfaction underlying the events. On the basis of thousands of service encounter stories, four common themes—recovery (after failure), adaptability, spontaneity, and coping—have been identified as the sources of customer satisfaction/dissatisfaction in memorable service encounters.[47] Each of the themes is discussed here, and sample stories of both satisfying and dissatisfying incidents are given in Exhibits 4.3 through 4.6. The themes encompass service behaviors in encounters spanning a wide variety of industries.

Recovery—Employee Response to Service Delivery System Failures The first theme includes all incidents in which there has been a failure of the service delivery

Satisfactory

They lost my room reservation but the manager gave me the V.P. suite for the same price. (external customer)

Even though I didn't make any complaint about the hour-and-a-half wait, the waitress kept apologizing and said the bill was on the house. (external customer)

I contacted the department that was responsible for correcting a problem in a monthly report that is prepared for a regulatory agency. The employee I was referred to dropped everything and worked to get a new report finished. I was favorably impressed because this employee cared, even though it [the report] was not her direct responsibility. (internal customer)

A gentleman left his shoes outside his room door to be shined. When he went to retrieve them, they were gone, and could not be found. The hotel staff took responsibility and within an hour a representative of Nordstrom had arrived with six pairs of shoes for the gentleman to choose from. (employee)

Dissatisfactory

We had made advance reservations at the hotel. When we arrived we found we had no room—no explanation, no apologies, and no assistance in finding another hotel. (external customer)

For weeks I had been waiting for my medical identification card and it had not arrived . . . so I went to the clinic. They told me to wait while they checked. After 10 minutes they gave me the excuse "It's in the mail." The reason I felt so dissatisfied was that nobody knew anything. They kept giving me the runaround. (external customer)

One of my suitcases was all dented up and looked like it had been dropped from 30,000 feet. When I tried to make a claim for my damaged luggage, the employee insinuated that I was lying and trying to rip them off. (external customer)

A loan officer's signature was missing on the application of a new VISA account. I contacted the loan officer who sent the paperwork. She stated that the paperwork had never been required and refused to fill it out. She had a very snippy attitude and refused to assist me. (internal customer)

system and an employee is required to respond in some way to consumer complaints and disappointments. The failure may be, for example, a hotel room that isn't available, an airplane flight that is delayed six hours, an incorrect item sent from a mail-order company, or a critical error on an internal document. The content or form of the employee's response is what causes the customer to remember the event either favorably or unfavorably. Examples of recovery incidents, both good and bad, are given in Exhibit 4.3. The source of the story is also identified: either an external customer, an internal customer, or an employee who has been asked to assume the point of view of the customer.

Adaptability—Employee Response to Customer Needs and Requests   A second theme underlying satisfaction/dissatisfaction in service encounters is how adaptable the service delivery system is when the customer has special needs or requests that place demands on the process. In these cases, customers judge service encounter quality in terms of the flexibility of the employees and the system. Incidents categorized within this theme all contain an implicit or explicit request for customization of the service to meet a need. Much of what customers see as special needs or requests may actually be rather routine from the employee's point of view; what is important is that the customer perceives that something special is being done for her based on her own individual needs. External customers and internal customers alike are pleased

Satisfactory

I didn't have an appointment to see a doctor; however, my allergy nurse spoke to a practitioner's assistant and worked me into the schedule. I received treatment after a 10-minute wait. I was very satisfied with the special treatment I received, the short wait, and the quality of the service. (external customer)

It was snowing outside—my car broke down. I checked 10 hotels and there were no rooms. Finally, one understood my situation and offered to rent me a bed and set it up in a small banquet room. (external customer)

Although it was not our regular order time, I needed some supplies that we did not have in stock. I called the supply office and the gentleman on the phone said, "No problem. I will send that to you through interbranch mail today." I received the supplies the next day. His word was as good as gold. (internal customer)

The weather was very cold and I got off work at 7 A.M. as night auditor. Three groups of hotel guests were having trouble starting their cars in the cold. I told them that if they would like to sit in the lobby and have some coffee, I would jump start their cars. (employee)

Dissatisfactory

My young son, flying alone, was to be assisted by the stewardess from start to finish. At the Albany airport she left him alone in the airport with no one to escort him to his connecting flight. (external customer)

Despite our repeated requests, the hotel staff wouldn't deal with the noisy people partying in the hall at 3 A.M. (external customer)

I called a branch to get the specifics on a customer's NSF notice. It turned out that a deposit slip was encoded improperly—our mistake—but the fee for the NSF was taken out at another branch. The employee said, "Oh, you made the mistake and we have to pay for it." Even though the mistake was made at our branch, I am still an employee of the same bank and should be treated with respect. (internal customer)

A guest explained to the bellman that he had to get to the airport in 10 minutes. This was very short notice. The employee contacted the hotel van driver, Chuck. Chuck says, "No way!" The bellman ends up having to call a cab for the guest. (employee)

when the service provider puts forth the effort to accommodate and adjust the system to meet their requirements. On the flip side, they are angered and frustrated by an unwillingness to try to accommodate and by promises that are never followed through. Contact employees also see their abilities to adapt the system as being a prominent source of customer satisfaction, and often they are equally frustrated by constraints that keep them from being flexible. Examples of adaptability incidents, both good and bad, are given in Exhibit 4.4.

Spontaneity—Unprompted and Unsolicited Employee Actions Even when there is no system failure and no special request or need, customers can still remember service encounters as being very satisfying or very dissatisfying. Employee spontaneity in delivering memorably good or poor service is the third theme. Satisfying incidents in this group represent very pleasant surprises for the customer (special attention, being treated like royalty, receiving something nice but not requested), whereas dissatisfying incidents in this group represent negative and unacceptable employee behaviors (rudeness, stealing, discrimination, ignoring the customer). Examples of spontaneity incidents are shown in Exhibit 4.5.

Satisfactory

We always travel with our teddy bears. When we got back to our room at the hotel we saw that the maid had arranged our bears very comfortably in a chair. The bears were holding hands. (external customer)

The anesthesiologist took extra time to explain exactly what I would be aware of and promised to take special care in making sure I did not wake up. It impressed me that the anesthesiologist came to settle my nerves and explain the difference in the medicine I was getting because of my cold. It was a nice bit of extra attention that he did not have to give. (external customer)

I was preparing a presentation and needed input from another department. An employee from the department provided the needed input and agreed to review the presentation. I was favorably impressed because of (1) the employee's enthusiasm in providing input and (2) the subsequent constructive criticism the employee made on improving the presentation. (internal customer)

A manager from the mall called in an order to go over the phone. She said she'd pick it up as soon as she could, but it might be a while because she was so busy. When her food was ready, I had a waitress cover my tables and I took her food to her personally. (employee)

Dissatisfactory

The lady at the front desk acted as if we were bothering her. She was watching TV and paying more attention to the TV than to the hotel guests. (external customer)

I needed a few more minutes to decide on a dinner. The waitress said, "If you would read the menu and not the road map, you would know what you want to order." (external customer)

Victoria never seemed to hear what I said. She asked me to repeat everything. After the first few times, I grew annoyed. Very calmly, I asked once again if she could tell me whether I'd keep the same number. "It all depends" was her stock answer. She offered me a service package (call waiting/forwarding), which I declined. She offered again, saying she couldn't understand why anyone wouldn't want call waiting. Now I was angry. (external customer)

There was a woman who came into the restaurant every morning. The one waitress on the floor didn't like this woman and gave her minimal service. The woman asked for a refill and marmalade, but the waitress wouldn't go back to the table. I brought her what she wanted, the waitress came back to the table and began to verbally abuse the customer. (employee)

Coping—Employee Response to Problem Customers The incidents categorized in this group came to light when employees were asked to describe service encounter incidents in which customers were either very satisfied or dissatisfied. In addition to describing incidents of the types outlined under the first three themes, employees described many incidents in which customers were the cause of their own dissatisfaction. Such customers were basically uncooperative—that is, unwilling to cooperate with the service provider, other customers, industry regulations, and/or laws. In these cases nothing the employee could do would result in the customer feeling pleased about the encounter. The term "coping" is used to describe these incidents because this is the behavior generally required of employees to handle problem customer encounters. As is apparent in the examples of these given in Exhibit 4.6, rarely are such encounters satisfying from the customers' point of view.[48] Also of interest is that customers themselves didn't relate any "problem customer" incidents. That is, customers either do not see, or choose not to remember or retell, stories of the times when they themselves were unreasonable to the point of causing their own dissatisfactory service encounter.

No problem customer incidents were reported by either external or internal customers. Only 3 percent of the incidents in this group were satisfactory.

Satisfactory

A person who became intoxicated on a flight started speaking loudly, annoying the other passengers. The flight attendant asked the passenger if he would be driving when the plane landed and offered him coffee. He accepted the coffee and became quieter and friendlier. (employee)

Dissatisfactory

An intoxicated man began pinching the female flight attendants. One attendant told him to stop, but he continued and then hit another passenger. The copilot was called and asked the man to sit down and leave the others alone, but the passenger refused. The copilot then "decked" the man, knocking him into his seat. (employee)

While a family of three were waiting to order dinner, the father began hitting his child. Another customer complained about this to the manager who then, in a friendly and sympathetic way, asked the family to leave. The father knocked all of the plates and glasses off the table before leaving. (employee)

Five guests were in a hotel room two hours past checkout time. Because they would not answer the phone calls or let the staff into the room, hotel security staff finally broke in. They found the guests using drugs and called the police. (employee)

General Service Behaviors

Table 4.3 summarizes the specific behaviors that cause satisfaction and dissatisfaction in service encounters according to the four themes just presented. The left side of the table suggests what employees do that results in positive encounters, whereas the right side summarizes negative behaviors within each theme.

This section of the chapter has examined in some depth the service encounter, or the "moment of truth," as the building block of consumer perceptions of service. Individual encounters are the most fundamental, concrete, and vivid events through which consumers can begin building their overall impressions of an organization. Because of the potential importance of these immediate events, many organizations have found it useful to capture customer impressions of service encounters on the spot before the memory of the event has faded.

Satisfaction with Technology-Based Service Encounters

All of the research on service encounters described thus far and the resulting themes underlying service encounter satisfaction are based on interpersonal services—that is, personal encounters between customers and employees of service organizations. Recently researchers have begun to look at the factors underlying satisfaction in technology-based service encounters.[49] These types of encounters involve customers interacting with Internet-based services, automated phone services, kiosk services, and services delivered via CD or video technology. Often these are referred to as *self-service technologies* because the customer essentially provides his or her own service.

TABLE 4.3   General Service Behaviors—Do's and Don'ts

Theme	Do	Don't
Recovery	Acknowledge problem	Ignore customer
	Explain causes	Blame customer
	Apologize	Leave customer to "fend for him/herself"
	Compensate/upgrade	Downgrade
	Lay out options	Act as if nothing is wrong
	Take responsibility	"Pass the buck"
Adaptability	Recognize the seriousness of the need	Ignore
	Acknowledge	Promise, but fail to follow through
	Anticipate	Show unwillingness to try
	Attempt to accommodate	Embarrass the customer
	Adjust the system	Laugh at the customer
	Explain rules/policies	Avoid responsibility
	Take responsibility	"Pass the buck"
Spontaneity	Take time	Exhibit impatience
	Be attentive	Ignore
	Anticipate needs	Yell/laugh/swear
	Listen	Steal from customers
	Provide information	Discriminate
	Show empathy	
Coping	Listen	Take customer's dissatisfaction personally
	Try to accommodate	Let customer's dissatisfaction affect others
	Explain	
	Let go of the customer	

The research reveals that customer experiences with self-service technologies (SSTs) suggest some different themes in terms of what drives customer satisfaction and dissatisfaction. Across a wide range of contexts, including Internet retailing, Internet-based services, ATMs, automated phone systems, and others, the following themes were identified from analysis of hundreds of critical incident stories:

For Satisfying SSTs

Solved an intensified need. Customers in this category were thrilled that the technology could bail them out of a difficult situation—for example, a cash machine that came to the rescue, allowing the customer to get cash to pay a cab driver and get to work on time when a car had broken down.

Better than the alternative. Many SST stories related to how the technology-based service was in some way better than the alternative—easy to use, saved time, available when and where the customer needed it, saved money.

Did its job. Because there are so many failures of technology, many customers are simply thrilled when the SST works as it should!

For Dissatisfying SSTs

Technology failure. Many dissatisfying SST stories relate to the technology simply not working as promised—it isn't available when needed, PIN numbers don't work, or systems are off line.

Process failure. Often the technology seems to work, but later the customer discovers that a back-office or follow-up process, which they assumed was connected, doesn't work. For example, a product order seems to be placed successfully, but it never arrives or the wrong product is delivered.

Poor design. Many stories relate to the customer's dissatisfaction with how the technology is designed, in terms of either the technical process (technology is confusing, menu options are unclear) or the actual service design (delivery takes too long, service is inflexible).

Customer-driven failure. In some cases the customers told stories of their own inabilities or failures to use the technology properly. These types of stories are (of course) much less common than stories blaming the technology or the company.

For all of the dissatisfying SST stories, there is clearly an element of service failure. Interestingly, the research revealed little attempt in these technology-based encounters to recover from the failure—unlike the interpersonal service situations described earlier, where excellent service recovery can be a foundation for retaining and even producing very satisfied customers. As companies progress further with SSTs and become better at delivering service this way, we expect that growing numbers will be able to deliver superior service via technology. Many are doing it already, as our Technology Spotlight on Amazon.com illustrates. In the future we believe that many firms will be able to deliver highly reliable, responsive, customized services via technology and will offer easy and effective means for service recovery when failure does occur.[50] This simply isn't as easy as it might appear on the surface, which is why there is still a long road ahead for many organizations.

The Evidence of Service

Because services are intangible, customers are searching for evidence of service in every interaction they have with an organization.[51] Figure 4.7 depicts the three major categories of evidence as experienced by the customer: people, process, and physical evidence. These categories together represent the service and provide the evidence that tangibilizes the offering. Note the parallels between the elements comprising evidence of service and the new marketing mix elements presented in Chapter 1. The new mix elements essentially *are* the evidence of service in each moment of truth.

FIGURE 4.7
The Evidence of Service (from the Customer's Point of View)

- Contact employees
- Customer him/herself
- Other customers

People

Process

Physical evidence

- Operational flow of activities
- Steps in process
- Flexibility versus standard
- Technology versus human

- Tangible communication
- Servicescape
- Guarantees
- Technology
- Website

All of these evidence elements, or a subset of them, are present in every service encounter a customer has with a service firm and are critically important in managing service encounter quality and creating customer satisfaction. For example, when an HMO patient has an appointment with a doctor in a health clinic, the first encounter of the visit is frequently with a receptionist in a clinic waiting area. The quality of that encounter will be judged by how the appointment registration *process* works (Is there a line? How long is the wait? Is the registration system computerized and accurate?), the actions and attitude of the *people* (Is the receptionist courteous, helpful, knowledgeable? Does he treat the patient as an individual? Does he handle inquiries fairly and efficiently?), and the *physical evidence* of the service (Is the waiting area clean and comfortable? Is the signage clear?). The three types of evidence may be differentially important depending on the type of service encounter (remote, phone, face-to-face). All three types will operate in face-to-face service encounters as in the one just described.

STRATEGIES FOR INFLUENCING CUSTOMER PERCEPTIONS

The primary purpose of this chapter is to orient you to the building blocks of customer perceptions and to show how these are organized around broader perceptions of quality and satisfaction. Now we describe management strategies used to influence perceptions of service directly. We cover these strategies only briefly here because much of the rest of the book is aimed at providing in-depth understanding of all of these approaches.

Measure and Manage Customer Satisfaction and Service Quality

It should be obvious from everything in this chapter that a key strategy for customer-focused firms is to measure and monitor customer satisfaction and service quality. Such measurements are needed to track trends, to diagnose problems, and to link to other customer-focused strategies. In examples provided throughout the text, you will see how companies have linked their measurement of customer satisfaction to strategies related to employee training, reward systems, internal process metrics, organizational structure, and leadership goals. Much of the rest of the book focuses on these types of strategies and the linkages among them, customer satisfaction, and quality. In Chapter 5 we look more closely at customer-focused research and the measurement of satisfaction and quality, and in Chapter 17 we look specifically at how to link measures of satisfaction and quality to specific financial outcomes.

Aim for Customer Quality and Satisfaction in Every Service Encounter

Because every service encounter is potentially critical to customer retention, many firms aim for "zero defects," or 100 percent satisfaction in every encounter. To achieve this requires, first, clear documentation of all of the points of contact between the organization and its customers. Development of understanding of customer expectations for each of these encounters is the next step, so that strategies can be built around meeting those expectations. Each of the four themes underlying satisfaction/dissatisfaction in service encounters presented earlier in the chapter—recovery, adaptability, spontaneity, and coping—suggests specific types of actions that would aid an organization aiming for zero defects.

Plan for Effective Recovery   The examples presented in Exhibit 4.3 illustrate that service failures and subsequent recovery efforts create strong memories for customers and for employees who empathize with their customers. When service customers have been disappointed on the first try, "doing it very right the second time" is essential to maintaining customer loyalty.[52] This implies a need for service process and system analysis to determine the root causes of failure so that a redesign can ensure higher reliability.[53] However, because of the inherent variability of services, failures are inevitable even for the best of firms. Thus organizations need recovery systems that allow employees to turn the failure around and leave the customer satisfied.[54] Recovery strategies are discussed fully in Chapter 7.

Facilitate Adaptability and Flexibility   As shown in Exhibit 4.4, customer perceptions of organizational adaptability and flexibility also create feelings of satisfaction or dissatisfaction in service encounters. The existence of this encounter theme suggests a need to know when and how the system can be flexed, and when and how to explain to customers why a particular request cannot be granted. Knowledge of the service concept, the service delivery system and its operation, and the system standards enables employees to inform customers about what happened, what can be done, and why their needs or requests can or cannot be accommodated. Such knowledge and willingness to explain can leave a lasting positive impression on customers even when their specific requests cannot be met.

Encourage Spontaneity   Memorable encounters occur for customers even when there is no system failure and no special request, as shown in Exhibit 4.5. Although employee behaviors within this third theme would appear to be somewhat random and relatively uncontrollable, there are things that organizations can do to encourage positive spontaneous behaviors and discourage negative behaviors. Recruitment and selection procedures can be used to hire employees with strong service orientation, whose natural tendency is to be service-minded.[55] A strong service culture, employee empowerment, effective supervision and monitoring, and quick feedback to employees also will control to some extent the seeming randomness of these behaviors. Because of their extreme importance for service quality, we discuss these human resource issues in depth in Chapter 11.

Help Employees Cope with Problem Customers   The service encounters classified within the coping theme (Exhibit 4.6) represent times when customers were the cause of their own dissatisfaction. Several management strategies are suggested by this last theme. First, managers and customers need to acknowledge that the customer isn't always right, nor will she always behave in acceptable ways. Contact employees who have been on the job any length of time know this, but freqently they are told that the "customer is king" and are not given the appropriate training and tools to deal with problem customers. Employees need appropriate coping and problem-solving skills to handle difficult customers as well as their own feelings in such situations. Another implication is the need for "training customers" so that they will know what to expect and know the appropriate behaviors in given situations. Issues relevant to this theme will be explored further in Chapters 11 and 12.

Manage the Dimensions of Quality at the Encounter Level   Although the five dimensions of service quality—reliability, responsiveness, assurance, empathy, and tangibles—are generally applied to the overall quality of the firm, it is certainly possible to relate them to each individual encounter. If we think of each encounter in terms of these five themes, we can formulate strategies for ensuring satisfaction in the "moment of truth" that will add to the broad strategies around the four themes just discussed. Many of the strategies related to the four encounter themes will reinforce the quality dimensions directly. For example, strategies aimed at improving adaptability of service employees should enhance customer perceptions of responsiveness and empathy.

Manage the Evidence of Service to Reinforce Perceptions

The evidence of service—people, process, physical evidence—shown in Figure 4.7 provides a framework for planning marketing strategies that address the expanded marketing mix elements for services. These new elements, or a subset of them, essentially tangibilize the service for the customer and thus represent important means for creating positive perceptions. Because of their importance, the new elements need to be treated as strategic marketing variables, as are product, price, place, and promotion, the traditional mix elements. Entire chapters of this book are devoted to strategies relevant to people (Chapters 11, 12), process (Chapter 8), and physical evidence (Chapter 10).

Summary

This chapter described customer perceptions of service by first introducing you to two critical concepts: customer satisfaction and service quality. These critical customer perceptions were defined and discussed in terms of the factors that influence each of them. You learned that customer satisfaction is a broad perception influenced by features and attributes of the product as well as by customers' emotional responses, their attributions, and their perceptions of fairness. Service quality, the customer's perception of the service component of a product, is also a critical determinant of customer satisfaction. Sometimes, as in the case of a pure service, service quality may be the *most* critical determinant of satisfaction. You learned that perceptions of service quality are based on five dimensions: reliability, assurance, empathy, responsiveness, and tangibles.

The second major purpose of the chapter was to introduce the notion of service encounters, or "moments of truth," as the foundations for both satisfaction and quality. You learned that every service encounter (whether remote, over the phone, or in person) is an opportunity to build perceptions of quality and satisfaction. The underlying themes of pleasure and displeasure in service encounters were also described. The importance of managing the evidence of service in each and every encounter was discussed. The evidence of service includes people, processes, and physical evidence.

Finally, we described strategies firms use to enhance customer perceptions of service quality and increase customer satisfaction. Broadly, these strategies include measuring and managing customer satisfaction and service quality and aiming for quality and satisfaction in every service encounter. Specific strategies were presented very briefly because the rest of the book provides more depth on all of the strategies mentioned.

Chapters 2, 3, and 4 have provided you with a grounding in customer issues relevant to services. The three chapters together are intended to give you a solid understanding of customer behavior issues and of service expectations and perceptions. We proceed through the rest of the book to illustrate strategies firms can use to close the gap between customer expectations and perceptions.

Discussion Questions

1. What is customer satisfaction, and why is it so important? Discuss how customer satisfaction can be influenced by each of the following: product attributes and features, customer emotions, attributions for success or failure, perceptions of fairness, and family members or other customers.

2. What is the ACSI? Do you believe that such national indicators of customer satisfaction should be included as benchmarks of national economic well-being similar to GDP, price indicators, and productivity measures?

3. Why do you believe service companies generally receive lower satisfaction ratings in the ACSI than nondurable and durable product companies?

4. Discuss the differences between perceptions of service quality and customer satisfaction.

5. List and define the five dimensions of service quality. Describe the services provided by a firm you do business with (your bank, your doctor, your favorite restaurant) on each of the dimensions. In your mind, has this organization distinguished itself from its competitors on any particular service quality dimension?

6. Describe a remote encounter, a phone encounter, and a face-to-face encounter that you have had recently. How did you evaluate the encounter, and what were the most important factors determining your satisfaction/dissatisfaction in each case?

7. Describe an "encounter cascade" for an airplane flight. In your opinion, what are the most important encounters in this cascade for determining your overall impression of the quality of the airline?

8. Why did the gentleman described in Exhibit 4.2 leave his bank after 30 years? What were the underlying causes of his dissatisfaction in that instance, and why do you think that would cause him to leave the bank?

9. Assume you are a manager of a health club. Discuss general strategies you might use to maximize customers' positive perceptions of your club. How would you know if you were successful?

Exercises

1. Keep a journal of your service encounters with different organizations (at least five) during the week. For each journal entry ask yourself the following questions: What circumstances led up to this encounter? What did the employee say or do? How did you evaluate this encounter? What exactly made you evaluate the encounter that way? What should they have done differently (if anything)? Categorize your encounters according to the four themes of service encounter satisfaction/dissatisfaction (recovery, adaptability, spontaneity, coping) identified in the text.

2. Interview someone with a non-U.S. cultural background. Ask the person about service quality, whether the five dimensions of quality are relevant, and which are most important in determining quality of banking services (or some other type of service) in the person's country.

3. Think of an important service experience you have had in the last several weeks. Analyze the encounter according to the "evidence of service" provided (see Figure 4.7). Which of the three evidence components was (or were) most important for you in evaluating the experience, and why?

4. Interview an employee of a local service business. Ask the person to discuss each of the five dimensions of quality with you as it relates to the person's company. Which dimensions are most important? Are any dimensions *not* relevant in this

context? Which dimensions does the company do best? Why? Which dimensions could benefit from improvement? Why?

5. Interview a manager, owner, or president of a business. Discuss with him or her the strategies he or she uses to ensure customer satisfaction. How does service quality enter into the strategies, or does it? Find out how he or she measures customer satisfaction and/or service quality.

6. Visit Amazon.com's website. Visit a traditional bookstore. How would you compare the two experiences? Compare and contrast the factors that most influenced your satisfaction and perceptions of service quality in the two different situations. When would you choose to use one versus the other?

Notes

1. K. Anderson and R. Zemke, *Tales of Knock Your Socks Off Service* (New York: AMACOM, 1998), pp. 56–57.

2. For more discussion of the debate on the distinctions between quality and satisfaction see A. Parasuraman, V. A. Zeithaml, and L. L. Berry, "Reassessment of Expectations as a Comparison Standard in Measuring Service Quality: Implications for Future Research," *Journal of Marketing* 58, no. 1 (January 1994), pp. 111–24; R. L. Oliver, "A Conceptual Model of Service Quality and Service Satisfaction: Compatible Goals, Different Concepts," in *Advances in Services Marketing and Management,* vol. 2, ed. T. A. Swartz, D. E. Bowen, and S. W. Brown (Greenwich, CT: JAI Press, 1994), pp. 65–85; M. J. Bitner and A. R. Hubbert, "Encounter Satisfaction vs. Overall Satisfaction vs. Quality: The Customer's Voice," in *Service Quality: New Directions in Theory and Practice,* ed. R. T. Rust and R. L. Oliver (Newbury Park, CA: Sage, 1993), pp. 71–93; and D. Iacobucci et al., "The Calculus of Service Quality and Customer Satisfaction: Theory and Empirical Differentiation and Integration," in *Advances in Services Marketing and Management,* vol. 3, ed. T. A. Swartz, D. E. Bowen, and S. W. Brown (Greenwich, CT: JAI Press, 1994), pp. 1–67; P. A. Dabholkar, C. D. Shepherd, and D. I. Thorpe, "A Comprehensive Framework for Service Quality: An Investigation of Critical Conceptual and Measurement Issues through a Longitudinal Study," *Journal of Retailing* 7 (2), Summer 2000, pp. 139–73; J. J. Cronin, Jr., M. K. Brady, and G. T. M. Hult, "Assessing the Effects of Quality, Value, and Customer Satisfaction on Consumer Behavioral Intentions in Service Environments," *Journal of Retailing* 7 (2), Summer 2000, pp. 193–218.

3. See in particular, Parasuraman, Zeithaml, and Berry, "Reassessment of Expectations"; Oliver, "A Conceptual Model of Service Quality"; and M. K. Brady and J. J. Cronin, Jr., "Some New Thoughts on Conceptualizing Perceived Service Quality: A Hierarchical Approach," *Journal of Marketing* 65 (July 2001), pp. 34–49.

4. Brady and Cronin, "Some New Thoughts."

5. A. Parasuraman, V. A. Zeithaml, and L. L. Berry, "SERVQUAL: A Multiple-Item Scale for Measuring Consumer Perceptions of Service Quality," *Journal of Retailing* 64 (Spring 1988), pp. 12–40.

6. Parasuraman, Zeithaml, and Berry, "Reassessment of Expectations."

7. Oliver, "A Conceptual Model of Service Quality."

8. R. L. Oliver, *Satisfaction, a Behavioral Perspective on the Consumer* (New York: McGraw-Hill, 1997).

9. Ibid, p. 13.

10. For a more detailed discussion of the different types of satisfaction, see

E. Arnould, L. Price, and G. Zinkhan, *Consumers,* chap. 17, "Consumer Satisfaction" (New York: McGraw-Hill, 2001), pp. 614–53.

11. S. Fournier and D. G. Mick, "Rediscovering Satisfaction," *Journal of Marketing* 63 (October 1999), pp. 5–23.

12. Oliver, *Satisfaction,* chap. 2.

13. A. Ostrom and D. Iacobucci, "Consumer Trade-Offs and the Evaluation of Services," *Journal of Marketing* 59 (January 1995), pp. 17–28.

14. For more on emotions and satisfaction, see Oliver, *Satisfaction,* chap. 11; and L. L. Price, E. J. Arnould, and S. L. Deibler, "Consumers' Emotional Responses to Service Encounters," *International Journal of Service Industry Management* 6, no. 3 (1995), pp. 34–63.

15. L. L. Price, E. J. Arnould, and P. Tierney, "Going to Extremes: Managing Service Encounters and Assessing Provider Performance," *Journal of Marketing* 59 (April 1995), pp. 83–97.

16. V. Liljander and T. Strandvik, "Emotions in Service Satisfaction," *International Journal of Service Industry Management* 8, no. 2 (1997), pp. 148–69.

17. For more on attributions and satisfaction, see V. S. Folkes, "Recent Attribution Research in Consumer Behavior: A Review and New Directions," *Journal of Consumer Research* 14 (March 1988), pp. 548–65; and Oliver, *Satisfaction,* chap. 10.

18. A. R. Hubbert, "Customer Co-Creation of Service Outcomes: Effects of Locus of Causality Attributions," doctoral dissertation, Arizona State University, Tempe, Arizona, 1995.

19. M. J. Bitner, "Evaluating Service Encounters: The Effects of Physical Surrounding and Employee Responses," *Journal of Marketing* 54 (April 1990), pp. 69–82.

20. For more on fairness and satisfaction, see E. C. Clemmer and B. Schneider, "Fair Service," in *Advances in Services Marketing and Management,* vol. 5, ed. T. A. Swartz, D. E. Bowen, and S. W. Brown (Greenwich, CT: JAI Press, 1996), pp. 109–26; and Oliver, *Satisfaction,* chap. 7.

21. As described in K. Seiders and L. L. Berry. "Service Fairness: What It Is and Why It Matters," *Academy of Management Executive* 12, no. 2 (1998), pp. 8–20.

22. Fournier and Mick, "Rediscovering Satisfaction."

23. C. Fornell, M. D. Johnson, E. W. Anderson, J. Cha, and B. E. Bryant, "The American Customer Satisfaction Index: Nature, Purpose, and Findings," *Journal of Marketing* 60 (October 1996), pp. 7–18.

24. E. W. Anderson, C. Fornell, and D. R. Lehmann, "Customer Satisfaction, Market Share, and Profitability: Findings from Sweden," *Journal of Marketing* 58 (July 1994), pp. 53–66.

25. M. Bruhn and M. A. Grund, "Theory, Development and Implementation of National Customer Satisfaction Indices: The Swiss Index of Customer Satisfaction (SWICS)," *Total Quality Management,* vol. 11, no. 7 (2000), pp. S1017–S1028; A. Meyer and F. Dornach, "The German Customer Barometer," http://www.servicebarometer.de.or.

26. Fornell et al., "The American Customer Satisfaction Index."

27. For a listing of companies and their scores go to the ACSI website at www.bus.mich.edu/research/nqrc/.

28. ACSI website, www.bus.umich.edu/research.nqrc/.

29. C. Fornell, "Customer Satisfaction and Corporate Earning," commentary appearing on ACSI website, May 21, 2001, www.bus.umich.edu/research/nqrc/Q1-01c.html.

30. J. L. Heskett, W. E. Sasser, Jr., and L. A. Schlesinger, *The Service Profit Chain* (New York: Free Press, 1997).

31. M. A. J. Menezes and J. Serbin, *Xerox Corporation: The Customer Satisfaction Program,* case no. 591-055 (Boston: Harvard Business School, 1991).

32. E. W. Anderson and V. Mittal, "Strengthening the Satisfaction–Profit Chain," *Journal of Service Research* 3 (November 2000), pp. 107–20.

33. M. K. Brady and J. J. Cronin, Jr., "Some New Thoughts on Conceptualizing Perceived Service Quality: A Hierarchical Approach," *Journal of Marketing* 65 (July 2001), pp. 34–49.

34. Ibid.

35. C. Gronroos, "A Service Quality Model and Its Marketing Implications," *European Journal of Marketing* 18 (4), pp. 36–44.

36. R. T. Rust and R. L. Oliver, "Service Quality Insights and Managerial Implications from the Frontier," in *Service Quality: New Directions in Theory and Practice,* ed. R. T. Rust and R. L. Oliver (Thousand Oaks, CA: Sage, 1994), pp. 1–19.

37. M. J. Bitner, "Managing the Evidence of Service," in *The Service Quality Handbook,* ed. E. E. Scheuing and W. F. Christopher (AMACOM, 1993), pp. 358–70.

38. A. Parasuraman, V. Z. Zeithaml, and L. L. Berry, "SERVQUAL: A Multiple-Item Scale for Measuring Consumer Perceptions of Service Quality," *Journal of Retailing* 64 (Spring 1988), pp. 12–40. Details on the SERVQUAL scale and the actual items used to assess the dimensions are provided in Chapter 5.

39. Ibid.

40. V. Zeithaml, A. Parasuraman, and A. Malhotra, "A Conceptual Framework for Understanding e-Service Quality: Implications for Future Research and Managerial Practice," Marketing Science Institute Working Paper, Report No. 00-115, 2001.

41. "How Marriott Makes a Great First Impression," *The Service Edge* 6, no. 5 (May 1993), p. 5.

42. A. G. Woodside, L. L. Frey, and R. T. Daly, "Linking Service Quality, Customer Satisfaction, and Behavioral Intention," *Journal of Health Care Marketing* 9, no. 4 (December 1989), pp. 5–17.

43. R. N. Bolton and J. H. Drew, "Mitigating the Effect of Service Encounters," *Marketing Letters* 3, no. 1 (1992), pp. 57–70.

44. G. L. Shostack, "Planning the Service Encounter," in *The Service Encounter,* ed. J. A. Czepiel, M. R. Solomon, and C. F. Surprenant (Lexington, MA: Lexington Books, 1985), pp. 243–54.

45. Ibid.

46. For detailed discussions of the Critical Incident Technique see J. C. Flanagan, "The Critical Incident Technique," *Psychological Bulletin* 51 (July 1954), pp. 327–58; M. J. Bitner, J. D. Nyquist, and B. H. Booms, "The Critical Incident as a Technique for Analyzing the Service Encounter," in *Services Marketing in a Changing Environment,* ed. T. M. Bloch, G. D. Upah, and V. A. Zeithaml (Chicago: American Marketing Association, 1985), pp. 48–51; S. Wilson-Pessano, "Defining Professional Competence: The Critical Incident Technique 40 Years Later," presentation to the Annual Meeting of the American Educational Research Association, New Orleans, 1988.

47. For a complete discussion of the research on which this section is based, see M. J. Bitner, B. H. Booms, and M. S. Tetreault, "The Service Encounter: Diagnosing Favorable and Unfavorable Incidents," *Journal of Marketing* 54 (January 1990), pp. 71–84; M. J. Bitner, B. H. Booms, and L. A. Mohr, "Critical Service

Encounters: The Employee's View," *Journal of Marketing* 58, no. 4 (1994), pp. 95–106; D. Gremler and M. J. Bitner, "Classifying Service Encounter Satisfaction across Industries," in *Marketing Theory and Applications,* ed. C. T. Allen et al. (Chicago: American Marketing Association, 1992), pp. 111–18; and D. Gremler, M. J. Bitner, and K. R. Evans, "The Internal Service Encounter," *International Journal of Service Industry Management* 5, no. 2 (1994), pp. 34–56.

48. Bitner, Booms, and Mohr, "Critical Service Encounters."

49. This discussion is based on research and results presented in M. L. Meuter, A. L. Ostrom, R. I. Roundtree, and M. J. Bitner, "Self-Service Technologies: Understanding Customer Satisfaction with Technology-Based Service Encounters," *Journal of Marketing* 64 (July 2000), pp. 50–64.

50. M. J. Bitner, S. W. Brown, and M. L. Meuter, "Technology Infusion in Service Encounters," *Journal of the Academy of Marketing Science* 28 (1), pp. 138–49.

51. M. J. Bitner, "Managing the Evidence of Service," in *The Service Quality Handbook,* ed. E. Scheuing and W. Christopher (New York: AMACOM, 1993), pp. 358–70.

52. L. L. Berry and A. Parasuraman, *Marketing Services* (New York: Free Press, 1991), chap. 3.

53. G. L. Shostack, "Designing Services That Deliver," *Harvard Business Review,* January–February 1984, pp. 133–39; G. L. Shostack, "Service Positioning through Structural Change," *Journal of Marketing* 51 (1987), pp. 34–43.

54. For good coverage of recovery strategies see Berry and Parasuraman, *Marketing Services;* and C. W. L. Hart, J. L. Heskett, and W. E. Sasser, Jr., "The Profitable Art of Service Recovery," *Harvard Business Review,* July–August 1990, pp. 148–56. Recovery strategies will also be discussed further in Chapter 7 of this book.

55. B. Schneider and D. Schechter, "Development of a Personnel System for Service Jobs," in *Service Quality: Multi-disciplinary and Multi-national Perspectives,* ed. S. W. Brown, E. Gummesson, and B. Edvardsson (Lexington, MA: Lexington Books, 1991), pp. 217–36.

Listening to Customer Requirements

Part 2

Not knowing what customers expect is one of the root causes of not delivering to customer expectations. Provider gap 1 is the difference between customer expectations of service and company understanding of those expectations. Note that in the accompanying figure we created a link between the customer and the company, showing customer expectations above the line that dissects the model and provider perceptions of those expectations below the line. When we use the term *company* in this gap, we refer to anyone in the organization who has the responsibility and authority to create or change service policies, procedures, and standards. This could include top executives, middle managers, supervisors, and—in many of the more innovative companies today—empowered teams. In earlier versions of the gaps model, the term *manager* was used rather than company because in the past most changes in service policies and procedures were established and approved by management.

In this text we have broadened the responsibility for the first provider gap from managers alone to any employee in the organization with the authority to change or influence service policies and procedures. In today's changing organizations, the authority to make adjustments in service delivery is delegated to empowered teams and front-line people.

Provider Gap 1

Why does this first provider gap occur? Many reasons exist: no direct interaction with customers, unwillingness to ask about expectations, and/or unpreparedness in addressing them. When people with the authority and responsibility for setting priorities do not fully understand customers' service expectations, they may trigger a chain of bad decisions and suboptimal resource allocations that result in perceptions of poor service quality. One example of misplaced priorities stemming from an inaccurate understanding of customers' expectations is spending far too much money on buildings and the appearance of a company's physical facilities when customers are more concerned with how convenient, comfortable, and functional the facilities are. Another example is health organizations training doctors in the latest surgical techniques but forgetting to educate them about patients' needs for concern and care.

An inaccurate understanding of what customers expect and what really matters to them leads to service performance that falls short of customer expectations. The necessary first step in improving quality of service is for management or empowered employees to acquire accurate information about customers' expectations (that is, close provider gap 1). Formal and informal methods to capture information about customer expectations can be developed through market research. Techniques involving a variety of traditional research approaches must be used to stay close to the customer, among them customer visits, survey research, complaint systems, and customer panels. More innovative techniques, such as quality function deployment, structured brainstorming, and service quality gap analysis, are often needed as well. Chapter 5 in this section discusses marketing research and other techniques that close provider gap 1.

Part of closing gap 1 is recognizing that not all customers are the same. *Market segmentation* is the grouping of customers sharing similar requirements, expectations, and demographic or psychographic profiles. Although marketers have used segmentation for decades, it may be more critical today than at any other time. Homogeneous products and services for the mass market no longer satisfy customers; now, more than ever before, they are seeking and buying services that fit their unique configuration of needs. Many marketers are achieving success with the concept of *mass customization*—creating services that can be customized or appear to be customized through technological innovations. Finally, service companies must manage the customer mix, an issue more critical in services marketing, where customers often interact with each other while receiving service, than in goods marketing. Managing the customer mix, in a broad sense, means determining and choosing a mix of customers to target that are compatible or at least separated from each other if incompatible.

Another trend related to provider gap 1 involves current company strategies to retain customers and strengthen relationships with them. The term *relationship marketing* is used to describe this approach, which emphasizes strengthening the bonds between companies and their existing customers. When organizations have strong relationships with their customers, gap 1 is less likely to occur. One of the major marketing factors that is leveraged in relationship marketing, particularly in manufacturing companies, is service. Technology affords companies the ability to acquire and integrate vast quantities of data on customers that can be used to build relationships. Frequent flyer travel programs conducted by airlines, car rental companies, and hotels are among the most familiar programs of this type. Frequent buyer programs used by bookstores such as Waldenbooks and B. Dalton Bookseller also encourage loyalty and frequent purchase among customers. Relationship marketing is distinct from *transactional marketing,* the term used to describe the more conventional emphasis on acquiring new customers rather than on retaining them. When companies focus too much on attracting new customers, they may fail to understand the changing needs and expectations of their current customers. Chapter 6 in this section discusses the growing emphasis on customer relationships and the ways that companies are strengthening their bonds with their most important assets.

Even the best companies, with the best of intentions and clear understanding of their customers' expectations, sometimes fail. Given the inherent characteristics of services—heterogeneity across providers, simultaneous production and consumption, and customer involvement—service failure is inevitable. Knowing what customers expect when things go wrong and executing strong service recovery efforts under these circumstances are critical strategies for closing gap 1. Many firms now recognize that the "customer who complains is your best friend." In fact, a complaining customer provides the company with the opportunity to make up to that customer, learn from its mistakes, and hopefully retain that customer's business in the future. Chapter 7 in this section discusses the importance of service recovery, why people complain, what they expect when they complain, and how to develop effective service recovery strategies for dealing with inevitable service failures. This might involve a well-defined complaint-handling procedure and empowering employees to react on the spot, in real time, to fix the failure; other times it involves a service guarantee or way to compensate the customer for the unfulfilled promise.

From the material in this section you will learn how to understand customers through multiple research strategies (Chapter 5), how to build strong relationships and understand customer needs over time (Chapter 6), and how to implement recovery strategies when things go wrong (Chapter 7). Through these strategies, provider gap 1—the customer expectations gap—will be minimized.

Chapter 5

Understanding Customer Expectations and Perceptions through Marketing Research

This chapter's objectives are to

1. Present the types of and guidelines for marketing research in services.

2. Show how marketing research information can and should be used for services.

3. Describe the strategies by which companies can facilitate interaction and communication between management and customers.

4. Present ways that companies can and do facilitate interaction between contact people and management.

Students and Recruiters Use Marketing Research to Select Business Schools

Until 1988, students contemplating a graduate business school education could find only limited information about the various schools, particularly about the experience and evaluations of students who had matriculated at the schools. Published ratings of schools rested on test scores of entering students and starting salaries of graduates. The only available school rankings used deans of business schools as judges, rather than the students attending the schools. Finding out student perceptions of schools required informal word-of-mouth communication

and networking, activities that were time-consuming and whose results were difficult to compare across schools.

Beginning in 1988, *Business Week* revolutionized business school choice by providing potential students with the information they wanted: opinions and attitudes of students themselves. In a pioneering marketing research study, the magazine began its semiannual rankings of business schools by their primary "customers"—recent graduates and corporate recruiters. The study ranks the institutions on the basis of customer satisfaction: how the schools determine and satisfy the needs of both graduates and the corporations who hire them.[1]

In the 2000 version of the study, *Business Week* mailed 16,843 surveys to recent master's of business administration graduates and 419 to corporate recruiters. A full 60 percent of the graduates and 59 percent of the corporate recruiters responded to the survey—a very high rate of return by research standards.[2]

Here's how the student survey worked. Questionnaires were mailed to a random sample of MBA candidates from 82 business schools. The recipients answered 37 questions about the school's performance, which were subsequently weighted to reflect how closely they related to overall satisfaction. A composite index was created from the results of the 2000 surveys (weighted 50 percent), the 1998 surveys (weighted 25 percent), and the 1996 surveys (weighted 25 percent). Graduates judged only their own schools on teaching quality, program content, and career placement.

The survey of recruiters polled companies that hired MBAs and asked them to rate their top 20 schools on the basis of the rate of success of a school's graduates in their companies. The 2000 rankings were:

1. Pennsylvania's Wharton
2. Northwestern's Kellogg School
3. Harvard
4. MIT (Sloan)
5. Duke (Fuqua)
6. Michigan
7. Columbia
8. Cornell (Johnson)
9. Virginia (Darden)
10. Chicago
11. Stanford
12. UCLA (Anderson)
13. NYU (Stern)
14. Carnegie Mellon
15. UNC–Chapel Hill
16. Dartmouth (Tuck)
17. Texas–Austin
18. UC Berkeley (Haas)
19. Yale
20. Indiana

The *Business Week* research-derived rankings have led to many changes in schools, including revamped curricula, refocusing of efforts to topics such as teamwork and global concerns, and greater emphasis on the satisfaction of students and corporations.

One reaction to the survey and its findings is a response that occurs frequently in market research: when managers do not like the findings, they question a study's accuracy and claim the results are biased. Students at five schools also tried to "game" the results by inflating responses on the student portion of the survey. *Business Week* adjusted the scores at these schools by decreasing their weight to adjust for these efforts.

Despite a genuine interest in meeting customer expectations, many companies miss the mark by thinking inside out—they believe they know what customers *should* want and deliver that, rather than finding out what they *do* want. When this happens, companies provide services that do not match customer expectations: important features are left out, and the levels of performance on features that are provided are inadequate. Because services have few clearly defined and tangible cues, this difficulty may be considerably larger than it is in manufacturing firms. A far better approach involves thinking outside in—determining customer expectations and then delivering to them. Thinking outside in involves using marketing research to understand customers and their requirements fully. Marketing research, the subject of this chapter, involves far more than conventional surveys. It consists of a portfolio of listening strategies that allow the company to deliver to expectations.

USING MARKETING RESEARCH TO UNDERSTAND CUSTOMER EXPECTATIONS

Finding out what customers expect is essential to providing service quality, and marketing research is a key vehicle for understanding customer expectations and perceptions of services. In services, as with any offering, a firm that does no marketing research at all is unlikely to understand its customers. A firm that does marketing research, but not on the topic of customer expectations, may also fail to know what is needed to stay in tune with changing customer requirements. Marketing research must focus on service issues such as what features are most important to customers, what levels of these features customers expect, and what customers think the company can and should do when problems occur in service delivery. Even when a service firm is small and has limited resources to conduct research, avenues are open to explore what the customer expects.

In this section we discuss the elements of services marketing research programs that help companies to identify customer expectations and perceptions. In the following sections we will discuss ways the tactics of general marketing research may need to be adjusted to maximize their effectiveness in services.

Research Objectives for Services

The first step in designing services marketing research is without doubt the most critical: defining the problem and research objectives. This is where the services marketer poses the questions to be answered or problems to be solved with the research. Does the company want to know how customers view the service provided by the company, what customer requirements are, how customers will respond to a new service introduction, or what customers will want from the company five years from now? Each of these research questions requires a different research strategy. Thus it is essential to devote time and resources to define the problem thoroughly and accurately. In spite of the importance of this first stage, many marketing research studies are initiated without adequate attention to objectives.

Research objectives translate into action questions. While many different questions are likely to be part of a marketing research program, the following are the most common research objectives in services:

- To identify dissatisfied customers, so that service recovery can be attempted.

- To discover customer requirements or expectations for service.

- To monitor and track service performance.

- To assess overall company performance compared with that of competition.

- To assess gaps between customer expectations and perceptions.

- To gauge effectiveness of changes in service delivery.

- To appraise the service performance of individuals and teams for evaluation, recognition, and rewards.

- To determine customer expectations for a new service.

- To monitor changing customer expectations in an industry.

- To forecast future expectations of customers.

These research objectives are similar in many ways to the research conducted for physical products: both aim to assess customer requirements, dissatisfaction, and demand. Services research, however, incorporates additional elements that require specific attention.

First, services research must continually monitor and track service performance because performance is subject to human variability and heterogeneity. Conducting performance research at a single point in time, as might be done for a physical product such as an automobile, would be insufficient in services. A major focus of services research involves capturing human performance—at the level of the individual employee, the team, the branch, the organization as a whole, and the competition. Another focus of services research is documenting the process by which service is performed. Even when service employees are performing well, a service provider must continue to track performance because the potential for variation in service delivery is always present.

A second distinction in services research is the need to consider and monitor the gap between expectations and perceptions. This gap is dynamic because both perceptions and expectations can fluctuate. Does the gap exist because performance is declining, because performance varies with demand and supply level, or because expectations are escalating?

Exhibit 5.1 (pages 128–129) lists a number of services research objectives. Once objectives such as these have been identified, they will point the way to decisions about the most appropriate type of research, methods of data collection, and ways to use the information. We will describe the additional columns in this table in the following sections of this chapter.

Criteria for an Effective Services Research Program

A **services research program** can be defined as *the composite of separate research studies and types needed to address research objectives and execute an overall measurement strategy.* Many types of research could be considered in a research program. Understanding the criteria for an effective services research program (see Figure 5.1) will help a company evaluate different types of research and choose the ones most appropriate for its research objectives. In this section we discuss these criteria.

Includes Qualitative and Quantitative Research[3]   Marketing research is not limited to surveys and statistics. Some forms of research are exploratory and preliminary, called *qualitative research,* and are conducted to clarify problem definition and prepare for more formal empirical research. *Quantitative research* in marketing, on the other hand, is designed to describe the nature, attitudes, or behaviors of customers empirically and to test specific hypotheses that a services marketer wants to examine. Both types of research are important and need to be included in services marketing research programs. Insights gained through qualitative methods such as customer focus groups, informal conversations with individual customers, critical incidents research (described in Chapter 4 and discussed more fully later in this chapter), and direct observation of

FIGURE 5.1
Criteria for an Effective Services Research Program

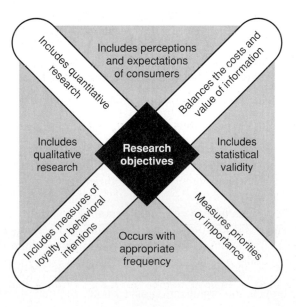

service transactions show the marketer the right questions to ask of consumers and make the numbers in computer printouts meaningful. Qualitative research also gives managers the perspective and sensitivity that are critical in interpreting the data and initiating improvement efforts.[4] Because the results of qualitative research play a major role in designing quantitative research, it often is the first type of research conducted.

Quantitative research clearly is important in assessing and improving service delivery and design. Quantitative research gives managers data from which they can make broad inferences about customer groups. These studies are essential for quantifying customer satisfaction, the importance of service attributes, the extent of service quality gaps, and perceptions of value. They also provide managers with yardsticks to evaluate and track the firm's service performance and show how the firm compares with competitors. Finally, results from empirical studies often trigger the need to conduct further qualitative research. Empirical data can highlight specific service deficiencies for deeper qualitative probing.

Includes Both Perceptions and Expectations of Customers As we discussed in Chapter 3, expectations serve as standards or reference points for customers. In evaluating service quality, customers compare what they perceive they get in a service encounter with their expectations of that encounter. For this reason, a measurement program that captures only perceptions of service is missing a critical part of the service quality equation. Companies need also to incorporate measures of customer expectations.

Measurement of expectations can be included in a research program in multiple ways. First, basic research that relates to customers' requirements—that identifies the service features or attributes that matter to customers—can be considered expectation research. In this form, the *content* of customer expectations is captured, initially in some form of qualitative research such as focus group interviews. Research on the *levels* of customer expectations also is needed. This type of research quantitatively assesses the levels of customer expectations and compares these with perception levels, usually by calculating the gap between expectations and perceptions.

Balances the Cost of the Research and the Value of the Information One of the major criteria for deciding the types of research to include in a services marketing research program is an assessment of the cost of the research compared with its benefits or value for the company. One type of cost is the monetary outlay in terms of direct costs to marketing research companies, payments to respondents, and internal company costs incurred by employees collecting the information (as in complaint solicitations). Time costs are also a factor, including the length of time between the start of a research study and the time the data are available for use by employees, as well as the time commitment needed internally by employees to administer the research. These and other costs must be traded off against the value of the information to the company in terms of better decision making, retained customers, and successful new service launches. As in many other marketing decisions, the costs are easier to estimate and track than the value of the information. For this reason, we include only costs in the columns of Exhibit 5.1. In later chapters we describe approaches to estimating the value of customers to a company, approaches that are useful as input to the trade-off analysis needed to address this criterion.

Includes Statistical Validity When Necessary We have already shown that research has multiple and diverse objectives. These objectives determine the appropriate type of research and methodology. To illustrate, some research is used within companies not so much to measure as to build relationships with customers—to allow

5.1 ELEMENTS IN AN EFFECTIVE MARKETING RESEARCH PROGRAM FOR SERVICES

Type of Research	Primary Research Objectives	Qualitative/Quantitative	Costs of Information		Frequency
			Monetary	Time	
Complaint solicitation	To identify/attend to dissatisfied customers To identify common service failure points	Qualitative	Low	Low	Continuous
Critical incident studies	To identify "best practices" at transaction level To identify customer requirements as input for quantitative studies To identify common service failure points To identify systemic strengths and weaknesses in customer-contact services	Qualitative	Low	Moderate	Periodic
Requirements research	To identify customer requirements as input for quantitative research	Qualitative	Moderate	Moderate	Periodic
Relationship surveys and SERVQUAL surveys	To monitor and track service performance To assess overall company performance compared with that of competition To determine links between satisfaction and behavioral intentions To assess gaps between customer expectations and perceptions	Quantitative	Moderate	Moderate	Annual
Trailer calls	To obtain immediate feedback on performance of service transactions To measure effectiveness of changes in service delivery To assess service performance of individuals and teams To use as input for process improvements To identify common service failure points	Quantitative	Low	Low	Continuous

Type of Research	Research Objective	Qualitative/ Quantitative	Cost	Cost	Frequency
Service expectation meetings and reviews	To create dialogue with important customers To identify what individual large customers expect and then to assure that it is delivered To close the loop with important customers	Qualitative	Moderate	Moderate	Annual
Process checkpoint evaluations	To determine customer perceptions of long-term professional services during service provision To identify service problems and solve them early in the service relationship	Quantitative	Moderate	Moderate	Periodic
Market-oriented ethnography	To research customers in natural settings To study customers from cultures other than America in an unbiased way	Qualitative	Moderate	High	Periodic
Mystery shopping	To measure individual employee performance for evaluation, recognition, and rewards To identify systemic strengths and weaknesses in customer-contact services	Quantitative	Low	Low	Quarterly
Customer panels	To monitor changing customer expectations To provide a forum for customers to suggest and evaluate new service ideas	Qualitative	Moderate	Moderate	Continuous
Lost customer research	To identify reasons for customer defection	Qualitative	Low	Low	Continuous
Future expectations research	To forecast future expectations of customers To develop and test new service ideas	Qualitative	High	High	Periodic
Database marketing research	To identify the individual requirements of customers using information technology and database information	Quantitative	High	High	Continuous

129

company contact people to learn what customers desire, to diagnose the strengths and weaknesses of their and the firm's efforts to address the desires, to prepare a plan to meet requirements, and to confirm after a period of time (usually one year) that the company has executed the plan. The underlying objective is to allow contact people to identify specific action items that will gain the maximum return in customer satisfaction for individual customers. This type of research does not need sophisticated quantitative analysis, anonymity of customers, careful control of sampling, or strong statistical validity.

On the other hand, research used to track overall service quality that will be used for bonuses and salary increases of salespeople must be carefully controlled for sampling bias and statistical validity. One of us (VZ) has worked with a company that paid salespeople on the basis of customers' satisfaction scores while allowing the salespeople to control the customers sampled. Obviously, the salespeople quickly learned that they could have surveys sent only to satisfied customers, artificially inflating the scores and—of course—undermining the confidence in the measurement system.

Not all forms of research have statistical validity, and not all forms need it. Most forms of qualitative research, for example, do not possess statistical validity.

Measures Priorities or Importance   Customers have many service requirements, but not all are equally important. One of the most common mistakes managers make in trying to improve service is spending resources on the wrong initiatives, only to become discouraged because the firm's service does not improve! Measuring the relative importance of service dimensions and attributes helps managers to channel resources effectively; therefore, research must document the priorities of the customer. Prioritization can be accomplished in multiple ways. First, *direct importance measures* ask customers to prioritize items or dimensions of service. Several alternatives are available for measuring importance directly, among them asking respondents to rank-order service dimensions or attributes, or to rate them on a scale from "not at all important" to "extremely important." One effective approach involves asking respondents to allocate a total of 100 points across the various service dimensions. *Indirect importance measures* are estimated using the statistical procedures of correlation and regression analysis, which show the relative contribution of questionnaire items or requirements to overall service quality. Both indirect and direct importance measures provide evidence of customer priorities, and the technique that is chosen depends on the nature of the study and the number of dimensions or attributes that are being evaluated.

Occurs with Appropriate Frequency   Because customer expectations and perceptions are dynamic, companies need to institute a service quality research process, not just do isolated studies. A single study of service provides only a "snapshot" view of one moment in time. For full understanding of the marketplace's acceptance of a company's service, marketing research must be ongoing. Without a pattern of studies repeated with appropriate frequency, managers cannot tell whether the firm is moving forward or falling back and which of their service improvement initiatives are working. Just what does "ongoing research" mean in terms of frequency? The answer is specific to the type of service and to the purpose and method of each type of service research a company might do.[5] As we discuss the different types in the following section, you will see the frequency with which each type of research could be conducted.

Includes Measures of Loyalty or Behavioral Intentions   An important trend in services research involves measuring the positive and negative consequences of service quality along with overall satisfaction or service quality scores. Among the most important generic behavioral intentions are willingness to recommend the service to others and repurchase intent. These behavioral intentions can be viewed as positive and negative consequences of service quality. Positive behavioral intentions include saying positive things about the company, recommending the company to others, remaining loyal, spending more with the company, and paying a price premium. Negative behavioral intentions include saying negative things to others, doing less business with the company, switching to another company, and complaining to outside organizations such as the Better Business Bureau. Other more specific behavioral intentions differ by service; for example, behavioral intentions related to medical care include following instructions from the doctor, taking medications, and returning for follow-up. Tracking these areas can help a company estimate the relative value of service improvements to the company and can also identify customers who are in danger of defecting.

Summary   The research criteria discussed here should be incorporated into a services marketing research program. As we discuss the elements in an effective services marketing research program, we will indicate how these approaches satisfy the criteria. In addition to the types and techniques of research shown in Exhibit 5.1, the boxes in this chapter show how electronic and other technologies add to the information managers can collect.

ELEMENTS IN AN EFFECTIVE SERVICES MARKETING RESEARCH PROGRAM

A good services marketing research program includes multiple types of research studies. The composite of studies and types of research will differ by company because the range of uses for service quality research—from employee performance assessment to advertising campaign development to strategic planning—requires a rich, multifaceted flow of information. The particular portfolio for any company will match company resources and address the key areas needed to understand the customers of the business. If a company were to engage in virtually all types of service research, the portfolio would look like Exhibit 5.1. So that it will be easier for you to identify the appropriate type of research for different research objectives, we list the objectives in column 2 of the table. In the following sections we describe each major type of research and show the way each type addresses the criteria associated with it. The Technology Spotlight discusses research conducted online.

Complaint Solicitation

Many of you have complained to employees of service organizations, only to find that nothing happens with your complaint. No one rushes to solve it, and the next time you experience the service the same problem is present. How frustrating! Good service organizations take complaints seriously. Not only do they listen to complaints—they also seek complaints as communications about what can be done to improve their service and their service employees.

Firms that use complaints as research collect and document them, then use the information to identify dissatisfied customers, correct individual problems where possible, and identify common service failure points. Although this research is used for both goods and services, it has a critical real-time purpose in services—to improve failure points and to improve or correct the performance of contact personnel. Research on complaints is one of the easiest types of research for firms to conduct,

Technology Spotlight
http://www.marketingresearch

Although only about 30 percent of U.S. residents are on the Internet, many companies want to reach that group because they are early adopters and leading-edge consumers. In 1996 less than $3 million was spent on online research efforts; but by 2000 Internet research accounted for $46 million globally. One of the most intriguing applications of the Internet is online research, replacing comment cards and intrusive telephone calls with cyber-surveys that are challenging and fun for consumers. The application is growing rapidly: more than 75 percent of the 165 members of the Council of American Survey Research Organization have their own websites, and more than 95 percent offer Internet-based data collection. The reasons are obvious—Internet research has been touted to have many benefits to marketers besides more willing respondents, including the following:

- *Speed.* Rather than three to four months required to collect data through mail questionnaires, or six to eight weeks needed to train interviewers and obtain data from telephone questionnaires, online surveys can be prepared and executed quickly. A sample of 300 to 400, large enough for many studies, can be completed in a weekend and available for viewing by clients on a secure website. One market research firm was able to complete 1,000 customer satisfaction surveys in only two hours.

- *Ability to target hard-to-reach populations.* One of the traditional difficulties in research, particularly segmentation research, is to identify and access respondents who fit a particular lifestyle or interest profile. Doctors, lawyers, professionals, and working mothers are all valuable but difficult-to-access groups of customers. These people might read special interest magazines (such as professional or hobby publica-

tions) that are expensive to advertise in. They could be reached in surveys only by having the service company purchase at great cost the mailing list of that magazine. However, online sites for special interests are quite simple to identify, access, and insert survey banners in.

- *Ability to target customers with money.* Online research allows service companies to reach customers who have higher incomes, higher education levels, and greater willingness to spend. Consumers with computers who use online services regularly tend to be in these demographic target groups, and they can be effectively surveyed with online research. Compared with the sample that would be obtained from traditional research using all telephone subscribers, the sample of online users is far better in terms of marketing potential.

- *Opportunity to use multimedia to present video and audio.* Telephone surveys are limited to voice alone, whereas mail surveys are constrained to two-dimensional visuals. In the past, to present the full range of audio and video needed to give respondents the true sense of a service being researched, surveys had to be conducted in person and were therefore very expensive ($30 to $150 per person depending on the topic and sample). Online research offers broader stimuli potential through all multimedia possibilities at a fraction of the cost.

- *No interviewers*—and therefore no interviewer errors or interviewer bias. Bias occurs when the interviewer is in a bad mood, tired, impatient, or not objective. These problems occur with human interviews but not cyber-interviews. Interviewer error is another

leading many companies to depend solely on complaints to stay in touch with customers. Unfortunately, research conducted by TARP, a research organization in Washington, has provided convincing evidence that customer complaints alone are a woefully inadequate source of information: only a small percentage of customers with problems actually complain to the company. The rest will stay dissatisfied, telling more than 10 other people about their dissatisfaction.[6]

To be effective, complaint solicitation requires rigorous recording of numbers and types of complaints through many channels, and then working to eliminate the most

Technology Spotlight
http://www.marketingresearch—continued

age-old research problem, described well by a research professional:

> The first survey I ever designed was on the subject of home heating systems. When I went to observe the first day of field, I was surprised and horrified to realize that most of my interviewers could not pronounce many of the technical terms that I had used in the survey, and virtually none of them knew what those terms meant. It wasn't exactly the best way to collect data.

• *Control over data quality,* which can eliminate contradictory or nonsensical answers. With traditional surveys, researchers need a step called "data cleaning and editing" in which all data are checked for such problems; electronic checks can be built into online surveys that take care of this problem as it occurs.

• *Inexpensive research.* Data collection costs can be the most expensive part of a study, and the most expensive part of data collection is paying subjects to participate. Online marketing research, astonishingly, is 10 to 80 percent less expensive than other approaches. The Internet also eliminates postage, phone, labor, and printing costs that are typical with other survey approaches. Respondents also seem to complete Web-based surveys in half the time it would take an interviewer to conduct the survey, perhaps contributing to the lack of need for incentives.

One additional but to date undersubstantiated benefit is higher response rate—reportedly as high as 70 percent—possibly stemming from the fact that the interactive nature of cyber-research can make answering surveys fun for respondents. While it is getting more difficult to get consumers to answer traditional surveys, the entertainment value of cyber-surveys makes it easy to recruit participants. One study shows that consumers are five times more likely to complete an electronic survey as they are to do the same survey with written materials and that researchers obtain the following three additional benefits: (1) consumers "play" an e-survey longer, answering more questions than in a traditional survey; (2) people tend to concentrate more fully on their answers; and (3) the entertainment value of an e-survey actually lowers the respondent's perceived time to complete the survey.

The advantages of online research likely far outnumber the disadvantages. However, marketers need to be aware of these drawbacks. Perhaps the major problem is the composition of the sample. Unlike the process used with most telephone and mail surveys, the population of responders is not usually selected but is a matter of convenience, consisting of whoever responds to the survey. This is a particular problem when respondents are recruited from other websites and click through to the survey. In these cases marketers may not even know who the responders are and whether they are in fact the right profile for answering the survey. To address this problem, companies are prequalifying respondents by telephone or e-mail, then asking for enough demographic information to ensure that the respondents meet the desired requirements.

Sources: A. Hogg, "Online Research Overview," MarketingPower.com, 2001; D. McCullough, "Web-Based Market Research Ushers in New Age," *Marketing News,* September 14, 1998, p. 28; R. Weible and J. Wallace, "Cyber Research: The Impact of the Internet on Data Collection," *Marketing Research,* Fall 1998, pp. 19–24; R. Nadilo, "On-Line Research Taps Consumers Who Spend," *Marketing News,* June 8, 1998, p. 12.

frequent ones. These channels include employees at the front line, intermediary organizations like retailers who deliver service, managers, and complaints to third parties such as customer advocate groups. Companies must both solve individual customer problems and seek overall patterns to eliminate failure points. More sophisticated forms of complaint resolution define "complaint" broadly to include all comments—both negative and positive—as well as questions from customers. The firm must build a depository for this information and report results frequently, perhaps weekly or monthly.

FIGURE 5.2

Participants in a focus group discuss services using the critical incidents technique.

Source: David Grossman/Photo Researchers, Inc.

Critical Incidents Studies

In Chapter 4 we discussed the Critical Incidents Technique, whereby customers provide verbatim stories about satisfying and dissatisfying service encounters they have experienced (Figure 5.2). Studies using critical incidents are appropriate to address many different research objectives. They are effective alternatives to complaint solicitation because they too identify dissatisfied customers and common service failure points. Critical incidents are powerful and vivid in eliciting customer requirements, particularly when the research is focused on behaviors of employees. The critical incidents technique is also an ideal way to have customers describe "best practices."

By providing verbatim stories about satisfying and dissatisfying service encounters they have experienced, customers reveal what they desire in service encounters. In Chapter 4 we summarized four broad categories or themes that cause satisfaction and dissatisfaction in service encounters across multiple industries (recovery, adaptability, spontaneity, and coping). This generic research provides a perspective from which to start, but the real benefit for any particular company is in using the critical incidents technique to identify customer requirements for individual service encounters. For example, the initial question might read, "Think of a time when you had a particularly satisfying visit from a salesperson from XYZ company." The remaining questions would be posed about that particular sales encounter rather than about the company or firms in general.

The critical incidents technique is powerful and vivid in eliciting customer requirements, particularly when the research is focused on behavioral dimensions of employee performance at the service encounter level. As a result of conducting a critical incidents study, the researcher emerges with a list of desirable and undesirable employee behaviors in those service encounters. These can be communicated to contact personnel quite clearly in terms of what behaviors satisfy customers.

Requirements Research

Requirements research involves identifying the benefits and attributes that customers expect in a service. This type of research is very basic and essential because it determines the type of questions that will be asked in surveys and ultimately the improvements that will be attempted by the firm. Because these studies are so foundational, qualitative techniques are appropriate to begin them. Quantitative techniques may follow, usually during a pretest stage of survey development. Unfortunately, many companies do inadequate requirements research, often developing surveys on the basis of intuition or company direction rather than thorough customer probing.

An example of requirements research is *structured brainstorming,* a technique developed by researchers in IBM's Advanced Business Systems unit.[7] In this technique a sample of customers and potential customers is assembled. A facilitator leads the group through a series of exercises on creativity and then has the customers describe the ideal provider of the service—what they would want if they could have their ideal service. The facilitator asks "what" customers want (to elicit fundamental requirements), "why" they want it (to elicit the underlying need or benefit sought), and "how" they will know when they receive it (to elicit specific service features).

Another approach to requirements research that has been effective in services industries is to examine existing research about customer requirements in similar service industries. The five dimensions of quality service are generalizable across industries, and sometimes the way these dimensions are manifest is also remarkably similar. Hospital patients and customers of hotels, for example, expect many of the same features when using these two services. Besides expert medical care, patients in hospitals expect comfortable rooms, courteous staff, and food that tastes good—the same features that are salient to hotel customers. In these and other industries that share common customer expectations, managers may find it helpful to seek knowledge from existing research in the related service industry. Because hotels have used marketing and marketing research longer than hospitals have, insights about hotel guests' expectations can inform about patients' expectations. Hospital administrators at Albert Einstein Medical Center in Philadelphia, for example, asked a group of nine local hotel executives for advice in understanding and handling patients. Many improvements resulted, including better food, easier-to-read name tags, more prominent information desks, and radios in many rooms.[8]

"Relationship" and SERVQUAL Surveys

One category of surveys could appropriately be named *relationship surveys* because they pose questions about all elements in the customer's relationship with the company (including service, product, and price). This comprehensive approach can help a company diagnose its relationship strengths and weaknesses. These surveys typically monitor and track service performance annually with an initial survey providing a baseline. Relationship surveys are also effective in comparing company performance with that of competitors, often focusing on the best competitor's performance as a benchmark. When used for this purpose, the sponsor of the survey is often not identified and questions are asked about both the focal company and one or more competitors.

A sound measure of service quality is necessary for identifying the aspects of service needing performance improvement, assessing how much improvement is needed on each aspect, and evaluating the impact of improvement efforts. Unlike goods quality, which can be measured objectively by such indicators as durability and number of defects, service quality is abstract and is best captured by surveys that measure customer evaluations of service. One of the first measures to be developed specifically to measure service quality was the SERVQUAL survey.

The SERVQUAL scale involves a survey containing 21 service attributes, grouped into the five service quality dimensions (discussed in Chapter 4) of reliability, responsiveness, assurance, empathy, and tangibles. The survey often asks customers to provide two different ratings on each attribute—one reflecting the level of service they would expect from excellent companies in a sector and the other reflecting their perception of the service delivered by a specific company within that sector. The difference between the expectation and perception ratings constitutes a quantified measure of service quality. Exhibit 5.2 shows the items on the basic SERVQUAL scale, as well as the phrasing of the expectations and perceptions portions of the scale.[9]

5.2 SERVQUAL: A MULTIDIMENSIONAL SCALE TO CAPTURE CUSTOMER PERCEPTIONS AND EXPECTATIONS OF SERVICE QUALITY

The SERVQUAL scale was first published in 1988 and has undergone numerous improvements and revisions since then. The scale currently contains 21 perception items that are distributed throughout the five service quality dimensions. The scale also contains expectation items. Although many different formats of the SERVQUAL scale are now in use, we show here the basic 21 perception items, as well as a sampling of ways the expectation items have been posed.

PERCEPTIONS

Perceptions Statements in the Reliability Dimension

	Strongly disagree						Strongly agree
1. When XYZ Company promises to do something by a certain time, it does so.	1	2	3	4	5	6	7
2. When you have a problem, XYZ Company shows a sincere interest in solving it.	1	2	3	4	5	6	7
3. XYZ Company performs the service right the first time.	1	2	3	4	5	6	7
4. XYZ Company provides its services at the time it promises to do so.	1	2	3	4	5	6	7
5. XYZ Company keeps customers informed about when services will be performed.	1	2	3	4	5	6	7

Statements in the Responsiveness Dimension

	Strongly disagree						Strongly agree
1. Employees in XYZ Company give you prompt service.	1	2	3	4	5	6	7
2. Employees in XYZ Company are always willing to help you.	1	2	3	4	5	6	7
3. Employees in XYZ Company are never too busy to respond to your request.	1	2	3	4	5	6	7

Statements in the Assurance Dimension

	Strongly disagree						Strongly agree
1. The behavior of employees in XYZ Company instills confidence in you.	1	2	3	4	5	6	7
2. You feel safe in your transactions with XYZ Company.	1	2	3	4	5	6	7
3. Employees in XYZ Company are consistently courteous with you.	1	2	3	4	5	6	7
4. Employees in XYZ Company have the knowledge to answer your questions.	1	2	3	4	5	6	7

Statements in the Empathy Dimension

	Strongly disagree						Strongly agree
1. XYZ Company gives you individual attention.	1	2	3	4	5	6	7
2. XYZ Company has employees who give you individual attention.	1	2	3	4	5	6	7
3. XYZ Company has your best interests at heart.	1	2	3	4	5	6	7
4. Employees of XYZ Company understand your specific needs.	1	2	3	4	5	6	7

Statements in the Tangibles Dimension

	Strongly disagree						Strongly agree
1. XYZ Company has modern-looking equipment.	1	2	3	4	5	6	7
2. XYZ Company's physical facilities are visually appealing.	1	2	3	4	5	6	7
3. XYZ Company's employees appear neat.	1	2	3	4	5	6	7
4. Materials associated with the service (such as pamphlets or statements) are visually appealing at XYZ Company.	1	2	3	4	5	6	7
5. XYZ Company has convenient business hours.	1	2	3	4	5	6	7

EXPECTATIONS: Several Formats for Measuring Customer Expectations Using Versions of SERVQUAL

Matching Expectations Statements (Paired with the Previous Perception Statements)

	Strongly disagree					Strongly agree
When customers have a problem, excellent firms will show a sincere interest in solving it.	1	2	3	4	5	6	7

Referent Expectations Formats

1. Considering a "world class" company to be a "7," how would you rate XYZ Company's performance on the following service features?

	Low						High
Sincere, interested employees	1	2	3	4	5	6	7
Service delivered right the first time	1	2	3	4	5	6	7

2. Compared with the level of service you expect from an excellent company, how would you rate XYZ Company's performance on the following?

	Low						High
Sincere, interested employees	1	2	3	4	5	6	7
Service delivered right the first time	1	2	3	4	5	6	7

Combined Expectations/Perceptions Statements

For each of the following statements, circle the number that indicates how XYZ Company's service compares with the level you expect:

	Lower than my desired service level			The same as my desired service level			Higher than my desired service level		
1. Prompt service	1	2	3	4	5	6	7	8	9
2. Courteous employees	1	2	3	4	5	6	7	8	9

Expectations Distinguishing between Desired Service and Adequate Service

For each of the following statements, circle the number that indicates how XYZ Company's performance compares with your *minimum service level* and with your *desired service level.*

When it comes to . . .	Compared with my *minimum* service level XYZ's service performance is:									Compared with my *desired* service level XYZ's service performance is:								
	Lower			Same			Higher			Lower			Same			Higher		
1. Prompt service	1	2	3	4	5	6	7	8	9	1	2	3	4	5	6	7	8	9
2. Employees who are consistently courteous	1	2	3	4	5	6	7	8	9	1	2	3	4	5	6	7	8	9

Source: Reprinted with permission of Elsevier Science Limited from A. Parasuraman, V. A. Zeithaml, and L. L. Berry, "SERVQUAL: A Multiple-Item Scale for Measuring Consumer Perceptions of Service Quality," *Journal of Retailing* 64, no. 1 (Spring 1988).

Data gathered through a SERVQUAL survey can be used for a variety of purposes:

- To determine the average gap score (between customers' perceptions and expectations) for each service attribute.

- To assess a company's service quality along each of the five SERVQUAL dimensions.

- To track customers' expectations and perceptions (on individual service attributes and/or on the SERVQUAL dimensions) over time.

- To compare a company's SERVQUAL scores against those of competitors.

- To identify and examine customer segments that differ significantly in their assessments of a company's service performance.

- To assess internal service quality (that is, the quality of service rendered by one department or division of a company to others within the same company).

This instrument spawned many studies focusing on service quality assessment and is used all over the world in service industries. Published studies have used SERVQUAL and adaptations of it in a variety of contexts: real estate brokers, physicians in private practice, public recreation programs, a dental school patient clinic, a business school placement center, a tire store, motor carrier companies, an accounting firm, discount and department stores, a gas and electric utility company, hospitals, banking, pest control, dry cleaning, fast food, and higher education.

SERVQUAL has been productively used in multiple contexts, cultures, and countries for measuring service quality in commercial as well as public-sector organizations. Many of the findings from these applications are unpublished and/or proprietary. However, based on the authors' knowledge of some of these applications, two samples are briefly described here.

Consumer Service Context

A large Australian bank used SERVQUAL to measure its quality of service as evaluated by several segments of individual customers.[10] The bank analyzed the data to assess service quality deficiencies on individual attributes and on the five SERVQUAL dimensions as well as to compute gap scores. The bank also benchmarked its SERVQUAL scores against those of two similar U.S. banks that had participated in previous studies. Although some differences between the results for the Australian and U.S. banks were found on specific service attributes, there were striking similarities in the overall pattern of results. For instance, the relative importance levels of the five dimensions (as measured by the point allocation question) were as follows:

	Points Allocated		
	Australian Bank	U.S. Bank 1	U.S. Bank 2
Tangibles	13	10	11
Reliability	28	31	32
Responsiveness	22	22	22
Assurance	19	20	19
Empathy	18	17	16

The Australian bank set up a measurement system to track service quality at regular intervals and to assess the impact of service improvement efforts.

Industrial Product Context

The Ceramic Products Division of Corning, Inc., a large U.S. manufacturing company, developed a systematic process for monitoring and improving its service quality as perceived by customer organizations to which it supplied its manufactured products. The SERVQUAL approach was an integral component of this process. Corning's Ceramic Products Division began its service improvement process by focusing on its largest client, a multinational company. This division modified the SERVQUAL instrument for assessing its service quality as perceived by multiple levels within this company. The SERVQUAL survey was re-administered a year later to assess the impact of the corrective actions. Results indicated significant improvements in most of the targeted attributes and also identified additional areas for further corrective action. The success of SERVQUAL in this pilot application prompted Corning to make this process an ongoing activity in the Ceramics Product Division and to expand its implementation to other divisions and customer groups.

Corning's use of SERVQUAL touches on virtually all of the potential applications of the instrument listed earlier. It also illustrates the fact that SERVQUAL is a generic, skeletal instrument that can be adapted for use in a variety of contexts, including industrial product and internal service contexts.

Trailer Calls or Posttransaction Surveys

Whereas the purpose of SERVQUAL surveys is usually to gauge the overall relationship with the customer, the purpose of transaction surveys is to capture information about one or all of the key service encounters with the customer. In this method, customers are asked a short list of questions immediately after a particular transaction (hence the name *trailer calls*) about their satisfaction with the transaction and contact personnel with whom they interacted. Because the surveys are administered continuously to a broad spectrum of customers, they are more effective than complaint solicitation (where the information comes only from dissatisfied customers).

At checkout, immediately after staying at Fairfield Inns, customers are asked to use a computer terminal to answer four or five questions about their stay in the hotel. This novel approach has obvious benefits over the ubiquitous comment cards left in rooms—the response rate is far higher because the process engages customers and takes only a few minutes. In other companies, transaction surveys are administered by telephone several days after a transaction such as installation of durable goods or claims adjustment in insurance. Because they are timed to occur close to service transactions, these surveys are useful in identifying sources of dissatisfaction and satisfaction. A strong benefit of this type of research is that it often appears to customers that the call is following up to assure that they are satisfied; consequently the call does double duty as a market research tool and as customer service. This type of research is simple and fresh and provides management with continuous information about interactions with customers. Further, the research allows management to associate service quality performance with individual contact personnel so that high performance can be rewarded and low performance corrected. It also serves as an incentive for employees to provide better service because they understand how and when they are being evaluated.

Service Expectation Meetings and Reviews

In business-to-business situations when large accounts are involved, a form of customer research that is highly effective involves eliciting the expectations of the client at a specified time of the year and then following up later (usually after a year) to determine whether the expectations were fulfilled. Even when the company produces a physical product, the meetings deal almost completely with the service expected and provided by an account or sales team assigned to the client. Unlike other forms of research we have discussed, these meetings are not conducted by objective and unbiased researchers but are instead initiated and facilitated by senior members of the account team so that they can listen carefully to the client's expectations. You may be surprised to find that this does not come naturally to sales teams who are used to talking *to* clients rather than listening carefully to their needs. Consequently, teams have to be carefully trained not to defend or explain but instead to comprehend. One company found that the only way it could teach its salespeople not to talk on these interviews was to take a marketing researcher along to gently kick the salesperson under the table whenever he or she strayed from the format!

The format, when appropriate, consists of (1) asking clients what they expect in terms of 8 to 10 basic requirements determined from focus group research, (2) inquiring what particular aspects of these requirements the account team performed well in the past as well as what aspects need improvement, and (3) requesting that the client rank the relative importance of the requirements. After getting the input, senior account members go back to their teams and plan their goals for the year around client requirements. The next step is verifying with the client that the account plan will satisfy requirements or, when it will not, managing expectations to let the client know what cannot be accomplished. After executing the plan for the year, the senior account personnel then return to the client, determine whether the plan has been successfully executed and expectations met, then establish a new set of expectations for the coming year.

Process Checkpoint Evaluations

With professional services such as consulting, construction, and architecture, services are provided over a long period, and there are not obvious ways or times to collect customer information. Waiting until the entire project is complete—which could last years—is undesirable because myriad unresolvable problems could have occurred by then. But discrete service encounters to calibrate customer perceptions are also not

In professional services, evaluations are made at important checkpoints in the process.

Source: Jiang Jin/SuperStock

usually available. In these situations, the smart service provider defines a process for delivering the services and then structures the feedback around the process, checking in at frequent points to ensure that the client's expectations are being met. For example, a management consulting firm might establish the following process for delivering its services to clients: (1) collect information, (2) diagnose problems, (3) recommend alternative solutions, (4) select alternatives, and (5) implement solutions. Next it could agree with the client up front that it will communicate at major process checkpoints—after diagnosing the problem, before selecting the alternative, and so on—to make certain that the job is progressing as planned.

Market-Oriented Ethnography

Many of the types of research we discuss in this section are particularly relevant for the United States and cultures similar to it. Structured questionnaires, for example, make key assumptions about what people are conscious of or can recall about their behavior and what they are willing to explain to researchers about their opinions. These assumptions are based on American culture. Even focus group interviews are inherently culture based because they depend on norms of participation, or what people are willing to say in front of others and to researchers. To fully understand how customers of other cultures assess and use services, it is necessary and effective to use other approaches, such as market-oriented ethnography. This set of approaches allows researchers to observe consumption behavior in natural settings. The goal is to enter the consumer's world as much as possible—observing how and when a service is used in an actual home environment or consumption environment, such as watching consumers eat in restaurants or attend concerts. Among the techniques used are observation, interviews, documents, and examination of material possessions such as artifacts. Observation involves entering the experience as a participant observer and watching what occurs rather than asking questions about it. One-on-one interviews, particularly with key informants in the culture rather than consumers themselves, can provide compelling insights about culture-based behavior. Studying existing documents and cultural artifacts can also provide valuable insights, especially about lifestyles and usage patterns.[11]

Best Western International recently used this technique to better understand its senior market. Rather than bringing participants into focus group facilities and asking them questions, it paid 25 over-55 couples to videotape themselves on cross-country journeys. The firm was able to listen to how couples actually made decisions, rather than the way they reported them. The insights they gained from this research were decidedly different from what they would have learned otherwise. Most noteworthy was the finding that seniors who talked hotel clerks into better deals on rooms didn't need the lower price to afford staying at the hotel—they were simply after the thrill of the deal, as illustrated in this description:

> The 60-ish woman caught on the grainy videotape is sitting on her hotel bed, addressing her husband after a long day spent on the road. "Good job!" she exults. "We beat the s—t out of the front desk and got a terrific room."[12]

These customers then spent their discount money on better dinners elsewhere, contributing nothing to Best Western. "The degree of discount clearly isn't what it used to be in importance—and we got that right out of the research," claimed the manager of programs for Best Western.[13] This finding would be highly unlikely using traditional research and asking customers directly, for few customers would admit to being willing to pay a higher price for a service!

"Mystery" Shopping

In this form of research, which is unique to services,[14] companies hire outside research organizations to send people into service establishments and experience the service as if they were customers. These "mystery" shoppers are trained in the criteria important to customers of the establishment. They deliver objective assessments about service performance by completing questionnaires about service standards. Questionnaires contain items that represent important quality or service issues to customers. Au Bon Pain, for example, sends mystery shoppers to its stores to buy meals and then complete questionnaires about the servers, the restaurant, and the food. Servers are evaluated on standards that include the following:

Acknowledged within three seconds after reaching first place in line.

Acknowledged pleasantly.

Server suggested additional items.

Server requested payment prior to delivering order.

Received receipt.

Received correct change.

Correct order received.

Au Bon Pain motivates workers to perform to service standards by using the mystery shopper program as a key element in its compensation and reward system. Individual workers who receive positive scores have their names posted on the store's bulletin board and receive letters of congratulations as well as bonuses. Managers whose stores earn high scores can receive on-the-spot bonuses of "Club Excellence" dollars that can be traded like green stamps for items in a company catalog. Perhaps more important, the overall scores received by shift and district managers qualify them for monthly profit-sharing cash bonuses. A score lower than 78 percent removes them from consideration for a bonus, whereas high numbers lead to good bonuses.

Mystery shopping keeps workers on their toes because they know they may be evaluated at any time. They know they are being judged on the company's service standards and therefore carry out the standards more consistently than if they were not going to be judged. Mystery shopping can be a very effective way of reinforcing service standards.

Customer Panels

Customer panels are ongoing groups of customers assembled to provide attitudes and perceptions about a service over time. They offer a company regular and timely customer information—virtually a pulse on the market. Firms can use customer panels to represent large segments of end customers. USAir, for example, instituted business traveler panels that meet several times a year. Panelists are frequent travelers of both USAir and other airlines and provide insights and suggestions about airline service and facilities.

Customer panels are used in the entertainment industry to screen movies before they are released to the public. After a rough cut of a film has been created, a panel of consumers that matches the demographic target views the movie. In the most basic of these panels, consumers participate in postscreening interviews or focus groups where they report on their responses to the movie. They may be asked questions as general as their reactions to the ending of the movie and as specific as whether they understood different aspects of the plot line. Based on these panels, movies are revised and edited to ensure that they are communicating the desired message and that they will succeed in the marketplace. In extreme situations, entire endings of movies have been changed to be more consistent with customer attitudes. In some of the most sophisticated consumer panel research on movies (also used for television shows and commercials) consumers have a digital device in their seat where they indicate their responses as they watch the film. This allows the producers, directors, and editors to make changes at the appropriate places in the film to ensure that the story line, characters, and scenery are "tracking."

Lost Customer Research

This type of research involves deliberately seeking customers who have dropped the company's service to inquire about their reasons for leaving. Some lost customer research is similar to "exit interviews" with employees in that it asks open-ended, indepth questions to expose the reasons for defection and the particular events that led to dissatisfaction. It is also possible to use more standard surveys on lost customers. For example, a Midwestern manufacturer used a mail survey to ask former customers about its performance during different stages of the customer–vendor relationship. The survey also sought specific reasons for customers' defections and asked customers to describe problems that triggered their decreases in purchases.[15]

One benefit of this type of research is that it identifies failure points and common problems in the service and can help establish an early-warning system for future defectors. Another benefit is that the research can be used to calculate the cost of lost customers.

Future Expectations Research

Customer expectations are dynamic and can change very rapidly in markets that are highly competitive and volatile. As competition increases, as tastes change, and as consumers become more knowledgeable, companies must continue to update their information and strategies. One such "industry" is interactive video, representing the merger of computer, telecommunications, and cable television. The technologies available in this industry are revolutionary. In situations such as these, companies want to understand not just current customer expectations but also future expectations—the service features desired in the future. This type of research is the newest and includes different types. First, *features research* involves environmental scanning and querying of customers about desirable features of possible services. *Lead user research* brings in customers who are opinion leaders/innovators and asks them what requirements are not currently being met by existing products or services. Another form of this research is the *synectics approach,* which defines lead users more broadly than in standard lead user research.

ANALYZING AND INTERPRETING MARKETING RESEARCH FINDINGS

One of the biggest challenges facing a marketing researcher is converting a complex set of data to a form that can be read and understood quickly by executives, managers, and other employees who will make decisions from the research (see Exhibit 5.3).

5.3 FROM GREETING CARDS TO GAMBLING, COMPANIES BET ON DATABASE MARKETING RESEARCH

Most of the marketing research approaches in this chapter study patterns of customers in groups. Surveys examine the service quality perceptions of the totality of a firm's customers to get a sense of how they feel as a group. Focus groups identify the needs of important service segments, and lost customer research pinpoints the primary reasons why exiting customers are dissatisfied enough to leave the company. However, an emerging and powerful form of research—called *database marketing* or *customer relationship management (CRM)*—studies customers one by one to develop profiles on their individual needs, behaviors, and responses to marketing. This approach allows a company to get very close to its customers and to tailor services uniquely to individuals.

Individual customer research is founded on a database, which allows a company to tell customers apart and remember them uniquely. You may be most familiar with this form of data collection in grocery store loyalty cards—like VIC for Harris Teeter or MVP for Food Lion—that capture information about your purchases and offer you tailored coupons and specials based on your buying patterns. One of the most familiar examples of using a technology database to remember customers is the Ritz-Carlton's frequent guest registry, which documents preferences of each frequent guest. (Does he like a smoking or nonsmoking room? Feather pillows? Does she take cinnamon on her room-service oatmeal?) Each time a guest visits, new observations about preferences are entered so that the institution itself comes to "know" each guest.

Here are two of the most innovative examples of database marketing and how they are applied to understand and market to individual customers:

Hallmark Gold Crown Hallmark's database, capable of recognizing customers in all 5,000 Hallmark retail stores, tracks purchases, contacts, and communications so that it learns what each customer individually values about the relationship with the company. This includes what core product or benefit has the most value to her and what differentiates Hallmark from its competition. The mechanism by which the company tracks this information is a Gold Crown Card that customers use to accumulate points for purchases. They receive personalized point statements, newsletters, reward certificates, and individualized news of new products and events at local stores. The top 10 percent of customers—who buy more cards and ornaments than others—get special amenities such as longer bonus periods and their own private priority toll-free number, as well as very targeted communication about the specific products they value:

> We are using our data to learn more about our customers and give them what they want. Ornament lovers want to hear all about new products. They want to hear a lot of product info, and they want it as soon as possible. Knowing this, we are able to isolate them and give them just what they want. Other segments represent busy women who want the shortened version—tell me the short notes, the highlights of what I need to know for Valentine's Day, is there a bonus offer, where is my reward certificate? Our whole goal is to respond to what our customers are telling us with their purchases. It really is a dialogue.

Several times a year Hallmark executives sit down with preferred and regular members to hear how they feel about the program, what they would like to see added or changed, and how they react to product offerings. Results of the program have been impressive. The program has

Many of the people who use marketing research findings have not been trained in statistics and have neither the time nor the expertise to analyze computer printouts and other technical research information. The goal in this stage of the marketing research process is to communicate information clearly to the right people in a timely fashion. Among considerations are the following: Who gets this information? Why do they need it? How will they use it? Does it mean the same thing across cultures? (See the Global Feature.) When users feel confident that they understand the data, they are far more likely to apply it appropriately. When managers do not understand how to interpret the data, or when they lack confidence in the research, the investment of time, skill, and effort will be lost.

more than 20 million permanent cardholders, 10 million who have purchased in the last 6-month period, and over 12 million who have purchased in the last 12 months. With 51 consecutive months of share gains since inception of the program, member sales represent 35 percent of total store transactions and 45 percent of total store sales.

Harrah's Entertainment, Inc. The gambling industry has long recognized that certain customers are better than others and that encouraging the "high rollers" to spend time in one's casinos is a worthwhile and profitable strategy. One of the main ways they encourage increased patronage is "comping"—giving free drinks, hotel rooms, limousines, and sometimes chips to top customers. The strategy has been limited in most casinos to customers that could be identified and followed, making the approach spotty and missing many potential repeat patrons. Harrah's Entertainment, which owns and operates more than 20 gambling casinos in places such as Las Vegas and Atlantic City, found a more systematic way to extend the practice to a wider group of customers. The company was the first in the industry to apply the database technology to gambling by developing a database that tracks the names and addresses of repeat visitors, along with what slot machines they play, for how long, and how much they gamble. Their approach uses a Total Rewards card that any customer can obtain—often with the incentive of covering their slot losses for half an hour up to $100. To earn points toward drinks, rooms, and other benefits, customers allow their cards to be swiped on the casino floor to monitor the sums gambled and time spent at slot machines and card tables. The company is also working to automate table games such as blackjack by inserting radio frequency transmitters into gaming chips and installing an antenna under the table felt to record the amount of each wager. The reaction of gamblers to this kind of intense scrutiny of their habits is still unknown, but Harrah's is counting on customers wanting the points enough to agree to be tracked.

While players can earn platinum or diamond status based on their gambling levels, the program is designed for mass markets. The average Harrah's customer gambles less than $3,000 annually and comes to Vegas just once or twice a year. This program allows Harrah's to determine how profitable all customers are as individuals and make special offers tailored to their casino behavior to keep them coming back.

Database marketing has applications in virtually any service where customers make repeat purchases. Underlying the approach is the necessity for the company to create customer information files (CIFs) that integrate different data sources on individual customers including demographics, segmentation, usage information, customer satisfaction data, and accounting and financial information. Although this approach raises privacy concerns with some customers, you can see the extent to which marketing research is enhanced under these conditions. A company no longer needs to depend on the customers' words on a survey about whether they intend to remain customers with a company—it can track their purchases and find out for certain. It no longer needs to guess which demographics are most related to psychographic segmentation information—the company can run an analysis to provide valid and reliable data on the topic.

Source: F. Newell, *loyalty.com* (New York: McGraw-Hill, 2000), pp. 232–38; C. T. Heun, "Harrah's Bets on IT to Understand Its Customers," *Informationweek*, December 11, 2000.

Depicting marketing research findings graphically is a powerful way to communicate research information. Here are a sample of graphic representations of the types of marketing research data we have discussed throughout this chapter.

Tracking of Performance, Gap Scores, and Competition[16]

A simple way of tracking performance is shown in Figure 5.3. Both expectations and perceptions are plotted and the gap between them shows the service quality shortfall. While any attribute or dimension of service can be tracked, Figure 5.3 shows the scores for service reliability. Competitor service performance is another frequently tracked service quality measurement. It allows managers to have a better grasp of service

The industry of customer satisfaction measurement and research started in the United States and spread to Europe and other countries largely when U.S. companies moved their businesses into Europe. Although it would seem that the need for customer satisfaction measurement is universal and that importing practices for effective programs would be easy, key differences have surfaced between U.S. and European programs.

First, European companies are less likely than U.S. companies to have quality departments and therefore less likely to use customer satisfaction measurement as a way to make improvements across organizations. Instead, customer satisfaction is largely a marketing issue—a way to calibrate how effective the marketing mix for a service is—rather than a central issue from which all decisions about services stem. One negative result of this orientation is that nonmarketing problems identified in customer satisfaction research (such as operations and delivery issues) are often left unaddressed, frustrating the customer. Imagine how you would feel providing input about aspects of service that displease you, then having no changes take place! It is probably no surprise that response rates to surveys are also lower in Europe than in the United States; if nothing positive occurs as a result of filling out a survey, why should a customer do it?

Second, few European companies measure employee satisfaction or link employee compensation to customer satisfaction scores. Top management in U.S. companies, who have learned the value of customer service programs and their impact on front-line employees, buy into the idea of motivating employees with monetary incentives. European companies are less inclined to do so, perhaps resulting in the well-documented lower levels of motivation to provide service on the part of front-line personnel. European labor law also protects employees from employers who might penalize them for delivering poor customer service. As you may remember, one of the central causes of the early failure of Euro Disney was the unwillingness of French employees to adhere to service standards of dress, friendliness, and responsiveness.

Third, European attitudes toward service quality training are very different from those in the United States. Standardized employee training that results in consistent service delivery is viewed as artificial and uniquely American. European managers see this "one-size-fits-all" style of greeting and dealing with customers as a packaged approach to service delivery. The European approach is more individualistic—perhaps more genuine at times but also less predictable.

Fourth, and very problematic in developing effective customer satisfaction research in Europe, is that customers across countries are very different and respond inconsistently to the same research. Using the same survey across countries is not the most effective technique because respondents of different cultures require customized questions geared to their unique values and attitudes (as discussed in Chapter 2). Language, its structure, and conversational habits also differ, making results difficult to compare. Furthermore, researchers have documented that consumers differ in their levels of response to satisfaction questions. For example, respondents in southern Europe tend to claim that their satisfaction is higher than it is, while those in northern European countries tend to understate it. Comparing scores across countries is therefore very difficult—". . . a 90 percent satisfaction rate in Italy probably reflects less good performance than an 80 percent satisfaction score in Germany."

Any service company that plans to extend its offerings in Europe or elsewhere should be warned: merely taking U.S. research practices abroad will not gather valid information unless it takes into account these and other potential differences. Other international locations have their idiosyncrasies as well. What is a U.S. researcher to do? One of the best strategies is the same one found to work well in all international business: to involve managers and market research firms from host countries when conducting customer satisfaction studies abroad.

Source: E. Sivadas, "Europeans Have a Different Take on CS [Customer Satisfaction] Programs," *Marketing News,* October 26, 1998, p. 39.

FIGURE 5.3
Tracking of Customer Expectations and Perceptions of Service Reliability

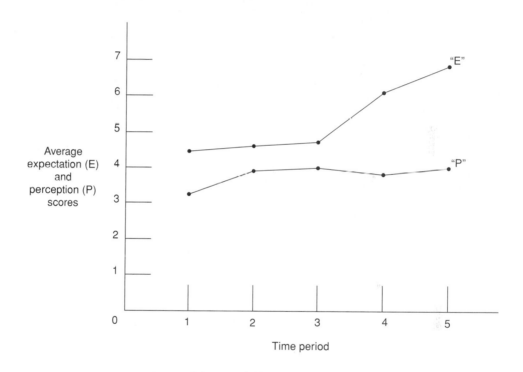

improvement priorities for their firm by comparing the firm's service strengths and weaknesses against those of key competitors.

Zones of Tolerance Charts[17]

When companies collect data on the dual expectation levels described in Chapter 3—desired service and adequate service—along with performance data, they can convey the information concisely on zones of tolerance charts. Figure 5.4 plots customer service quality perceptions relative to customers' zones of tolerance. Perceptions of company performance are indicated by the circles, and the zones of tolerance boxes are bounded on the top by the desired service score and on the bottom by the adequate service score. When the perception scores are within the boxes, as in Figure 5.4, the company is delivering service that is above customers' minimum level of expectations.

FIGURE 5.4
Service Quality Perceptions Relative to Zones of Tolerance by Dimensions

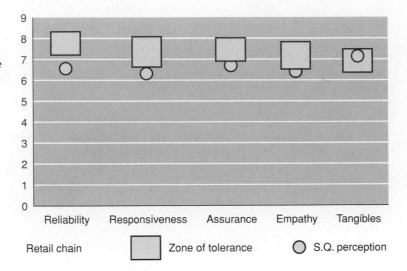

Retail chain — Zone of tolerance — S.Q. perception

When the perception scores are below the boxes, the company's service performance is lower than the minimum level, and customers are dissatisfied with the company's service.

Importance/Performance Matrices

One of the most useful forms of analysis in marketing research is the importance/performance matrix. This chart combines information about customer perceptions and importance ratings. An example is shown in Figure 5.5. Attribute importance is represented on the vertical axis from high (top) to low (bottom). Performance is shown on the horizontal axis from low (left) to high (right). There are many variations of these matrices: Some companies define the horizontal axis as the gap between expectations and perceptions, or as performance relative to competition. The shading on the chart indicates the area of highest leverage for service quality improvements—where importance is high and performance is low. In this quadrant are the attributes that most need to be improved. In the adjacent upper quadrant are attributes to be maintained, ones that a company performs well and that are very important to customers. The lower two quadrants contain attributes that are less important, some of which are per-

FIGURE 5.5
Importance/ Performance Matrix

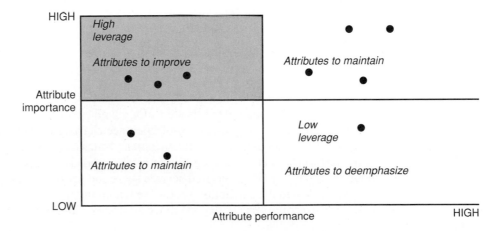

formed well and others poorly. Neither of these quadrants merit as much attention in terms of service improvements as the upper quadrants because customers are not as concerned about the attributes that are plotted in them as they are the attributes in the upper quadrants.

Model Services Marketing Research Programs

We have chosen three companies to illustrate comprehensive and effective programs that have sustained close customer–company relationships.

Disney   Most visitors to Walt Disney theme parks see magic, but the magic is based on solid research discipline. Disney conducts over 200 different external surveys a year, tracking satisfaction along with demographic profiles of its customers. The company also conducts price sensitivity analysis to determine the tolerance of guests for various levels of pricing. One recent outcome of this price sensitivity analysis was the FastPass, a premium-priced ticket to the park that allows its purchasers to avoid lines and expedite their access to rides and other attractions. The company also has guests evaluate its different attractions, noting the aspects that are pleasing or troublesome and changing aspects to ensure that the attractions run as smoothly as possible. In addition, the company monitors tens of thousands of letters and comment cards it receives and practices "management by walking around." By doing so, Disney gathers critical information that enables the design of a service experience that delights its guests.[18]

Intuit   Intuit, maker of the software *Quicken* and *Turbo Tax,* became successful in the extremely competitive software market by using a comprehensive marketing research strategy. The approach included focus groups of potential users, annual customer satisfaction surveys, new product feature testing, mystery shopping of dealers, intense listening to complaints, and a lifetime guarantee that served as a constant line of communication to find out what problems customers were having with their software. One of the more innovative approaches they used early in software development was a "follow me home" program, in which observers went to customers' homes and watched them install and use the program. The company involved customers in the design of its products, thereby opening a dialogue between customers and design engineers. Engineers also listened to technical support calls so that they fully understood problems in the words of the customer.

Federal Express   Federal Express, the first major service company to win the Malcolm Baldrige National Quality Award, has a strong and comprehensive program of marketing and customer satisfaction research.[19] Its program includes

- Customer requirements and expectations, gleaned from multiple qualitative and quantitative research studies, feedback from sales professionals, and feedback from customer service professionals.

- Toll-free numbers for complaints, which are systematically captured and dispatched to responsible parties. Trends are also tracked and analyzed.

- Customer satisfaction studies, with objectives of assessing satisfaction, identifying reasons for dissatisfaction, and monitoring satisfaction over time. This involves 2,400 telephone interviews per quarter measuring 17 domestic service attributes, 22 export service attributes, eight drop-box attributes, and eight service center attributes.

- Ten targeted satisfaction studies on specialized business functions. These are direct-mail, self-administered surveys.

- Satisfaction monitoring at every point of interaction with the customer, some through transaction-based studies and others using operational measures driven by customer requirements.

- A comment card program, monitoring satisfaction with counter service.

- Customer satisfaction studies in world markets, focusing on understanding how service delivery must be adapted to global markets.

USING MARKETING RESEARCH INFORMATION

Conducting research about customer expectations is only the first part of understanding the customer, even if the research is appropriately designed, executed, and presented. A service firm must also use the research findings in a meaningful way—to drive change or improvement in the way service is delivered. The misuse (or even nonuse) of research data can lead to a large gap in understanding customer expectations. When managers do not read research reports because they are too busy dealing with the day-to-day challenges of the business, companies fail to use the resources available to them. And when customers participate in marketing research studies but never see changes in the way the company does business, they feel frustrated and annoyed with the company. Understanding how to make the best use of research—to apply what has been learned to the business—is a key way to close the gap between customer expectations and management perceptions of customer expectations. Managers must learn to turn research information and insights into action, to recognize that the purpose of research is to drive improvement and customer satisfaction.

The research plan should specify the mechanism by which customer data will be used. The research should be actionable: timely, specific, and credible. It can also have a mechanism that allows a company to respond to dissatisfied customers immediately.

UPWARD COMMUNICATION

In some service firms, especially small and localized firms, owners or managers may be in constant contact with customers, thereby gaining firsthand knowledge of customer expectations and perceptions. But in large service organizations, managers do not always get the opportunity to experience firsthand what their customers want.

The larger a company is, the more difficult it will be for managers to interact directly with the customer and the less firsthand information they will have about customer expectations. Even when they read and digest research reports, managers can lose the reality of the customer if they never get the opportunity to experience the actual service. A theoretical view of how things are supposed to work cannot provide the richness of the service encounter. To truly understand customer needs, management benefits from hands-on knowledge of what really happens in stores, on customer service telephone lines, in service queues, and in face-to-face service encounters. If gap 1 is to be closed, managers in large firms need some form of customer contact.

Objectives for Upward Communication

Exhibit 5.4 shows the major research objectives for improving upward communication in an organization. They include gaining firsthand knowledge about customers, improving internal service quality, gaining firsthand knowledge of employees, and ob-

5.4 ELEMENTS IN AN EFFECTIVE PROGRAM OF UPWARD COMMUNICATION

Type of Interaction or Research	Research Objective	Qualitative/ Quantitative	Cost of Information		
			Money	Time	Frequency
Executive visits to customers	To gain firsthand knowledge about customers	Qualitative	Moderate	Moderate	Continuous
Executive listenings	To gain firsthand knowledge about customers	Qualitative	Low	Low	Continuous
Research on intermediate customers	To gain in-depth information on end customers	Quantitative	Moderate	Moderate	Annual
Employee internal satisfaction surveys	To improve internal service quality	Quantitative	Moderate	Moderate	Annual
Employee visits or listenings	To gain firsthand knowledge about employees	Qualitative	Moderate	Moderate	Continuous
Employee suggestions	To obtain ideas for service improvements	Qualitative	Low	Low	Continuous

taining ideas for service improvement. These objectives can be met by two types of interactive activities in the organization: one designed to improve the type and effectiveness of communications from customers to management, and the other designed to improve communications between employees and management.

Research for Upward Communication

Executive Visits to Customers   This approach is frequently used in business-to-business services marketing. In some visits, executives of the company make sales or service calls with customer contact personnel (salespeople). In other situations, executives of the selling company arrange meetings with executives at a similar level in client companies. When Lou Gerstner became CEO of IBM, one of his first actions was to arrange a meeting with 175 of the company's biggest customers for a discussion of how IBM can better meet their needs. The meeting was viewed as a signal that the new IBM would be more responsive and focused on the customer than it had become in the late 1980s and early 1990s.

Executive or Management Listening Approaches (Customers)   The marketing director at Milliken called his experience working the swing shift "naive listening," and he described its benefits as follows:

> Getting close to the customer is a winner! . . . I worked the second shift (3:00 P.M. to midnight) and actually cleaned carpeting as well as hard-surface floors. I operated all the machinery they used daily, plus handled the same housekeeping problems. . . . Now I can

put together my trade advertising as well as my entire merchandising program based directly upon the needs of my customers as I observed them. . . . I'm learning—from new-product introduction to maintenance of existing products—exactly what our health care customers require.[20]

As this example illustrates, direct interaction with customers adds clarity and depth to the manager's understanding of customer expectations and needs.

Managers can also spend time on the line, interacting with customers and experiencing service delivery. A formal program for encouraging informal interaction is often the best way to ensure that the contact takes place. First National Bank of Chicago's survey process involves having senior managers, among them the senior vice president and his department heads, trained and certified to conduct survey interviews.

Research on Intermediate Customers Intermediate customers (such as contact employees, dealers, distributors, agents, and brokers) are people the company serves who serve the end customer. Researching the needs and expectations of these customers *in serving the end customer* can be a useful and efficient way to both improve service to and obtain information about end users. The interaction with intermediate customers provides opportunities for understanding end customers' expectations and problems. It can also help the company learn about and satisfy the service expectations of intermediate customers, a process critical in their providing quality service to end customers.

Research on Internal Customers Employees who perform services are themselves customers of internal services on which they depend heavily to do their jobs well. There is a strong and direct link between the quality of internal service that employees receive and the quality of service they provide to their own customers. For this reason it is important to conduct employee research that focuses on the service internal customers give and receive. In many companies this requires adapting existing employee opinion research to focus on service satisfaction. Employee research complements customer research when service quality is the issue being investigated. Customer research provides insight into what is occurring, whereas employee research provides insight into why. The two types of research play unique and equally important roles in improving service quality. Companies that focus service quality research exclusively on external customers are missing a rich and vital source of information.[21]

Executive or Management Listening Approaches (Employees) Employees who actually perform the service have the best possible vantage point for observing the service and identifying impediments to its quality. Customer-contact personnel are in regular contact with customers and thereby come to understand a great deal about customer expectations and perceptions.[22] If the information they know can be passed on to top management, top managers' understanding of the customer may improve. In fact, it could be said that in many companies, top management's understanding of the customer depends largely on the extent and types of communication received from customer contact personnel and from noncompany contact personnel (like independent insurance agents and retailers) who represent the company and its services. When these channels of communication are closed, management may not get feedback about problems encountered in service delivery and about how customer expectations are changing.

Sam Walton, the late founder of Wal-Mart, the highly successful discount retailer, once remarked, "Our best ideas come from delivery and stock boys."[23] To stay in touch with the source of new ideas, he spent endless hours in stores working the floor, helping clerks, or approving personal checks, even showing up at the loading dock with a bag of doughnuts for a surprised crew of workers.[24] He was well known for having his plane drop him next to a wheat field where he would meet a Wal-Mart truck driver. Giving his pilot instructions to meet him at another landing strip 200 miles down the road, he would make the trip with the Wal-Mart driver, listening to what he had to say about the company.

Upward communication of this sort provides information to upper-level managers about activities and performances throughout the organization. Specific types of communication that may be relevant are formal (such as reports of problems and exceptions in service delivery) and informal (like discussions between contact personnel and upper-level managers). Managers who stay close to their contact people benefit not only by keeping their employees happy but also by learning more about their customers.[25] These companies encourage, appreciate, and reward upward communication from contact people. Through this important channel, management learns about customer expectations from employees in regular contact with customers and can thereby reduce the size of gap 1.

Employee Suggestions   Most companies have some form of employee suggestion program whereby contact personnel can communicate to management their ideas for improving work. Suggestion systems have come a long way from the traditional suggestion box. Effective suggestion systems are ones in which employees are empowered to see their suggestions through, where supervisors can implement proposals immediately, where employees participate for continuous improvement in their jobs, where supervisors respond quickly to ideas, and where coaching is provided in ways to handle suggestions. The National Association of Suggestion Systems (NASS) reports that U.S. companies receive fewer suggestions than their counterparts in Japan, and that the typical financial return for an idea is much higher than the return in Japan.[26] In today's companies, suggestions from employees are facilitated by self-directed work teams that encourage employees to identify problems and then work to develop solutions to those problems.

Summary

This chapter discussed the role of marketing research in understanding customer perceptions and expectations. After first describing criteria for effective services research, the chapter defined key forms of services research including critical incidents studies, mystery shopping, service expectation meetings and reviews, process checkpoint evaluations, and database research. Important topics in researching services—including developing research objectives and presenting data—were also described. Finally, upward communication, ways in which management obtains and uses information from customers and customer contact personnel, was discussed. These topics combine to close gap 1 between customer expectations and company understanding of customer expectations, the first of four provider gaps in the gaps model of service quality.

Discussion Questions

1. Give five reasons research objectives must be established before marketing research is conducted.
2. Why are both qualitative and quantitative research methods needed in a services marketing research program?
3. Why does the frequency of research differ across the research methods shown in Exhibit 5.1?

4. Compare and contrast the types of research that help a company identify common failure points (see column 2 in Exhibit 5.1). Which of the types do you think produces better information? Why?

5. In what situations does a service company need requirements research?

6. What reasons can you give for companies' lack of use of research information? How might you motivate managers to use the information to a greater extent? How might you motivate front-line workers to use the information?

7. Given a specific marketing research budget, what would be your recommendations for the percentage to be spent on customer research versus upward communication? Why?

8. What kinds of information could be gleaned from research on intermediate customers? What would intermediate customers know that service providers might not?

9. For what types of products and services would research on the Internet be preferable to traditional research?

Exercises

1. Choose a local services organization to interview about marketing research. Find out what the firm's objectives are and the types of marketing research it currently uses. Using the information in this chapter, think about the effectiveness of its marketing research. What are the strengths? Weaknesses?

2. Choose one of the services you consume. If you were in charge of creating a survey for that service, what questions would you ask on the survey? Give several examples. What type of survey (relationship versus transaction based) would be most appropriate for the service? What recommendations would you give to management of the company about making such a survey actionable?

3. If you were the marketing director of your college or university, what types of research (see Exhibit 5.1) would be essential for understanding both external and internal customers? If you could choose only three types of research, which ones would you select? Why?

4. Using the SERVQUAL scale in this chapter, create a questionnaire for a service firm that you use. Give the questionnaire to 10 people, and describe what you learn.

5. To get an idea of the power of the critical incidents technique, try it yourself with reference to restaurant service. Think of a time when, as a customer, you had a particularly satisfying interaction with a restaurant. Follow the instructions here, which are identical to the instructions in an actual study, and observe the insights you obtain about your requirements in restaurant service:
   a. When did the incident happen?
   b. What specific circumstances led up to this situation?
   c. Exactly what did the employee (or firm) say or do?
   d. What resulted that made you feel the interaction was satisfying?
   e. What could or should have been done differently?

Notes

1. "The Best B Schools," *Business Week,* October 2, 2000, pp. 75–100.
2. Ibid.
3. A. Parasuraman, L. L. Berry, and V. A. Zeithaml, "Guidelines for Conducting Service Quality Research," *Marketing Research: A Magazine of Management and Applications,* December 1990, pp. 34–44.

4. Ibid., p. 35.
5. L. L. Berry, A. Parasuraman, and V. A. Zeithaml, "Ten Lessons for Improving Service Quality," Marketing Science Institute Report No. 93-104, May 1993.
6. K. Albrecht and R. Zemke, *Service America! Doing Business in the New Economy* (Homewood, IL: Dow Jones–Irwin, 1985).
7. E. E. Lueke and T. W. Suther III, "Market-Driven Quality: A Market Research and Product Requirements Methodology," *IBM Technical Report* (June 1991).
8. J. Carey, J. Buckley, and J. Smith, "Hospital Hospitality," *Newsweek,* February 11, 1985, p. 78.
9. See A. Parasuraman and V. A. Zeithaml, "Understanding and Improving Service Quality: A Literature Review and Research Agenda," *Marketing Handbook* (Sage Publications, 2002) for a complete review of this research, including the many publications by the original authors of SERVQUAL and the extensions by other authors.
10. J. M. Farley, C. F. Daniels, and D. H. Pearl, "Service Quality in a Multinational Environment," *Proceedings of the ASQC Quality Congress Transcatios,* San Francisco, CA, 1990.
11. E. Day, "Researchers Must Enter Consumer's World," *Marketing News,* August 17, 1998, p. 17.
12. G. Khermouch, "Consumers in the Mist," *Business Week,* February 26, 2001, pp. 92–93.
13. Ibid., p. 92.
14. For examples, see S. J. Grove and R. P. Fiske, "Observational Data Collection Methods for Services Marketing: An Overview," *Journal of the Academy of Marketing Science* 20 (Summer 1992), pp. 117–214.
15. "Knowing What It Takes to Keep (or Lose) Your Best Customers," *Executive Report on Customer Satisfaction* 5 (October 30, 1992).
16. V. A. Zeithaml, A. Parasuraman, and L. L. Berry, *Delivering Quality Service: Balancing Customer Perceptions and Expectations* (New York: Free Press, 1990), p. 28.
17. A. Parasuraman, V. A. Zeithaml, and L. L. Berry, "Moving Forward in Service Quality Research," *Marketing Science Institute Report No. 94-114,* September 1994.
18. R. Johnson, "A Strategy for Service—Disney Style," *Journal of Business Strategy* (September–October 1991), pp. 38–43.
19. "Multiple Measures Give FedEx Its 'Good' Data," *The Service Edge,* June 1991, p. 6.
20. T. J. Peters and N. Austin, *A Passion for Excellence* (New York: Random House, 1985), p. 16.
21. "Baldridge Winner Co-Convenes Quality Summit," *Executive Report on Customer Satisfaction,* October 30, 1992.
22. M. J. Bitner, B. Booms, and L. Mohr, "Critical Service Encounters: The Employee's Viewpoint," *Journal of Marketing* 58, no. 4 (October 1994), pp. 95–106.
23. S. Koepp, "Make That Sale, Mr. Sam," *Time,* May 18, 1987.
24. Ibid.
25. Zeithaml, Parasuraman, and Berry, *Delivering Quality Service,* p. 64.
26. "Empowerment Is the Strength of Effective Suggestion Systems," *Total Quality Newsletter,* August 1991.

Chapter 6

BUILDING CUSTOMER RELATIONSHIPS

This chapter's objectives are to

1. Explain relationship marketing, its goals, and the benefits of long-term relationships for firms and customers.

2. Explain why and how to estimate customer relationship value.

3. Specify the foundations for successful relationship marketing—namely, quality core services and careful market segmentation.

4. Introduce the somewhat controversial idea that "the customer isn't always right," and the related strategy of customer profitability segmentation.

5. Provide examples of successful customer retention strategies.

USAA Focuses on Long-Term Relationships

USAA is a preeminent example of a company focused on building long-term relationships with customers.[1] Customer retention has been a core value of the company since long before customer loyalty became a popular business concept. In business since 1922, USAA provides for the insurance needs of a highly targeted market segment: current and former U.S. military personnel and their families. Headquartered in San Antonio, Texas, USAA owns and manages more than $60 billion in assets. It consistently appears on *Fortune* magazine's list of the 100 best companies to work for in America, and customer retention figures approach 100 percent. In fact, the most likely reason for a customer to leave the company is death.

The goal of the company is to "think about the events in the life of a career officer and then work out ways to help him get through them." The company is intent on serving its current customer base and growing with them. To do this, USAA relies heavily on extensive customer research through surveys and a member advisory board that meets regularly with executives. The company also focuses on retaining the best employees and rewarding them for customer-oriented objectives such as percentage of customer questions or requests that are handled on the first call with no need for follow-up. They believe so strongly in the importance of customer retention that managers' and executives' own bonuses are based on this metric.

A striking example of how USAA gives priority to the needs of its existing customers occurred during the Gulf War. Anticipating the needs of those who were sent to the Gulf, the company encouraged them to *downgrade* their automobile insurance to save themselves money. For instance, if their cars were just going to sit in garages while they were gone, they wouldn't need liability coverage. And when two-car families had one spouse in the Gulf, USAA gave them the rates for a single person with two cars. Although this approach obviously cost USAA immediate dollars, actions such as these clearly indicate USAA's commitment to its current members, serving to ensure their loyalty and grow their business over time.

The commitment to customer retention and employees is reflected in what USAA refers to as the *loyalty chain:*

> If you don't take care of the employees, they can't take care of the customers. We give employees all they need to be happy and absolutely enthralled to be here. If they are unhappy, we will not have satisfied customers in the long run. . . . We must have a passion for customers. If we don't, we are in the wrong business. Our members have served our country, and we want to serve them. We take them seriously. We always ask, "What is the impact on our members?[2]

USAA provides a strong example of a company that has focused on keeping its customers and building long-term relationships with them. Unlike the USAA example, however, many companies fail to understand customers accurately because they fail to focus on customer relationships. They tend to fixate on acquiring new customers rather than viewing customers as assets they need to nurture and retain. By concentrating on new customers, firms can easily fall into the traps of short-term promotions, price discounts, or catchy ads that bring customers in but are not enough to bring them back. By adopting a relationship philosophy, on the other hand, companies begin to understand customers over time and in great depth, and are better able to meet their changing needs and expectations.

Marketing strategies for understanding customers over time and building long-term relationships are the subjects of this chapter.

RELATIONSHIP MARKETING

> There has been a shift from a transactions to a relationship focus in marketing. Customers become partners and the firm must make long-term commitments to maintaining those relationships with quality, service and innovation.[3]

Relationship marketing essentially represents a paradigm shift within marketing—away from an acquisitions/transaction focus toward a retention/relationship focus.[4] Relationship marketing (or relationship management) is a philosophy of doing business, a strategic orientation, that focuses on *keeping and improving* current customers rather than on acquiring new customers. This philosophy assumes that many consumers and business customers prefer to have an ongoing relationship with one organization than to switch continually among providers in their search for value. Building on this assumption and the fact that it is usually much cheaper to keep a current customer than to attract a new one, successful marketers are working on effective strategies for retaining customers. Our opening example showed how USAA has built its business around a relationship philosophy.

It has been suggested that firms frequently focus on attracting customers (the "first act") but then pay little attention to what they should do to keep them (the "second act").[5] Ideas expressed in an interview with James L. Schorr, then executive vice president of marketing at Holiday Inns, illustrate this point.[6] In the interview he stated that he was famous at Holiday Inns for what's called the "bucket theory of marketing." By this he meant that marketing can be thought of as a big bucket: It's what the sales, advertising, and promotion programs do that pours business in to the top of the bucket. As long as these programs are effective, the bucket stays full. However, "There's only one problem," he said, "there's a hole in the bucket." When the business is running well and the hotel is delivering on its promises, the hole is small and few customers are leaving. When the operation is weak and customers are not satisfied with what they get, however, people start falling out of the bucket through the holes faster than they can be poured in through the top.

The bucket theory illustrates why a relationship strategy that focuses on plugging the holes in the bucket makes so much sense. Historically, marketers have been more concerned with acquisition of customers, so a shift to a relationship strategy often represents changes in mind set, organizational culture, and employee reward systems. For example, the sales incentive systems in many organizations are set up to reward bringing in new customers. There are often fewer (or no) rewards for retaining current accounts. Thus, even when people see the logic of customer retention, the existing organizational systems may not support its implementation.

Goals of Relationship Marketing

The primary goal of relationship marketing is to *build and maintain a base of committed customers who are profitable for the organization.* To achieve this goal, the firm will focus on the *attraction, retention, and enhancement of customer relationships.*[7] First the firm will seek to attract customers who are likely to become long-term relationship customers. Through market segmentation (discussed later in the chapter), the company can come to understand the best target markets for building lasting customer relationships. As the number of these relationships grows, the loyal customers themselves will frequently help to attract (through word of mouth) new customers with similar relationship potential.

Once they are attracted to begin a relationship with the company, customers will be more likely to stay in the relationship when they are consistently provided with quality products and services and good value over time. They are less likely to be pulled away by competitors if they feel the company understands their changing needs and seems willing to invest in the relationship by constantly improving and evolving its product and service mix.

Finally, the goal of customer enhancement suggests that loyal customers can be even better customers if they buy more products and services from the company over time. Loyal customers not only provide a solid base for the organization, they may represent growth potential. This is certainly true for USAA, our opening example in this chapter, whose officer members' needs for insurance increase over their lifetimes as well as the lifetimes of their children. Other examples abound. A bank checking account customer becomes a better customer when she sets up a savings account, takes out a loan, and/or uses the financial advising services of the bank. And a corporate account becomes a better customer when it chooses to do 75 percent of its business with a particular supplier rather than splitting the business equally among three suppliers. In recent years, in fact, many companies have aspired to be the "exclusive supplier" of

FIGURE 6.1

Customer goals of relationship marketing: getting customers, satisfying customers, retaining customers, and enhancing customers.

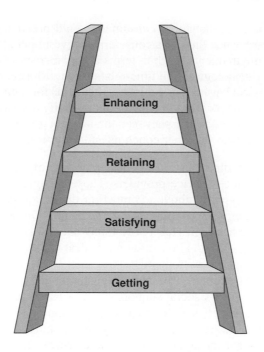

a particular product or service for their customers. Over time these enhanced relationships can increase market share and profits for the organization.

Figure 6.1 illustrates the goals of relationship marketing graphically. The overriding goal is to move as many profitable customers up the ladder, from the base where they are newly attracted customers through to being highly valued, enhanced customers.

Benefits for Customers and Firms

Both parties in the customer–firm relationship can benefit from customer retention. That is, it is not only in the best interest of the organization to build and maintain a loyal customer base, but customers themselves also benefit from long-term associations.

Benefits for Customers

Assuming they have a choice, customers will remain loyal to a firm when they receive greater value relative to what they expect from competing firms. *Value* represents a trade-off for the consumer between the "give" and the "get" components. Consumers are more likely to stay in a relationship when the gets (quality, satisfaction, specific benefits) exceed the gives (monetary and nonmonetary costs). When firms can consistently deliver value from the customer's point of view, clearly the customer benefits and has an incentive to stay in the relationship.

Beyond the specific inherent benefits of receiving service value, customers also benefit in other ways from long-term associations with firms. Sometimes these relationship benefits keep customers loyal to a firm more than the attributes of the core service. Research has uncovered specific types of relational benefits that customers experience in long-term service relationships including confidence benefits, social benefits, and special treatment benefits.[8]

Confidence Benefits These benefits comprise feelings of trust or confidence in the provider, along with a sense of reduced anxiety and comfort in knowing what to expect. Across all of the services studied in the research just cited, confidence benefits were the most important to customers.

Human nature is such that most consumers would prefer not to change service providers, particularly when there is a considerable investment in the relationship. The costs of switching are frequently high in terms of dollar costs of transferring business and the associated psychological and time-related costs. Most consumers (whether individuals or businesses) have many competing demands for their time and money and are continually searching for ways to balance and simplify decision making to improve the quality of their lives. When they can maintain a relationship with a service provider, they free up time for other concerns and priorities.

Social Benefits   Over time, customers develop a sense of familiarity and even a social relationship with their service providers. These ties make it less likely that they will switch, even if they learn about a competitor that might have better quality or a lower price. A quote from the research just cited illustrates this as a customer describes her hair stylist: "I like him. . . . He's really funny and always has lots of good jokes. He's kind of like a friend now. . . . It's more fun to deal with somebody that you're used to. You enjoy doing business with them."

In some long-term customer–firm relationships a service provider may actually become part of the consumer's social support system.[9] Hairdressers, as in the example just cited, often serve as personal confidants. Less common examples include proprietors of local retail stores who become central figures in neighborhood networks; the health club or restaurant manager who knows her customers personally; the private school principal who knows an entire family and its special needs; or the river guide who befriends patrons on a long rafting trip.[10]

These types of personal relationships can develop for business-to-business customers as well as for end consumers of services. The social support benefits resulting from these relationships are important to the consumer's quality of life (personal and/or work life) above and beyond the technical benefits of the service provided. Many times the close personal and professional relationships that develop between service providers and clients are the basis for the customer's loyalty. The flip side of this customer benefit is the risk to the firm of losing customers when a valued employee leaves the firm and takes customers with him or her.[11]

Special Treatment Benefits   Special treatment includes such things as getting the benefit of the doubt, being given a special deal or price, or getting preferential treatment as exemplified by the following quotes from the research:

> I think you get special treatment [when you have established a relationship]. My pediatrician allowed me to use the back door to the office so my daughter could avoid contact with other sick children. Other times I have been in a hurry and they take me right back.

> You should get the benefit of the doubt in many situations. For example, I always pay my VISA bill on time, before a service charge is assessed. One time my payment didn't quite arrive on time. When I called them, by looking at my past history, they realized that I always make an early payment. Therefore, they waived the service charge.

Interestingly, the special treatment benefits, while important, were less important than the other types of benefits received in service relationships. Although special treatment benefits can clearly be critical for customer loyalty in some industries (think of frequent flyer benefits in the airline industry), they seem to be less important to customers overall.

Benefits for the Organization

The benefits to an organization of maintaining and developing a loyal customer base are numerous. In fact, research based on information contained in the Compustat and

Compact Disclosure databases reveals that over the long run, relationship-oriented business-to-business service firms achieve higher overall returns on their investments than do transaction-oriented firms.[12] These bottom-line benefits come from a variety of sources including increased revenues over time from the customer, reduced marketing and administrative costs, and the ability to maintain margins without reducing prices. Here we highlight some of the benefits firms receive from long-term customer relationships.[13] In Chapter 17 we will provide more specifics on the financial impact of customer retention.

One of the most commonly cited benefits of customer retention is increased purchases over time, as illustrated in Figure 6.2. The figure summarizes results of studies reported by Frederick Reichheld and W. Earl Sasser showing that across industries customers tend to spend more each year with a particular relationship partner than they did in the preceding period.[14] As consumers get to know a firm and are satisfied with the quality of its services relative to that of its competitors, they tend to give more of their business to the firm.

Another benefit of long-term relationships is lower costs. There are many start-up costs associated with attracting new customers. They include advertising and other promotion costs, operating costs of setting up accounts and systems, and time costs of getting to know the customers. Sometimes these initial costs can outweigh the revenue expected from the new customers in the short term. Even ongoing relationship maintenance costs are likely to drop over time. For example, early in a relationship a

FIGURE 6.2
Profit Generated by a Customer over Time

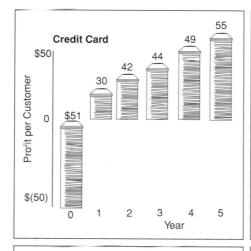

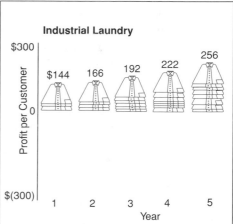

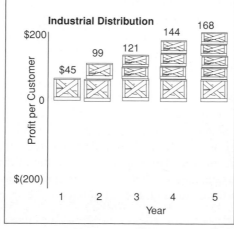

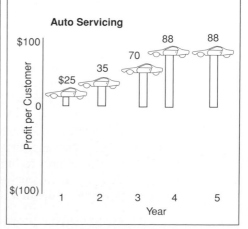

customer is likely to have questions and to encounter problems as he or she learns to use the service. Once learning has taken place the customer will have fewer problems and questions (assuming the quality of service is maintained at a high level), and the service provider will incur fewer costs in serving the customer.

Another benefit to firms is free advertising through word of mouth. When a product is complex and difficult to evaluate, and there is risk involved in the decision to buy it—as is the case with many services—consumers most often look to others for advice on which providers to consider. Satisfied, loyal customers are likely to provide a firm with strong word-of-mouth endorsements. This form of advertising can be more effective than any paid advertising the firm might use, and it has the added benefit of reducing the costs of attracting new customers.

An indirect benefit of customer retention is employee retention. It is easier for a firm to retain employees when it has a stable base of satisfied customers. People like to work for companies whose customers are happy and loyal. Their jobs are more satisfying, and they are able to spend more of their time fostering relationships than scrambling for new customers. In turn, customers are more satisfied and become even better customers—a positive upward spiral. Because employees stay with the firm longer, service quality improves and costs of turnover are reduced, adding further to profits.

RELATIONSHIP VALUE OF CUSTOMERS

Relationship value of a customer is a concept or calculation that looks at customers from the point of view of their lifetime revenue and/or profitability contributions to a company. This type of calculation is obviously needed when companies start thinking of building long-term relationships with their customers. Just what is the potential financial value of those long-term relationships? And what are the financial implications of *losing* a customer? Here we'll first overview the factors that influence a customer's relationship value, and then show some ways it can be estimated. In Chapter 17 we provide more detail on lifetime value financial calculations.

Factors That Influence Relationship Value

The lifetime or relationship value of a customer is influenced by the length of an average "lifetime," the average revenues generated per relevant time period over the lifetime, sales of additional products and services over time, referrals generated by the customer over time, and costs associated with serving the customer. *Lifetime value* sometimes refers to lifetime revenue stream only; but most often when costs are considered, lifetime value truly means "lifetime profitability."

An example will help. Intuit Corporation's *Quicken* software for personal finance and bill paying costs a modest $30. However, the lifetime value of a *Quicken* customer is potentially thousands of dollars. How can this be? First, as customers become hooked on the product, they purchase software updates, generating an annual revenue stream. They may also buy special check blanks needed to pay their bills using *Quicken*'s system. Or they may use an electronic bill-paying service by paying a small fee to Intuit. They may also choose to purchase related products such as *Turbotax* over time, generating further revenue. Finally, Intuit's satisfied customers are likely to refer new customers to Intuit, thus further enhancing the value of the initial customer relationship. Even one new customer referral per year can increase the lifetime revenue potential of the first customer to thousands of dollars in the space of just a few years.[15]

By looking at customers in this way, even the most skeptical of managers will begin to see the value of customer retention! The true costs of losing a customer will also be apparent, resulting in renewed energy directed at retaining them.

Estimating Customer Lifetime Value

If companies knew how much it really costs to lose a customer, they would be able to accurately evaluate investments designed to retain customers. One way of documenting the dollar value of loyal customers is to estimate the increased value or profits that accrue for each additional customer who remains loyal to the company rather than defecting to the competition. This is what Bain & Co. has done for a number of industries, as shown in Figure 6.3.[16] The figure shows the percentage increase in total firm profits when the retention or loyalty rate rises by 5 percentage points. The increases are dramatic, ranging from 35 to 95 percent. These increases were calculated by comparing the net present values of the profit streams for the average customer life at current retention rates with the net present values of the profit streams for the average customer life at 5 percent higher retention rates.

With sophisticated accounting systems to document actual costs and revenue streams over time, a firm can be quite precise in documenting the dollar value and costs of retaining customers. These systems attempt to estimate the dollar value of *all* the benefits and costs associated with a loyal customer, not just the long-term revenue stream. The value of word-of-mouth advertising, employee retention, and declining account maintenance costs can also enter into the calculation.

For example, Table 6.1 shows how First Data Corporation estimates the lifetime value of an average business customer at its TeleCheck International subsidiary (product names and data are disguised in the table). TeleCheck is a large check acceptance company, providing a range of financial services for business customers related to check guarantees, verifications, and collection services. By including estimates over a five-year lifetime of increased revenues from its core product (QuickResponse), declining per-unit service costs, increasing revenues from a new product (FastTrack), and profit from referrals, the company estimated that an annual increase in revenue of 20 percent on its base product would result in a 33 percent annual increase in operating profit over a five-year customer life.[17]

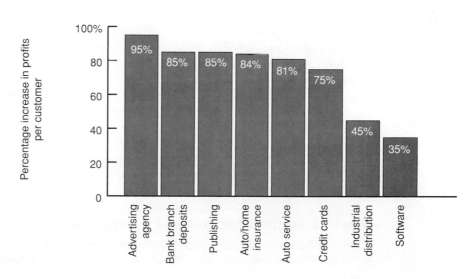

FIGURE 6.3
Profit Impact of 5 Percent Increase in Retention Rate

Source: Reprinted with permission of the American Marketing Association. From F. E. Reichheld, "Loyalty and the Renaissance of Marketing," *Marketing Management*, vol. 2, no. 4 (1994), p. 15.

TABLE 6.1 **Lifetime Value of an Average Business Customer at Telecheck International, Inc.***

	Year 0	Year 1	Year 2	Year 3	Year 4	Year 5
Revenue:[a]						
QuickResponse	—	$33,000	$39,600	$47,520	$57,024	$68,429
FastTrack	—	—	5,500	6,600	7,920	9,504
Costs:						
QuickResponse	$6,600	$24,090	$28,908	$34,690	$41,627	$49,953
FastTrack	—	—	4,152	4,983	5,980	7,175
Lifetime customer value:						
QuickResponse profit	($6,600)	$ 8,910	$10,692	$12,830	$15,397	$18,476
Increased purchases of QuickResponse	—	—	1,782	3,920	6,487	9,566
Profit from added products (FastTrack)	—	—	1,348	1,617	1,940	2,329
Reduced overhead allocation[b]	—	—	1,155	1,486	1,663	1,995
Profit from referrals[c]	—	—	1,100	1,650	3,300	6,600
Total profit	($6,600)	$ 8,910	$16,077	$21,503	$28,787	$38,966

*Product names and data have been disguised. As a result, profit on these products is overstated.

[a]Assuming revenue increases on both products of 20 percent per year.

[b]Declining at the rate of 15 percent per year in relation to revenue, to reflect lower costs of customer relationship associated with both customer and supplier learning curve effects.

[c]Estimated, based on assumptions concerning (1) the importance of referrals to new customers from old customers, (2) the frequency with which satisfied customers refer new customers, (3) the size of customers referred, and (4) the lifetime value calculations for new customers.

Source: Reprinted with permission of The Free Press, a Division of Simon & Schuster, Inc., from J. L. Heskett, W. E. Sasser, Jr., and L. A. Schlesinger, *The Service Profit Chain: How Leading Companies Link Profit and Growth to Loyalty* (New York: The Free Press, 1997), p. 201. Copyright © 1997 by J. L. Heskett, W. E. Sasser, and L. A. Schlesinger.

FOUNDATIONS FOR RELATIONSHIP STRATEGIES

The preceding discussion should have you convinced that it is good business to focus on current customers, to understand them, and to build strategies around retaining their business. Later in the chapter we describe specific retention strategies that firms use to keep their current customers. But first, in this section, we discuss the foundations needed to begin focusing on retention strategies: (1) quality offered in the core service, (2) careful market segmentation and targeting, and (3) continuous monitoring of relationships.

Quality in the Core Service

Retention strategies will have little long-term success unless there is a solid base of service quality and customer satisfaction to build on. This doesn't necessarily mean that the firm has to be the very best among its competitors, or "world class" in terms of quality and customer satisfaction. It must be competitive, however, and frequently better than that. All of the retention strategies we describe later are built on the assumption of competitive quality being offered. It does no good to design relationship strategies for inferior services. Two earlier examples, Intuit and USAA, provide convincing support for the argument that excellence in the core service or product offered is essential to a successful relationship strategy. Both of these companies have benefited tremendously from their loyal customer base; both offer excellent quality; both use relationship strategies to enhance their success.

Market Segmentation and Targeting

A second basic foundation of relationship marketing is market segmentation—learning and defining who the organization wants to have relationships with. In earlier

6.1 REVIEW OF BASIC MARKETING PRINCIPLES: MARKET SEGMENTATION AND MARKET TARGETING

Bases for Market Segmentation

Demographic segmentation: Dividing the market to form groups based on variables such as age, sex, family size, income, occupation, or religion.

Geographic segmentation: Dividing the market to form different geographic units such as nations, counties, or states.

Psychographic segmentation: Dividing buyers to form groups based on social class, lifestyle, or personality characteristics.

Behavioral segmentation: Dividing buyers to form groups based on knowledge, attitude, uses, or responses to a service.

Requirements for Effective Segmentation

Measurability: The degree to which the size and purchasing power of the segments can be measured.

Accessibility: The degree to which the segments can be reached and served.

Substantiality: The degree to which the segments are large or profitable enough.

Actionability: The degree to which effective programs can be designed for attracting and servicing of the segments.

Criteria for Evaluating Market Segments for Market Targeting

Segment size and growth: Includes information on current dollar sales, projected growth rates, and expected profit margins.

Segment structural attractiveness: Includes current and potential competitors, substitute products and services, relative power of buyers, and relative power of suppliers.

Company objectives and resources: Involves whether the segment fits the company's objectives.

---

chapters we discussed consumers of services and described their behavior, expectations, and perceptions. If we were to aggregate all the behavior, expectation, and perception information for all the customers in a particular market, we would probably be overwhelmed with the variations across customers. At one extreme, service firms—historically those with a relatively small number of customers, each of whom is vitally important—treat customers as individuals and develop individual marketing plans for each customer. For example, a law firm, an advertising agency, or even a large manufacturer like the Boeing Airplane Company will develop service offerings customized specifically and individually for their large corporate clients.

At the other extreme, some service firms offer one service to all potential customers as if their expectations, needs, and preferences were homogeneous. Providers of gas or electricity, for example, often view the needs of customers as varying only in terms of quantity purchased; for this reason their marketing approach is standardized. Between these two extremes are options that most service marketers choose—offering different services to different *groups* of customers. To do this effectively, companies need market segmentation and targeting.

Process for Market Segmentation and Targeting in Services

Many aspects of segmentation and targeting for services are the same as those for manufactured goods. For that reason we include Exhibit 6.1 as a review of basic marketing principles for segmentation and targeting.[18] There are differences, however. The most powerful difference involves the need for compatibility in market segments. Because

FIGURE 6.4
Steps in Market Segmentation and Targeting for Services

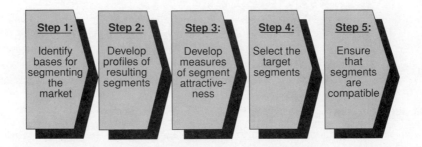

Step 1: Identify bases for segmenting the market

Step 2: Develop profiles of resulting segments

Step 3: Develop measures of segment attractiveness

Step 4: Select the target segments

Step 5: Ensure that segments are compatible

other customers are often present when a service is delivered, service providers must recognize the need to choose compatible segments or to ensure that incompatible segments are not receiving service at the same time. A second difference between goods and services is that service providers have a far greater ability to customize service offerings in real time than manufacturing firms have. Figure 6.4 illustrates the steps involved in segmenting and targeting services, and a brief discussion of each step follows.

Identify Bases for Segmenting the Market   Market segments are formed by grouping customers who share common characteristics that are in some way meaningful to the design, delivery, promotion, or pricing of the service. Common segmentation bases for consumer markets are shown in Exhibit 6.1, including demographic segmentation, geographic segmentation, psychographic segmentation, and behavioral segmentation. Segments may be identified on the basis of one of these characteristics or a combination. For instance, an urban YMCA may provide services for demographic segments determined by age: preschool and gymnastics for those under 6; basketball for boys and girls ages 5 to 16; and weight training and fitness classes for adults. Within these demographic segments there may be more finely defined services based on lifestyle or usage, for example, fitness classes offered at 5 A.M. and 5:30 P.M. for adults who work from 8 A.M. to 5 P.M.

Develop Profiles of Resulting Segments   Once the segments have been identified it is critical to develop profiles of them. In consumer markets these profiles usually involve demographic characterizations or psychographic or usage segments. Of most importance in this stage is clearly understanding how and whether the segments differ from each other in terms of their profiles. If they arc not different from each other, the benefits to be derived from segmentation, that is, from more precisely identifying sets of customers, will not be realized.

Develop Measures of Segment Attractiveness   The fact that segments of customers exist does not justify a firm's choice of them as targets. Segments must be evaluated in terms of their attractiveness, some aspects of which are shown in Exhibit 6.1. The size and purchasing power of the segments must be measurable so that the company can determine if the segments are worth the investment in marketing and relationship costs associated with the group. Later in this chapter, the idea of customer profitability segmentation is presented as an approach for defining and selecting target segments. The chosen segments also must be accessible, meaning that advertising or marketing vehicles must exist to allow the company to reach the customers in the segments.

Select the Target Segments   Based in part on the evaluation criteria just discussed, the services marketer will select the target segment or segments for the service. The firm must decide if the segment is large enough and trending toward growth. Market size will be estimated and demand forecasts completed to determine whether the segment provides strong potential. Competitive analysis, including an evaluation of current and potential competitors, substitute products and services, and relative power of buyers and suppliers, will also help in the final selection of target segments. Finally, the firm must decide whether serving the segment is consistent with company objectives and resources.

Ensure That the Target Segments Are Compatible This step, of all the steps in segmentation strategy, is arguably more critical for service companies than for goods companies. Because services are often performed in the presence of the customer, the services marketer must be certain that the customers are compatible with each other. If during the nonpeak season a hotel chooses to serve two segments that are incompatible with each other—for example, families who are attracted by the discounted prices and college students on their spring break—it may find that the two groups do not merge well. It may be possible to manage the segments in this example so that they do not directly interact with each other, but if not, they may negatively influence each others' experiences, hurting the hotel's future business. In identifying segments it is thus important to think through how they will use the service and whether segments will be compatible. Later in the book (in Chapters 12 and 14) we will examine specific strategies for balancing demand for service while serving the right segments and strategies for managing the customer mix.

Individualized Service: Segments of One

When carried to their logical conclusions, both segmentation and customization lead to "segments of one" or "mass customization"—products and services designed to fit each individual's needs. The inherent characteristics of services lend themselves to customization and support the possibility of segmenting to the individual level. That is, because services are delivered to people by people, they are difficult to standardize and their outcomes and processes may be inconsistent from provider to provider, from customer to customer, and even from one time period to the next. This inherent heterogeneity is at once a curse and a blessing. On the one hand it means that service delivery is difficult to control and predict, and the resulting inconsistencies may cause customers to question a firm's reliability. On the other hand it presents opportunities to customize and tailor the service in ways typically not possible for manufacturers of goods. Because the service itself is frequently delivered in "real time" by "real people" there is an opportunity for one-to-one customization of the offering. Heterogeneity pursued in a purposeful manner can be turned into an effective customization strategy.

While segments of one may be practically unrealistic in some cases, the underlying idea of crafting a customized service to fit each individual's needs fits very well with today's consumers, who demand to be treated as individuals and who want their own particular needs satisfied. (Remember from Chapter 4 that customer perceptions of service are clearly linked to adaptability, flexibility, and responsiveness of the service.)

For service providers who have a limited number of large customers, the segment of one marketing strategy may be obvious. For example, a food management company that provides cafeteria and other types of food service for large manufacturing facilities will customize its services for each large account on the basis of the specific needs of the organization. Or an advertising agency that specializes in providing communication services for *Fortune* 500 companies will develop individualized plans for each client. In such situations, a relationship manager or an account manager will likely be assigned to a particular customer or client to develop a marketing plan tailored to that client's needs.

Technology Spotlight
Customer Information Systems Allow Customization of Services

The potential of today's customer information systems far exceeds any traditional marketing information system that has gone before. These new systems differ from the old in their scale (thousands of bits of information on tens of millions of customers), the depth of information that can be captured on each individual or household, and the ways in which the information can be used. In many cases, access to this type of information about individual customers allows the organization to customize to the individual level what previously would have been undifferentiated services.

For example, the Ritz-Carlton Hotel Company, winner of the 1992 Malcolm Baldrige National Quality Award, targets its services to industry executives, meeting and corporate travel planners, and affluent travelers. Although there are many dimensions to their success, one of the keys is the quality of their customer database. By training each employee to note the likes and dislikes of regular guests and to enter this information immediately into the customer's file, employees at any Ritz-Carlton Hotel are able to personalize services to the Ritz-Carlton's 240,000 repeat customers. They can know in advance the guest's preferences and be prepared to provide individualized service even before the guest's arrival. For example, if a guest prefers a feather pillow, wants extra brown sugar with her oatmeal, or always orders a glass of sherry before retiring, this information can be entered into the database and these needs anticipated—often much to the guest's surprise.

In a very different realm, NewsEdge is a leader in an industry that gives business customers customized news and information based on individual client needs and preferences. NewsEdge is a $71 million company that provides real-time news and information products and services to approximately 1,500 corporations and professional service firms worldwide. This information can be provided to websites, company intranets, or directly to employees. The need addressed by this industry is the "information overload" that exists in our modern world, combined with corporations' desires for their people to be up-to-date on industry-specific news. (Note that while NewsEdge focuses on corporate clients, Dow Jones provides a similar service for individual consumers.) NewsEdge content is individually tailored to their corporate clients' specified needs as identified and tracked in their customer database. Using sophisticated technology as well as human content experts, NewsEdge sifts through hundreds of premier information sources in thousands of topic categories and then provides tailored real-time content to clients. Clients are corporations or professional service firms who want their employees to have access to particular types of breaking news. In addition to individual corporate clients, other customers of NewsEdge include online information providers such as Lycos Small Business (a comprehensive online resource for small businesses) that purchase NewsEdge services to provide relevant news and information for small businesses that they could not afford to supply individually. In 2001 The Thomson Corporation acquired NewsEdge.

Sources: "1992 Award Winner," publication of the Ritz-Carlton Hotel Company; *www.newsedge.com*, 2001.

But even in consumer markets where a company may have hundreds, thousands, or even millions of moments of truth per day, technology combined with employee empowerment is leading the way to mass customization. Our Technology Spotlight features two very different companies that are successfully using information technologies to customize their offerings: NewsEdge, a customized news search service, and the Ritz-Carlton, a high-end luxury hotel.

Monitoring Relationships

A thorough means of monitoring and evaluating relationship quality over time is another foundation for relationship marketing. Basic market research in the form of (at a minimum) annual customer relationship surveys can be the foundation for such a monitoring strategy. Current customers should be surveyed to determine their perceptions of value received, quality, satisfaction with services, and satisfaction with the provider relative to competitors. The organization should also regularly communicate with its best customers in person or over the telephone. In a competitive market it is difficult to retain customers unless they are receiving a base level of quality and value.

A well-designed customer database is critical. Knowing who the organization's current customers are (names, addresses, phone numbers, and so on), what their buying behavior is, the revenue they generate, the related costs to serve them, their preferences, and relevant segmentation information (like demographics, lifestyle, and usage patterns) forms the foundation of a customer database. In cases of customers leaving the organization, information on termination would also exist in the database. By having such a detailed database on its customers, American Express is able to tailor its corporate card member newsletter on the basis of cardholders' spending patterns and preferences. The result of this tailoring is 1,349 versions of the newsletter, targeted at specific customer needs and interests.[19]

These two basics (relationship survey and customer database) are combined with a variety of other types of marketing research as described in Chapter 5 (for example, trailer calls, complaint monitoring, lost customer surveys, and customer visits) to develop a profile of the organization's customer relationships. With a foundation of customer knowledge combined with quality offerings and value, a firm can engage in retention strategies to hold onto its best customers.

THE CUSTOMER ISN'T ALWAYS RIGHT

Given the many benefits of long-term customer relationships, it would seem that a company would not want to refuse or terminate a relationship with any customer. The assumption that all customers are good customers is also very compatible with the belief that "the customer is always right," an almost sacrosanct tenet of business. Yet any service worker can tell you that this statement isn't always true, and in some cases it may be preferable for the firm and the customer to not continue their relationship. This section presents a view of customer relationships suggesting that all relationships may not be beneficial, and that every customer is not right all of the time.

The Wrong Segment

A company cannot target its services to all customers; some segments will be more appropriate than others. It would not be beneficial to either the company or the customer for a company to establish a relationship with a customer whose needs the company cannot meet. For example, a school offering a lock-step, daytime MBA program would not encourage full-time working people to apply for its program, nor would a law firm specializing in government issues establish a relationship with individuals seeking advice on trusts and estates. These examples seem obvious. Yet firms frequently do give in to the temptation to make a sale by agreeing to serve a customer who would be better served by someone else.

Similarly, it would not be wise to forge relationships simultaneously with incompatible market segments. In many service businesses (such as restaurants, hotels, tour package operators, entertainment, and education), customers experience the service together and can influence each other's perceptions about value received. Thus, to maximize service to core segments an organization may choose to turn away marginally profitable segments that would be incompatible. For example, a conference hotel may find that mixing executives in town for a serious educational program with students in town for a regional track meet may not be wise. If the executive group is a key long-term customer, the hotel may choose to pass up the sports group in the interest of retaining the executives.

Not Profitable in the Long Term

In the absence of ethical or legal mandates, organizations will prefer *not* to have long-term relationships with unprofitable customers. Some segments of customers will not be profitable for the company even if their needs can be met by the services offered. This may be the case when there are not enough customers in the segment to make it profitable to develop a marketing approach, when the segment cannot afford to pay the cost of the service, or when the projected revenue flows from the segment would not cover the costs incurred to originate and maintain the business. For example, in the banking industry it has been estimated that 40 to 70 percent of customers served in a typical bank are not profitable in the sense that the costs of serving these customers exceed the revenues generated.[20]

At the individual customer level, it may not be profitable for a firm to engage in a relationship with a particular customer who has bad credit or who is a poor risk for some other reason. Retailers, banks, mortgage companies, and credit card companies routinely refuse to do business with individuals whose credit histories are unreliable. Although the short-term sale may be beneficial, the long-term risk of nonpayment makes the relationship unwise from the company's point of view. Similarly, some car rental companies have begun to check into the driving records of customers and are rejecting bad-risk drivers.[21] This practice, while controversial, is logical from the car rental companies' point of view because they can cut back on insurance costs and accident claims (thus reducing rental costs for good drivers) by not doing business with accident-prone drivers.

Beyond the monetary costs associated with serving the wrong customers, there can be substantial time investments in some customers that, if actually computed, would make them unprofitable for the organization. Everyone has had the experience of waiting in a bank, a retail store, or even in an education setting while a particularly demanding customer seems to use more than his share of the service provider's time. The dollar value of the time spent with a specific customer is typically not computed or calculated into the price of the service.

In a business-to-business relationship, the variability in time commitment to customers is even more apparent. Some customers may use considerable resources of the supplier organization through inordinate numbers of phone calls, excessive requests for information, and other time-consuming activities. In the legal profession, clients are billed for every hour of the firm's time that they use in this way because time is essentially the only resource the firm has. Yet in other service businesses all clients essentially pay the same regardless of the time demands they place on the organization.

It should be noted that the best customers are not just the ones that generate the most profit. Especially in business-to-business settings, those customers that inspire the best ideas and innovations are also good relationship customers even if they don't necessarily generate the highest profits.[22] Customers who are willing to be involved in new service development or who are on the cutting edges of their own industries can help the organization develop and maintain quality services for the entire marketplace. These customers benefit the organization beyond the profits they generate.

Difficult Customers

Managers have repeated the phrase "the customer is always right" so often that it should be accepted by every employee in every service organization. Why isn't it? Perhaps because it simply isn't true. The customer isn't always right. No matter how frequently it is said, it doesn't become reality, and service employees know it.

Employees recognize that beyond the monetary and time loss that can be traced to some customers, there are customers who are simply difficult to work with for a variety of reasons. Because of the stress they place on the organization and its employees, some organizations may choose to avoid relationships with these customers.

Although often these difficult customers will be accommodated and employees can be trained to recognize and deal with them appropriately, at times the best choice may be to not maintain the relationship at all—especially at the business-to-business level where long-term costs to the firm can be substantial. Take, for example, the view of some of Madison Avenue's major ad agencies. "Some ad agencies say some accounts are so difficult to work with that they simply cannot—or will not—service them."[23] Difficult clients paralyze the ad agency for a variety of reasons. Some ask that a particular ad campaign work for all of their diverse constituencies at the same time, which in some cases may be next to impossible. Others require so much up-front work and ad testing before selecting the agency that the work is essentially done for free by those agencies not selected. Other clients are stingy; require dozens of storyboards before settling on a concept; or require a lot of direct, frequently disruptive, involvement in the production process. As a result agencies have become more wary of chasing every client that comes along. "As in a marriage, all agencies and all clients don't work well together."[24]

Should Firms "Fire" Their Customers?

A logical conclusion to be drawn from the preceding sections is that firms should somehow get rid of those customers who are not right for the company. More and more companies are making these types of decisions based on the belief that troublesome customers are usually less profitable and less loyal, and that it may be counterproductive to attempt to retain their business. Another reason for firing a customer is the negative effect that these customers can have on employee quality of life and morale.

This is exactly what one company concluded when a client, the CEO of an Internet start-up company, paged one of their employees at her home on the West Coast at 4 A.M. asking her to order a limousine for him in New York City.[25] This was enough to push the employee over the edge and cause her boss to agree that they should "fire" this client. They did so by directly telling him the relationship wasn't working out and to take his business elsewhere.

Another company that took reducing its customer base to the extreme is Nypro—a global, employee-owned company specializing in molded plastics applications for such clients as Gillette, Abbott Laboratories, Hewlett-Packard, and other large organizations.[26] In the 1980s Nypro reduced its customer base from 800 to approximately 30 clients on the belief that it could better serve those clients and grow more effectively if it focused on fewer relationships. Nypro adopted a customer intimacy strategy and tied itself closely to this much smaller number of clients. Some of these clients have now been with Nypro for over 40 years. Over time Nypro has selectively added clients to this base, and the company has enjoyed 15 consecutive years of record sales and profit growth with profits up 41 percent in 2000 over the preceding year.

Although it may sound like a good idea, "firing" customers is not that simple and needs to be done in a way that avoids negative publicity or negative word of mouth. Sometimes raising prices or charging for services that previously had been given away for free can move unprofitable customers out of the company. Helping a client find a new supplier who can better meet its needs is another way to gracefully exit a nonproductive relationship. If the customer has become too demanding, negotiating expectations or finding more efficient ways to serve the client can also salvage the relationship. If not, both parties may find an agreeable way to end the relationship.

CUSTOMER PROFITABILITY SEGMENTS[27]

Service companies today are beginning to recognize, as we just discussed, that not all customers are worth attracting and keeping. Federal Express Corporation, for example, has revolutionized its marketing philosophy by categorizing its customers internally as the good, the bad, and the ugly—based on their profitability. Rather than marketing to all customers in a similar manner, the company now puts its efforts into the good, tries to move the bad to the good, and discourages the ugly.[28]

Companies may want to treat all customers with superior service, but they find it is neither practical nor profitable to meet (and certainly not to exceed) all customers' expectations. To build and improve upon traditional segmentation, companies are now trying to identify segments—or, more appropriately, tiers of customers—that differ in current and/or future profitability to a firm. This approach goes beyond usage or volume segmentation because it tracks costs and revenues for segments of customers, thereby capturing their financial worth to companies. After identifying profitability bands, the firm offers services and service levels in line with the identified segments. Building a high-loyalty customer base of the right customers increase profits. At MBNA, a leading financial services firm, a 5 percent jump in retention of the right customers increased the company profits 60 percent by the fifth year.[29]

The 80/20 Customer Pyramid

Although some may view the FedEx grouping of customers into "the good, the bad, and the ugly" as negative, it can be very useful internally to provide descriptive labels of the tiers. This is especially true if it helps the company keep track of which customers are profitable.

Virtually all firms are aware at some level that their customers differ in profitability—in particular that a minority of their customers accounts for the highest proportion of sales or profit. This has often been called the "80/20 rule"—20 percent of customers produce 80 percent of sales or profit. This 80/20 customer pyramid is shown in Figure 6.5.

FIGURE 6.5
The 80/20 Customer Pyramid

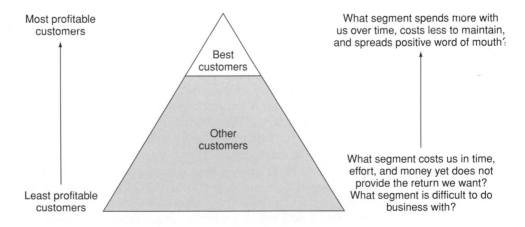

In this version of tiering, 20 percent of the customers constitute the top tier, those who can be identified as the most profitable in the company. The rest are indistinguishable from each other but differ from the top tier in profitability. Most companies realize that there are differences among customers within this tier but do not possess the data or capabilities to analyze the distinctions. The 80/20 customer pyramid is a two-tier scheme that assumes that consumers within the two tiers are similar, just as conventional market segmentation schemes typically assume consumers within segments are similar.

The Expanded Customer Pyramid

More than two tiers are likely and can be used if the company has sufficient data to analyze customer tiers more finely. Different systems and labels can be useful. One useful four-tier system, shown in Figure 6.6, might be the following:

1. The *platinum tier* describes the company's most profitable customers, typically those who are heavy users of the product, are not overly price sensitive, are willing to invest in and try new offerings, and are committed customers of the firm.

2. The *gold tier* differs from the platinum tier in that profitability levels are not as high, perhaps because the customers want price discounts that limit margins or are not as loyal. They may be heavy users who minimize risk by working with multiple vendors rather than just the focal company.

3. The *iron tier* contains essential customers who provide the volume needed to utilize the firm's capacity; but their spending levels, loyalty, and profitability are not substantial enough for special treatment.

4. The *lead tier* consists of customers who are costing the company money. They demand more attention than they are due given their spending and profitability and are sometimes problem customers—complaining about the firm to others and tying up the firm's resources.

Note that this classification is superficially reminiscent of but very different from traditional usage segmentation performed by airlines such as American Airlines. Two differences are obvious. First, in the customer pyramid profitability rather than usage defines all levels. Second, the lower levels actually articulate classes of customers who require a different sort of attention. The firm must work either to change the customers' behavior—to make them more profitable through increases in revenue—or to

FIGURE 6.6
The Expanded Customer Pyramid

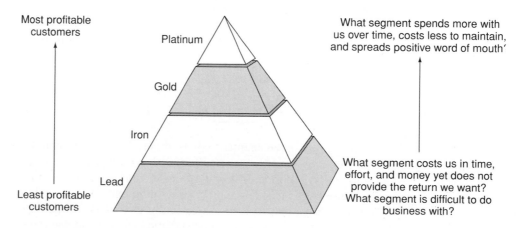

change the firm's cost structure to make them more profitable through decreases in costs.

Examples of effective use of the customer pyramid approach exist in a number of business contexts. Financial services firms are leading the way, perhaps because of the vast amounts of data already housed in those firms. In 1994 Bank One realized that all financial institutions had grossly overcharged their best customers to subsidize others who were not paying their way. Determined to grow its top-profit customers, who were vulnerable because they were being underserved, Bank One implemented a set of measures to focus resources on their most productive use. Next it identified the profit drivers in this top segment and thereby stabilized its relationships with key customers.[30]

Once a system has been established for categorizing customers, the multiple levels can be identified, motivated, served, and expected to deliver differential levels of profit. Companies improve their opportunities for profit when they increase shares of purchases by customers who either have the greatest need for the services or show the greatest loyalty to a single provider. By lengthening relationships with the loyal customers, increasing sales with existing customers, and increasing the profitability on each sale opportunity, they thereby increase the potential of each customer.

The Customer's View of Profitability Tiers

Whereas profitability tiers make sense from the company's point of view, customers are not always understanding, nor do they appreciate being categorized into a less desirable segment.[31] For example, at some companies the top clients have their own individual account representative whom they can contact personally. The next tier of clients may be handled by representatives who each have 100 clients. Meanwhile, most clients are served by an 800 number, an automated voice response system, or referral to a website. Customers are aware of this unequal treatment, and many resist and resent it. It makes perfect sense from a business perspective, but customers are often disappointed in the level of service they receive and give firms poor marks for quality as a result.

Therefore, it is increasingly important that firms communicate with customers so they understand the level of service they can expect and what they would need to do or pay to receive faster or more personalized service. The most significant issues result when customers don't understand, believe they have been singled out for poor service, or feel that the system is unfair. While many customers refuse to pay for quality service, they react negatively if they believe it has been taken away from them unfairly.

The ability to segment customers narrowly based on profitability implications also raises questions of privacy for customers. In order to know who is profitable and who is not, companies must collect large amounts of individualized behavioral and personal data on consumers. Many consumers today resent what they perceive as an intrusion into their lives in this way, especially when it results in differential treatment that they perceive is unfair.

LEVELS OF RELATIONSHIP STRATEGIES

To this point in the chapter we have focused on the rationale for relationship marketing, the benefits of customer retention, and the importance of identifying the right market segment(s) for relationship building. In this section we look at some of the specific strategies and tactics used by firms to build relationships and tie customers closer to the firm. That is, once a firm has carefully identified its market segments and developed quality services, what are some specific tactics it can use to retain its customers?

FIGURE 6.7
Levels of Relationship Strategies

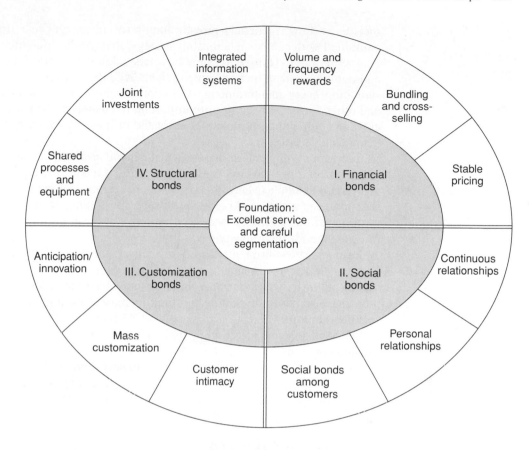

Leonard Berry and A. Parasuraman have developed a framework for understanding types of retention strategies.[32] The framework suggests that relationship marketing can occur at different levels and that each successive level of strategy results in ties that bind the customer a little closer to the firm. At each successive level, the potential for sustained competitive advantage is also increased. Building on the levels of the retention strategy idea, Figure 6.7 illustrates four types of retention strategies, which are discussed in the following sections. Recall from the material presented earlier in the chapter, however, that the most successful retention strategies will be built on foundations of quality service, market segmentation, and monitoring of changing relationship needs over time.

Level 1—Financial Bonds

At level 1, the customer is tied to the firm primarily through financial incentives— lower prices for greater volume purchases or lower prices for customers who have been with the firm a long time. Examples of level 1 relationship marketing are not hard to find. Think about the airline industry and related travel service industries like hotels and car rental companies. Frequent flyer programs provide financial incentives and rewards for travelers who bring more of their business to a particular airline. Hotels and car rental companies do the same. Long-distance telephone companies in the United States have engaged in a similar battle, trying to provide volume discounts and other price incentives to retain market share and build a loyal customer base. One reason these financial incentive programs proliferate is that they are not difficult to initiate and frequently result in at least short-term profit gains. Unfortunately, financial incentives do not generally provide long-term advantages to a firm because, unless combined with another relationship strategy, they don't differentiate the firm from its competitors in the long run. Many travelers belong to several frequent flyer programs and don't hesitate to trade off among them. And there has been considerable customer switching every month among the major telecommunication suppliers. While price and other financial incentives are important to customers, they are generally not difficult for competitors to imitate because the primary customized element of the marketing mix is price.

Other types of retention strategies that depend primarily on financial rewards are focused on bundling and cross-selling of services. Frequent flyer programs again provide a common example. Many airlines link their reward programs with hotel chains, auto rental, and in some cases credit card usage. By linking airline mileage points earned to usage of other firm's services, customers can enjoy even greater financial benefits in exchange for their loyalty.

In other cases, firms aim to retain their customers by simply offering their most loyal customers the assurance of stable prices, or at least lower price increases than those paid by new customers. In this way they reward their loyal customers by sharing with them some of the cost savings and increased revenue the firm receives through serving them over time.

While widely and increasingly used as retention tactics, loyalty programs based on financial rewards merit caution.[33] As pointed out earlier, these programs are often easily imitated. Thus any increased usage or loyalty from customers may be short-lived. Second, these strategies are not likely to be successful unless they are structured so that they truly lead to repeat or increased usage rather than serving as means to attract new customers and potentially causing endless switching among competitors.

Level 2—Social Bonds

Level 2 strategies bind customers to the firm through more than financial incentives. Although price is still assumed to be important, level 2 retention marketers build long-term relationships through social and interpersonal as well as financial bonds. Customers are viewed as "clients," not nameless faces, and become individuals whose needs and wants the firm seeks to understand.

Social, interpersonal bonds are common among professional service providers (lawyers, accountants, teachers) and their clients as well as among personal care providers (hairdressers, counselors, health care providers) and their clients. A dentist who takes a few minutes to review her patient's file before coming into the exam room is able to jog her memory on personal facts about the patient (occupation, family details, interests, dental health history). By bringing these personal details into the conversation, the dentist reveals her genuine interest in the patient as an individual and builds social bonds.

Interpersonal bonds are also common in business-to-business relationships where customers develop relationships with salespeople and/or relationship managers working with their firms.[34] Recognizing the value of continuous relationships in building loyalty, Caterpillar Corporation credits much of its noted success to its extensive, stable distribution organization worldwide. Caterpillar is the world's largest manufacturer of mining, construction, and agriculture heavy equipment. Although its engineering and product quality are superior, the company attributes much of its success to its strong dealer network and product support services offered throughout the world. CEO David Fites contends that knowledge of the local market and close relationships with customers that Caterpillar's dealers provide is invaluable: "Our dealers tend to be promi-

FIGURE 6.8
Harley Davidson riders develop customer-to-customer bonds through Harley Owners Group (HOG) activities.

Source: EyeWire Collection/Getty Images

nent business leaders in their service territories who are deeply involved in community activities and who are committed to living in the area. Their reputations and long-term relationships are important because selling our products is a personal business."[35]

Sometimes relationships are formed with the organization due to the social bonds that develop *among customers* rather than between customers and the provider of the service. This is frequently the case in health clubs, country clubs, educational settings, and other service environments where customers interact with each other. Over time the social relationships they have with other customers are important factors that keep them from switching to another organization. One company that has built a significant strategy around customer-to-customer bonds is Harley Davidson with its local Harley Owners Groups, or HOGs. HOGs are involved in local rallies, tours, and parties, as well as participating in national HOG events organized by the company. Through the HOGs, Harley customers come to know each other and develop a sense of community around their common interest—motorcycle riding— as illustrated in Figure 6.8.

Social bonds alone may not tie the customer permanently to the firm, but they are much more difficult for competitors to imitate than are price incentives. In the absence of strong reasons to shift to another provider, interpersonal bonds can encourage customers to stay in a relationship. In combination with financial incentives, social bonding strategies may be very effective.

Level 3—Customization Bonds

Level 3 strategies involve more than social ties and financial incentives, although there are commonly elements of level 1 and 2 strategies encompassed within a customization strategy and vice versa. For example, in the Caterpillar dealership strategy just described, dealers are relied on not just to form strong personal commitments to customers. They are also relied on to feed information back into the system to help Caterpillar customize services to fit developing customer needs.[36]

Two commonly used terms fit within the customization bonds approach: *mass customization* and *customer intimacy.* Both of these strategies suggest that customer loyalty can be encouraged through intimate knowledge of individual customers and through the development of "one-to-one" solutions that fit the individual customers' needs.

Boots The Chemists is one of the best-known and trusted brands in the United Kingdom and is the UK's leading health and beauty retailer. The company was founded in 1887, spanning three centuries of successful operations. Currently offering its products through 1,400 retail stores as well as an online store at www.wellbeing.com, the company is deservedly called the "Chemist to the Nation." On its website, the Boots Company states that it intends to become the global leader in well being products and services and is expanding globally through Boots Healthcare International.

A foundation for Boots' success in recent years is its increased focus on the customer and its desire to develop customer loyalty through a number of retention and relationship strategies. At the heart of the company's loyalty strategy is its Advantage Card, started in 1997. The Advantage Card is right now the world's largest smart card loyalty scheme with close to 13 million members. Over 50 percent of Boots' current sales are now linked to the card. The card offers a number of benefits to customers and has helped the company to increase sales, but, more than that, it has been the foundation for building greater loyalty among Boots' best customers.

Using the card for purchases, Boots' customers receive 4 points for every pound spent. These points can be redeemed for selected products, aimed to treat customers to something special, rather than simply to offer discounts off purchases. In fact the card is *not* about discounts, but rather it is about treating oneself. Customers can use their points to treat themselves to a simple lunch or to a full day of pampering at a spa. From a financial perspective, the company has seen increasing average transaction values among higher-spending customers. Boots managers say that they have increased loyalty and spending from those who were already good and profitable customers—a clear win for the company.

A number of initiatives are tied to the Advantage Card, taking it beyond a pure points reward program from the customer's perspective. For example, Boots now mails a first-class health and beauty magazine to the top spending 3 million Advantage Card holders. The magazine is Britain's biggest health and beauty magazine, and is not viewed as a "Boots"

Mass customization has been defined as "the use of flexible processes and organizational structures to produce varied and often individually customized products and services at the price of standardized, mass-produced alternatives."[37] Mass customization does not mean providing customers with endless solutions or choices that only make them work harder for what they want; rather, it means providing them through little effort on their part with tailored services to fit their individual needs. The earlier Technology Spotlight provides examples of companies who are using technology to customize services to large numbers of individual customers. Our Global Feature illustrates how Boots The Chemists in the UK has used technology to understand its customers and build the world's largest smart card loyalty scheme.

Level 4—Structural Bonds

Level 4 strategies are the most difficult to imitate and involve structural as well as financial, social, and customization bonds between the customer and the firm. Structural

magazine, but rather a health and beauty magazine sent by Boots. Cardholders also have access to additional benefits and discounts using interactive kiosks in over 380 stores. The card can be used for purchases at the online store through the www.wellbeing.com site that was launched jointly with Granada Media in 2001. Many products are offered on the site that are not available in Boots stores. In addition, the site provides access to an online magazine, answers to questions, a chat room, and other features and services. A credit card version of the Advantage Card was launched in 2001. And, Boots joined with the Department of Health to enable Advantage Card holders to register with the National Health Service Organ Donor program and carry an Advantage Card featuring the program's logo.

From the company's perspective, the card is much more than a reward program as well. Data generated through the card is used to understand customers, to anticipate, and to identify individual needs in health and beauty care products. In fact, the goals with the Advantage Card program back in 1997 were to: gain customer insight; build a database that would allow the company to tailor offerings to individual customer's needs; develop incremental sales by building customer loyalty; and use the customer knowledge to develop and introduce new products and services. A great deal of planning and testing went into developing the program, and this planning paid off in developing customer loyalty. Buy-in from the company's 60,000 staff members also aided in the rapid success of the program. All associates were signed up as members six months before the launch of the card. After experiencing the benefits of the card first hand, they became enthusiastic advocates, encouraging customers to sign up.

Through the program, Boots has learned that the more broadly customers buy, in more categories over time, the more they increase visits to Boots stores. The result has been customization of product and service offerings and more sales and greater loyalty from its best customers.

Sources: Frederick Newell, *Loyalty.com*, New York: McGraw-Hill, 2000, Chapter 24, pp. 239–45; *www.boots-plc.com*, 2002; *www.wellbeing.com*, 2002.

bonds are created by providing services to the client that are frequently designed right into the service delivery system for that client. Often structural bonds are created by providing customized services to the client that are technology based and make the customer more productive.

An example of structural bonds can be seen in a business-to-business context with Allegiance Healthcare Corporation. By working closely with its hospital customers, Allegiance (a Cardinal Health company) has developed ways to improve hospital supply ordering, delivery, and billing that have greatly enhanced its value as a supplier. For example, Allegiance developed "hospital-specific pallet architecture," which meant all items arriving at a particular hospital were shrink-wrapped with labels visible for easy identification. Separate pallets were assembled to reflect the individual hospital's storage system so that instead of miscellaneous supplies arriving in boxes sorted at the convenience of Allegiance's internal needs, they arrived on "client-friendly" pallets designed to suit the distribution needs of the individual hospital. By linking the hospital through its ValueLink service into a database ordering system, and providing enhanced value in the actual delivery, Allegiance has structurally tied itself to its more than 150 acute care hospitals in the United States. In addition to the enhanced service ValueLink provides, Allegiance estimates that the system saves its customers an average of $500,000 or more each year.[38]

Another example of level 4 strategy can be seen in the long competitive battle between UPS and Federal Express.[39] In the mid 1990s, both firms attempted to tie their

FIGURE 6.9
UPS uses technology to build ties to customers.

Source: Courtesy of UPS; Photo by William Howard © The Martin Agency

clients closer to them by providing them with free computers—Federal Express's Pow-erShips and UPS's MaxiShips—that stored addresses and shipping data, printed mail-ing labels, and helped track packages. By tying into one of the systems a company saved time overall and could better track daily shipping records. As technology has continued to advance, the two companies have tied their customers to them through the Web and now through wireless technology, as shown in the UPS ad in Figure 6.9.

But there is also a potential downside to this arrangement from the customer's per-spective. Customers may fear that tieing themselves too closely to one provider may not allow them to take advantage of potential price savings from other providers in the future.

Customer Appreciation

We end our retention strategies discussion with an obvious, but often neglected, way to retain customers: showing appreciation for their business. By first providing the services as promised, and then thanking the customer for the business, firms can go a long way toward retaining individual customers. Especially in business-to-business situations, customers would like their suppliers to extend appreciation either in person or over the phone, and not just take their business for granted. Letters addressed to "Dear Valued Customer" are not really the answer, especially for the organization's best customers. Such an impersonal approach may well communicate exactly the op-posite of what was intended. Instead, a personal letter (addressed to the right person with correct spelling and current title), or a personal phone call will have greater im-pact. For example, at IBM Global Services, customers who take the time to recognize the special actions of an employee are themselves thanked personally for the recogni-tion and for their business.

Summary

In this chapter we focused on the rationale for, benefits of, and strategies for develop-ing long-term relationships with customers. It should be obvious by now that organi-zations that focus only on getting new customers may well fail to understand their cur-rent customers and thus may be bringing customers through the front door while equal or greater numbers are exiting. Estimates of lifetime relationship value accentuate the importance of retaining current customers.

The particular strategy an organization uses to retain its current customers can and should be customized to fit the industry, the culture, and the customer needs of the or-ganization. However, the basics of a good relationship strategy require (1) effective market segmentation to identify who the organization wants to have relationships with, (2) continuous development of services that evolve to suit the needs of these relation-ship customers, and (3) monitoring of current customer relationships through rela-tionship surveys and an up-to-date customer database. By working with current cus-tomers in these ways, the organization has a good chance of accurately understanding current customer expectations and of narrowing service quality gap 1.

The chapter continues with a discussion of the idea that, although long-term cus-tomer relationships are critical and can be extremely profitable, firms should not at-tempt to build relationships with just any customer. In other words, "the customer isn't always right." Building from these foundations, the chapter detailed four levels of spe-cific retention strategies offering increasing levels of competitive advantage. Each strategic approach focuses on a different type of bond between the customer and the firm: financial bonds, social bonds, customization bonds, and structural bonds.

Discussion Questions

1. Discuss how relationship marketing or retention marketing is different from the traditional emphasis in marketing.

2. Think about a service organization that retains you as a loyal customer. Why are you loyal to this provider? What are the benefits to you of staying loyal and not switching to another provider? What would it take for you to switch?

3. With regard to the same service organization, what are the benefits to the organization of keeping you as a customer? Calculate your "lifetime value" to the organization.

4. What are the basic steps in market segmentation? What specific challenges exist for service organizations when it comes to segmentation?

5. Explain the logic behind the "segments of one" idea. Why are services particularly amenable to this form of segmentation?

6. Describe the logic behind "customer profitability segmentation" from the company's point of view. Also discuss what customers think of the practice.

7. Describe the four levels of retention strategies, and give examples of each type. Again, think of a service organization to which you are loyal. Can you describe the reason(s) you are loyal in terms of the different levels? In other words, what ties you to the organization?

8. Have you ever worked as a front-line service employee? Can you remember having to deal with difficult or "problem" customers? Discuss how you handled such situations. As a manager of front-line employees, how would you help your employees deal with difficult customers?

Exercises

1. Interview the manager of a local service organization. Discuss with the manager the target market(s) for the service. Estimate the lifetime value of a customer in one or more of the target segments. To do this you will need to get as much information from the manager as you can. If the manager cannot answer your questions, make some assumptions.

2. In small groups in class debate the question, "Is the customer always right?" In other words, are there times when the customer may be the wrong customer for the organization?

3. Design a "customer appreciation" program for the organization you currently work for. Why would you have such a program, and whom would it be directed toward?

4. Choose a specific company context (your class project company, the company you work for, or a company in an industry you are familiar with). Calculate the lifetime value of a customer for this company. You will need to make assumptions to do this, so make your assumptions clear. Using ideas and concepts from this chapter, describe a relationship marketing strategy to increase the number of lifetime customers for this firm.

Notes

1. USAA is featured in the following two books, and material in this section is drawn from them: L. L. Berry, *Discovering the Soul of Service* (New York: The Free Press, 1999); F. F. Reichheld, *Loyalty Rules!* (Boston: Harvard Business School Press, 2001).

2. A quote from Bill Cooney, deputy CEO for USAA's Property and Casualty Insurance operations as it appeared in L. L. Berry, *Discovering the Soul of Service,* p. 32.

3. F. E. Webster, Jr., "The Changing Role of Marketing in the Corporation," *Journal of Marketing,* October 1992, pp. 1–17.

4. For discussions of relationship marketing and its influence on the marketing of services, consumer goods, strategic alliances, distribution channels, and buyer–seller interactions, see *Journal of the Academy of Marketing Science,* Special Issue on Relationship Marketing (vol. 23, no. 4, Fall 1995). Some of the early roots of this paradigm shift can be found in C. Gronroos, *Service Management and Marketing* (New York: Lexington Books, 1990); and E. Gummesson, "The New Marketing—Developing Long-Term Interactive Relationships," *Long Range Planning* 20 (1987), pp. 10–20. For current thinking and excellent reviews of relationship marketing across a spectrum of topics, see J. N. Sheth, *Handbook of Relationship Marketing* (Thousand Oaks, CA: Sage Publications, 2000).

5. L. L. Berry and A. Parasuraman, *Marketing Services* (New York: Free Press, 1991), chap. 8.

6. G. Knisely, "Comparing Marketing Management in Package Goods and Service Organizations," a series of interviews appearing in *Advertising Age,* January 15, February 19, March 19, and May 14, 1979.

7. L. L. Berry, "Relationship Marketing," in *Emerging Perspectives on Services Marketing,* ed. L. L. Berry, G. L. Shostack, and G. D. Upah (Chicago: American Marketing Association, 1983), pp. 25–28.

8. The three types of relational benefits discussed in this section are drawn from K. P. Gwinner, D. D. Gremler, and M. J. Bitner, "Relational Benefits in Service Industries: The Customer's Perspective," *Journal of the Academy of Marketing Science* 26, no. 2 (Spring 1998), pp. 101–14.

9. See M. B. Adelman, A. Ahuvia, and C. Goodwin, "Beyond Smiling: Social Support and Service Quality," in *Service Quality, New Directions in Theory and Practice,* ed. R. T. Rust and R. L. Oliver (Thousand Oaks, CA: Sage Publications, 1994), pp. 139–72; and C. Goodwin, "Private Roles in Public Encounters: Communal Relationships in Service Exchanges," unpublished manuscript, University of Manitoba, 1993.

10. E. J. Arnould and L. L. Price, "River Magic: Extraordinary Experience and the Extended Service Encounter," *Journal of Consumer Research* 20, no. 1 (1993), pp. 24–45.

11. N. Bendapudi and R. P. Leone, "How to Lose Your Star Performer Without Losing Customers, Too," *Harvard Business Review,* November 2001, pp. 104–15.

12. P. Kumar, "The Impact of Long-Term Client Relationships on the Performance of Business Service Firms," *Journal of Service Research,* vol. 2, no. 1, August 1999, pp. 4–18.

13. F. F. Reichheld, *Loyalty Rules!* (Boston: Harvard Business School Press, 2001).

14. F. F. Reichheld and W. E. Sasser, Jr., "Zero Defections: Quality Comes to Services," *Harvard Business Review,* September–October 1990, pp. 105–11; and F. F. Reichheld, *The Loyalty Effect* (Boston: Harvard Business School Press, 1996).

15. This example is cited in J. L. Heskett, W. E. Sasser, Jr., and L. A. Schlesinger, *The Service Profit Chain* (New York: The Free Press, 1997), pp. 60–63.

16. Reichheld and Sasser, Jr., "Zero Defections."

17. Example adapted from Heskett, Sasser, Jr., and Schlesinger, *The Service Profit Chain,* pp. 200–1.

18. See P. Kotler and G. Armstrong, "Marketing Segmentation, Targeting and Positioning," *Principles of Marketing,* 5th ed. (Englewood Cliffs, NJ: Prentice Hall, 1991), pp. 216–49.

19. W. Marx, "The New Segment of One," *Direct Magazine,* September 1994, pp. 45–48.
20. R. Brooks, "Alienating Customers Isn't Always a Bad Idea, Many Firms Discover," *The Wall Street Journal,* January 7, 1999, p. A1; P. Carroll and S. Rose, "Revisiting Customer Retention," *Journal of Retail Banking* 15, no. 1 (1993), pp. 5–13.
21. J. Dahl, "Rental Counters Reject Drivers without Good Records," *The Wall Street Journal,* October 23, 1992, p. B1.
22. M. Schrage, "Fire Your Customers," *The Wall Street Journal,* March 16, 1992, p. A8.
23. L. Bird, "The Clients That Exasperate Madison Avenue," *The Wall Street Journal,* November 2, 1993, p. B1.
24. Ibid.
25. S. Shellenbarger, "More Firms, Siding with Employees, Bid Bad Clients Farewell," *The Wall Street Journal,* February 16, 2000, p. B1.
26. "Service with Soul" video, hosted by Tom Peters (Chicago: Video Publishing House, 1995); and http://www.nypro.com.
27. For more on customer profitability segments and related strategies, see V. A. Zeithaml, R. T. Rust, and K. N. Lemon, "The Customer Pyramid: Creating and Serving Profitable Customers," *California Management Review,* vol. 43, no. 4 (Summer 2001), pp. 118–42.
28. Brooks, "Alienating Customers Isn't Always a Bad Idea, Many Firms Discover."
29. F. Reichheld, "Loyalty-Based Management," *Harvard Business Review,* March–April 1993, pp. 64–74.
30. G. Hartfeil, "Bank One Measures Profitability of Customers, Not Just Products," *Journal of Retail Banking Services,* vol. 18, no. 2 (1996), pp. 24–31.
31. D. Brady, "Why Service Stinks," *Business Week,* October 23, 2000, pp. 118–28.
32. Berry and Parasuraman, *Marketing Services,* pp. 136–42.
33. For more information on cautions to be considered in implementing rewards strategies, see L. O'Brien and C. Jones, "Do Rewards Really Create Loyalty?" *Harvard Business Review,* May–June 1995, pp. 75–82; and G. R. Dowling and M. Uncles, "Do Customer Loyalty Programs Really Work?" *Sloan Management Review,* Summer 1997, pp. 71–82.
34. Bendapudi and Leone, "How to Lose Your Star Performer Without Losing Customers."
35. D. V. Fites, "Make Your Dealers Your Partners," *Harvard Business Review,* March–April 1996, pp. 84–95.
36. See J. Pine, *Mass Customization: The New Frontier in Business Competition* (Boston: Harvard Business School Press, 1993); and M. Treacy and F. Wiersema, "Customer Intimacy and Other Value Disciplines," *Harvard Business Review,* January–February 1993, pp. 84–93.
37. C. W. Hart, "Made to Order," *Marketing Management* 5, no. 2 (Summer 1996), pp. 11–23.
38. Arthur Andersen, *Best Practices—Building Your Business with Customer-Focused Solutions* (New York: Simon & Schuster, 1998), pp. 125–27.
39. L. M. Grossman, "Federal Express, UPS Face Off on Computers," *The Wall Street Journal,* September 17, 1993, p. B1.

Chapter 7

SERVICE RECOVERY

This chapter's objectives are to

1. Illustrate the importance of recovery from service failures in keeping customers and building loyalty.

2. Discuss the nature of consumer complaints and why people do and do not complain.

3. Provide evidence of what customers expect and the kind of responses they want when they do complain.

4. Provide strategies for effective service recovery, together with examples of what does and does not work.

5. Discuss service guarantees—what they are, the benefits of guarantees, and when to use them—as a particular type of service recovery strategy.

September 11, 2001:
Rebuilding a Firm—The Ultimate Service Recovery

"As I watched TV on September 11, 2001, I was struck with horror along with the rest of the world at the sight of the World Trade Center towers in New York City collapsing. My immediate thoughts that morning were, as for many, of friends and loved ones who worked in those towers, wondering where they were and if they were all right. In my case, it was a friend of over 30 years who worked in the North Tower of the World Trade Center, on the 55th floor, in a law firm where he is a partner. Other friends and I immediately started to think of ways to reach him, and eventually one of us did, that afternoon. He was safe."

M.J.B.

The story of how Sidley Austin Brown & Wood was able to rebuild itself and serve its clients and employees was reported in *The New York Times* the following Sunday, September 16.[1] A remarkable story, it is the ultimate example of service recovery in its most monumental proportions. All but one of the firm's 600 employees who worked in the WTC survived the disaster, and they were back in business, able to serve their clients, within six days.

Sidley Austin Brown & Wood is the fourth largest law firm in the United States, employing 1,325 attorneys and serving large corporate, financial, and government clients. The firm is the result of a merger in 2001 of two firms with long histories—Sidley & Austin founded in 1866 in Chicago and Brown & Wood founded in 1914 in New York. The firm has primary offices in New York and Chicago and additional offices in San Francisco; Los Angeles; Washington, D.C.; Seattle; Dallas; Shanghai; Tokyo; Hong Kong; Beijing; Singapore; and London.

How was the firm's remarkable recovery following September 11 achieved? Some of it had to do with careful planning as a result of surviving the WTC bombing in 1993. A lot of it had to do with courageous, focused employees, as well as cooperative, helpful suppliers and understanding clients. We can capture only a tiny bit of what happened here.

The first and highest priority of the firm was of course its employees and their safety. All 13 offices of the firm around the world were shut down the day following the collapse of the twin towers, and three centers of activity were established to deal with the aftermath. Once it was learned that most employees were accounted for and out of the building, the firm's administrators and managing partners focused on reestablishing the New York office and beginning what it needed to do to serve its employees and its corporate and government clients.[2]

Within three hours of the disaster, a partner in the firm had secured leases on four additional floors of a building in midtown New York where the firm already had some space. The cost of the space was not discussed, and a firm that was due to move into the space agreed to delay its move to give the space to Sidley, at least temporarily. By the end of the day, others had arranged for the delivery of 800 desks, 300 computers, and hundreds of cell phones. Contractors were hired that day to string cable and reestablish the firm's computer network. Normal rules of business were bypassed as suppliers and even competitors offered to help. Nightly backups of the firm's entire electronic network enabled everything up to the night before the attacks to be restored. The backup tapes were stored in New Jersey by two independent firms and needed to be shipped immediately to Chicago so they could be restored and readied for use. Because no planes were flying for several days, these companies offered to have their own employees drive the tapes to Chicago from New Jersey.

On September 12 a letter to "our colleagues, clients, and friends" appeared on the firm's website to assure clients of the progress being made to serve them without interruption, ending with the following statement: "We will not let down our predecessors, or our current colleagues, clients, and friends. From this tragedy, we have the opportunity to build something stronger and more energized than ever before, and we intend to do so. Thank you for your thoughts and prayers. We will keep you informed."[3] The firm was back in business, serving its clients, in its new midtown offices on September 17.

During and following all of the hectic efforts to reopen the firm for business, people remained a primary concern. Once the safety of employees, friends, and loved ones was assured, the firm turned to providing counseling, to ensuring that employees' pay was not interrupted, to bringing people together to see each other and share their feelings, and to ensuring the security of the workplace. Heroic stories of employee actions and sad accounts of the things they felt and saw in those days in September have become part of the fabric and culture of the firm. Six hundred of its employees worked in the WTC and were displaced on that day in September. All but one of those employees survived the disaster.

The preceding two chapters have given you grounding in understanding customers through research as well as through knowing them as individuals and developing strong relationships with them. These strategies, matched with effective service design, delivery, and communication—treated in other parts of the text—form the foundations for service success. But, in all service contexts—whether customer service, consumer services, or business-to-business services—service failure is inevitable. Failure is inevitable even for the best of firms with the best of intentions, even for those with world-class service systems.

To fully understand and retain their customers, firms must understand what customers expect when service failures occur, and implement effective strategies for service recovery. Our chapter opening vignette illustrates how one firm was able to recover even under the most unexpected and dire circumstances.

THE IMPACT OF SERVICE FAILURE AND RECOVERY

Service recovery refers to the actions taken by an organization in response to a service failure. Failures occur for all kinds of reasons—the service may be unavailable when promised, it may be delivered late or too slowly, the outcome may be incorrect or poorly executed, or employees may be rude or uncaring.[4] All of these types of failures bring about negative feelings and responses from customers. Left unfixed, they can result in customers leaving, telling other customers about their negative experiences, and even challenging the organization through consumer rights organizations or legal channels.

Research has shown that resolving customer problems effectively has a strong impact on customer satisfaction, loyalty, and bottom-line performance.[5] That is, customers who experience service failures, but are ultimately satisfied based on recovery efforts by the firm, will be more loyal than those whose problems are not resolved. That loyalty translates into profitability as you learned in Chapter 6. Data from the Technical Assistance Research Program (TARP) verifies this relationship, as shown in Figure 7.1.[6] Those who complain and have their problems resolved quickly are much

FIGURE 7.1
Unhappy Customers' Repurchase Intentions

Source: Adapted from data reported by the Technical Assistance Research Program.

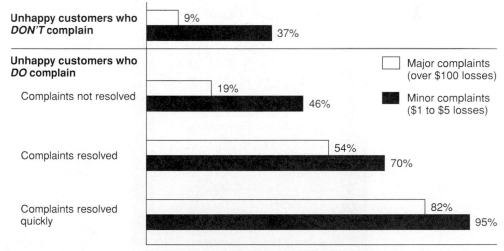

Unhappy customers who **DON'T** complain
- 9%
- 37%

Unhappy customers who **DO** complain

☐ Major complaints (over $100 losses)
■ Minor complaints ($1 to $5 losses)

Complaints not resolved
- 19%
- 46%

Complaints resolved
- 54%
- 70%

Complaints resolved quickly
- 82%
- 95%

Percentage of customers who will buy again

more likely to repurchase than are those whose complaints are not resolved. Those who never complain are *least* likely to repurchase.

Similar results were reported in a study of 720 HMO members, in which researchers found that those who were not satisfied with service recovery were much more likely to switch to a different health care provider than were those who were happy with how their problems were addressed.[7] The study also found that satisfaction with service recovery was the second most important factor out of 11 service attributes in predicting overall customer satisfaction. The most important factor, not surprisingly, was perceived medical outcome.

Hampton Inns directly realized the benefits of effective service recovery through their service guarantee. They achieved $11 million in additional annual revenue and the highest customer retention rate in their industry after implementing the 100 percent customer satisfaction guarantee shown in Figure 7.2.[8] The guarantee reimburses customers who experience service failures in their hotels—and is part of an overall service recovery and customer retention strategy.

An effective service recovery strategy has multiple potential impacts. It can increase customer satisfaction and loyalty and generate positive word of mouth as noted earlier. A well-designed, well-documented service recovery strategy also provides information that can be used to improve service as part of a continuous improvement effort. By making adjustments to service processes, systems, and outcomes based on learning from service recovery experiences, companies increase the likelihood of "doing it right the first time." In turn, this reduces costs of failures and increases initial customer satisfaction.

FIGURE 7.2
The Hampton Inn 100 Percent Satisfaction Guarantee

Source: Courtesy of Hampton Inn Hotels.

There are tremendous downsides to having no service recovery or ineffective service recovery strategies. Poor recovery following a bad service experience can lead to customers who are so dissatisfied they become "terrorists," actively pursuing opportunities to openly criticize the company.[9] Further, repeated service failures without an effective recovery strategy in place can aggravate even the best employees. The costs in employee morale and even lost employees can be huge, but often overlooked, costs of not having an effective service recovery strategy.

The Recovery Paradox

Some have suggested that customers who are dissatisfied, but experience a high level of excellent service recovery, may ultimately be even more satisfied and more likely to repurchase than are those who were satisfied in the first place.[10] For example, think of a hotel customer who arrives to check in and finds there is no room available. In an effort to recover, the hotel front desk person immediately upgrades this guest to a better room at the same original price. The customer is so thrilled with this compensation that she is extremely satisfied with this experience, is even more impressed with the hotel than she was before, and vows to be loyal into the future. The logical, but not very rational, conclusion is that companies should plan to disappoint customers so they can recover and gain even greater loyalty from them as a result! This idea has become known as *the recovery paradox.*

Certainly, the recovery paradox is more complex than it may seem on the surface. First of all, it is expensive to fix mistakes, and it would appear somewhat ludicrous to encourage service failures—after all, we know that reliability ("doing it right the first time") is the most critical determinant of service quality across industries. Second, empirical research suggests that only under the very highest levels of customers' service recovery ratings will we observe increased satisfaction and loyalty.[11] This research suggests that customers weight their most recent experiences heavily in their determination of whether to buy again. If the experience is negative, overall feelings about the company will decrease and repurchase intentions will also diminish significantly. Unless the recovery effort is absolutely superlative, it cannot overcome the negative impression of the initial experience enough to build repurchase intentions beyond where they would be if the service had been provided correctly in the first place.

These conclusions are somewhat complicated by a recent study that shows no support at all for the recovery paradox. In the context of that study, overall satisfaction was consistently lower for those customers who had experienced a service failure than for those who had experienced no failure, no matter what the recovery effort.[12] An explanation for why no recovery paradox occurred is suggested by the magnitude of the service failure in this study—a three-hour airplane flight delay. This type of failure may be too much to be overcome by any recovery effort. Even in this study, however, strong service recovery was able to mitigate, if not reverse, the effects of the failure by reducing overall dissatisfaction.

Given the somewhat mixed opinions on whether a recovery paradox exists, it is safe to say "doing it right the first time" is still the best and safest strategy. However, when a failure does occur, then every effort at a superior recovery should be made to mitigate its negative effects. In cases where the failure can be fully overcome, the failure is less critical, or the recovery effort is clearly superlative, it may be possible to observe evidence of the recovery paradox.

HOW CUSTOMERS RESPOND TO SERVICE FAILURES

When there is a service failure, customers can respond in a variety of ways as illustrated in Figure 7.3.[13] It is assumed that following a failure, dissatisfaction at some level will occur for the customer. In fact, research suggests that a variety of negative emotions can occur following a service failure, including such feelings as anger, discontent, disappointment, self-pity, and anxiety.[14] These initial negative responses will affect how customers evaluate the service recovery effort and presumably their ultimate decision to return to the provider or not.[15]

Many customers are very passive about their dissatisfaction, simply saying or doing nothing. Whether they take action or not, at some point the customers will decide whether to stay with that provider or switch to a competitor. As we already have seen, those who do not complain are least likely to return. For companies, customer passivity in the face of dissatisfaction is a threat to future success.

Types of Customer Complaint Actions

If customers initiate actions following service failure, the action can be of various types. A dissatisfied customer can choose to complain on the spot to the service provider, giving the company the opportunity to respond immediately. This is often the best-case scenario for the company because it has a second chance right at that moment to satisfy the customer, keep his or her business in the future, and potentially avoid any negative word of mouth. If they don't complain immediately, customers may choose to complain later to the provider by phone or in writing, or even to write or call the corporate offices of the company. Again, the company has a chance to recover. Researchers refer to these proactive types of complaining behavior as *voice* responses or *seeking redress*.

FIGURE 7.3   **Customer Complaint Actions Following Service Failure**

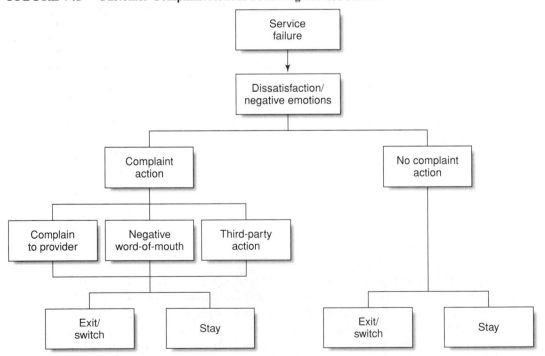

Some customers choose not to complain directly to the provider but rather spread negative word of mouth about the company to friends, relatives, and coworkers. This negative word of mouth can be extremely detrimental because it can reinforce the customer's feelings of negativism and spread that negative impression to others as well. Further, the company has no chance to recover unless the negative word of mouth is accompanied by a complaint directly to the company.

Finally, customers may choose to complain to third parties such as the Better Business Bureau, to consumer affairs arms of the government, to a licensing authority, to a professional association, or potentially to a private attorney. No matter the action (or inaction), ultimately the customers determine whether to patronize the service provider again or to switch to another provider.

Types of Complainers

Research suggests that people can be grouped into categories based on how they respond to failures. Four categories of response types were identified in a study that focused on grocery stores, automotive repair services, medical care, and banking and financial services[16]: *passives, voicers, irates,* and *activists.* Although the proportion of the types of complainers is likely to vary across industries and contexts, it is likely that these four categories of complainer types will be relatively consistent and that each type can be found in all companies and industries.

Passives   This group of customers is least likely to take any action. They are unlikely to say anything to the provider, less likely than others to spread negative word of mouth, and unlikely to complain to a third party. They often doubt the effectiveness of complaining, thinking the consequences will not merit the time and effort they will expend. Sometimes their personal values or norms argue against complaining. These folks tend to feel less alienated from the marketplace than irates and activists.

Voicers   These customers actively complain to the service provider, but they are less likely to spread negative word of mouth, to switch patronage, or to go to third parties with their complaints. These customers should be viewed as the service provider's best friends! They actively complain and thus give the company a second chance. As with the passives, these customers are less alienated from the marketplace than those in the other two groups. They tend to believe complaining has social benefits and therefore don't hesitate to voice their opinions. They believe the consequences of complaining to the provider can be very positive, and they believe less in other types of complaining such as spreading word of mouth or talking to third parties. Their personal norms are consistent with complaining.

Irates   These consumers are more likely to engage in negative word of mouth to friends and relatives and to switch providers than are others. They are about average in their propensity to complain to the provider. They are unlikely to complain to third parties. These folks tend to feel somewhat alienated from the marketplace. As their label suggests, they are more angry with the provider, although they do believe that complaining to the provider can have social benefits. They are less likely to give the service provider a second chance and instead will switch to a competitor, spreading the word to friends and relatives along the way.

Activists   These consumers are characterized by above average propensity to complain on all dimensions: they will complain to the provider, they will tell others, and they are more likely than any other group to complain to third parties. Complaining

Starbucks Coffee has set the pace in its industry—from its humble beginnings in Seattle, Washington, in the early 1970s, this coffee retail giant has grown to approximately 4,000 outlets in the United States and over 1,000 in other parts of the world including the Middle East, Europe, and the Pacific Rim. The company and its legendary CEO, Howard Schulz, have a reputation for world-class service and outstanding employee relations and benefits. (Look ahead to Chapter 13, Exhibit 13.1, for a full description of the Starbucks success story.) But even giants like Starbucks can stumble—no one in the service industry can escape failures from time to time. And sometimes a seemingly innocent failure can escalate, as it did for Starbucks in the following story.

The story began when a Starbucks customer bought a defective cappuccino maker, which he returned for a replacement. While returning the machine, he bought another for a friend as a gift—however, he did not receive the ½-pound free coffee promised with the machine. And, the customer claims, the employee was rude besides. Unfortunately, the gift machine also turned out to be defective, so the customer demanded that Starbucks replace it with its top-of-the-line cappuccino machine, worth approximately $2,000 more than he had paid for the gift. The customer threatened to take out a full-page ad in *The Wall Street Journal* denouncing the company if his request were refused. The company refused. A full-page ad against Starbucks appeared in the *Journal,* with the customer soliciting others to complain through his own 800 number. When Starbucks apologized and attempted to replace both machines, the customer claimed that was not enough and placed even more demands on Starbucks. He demanded it place a full-page ad in the *Journal* apologizing to him and that it fund his favorite charity. Needless to say, the whole issue received national media attention.

Although these types of customer terrorism are rare indeed, the example points to what can happen, and the lengths some customer terrorists are willing to go to.

Experts were asked at the time of the incident to comment on the situation at Starbucks. All experts noted how critical that first encounter with the Starbucks employee was in setting the stage and tone for the rest of the story. One expert believed Starbucks should have given the customer two pounds of coffee when he came to return the first defective machine, and then followed up with a call within a week to determine whether both machines were working. Another expert suggested that customers with problems be put on a VIP list to alert employees and management to treat subsequent transactions with extreme care and priority. Still another felt Starbucks should have replaced the defective machine with the $2,000+ machine immediately—no questions. This expert believes the percentage of customers who are this demanding is so small that it is worth it to spend whatever is necessary to avoid potential acts of customer terrorism such as this one. Another expert felt that as soon as the *Journal* ad appeared the company should have flown someone out to talk to the customer face-to-face, apologize, listen to the customer, and find out what he wanted. Several of the experts acknowledged that past a certain point damage control is the only option, but escalation to that point can often be avoided.

This story illustrates how even world-class service providers can be caught in tough situations.

Sources: "Customers from Hell: Nightmare or Opportunity," *On Achieving Excellence,* December 1995, pp. 2–3; and A. Lucas, "Trouble Brews for Starbucks," *Sales and Marketing Management* 147, no. 8 (August 1995), p. 15; www.starbucks.com.

fits with their personal norms. As with the irates, these consumers are more alienated from the marketplace than the other groups. They have a very optimistic sense of the potential positive consequences of all types of complaining.

In extreme cases these consumers can become "terrorists," as in the Starbuck's Coffee case described in Exhibit 7.1.

WHY DO (AND DON'T) PEOPLE COMPLAIN?

The categories just described suggest that some customers are more likely to complain than others. As individuals, these consumers believe that positive consequences may occur and that there are social benefits of complaining, and their personal norms support their complaining behavior. They believe they will and should be provided compensation for the service failure in some form. They believe that fair treatment and good service are their due, and that in cases of service failure, someone should make good. In some cases they feel a social obligation to complain—to help others avoid similar situations or to punish the service provider. A very small number of consumers have "complaining" personalities—they just like to complain or cause trouble.

Those who are unlikely to take any action hold the opposite beliefs. They often see complaining as a waste of their time and effort. They don't believe anything positive will occur for them or others based on their actions. Sometimes they don't know how to complain—they don't understand the process or may not realize there are avenues open to them to voice their complaints. In some cases noncomplainers may engage in "emotion-focused coping" to deal with their negative experiences. This type of coping involves self-blame, denial, and possibly seeking social support.[17] They may feel that the failure was somehow their fault and that they don't deserve redress.

Personal relevance of the failure can also influence whether people complain.[18] If the service failure is not really important, if the failure had no critical consequences for the consumer, or if the consumer has little ego involvement in the service experience, then he or she is less likely to complain. For example, consumers are more likely to complain about services that are expensive, high risk, and ego involving (like vacation packages, airline travel, and medical services) than they are about less expensive, frequently purchased services (fast-food drive-through service, a cab ride, a call to a customer service help line). These latter services are simply not important enough to warrant the time to complain. Unfortunately, even though the experience may not be important to the consumer at the moment, a dissatisfying encounter can still drive him or her to a competitor next time the service is needed.

WHEN THEY COMPLAIN, WHAT DO CUSTOMERS EXPECT?

When they take the time and effort to complain, customers generally have high expectations. They expect to be helped quickly. They expect to be compensated for their grief and for the hassle of being inconvenienced. And they expect to be treated nicely in the process. Our "Story of a Service Hero," Exhibit 7.2, epitomizes this kind of service recovery.

Customers Expect Fair Treatment

Specifically, customers want justice and fairness in handling their complaints. Service recovery experts Steve Brown and Steve Tax have documented three specific types of justice that customers are looking for following their complaints: *outcome fairness, procedural fairness,* and *interactional fairness.*[19] Exhibit 7.3 shows examples of each type of fairness taken from their study of consumers who reported on their experiences with complaint resolution.

Outcome Fairness

Customers expect outcomes, or compensation, that match the level of their dissatisfaction. This compensation can take the form of actual monetary compensation, an apology, future free services, reduced charges, repairs, and/or replacements. They expect equity in the exchange—that is, they want to feel that the company has "paid" for its mistakes in a manner at least equal to what the customer has suffered. The company's "punishment should fit the crime." They expect equality—that is, they want to be compensated no more or less than other customers who have experienced the same

A good recovery can turn angry, frustrated customers into loyal ones. It can, in fact, create more goodwill than if things had gone smoothly in the first place. Consider how Club Med–Cancun, part of the Paris-based Club Mediterranée, recovered from a service nightmare and won the loyalty of one group of vacationers.

The vacationers had nothing but trouble getting from New York to their Mexican destination. The flight took off six hours late, made two unexpected stops, and circled 30 minutes before it could land. Because of all the delays and mishaps, the plane was en route for 10 hours more than planned and ran out of food and drinks. It finally arrived at two o'clock in the morning, with a landing so rough that oxygen masks and luggage dropped from overhead. By the time the plane pulled up to the gate, the soured passengers were faint with hunger and convinced that their vacation was ruined before it had even started. One lawyer on board was already collecting names and addresses for a class-action lawsuit.

Silvio de Bortoli, the general manager of the Cancun resort and a legend throughout the organization for his ability to satisfy customers, got word of the horrendous flight and immediately created an antidote. He took half the staff

to the airport, where they laid out a table of snacks and drinks and set up a stereo system to play lively music. As the guests filed through the gate, they received personal greetings, help with their bags, a sympathetic ear, and a chauffeured ride to the resort. Waiting for them at Club Med was a lavish banquet, complete with mariachi band and champagne. Moreover, the staff had rallied other guests to wake up and greet the newcomers, and the partying continued until sunrise. Many guests said it was the most fun they'd had since college.

In the end, the vacationers had a better experience than if their flight from New York had gone like clockwork. Although the company probably couldn't measure it, Club Mediterranée won market share that night. After all, the battle for market share is won not by analyzing demographic trends, ratings points, and other global measures, but rather by pleasing customers one at a time.

Source: Reprinted by permission of *Harvard Business Review.* An excerpt from C. W. L. Hart, J. L. Heskett, and W. E. Sasser, Jr., "The Profitable Art of Service Recovery," *Harvard Business Review,* July–August 1990, pp. 148, 149. Copyright © 1990 by the President and Fellows of Harvard College. All rights reserved.

type of service failure. They also appreciate it when a company gives them choices in terms of compensation. For example, a hotel guest could be offered the choice of a refund or a free upgrade to a better room in compensation for a room not being available on arrival.

In the Club Med example in Exhibit 7.2, customers were compensated by being met at the airport with snacks and drinks, being chauffeured to the resort, being served a lavish buffet, and being treated to an all-night party that was not part of the package initially. These guests had suffered a lot through the delay of their long-awaited vacation, and the compensation definitely was adequate. Note that in this case the service failure wasn't even Club Med's fault.

On the other hand, customers can be uncomfortable if they are overly compensated. Early in its experience with service guarantees, Domino's Pizza offered not to charge for the pizza if the driver arrived after the 30-minute guaranteed delivery time. Many customers were not comfortable asking for this level of compensation, especially if the driver was only a few minutes late. In this case "the punishment was greater than the crime." For a while Domino's changed the compensation to a more reasonable $3 off for late deliveries. Later the time guarantee was dropped altogether because of problems it caused with employees who were driving too fast in order to make their deliveries.

Procedural Fairness

In addition to fair compensation, customers expect fairness in terms of policies, rules, and timeliness of the complaint process. They want easy access to the complaint process, and they want things handled quickly, preferably by the first person they con-

	Fair	Unfair
Outcome fairness	"The waitress agreed that there was a problem. She took the sandwiches back to the kitchen and had them replaced. We were also given a free drink." "They were very thorough with my complaint. One week later I received a coupon for a free oil change and an apology from the shop owner." "Since I had to come back to the store a third time, they not only gave me an exchange, they also apologized repeatedly and gave me a $25 store coupon."	"Their refusal to refund our money or make up for the inconvenience and cold food was inexcusable." "The situation was never remedied. Once they had my money, they disappeared when I had problems." "If I wanted a refund, I had to go back to the store the next day. It's a 20-minute drive; the refund was barely worth the trouble." "All I wanted was for the ticket agent to apologize for doubting my story. I never got the apology."
Procedural fairness	"The hotel manager said that it didn't matter to her who was at fault, she would take responsibility for the problem immediately." "The representative was pleasant and quick to resolve the problem." "The sales manager called me back one week after my complaint to check if the problem was taken care of to my satisfaction."	"They should have assisted me with the problem instead of giving me a phone number to call. No one returned my calls, and I never had a chance to speak to a real person." "I had to tell my problem to too many people. I had to become irate in order to talk with the manager, who was apparently the only one who could provide a solution." "Not only did the hotel ruin my vacation, I was accused of causing the problem! It was their fault and they should have taken care of it."
Interactional fairness	"The loan officer was very courteous, knowledgeable, and considerate—he kept me informed about the progress of the complaint." "The manager had a good attitude. She wanted to make sure I left satisfied." "The teller explained that they had a power outage that morning so things were delayed. He went through a lot of files [effort] so that I would not have to come back the next day."	"The person who handled my complaint about the faulty air conditioner repair wasn't going to do anything about it and didn't seem to care." "They lied to me about the free Pepsi and they wouldn't give me a clear explanation why the pizza was so late to begin with." "The receptionist was very rude; she made it seem like the doctor's time was important but mine was not."

Source: Reprinted from S. S. Tax and S. W. Brown, "Recovering and Learning from Service Failure," *Sloan Management Review, Fall 1998*, p. 79, by permission of the publisher. Copyright 1998 by Sloan Management Review Association. All rights reserved.

tact. They appreciate companies that can be adaptable in their procedures so that the recovery effort can match their individual circumstances. In some cases, particularly in business-to-business services, companies actually ask the customer, "What can we do to compensate you for our failure?" Many times what the customer asks for is actually less than the company might have expected.

Fair procedures are characterized by clarity, speed, and absence of hassles. Unfair procedures are those customers perceive as slow, prolonged, and inconvenient. Customers also feel it is unfair if they have to prove their case—when the assumption seems to be they are wrong or lying until they can prove otherwise.

In the Club Med case in Exhibit 7.2, the recovery happened as quickly as possible when the passengers landed in Mexico. Even though it wasn't Club Med's fault, the company went out of its way to compensate the delayed guests immediately on arrival. There were no more hassles once they were on the ground.

Interaction Fairness Above and beyond their expectations of fair compensation and hassle-free, quick procedures, customers expect to be treated politely, with care and honesty. This form of fairness can dominate the others if customers feel the company and its employees have uncaring attitudes and have done little to try to resolve the problem. This type of behavior on the part of employees may seem strange—why would they treat customers rudely or in an uncaring manner under these circumstances? Often it is due to lack of training and empowerment—a frustrated, front-line employee who has no authority to compensate the customer may easily respond in an aloof or uncaring manner, especially if the customer is angry and/or rude.

In the Club Med case in Exhibit 7.2, Silvio de Bortoli and his staff were gracious, caring, and upbeat when they greeted the long-delayed passengers. They personally met them at the airport even though it was late at night. They even involved other guests already staying at the resort to greet the new arrivals and party with them, making them feel welcome and helping to give their vacation a jump start.

How Are Companies Doing?

Unfortunately, research suggests that customers are not generally happy with the way their complaints are handled or with the levels of outcome, procedural, and interactional justice they receive.[20] There is tremendous room for improvement in service recovery effectiveness across industries. Figure 7.4 illustrates the percentage of customers who felt they were fairly and unfairly treated on the three different dimensions of fairness. The figure also shows that a majority of customers are dissatisfied with the way their complaints are handled overall.

FIGURE 7.4 **Fairness and Satisfaction**

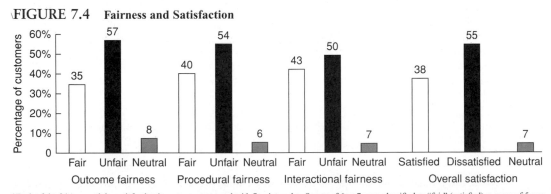

*Each of the fairness and the satisfaction items were measured with 7-point scales. Scores of 6 or 7 were classified as "fair" (satisfied), a score of 5 was classified as "neutral," and scores of 1 to 4 were classified as "unfair" (dissatisfied). This classification was based on comparing the open-ended comments with the quantitative measures. When customers rated the fairness or satisfaction as 6 or 7, their comments were generally favorable. Scores below 5 coincided with negative comments, and scores of 5 led to mostly neutral comments.

Source: Reprinted from S. S. Tax and S. W. Brown, "Recovering and Learning from Service Failure," *Sloan Management Review,* Fall 1998, p. 80, by permission of the publisher. Copyright 1998 by the Sloan Management Review Association. All rights reserved.

SWITCHING VERSUS STAYING FOLLOWING SERVICE RECOVERY

Ultimately, how a service failure is handled and the customer's reaction to the recovery effort can influence future decisions to remain loyal to the service provider or to switch to another provider. Whether or not customers switch to a new provider following service failure will depend in addition on a number of other factors. The magnitude and criticality of the failure will clearly be a factor in future repurchase decisions. The more serious the failure, the more likely the customer is to switch no matter what the recovery effort.[21]

The nature of the customer's relationship with the firm may also influence whether the customer stays or switches providers. Research suggests that customers who have "true relationships" with their service providers are more forgiving of poorly handled service failures and are less likely to switch than are those who have a "pseudo-relationship" or a "first-time encounter" type of relationship.[22] A true relationship is one where the customer has had repeated contact over time with the same service provider. A first-time encounter relationship is where the customer has had only one contact, on a transaction basis, with the provider. And a pseudo-relationship is one where the customer has interacted many times with the same company, but with different service providers each time.

Other research reveals that the individual customer's attitude toward switching will strongly influence whether he or she ultimately stays with the provider, and that this attitude toward switching will be even more influential than basic satisfaction with the service.[23] This suggests that certain customers will have a greater propensity to switch service providers no matter how their service failure situations are handled. Research in an online service context, for example, shows that demographic factors such as age and income as well as individual factors such as risk aversion will influence whether a customer continues to use an online service or switches to another provider.[24] The profile of an "online service switcher" emerged in the research as one who was influenced to subscribe to the service through word of mouth; who used the service less; who was less satisfied and less involved with the service; who had a lower income and education level; and who also had a lower propensity for taking risks.

Finally, the decision to switch to a different service provider may not occur immediately following service failure or poor service recovery, but may follow an accumulation of events. That is, service switching can be viewed as a process resulting from a series of decisions and critical service encounters over time, rather than one specific moment in time when a decision is made.[25] This process orientation suggests that companies could potentially track customer interactions and predict the likelihood of defection based on a series of events, intervening earlier in the process to head off the customer's decision to switch.

SERVICE RECOVERY STRATEGIES

Not all companies are doing poorly at service recovery. Many have learned the importance of providing excellent recovery for disappointed customers. In this section we examine their strategies and share examples of benchmark companies and what they are doing. It will become clear that excellent service recovery is really a combination of a variety of strategies that need to work together, as illustrated in Figure 7.5. Each of the strategies shown in the figure will be discussed, starting with the basic "do it right the first time."

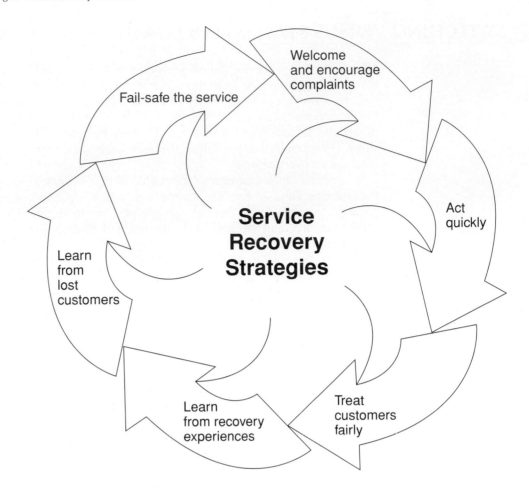

FIGURE 7.5
Service Recovery Strategies

Fail-Safe Your Service—Do It Right the First Time!

The first rule of service quality is to do it right the first time. In this way recovery is unnecessary, customers get what they expect, and the costs of redoing the service and compensating for errors can be avoided. As you have already learned, reliability, or doing it right the first time, is the most important dimension of service quality across industry contexts.[26] As the figure suggests, elements of a total service recovery strategy will lead in a circular fashion back to this most basic and fundamental of all service strategies—service reliability.

What specific strategies do firms employ to achieve reliability? TQM, or total quality management, practices aimed at "zero defects" are commonly used. However, given the inherent differences between services and manufactured products, these tools typically require considerable adaptation to work well in service contexts. Firms that blindly adopt TQM practices, without considering services implications, often fail in their efforts.

Dick Chase, noted service operations expert, suggests that services adopt the TQM notion of *poka yokes* to improve service reliability.[27] Poka yokes are automatic warnings or controls in place to ensure mistakes are not made; essentially they are quality control mechanisms, typically used on assembly lines. Chase suggests that poka yokes can be devised in service settings to "mistakeproof" the service, to ensure that essential procedures are followed, and to ensure that service steps are carried out in the proper order and in a timely manner. In a hospital setting numerous poka yokes ensure that procedures are followed to avoid potentially life-threatening mistakes. For example, trays for surgical instruments have indentations for specific instruments, and each instrument is nested in its appropriate spot. In this way surgeons and their staff know that all instruments are in their places prior to closing the patient's incision.[28]

Similarly, poka yokes can be devised to ensure that the tangibles associated with the service are clean and well maintained, and that documents are accurate and up-to-date. Poka yokes can also be implemented for employee behaviors (checklists, role-playing and practice, reminder signs) and even for ensuring that customers perform effectively. Many of the strategies we discuss in Parts 3 and 4 of the text ("Aligning Strategy, Service Design, and Standards" and "Delivering and Performing Service") are aimed at ensuring service reliability and can be viewed as applications of the basic fail-safing notion of poka yokes.

Even more fundamentally, it is important to create a culture of zero defections to ensure doing it right the first time.[29] Within a zero defections culture, everyone understands the importance of reliability. Employees and managers aim to satisfy every customer and look for ways to improve service. Employees in a zero defections culture fully understand and appreciate the "lifetime value of a customer" concept that was presented in Chapter 6. Thus they are motivated to provide quality service *every time* and to *every customer.*

Welcome and Encourage Complaints

Even in a zero defections organization that aims for 100 percent service quality, failures occur. A critical component of a service recovery strategy is thus to welcome and encourage complaints. Complaints should be anticipated, encouraged, and tracked. The complaining customer should truly be viewed as a friend.

There are a number of ways to encourage and track complaints. Customer research can be designed specifically to do this through satisfaction surveys, critical incidents studies, and lost customer research as discussed in Chapter 5. In a less formal manner, employees can be important listening posts, discovering sources of customer dissatisfaction and service failure on the front line. They should be encouraged to report this type of information. For example, at Ritz-Carlton hotels, all employees carry service recovery forms called "instant action forms" with them at all times so that they can immediately record service failures and actions to address them. Each individual employee "owns" any complaint that he or she receives and is responsible for seeing that service recovery occurs. In turn, the employees report these sources of service failure and the remedies. If common themes are observed across a number of failure situations, changes are made to service processes or attributes.

Part of encouraging complaints also involves teaching customers *how* to complain. Sometimes they have no idea whom to speak to, what the process is, or what will be involved. It is best to make this process as simple as possible—the last thing customers want when they are dissatisfied is to face a complex, difficult-to-access process for complaining.

One way that the complaining process has been simplified for customers is through technology. New technologies have resulted in easier access for customers to sales and service representatives. Toll-free call centers, e-mail, and pagers are all used to facilitate, encourage, and track complaints. Software applications in a number of companies also allow complaints to be analyzed, sorted, responded to, and tracked automatically.[30]

Ads for British Airways (BA) reinforce the company's branding strategy as the "World's Favourite Airline." Indeed, British Airways is a favorite among world travelers—but it wasn't always so. The success in turning BA around from a bureaucratic institution that regarded itself as doing the public a favor by allowing them to fly on its planes to a customer-responsive, world-class service provider can be attributed to its CEO at the time, Sir Colin Marshall. Marshall (currently chairman of the board) was brought in to head up a major change for BA in the 1980s—and he did. His legacy has sustained and further propelled the airline to its current level of success.

A big part of this success was achieved in new ways of listening to customers and new approaches to dealing with customer complaints. One of the first things Marshall did was to install video booths at Heathrow airport so that upset customers could immediately go to the video booth while still at the airport and complain directly to him. In addition to this type of innovative action, Marshall instituted a series of systems and training changes to encourage and be responsive to customer complaints. To quote him directly, "I ardently believe that customer complaints are precious opportunities to hold on to customers who otherwise might take their business elsewhere and to learn about problems that need to be fixed."

Initially BA did research to understand the effect dissatisfied or defecting customers had on the business. It learned that 50 percent of the dissatisfied customers who did *not* tell BA about their problems left the airline for a competitor. However, of those who *did* tell them of their problems, 87 percent remained loyal to BA. It quickly became obvious that complaints should be encouraged! Considering that an average business class passenger has a lifetime value of $150,000, encouraging complaints and retaining their business was obviously critical.

BA responded by building a model for "Making Customers into Champions." Goals of the new system were to (1) use customer feedback more effectively to improve quality; (2) strive to prevent future service problems through teamwork; (3) compensate customers on their terms, not the company's; and (4) practice customer retention, not adjudication. The bottom-line objective: to prevent customer defections.

To accomplish this objective, BA set up a four-step process to guide development of its technical and human delivery systems. This process was based on knowledge of how customers would like their complaints handled. The first step in the process was to *apologize and own the customer's problem*—not to search for someone to blame but rather to become the customer's advocate. The second essential was to *respond quickly*—taking absolutely no longer than 72 hours, and preferably providing an immediate solution. The third step was

Our Global Feature shows how a world-class airline, British Airways, encourages, facilitates, and tracks customer complaints as a critical component of its effective service recovery process. It is apparent that British Airways is highly dependent on information technology to implement its strategy.

In some cases technology can anticipate problems and complaints before they happen, allowing service employees to diagnose problems before the customer recognizes they exist. This is the case at companies such as IBM and Caterpillar, where information systems are being implemented to anticipate equipment failures and send out an

to *assure the customer the problem is being fixed.* Finally, as much as possible, *handle complaints by phone.* BA found that customers with problems were delighted to speak personally to a customer service representative who could solve their problems.

To facilitate the process just described required major investments in systems and people. First, BA invested in a computer system called *Caress* that eliminated all paper by scanning or manually entering all customer information relevant to a complaint into a customer complaint database. A particular customer's information was thus easily accessed, and the data could be analyzed for patterns as well. The process for dealing with a complaint was also shortened by eliminating a number of unnecessary and redundant steps: the number of steps required to deal with a complaint was reduced from 13 to 3. Further, customer service representatives were given the tools and authority—they were empowered—to use whatever resources were needed to retain the customer's business. New training on listening skills, how to handle anger, and how to negotiate win–win solutions were put in place for customer service representatives. Finally, customers were encouraged to complain. Previous to the new initiatives, BA knew that only about 10 percent of its customers ever communicated with the airline directly—whether for good or bad reasons. The airline thus worked hard to get customers to complain and provide input by establishing 12 different "listening posts" or ways of communicating, including postage-paid cards, customer forums, surveys, and a "Fly with Me" program, where customer service representatives flew with customers to experience and hear their responses firsthand.

Not only did BA use the information and systems it developed to directly retain dissatisfied customers, it also built systems to use the data and information to improve systems for the future. It used the information to design out common failure patterns and to design early-warning mechanisms to alert the company to potential future failures.

BA found that all of its efforts toward complaint management paid off. For every £1 spent in customer retention efforts, BA found it had a £2 return. BA continues to take great pride in delivering the highest levels of customer service. In January 2000 the company unveiled £600,000,000 worth of new customer service initiatives to be rolled out over the following two years.

Sources: J. Barlow and C. Moller, *A Complaint Is a Gift* (San Francisco: Berrett-Koehler Publishers, 1996), pp. 16–18; C. R. Weiser, "Championing the Customer," *Harvard Business Review,* November–December 1995, pp. 113–15; and S. E. Prokesch, "Competing on Service: An Interview with British Airways' Sir Colin Marshall," *Harvard Business Review,* November–December 1995, pp. 101–16; www.BritishAirways.com, 2002.

electronic alert to the local field technician with the nature of the problem as well as which parts and tools will be needed to make the repair—a repair the customer doesn't yet know is needed.[31]

Act Quickly

Complaining customers want quick responses. Thus if the company welcomes, even encourages, complaints, it must be prepared to act on them quickly. This requires systems and procedures that allow quick action, as well as empowered employees.

Take Care of Problems on the Front Line

Customers want the persons who hear their complaints to solve their problems whether a complaint is registered in person, over the phone, or via the Internet. In the example given earlier, the Ritz-Carlton insists that the first person to hear a complaint from a customer "owns" that complaint until he or she is sure it is resolved. That means that if a maintenance employee hears a complaint from a customer while the employee is in the middle of fixing a light in the hotel corridor, he owns that complaint and must be sure that it is handled appropriately before returning to his work.

Another obvious way to speed complaint handling is to call (or in some cases electronically respond to) customers, rather then send responses in the mail. Even customers who take the time to write can be called back. Smith and Hawken, a garden supply mail-order company based in California, found that this strategy of phoning customers worked well for them—they were quicker to respond to their customers, and the costs of the phone calls were offset by the reduced costs and time involved with paperwork.[32]

Empower Employees

Employees must be trained and empowered to solve problems as they occur. At Advance PCS, a large pharmacy benefits provider covering 75,000,000 patients, the goal is to solve the customer's problem on the first call. The company uses customer-knowledge databases as the key source for immediate problem solving by its customer service representatives. These representatives are empowered to solve the customer's problem, but at the same time they must adhere to stringent requirements necessary in the health and pharmaceutical administration business.

A problem not solved can quickly escalate. Take, for example, a true story of a corporate vice president who sent an e-mail to his bank to register a complaint as he was attempting a transaction through its Internet banking service. The e-mail was never answered. The customer then sent an e-mail directly to the president of the bank. That e-mail was never answered either. Ultimately the customer withdrew his approximately $70,000 account because his complaint was not handled in a timely manner. In this case the technology was not effectively linked to other systems, nor ultimately to employees. The Internet access encouraged the complaint, but the response never occurred.

Sometimes employees can even anticipate problems before they arise and surprise customers with a solution. For example, flight attendants on a flight severely delayed due to weather anticipated everyone's hunger, particularly the young children's. Once in flight, they announced to the harried travelers, "Thank you for your extreme patience in waiting with us. Now that we're on our way, we'd like to offer you complimentary beverages and dinner. Because we have a number of very hungry children on board, we'd like to serve them first, if that's OK with all of you." The passengers nodded and applauded their efforts, knowing that hungry, crying children could make the situation even worse. The flight attendants had anticipated a problem and solved it before it escalated.

For service employees, there is a specific and real need for recovery training. Because customers demand that service recovery take place on the spot and quickly, front-line employees need the skills, authority, and incentives to engage in effective recovery. Effective recovery skills include hearing the customer's problems, taking initiative, identifying solutions, improvising, and perhaps bending the rules from time to time.

Employees not only need the authority to act (usually within certain defined limits), but they should not be punished for taking action. In fact, incentives should exist that encourage employees to exercise their recovery authority. At the Ritz-Carlton, employees are authorized to spend $2,000 on behalf of the customer to solve a problem.

This amount of money is rarely needed, but knowing that they have it encourages employees to be responsive without fear of retribution.

Allow Customers to Solve Their Own Problems

Another way that problems or complaints can be handled quickly is by building systems that allow customers to actually solve their own service needs and fix their own problems. Typically this is done through technology. Customers directly interface with the company's technology to perform their own customer service, providing them with instant answers. This is the case with FedEx's package tracking services, for example. Our Technology Spotlight features a company that is a master at online customer service—Cisco Systems.

Treat Customers Fairly

In responding quickly, it is also critical to treat each customer fairly. As discussed in an earlier section, customers expect to be treated fairly in terms of the outcome they receive, the process by which the service recovery takes place, and the interpersonal treatment they receive. Examples, strategies, and results of research focused on fairness in service recovery were discussed earlier. Here you are reminded that this fair treatment is an essential component of an effective service recovery strategy.

Learn from Recovery Experiences

"Problem-resolution situations are more than just opportunities to fix flawed services and strengthen ties with customers. They are also a valuable—but frequently ignored or underutilized—source of diagnostic, prescriptive information for improving customer service."[33] By tracking service recovery efforts and solutions, managers can often learn about systematic problems in the delivery system that need fixing. By conducting root-cause analysis, firms can identify the sources of the problems and modify processes, sometimes eliminating almost completely the need for recovery. At the Ritz-Carlton, employees record every service recovery opportunity and how it was handled; the employee who gets the complaint is required to do this. This information is then entered into the customer database and analyzed for patterns and systemic service issues that need to be fixed. If needed, a project team is assigned to a problematic area to develop a solution. In addition, the information is entered into the customer's personal data file so that when that customer stays at the Ritz-Carlton again (no matter what hotel), employees can be aware of the previous experience, ensuring that it doesn't happen again for that particular customer.

Learn from Lost Customers

Another key component of an effective service recovery strategy is to learn from the customers who defect or decide to leave. Formal market research to discover the reasons customers have left can assist in preventing failures in the future. This type of research is difficult, even painful for companies, however. No one really likes to examine their failures. Yet this is essential for preventing the same mistakes and losing more customers in the future.[34]

As presented in Chapter 5, lost customer research typically involves in-depth probing of customers to determine their true reasons for leaving. This is most effectively done by depth interviews, administered by skilled interviewers who truly understand the business. It may be best to have this type of research done by senior people in the company, particularly in business-to-business contexts where customers are large and the impact of even one lost customer is great. The type of depth analysis often requires

Technology Spotlight
Cisco Systems, Inc.—Customers Recover for Themselves

One of the challenges of 90 percent growth per year is learning how to handle customers' service needs quickly. This is the case for Cisco Systems, Inc., a worldwide leader in the networking equipment business. Cisco provides the equipment, builds the factories, and produces networking devices that keep businesses running. If the network is not working, the business is not working. Failures in this environment become extremely costly, very quickly. Customers want to know that their problems can be solved immediately, and they want a sense of control over the solution.

To address these issues—extremely high growth coupled with the critical nature of the business—Cisco Systems turned to the Internet. It built a world-class model of customer service using the Internet. The system described here has set Cisco apart in its industry and helped the company to build customer loyalty in a highly competitive environment.

Essentially, Cisco has put customers in charge of their own service through the Internet. In many cases customers now solve their own service problems totally, with no intervention of Cisco personnel. Access to information is immediate, and solutions can be highly customized for the individual customer. Called "Cisco Connection Online," the system includes the following types of services:

- *Open forum*—A searchable database for answers to networking questions. If the question is too complex, the customer can escalate the request to a highly trained service representative. However, most questions can be answered without human intervention. Further, the questions asked are used to further enhance and develop the information system to answer questions in the future.

- *Troubleshooting engine*—An expert system that takes the user through the problem identification and resolution process. Here customers actually solve problems and are instructed on how to fix their systems. This saves time for customers and gives them a much

greater sense of control, particularly in critical situations where every minute of downtime is extremely costly.

- *Bug toolkit*—A collection of interactive tools for identifying, tracking, and resolving software bugs.

- *Software center*—A comprehensive vending machine for Cisco software. This system provides one-stop shopping for Cisco software and helps customers to upgrade in a timely manner and be sure that they have the right release of a particular software.

- *Service order agent*—A parts information, ordering, and tracking system that allows customers to conduct transactions online. This system provides fast service for orders and saves on administrative costs for both Cisco and its customers.

- *Service contract center*—A system that allows customers to view the contents and/or status of their contracts with Cisco.

Through its continual innovation in providing service to its customers through the Internet, Cisco has recognized tremendous benefits. Currently 80 percent of customer problems are handled via the Internet through information provided by Cisco and self-help tools that allow customers to diagnose and solve their own problems. Customer satisfaction increased with the introduction of Internet-based customer service, productivity increased at the rate of 200 percent, and the company saves over $500 million per year. This is truly a win–win situation for Cisco's bottom line, for its employees, and for its business customers.

Sources: www.cisco.com, 2002. "The Globally Networked Business," Cisco presentation at "Activating Your Firm's Service Culture" symposium, Arizona State University, 1997; R. L. Nolan, "Cisco Systems Architecture: ERP and Web-Enabled IT," Harvard Business School Case #9-301-099, 2001; "Ten Minutes with John Chambers," *NASDAQ: The International Magazine* 29, January 2001.

a series of "why" questions or "tell me more about that" questions to get at the actual, core reason for the customer's defection.[35]

In conducting this kind of research, it is important to focus on important or profitable customers who have left—not just everyone who has left the company. An insurance company in Australia once began this type of research to learn about their lost

FIGURE 7.6
Causes Behind Service Switching

Source: Reprinted with permission of the American Marketing Association. From S. Keaveney, "Customer Switching Behavior in Service Industries: An Exploratory Study," *Journal of Marketing* 59 (April 1995), pp. 71–82.

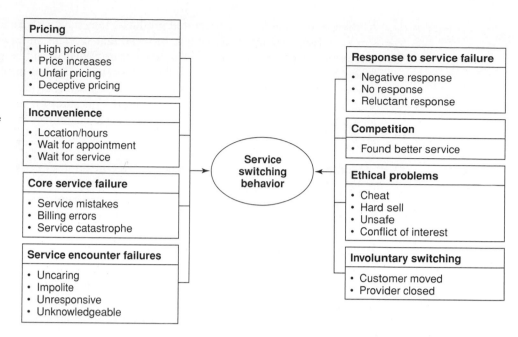

customers, only to find that the customers they were losing tended to be their least profitable customers anyway. They quickly determined that depth research on how to keep these unprofitable customers would not be a good investment!

Although the specific causes of customer defection will surely vary across industries and companies, some common themes have been observed in academic research. In a study of approximately 500 service-switching incidents, eight broad themes underlying the decision to defect were identified.[36] These themes (pricing, inconvenience, core service failure, service encounter failure, response to service failure, competition, ethical problems, and involuntary switching) and their subthemes are shown in Figure 7.6. In more than 300 of these switching incidents, more than one theme was represented. For example, one of the largest categories was "core service failure." In fact, 25 percent of the incidents with only one cause cited core service failure as the reason for switching. In incidents where there were two themes, 29 percent had core service failure as one of the causes for switching, and 22 percent of the three-theme incidents included this cause.

Return to "Doing It Right"

The set of strategies described follows Figure 7.5 and leads directly back to the beginning: "fail-safe the service and do it right the first time." By integrating all of the strategies, companies will find less and less of a need for service recovery. Yet, when those situations do occur, they will be prepared to impress the customer and keep their business anyway.

SERVICE GUARANTEES

A guarantee is a particular type of recovery tool. It is, according to the dictionary definition, "an assurance of the quality of or length of use to be expected from product offered for sale, often with a promise of reimbursement." Although guarantees are relatively common for manufactured products, they have only recently been used for services. Traditionally, many people believed that services simply could not be guaranteed given their intangible and variable nature. What would be guaranteed? With a product, the customer is guaranteed that it will perform as promised and if not, that it can be returned. With services, it is generally not possible to take returns or to "undo" what has been performed. Again, this raised the question for many of what could be guaranteed, and how. The skepticism about service guarantees is being dispelled, however, as more and more companies find they can guarantee their services and that there are tremendous benefits for doing so.

Companies are finding that effective service guarantees can complement the company's service recovery strategy—serving as one tool to help accomplish the service recovery strategies depicted in Figure 7.5. The Hampton Inn guarantee shown at the beginning of the chapter is an example of such an effective guarantee.

Benefits of Service Guarantees

"Service organizations, in particular, are beginning to recognize that guarantees can serve not only as a marketing tool but as a means for defining, cultivating, and maintaining quality throughout an organization."[37] As suggested by this quotation, the benefits to the company of an effective service guarantee are numerous:[38]

- *A good guarantee forces the company to focus on its customers.* To develop a meaningful guarantee, the company must know what is important to its customers—what they expect and value. In many cases "satisfaction" is guaranteed, but in order for the guarantee to work effectively, the company must clearly understand what satisfaction means for its customers (what they value and expect).

- *An effective guarantee sets clear standards for the organization.* It prompts the company to clearly define what it expects of its employees and to communicate that to them. The guarantee gives employees service-oriented goals that can quickly align employee behaviors around customer strategies. For example, Pizza Hut's guarantee that "If you're not satisfied with your pizza, let our restaurant know. We'll make it right or give you your money back" lets employees know exactly what they should do if a customer complains. It is also clear to employees that making it right for the customer is an important company goal.

- *A good guarantee generates immediate and relevant feedback from customers.* It provides an incentive for customers to complain and thereby provides more representative feedback to the company than simply relying on the relatively few customers who typically voice their concerns. The guarantee communicates to customers that they have the right to complain.

- *When the guarantee is invoked there is an instant opportunity to recover,* thus satisfying the customer and helping to retain loyalty.

- *Information generated through the guarantee can be tracked and integrated into continuous improvement efforts.* A feedback link between customers and service operations decisions can be strengthened through the guarantee.

- *Studies of the impact of service guarantees suggest that employee morale and loyalty can be enhanced as a result.* A guarantee generates pride among employees. Through feedback from the guarantee, improvements can be made in the service that benefit customers, and indirectly employees.

• *For customers, the guarantee reduces their sense of risk* and builds confidence in the organization. Because services are intangible and often highly personal or ego-involving, customers seek information and cues that will help reduce their sense of uncertainty. Guarantees have been shown to reduce risk and increase positive evaluation of the service prior to purchase.[39]

The Bottom Line   The bottom line for the company is that an effective guarantee can affect profitability through building customer awareness and loyalty, through positive word of mouth, and through reduction in costs as service improvements are made and service recovery expenses are reduced. Indirectly, the guarantee can reduce costs of employee turnover through creating a more positive service culture.

A Cautionary Note   Given all the positive benefits of service guarantees, a cautionary note is in order. Service guarantees are not appropriate for every company and certainly not in every service situation. Later in this section we provide hints as to when and how to employ a service guarantee strategy. First we discuss different types of guarantees and the characteristics of an effective guarantee.

Types of Service Guarantees

Satisfaction versus Service Attribute Guarantees   Service guarantees can be *unconditional satisfaction guarantees* or *service attribute guarantees.* Hampton Inns' guarantee is an unconditional satisfaction guarantee. In another context, Bain & Company, a management consulting firm, has offered some clients an unconditional guarantee for its services.[40] If clients are unhappy, they don't pay for the services. Bank One Corporation offers an unconditional guarantee to return fees to any client that is dissatisfied with its trust services. Lands End, a catalog retailer, has abbreviated its guarantee to "Guaranteed. Period."

In other cases, firms offer guarantees of particular aspects of the service that are important to customers. Wells Fargo, for example, guarantees that customers will not wait longer than five minutes in a teller line. If they do, they are given $5. FedEx guarantees package delivery by a certain time. In introducing a new seat design in first class, British Airways advertised "Comfort guaranteed or you get 25,000 miles." McDonald's advertised a guarantee that stated "Hot Food; Fast, Friendly Delivery; Double-Check Drive-Thru Accuracy . . . We'll make it right, or your next meal is on us." In all of these cases, the companies have guaranteed elements of the service that they know are important to customers.

Another type of service guarantee, a *combined guarantee,* combines the wide scope of the total satisfaction guarantee with specific attribute performance standards. Research suggests that this type of guarantee can be more effective than either of the other two types.[41] Exhibit 7.4 provides an example of a successful combined service guarantee offered by Datapro in Singapore.

External versus Internal Guarantees   Interestingly, guarantees don't have to be just for external customers. Some companies are finding that internal service guarantees—one part of the organization guaranteeing its services to others—are effective ways of aligning internal service operations. For example, at Embassy Suites the housekeeping supplies department guarantees its internal customer, the housekeeping staff, that they can get supplies on the day requested. If not, the supply department pays $5 to the housekeeper. At one direct-mail firm, the sales force guarantees to give

7.4 SERVICE GUARANTEE—DATAPRO SINGAPORE

Datapro Information Services provided IT and telecommunications information and consulting services around the world in the early 1990s. It employed over 400 analysts and consultants. Although having been in Asia for many years selling its prepackaged information services, only in 1993 did Datapro start offering consulting services throughout Southeast Asia via its Singapore office. Being confident about the high quality of its work, but at the same time somewhat lacking the brand equity other providers of similar services enjoyed, Datapro decided to become Asia's first IT consulting firm that explicitly guaranteed its services. In 1994 the company developed and introduced the guarantee described here in collaboration with the author of this case. Every proposal contained this guarantee in this last section just before the acceptance form:

> Datapro guarantees to deliver the report on time, to high quality standards, and to the contents outlined in this proposal. Should we fail to deliver according to this guarantee, or should you be dissatisfied with any aspect of our work, you can deduct any amount from the final payment which it deems as fair, subject to a maximum of 30%.
>
> In the event Datapro should fail to deliver the commissioned report in its entirety at the end of the period, you will have the option to deduct 10% off the price of the study for each week the said study is overdue subject to a maximum of 20%.
>
> We are able to offer this guarantee as we are confident about the good quality and professionalism of our work. We have secured a large number of blue-chip clients who have been completely satisfied with our services. Our clients in the last twelve months have included: Fujitsu, Hewlett-Packard, Intel, Northern Telecom, Philips, Sony, etc.

Datapro had ideally wanted to provide a 100 percent money-back guarantee, but at the same time wanted to limit the potential financial risks inherent in the introduction of such guarantees. These risks were considerable, with typical projects exceeding a value of well over $100,000. The guarantee contained a full satisfaction clause, as well as concrete promises like on-time delivery.

The marketing impact was dramatic. Clients were delighted that Datapro was willing to stand by its word and guarantee deadlines as well as content quality—especially because deadlines were a thorny issue in Asia's rapidly growing IT markets, and clients were often promised the sky during the proposal stage only to be confronted with late deliveries subsequently. The guarantee allowed Datapro to credibly promise delivery dates that otherwise might have been discounted by its clients. Datapro's management felt that the guarantee was an effective marketing tool that helped to sell a number of projects, and Datapro's consulting unit was extremely successful with an annual revenue and profit growth of around 100 percent for a number of successive years.

On the operations side, the guarantee pushed Datapro to keep up its quality. For example, it did not have a single late delivery after the introduction of the guarantee, mainly for two reasons. First, case leaders were cautious not to promise delivery dates they knew they could not keep. Second, in the case of unforeseen problems or delays, case leaders would try to bring the case back on track. Similar pressure was on the case teams to keep their clients happy because a dissatisfied client could mean a significant reduction in revenue and profit for that case, resulting in a steep reduction in staff bonuses.

Datapro was very successful, especially in breaking into the high-growth telecommunications consulting market, and was taken over at the end of 1997 by the Gartner Group, the world's largest IT consulting firm.

the production department all of the specifications needed to provide service to the external customer, or will personally the offending salesperson will take the production department to lunch, will sing a song at their next department meeting, or will personally input all of the specs into the computer.[42]

Characteristics of Effective Guarantees No matter the type of guarantee, certain characteristics make some more effective than others. Characteristics of effective

FIGURE 7.7
Characteristics of an Effective Service Guarantee

Source: C. W. L. Hart, "The Power of Unconditional Guarantees," *Harvard Business Review,* July–August 1988, pp. 54–62.

Unconditional

- The guarantee should make its promise unconditionally—no strings attached.

Meaningful

- It should guarantee elements of the service that are important to the customer.
- The payout should cover fully the customer's dissatisfaction.

Easy to understand and communicate

- Customers need to understand what to expect.
- Employees need to understand what to do.

Easy to invoke and collect

- There should not be a lot of hoops or red tape in the way of accessing or collecting on the guarantee.

guarantees are shown in Figure 7.7. The guarantee should be unconditional—no strings attached. Some guarantees can appear as if they were written by the legal department (and often are), with all kinds of restrictions, proof required, and limitations. These are generally not effective. The guarantee should be meaningful. Guaranteeing what is obvious or expected is not meaningful to customers. For example, a water delivery company offered a guarantee to deliver water on the day promised, or a free jug of water would be provided next time. In that industry, delivery on the day scheduled was an expectation nearly always met by every competitor—thus the guarantee was not meaningful to the customer. It was a bit like guaranteeing four wheels on an automobile! The payout should also be meaningful. Customers expect to be reimbursed in a manner that fully compensates them for their dissatisfaction, their time, and even for the hassle involved. The guarantee should also be easy to understand and communicate to both customers and employees. Sometimes the wording is confusing, the guarantee language is verbose, or there are so many restrictions and conditions that neither customers or employees are certain what is being guaranteed. Similarly, the guarantee should be easy to invoke and easy to collect on. Requiring customers to write a letter and/or provide documented proof of service failure are common pitfalls that make invoking the guarantee time-consuming and not worth it to the customer, particularly if the dollar value of the service is relatively low.

When to Use (or Not Use) a Guarantee

As noted earlier, guarantees are not always appropriate. Before putting a guarantee strategy in place, a number of important questions should be addressed, as suggested in Figure 7.8. A guarantee is probably *not* the right strategy when

- *Existing service quality in the company is poor.* Before instituting a guarantee, the company should fix any significant quality problems. While a guarantee will certainly draw attention to these failures and the poor quality, the costs of implementing the guarantee could easily outweigh any benefits. These costs include actually monetary payouts to customers for poor service as well as costs associated with customer goodwill.

- *A guarantee doesn't fit the company's image.* If the company already has a reputation for very high quality, and in fact implicitly guarantees its service, then a formal guarantee is most likely unnecessary. For example, if the Four Seasons Hotel were to offer an explicit guarantee, it could potentially confuse customers who already expect the highest of quality, implicitly guaranteed, from this high-end hotel

FIGURE 7.8
Questions to Consider in Implementing a Service Guarantee

Source: A. L. Ostrom and C. W. L. Hart, "Service Guarantees: Research and Practice," in *Handbook of Services Marketing and Management,* ed. D. Iacobucci and T. Swartz (Thousand Oaks, CA: Sage Publications, 2000). © 2000 by Sage Publications. Reprinted by permission of Sage Publications.

Deciding who decides

- Is there a guarantee champion in the company?
- Is senior management committed to a guarantee?
- Is the guarantee design a team effort?
- Are customers providing input?

When does a guarantee make sense?

- How high are quality standards?
- Can we afford a guarantee?
- How high is customer risk?
- Are competitors offering a guarantee?
- Is the company's culture compatible with a guarantee?

What type of guarantee should we offer?

- Should we offer an unconditional guarantee or a specific-outcome one?
- Is our service measurable?
- What should our specific guarantee be about?
- What are the uncontrollables?
- Is the company particularly susceptible to unreasonable triggerings?
- What should the payout be?
- Will a refund send the wrong message?
- Could a full refund make customers feel guilty?
- Is the guarantee easy to invoke?

chain. Research suggests that the benefits of offering a guarantee for a high-end hotel like the Four Seasons or the Ritz-Carlton may be significantly less than the benefits that a hotel of lesser quality would enjoy, and in fact the benefits might not be justified by the costs.[43]

- *Service quality is truly uncontrollable.* This is often an excuse for not employing a guarantee, but there are few situations where service quality is truly uncontrollable. However, a couple of examples may illustrate situations where this is the case. It would not be a good practice for a training organization to guarantee that all participants would pass a particular certification exam on completion of the training course if passing depends too much on the participants' own effort. The company could, however, guarantee satisfaction with the training or particular aspects of the training process. Similarly, an airline flying out of Chicago in the winter would probably not guarantee on-time departure, due to the unpredictability and uncontrollability of the weather.

- *Costs of the guarantee outweigh the benefits.* As with any quality investment, the company will want to carefully calculate expected costs (payouts for failures and costs of making improvements) against anticipated benefits (customer loyalty, quality improvements, attraction of new customers, word-of-mouth advertising).

- *Customers perceive little risk in the service.* Guarantees are usually most effective when customers are uncertain about the company and/or the quality of its services. The guarantee can allay uncertainties and help to reduce risk.[44] If customers perceive little risk, if the service is relatively inexpensive with lots of potential alternative providers, and if quality is relatively invariable, then a guarantee will likely produce little effectiveness for the company, other than perhaps some promotional value.

- *There is little perceived variability in service quality among competitors.* In some industries there is extreme variability in quality among competitors. In these cases a guarantee may be quite effective, particularly for the first company to offer one. This is also true in industries where quality is perceived to be low overall, across competitors. The first with a guarantee can often distinguish itself from competitors. In a study of guarantees offered by several service firms in Singapore, it was found that companies that were the only competitor offering a guarantee in their industry attributed more of their success to the guarantee than did companies in industries where guarantees were more common.[45]

Summary

Part 2 of this text (Chapters 5, 6, and 7) focused on the critical importance of understanding customer expectations, as well as many of the strategies firms use to accomplish this. Part of understanding customer expectations is being prepared for and knowing what to do when things go wrong or when the service fails. In this chapter we focused on service recovery, the actions taken by an organization in response to a service failure.

You learned in this chapter the importance of an effective service recovery strategy for retaining customers and increasing positive word of mouth. Another major benefit of an effective service recovery strategy is the information it provides that can be useful for service improvement. The potential downsides of poor service recovery are tremendous—negative word of mouth, lost customers, and declining business when quality issues are not addressed.

In this chapter you learned how customers respond to service failures and why some complain while others do not. You learned that customers expect to be treated fairly when they complain—not just in terms of the actual outcome or compensation they receive, but also in terms of the procedures that are used and how they are treated interpersonally. It is also clear from the chapter that there is tremendous room for improvement in service recovery effectiveness across firms and industries.

The second half of the chapter focused on specific strategies that firms are using for service recovery: (1) fail-safing the service or doing it right the first time, (2) welcoming and encouraging complaints, (3) acting quickly, (4) treating customers fairly, (5) learning from recovery experiences, and (6) learning from lost customers. The chapter ended with a discussion of service guarantees as a tool used by many firms as a foundation for service recovery. The benefits of service guarantees, the elements of a good guarantee, and the pros and cons of using guarantees under various circumstances were presented.

Discussion Questions

1. Why is it important for a service firm to have a strong recovery strategy? Think of a time when you received less-than-desirable service from a particular service organization. Was any effort made to recover? What should/could have been done differently? Do you still buy services from the organization? Why or why not? Did you tell others about your experience?

2. Discuss the benefits to a company of having an effective service recovery strategy. Describe an instance where you experienced (or delivered as an employee) an effective service recovery. In what ways did the company benefit in this particular situation?

3. Explain the "recovery paradox," and discuss the implications for a service firm manager.

4. Discuss the types of actions customers can take in response to a service failure. What type of complainer are you? Why? As a manager, how could you encourage your customers to be "voicers"? Would you want to do this?

5. Review Exhibit 7.1. What would you have done if you were on Starbucks' management team?

6. Explain the logic behind these two quotes: "a complaint is a gift" and "the customer who complains is your friend."

7. Choose a firm you are familiar with. Describe how you would design an ideal service recovery strategy for that organization.

8. What are the benefits to the company of an effective service guarantee? Should every service organization have one?

9. Describe three service guarantees that are currently offered by companies or organizations in addition to the ones already described in the chapter. Are these good or poor guarantees based on the criteria presented in this chapter?

Exercises

1. Write a letter of complaint to a service organization (or voice your complaint in person) where you have experienced less-than-desirable service. What do you expect the organization to do to recover? (Later, report to the class the results of your complaint, whether you were satisfied with the recovery, what could/should have been done differently, and whether you will continue using the service.)

2. Choose a service you are familiar with. Explain the service offered and develop a good service guarantee for it. Discuss why your guarantee is a good one, and the benefits to the company of implementing it.

3. Reread the Technology Spotlight in this chapter featuring Cisco Systems. Visit Cisco System's website (www.cisco.com). Review what it is currently doing to help its customers solve their own problems. Compare what Cisco is doing with the self-service efforts to another service provider of your choice.

4. Interview five people about their service recovery experiences. What happened, and what did they expect the firm to do? Were they treated fairly based on the definition of recovery fairness presented in the chapter? Will they return to the company in the future?

5. Interview a manager about service recovery strategies used in his/her firm. Use the strategies shown in Figure 7.5 to frame your questions.

Notes

1. J. Schwartz, "Up from the Ashes, One Firm Rebuilds," *The New York Times,* September 16, 2001, section 3, p. 1. For a follow-up story see John Schwartz, "Rebuilding a Day at a Time; Law Firm Pushes Two Steps Forward for Every Step Back," *The New York Times,* December 14, 2001, p. C1.

2. "Our Test," a personal account of the events surrounding September 11, 2001, by Thomas Cole, chairman of the executive committee of Sidley Austin Brown & Wood, at www.sidley.com, news and events.

3. Sidley Austin Brown & Wood website; www.sidley.com

4. For research that shows different types of service failures, see M. J. Bitner, B. H. Booms, and M. S. Tetreault, "The Service Encounter: Diagnosing Favorable and

Unfavorable Incidents," *Journal of Marketing* 54 (January 1990), pp. 71–84; and S. M. Keaveney, "Customer Switching Behavior in Service Industries: An Exploratory Study," *Journal of Marketing* 59 (April 1995), pp. 71–82.

5. For research on important outcomes associated with service recovery, see S. S. Tax, S. W. Brown, and M. Chandrashekaran, "Customer Evaluations of Service Complaint Experiences: Implications for Relationship Marketing," *Journal of Marketing* 62 (April 1998), pp. 60–76; S. S. Tax and S. W. Brown, "Recovering and Learning from Service Failure," *Sloan Management Review,* Fall 1998, pp. 75–88; A. K. Smith and R. N. Bolton, "An Experimental Investigation of Customer Reactions to Service Failure and Recovery Encounters," *Journal of Service Research* 1 (August 1998), pp. 65–81; S. W. Kelley, K. D. Hoffman, and M. A. Davis, "A Typology of Retail Failures and Recoveries," *Journal of Retailing* 69 (Winter 1993), pp. 429–52; R. N. Bolton, "A Dynamic Model of the Customer's Relationship with a Continuous Service Provider: The Role of Satisfaction," *Marketing Science* 17, no. 1 (1998), pp. 45–65; A. K. Smith and R. N. Bolton, "The Effect of Customers' Emotional Responses to Service Failures on Their Recovery Effort Evaluations and Satisfaction Judgments," *Journal of the Academy of Marketing Science,* 30, no. 1 (Winter 2002), pp. 5–23.

6. Technical Assistance Research Program, "Consumer Complaint Handling in America: An Update Study" (Washington, DC: Department of Consumer Affairs, 1986).

7. D. Sarel and H. Marmorstein, "The Role of Service Recovery in HMO Satisfaction," *Marketing Healthcare Services* 19:1 (Spring 1999), pp. 6–12.

8. B. Ettorre, "Phenomenal Promises That Mean Business," *Management Review,* March 1994, pp. 18–23.

9. Tax and Brown, "Recovering and Learning from Service Failure."

10. See C. W. Hart, J. L. Heskett, and W. E. Sasser, Jr., "The Profitable Art of Service Recovery," *Harvard Business Review* 68 (July–August 1990), pp. 148–56; M. A. McCollough and S. G. Bharadwaj, "The Recovery Paradox: An Examination of Consumer Satisfaction in Relation to Disconfirmation, Service Quality, and Attribution Based Theories," in *Marketing Theory and Applications,* ed. C. T. Allen et al. (Chicago: American Marketing Association, 1992), p. 119.

11. A. K. Smith and R. N. Bolton, "An Experimental Investigation of Customer Reactions to Service Failure and Recovery Encounters, Paradox or Peril?" *Journal of Service Research* 1, no. 1 (August 1998), pp. 65–81.

12. M. A. McCullough, L. L. Berry, and M. S. Yadav, "An Empirical Investigation of Customer Satisfaction after Service Failure and Recovery," *Journal of Service Research,* 3, no. 2 (November 2000), pp. 121–37.

13. For research foundations on typologies of customer responses to failures, see R. L. Day and E. L. Landon, Jr., "Towards a Theory of Consumer Complaining Behavior," in *Consumer and Industrial Buying Behavior,* ed. A. Woodside, J. Sheth, and P. Bennett (Amsterdam: North-Holland Publishing Company, 1977); J. Singh, "Consumer Complaint Intentions and Behavior: Definitional and Taxonomical Issues," *Journal of Marketing* 52 (January 1988), pp. 93–107; and J. Singh, "Voice, Exit, and Negative Word-of-Mouth Behaviors: An Investigation across Three Service Categories," *Journal of the Academy of Marketing Science* 18, no. 1 (Winter 1990), pp. 1–15.

14. Smith and Bolton, "The Effect of Customers' Emotional Responses to Service Failures."

15. Ibid.
16. J. Singh, " A Typology of Consumer Dissatisfaction Response Styles," *Journal of Retailing* 66, no. 1 (Spring 1990), pp. 57–99.
17. N. Stephens and K. P. Gwinner, "Why Don't Some People Complain? A Cognitive–Emotive Process Model of Consumer Complaining Behavior," *Journal of the Academy of Marketing Science* 26, no. 3 (1998), pp. 172–89.
18. Ibid.
19. See Tax, Brown, and Chandrashekaran, "Customer Evaluations of Service Complaint Experiences"; Tax and Brown, "Recovering and Learning from Service Failure."
20. Ibid.
21. McCullough et al., "An Empirical Investigation of Customer Satisfaction after Service Failure and Recovery."
22. A. S. Mattila, "The Impact of Relationship Type on Customer Loyalty in a Context of Service Failures," *Journal of Service Research,* 4, no. 2 (November 2001), pp. 91–101.
23. H. S. Bansal and S. F. Taylor, "The Service Provider Switching Model (SPSM)," *Journal of Service Research,* 2, no. 2 (November 1999), pp. 200–18.
24. S. M. Keaveney and M. Parthasarathy, "Customer Switching Behavior in Online Services: An Exploratory Study of the Role of Selected Attitudinal, Behavioral, and Demographic Factors," *Journal of the Academy of Marketing Science,* vol. 29, no. 4 (2001), pp. 374–90.
25. I. Roos, "Switching Processes in Customer Relationships," *Journal of Service Research,* 2, no. 1 (August 1999), pp. 68–85.
26. A. Parasuraman, V. A. Zeithaml, and L. L. Berry, "SERVQUAL: A Multiple-Item Scale for Measuring Consumer Perceptions of Service Quality," *Journal of Retailing* 64 (Spring 1988), pp. 64–79.
27. R. B. Chase and D. M. Stewart, "Make Your Service Fail-Safe," *Sloan Management Review,* Spring 1994, pp. 35–44.
28. Ibid.
29. F. R. Reichheld and W. E. Sasser, Jr., "Zero Defections: Quality Comes to Services," *Harvard Business Review,* September–October 1990, pp. 105–7.
30. L. M. Fisher, "Here Comes Front-Office Automation," *Strategy and Business* 13 (Fourth Quarter, 1999), pp. 53–65; and R. A. Shaffer, "Handling Customer Service on the Web," *Fortune,* March 1, 1999, pp. 204, 208.
31. S. W. Brown, "Service Recovery through IT," *Marketing Management,* Fall 1997, pp. 25–27.
32. Hart, Heskett, and Sasser, 1990.
33. L. L. Berry and A. Parasuraman, *Marketing Services* (New York: Free Press, 1991), p. 52.
34. F. F. Reichheld, "Learning from Customer Defections," *Harvard Business Review,* March–April 1996, pp. 56–69.
35. Ibid.
36. Keaveney, "Customer Switching Behavior in Service Industries."
37. A. L. Ostrom and C. W. L. Hart, "Service Guarantees: Research and Practice," in *Handbook of Services Marketing and Management,* ed. D. Iacobucci and T. Swartz (Thousand Oaks, CA: Sage Publications, 2000), pp. 299–316.
38. See ibid.; C. W. L. Hart, "The Power of Unconditional Guarantees," *Harvard Business Review,* July–August 1988, pp. 54–62; and C. W. L. Hart, *Extraordinary Guarantees* (New York: AMACOM, 1993).

39. A. L. Ostrom and D. Iacobucci, "The Effect of Guarantees on Consumers' Evaluation of Services," *Journal of Services Marketing* 12, no. 5 (1998), pp. 362–78.
40. Ostrom and Hart, "Service Guarantees."
41. J. Wirtz and D. Kum, "Designing Service Guarantees—Is Full Satisfaction the Best You Can Guarantee?" *Journal of Services Marketing,* 15, no. 4 (2001), pp. 282–99.
42. Example cited in Ostrom and Hart, "Service Guarantees."
43. J. Wirtz, D. Kum, and K. S. Lee, "Should a Firm with a Reputation for Outstanding Service Quality Offer a Service Guarantee?" *Journal of Services Marketing,* 14, no. 6 (2000), pp. 502–12.
44. Ostrom and Iacobucci, "The Effect of Guarantees."
45. J. Wirtz, "Development of a Service Guarantee Model," *Asia-Pacific Journal of Management* 15 (1998), pp. 51–75.

ALIGNING STRATEGY, SERVICE DESIGN, AND STANDARDS

Accurate perceptions of customers' expectations are necessary, but not sufficient, for delivering superior quality service. Another prerequisite is the presence of service designs and performance standards that reflect those accurate perceptions. A recurring theme in service companies is the difficulty executives, managers, and other policy setters experience in translating their understanding of customers' expectations into service quality specifications that employees can understand and execute.

Provider Gap 2

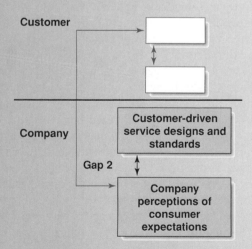

Provider gap 2 is the difference between company understanding of customer expectations and development of customer-driven designs and standards (see the accompanying figure). Provider gap 2 exists in service organizations for a variety of reasons. Those responsible for setting standards, typically management, sometimes believe that customer expectations are unreasonable or unrealistic. They may also believe that the degree of variability inherent in service defies standardization; therefore, creating designs and setting standards will not achieve the desired goal of meeting customer expectations. Further, they may contend that the demand for service is too hard to predict or that the way the company and its personnel operate cannot be changed. Although some of these assumptions are valid in some situations, they are often only rationalizations of management's reluctance to tackle head-on the difficult challenges of creating service designs and setting service standards to deliver excellent service.

Because services are intangible, they are difficult to describe and communicate. This is particularly true when new services are being developed. It is critical that all people involved (managers, front-line employees, and behind-the-scenes support staff) be working with the same concepts of the new service based on customer needs and expectations. For a service that already exists, any attempt to improve it will also suffer unless everyone has the same vision of the service and associated issues. One of the most important ways to avoid gap 2 is to clearly design services without oversimplification, incompleteness, subjectivity, and bias. To do this, tools are needed to ensure that new and existing services are developed and improved in as careful a manner as possible. Chapter 8 in this section describes the tools that are most effective in service development and design.

The quality of service delivered by customer contact personnel is critically influenced by the standards against which they are evaluated and compensated. Standards signal to contact personnel what management priorities are and which types of performance really count. When service standards are absent or when the standards in place do not reflect customers' expectations, quality of service as perceived by customers is likely to suffer. *Customer-defined standards* are different from the conventional performance standards that most services companies establish (called *company-defined standards*) in that they are based on pivotal customer requirements that are visible to and measured by customers. They are operations standards set to correspond to customer expectations and priorities rather than to company concerns such as productivity and efficiency. When standards reflect what customers expect, the quality of service they receive is likely to be enhanced. Chapter 9 deals with customer-defined service standards that, if developed appropriately, have a powerful positive impact on closing both provider gap 2 and the customer gap.

Because services are intangible, physical evidence—the tangibles surrounding the service—take on critical importance in service design. In Chapter 10 we focus on the roles of physical evidence in service design and in meeting customer expectations. By *physical evidence* we mean everything from business cards to reports, signage, Internet presence, equipment, and facilities used to deliver the service. The *servicescape,* the physical setting where the service is delivered, is a particular focus of this chapter. Think of a restaurant, a hotel, a theme park, a health club, a hospital, or a school. The servicescape—the physical facility—is critical in these industries in terms of communicating about the service and making the entire experience pleasurable. In these cases the servicescape plays a variety of roles from serving as a "visual metaphor" for what the company stands for to actually facilitating the activities of both consumers and employees. In Chapter 10 we explore the importance of physical evidence, the variety of roles it plays, and strategies for effectively designing physical evidence and the servicescape to meet customer expectations.

In Part 3 you learn to develop effective strategies for new services and to use service blueprinting as an implementation tool (Chapter 8), to develop customer-defined (as opposed to company-defined) service standards (Chapter 9), and to effectively design physical evidence and the servicescape to meet customer expectations (Chapter 10). Through these strategies, provider gap 2—the service design and standards gap—will be minimized.

Chapter 8

SERVICE DEVELOPMENT AND DESIGN

This chapter's objectives are to

1. Describe the challenges inherent in service design.

2. Present steps in the new-service development process.

3. Show the value of service blueprinting and quality function deployment (QFD) in new service design and service improvement.

4. Present lessons learned in choosing and implementing high-performance service innovations.

Innovative New Services at Wells Fargo Bank

Have you ever considered starting your own service business? What type of service would it be? What would you do first? Assuming you understood your market and had a good feel for potential customers' needs and expectations, how would you go about designing the service to meet those needs? If you were starting a business to manufacture a new product, you would most likely begin by designing and building a prototype of your new product. But how could you do this for a service?

These are the types of questions Wells Fargo Bank, fifth largest bank holding company in the United States, asks when it introduces new services to the marketplace. Wells Fargo is recognized as the industry leader in the United States for alternative delivery strategies of banking services. As such, it constantly introduces new services that allow customers to reach the bank when and where they want to—meeting expectations for speed and accessibility. Its strategy depends on a range of services from a vast automated teller machine (ATM) system (one of its ATMs was installed in Antarctica in 1998) to providing extensive banking services in supermarkets to highly accessible phone banking systems and call centers to online, Internet-based services. Wells was the first U.S. bank to offer online services (in 1989) and Internet banking (1995). Wireless banking was introduced in 2001. Wells has over 3 million Internet banking customers and leads U.S. banks in market share for Internet banking. To succeed in these pioneering efforts, Wells has had to anticipate its customers needs, develop effective delivery systems, and be willing to constantly change.

One of Wells's efforts involves locations equipped with only computer terminals and no human tellers, where customers who don't have their own computers can come in during extended hours to bank online and access the Internet. In 2001 the bank launched a service called "WellsFargo.com Bus" as a mobile financial education center. The service, literally housed in a bus, rolls across the western United States bringing Internet banking and online brokerage to consumers and small business customers. At each stop the bus crew demonstrates WellsFargo.com tools, calculators, and financial services using three servers, satellite-enabled Internet access, and a virtual private network. In 1998 Wells introduced WellsTrade, an online discount trading service. This service has evolved into WellsChoice online, a full-service brokerage account, combining high tech and high touch. The service is designed to combine the convenience of online trading with the guidance of a human financial consultant. In 2000 Wells had 178 Web-related projects under way in the bank, partnering with companies like eBay to develop unique services for customers.

All of these efforts and new service introductions are initiated to support the company's vision of providing "every channel our customers want, every product our customers need, anytime our customers choose." Through developing new services and being a leader in its industry, Wells has learned some important lessons. According to one of Wells's executive vice presidents, it has learned (1) the importance of having integrated marketing, sales, and support infrastructure to support the new services and (2) that nothing every happens as quickly as you'd like it too—it's hard work being the one that blazes the trail.[1]

So what causes new products and services such as those offered by Wells Fargo to fail or succeed? If you decide to start your own business, what can you do to protect yourself as much as possible from failure?

A study of 11,000 new products launched by 77 manufacturing, service, and consumer products companies found that only 56 percent of new offerings are still on the market five years later.[2] Failures can be traced to a number of causes: no unique benefits offered, insufficient demand, unrealistic goals for the new product/service, poor fit between the new service and others within the organization's portfolio, poor location, insufficient financial backing, or failure to take the necessary time to develop and introduce the product.[3] An analysis of over 60 studies on new product and service success showed that the dominant and most reliable predictors of success for new introductions relate to *product/service characteristics* (product meeting customer needs, product advantage over competing products, technological sophistication); *strategy characteristics* (dedicated human resources to support the initiative, dedicated R&D focused on the new product initiative), *process characteristics* (marketing, predevelopment, technological and launch proficiencies); and *marketplace characteristics* (market potential).[4]

Frequently a good service idea fails due to development, design, and specification flaws, as emphasized in this chapter.

CHALLENGES OF SERVICE DESIGN

Because services are intangible, such as a hospital stay, a golf lesson, or an NBA basketball game, they are difficult to describe and communicate. When services are delivered over a long period—a week's resort vacation, a six-month consulting engage-

FIGURE 8.1
Risks of Relying on Words Alone to Describe Services

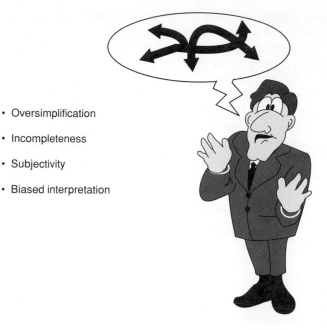

- Oversimplification

- Incompleteness

- Subjectivity

- Biased interpretation

ment, 10 weeks on a Weight Watchers program—their complexity increases, and they become even more difficult to define and describe. Further, because services are delivered by employees to customers, they are heterogeneous: rarely are two services alike or experienced in the same way. These characteristics of services, which we explored in the first chapter of this book, are the heart of the challenge involved in designing services.

Because services cannot be touched, examined, or tried out, people frequently resort to words in their efforts to describe them. Lynn Shostack, a pioneer in developing design concepts for services, has pointed out four risks of attempting to describe services in words alone, as illustrated in Figure 8.1.[5] The first risk is *oversimplification.* Shostack points out that "to say that 'portfolio management' means 'buying and selling stocks' is like describing the space shuttle as 'something that flies.' Some people will picture a bird, some a helicopter, and some an angel" (p. 76). Words are simply inadequate to describe a whole complex service system.

The second risk is *incompleteness.* In describing services, people (employees, managers, customers) tend to omit details or elements of the service with which they are not familiar. A person might do a fairly credible job of describing how a discount stock brokerage service takes orders from customers. But would that person be able to describe fully how the monthly statements are created, how the interactive computer system works, and how these two elements of the service are integrated into the order-taking process?

The third risk is *subjectivity.* Any one person describing a service in words will be biased by personal experiences and degree of exposure to the service. There is a natural (and mistaken) tendency to assume that because all people have gone to a fast-food restaurant, they all understand what that service is. Persons working in different functional areas of the same service organization (a marketing person, an operations person, a finance person) are likely to describe the service very differently as well, biased by their own functional blinders.

A final risk of describing services using words alone is *biased interpretation.* No two people will define "responsive," "quick," or "flexible" in exactly the same way. For example, a supervisor or manager may suggest to a front-line service employee that the employee should try to be more flexible or responsive in providing service to the customer. Unless flexibility is further defined, the employee is likely to interpret the word differently from the manager.

All of these risks become very apparent in the new service development process, when organizations may be attempting to design services never before experienced by customers. It is critical that all involved (managers, front-line employees, and behind-the-scenes support staff) be working with the same concepts of the new service, based on customer needs and expectations. For a service that already exists, any attempt to improve it will also suffer unless everyone has a shared vision of the service and associated issues.

In the following sections of this chapter we present approaches for new service development and design to address these unique challenges.

NEW SERVICE DEVELOPMENT

Research suggests that products that are designed and introduced via the steps in a structured planning framework have a greater likelihood of ultimate success than those not developed within a framework.[6] The fact that services are intangible makes it even more imperative for a new service development system to have four basic characteristics. (1) It must be objective, not subjective. (2) It must be precise, not vague. (3) It must be fact driven, not opinion driven. (4) It must be methodological, not philosophical.[7]

Often new services are introduced on the basis of managers' and employees' subjective opinions about what the services should be and whether they will succeed, rather than on objective designs incorporating data about customer perceptions, market needs, and feasibility. A new service design process may be imprecise in defining the nature of the service concept because the people involved believe either that intangible processes cannot be defined precisely or that "everyone knows what we mean." Neither of these explanations or defenses for imprecision is justifiable, as we illustrate in the model for new service development described in this chapter.

Because services are produced and consumed simultaneously and often involve interaction between employees and customers, it is also critical that the new service development process involve both employees and customers. Employees frequently *are* the service, or at least they perform or deliver the service, and thus their involvement in choosing which new services to develop and how these services should be designed and implemented can be very beneficial. Contact employees are psychologically and physically close to customers and can be very helpful in identifying customer needs for which new services can be offered. Involving employees in the design and development process also increases the likelihood of new service success because employees can identify the organizational issues that need to be addressed to support the delivery of the service to customers.[8] For example, at Metropolitan Life Insurance Co., cross-functional teams comprising representatives from administration, claims, marketing, and information systems are included to ensure that all aspects of the service and delivery process are considered before full-scale development of a new insurance service concept begins.

Because customers often actively participate in service delivery, they too should be involved in the new service development process. Beyond just providing input on their own needs, customers can help design the service concept and the delivery process, particularly in cases where the customer personally carries out part of the service process.

Marriott Corporation is well known for involving its guests in the design of its hotel rooms to ensure that the features and placement of furnishings in the rooms will work for the guests and not just for the staff or the architects who design the rooms.

TYPES OF NEW SERVICES

As we build the new service development process, remember that not all new services are "new" to the same degree. The types of new service options can run the gamut from major innovations to minor style changes:[9]

- *Major innovations* are new services for markets as yet undefined. Past examples include the first broadcast television services and Federal Express's introduction of nationwide, overnight small package delivery. Many innovations now and in the future will evolve from information, computer, and Internet-based technologies. Examples are highlighted in this chapter's Technology Spotlight.

- *Start-up businesses* consist of new services for a market that is already served by existing products that meet the same generic needs. Service examples include the creation of health maintenance organizations to provide an alternative form of health care delivery, online banking for financial transactions, and door-to-door airport shuttle services that compete with traditional taxi and limousine services.

- *New services for the currently served market* represent attempts to offer existing customers of the organization a service not previously available from the company (although it may be available from other companies). Examples include Barnes and Noble offering coffee service, a health club offering nutrition classes, and airlines offering fax, phone, and Internet service during flights.

- *Service line extensions* represent augmentations of the existing service line, such as a restaurant adding new menu items, an airline offering new routes, a law firm offering additional legal services, and a university adding new courses or degrees.

- *Service improvements* represent perhaps the most common type of service innovation. Changes in features of services that are already offered might involve faster execution of an existing service process, extended hours of service, or augmentations such as added amenities in a hotel room.

- *Style changes* represent the most modest service innovations, although they are often highly visible and can have significant effects on customer perceptions, emotions, and attitudes. Changing the color scheme of a restaurant, revising the logo for an organization, website redesign, or painting aircraft a different color all represent style changes. These do not fundamentally change the service, only its appearance, similar to how packaging changes are used for consumer products.

SERVICE REDESIGN

Instead of jettisoning outdated or declining services in favor of new service innovations, many firms have discovered that redesigning existing services is another viable approach to service development and growth. Based on their extensive research, Len Berry and Sandra Lampo have suggested five types of service redesign as potential ways of increasing customer benefits or reducing customers' costs.[10]

Technology Spotlight
Technology Makes New Service Offerings Possible

TECHNOLOGY MAKES NEW SERVICES POSSIBLE FOR OFFICE DEPOT AND ERNST & YOUNG

Technology is driving revolutionary changes in the types of services offered in almost every industry. Let's look at two examples in very different contexts: Office Depot's business sales and service, and Ernst & Young's online consulting services.

Business-to-Business Services at Office Depot

Office Depot is the biggest online retailer after amazon.com, booking $982 million in sales in 2000 through an online network for its business customers. According to Office Depot, its online unit is profitable. The company sells everything from paper clips and writing supplies to office furnishings and computer accessories. Office Depot is a bricks and mortar business-to-business retailer that has expanded into online sales and related services for its customers. What is so special about this service, and how did it develop and evolve?

First, unlike those of its competitors, Office Depot's online operations are woven into its existing businesses rather than operating independently of its stores. The online systems have been incorporated as essential components of the company's supply chain. They use a seamless network to track inventory and sales whether the customer buys online, in the store, or from a catalog. A new wireless service also allows customers to access the company anywhere, anytime.

A second element of success comes from listening to customers who tell them that they care more about ease of use than about hot new technologies. The desire to grow by meeting customers' service needs has resulted in Office Depot expanding into new areas—including accounting and payroll for small and midsize businesses, and partnerships with Stamps.com, Intuit, and Schedule Online to provide its 13 million small business customers with additional services.

Technology has allowed Office Depot to increase revenues and grow through new services at a time when its in-store sales are suffering.

Online Consulting at Ernst & Young

In another industry advances in technology are again making dramatically new services possible. The management consulting industry where Ernst & Young operates is traditionally highly labor-intensive, people-to-people, and customized in its service offerings. Further, the offerings tend to be highly intangible, and capacity of consulting companies is historically limited by the human resources they employ. Taking advantage of advances in information technology, Ernst & Young launched the first-ever online consulting service, "Ernie," in 1996. Goals with Ernie were to expand Ernst & Young's capacity, to make the expertise of its consultants available to a wider audience, and to make its information databases and internal expertise easily and quickly accessible to senior executives. When Ernst & Young split its tax and auditing business from its consulting arm in 2000, Ernie evolved into E&Y's current offering, "Ernst&Young Online" (EYO). Through EYO, offered via the Internet, E&Y's tax and audit clients can easily connect to the organization's resources and the expertise of its consultants. Through "Ask Ernst & Young," clients can ask direct questions of subject matter specialists who can be located in any part of the world. Customized answers are routed back to the client within a guaranteed time frame. Another EYO service is the Team Room, where clients and their colleagues can work closely with Ernst & Young professionals to share ideas and knowledge in real time. Beyond these services, EYO also offers a host of online "toolkits" for various tax and audit specialty areas and also provides up-to-date news and information on evolving business issues. E & Y's online services were truly revolutionary in the management consulting arena, and Ernst & Young has been a leader in this industry.

Sources: C. Haddad, "Office Depot's E-Diva," *Business Week, e.biz,* August 6, 2001, pp. EB22–24; Information Technology Services Marketing Association (ITSMA), Best Practice Case Study, "Ernst & Young LLP: The Evolution of a Revolutionary Idea," 1998; www.ey.com, 2002.

Self-service. One approach to redesign is to move the customer into a production mode rather than a passive, receiving mode. Redesigning the service process in this way increases benefits for the customer in terms of personal control, accessibility, and timing. Prime examples of self-service occur when companies offer their services via the Internet, as in the case of Internet banking in our opening vignette.

Direct service. Direct service means bringing the service to the customer rather than asking the customer to come to the provider. This might mean delivering the service to the customer in his or her home or workplace. Restaurant food and dry cleaning delivery to the office, pet grooming in the home, auto repair in one's driveway, and computer distance education and training services are examples of firms bringing services directly to their customers rather than customers traveling to the service provider.

Pre service. This type of redesign involves streamlining or improving the activation of the service, focusing on the front-end processes. Express check-in at a hotel or car rental, preadmission processing at a hospital, and prepayment of tolls on highways are examples. Making the front end of the service more efficient can dramatically change the customer experience during actual service delivery.

Bundled service. Grouping, or bundling, multiple services together is another way to redesign current offerings. The benefit to customers is in receiving greater value, combined with convenience, than they might have received by purchasing each service independently. Charles Schwab is a master at this approach, bundling different types of trading-related services for designated market segments.

Physical service. Physical redesign involves changing the customer's experience through the tangibles associated with the service or the physical surroundings of the service. Midway Express Airlines has changed the entire airline flight experience primarily through redesigning the interior of its airplanes. Leather seats, two-by-two seating, china plates, and cloth napkins are all ways of creating a new experience through tangibles and servicescape redesign.

STAGES IN NEW SERVICE DEVELOPMENT

Here we focus on the actual steps to be followed in new service development. The steps can be applied to any of the types of new services or service redesign efforts just described. Much of what is presented in this section has direct parallels in the new product development process for manufactured goods.[11] Because of the inherent characteristics of services, however, the development process for new services requires adaptations.[12] Figure 8.2 shows the basic principles and steps in new service development. Although these may be similar to those for manufactured goods, their implementation is significantly different.[13] In addition, for many service industries (like telecommunications, transportation, utilities, and banking), government agencies that regulate the industries greatly influence the nature and speed of new service development.

An underlying assumption of new product development process models is that new product ideas can be dropped at any stage of the process if they do not satisfy the criteria for success at that particular stage.[14] Figure 8.2 shows the checkpoints (represented by stop signs) that precede critical stages of the development process. The checkpoints specify requirements that a new service must meet before it can proceed to the next stage of development.

New service or product development is rarely a completely linear process. Many companies are finding that to speed up new service development, some steps can be

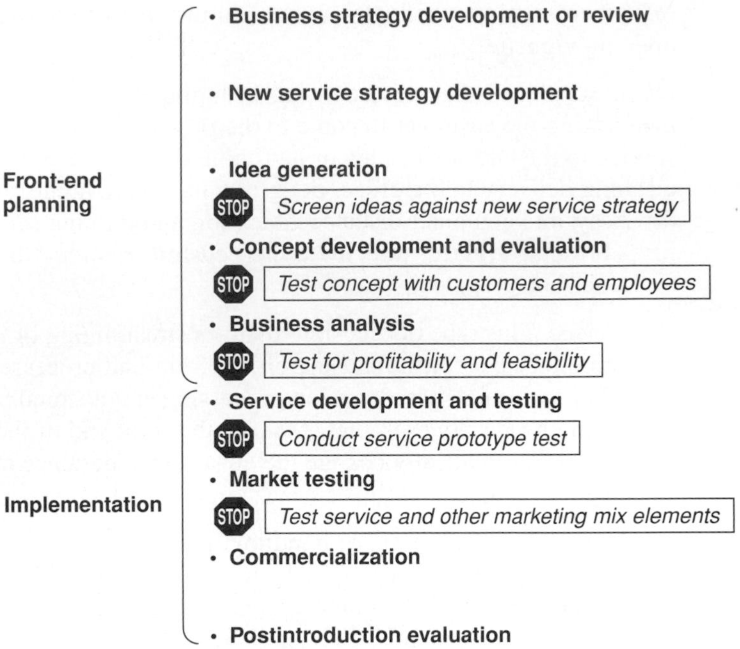

FIGURE 8.2
New Service
Development Process

Sources: Booz-Allen &
Hamilton, *New Product
Management for the 1980s*
(New York: Booz-Allen &
Hamilton, 1982); M. J. Bowers,
"An Exploration into New
Service Development:
Organization, Process and
Structure," doctoral
dissertation, Texas A&M
University, 1985; A. Khurana
and S. R. Rosenthal,
"Integrating the Fuzzy Front
End of New Product
Development," *Sloan
Management Review,* Winter
1997, pp. 103–20; and R. G.
Cooper, *Winning at New
Products,* 3rd ed. (Cambridge,
MA: Perseus Publishing, 2001).

Front-end planning

- Business strategy development or review
- New service strategy development
- Idea generation
  - [STOP] Screen ideas against new service strategy
- Concept development and evaluation
  - [STOP] Test concept with customers and employees
- Business analysis
  - [STOP] Test for profitability and feasibility

Implementation

- Service development and testing
  - [STOP] Conduct service prototype test
- Market testing
  - [STOP] Test service and other marketing mix elements
- Commercialization
- Postintroduction evaluation

worked on simultaneously, and in some instances a step may even be skipped. The overlapping of steps and simultaneous development of various pieces of the new service/product development process has been referred to as "flexible product development." This type of flexible, speedy process is particularly important in technology industries, where products and services evolve extremely quickly. In these environments, computer technology lets companies monitor customer opinions and needs during development and change the final offering right up until it is launched. In these cases the next version of the service is often in planning stages at the same time the current version is being launched.[15] Even if the stages are handled simultaneously, however, the important checkpoints noted in Figure 8.2 must be passed along the way to maximize chances of success.

The process shown in Figure 8.2 is divided into two sections: front-end planning and implementation. The front end determines what service concepts will be developed, whereas the back end executes or implements the service concept. When asked where the greatest weaknesses in product and service innovation occur, managers typically report problems with the "fuzzy front end."[16] The front end is called "fuzzy" because of its relative abstractness, which is even more apparent with services than with manufactured products.

Front-End Planning

Business Strategy Development

It is assumed that an organization will have an overall strategic vision and mission. Clearly a first step in new service development is to review that vision and mission. If these are not clear, the overall strategic direction of the organization must be determined and agreed on. The new services strategy and specific new service ideas must fit within the larger strategic picture of the organization.

FIGURE 8.3
New Service Strategy
Matrix for
Identifying Growth
Opportunities

Offerings	Markets	
	Current Customers	New Customers
Existing Services	Share building	Market development
New Services	Service development	Diversification

New Service Strategy Development

Research suggests that without a clear new product or service strategy, a well-planned portfolio of new products and services, and an organizational structure that facilitates product development via ongoing communications and cross-functional sharing of responsibilities, front-end decisions become ineffective.[17] Thus a product portfolio strategy and a defined organizational structure for new product or service development are critical—and are the foundations—for success.

The types of new services that will be appropriate will depend on the organization's goals, vision, capabilities, and growth plans. By defining a new service strategy (possibly in terms of markets, types of services, time horizon for development, profit criteria, or other relevant factors), the organization will be in a better position to begin generating specific ideas. For example, it may focus its growth on new services at a particular level of the described continuum from major innovations to style changes. Or the organization may define its new services strategy even more specifically in terms of particular markets or market segments or in terms of specific profit generation goals.

One way to begin formulating a new service strategy is to use the framework shown in Figure 8.3 for identifying growth opportunities.[18] The framework allows an organization to identify possible directions for growth and can be helpful as a catalyst for creative ideas. The framework may also later serve as an initial idea screen if, for example, the organization chooses to focus its growth efforts on one or two of the four cells in the matrix. The matrix suggests that companies can develop a growth strategy around current customers or for new customers, and can focus on current offerings or new service offerings. Figure 8.4 illustrates how Taco Bell has grown through market development in expanding its existing service offering to new locations such as universities and airports. Exhibit 8.1 further explains how Taco Bell has pursued growth in all four areas of the matrix.

Idea Generation

The next step in the process is the formal solicitation of new ideas. The ideas generated at this phase can be passed through the new service strategy screen described in the preceding step. Many methods and avenues are available for searching out new service ideas. Formal brainstorming, solicitation of ideas from employees and customers, lead user research, and learning about competitors' offerings are some of the most common approaches. Observing customers and how they use the firm's products and services can also generate creative ideas for new innovations. Sometimes referred to

FIGURE 8.4   Taco Bell Has Grown Through Market Development on University Campuses

Source: Fritz Hoffman/Image Works/TimePix

as *empathic design,* observation is particularly effective in situations where customers may not be able to recognize or verbalize their needs.[19]

In service businesses, contact personnel, who actually deliver the services and interact directly with consumers, can be particularly good sources of ideas for complementary services to those already in the marketplace and ways to improve current offerings.

Whether the source of a new idea is inside or outside the organization, there should exist some established mechanism for ensuring an ongoing stream of new service possibilities. This mechanism might include a formal new service development department or function with responsibility for generating new ideas, suggestion boxes for employees and customers, new service development teams that meet regularly, surveys and focus groups with customers and employees, or formal competitive analysis to identify new services. Although new service ideas may arise outside the formal mechanism, total dependence on luck is not a good strategy.

In listening to their customers, many manufacturers around the world have discovered ideas for new *services,* rather than product enhancements. These new services allow the manufacturer to move in the direction of becoming a solutions provider, as is the case with Volvo Truck, discussed in our Global Feature.

Service Concept Development and Evaluation

Once an idea surfaces that is regarded as a good fit with both the basic business and the new service strategies, it is ready for initial development. In the case of a tangible

8.1 TACO BELL EXPANDS MARKETS AND OFFERINGS

To illustrate how the matrix shown in Figure 8.3 might function as a catalyst for idea generation, consider growth strategies pursued by Taco Bell, one of the world's fastest-growing fast-food chains, specializing in Mexican food.

Share Building (Current Customers, Existing Services)

Share building is another term for market penetration—gaining a greater proportion of sales from existing markets. This strategy is pursued by Taco Bell in the rapid expansion of Taco Bell outlets throughout the United States. In the late 1990s Taco Bell stepped up its efforts to gain market share among Hispanic consumers, another share-building strategy.

Market Development (New Customers, Existing Services)

Taco Bell has expanded by offering its existing services in nontraditional locations, using creative formats to reach new customers. For example, Taco Bells can now be found in airports, universities, and schools. Taco Bell has also opened Taco Bell Express units in gas stations around the United States. Often the outlets in these locations are scaled-back "express" versions of the service with a limited menu and small space requirement. Another form of market development is expansion into international markets, taking existing services to other countries.

Service Development (Current Customers, New Services)

This type of growth is possible when current customers are offered additional new services or service improvements. In Taco Bell's case, it has new menu items—for example, its Gordita beef steak and chicken wraps—improved service delivery, and lower prices to better serve its current customers.

Diversification (New Customers, New Services)

This growth option, involving new services for consumers not currently served, is frequently the most challenging because it takes the organization into unfamiliar territories on both the product and market dimensions. Taco Bell has pursued this type of growth by selling its branded products in grocery stores and by buying significant interests in other restaurant chains. Another diversification strategy involves licensing its name to Salton/Maxim Housewares, which produces kitchen products such as tortilla makers under the Taco Bell name.

Sources: "It's No Longer Just 'Fill 'Er Up,'" *Franchise Times*, August 1997, pp. 27ff; "Taco Bell's Hispanic Strategy," *Advertising Age*, October 20, 1997, p. 12; "Taco Bell Takes Wraps Off Higher-End Items," *Brandweek*, March 30, 1998, p. 5; and "Salton/Mazim's Taco Bell Tack" *HFN*, January 12, 1998, p. 102.

---

product, this would mean formulating the basic product definition and then presenting consumers with descriptions and drawings to get their reactions.

The inherent characteristics of services, particularly intangibility and simultaneous production and consumption, place complex demands on this phase of the process. Drawing pictures and describing an intangible service in concrete terms are difficult. It is therefore important that agreement be reached at this stage on exactly what the concept is. By involving multiple parties in sharpening the concept definition, it often becomes apparent that individual views of the concept are not the same. For example, in describing the design and development of a new discount brokerage service, Lynn Shostack relates that initially the bank described the concept as a way "to buy and sell stocks for customers at low prices."[20] Through the initial concept development phase it became clear that not everyone in the organization had the same idea about how this description would translate into an actual service and that there were a variety of ways the concept could be developed. Only through multiple iterations of the service—and the raising of hundreds of issues, large and small—was an agreement finally reached on the discount brokerage concept.

After clear definition of the concept, it is important to produce a description of the service that represents its specific features and characteristics and then to determine initial customer and employee responses to the concept. The service design document would

Volvo, headquartered in Sweden, is one of the world's largest producers of trucks. In fact, two-thirds of Volvo's total 2000 sales of 130 billion SEK came from its Global Trucks group. But, as with many manufacturers worldwide, Volvo is much more than an equipment company. It views itself as a total customer solution company offering a variety of services to enhance the value of its products and to provide revenue growth.

By listening to its truck fleet customers, Volvo has identified ideas for new services that can enhance the value of its trucks. The physical product, the truck, has become a component of Volvo's service concept, and the company is moving in the direction of becoming a service company instead of purely a heavy truck manufacturer.

One of Volvo's recent service offerings, Dynafleet 2.0, provides a good example of how Volvo is enhancing the value it offers to its business customers. Dynafleet 2.0 is an extensive transportation information system that Volvo can customize for its truck transportation business customers. The system is composed of three separate modules that are installed in the company's fleet of trucks to provide exact information and direct communication resulting in more efficient operations and reduced costs for the company. One of the modules is the "logger tool" that gathers information on a vehicle and its driver. Some information is stored on the driver's smart card, and some information is logged in by the driver. The second module is the "communication tool," which transmits and receives text messages and also sends out information about the vehicle's location, fuel consumption, and other details to the company's fleet office. Drivers can also communicate directly with the office or send messages to other drivers through this communication system. The third module is the "information tool," providing maps and traffic information to the driver of the vehicle via a color display.

Back in the office, the fleet manager utilizes a "logger manager" that provides reports on vehicle fuel consumption, hour-by-hour information on workday activities of each vehicle and driver, and start and stop times. This information is useful for wage calculations and keeping track of work hours. The "transport manager," used to track exactly where each vehicle is at all times, generates reports that can be used in traffic planning and other operational decisions.

This example illustrates how Volvo has expanded far beyond simply providing trucks for its business customers. Other services, such as maintenance agreements, training, and financing, further enhance Dynafleet's offering.

The services available through Dynafleet address more fully the total customer value chain, allowing Volvo to move toward its goal of being a customer solution provider rather than a truck manufacturer. The benefits accrue directly to the drivers of the trucks as well as the transportation companies that buy the trucks. Administrative work is simplified, and fleet managers and traffic planners become more efficient. Volvo aims to maintain its leadership and compete effectively through offering Dynafleet 2.0 and other services aimed at improving their customers' efficiency, service reliability, and economic returns.

Sources: "Volvo Dynafleet 2.0—Applying a Service Perspective," in B. Edvardsson, A. Gustafsson, M. D. Johnson, and B. Sanden, *New Service Development & Innovation in the New Economy* (University of Karlstad, Sweden: Service Research Center, 2001), pp. 52–55; www.volvo.com, 2002.

describe the problem addressed by the service, discuss the reasons for offering the new service, itemize the service process and its benefits, and provide a rationale for purchasing the service.[21] The roles of customers and employees in the delivery process would also be described. The new service concept would then be evaluated by asking employees and customers whether they understand the idea of the proposed service, whether they are favorable to the concept, and whether they feel it satisfies an unmet need.

Business Analysis

Assuming the service concept is favorably evaluated by customers and employees at the concept development stage, the next step is to determine its feasibility and potential profit implications. Demand analysis, revenue projections, cost analyses, and operational feasibility are assessed at this stage. Because the development of service concepts is so closely tied to the operational system of the organization, this stage will involve preliminary assumptions about the costs of hiring and training personnel, delivery system enhancements, facility changes, and any other projected operations costs.

The organization will pass the results of the business analysis through its profitability and feasibility screen to determine whether the new service idea meets the minimum requirements.

Implementation

Once the new service concept has passed all of the front-end planning hurdles, it is ready for the implementation stages of the process.

Service Development and Testing

In the development of new tangible products, this stage involves construction of product prototypes and testing for consumer acceptance. Again, because services are intangible and largely produced and consumed simultaneously, this step is difficult. To address the challenge, this stage of service development should involve all who have a stake in the new service: customers and contact employees as well as functional representatives from marketing, operations, and human resources. During this phase, the concept is refined to the point where a detailed service blueprint representing the implementation plan for the service can be produced. The blueprint is likely to evolve over a series of iterations on the basis of input from all of the parties listed. For example, when a large state hospital was planning a new computer-based information service for doctors throughout its state, it involved many groups in the service development and evaluation stage, including medical researchers, computer programmers and operators, librarians, telecommunications experts, and records clerks as well as the physician customers.[22]

A final step is for each area involved in rendering the service to translate the final blueprint into specific implementation plans for its part of the service delivery process. Because service development, design, and delivery are so intricately intertwined, all parties involved in any aspect of the new service must work together at this stage to delineate the details of the new service. If not, seemingly minor operational details can cause an otherwise good new service idea to fail. For example, careful service development and lots of testing are the rules at Expedia.com, the giant travel information and transportation-booking website. Customers who use Expedia's website potentially have a lot to lose—a $1,000 trip may be at stake, or it may be the only week of vacation the person has in a whole year. So before launching any new software onto the site or redesigning the site itself, Expedia holds dozens of meetings with the design team to consider customer requirements. It then builds and tests prototypes of the software or website changes, conducts usability tests, and gathers customer feedback on designs. Feedback is reviewed and integrated into the design constantly before, during, and after the launch.[23]

Market Testing

It is at this stage of the development process that a tangible product might be test marketed in a limited number of trading areas to determine marketplace acceptance of the product as well as other marketing mix variables such as promotion, pricing, and distribution systems. Again, the standard approach for a new manufactured product is typically not possible for a new service due to its inherent characteristics. Because new service offerings are often intertwined with the delivery system for existing services, it is difficult to test new services in isolation. And in some cases, such as a one-site hospital, it may not be possible to introduce the service to an isolated market area because the organization has only one point of delivery. There are alternative ways of testing the response to marketing mix variables, however. The new service might be offered to employees of the organization and their families for a time to assess their responses to variations in the marketing mix. Or the organization might decide to test variations in pricing and promotion in less realistic contexts by presenting customers with hypothetical mixes and getting their responses in terms of intentions to try the service under varying circumstances. While this approach certainly has limitations compared with an actual market test, it is better than not assessing market response at all.

It is also extremely important at this stage in the development process to pilot run the service to be sure that the operational details are functioning smoothly. Frequently this purpose is overlooked and the actual market introduction may be the first test of whether the service system functions as planned. By this point, mistakes in design are harder to correct. As one noted service expert says, "There is simply no substitute for a proper rehearsal" when introducing a new service.[24] In the case of the discount brokerage service described earlier, a pilot test was run by offering employees a special price for one month. The offer was marketed internally, allowing the bank to observe the service process in action before it was actually introduced to the external market.

Commercialization

At this stage in the process, the service goes live and is introduced to the marketplace. This stage has two primary objectives. The first is to build and maintain acceptance of the new service among large numbers of service delivery personnel who will be responsible day to day for service quality. This task is made easier if acceptance has been built in by involving key groups in the design and development process all along. However, it will still be a challenge to maintain enthusiasm and communicate the new service throughout the system; excellent internal marketing will help.

The second objective is to monitor all aspects of the service during introduction and through the complete service cycle. If the customer needs six months to experience the entire service, then careful monitoring must be maintained through at least six months. Every detail of the service should be assessed—phone calls, face-to-face transactions, billing, complaints, and delivery problems. Operating efficiency and costs should also be tracked.

Postintroduction Evaluation

At this point, the information gathered during commercialization of the service can be reviewed and changes made to the delivery process, staffing, or marketing mix variables on the basis of actual market response to the offering. For example, in the case of Expedia.com, mentioned earlier, it became clear, despite prelaunch testing, that restrictions on Expedia bargain fares were confusing to customers. A "hot fix" team was called in to repair the problem.[25] Within a day, the project team redesigned the presentation of information so the fare restrictions would be clear to customers.

No service will ever stay the same. Whether deliberate or unplanned, changes will always occur. Therefore, formalizing the review process to make those changes that enhance service quality from the customer's point of view is critical. The service blueprint serves a valuable purpose in providing a focal point for discussing and planning changes in the offering.

SERVICE BLUEPRINTING

A stumbling block in developing new services (and in improving existing services) is seeming inability to describe and depict the service at the concept development, product development, and market test stages. One of the keys to matching service specifications to customer expectations is the ability to describe critical service process characteristics objectively and to depict them so that employees, customers, and managers alike know what the service is, can see their role in its delivery, and understand all of the steps and flows involved in the service process. In this section of the chapter we look in depth at service blueprinting, a tool that addresses the challenges of designing and specifying intangible service processes.[26]

What Is a Service Blueprint?

The manufacturing and construction industries have a long tradition of engineering and design. Can you imagine a house being built without detailed specifications? Can you imagine a car, a computer, or even a simple product like a child's toy or a shampoo being produced without concrete and detailed plans, written specifications, and engineering drawings? Yet services commonly lack concrete specifications. A service, even a complex one, might be introduced without any formal, objective depiction of the process.

A service blueprint is a picture or map that accurately portrays the service system so that the different people involved in providing it can understand and deal with it objectively regardless of their roles or their individual points of view. Blueprints are particularly useful at the design and redesign stages of service development. A service blueprint visually displays the service by simultaneously depicting the process of service delivery, the points of customer contact, the roles of customers and employees, and the visible elements of the service (see Figure 8.5). It provides a way to break a service down into its logical components and to depict the steps or tasks in the process, the means by which the tasks are executed, and the evidence of service as the customer experiences it.

Blueprinting has its origins in a variety of fields and techniques, including logistics, industrial engineering, decision theory, and computer systems analysis—all of which deal with the definition and explanation of processes.[27]

FIGURE 8.5
Service Blueprinting

A tool for simultaneously depicting the service process, the points of customer contact, and the evidence of service from the customer's point of view.

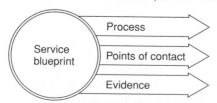

Blueprint Components

The key components of service blueprints are shown in Figure 8.6.[28] They are customer actions, "onstage" contact employee actions, "backstage" contact employee actions, and support processes. The conventions for drawing service blueprints are not rigidly defined, and thus the particular symbols used, the number of horizontal lines in the blueprint, and the particular labels for each part of the blueprint may vary somewhat depending on what you read and the complexity of the blueprint being described. This is not a problem as long as you keep in mind the purpose of the blueprint and view it as a useful tool, rather than as a set of rigid rules for designing services.

The *customer actions* area encompasses the steps, choices, activities, and interactions that the customer performs in the process of purchasing, consuming, and evaluating the service. In a legal services example, the customer actions might include a decision to contact an attorney, phone calls to the attorney, face-to-face meetings, receipt of documents, and receipt of a bill.

Paralleling the customer actions are two areas of contact employee actions. The steps and activities that the contact employee performs that are visible to the customer are the *onstage employee actions*. In the legal services setting, the actions of the attorney (the contact employee) that are visible to the client are, for example, the initial interview, intermediate meetings, and final delivery of legal documents.

Those contact employee actions that occur behind the scenes to support the onstage activities are the backstage *contact employee actions*. In the example, anything the attorney does behind the scenes to prepare for the meetings or to prepare the final documents will appear in this section of the blueprint, together with phone call contacts the customer has with the attorney or other front-line staff in the firm.

The *support processes* section of the blueprint covers the internal services, steps, and interactions that take place to support the contact employees in delivering the service. Again in the legal example, any service support activities such as legal research by staff, preparation of documents, and secretarial support to set up meetings will be shown in the support processes area of the blueprint.

FIGURE 8.6
Service Blueprint Components

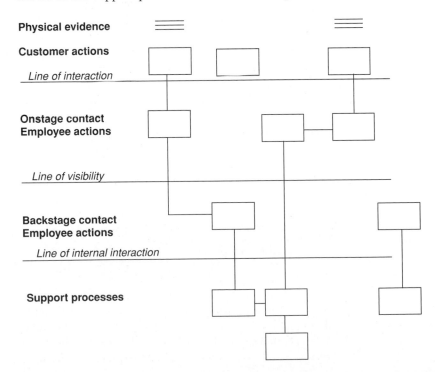

One of the most significant differences in service blueprints compared with other types of process flow diagrams is the inclusion of customers and their views of the service process. In fact, in designing effective service blueprints it is recommended that the diagramming start with the customer's view of the process and work backward into the delivery system. The boxes shown within each action area depict steps performed or experienced by the actors at that level.

The four key action areas are separated by three horizontal lines. First is the *line of interaction,* representing direct interactions between the customer and the organization. Anytime a vertical line crosses the horizontal line of interaction, a direct contact between the customer and the organization, or a service encounter, has occurred. The next horizontal line is the critically important *line of visibility.* This line separates all service activities that are visible to the customer from those that are not visible. In reading blueprints it is immediately obvious whether the consumer is provided with much visible evidence of the service simply by analyzing how much of the service occurs above the line of visibility versus the activities carried out below the line. This line also separates what the contact employees do onstage from what they do backstage. For example, in a medical examination situation, the doctor would perform the actual exam and answer the patient's questions above the line of visibility, or onstage, whereas she might read the patient's chart in advance and transcribe notes following the exam below the line of visibility, or backstage. The third line is the *line of internal interaction,* which separates contact employee activities from those of other service support activities and people. Vertical lines cutting across the line of internal interaction represent internal service encounters.

At the very top of the blueprint you see the *physical evidence* of the service. Typically, above each point of contact the actual physical evidence of the service is listed. Again using the legal example, above the encounter depicting the face-to-face meeting with the attorney you would see listed such things as office decor, written documents, lawyer's clothing, and so forth.

Service Blueprint Examples

Figures 8.7 and 8.8 show service blueprints for two different services: express mail and an overnight hotel stay.[29] These blueprints are deliberately kept very simple, showing only the most basic steps in the services. Complex diagrams could be developed for each step, and the internal processes could be much more fully developed. In addition to the four action areas separated by the three horizontal lines, these blueprints also show the physical evidence of the service from the customer's point of view at each step of the process.

In examining the express mail blueprint in Figure 8.7, it is clear that from the customer's point of view there are only three steps in the service process: the phone call, the package pickup, and the package delivery. The process is relatively standardized; the people that perform the service are the phone order-taker and the delivery person; and the physical evidence is the document package, the transmittal forms, the truck, and the handheld computer. The complex process that occurs behind the line of visibility is of little interest or concern to the customer. However, for the three visible-to-the-customer steps to proceed effectively, invisible internal services are needed. What these steps are and the fact that they support the delivery of the service to the external customer are apparent from the blueprint.

Any of the steps in the blueprint could be exploded into a detailed blueprint if needed for a particular purpose. For example, if it were learned that the "unload and sort" step was taking too long and causing unacceptable delays in delivery, that step could be blueprinted in much greater detail to isolate the problems.

In the case of the overnight hotel stay depicted in Figure 8.8, the customer obvi-

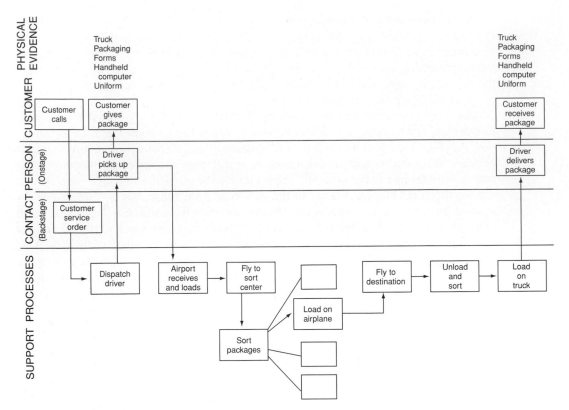

FIGURE 8.7 **Blueprint for Express Mail Delivery Service**

Source: Reprinted from M. J. Bitner, "Managing the Evidence of Service," in *The Service Quarterly Handbook,* ed. E. E. Scheuing and W. F. Christopher (New York: AMACOM, 1993), p. 359. Reprinted by permission of AMACOM, a division of American Management Association International, New York, NY. All rights reserved. http://www.amanet.org.

ously is more actively involved in the service than he or she is in the express mail service just described. The guest first checks in, then goes to the hotel room where a variety of steps take place (receiving bags, sleeping, showering, eating breakfast, and so on), and finally checks out. Imagine how much more complex this process could be and how many more interactions might occur if the service map depicted a week-long vacation at the hotel, or even a three-day business conference. From the service map it is also clear (by reading across the line of interaction) with whom the guest interacts and thus who provides evidence of the service to the customer. Several interactions occur with a variety of hotel employees including the bellperson, the front desk clerk, the food service order-taker, and the food delivery person. Each of the steps in the customer action area is also associated with various forms of physical evidence, from the hotel parking area and hotel exterior and interior to the forms used at guest registration, the lobby, the room, and the food. The hotel facility itself is critical in communicating the image of the hotel company, in providing satisfaction for the guest through the manner in which the hotel room is designed and maintained, and in facilitating the actions and interactions of both the guest and the employees of the hotel. In the hotel case, the process is relatively complex (although again somewhat standardized), the people providing the service are a variety of front-line employees, and the physical evidence includes everything from the guest registration form to the design of the lobby and room to the uniforms worn by front-line employees.

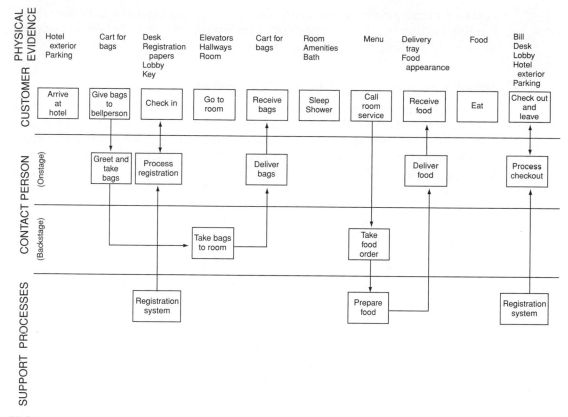

FIGURE 8.8 **Blueprint for Overnight Hotel Stay Service**

Blueprints for Technology-Delivered Self-Service

To this point all of our discussion of service blueprints has related to services that are delivered in person, where there are employees interacting directly at some point in the process with customers. But what about technology-delivered services like self-service websites (Expedia's travel information site, Cisco Systems customer self-service site) and interactive kiosks (ATMs, movie ticket ordering)? Can service blue-printing be used effectively to design these types of services? Certainly it can, but the lines of demarcation may need to change, and some of the blueprint labels can be adapted to fit this context.

If there are truly no employees involved in the service (except when there is a prob-lem or the service doesn't function as planned), the contact person areas of the blue-print are not needed. Instead, the area above the line of visibility can be used to illus-trate the interface between the customer and the computer website or the physical interaction with the kiosk. This area can be relabeled onstage technology. The back-stage contact person actions area would be irrelevant in this case.

If the service involves a combination of human and technology interfaces, as with airline self-check-in, then the onstage area can be cut into two distinct spaces divided by an additional horizontal line. In the airline self-check-in example, the human contact with the airline employee who takes the bags and checks identification would be shown in one area and the technology interactions with the self-check-in computer kiosk in the second area, both above the line of visibility.

Reading and Using Service Blueprints

A service blueprint can be read in a variety of ways, depending on your purpose. If the purpose is to understand the customer's view of the process, the blueprint can be read from left to right, tracking the events in the customer action area. Questions that might be asked include these: How is the service initiated by the customer? What choices does the customer make? Is the customer highly involved in creating the service, or are few actions required of the customer? What is the physical evidence of the service from the customer's point of view? Is the evidence consistent with the organization's strategy and positioning?

If the purpose is to understand the contact employees' roles, the blueprint can also be read horizontally but this time focusing on the activities directly above and below the line of visibility. Questions that might be asked include these: How rational, efficient, and effective is the process? Who interacts with our customers, when, and how often? Is one person responsible for the customer, or is the customer passed off from one contact employee to another? Recognition that the patient was passed from one employee to another with little or no individual attention resulted in a hospital in Florida reorganizing itself so that each patient was assigned to a "care pair" (usually a nurse and an assistant) that serves the patient's needs from check-in to discharge. The result was a reduction in operating costs of greater than 9 percent, along with higher patient satisfaction.[30]

If the purpose is to understand the integration of the various elements of the service process, or to identify where particular employees fit into the bigger picture, the blueprint can be analyzed vertically. In doing this, it becomes clear what tasks and which employees are essential in the delivery of service to the customer. The linkages from internal actions deep within the organization to front-line effects on the customer can also be seen in the blueprint. Questions that might be asked include these: What actions are being performed backstage to support critical customer interaction points? What are the associated support actions? How are hand-offs from one employee to another taking place?

If the purpose is service redesign, the blueprint can be looked at as a whole to assess the complexity of the process, how it might be changed, and how changes from the customer's point of view would impact the contact employee and other internal processes, and vice versa. The evidence of service can also be analyzed to determine if it is consistent with goals for the service. Blueprints can be used to isolate failure points or bottlenecks in the service process. When such points are discovered, the blueprint can be exploded to focus in much greater detail on that particular piece of the system.

On the basis of a blueprinting application in the design and fine-tuning of a new rapid train service between Stockholm and Gothenburg, the two largest cities in Sweden, a number of benefits were noted, as presented in Exhibit 8.2.[31] Clearly, one of the greatest benefits of blueprinting is education.[32] When people begin to develop a blueprint, it quickly becomes apparent what is actually known about the service. Sometimes the shared knowledge is very little. Biases and prejudices are made explicit, and agreements and compromises must be reached. The process itself promotes cross-functional integration and understanding. In the attempt to visualize the entire service system, people are forced to consider the service in new and more comprehensive ways.

1. Provides an overview so employees can relate "what I do" to the service viewed as an integrated whole, thus reinforcing a customer-oriented focus among employees.

2. Identifies fail points—that is, weak links of the chain of service activities, which can be the target of continuous quality improvement.

3. Line of interaction between external customers and employees illuminates the customer's role and demonstrates where the customer experiences quality, thus contributing to informed service design.

4. Line of visibility promotes a conscious decision on what customers should see and which employees will be in contact with customers, thus facilitating rational service design.

5. Line of internal interaction clarifies interfaces across departmental lines, with their inherent interdependencies, thus strengthening continuous quality improvement.

6. Stimulates strategic discussions by illuminating the elements and connections that constitute the service. Those who participate in strategic sessions tend to exaggerate the significance of their own special function and perspective unless a common ground for an integrated view of the service is provided.

7. Provides a basis for identifying and assessing cost, revenue, and capital invested in each element of the service.

8. Constitutes a rational basis for both external and internal marketing. For example, the service map makes it easier for an advertising agency or an in-house promotion team to overview a service and select essential messages for communication.

9. Facilitates top-down, bottom-up approach to quality improvement. It enables managers to identify, channel, and support quality improvement efforts of grass-roots employees working on both front-line and support teams. Employee work teams can create service maps and thus more clearly apply and communicate their experience and suggestions for improvements.

Source: Reprinted with permission, from E. Gummesson and J. Kingman-Brundage, "Service Design and Quality: Applying Service Blueprinting and Service Mapping to Railroad Services," in *Quality Management in Services,* ed. P. Kunst and J. Lemmink (Assen/Maastricht, Netherlands: Van Gorcum, 1991).

Building a Blueprint

Recall that many of the benefits and purposes of building a blueprint evolve from the process of doing it. Thus the final product is not necessarily the only goal. Through the process of developing the blueprint, many intermediate goals can be achieved: clarification of the concept, development of a shared service vision, recognition of complexities and intricacies of the service that are not initially apparent, and delineation of roles and responsibilities, to name a few. The development of the blueprint needs to involve a variety of functional representatives as well as information from customers. Drawing or building a blueprint is not a task that should be assigned to one person or one functional area. Figure 8.9 identifies the basic steps in building a blueprint.

FIGURE 8.9
Building a Service Blueprint

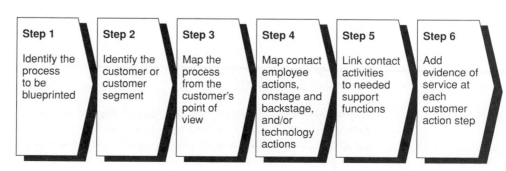

Step 1	Step 2	Step 3	Step 4	Step 5	Step 6
Identify the process to be blueprinted	Identify the customer or customer segment	Map the process from the customer's point of view	Map contact employee actions, onstage and backstage, and/or technology actions	Link contact activities to needed support functions	Add evidence of service at each customer action step

Step 1: Identify the Service Process to Be Blueprinted.   Blueprints can be developed at a variety of levels, and there needs to be agreement on the starting point. For example, the express mail blueprint shown earlier is at the basic service concept level. Little detail is shown, and variations based on market segment or specific services are not shown. Specific blueprints could be developed for two-day express mail, large accounts, Internet-facilitated services, and/or store-front drop-off centers. Each of these blueprints would share some features with the concept blueprint but would also include unique features. Or if the "sort packages" and "loading" elements of the process were found to be problem areas or bottlenecks that were slowing service to customers, a detailed blueprint of the subprocesses at work in those two steps could be developed. Identifying the process to be mapped will be determined by the underlying purpose for building the blueprint in the first place.

Step 2: Identify the Customer or Customer Segment Experiencing the Service. A common rationale for market segmentation is that each segment's needs are different and therefore will require variations in the service or product features. Thus, blueprints are most useful when developed for a particular customer or customer segment, assuming that the service process varies across segments. At a very abstract or conceptual level it may be possible to combine customer segments on one blueprint. However, once almost any level of detail is reached, separate blueprints should be developed to avoid confusion and maximize their usefulness.

Step 3: Map the Service Process from the Customer's Point of View.   This step involves charting the choices and actions that the customer performs or experiences in purchasing, consuming, and evaluating the service. Identifying the service from the customer's point of view first will help to avoid focusing on processes and steps that have no customer impact. This step forces agreement on who the customer is (sometimes no small task) and may involve considerable research to determine exactly how the customer experiences the service. In mapping the Margaret River Masters surfing event in Australia, researchers used a team of participant observers who involved themselves in the event while recording details about each stage and encounter in the total experience. These detailed observations, combined with customer surveys, allowed them to identify the important actions and activities of this unique event from a customer's point of view. The blueprint was then used to identify points for improvement in this competitive event that attracts the world's best surfers.[33]

Sometimes the beginning and ending of the service from the customer's point of view may not be obvious. For example, research in a hair-cutting context revealed that customers viewed the process as beginning with the phone call to the salon and setting of the appointment, whereas the hair stylists did not typically view the making of appointments as part of the service process.[34] Similarly, in a mammography screening service, patients viewed driving to the clinic, parking, and locating the screening office as part of the service experience. If the blueprint is being developed for an existing service, it may be helpful at this point in the process to videotape or photograph the service process from the customer's point of view. Often managers and others who are not on the front lines do not actually know what the customers are experiencing and what it all looks like from their points of view.

Step 4: Map Contact Employee Actions, Both Onstage and Backstage, and/or Technology Actions.   First the lines of interaction and visibility are drawn, and then the process from the customer contact person's point of view is mapped, distinguishing visible or onstage activities from invisible backstage activities. For existing services this will involve questioning front-line operations employees to learn what they do and which activities are performed in full view of the customer versus which activities are carried out behind the scenes.

In the case of technology-delivered services or those that combine technology and human delivery, the required actions of the technology interface will be mapped above the line of visibility as well. If no employees are involved in the service at all, then the area can be relabeled "onstage technology actions." If there are both human and technology interactions, those activities can be separated by an additional horizontal line to separate "onstage contact employee actions" from "onstage technology actions." Using the additional line will facilitate reading and interpretation of the service blueprint.

Step 5: Link Contact Activities to Needed Support Functions. The line of internal interaction can then be drawn and linkages from contact activities to internal support functions can be identified. It is in this process that the direct and indirect impact of internal actions on customers becomes apparent. Internal service processes take on added importance when viewed in connection with their link to the customer. Alternatively, certain steps in the process may be viewed as unnecessary if there is no clear link to the customer's experience or to an essential internal support service.

Step 6: Add Evidence of Service at Each Customer Action Step. Finally, the evidence of service can be added to the blueprint to illustrate what it is that the customer sees and receives as tangible evidence of the service at each step in the customer experience. The photographic blueprint including photos, slides, or video of the process can be very useful at this stage as well to aid in analyzing the impact of tangible evidence and its consistency with the overall strategy and service positioning.

Exhibit 8.3 provides answers to frequently asked questions about service blueprinting.

QUALITY FUNCTION DEPLOYMENT

In addition to service blueprinting, another approach that can be used to develop a service architecture is *quality function deployment (QFD)*. QFD has been defined as "a system for translating customer requirements into appropriate company requirements at every stage, from research through production design and development to manufacture; distribution; installation; and marketing, sales, and services."[35] QFD has more applications in manufacturing than in services, being used as a means of integrating marketing and engineering personnel in the development process. The ideas are also applicable to services, however. QFD is implemented via what is known as the "house of quality," which links customer requirements to design characteristics of the product or service.[36] These are then linked to internal processes such as product planning, process planning, production planning, and parts deployment. The house of quality is a diagrammatic representation of the service, its attributes, the customers' requirements, and the company's capabilities.

For services, the concept of service quality deployment has been suggested as a means of adapting QFD tools for service development and design.[37] The resulting house of service quality (see Figure 8.10 for an example) comprises three distinct sections: customer quality criteria (what customers perceive), service company facets (how these criteria are created by the firm), and the relationship grid (how the two are

8.3 FREQUENTLY ASKED QUESTIONS ABOUT SERVICE BLUEPRINTING

What process should be mapped?

What process to map depends on the team or organization's objectives. If these are not clearly defined, then identifying the process can present a challenge. Questions to ask: Why are we mapping the service? What is our objective? Where does the service process begin and end? Are we focusing on the entire service, a component of the service, or a period of time?

Can multiple market segments be included on one blueprint?

Generally the answer to this question is no. Assuming that market segments require different service processes or attributes, the blueprint for one segment may look very different from the blueprint for another. Only at a very high level (sometimes called a *concept blueprint*) might it be relevant to map multiple segments simultaneously.

Who should "draw" the blueprint?

A blueprint is a team effort. It should not be assigned as an individual task, certainly not in the development stages. All relevant parties should be involved or represented in the development effort. This might include employees across multiple functions in the organization (marketing, operations, human resources, facilities design) as well as customers in some cases.

Should the actual or desired service process be blueprinted?

If a new service is being designed, then clearly it is important to start with the desired service process. However, in cases of service improvement or service redesign, it is very important to map (at least at a conceptual level) the actual service process first. Once the group knows how the service is actually functioning, then the blueprint can be modified or used as a base for changes and improvements.

Should exceptions or recovery processes be incorporated within the blueprint?

It may be possible to map relatively simple, commonly occurring recovery processes onto a blueprint, assuming there aren't a lot of these. However, this can quickly become complex and cause the blueprint to be confusing or unreadable. Often a better strategy is to indicate common fail points on the blueprint and if needed develop sub-blueprints for the service recovery processes.

What is the appropriate level of detail?

The answer to this question depends again on the objective or purpose for doing the blueprint in the first place. If it is to be used primarily to communicate the general nature of the service, then a concept blueprint with few details is best. If it is being used to focus on diagnosing and improving the service process, then more detail is needed. Because some people are more detail oriented than others, this particular question will always arise and needs to be resolved in any team blueprinting effort.

What symbols should be used?

At this point in time, there is not a lexicon of blueprinting symbols that is commonly used or accepted across companies. It is most important that the symbols be defined, kept relatively simple, and be used consistently by the team and across the organization if blueprints are being shared internally.

Should time or dollar costs be included on the blueprint?

Blueprints are very versatile. If reducing the time taken for various parts of the service process is an objective of the blueprinting effort, then time can definitely be included. The same is true for dollar costs or anything else that is relevant as an objective. However, it is not advisable to put these types of things on the blueprint unless they are of central concern.

related). This matrix is extended to include quantitative information so that relative importance of relationships among different functions of the firm can be highlighted.

Figure 8.10 provides an example of QFD applied to Village Volvo, a Volvo service garage, to create a house of service quality.[38] The following paragraphs explain elements of the house of service quality shown in Figure 8.10:

1. *Customer expectations.* On the far left of the house are listed the customer's expectations of Village Volvo's customer service. In this case the customers' expectations correspond to the five service quality dimensions presented in Chapter 4.
2. *Importance of expectations.* Next to each expectation (on the chimney of the house) is listed the importance of that particular attribute to customers on a scale from 1 to 9,

FIGURE 8.10
House of Service Quality for Village Volvo

Source: Reprinted from J. A. Fitzsimmons and M. J. Fitzsimmons, *Service Management,* 3rd ed. (New York: Irwin McGraw-Hill, 2000), p. 58. © 2000 by The McGraw-Hill Companies, Inc. Reprinted by permission of The McGraw-Hill Companies.

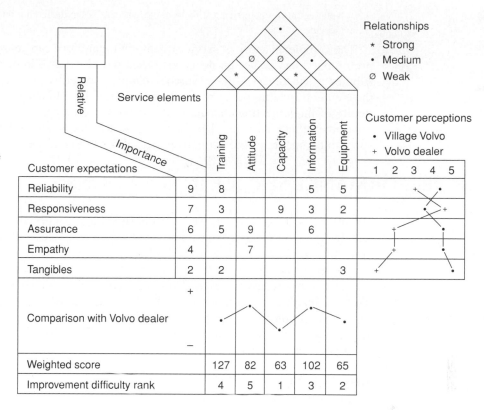

Customer expectations	Relative Importance	Training	Attitude	Capacity	Information	Equipment	Customer perceptions
Reliability	9	8			5	5	
Responsiveness	7	3		9	3	2	
Assurance	6	5	9		6		
Empathy	4		7				
Tangibles	2	2				3	
Comparison with Volvo dealer							
Weighted score		127	82	63	102	65	
Improvement difficulty rank		4	5	1	3	2	

Relationships
* Strong
• Medium
∅ Weak

Customer perceptions
• Village Volvo
+ Volvo dealer

with 9 being the most important. These importance weights are determined by customer research.

3. *Controllable elements of service.* The columns of the house represent the elements of service that the company has control over such as training, capacity, equipment, attitude, and information.

4. *Relationship among elements.* The relationships among the elements of service are shown in the roof of the house. The relationship among elements can be strong, medium, or weak. For example, the relationship between training and attitude is strong, whereas the relationship between training and capacity is weak.

5. *Association between expectations and service elements.* In the body of the matrix are listed numbers representing the strength of the relationship between each expectation and the related service element. The numbers reflect (from the service team's perspective) how various elements affect the company's ability to satisfy the particular customer expectation. A 0 suggests no effect, whereas a 9 suggest a very strong effect.

6. *Overall importance of service elements for meeting customer expectations.* The weighted score on the floor of the house represents the total points for each element, calculated by multiplying the importance weights by the element association ratings and adding all of the scores for each element together [e.g., training = (9)(8) + (7)(3) + (6)(5) + (4)(0) + (2)(2) = 127]. These scores should be treated relatively, however, and not as absolutes because they are determined based on some subjectivity and judgment.

7. *Difficulty rankings.* In the basement of the house are listed the difficulty rankings assigned to each element in terms of how difficult it would be to make improvements in that element, with the ranking of 1 being the most difficult.

8. *Competitive assessment.* Two areas of the house suggest some comparisons of Village Volvo with the competing Volvo dealership. On the right are shown comparisons of the two on the dimensions of service quality. Just above the floor of the house are shown

relative ratings comparing Village Volvo with the Volvo dealership on the elements of service.

The completed house of service quality in Figure 8.10 can be used to begin to make preliminary service design decisions based on the relative importance of various attributes to customers, Village Volvo's relative competitive position, the weighting of the elements in terms of their contribution overall to customer satisfaction, and the difficulty of implementing change. In this case it would appear that training would be a good investment because it has the strongest weight, is rated relatively weak with respect to competition, and is relatively less difficult to change.

HIGH-PERFORMANCE SERVICE INNOVATIONS

To this point in the chapter, we have discussed approaches and tools for developing and designing new services. A dilemma in most companies is that there are too many new ideas to choose from. New technologies, changing customer needs, deregulation, competitors' actions—all of these result in myriad potential new offerings to consider. The question is which to pursue. How can a company decide which new offerings will likely be major successes, and which may be less successful or even fail?

In this section we summarize some of what has been learned about successful new services in terms of measures of success, key success drivers, and the importance of integrating new services.

Choose the Right Projects

Success with new services is going to be determined by two things: choosing the right projects and doing the projects right.[39] Researchers confirm that following the new service development process discussed earlier in the chapter (Figure 8.2) will help with both these goals.[40] Service blueprinting and QFD, also presented in this chapter, will help as well, primarily with the second goal.

Another concept, *portfolio management for new products,* is very useful in helping companies choose the right projects in the first place.[41] Using this approach, companies manage their product portfolio similarly to their financial portfolio. The approach helps companies prioritize projects; choose which ones to accelerate; and determine the best balance between risk versus return, maintenance versus growth, and short-term versus long-term projects. There are a number of methods for doing this including financial models, scoring models and checklists, mapping approaches, and behavioral approaches.[42]

Integrate New Services

Because of the nature of services—they are processes, typically delivered at least in part by people, consumed and produced simultaneously—any new service introduction will affect the existing systems and services. Unlike when a manufacturer adds a new product to its production facility, new service introductions are frequently visible to customers and may even require their participation. Explicit recognition of these potential impacts, and planning for the integration of people, processes, and physical evidence, will encourage success.[43] This recognition will help in both (1) deciding which projects to pursue—sometimes the disruptive effect on existing systems is too great to warrant the investment—and (2) knowing how to proceed with implementation—what elements of existing processes, people, and physical facilities will need to be adjusted, added, or changed.

Consider Multiple Measures of Success

In predicting the success of a new service, multiple measures may be considered.[44] First, and most commonly used, is near-term *financial performance* including revenue growth, profitability, market share, and return on investment (ROI). In other cases, *relationship enhancement* may be a more appropriate measure of success. This might include the new service's effect on customer loyalty, image enhancement, and the effect on the success of other products and services. Or success may be measured in terms of *market development*—the degree to which the new service opens up new markets or new customer segments. Successful projects will lead to increases in one, or perhaps more than one, of these measures.

Learn from Major Successes

In investing in new products and services, most companies are looking for big winners rather than modest improvements.[45] In a study of financial services the following factors were found to distinguish major successes from moderate or small successes:[46]

Market synergy. There is a strong fit between the new service and the company's marketing, promotion, sales, and distribution expertise and resources.

Market-driven new-product process. The company has a well-planned and executed new service development process including customer input, research and development, customer testing, and competitive analysis.

Effective marketing communications. The company has an effective strategy for raising customer awareness, explaining service benefits, and establishing a unique positioning and distinct brand image.

Customer service. The most successful new financial products were linked to excellent customer service support.

Managerial and financial synergy. There is a strong fit between the new project and the company's management and financial expertise and resources.

Launch preparation. The company provides extensive training and preparation of front-line personnel to support the product prior to launch.

Product responsiveness. Major successes are new services that truly offer improvements from the customers' point of view—better than competition, responsive to a new need, or offering greater flexibility.

Product advantage. Major successes are better than alternatives in terms of benefits, quality, and distinct branding.

Innovative technology. Technology is instrumental in providing a superior product, or it provides innovation for the delivery system, or the company uses hardware and software to develop significant new offerings. (This factor is particularly important for market development.)

Maintain Some Flexibility

From the preceding research and the work of others, it becomes clear that new-service success depends on (1) market-driven, customer-focused new-product processes; (2) emphasis on planning for and executing the launch; (3) integration of services within existing processes (including staff training); and (4) strong marketing communications, both external and internal. Yet, at the same time, we are cautioned about being too rigid in the new service development approach. Steps in the development process should be allowed some flexibility, and there will no doubt be overlapping processes. Initial service development, for example, can be occurring simultaneously with additional gathering of customer information. Because services, particularly business-to-business services, are often very complex, some creativity and "out of order" decisions will be needed. There must be some elements of improvisation, anarchy, and internal competition in the development of new services. "Consequently, the innovation and adoption of new services must be both a planned process and a happening!"[47]

Summary

Service providers must effectively match customer expectations to new service innovations and actual service process designs. However, because of the very nature of services—their intangibility and heterogeneity specifically—the design and development of service offerings are complex and challenging. Many services are only vaguely defined before their introduction to the marketplace. This chapter has outlined some of the challenges involved in designing services and some strategies for effectively overcoming the challenges.

Through adaptations of the new product development process that is commonplace in goods production and manufacturing companies, service providers can begin to make their offerings more explicit and avoid failures. The new service development process presented in the chapter includes nine stages, beginning with the development of a business and new service strategy and ending with postintroduction evaluation of the new service. Between these initial and ending stages are a number of steps and checkpoints designed to maximize the likelihood of new service success. Carrying out the stages requires the inclusion of customers, contact employees, and anyone else who will affect or be affected by the new service. Because successful new service introduction is often highly dependent on service employees (often they are the service), integration of employees at each stage is critical.

Service blueprinting is a particularly useful technique in the new service development process. A blueprint can make a complex and intangible service concrete through its visual depiction of all of the steps, actors, processes, and physical evidence of the service. The key feature of service blueprints is their focus on the customer—the customer's experience is documented first and is kept fully in view as the other features of the blueprint are developed. This chapter has provided the basic tools needed to build, use, and evaluate service blueprints. Quality function deployment (QFD) was introduced as another tool for linking customer requirements to internal elements of service design.

The final section of the chapter summarized some of the key factors driving successful new service innovations, including the need for portfolio planning and integration of new services with existing processes and systems. The need to consider multiple measures of success was highlighted as well as the importance of maintaining flexibility in the new service development process.

Discussion Questions

1. Why is it challenging to design and develop services?
2. What are the risks of attempting to describe services in words alone?
3. Compare and contrast the blueprints in Figures 8.7 and 8.8.
4. How might a service blueprint be used for marketing, human resource, and op-

erations decisions? Focus on one of the blueprint examples shown in the text as a context for your answer.

5. Assume that you are a multiproduct service company that wants to grow through adding new services. Describe a logical process you might use to introduce a new service to the marketplace. What steps in the process might be most difficult and why? How might you incorporate service blueprinting into the process?

6. Discuss Figure 8.3 in terms of the four types of opportunities for growth represented there. Choose a company or service, and explain how it could grow by developing new services in each of the four cells (see the Taco Bell example in Exhibit 8.1).

7. Explain the house of service quality as shown in Figure 8.10. Based on the information shown in that figure for Village Volvo, what might you do to improve service if you were the manager of that organization?

Exercises

1. Think of a new service you would like to develop if you were an entrepreneur. How would you go about it? Describe what you would do and where you would get your information.

2. Find a new and interesting service in your local area, or a service offered on your campus. Document the service process via a service blueprint. To do this you will probably need to interview one of the service employees. After you have documented the existing service, use blueprinting concepts to redesign the service or change it in some way.

3. Choose a service you are familiar with and document the customer action steps through a photographic blueprint. What is the "evidence of service" from your point of view as a customer?

4. Develop a service blueprint for a technology-delivered service (such as an Internet-based travel service). Compare and contrast this blueprint to one for the same service delivered via more traditional channels (such as a personal travel agent).

5. Interview customers and employees of a service of your choice. Construct a basic house of service quality. What would you recommend to the manager of the service based on your analysis?

6. Compare two services on the Internet. Discuss the design of each in terms of whether it meets your expectations. How could the design or the service process be changed? Which one is most effective, and why?

Notes

1. Wells Fargo website, 2001 (www.wellsfargo.com); G. Anders, "Power Partners," *Fast Company,* September 2000, pp. 146–48; *Newsbytes News Network,* November 6, 1998; P. Beckett, "Banks Still Seek Big Payoff in Online Services," *The Wall Street Journal,* January 21, 2000, p. C1.

2. "Flops, Too Many New Products Fail. Here's Why—and How to Do Better," cover story, *Business Week,* August 16, 1993, pp. 76–82.

3. Ibid.; and R. G. Cooper, *Winning at New Products,* 3rd ed. (Cambridge, MA: Perseus Publishing, 2001); R. G. Cooper and S. J. Edgett, *Product Development for the Service Sector* (Cambridge, MA: Perseus Books, 1999).

4. D. H. Henard and D. M. Szymanski, "Why Some New Products Are More Successful Than Others," *Journal of Marketing Research,* August 2001, pp. 362–75.

5. G. L. Shostack, "Understanding Services through Blueprinting," in *Advances in Services Marketing and Management,* vol. 1, ed. T. A. Swartz, D. E. Bowen, and S. W. Brown (Greenwich, CT: JAI Press, 1992), pp. 75–90.

6. Cooper, *Winning at New Products;* Cooper and Edgett, *Product Development for the Service Sector;* Henard and Szymanski, "Why Some New Products Are More Successful Than Others."

7. G. L. Shostack, "Service Design in the Operating Environment," in *Developing New Services,* ed. W. R. George and C. Marshall (Chicago: American Marketing Association, 1984), pp. 27–43.

8. B. Schneider and D. E. Bowen, "New Services Design, Development and Implementation and the Employee," in *Developing New Services,* ed. W. R. George and C. Marshall, pp. 82–101.

9. Adapted from D. F. Heany, "Degrees of Product Innovation," *Journal of Business Strategy,* Spring 1983, pp. 3–14, appearing in C. H. Lovelock, "Developing and Implementing New Services," in *Developing New Services,* ed. W. R. George and C. Marshall, pp. 44–64.

10. L. L. Berry and S. K. Lamp, "Teaching an Old Service New Tricks, The Promise of Service Redesign," *Journal of Service Research,* 2, no. 3 (February 2000), pp. 265–75.

11. Cooper, *Winning at New Products.*

12. For a discussion of these adaptations and related research issues, see M. V. Tatikonda and V. A. Zeithaml, "Managing the New Service Development Process: Synthesis of Multidisciplinary Literature and Directions for Future Research," in *New Directions in Supply Chain Management: Technology, Strategy and Implementation,* ed. Boone and Ganeshan (AMACOM, 2001); B. Edvardsson, A. Gustafsson, M. D. Johnson, and B. Sanden, *New Service Development and Innovation in the New Economy* (University of Karlstad, Sweden: Service Research Center, 2001).

13. The steps shown in Figure 8.2 and discussed in the text are based primarily on the model developed by M. J. Bowers, "An Exploration into New Service Development: Organization, Process and Structure," doctoral dissertation, Texas A&M University, 1985. Bowers's model is adapted from Booz-Allen & Hamilton, *New Product Management for the 1980s* (New York: Booz-Allen & Hamilton, 1982).

14. R. G. Cooper, "Stage Gate Systems for New Product Success," *Marketing Management* 1, no. 4 (1992), pp. 20–29.

15. M. Iansiti and A. MacCormack, "Developing Products on Internet Time," *Harvard Business Review,* September–October 1997, pp. 108–17.

16. A. Khurana and S. R. Rosenthal, "Integrating the Fuzzy Front End of New Product Development," *Sloan Management Review,* Winter 1997, pp. 103–20.

17. Ibid, p. 104; see also R. G. Cooper, S. J. Edgett, and E. J. Kleinschmidt, *Portfolio Management for New Products* (Reading, MA: Addison-Wesley, 1998).

18. While the basic framework shown in Figure 8.3 has been developed and adapted by many researchers and authors over the last 30 years, its original form can be found in H. I. Ansoff, *Corporate Strategy* (New York: McGraw-Hill, 1965)

19. D. Leonard and J. F. Rayport, "Spark Innovation through Empathic Design," *Harvard Business Review,* November–December 1997, pp. 103–13.

20. G. L. Shostack, "Service Design."

21. E. E. Scheuing and E. M. Johnson, "A Proposed Model for New Service Development," *Journal of Services Marketing* 3, no. 2 (1989), pp. 25–34.

22. M. R. Bowers, "Developing New Services for Hospitals: A Suggested Model," *Journal of Health Care Marketing* 7, no. 2 (June 1987), pp. 35–44.

23. D. Maxey, "Testing, Testing, Testing." *The Wall Street Journal,* December 10, 2001, p. R8.

24. Shostack, "Service Design," p. 35.

25. Maxey, "Testing, Testing, Testing."

26. The service blueprinting section of the chapter draws from the pioneering works in this area: G. L. Shostack, "Designing Services That Deliver," *Harvard Business Review,* January–February 1984, pp. 133–39; G. L. Shostack, "Service Positioning through Structural Change," *Journal of Marketing* 51 (January 1987), pp. 34–43; J. Kingman-Brundage, "The ABC's of Service System Blueprinting," in *Designing a Winning Service Strategy,* ed. M. J. Bitner and L. A. Crosby (Chicago: American Marketing Association, 1989), pp. 30–33.

27. Shostack, "Understanding Services through Blueprinting," pp. 75–90.

28. These key components are drawn from Kingman-Brundage, "The ABC's."

29. The text explaining Figures 8.7 and 8.8 relies on M. J. Bitner, "Managing the Evidence of Service," in *The Service Quality Handbook,* ed. E. E. Scheuing and W. F. Christopher (New York: American Management Association, 1993), pp. 358–70.

30. "Hospital, Heal Thyself," *Business Week,* August 27, 1990, pp. 66–68.

31. E. Gummesson and J. Kingman-Brundage, "Service Design and Quality: Applying Service Blueprinting and Service Mapping to Railroad Services," in *Quality Management in Services,* ed. P. Kunst and J. Lemmink (Assen/Maastricht, Netherlands: Van Gorcum, 1991).

32. Shostack, "Understanding Services through Blueprinting."

33. D. Getz, M. O'Neill, and J. Carlsen, "Service Quality Evaluation at Events through Service Mapping," *Journal of Travel Research,* 39, no. 4 (May 2001), pp. 380–90.

34. A. R. Hubbert, A. Garcia Sehorn, and S. W. Brown, "Service Expectations: The Consumer vs. The Provider," *International Journal of Service Industry Management* 6, no. 1 (1995), pp. 6–21.

35. American Supplier Institute, 1987, as quoted in R. S. Behara and R. B. Chase, "Service Quality Deployment: Quality Service by Design," in *Perspectives in Operations Management: Essays in Honor of Elwood Buffa,* ed. R. V. Sarin (Norwell, MA: Kluwer Academic Publisher, 1993).

36. J. R. Hauser and D. Clausing, "The House of Quality," *Harvard Business Review,* May–June 1988, pp. 63–73.

37. Behara and Chase, "Service Quality Deployment." See also F. I. Stuart and S. S. Tax, "Planning for Service Quality: An Integrative Approach," *International Journal of Service Industry Management* 7, no. 4 (1996), pp. 58–77.

38. J. A. Fitzsimmons and M. J. Fitzsimmons, *Service Management,* 3rd ed. (New York: McGraw-Hill/Irwin, 2000), pp. 57–59.

39. R. G. Cooper, S. J. Edgett, and E. J. Kleinschmidt, *Portfolio Management for New Products* (Reading, MA: Addison-Wesley, 1998).

40. C. M. Froehle, A. V. Roth, R. B. Chase, and C. A. Voss, "Antecedents of New Service Development Effectiveness," *Journal of Service Research,* 3, no. 1 (August 2000), pp. 3–17; Henard and Szymanski, "Why Some New Products Are More Successful Than Others"; Edvardsson et al., *New Service Development and Innovation in the New Economy.*

41. Cooper et al., *Portfolio Management for New Products.*

42. See ibid. for an excellent discussion and coverage of multiple methods for managing product and service portfolios.

43. S. S. Tax and I. Stuart, "Designing and Implementing New Services: The Challenges of Integrating Service Systems," *Journal of Retailing* 73, no. 1 (1997), pp. 105–34.

44. R. G. Cooper, C. J. Easingwood, S. Edgett, E. J. Kleinschmidt, and C. Storey, "What Distinguishes the Top Performing New Products in Financial Services," *Journal of Product Innovation Management* 11(1994), pp. 281–99.

45. For information on success and failure of new services, see Cooper et al., "What Distinguishes the Top Performing New Products"; Ulrike de Brentani, "New Industrial Service Development: Scenarios for Success and Failure," *Journal of Business Research* 32 (1995), pp. 93–103; C. R. Martin, Jr., and D. A. Horne, "Services Innovation: Successful versus Unsuccessful Firms," *International Journal of Service Industry Management* 4, no. 1 (1993), pp. 49–65; B. Edvardsson, L. Haglund, and J. Mattsson, "Analysis, Planning, Improvisation and Control in the Development of New Services," *International Journal of Service Industry Management* 6, no. 2 (1995), pp. 24–35; Froele et al., "Antecedents of New Service Development Effectiveness"; Henard and Szymanski, "Why Some New Products Are More Successful Than Others"; Cooper and Edgett, *Product Development for the Service Sector.*

46. Cooper et al., "What Distinguishes the Top Performing New Product in Financial Services."

47. Edvardsson, Haglund, and Mattsson, "Analysis, Planning, Improvisation and Control," p. 34.

Chapter 9

CUSTOMER-DEFINED SERVICE STANDARDS

This chapter's objectives are to

1. Differentiate between company-defined and customer-defined service standards.

2. Distinguish among one-time service fixes and "hard" and "soft" customer-defined standards.

3. Explain the critical role of the service encounter sequence (discussed in Chapter 4) in developing customer-defined standards.

4. Illustrate how to translate customer expectations into behaviors and actions that are definable, repeatable, and actionable.

5. Explain the process of developing customer-defined service standards.

6. Emphasize the importance of service performance indexes in implementing strategy for service delivery.

FedEx Sets Standards through SQI

Marketing research data aren't the only numbers Federal Express tracks to run its business. The company drives its operations with the aid of the most comprehensive, customer-defined index of service standards and measures in the world. FedEx's service quality indicator (SQI) was designed as "unforgiving internal performance measurement" to ensure that the company delivered to its goal of "100 percent customer satisfaction after every interaction and transaction and 100 percent service performance on every package handled."[1] The development and implementation of SQI led to a Malcolm Baldrige National Quality Award.

What makes this service index different from those of other companies is its foundation in customer feedback. Since the 1980s, FedEx has documented customer complaints and used the information to improve internal processes. Its composite listing of the eight most common customer complaints, called the "Hierarchy of Horrors," included wrong day delivery, right day late delivery, pickup not made, lost package, customer misinformed by Federal Express, billing and paperwork mistakes, employee performance failures, and damaged packages. Although this list was useful, it fell short of giving management the ability to anticipate and eliminate customer complaints before they occurred.

Indicator	Weight
Right day late deliveries	1
Wrong day late deliveries	5
Traces not answered	1
Complaints reopened	5
Missing proofs of delivery	1
Invoice adjustments	1
Missed pickups	10
Damaged packages	10
Lost packages	10
Aircraft delay minutes	5
Overgoods	5
Abandoned calls	1
International	1

In 1988 the company developed the 12-item statistical SQI to be a more "comprehensive, pro-active, customer-oriented measure of customer satisfaction and service quality."[2] The SQI consists of the following components and weighting (based on relative importance of each component to customers):

Another distinguishing feature of the SQI is its reporting in terms of *numbers* of errors rather than percentages. Management of the company strongly believed that percentages distanced the company from the consumer: to report 1 percent of packages late diminished the reality of 15,000 unhappy customers (1 percent of the approximately 1.5 million packages shipped a day). The service quality indicator report is disseminated weekly to everyone in the company. On receipt of the report, root causes of service failures are investigated. With a senior officer assigned to each component, and with bonuses for everyone in the company tied to performance on the SQI, the company drives continuously closer to its goal of 100 percent satisfaction with every transaction.[3]

As we saw in Chapters 2, 3, and 4, understanding customer expectations and perceptions is the first step in delivering high service quality. Once managers of service businesses accurately understand what customers expect, they face a second critical challenge: using this knowledge to set service quality standards and goals for the organization. Service companies often experience difficulty in setting standards to match or exceed customer expectations partly because doing so requires that the marketing and operations departments within a company work together. In most service companies, integrating the work of the marketing function and the operations function (appropriately called *functional integration*) is not a typical approach; more frequently these two functions operate separately—setting and achieving their own internal goals—rather than pursuing a joint goal of developing the operations standards that best meet customer expectations.

Creating service standards that address customer expectations is not a common practice in U.S. firms. Doing so often requires altering the very process by which work is accomplished, which is ingrained in tradition in most companies. Often change requires new equipment or technology. Change also necessitates aligning executives from different parts of the firm to understand collectively the comprehensive view of service quality from the customer's perspective. And almost always, change requires a willingness to be open to different ways of structuring, calibrating, and monitoring the way service is provided.

FACTORS NECESSARY FOR APPROPRIATE SERVICE STANDARDS

Standardization of Service Behaviors and Actions

The translation of customer expectations into specific service quality standards depends on the degree to which tasks and behaviors to be performed can be standardized or routinized (Figure 9.1). Some executives and managers believe that services cannot be standardized—that customization is essential for providing high-quality service. In certain "expert" services such as accounting, consulting, engineering, and dentistry, for example, professionals provide customized and individualized services; standardizing of the tasks is perceived as being impersonal, inadequate, and not in the customer's best interests. Managers also may feel that standardizing tasks is inconsistent with employee empowerment—that employees will feel controlled by the company if tasks are standardized. Further, they feel that services are too intangible to be measured. This view leads to vague and loose standard setting with little or no measurement or feedback.

In reality, many service tasks are routine (such as those needed for opening checking accounts or spraying lawns for pests), and for these, specific rules and standards

FIGURE 9.1 Federal Express has standardized service behaviors and actions, resulting in superior employee performance. Source: © 1995–2002 FedEx. All Rights Reserved.

can be fairly easily established and effectively executed. Employees may welcome knowing how to perform actions most efficiently: it frees them to use their ingenuity in the more personal and individual aspects of their jobs. If services are customized for individual customers (as in investment portfolio management or estate planning), specific standards (such as those relating to time spent with the customer) may not be appropriate. Even in highly customized services, however, many aspects of service provision can be routinized. Physicians and dentists, for example, can and do standardize recurring and nontechnical aspects of the service such as checking patients in, weighing patients, billing patients, collecting payment, and taking routine measurements. In delegating these routine tasks to assistants, physicians and dentists can spend more of their time on the expert services of diagnosis or patient care.

According to one long-term observer of service industries, standardization of service can take three forms: (1) substitution of technology for personal contact and human effort, (2) improvement in work methods, and (3) combinations of these two methods.[4] Examples of technology substitution include automatic teller machines, automatic car washes, and airport X-ray machines. Improvements in work methods are illustrated by restaurant salad bars and routinized tax and accounting services developed by firms such as H&R Block and Comprehensive Accounting Corporation.

Technology and work improvement methods facilitate the standardization of service necessary to provide consistent delivery to customers. By breaking tasks down and providing them efficiently, technology also allows the firm to calibrate service standards such as the length of time a transaction takes, the accuracy with which operations are performed, and the number of problems that occur. In developing work improvements, the firm comes to understand completely the process by which the service is delivered. With this understanding, the firm more easily establishes appropriate service standards.

Standardization, whether accomplished by technology or by improvements in work processes, reduces gap 2. Both technology and improved work processes structure important elements of service provision and also facilitate goal setting. It is important to recognize that standardization does not mean that service is performed in a rigid, mechanical way. Customer-defined standardization ensures that the most critical elements of a service are performed as expected by customers, not that every action in a service is executed in a uniform manner. Using customer-defined standardization can, in fact, allow for and be compatible with employee empowerment. One example of this compatibility involves the time limits many companies establish for customer service calls. If their customers' highest priorities involve feeling good about the call or resolving problems, then setting a limit for calls would be decidedly company defined and not in customers' best interests. In other words, this would be standardization that both constrains employees and works against customer priorities. Companies such as American Express and L. L. Bean, in using customer priorities rather than company priorities, have no set standard for the amount of time an employee spends on the telephone with a customer. Instead, they have standards that focus on making the customer satisfied and comfortable, allowing telephone representatives to use their own judgment about the time limits.

Formal Service Targets and Goals

Companies that have been successful in delivering consistently high service quality are noted for establishing formal standards to guide employees in providing service. These companies have an accurate sense of how well they are performing service that is critical to their customers—how long it takes to conduct transactions, how frequently service fails, how quickly they settle customer complaints—and strive to improve by defining goals that lead them to meet or exceed customer expectations.

Several types of formal goal setting are relevant in service businesses. First, there are specific targets for individual behaviors or actions. As an example, consider the behavior "calls the customer back quickly," an action that signals responsiveness in contact employees. If the service goal for employee behavior is stated in such a general term as "call the customer back quickly," the standard provides little direction for service employees. Different employees will interpret this vague objective in their own ways, leading to inconsistent service: some may call the customer back in 10 minutes whereas others may wait two to four days. And the firm itself will not be able to determine when or if individual employees meet the goal because its expression is not measurable—one could justify virtually any amount of time as "quickly." On the other hand, if the individual employee's service goal is to call each customer back within four hours, employees have a specific, unambiguous guideline about how quickly they should execute the action (four hours). Whether the goal is met is also unequivocal: if it occurs within four hours it meets the goal, otherwise it does not.

Another type of formal goal setting involves the overall department or company target, most frequently expressed as a percentage, across all executions of the behavior or action. For example, a department might set as its overall goal "to call the customer back within four hours 97 percent of the time" and collect data over a month's or year's time to evaluate the extent to which it meets the target.

Service firms that produce consistently excellent service—firms such as Walt Disney, Federal Express, and Merrill Lynch—have very specific, quantified, measurable service goals. Walt Disney calibrates employee performance on myriad behaviors and actions that contribute to guest perceptions of high service quality. Whether they are set and monitored using audits (such as timed actions) or customer perceptions (such as opinions about courtesy), service standards provide a means for formal goal setting.

Customer—Not *Company*—Defined Standards

Virtually all companies possess service standards and measures that are *company defined*—they are established to reach internal company goals for productivity, efficiency, cost, or technical quality. To close gap 2, standards set by companies must be based on customer requirements and expectations rather than just on internal company goals. In this chapter we make the case that company-defined standards are not typically successful in driving behaviors that close provider gap 2. Instead, a company must set *customer-defined standards:* operational standards based on pivotal customer requirements that are visible to and measured by customers. These standards are deliberately chosen to match customer expectations and to be calibrated the way the customer views and expresses them. Because these are the goals that are essential to the provision of excellent service, the rest of this chapter focuses on customer-defined standards.

Knowing customer requirements, priorities, and expectation levels can be both effective and efficient. Anchoring service standards on customers can save money by identifying what the customer values, thus eliminating activities and features that the customer either does not notice or will not pay for. Through precise measurement of expectations, the company often discovers that it has been overdelivering to many customer needs:

> . . . a bank might add several extra tellers and reduce the average peak waiting time in line from 7 minutes to 5 minutes. If customers expect, however, to wait up to 8 minutes during peak time, the investment in extra tellers may not be effective. An opportunity thus exists to capture the value of this information through reduced teller costs and higher profits.[5]

On the other hand, many firms create standards and policies to suit their own needs that are so counter to the wishes of customers that the companies endanger their customer relationships. In late 1998, when the hotel industry was booming, many hotels initiated policies penalizing late arrivals and early departures as well as imposing minimum-stay requirements. The Hilton San Francisco and Towers Hotel began to charge guests $50 when they stayed fewer days than agreed to at check-in. The Peabody Orlando kept guests' one-night deposits unless they canceled at least three days prior to arrival. And a Chicago hotel required a business customer to buy four nights' lodging when all she needed was three, putting the customer out an extra cost of $2,700![6] Hotels defend these policies on the basis of self-protection, but they are clearly not customer oriented.

While customer-defined standards need not conflict with productivity and efficiency, they do not originate with these company concerns. Rather they are anchored in and steered by customer perceptual measures of service quality or satisfaction. The service standards that evolve from a customer perspective are likely to be different from company-defined service standards.

Virtually all organizations have lists of things they measure regularly, most of which fall into the category of company-defined standards. Often these standards deal with activities or actions that reflect the history of the business rather than the reality of today's competitive marketplace or the needs of current customers.

CUSTOMER-DEFINED SERVICE STANDARDS

The type of standards that close provider gap 2 are *customer-defined standards:* operational goals and measures based on pivotal customer requirements that are visible to and measured by customers. They are operations standards set to correspond to customer expectations and priorities rather than to company concerns such as productivity or efficiency. Take a typical operations standard such as inventory control. Most firms measure inventory control from the company's point of view. However, the highly successful office supply retailer Office Depot captures every single service measurement related to inventory control *from the customer's point of view.* The company began with the question, "What does the customer see?" and answered, "The average number of stockouts per week." Office Depot then designed a customer-focused measurement system based on measures such as the number of complaints and compliments it received about inventory as well as a transaction-based survey with the customer about its performance in this area. These and other customer-defined standards allow for the translation of customer requirements into goals and guidelines for employee performance.

"Hard" Customer-Defined Standards

Two major types of customer-defined service standards can be distinguished. All of the Federal Express standards that comprise the SQI fall into the category of "hard" standards and measures: *things that can be counted, timed, or observed through audits.* Many of Federal Express's standards relate to on-time delivery and not making mistakes, and for good reason. As we stressed earlier in this text, customer expectations of reliability—fulfillment of service promises—are high. A series of 35 studies across numerous industries from the Arthur D. Little management consulting firm found that the most frequently cited customer complaint was late product and service delivery (44 percent), followed by product and service quality mistakes (31 percent).[7]

To address the need for reliability, companies can institute a "do it right the first time" and an "honor your promises" value system by establishing reliability standards. An example of a generic reliability standard that would be relevant to virtually any service company is "right first time," which means that the service performed is done correctly the first time according to the customer's assessment. If the service involves delivery of products, "right first time" to the customer might mean that the shipment is accurate—that it contains all that the customer ordered and nothing that the customer did not order. If the service involves installation of equipment, "right first time" would likely mean that the equipment was installed correctly and was able to be used immediately by the customer. Another example of a reliability standard is "right on time," which means that the service is performed at the scheduled time. The company representative arrives when promised or the delivery is made at the time the customer expects it. In more complex services, such as disaster recovery or systems integration in computer service, "right on time" would likely mean that the service was completed by the promised date.

As we have discussed in previous chapters, reliability is the single most important concern of service customers. In electronic retailing, on-time, accurate fulfillment of orders is one of the most important aspects of reliability. One of the best examples of customer-defined hard standards in the Internet context is the set of summary metrics that Dell Computer uses for fulfillment.[8] They include

- *Ship to target (SSTT)*—the percentage of orders delivered on time with complete accuracy.

- *Initial field incident rate (IFIR)*—the frequency of customer problems.

- *On time first time fix (OTFTF)*—the percentage of problems fixed on the first visit by a service representative arriving at the time promised.

Dell tracks its performance to these standards and rewards employees on the basis of their "met promises" or reliability, which is often higher than 98 percent.

When it comes to providing service across cultures and continents, service providers need to recognize that customer-defined service standards often need to be adapted (see Global Feature). In the United States we expect waiters to bring the check promptly. In fact, if we do not receive it shortly after the last course, and without our asking for it, we evaluate the service as slow and nonresponsive. In Spain, however, customers consider it rude for the waiter to bring the check to the table without being asked to do so. They feel rushed, a state they dislike during meals. Although bringing the check to the table (whether sooner or later, requested or not) is an activity that restaurants need to incorporate as a customer-defined service standard, the parameters of the standard must be adapted to the culture.

Hard service standards for responsiveness are set to ensure the speed or promptness with which companies deliver products (within two working days), handle complaints (by sundown each day), answer questions (within two hours), answer the telephone (see the Technology Spotlight), and arrive for repair calls (within 30 minutes of the estimated time). In addition to standard setting that specifies levels of response, companies must have well-staffed customer service departments. Responsiveness perceptions diminish when customers wait to get through to the company by telephone, are put on hold, or are dumped into a phone mail system.

Table 9.1 shows a sampling of the hard standards that have been established by service companies. This list is a small subset of all of these standards because we include only those that are customer defined—based on customers' requirements and

As service companies expand their offerings to international stages, they face a critical question about service delivery: Do we provide the same level of service in other countries as we do in our home country? The answer to this question depends on the answers to several other questions. First, are customer expectations of service delivery uniform across international locations, or do cultural influences lead to different service delivery expectations? Second, what is the performance of competing firms in the countries where expansion is to take place? Third, do personnel and infrastructure constraints exist in other countries that prevent meeting service performance expectations? All of these questions are important, but we discuss the answer to the first most fully because it strongly influences the other two questions.

Responsiveness Varies by Cultures

It has been shown that customers from different cultures have different tolerances for service responsiveness and timeliness. As we discussed in this chapter, Spanish and American customers have different expectations of the speed with which a check is brought to the table following a meal. Whereas Americans consider bringing the check to the table quickly to be good service, Spanish customers are insulted—believing that the service establishment is rushing them out the door.

Larry Crosby, a renowned marketing researcher who has focused on international customer expectations, has provided research evidence of differences in international customer expectations that lead directly to implications for service standards. In his work on customer expectations of service perceptions across countries, he developed the accompanying exhibits, which are helpful and revealing. Two of the exhibits, one for mail delivery (A) and one for a supplier's follow-through on requests (B), provide evidence of how differently customers view levels of responsiveness. In Italy, more than 70 percent of customers rate receiving a letter mailed in their country within three days good, very good, or excellent. In contrast, in the United Kingdom or the Netherlands, more than 90 percent consider that level of responsiveness fair or poor. As business-to-business customers of suppliers (B), Italians consider 75 percent follow-through on requests to be quite good (nearly 50 percent rating that level good, very good, or excellent), whereas almost 60 percent of Australians consider that same service level fair or poor. As you can see, there is a great difference in tolerances for responsiveness across countries.

Reliability Varies by Cultures

Other cultural expectation differences discussed in earlier chapters have a major effect on the service standards set in different countries. Asians are more sensitive to reliability than many other cultural groups, making it important that service standards focus on this area and ensure that performance is as promised. This sensitivity is demonstrated in Exhibit C. The ratings of a concert pianist who makes one noticeable mistake in a one-hour

A. A letter mailed in your country takes three days to reach you.

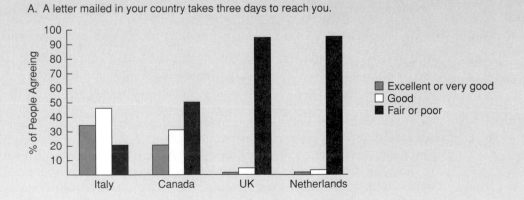

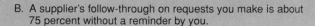

B. A supplier's follow-through on requests you make is about 75 percent without a reminder by you.

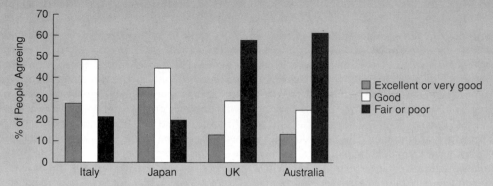

C. A concert pianist makes one noticeable mistake in a one-hour solo performance.

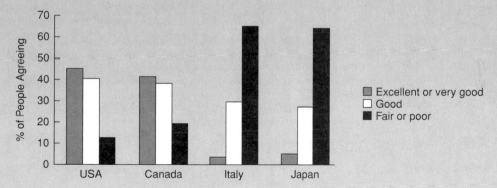

solo performance are shown for people from the United States, Canada, Italy, and Japan. While 45 percent of Americans and 40 percent of Canadians still consider the performance to be good, very good, or excellent, only 30 percent of the Japanese rated it that highly—in fact, around 65 percent devalued the performance to fair or poor based on one mistake! In this particular entertainment service, the ratings of Italians were similar to the ratings of the Japanese; however, in many other services Europeans are more forgiving than Asians of reliability problems.

Implications for Service Standards

Consider the implications of the data about responsiveness differences for services created in America and differentiated on the basis of speed and responsiveness—services such as overnight package delivery, Jiffy Lube,

fast food, "while you wait" shoe repair, and 15-minute haircuts. The lack of importance of responsiveness in some other cultures undermines the very positioning of these responsiveness-based services. Unless other aspects of the services make them competitive in other cultures, they may not be as successful as they are in the United States. On the other hand, if the services are well accepted in other countries, one implication may be that companies can relax U.S.-based responsiveness standards. In any case, companies from around the world need to recognize that universal service expectations are probably not the norm and that the best service offerings acknowledge differences across cultures and geographies.

Source: L. A. Crosby, "Factors Affecting the Comparability of Multicountry CSM Information," QUIS 3, Karlsbad, Sweden, April 1994, pp. 273–86; figures reprinted with permission.

Technology Spotlight
The Power of a Good Telephone Responsiveness Standard

In 1993, at the National Performance Review's recommendation, President Clinton issued an executive order requiring all government agencies that deal directly with the public to survey their customers and establish customer service standards. By 1998 this order resulted in more than 4,000 customer service standards from 570 agencies. One of the most successful came from the Social Security Administration (SSA) and illustrates a customer-defined hard standard relating to a technology issue that all customers face in dealing with public and private companies alike: telephone responsiveness.

The SSA knew that access—getting through to the agency on its 800 number—was the single biggest driver of customer satisfaction and public perception of the agency's competency. Unfortunately, customers more often than not repeatedly encountered busy signals on the 60 million calls they placed to the SSA's high-volume 800 number. The National Performance Review suggested to the agency that its service standard ought to be that everyone who called its 800 number would get through on the first try: 100 percent access! The SSA balked, recognizing that its telephone technology, limited employee resources, and wide fluctuations in demand would prevent the standard from being met.

The agency ultimately settled on a more reasonable standard: 95 percent of all callers would be served within five minutes. This standard became a very clear and focused goal that "everybody knew and everybody was shooting for," according to an SSA manager. Early measurements indicated less-than-stellar performance; in 1995 only 73.5 percent of callers got through in five minutes.

What followed was an impressive effort of technology, people, and measurement. According to an expert,

"SSA endured tremendous expense, dislocation, pain—and even failure—to meet its standard." First, SSA officials developed a new phone system with AT&T that involved a sophisticated call-routing approach. Second, the organization trained virtually all technical people who held jobs other than in teleservices in those skills so that they could be shifted during peak hours to help with the volume. Third, the agency restricted leave for teleservice representatives at peak time, increased the use of overtime, and worked with employees to change processes and rules to improve performance.

The low point in performance to the standard was during the transition to the new system. In November 1995 only 57.2 percent of callers got through within five minutes. Even worse was that on the first day back to work in January 1996, the AT&T 800-number system crashed, leading to even more busy signals. By February, after AT&T fixed the system and the organization got used to its changes, performance improved significantly. The five-minute access rate was 92.1 percent in February, 95.9 percent in November, and above 95 percent ever since.

The SSA standard was successful because it was specific, measurable, and meaningful to customers. Because its results were documented and publicized both within and outside the agency, both employees and management were accountable for performance. Unlike many of the vague, meaningless standards that resulted from the NPR's work with government agencies, this one was a winner.

Source: D. Osborne, "Higher Standards," *Government Executive,* July 2000, pp. 63–71.

perspectives. Because Federal Express has a relatively simple and standard set of services, it can translate most of its customers' requirements into hard standards and measures. Not all standards, however, are as easily quantifiable as those at FedEx.

"Soft" Customer-Defined Standards

Not all customer priorities can be counted, timed, or observed through audits. As Albert Einstein once said, "Not everything that counts can be counted, and not everything that can be counted, counts." For example, "understanding and knowing the customer" is not a customer priority that a standard that counts, times, or observes employees can adequately capture. In contrast to hard measures, soft measures are those that must be documented using perceptual measures. We call the second category of customer-defined standards *soft standards and measures* because they are opinion-based measures that cannot be observed and must be collected by talking to customers, employees, or others. Soft standards provide direction, guidance, and feedback to employees in ways to achieve customer satisfaction and can be quantified by measuring customer perceptions and beliefs. These are especially important for person-to-person interactions such as the selling process and the delivery process for professional services. Table 9.2 shows examples of soft customer-defined standards.

Mini Maid Services, a firm that franchises home and office janitorial services, successfully built a business by developing a repertoire of 22 customer-defined soft standards for daily cleaning chores. The company sends out crews of four who perform these 22 tasks in an average time of 55 minutes for a fee ranging from approximately $45 to $55. Follow-up trailer calls survey customer perceptions of the effectiveness of these soft standards.

The Ritz-Carlton, winner of a Malcolm Baldrige Award, uses a set of "Gold Standards" to drive the service performance it wants. The soft standards established are included in Table 9.2.

The differences between hard and soft standards are illustrated in Exhibit 9.1 using the customer care standards developed at Ford Motor Company.

One-Time Fixes

When customer research is undertaken to find out what aspects of service need to be changed, requirements can sometimes be met using *one-time fixes*. One-time fixes are *technology, policy, or procedure changes that, when instituted, address customer requirements* (see Exhibit 9.2). Performance standards do not typically need to be developed for these dissatisfiers because the one-time change in technology, policy, or procedures accomplishes the desired change.

To illustrate policy and procedure changes in an international context, consider London's Central Middlesex Hospital. At one time almost everything about Central Middlesex, from the architectural design of the buildings to staff processes and activities, centered on the inpatient aspects of the business, despite the fact that 90 percent of the hospital's patients were outpatients. When the hospital became a self-governing trust under the British government's National Health Service reforms, plans were announced to convert it to a patient-focused hospital. The most important one-time fix was to reverse the emphasis from inpatients to outpatients. With the recognition for this change, the hospital was reorganized around 14 ambulatory centers such as rehabilitation services and a family care center that combined obstetrics, pediatrics, and gynecology.

Examples of successful one-time fixes include Marriott Hotel's express checkout and check-in, Hertz and other rental car companies' express check-in, GM Saturn's one-price policy for automobiles, and Granite Rock's 24-hour express service. In each of these examples, customers had expressed a desire to be served in ways different from the past. Marriott's customers had clearly indicated their frustration at waiting in long checkout lines. Saturn customers disliked haggling over car prices in dealer showrooms. And Granite Rock, a Malcolm Baldrige National Quality Award winner with a "commodity" product, had customers who desired 24-hour availability of ground rock from its quarry.

Where most companies in their industries decided for various reasons not to address these customer requirements, Marriott, Saturn, and Granite Rock each responded with one-time fixes that virtually revolutionized the service quality delivered by their companies. Marriott used technology to create Express Checkout, a one-time fix that also resulted in productivity improvements and cost reductions. The company

TABLE 9.1 Examples of Hard Customer-Defined Standards

Company	Customer Priorities	Customer-Defined Standards
Federal Express	On-time delivery	Number of packages right day late Number of packages wrong day late Number of missed pickups
Dell Computer	On-time delivery Computer works properly	Ship to target Initial field incident rate Missing, wrong, and damaged rate
	Problems fixed right first time	Service delivery on time first time fix
Social Security Administration	Telephone access	95 percent of calls served within five minutes (see Technology Spotlight)
Southwest Airlines	Reliability Responsiveness to complaints	On-time arrival Two-week reply to letters
Lenscrafters (optical retailer)	Quick turnaround on eyeglasses	Glasses ready in one hour
Fotomat (photograph-developing retailer)	Quick developing of photographs	Photographs developed within one hour
Aetna/U.S. Healthcare	Fast response to calls and problems	Calls answered within 20 seconds Same-day complaint resolution Two-hour response time for requests
	Regular contact with customers	Proactive service calls three times per year
Honeywell Home and Building Division	Fast delivery On-time delivery Order accuracy	Orders entered same day received Orders delivered when promised Order 100 percent accurate
Southern Pacific	19 key customer-defined attributes	Operational measures to correspond with the 19 key attributes
Universal Card (credit card)	Access	Calls answered within 20 seconds Abandon rate lower than 3 percent of incoming calls
Texas Instruments Defense System	Compliance with commitments	On-time delivery Product compliance to requirements
	More personal contact	Increased number of personal visits

also pioneered a similar one-time fix for hotel Express Check-In, again in response to customers' expressed desires. Saturn countered industry tradition and offered customers a one-price policy that eliminated the haggling characteristics of automobile dealerships. And Granite Rock created an ATM-like system for 24-hour customer access to rock ground to the 14 most popular consistencies. The company created its own Granite Xpress Card that allowed customers to enter, select, and receive their supplies at any time of the day or night.

One-time fixes are often accomplished by hard technology. Hard technology can simplify and improve customer service, particularly when it frees company personnel by handling routine, repetitive tasks and transactions. Customer service employees can then spend more time on the personal and possibly more essential portions of the job. Some hard technology, in particular computer databases that contain information on individual needs and interests of customers, allows the company to standardize the essential elements of service delivery. Basic delivery standards can then be established and measured. Some types of hard technology useful in standard setting include in-

TABLE 9.2 **Examples of Soft Customer-Defined Standards**

Company	Customer Priorities	Customer-Defined Standards
General Electric	Interpersonal skills of operators: Tone of voice, Problem solving, Summarizing actions, Closing	Taking ownership of the call; following through with promises made; being courteous and knowledgeable; understanding the customer's question or request
Ritz-Carlton[a]	Treat me with respect	"Gold Standards" Uniforms are to be immaculate, Wear proper and safe footware, Wear name tag, Adhere to grooming standards, Notify supervisor immediately of hazards, Use proper telephone etiquette, Ask the caller, "May I place you on hold?", Do not screen calls, Eliminate call transfers where possible
Nationwide Insurance	Responsiveness	Human voice on the line when customers report problems
L. L. Bean	Calming human voice; minimize customer anxiety	Tone of voice; other tasks not done (arranging gift boxes) while on the telephone with customers
BellSouth	Telephone responsiveness	Customers not put on hold or transferred; ability to answer questions; courteous and professional; caring and concern
American Express	Resolution of problems	Resolve problem at first contact (no transfers, other calls, or multiple contacts); communicate and give adequate instructions; take all the time necessary
	Treatment	Listen; do everything possible to help; be appropriately reassuring (open and honest)
	Courtesy of representative	Put card member at ease; be patient in explaining billing process; display sincere interest in helping card member; listen attentively; address card member by name; thank card member at end of call

[a]"The Ritz-Carlton Basics," flyer distributed by the Ritz-Carlton to all employees.

formation databases, automated transactions, and scheduling and delivery systems. Effective use of information databases is illustrated in this example from Pizza Hut:

> Pizza Hut centralized and computerized its home delivery operations. Rather than having the separate tasks of order taking, baking, and delivery all in the same location, the company developed a system that works more effectively for both the company and the customer. Operators in a customer service center (not a bakery) take requests for pizza. Working from a database that shows past orders, trained operators take an average of 17 seconds to verify directions to a caller's home and enter his or her request. Operators then route the orders to the closest bake shops, which are strategically located throughout cities to ensure fast deliveries. Cooks in the satellite bake shops prepare pizzas on instructions sent to bake shop printers from order-takers' computers. Drivers aim to complete their deliveries within a half hour of a customer's call, and usually succeed.

9.1 HARD AND SOFT STANDARDS AT FORD MOTOR COMPANY

As we discuss in this chapter, there are two types of customer-defined service standards. "Hard" standards and measures are operational measures that can be counted, timed, or observed through audits. The other category, "soft" standards, are opinion-based measures that cannot be obtained by counting or timing but instead must be asked of the customer. A real example of the difference between hard and soft standards might help distinguish between them. We use Ford Motor Company's Customer Care standards for service at their dealerships. Marketing research involving 2,400 customers asked them about specific expectations for automobile sales and service; the following seven specific service standards were established as most critical to customers:

1. Appointment available within one day of customer's requested service day.

2. Write-up begins within four minutes or less.

3. Service needs are courteously identified, accurately recorded on repair order, and verified with customer.

4. Vehicle serviced right on the first visit.

5. Service status provided within one minute of inquiry.

6. Vehicle ready at agreed-upon time.

7. Thorough explanation given of work done, coverage, and charges.

Hard Standards and Measures

Several of these standards fall into the category of hard standards—they can be counted, timed, or observed through audits. Standards 2 and 5, for example, could be timed by an employee in the service establishment. The hard measure could be either (1) the frequency or percentage of times that the standard's time periods are met or (2) the average times themselves (e.g., average time that write-ups begin). Other standards could be counted or audited, such as standards 1, 4, and 6. The service clerk who answers the telephone could record the number of times that appointments were available within one day of the customer's request. The number of repeat visits could be counted to measure standard 4. And the number of vehicles ready at the agreed-upon time could be tallied as customers come in to pick up their cars.

Soft Standards and Measures

Consider standards 3 and 7 and note how they differ from the ones we have just discussed. These represent desired behaviors that are soft and therefore cannot be counted or timed. Standard 7 requires a different type of measure—the customer's perception or opinion about whether this behavior was performed appropriately. It is not that soft standards cannot be measured; instead, they must be measured in different ways.

Soft standards provide direction, guidance, and feedback to employees in ways to achieve customer satisfaction and can be quantified by measuring customer perceptions and beliefs. These are especially important for person-to-person interactions such as the selling process and the delivery process for professional services. To be effective, companies must provide feedback to employees about customer perceptions of their performance.

Source: Benelux Press/Getty Images

9.2 ONE-TIME FIXES AND WAITING IN LINE

Few customers like to wait in line, and many of us measure the responsiveness and service of an organization by how long it takes us to get to the teller or the counter or our table in a restaurant. Because customers so often wait so long, it may surprise you to know that the subject is a source of constant study and one-time fixes in service companies! Take McDonald's, for example. In the late 1990s, an experiment conducted in 70 McDonald's restaurants in California tested whether it should change its age-old process of multiple waiting lines into a "serpentine-style" single line. Both Wendy's and Burger King already use the single-line system, as do airlines, banks, many hotels, and even the U.S. Postal Service. McDonald's research was conducted because the company was not certain that customers were served best by a single line. Let's visit the single-versus-multiple-line question to see which creates the better standard for customer service.

The Single Line Is Better

Fairness, speed, and lack of stress and frustration top the reasons many companies and behavioral researchers favor a single line. Consider the following scenario:

> You fling open the door to a McDonald's, size up how fast the various lines are moving, trying to avoid any megaorders in the works. When you pick a line, you keep glancing from side to side to see if others are gaining on you. Inevitably, people who jump from line to line jostle one another. These queue hoppers also sometimes arrive at the register clueless about what they want to order.

Multiple lines have been found to create tremendous stress on customers because they require effort to be sure the "right" line is chosen. How many times have you been frustrated in lines and wondered how it is that you always choose the slow cashier/teller/order-taker?

Multiple Lines Are Better

Those who oppose a single line do so on three counts. First, some critics claim they are "dehumanizing, because [the] velvet ropes corral customers like cattle." Second, one line can appear to be much longer than several short ones, a perception that is incorrect based on actual time measurements but is nevertheless sufficient to drive customers away in search of an establishment with a shorter-appearing wait. Finally, many of them are difficult to use by the disabled.

Experts claim that most customers prefer the single line over the multiple lines, but innovative and customer-focused firms are going further than just making that decision. Some are managing customer perceptions in lines, giving them something to watch or read or otherwise focus on to get their minds off the waits. Others are removing lines altogether, as is the case with restaurants (and some doctor's offices) that give customers pagers so that they can shop or go elsewhere until it is time for them to be served. Still others are letting customers know how long the wait is. Digital signs in the lobby of First Chicago NBD Corporation tell customers the anticipated length of their wait, an up-to-date electronic version of the signs at Walt Disney theme parks that let little customers know how many minutes until they ride Space Mountain.

Source: R. Gibson, "Merchants Mull the Long and the Short of Lines," *The Wall Street Journal*, September 3, 1998, pp. B1ff. Republished by permission of Dow Jones, Inc. via Copyright Clearance Center, Inc., © 1998 Dow Jones and Company, Inc. All Rights Reserved Worldwide.

P.C. Vey

One-time fixes also deal with the aspects of service that are affected by things other than human performance: rules and policies, operating hours, product quality, and price. An example of a one-time fix involving a policy change is that of allowing front-line employees to refund money to dissatisfied customers. An example of operating hour changes is one allowing retail establishments to be open on Sundays.

Building Blocks: The Service Encounter Sequence

Customer-defined standards are established to define processes or human performance operationally to meet the expectations of customers. Performance requirements are rarely the same across all parts of a company; instead, they are associated with particular service processes and encounters. Consider Figure 9.2, a representation of AT&T General Business Systems' customer contact processes, which decomposes the relationship between the customer and AT&T across the entire business.[9] Except for the top branch, labeled "Product" (which reflects the tangible equipment the company sells), each of the business process branches represents a company process during which customers and the firm interact. The first customer–firm interaction point is sales, followed by installation, repair, and billing. AT&T recognized that its customers' requirements and priorities differed across these processes. Because of these differences, internal measurements chosen to drive behavior differ across the processes and correspond to customers' priorities in each individual encounter.

A customer's overall service quality evaluation is the accumulation of evaluations of multiple service experiences. Service encounters, therefore, are the building blocks for service quality and the component pieces needed to establish service standards in a company. In establishing standards we are concerned with service encounter quality, because we want to understand for each service encounter the specific requirements and priorities of the customer. When we know these priorities we can focus on them as the aspects of service encounters for which standards should be established. Therefore, one of the first steps in establishing customer-defined standards is to delineate the service encounter sequence. Identifying the sequence can be done by listing the sequential steps and activities that the customer experiences in receiving the service. Alternatively,

FIGURE 9.2
AT&T's Process Map for Measurements

Source: From R. E. Kordupleski, R. T. Rust, and A. J. Zaharik, "Why Improving Quality Doesn't Improve Quality (or Whatever Happened to Marketing?)," *California Management Review* 35, no. 3 (Spring 1993). Copyright © 1993 by The Regents of the University of California. By permission of The Regents.

Business Process	Customer Need		Internal Metric
30% Product	Reliability	(40%)	% Repair Call
	Easy to Use	(20%)	% Calls for Help
	Features / Functions	(40%)	Functional Performance Test
30% Sales	Knowledge	(30%)	Supervisor Observations
	Responsive	(25%)	% Proposal Made on Time
	Follow-Up	(10%)	% Follow-Up Made
10% Installation	Delivery Interval Meets Needs	(30%)	Average Order Interval
	Does Not Break	(25%)	% Repair Reports
	Installed When Promised	(10%)	% Installed on Due Date
15% Repair	No Repeat Trouble	(30%)	% Repeat Reports
	Fixed Fast	(25%)	Average Speed of Repair
	Kept Informed	(10%)	% Customers Informed
15% Billing	Accuracy, No Surprise	(45%)	% Billing Inquiries
	Resolve on First Call	(35%)	% Resolved First Call
	Easy to Understand	(10%)	% Billing Inquiries

Total Quality

service blueprints (see Chapter 8) can be used to identify the sequence by noting all of the customers' activities across the top of the blueprint. Vertical lines from customer activities into the lower levels of the blueprint signal the points at which service encounters take place. Standards that meet customer expectations can then be established.

Because many services have multiple encounters, companies and researchers have examined whether some encounters (for example, the first or the last) are more important than others. The Marriott Corporation identified the encounters that occur in the first 10 minutes of a hotel stay as the most critical, leading the hospitality company to focus on hotel front desk experiences (such as Express Check-In) when making improvements. As you can see from the AT&T data in Figure 9.2, the sales experience was considered by customers to be the most important service encounter for AT&T, which suggests that management should focus on the initial encounter. Although service practice and management literature have emphasized strong starts, recent research indicates that strong finishes in the final event of the encounter have a bigger impact on overall satisfaction. Further, the research shows that consistent performance throughout the encounter—widely held to produce the most favorable evaluations—is not as effective as a pattern of improving performance that culminates in a strong finish.[10] An implication of this research for hotels is that managers should focus on the "back end" of the hotel experience—checkout, parking, bellperson services—to leave a strong final impression.

Expressing Customer Requirements as Specific Behaviors and Actions

Setting a standard in broad conceptual terms, such as "improve skills in the company," is ineffective because the standard is difficult to interpret, measure, and achieve. When a company collects data, it often captures customer requirements in very abstract terms. In general, contact or field people often find that data are not diagnostic—they are too broad and general. Research neither tells them specifically what is wrong and right in their customer relationships nor helps them understand what activities can be eliminated so that the most important actions can be accomplished. In most cases, field people need help translating the data into specific actions to deliver better customer service.

Effective service standards are defined in very specific ways that enable employees to understand what they are being asked to deliver. At best, these standards are set and measured in terms of specific responses of human behaviors and actions, as illustrated by the following quotation from an American Airlines executive:

> We have standards for almost every area of the operation, and we check them on a regular basis. We are constantly measuring how long it takes us to answer a reservations call, or process a customer in a ticket line, or get a plane-load of passengers on board the aircraft, or open the door of the airplane once it reaches its destination, or get food on, or get trash off.[11]

Although all of the examples in this quotation are hard standards, soft standards can also be described and measured using perceptions data. The measures of these activities form the baseline for performance at American Airlines and the standard against which all ensuing transactions are measured.

Figure 9.3 shows different levels of abstraction/concreteness for standards in a service firm, arrayed from top (most abstract) to bottom (most concrete and specific). At the very abstract level are customer requirements that are too general to be useful to employees: customers want satisfaction, value, and relationships. One level under these very general requirements are abstract dimensions of service quality already

FIGURE 9.3 **What Customers Expect: Getting to Actionable Steps**

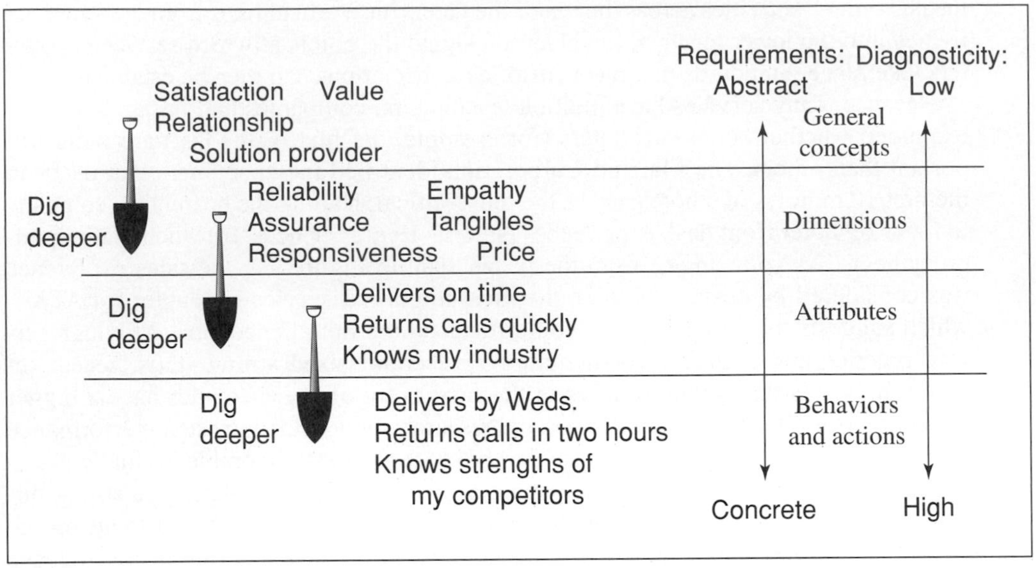

discussed in this text: reliability, responsiveness, empathy, assurance, and tangibles. One level further are attributes more specific in describing requirements. If we dig still deeper beneath the attribute level, we get to specific behaviors and actions that are at the right level of specificity for setting standards. Exhibit 9.3 defines and describes the concepts related to these levels of abstraction and customer-defined standards.

A real-world example of the difference in requirements across these levels will illustrate the practical significance of these levels. In a traditional measurement system for a major company's training division, only one aspect of the instructor was included in its class evaluation: ability of instructor. During qualitative research relating to the attributes that satisfy students, three somewhat more specific requirements were elicited: (1) instructor's style, (2) instructor's expertise, and (3) instructor's management of class. Although the articulation of the three attributes was more helpful to instructors than the broad "ability of instructor," management found that the attributes were still too broad to help instructors wanting to improve their course delivery. When the company invested in a customer-defined standards project, the resulting measurement system was far more useful in diagnosing student requirements because the research focused on *specific behaviors and actions* of instructors that met student requirements. Instead of a single broad requirement or three general attributes, the requirements of students were articulated in 14 specific behaviors and actions that related to the instructor and 11 specific behaviors and actions that related to the course content. These behaviors and actions were clearly more diagnostic for communicating what was good and bad in the courses. An additional benefit of this approach was that feedback on behaviors and actions was less personal than feedback on traits or personal characteristics. It was also easier for employees of the company to make changes that related to behaviors rather than to personality traits.

In summary, the level of customer requirements appropriate for customer-defined standards is concrete behaviors and actions. These are equivalent to features and functions in products, whereas the most abstract level is equivalent to product benefits. It is relatively easy to distinguish between a product feature (the color is red and the instrument panel has 25 buttons) and a benefit (the car has prestige or high perfor-

9.3 Concepts Relevant to Customer-Defined Standards

General, Abstract Concepts: Broad, vague terms that could incorporate many or most different aspects of what a customer wants and are therefore not diagnostic. Examples:

Solution provider	Service quality
Relationship	Partnership
Quality	Value
Total solution	Value for the investment

Service Dimensions: More specific (and therefore more diagnostic) than general abstract concepts, *dimensions* are subgroups of similar features or attributes. Examples:

Reliability	Responsiveness
Empathy	Tangibles
Courtesy	Competence
Assurance	Understanding the customer

Attributes: Specific features or characteristics that describe aspects of service. Because attributes are more specific than the terms listed, they are more diagnostic. Examples:

Answers calls quickly	Respects my point of view
Meets deadlines	Acknowledges problems
Delivers on time	Shares knowledge with me
Asks me what I want	Keeps me informed
Adjusts the system	Apologizes
Listens	Provides information

Behaviors and Actions: Concrete and tangible representations of requirements that fully define the performance expected. Examples:

- Delivers or installs on promised date
- Gets price we had originally agreed upon
- Tells me cost ahead of time
- Fixes the product the first time
- Greets me within five minutes of entering store

Standards: Guidelines set for behaviors, actions, and activities of employees. Examples:

- Delivers by 10:30 A.M.
- Sends a follow-up letter
- Calls me back within four hours
- Resolves every complaint by end of day
- Opens airplane door within 16 seconds
- Proposals have fewer than 10 pages

Measures: Metrics that allow tracking of conformance to standards. Examples:

- Number of times packages are delivered late
- Percentage of total packages delivered late
- Number of complaints resolved by end of day
- Percentage of complaints resolved by end of day
- Percentage of proposals with correct number of pages

mance). But distinguishing between behaviors and actions and attributes or dimensions of service is more complicated, and requires a researcher's experience and familiarity with services. The difficulty in distinguishing among these levels is one of the main reasons quality approaches used in manufacturing (e.g., "voice of the customer" and a widely used method of quality analysis called "quality function deployment," discussed in Chapter 8) have been more difficult to apply in service companies than in product companies.

Measurements of Behaviors and Actions

Hard Measurements

Hard measurements consist of counts or audits or timed actions that provide feedback about the operational performance of a service standard. What distinguishes these data

from soft measurements is that they can be captured continuously and operationally without asking the customer's opinion about them. To demonstrate, here are some of the actual hard measurements for components of the FedEx SQI:

Missing proofs of delivery: the number of invoices that do not include proof-of-delivery paperwork.

Overgoods: lost and found packages that lack, or have lost, identifying labels for the sender and the addressee and are sent to the Overgoods Department.

Wrong day late deliveries: number of packages delivered after the commitment date.

Traces: the number of "proof of performance" requests from customers that cannot be answered through data contained in the computer system.[12]

In these and other hard measurements, the actual gauge involves a count of the number and type of actions or behaviors that are correct or incorrect. Somewhere in the operation system these actions and behaviors are tabulated, frequently through information technology. Other gauges of hard measures include service guarantee lapses (the number of times a service guarantee is invoked because the service did not meet the promise), amounts of time (as in the number of hours or days to respond to a question or complaint or minutes waited in line), and frequencies associated with relevant standards (such as the number of visits made to customers).

Computer information systems are often the basis for setting standards to improve customer service. L. L. Bean, the direct marketer, earned its reputation for outstanding customer service using a computer database that supplies moment-to-moment information about models, colors, and sizes of products in stock. With this system the company can set and achieve high standards of customer service. The database enables L. L. Bean to fill an incredible 99.8 percent of orders accurately.[13]

The appropriate hard measure to deliver to customer requirements is not always intuitive or obvious, and the potential for counting or tracking an irrelevant aspect of operations is high. For this reason it is desirable to link the measure of operational performance with soft measures (surveys or trailer calls) to be sure that they are strongly correlated.

Soft Measurements

Two types of perceptual measurement that were described in Chapter 5 can document customers' opinions about whether performance met the standards established: trailer calls and relationship surveys. Relationship and SERVQUAL surveys cover all aspects of the customer's relationship with the company, are typically expressed in attributes, and are usually completed once per year. Trailer calls are associated with specific service encounters, are short (approximately six or seven questions), and are administered as close in time to a specific service encounter as possible. Trailer calls can be administered in various ways: company-initiated telephone calls following the interactions, postcards to be mailed, letters requesting feedback, customer-initiated calls to an 800 number, or online electronic surveys. For requirements that are longer term and at a higher level of abstraction (such as at the attribute level), annual relationship surveys can document customer perceptions on a periodic basis. Trailer calls are administered continuously, whenever a customer experiences a service encounter of the type being considered, and they provide data on a continuous basis. The company must decide on a survey strategy combining relationship surveys and trailer calls to provide soft measurement feedback.

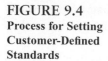

FIGURE 9.4
Process for Setting Customer-Defined Standards

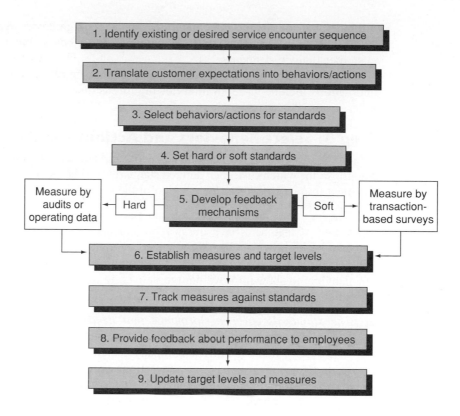

PROCESS FOR DEVELOPING CUSTOMER-DEFINED STANDARDS

Figure 9.4 shows the general process for setting customer-defined service standards.

Step 1: Identify Existing or Desired Service Encounter Sequence

The first step involves delineating the service encounter sequence. Some companies will view this sequence as AT&T General Business Systems did in Figure 9.2. Other times a service blueprint may be used to identify the service encounter sequence. Ideally, the company would be open to discovering customers' desired service encounter sequences, exploring the ways customers want to do business with the firm.

Step 2: Translate Customer Expectations into Behaviors and Actions for Each Service Encounter

The input to step 2 is existing research on customer expectations. In this step, abstract customer requirements and expectations must be translated into concrete, specific behaviors and actions associated with each service encounter. Abstract requirements (like reliability) can call for a different behavior or action in each service encounter, and these differences must be probed. Eliciting these behaviors and actions is likely to require additional qualitative research because most service companies' marketing information has not been collected for this purpose.

Information on behaviors and actions must be gathered and interpreted by an objective source such as a research firm or an inside department with no stake in the ultimate decisions. If the information is filtered through company managers or front-line people with an internal bias, the outcome would be company-defined rather than customer-defined standards.

Research techniques discussed in Chapter 5 that are relevant for eliciting behaviors and actions include in-depth interviewing of customers, focus group interviews, and other forms of research such as partnering.

Step 3: Select Behaviors and Actions for Standards

This stage involves prioritizing the behaviors and actions, of which there will be many, into those for which customer-defined standards will be established. The following are the most important criteria for creation of the standards.

1. *The standards are based on behaviors and actions that are very important to customers.* Customers have many requirements for the products and services that companies provide. Customer-defined standards need to focus on what is very *important* to customers. Unless very important behaviors/actions are chosen, a company could show improvement in delivering to standards with no impact on overall customer satisfaction or business goals.

2. *The standards cover performance that needs to be improved or maintained.* Customer-defined standards should be established for behavior that needs to be improved or maintained. The company gets the highest leverage or biggest impact from focusing on behaviors and actions that need to be improved. Figure 9.5 shows an importance/performance matrix for a computer manufacturer. It combines the importance and performance criteria and indicates by shading in the

FIGURE 9.5
**Importance/
Performance Matrix:
Delivery, Installing,
Performing**

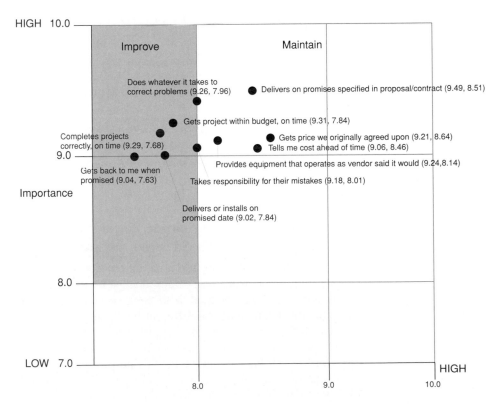

Large Customers

    Assigned an individual to call with complaints.

    Four-hour standard for resolving problems.

Small Customers

    Can call service center or individual.

    Eight-hour standard for resolving problems.

All Complaint-Handling Personnel Trained to

    Paraphrase problems.

    Ask customers what solution they prefer.

    Verify that problem has been fixed.

cell in the matrix where behaviors and actions should be selected to meet those criteria.

3. *The standards cover behaviors and actions employees can improve.* Employees perform according to standards consistently only if they understand, accept, and have control over the behaviors and actions specified in the standards. Holding contact people to standards that they cannot control (such as product quality or time lag in introduction of new products) does not result in improvement. For this reason, service standards should cover controllable aspects of employees' jobs.

4. *The standards are accepted by employees.* Employees will perform to standards consistently only if they understand and accept the standards. Imposing standards on unwilling employees often leads to resistance, resentment, absenteeism, even turnover. Many companies establish standards for the amount of time it should take (rather than for the time it does take) for each service job and gradually cut back on the time to reduce labor costs. This practice inevitably leads to increasing tensions among employees. In these situations, managers, financial personnel, and union employees can work together to determine new standards for the tasks.

5. *The standards are predictive rather than reactive.* Customer-defined standards should not be established on the basis of complaints or other forms of reactive feedback. Reactive feedback deals with past concerns of customers, rather than with current and future customer expectations. Rather than waiting for dissatisfied customers to complain, the company should actively seek both positive and negative perceptions of customers in advance of complaints.

6. *The standards are challenging but realistic.* A large number of studies on goal setting show that highest performance levels are obtained when standards are challenging but realistic. If standards are not challenging, employees get little reinforcement for mastering them. On the other hand, unrealistically high standards leave an employee feeling dissatisfied with performance and frustrated by not being able to attain the goal.

Exhibit 9.4 shows an example of the set of behaviors and actions selected by a company for its complaint-handling service encounter. Some of these are different across the two segments of customers for which standards were set (small and large customers). Three other behaviors were chosen for standards across all customers.

FIGURE 9.6
Linkage between Soft and Hard Measures for Speed of Complaint Handling

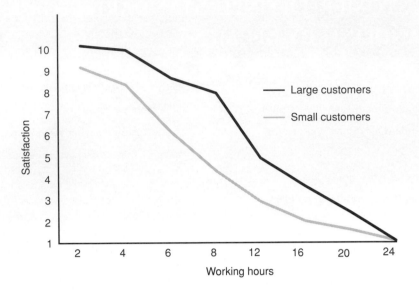

Step 4: Decide Whether Hard or Soft Standards Are Appropriate

The next step involves deciding whether hard or soft standards should be used to capture the behavior and action. One of the biggest mistakes companies make in this step is to choose a hard standard hastily. Companies are accustomed to operational measures and have a bias toward them. However, unless the hard standard adequately captures the expected behavior and action, it is not customer defined. The best way to decide whether a hard standard is appropriate is to first establish a soft standard by means of trailer calls and then determine over time which operational aspect most correlates to this soft measure. Figure 9.6 shows the linkage between speed of complaint handling (a hard measure) and satisfaction (a soft measure); the figure illustrates that satisfaction strongly depends on the number of hours it takes to resolve a complaint.

Step 5: Develop Feedback Mechanisms for Measurement to Standards

Once companies have determined whether hard or soft standards are appropriate, and which specific standards best capture customer requirements, they must develop feedback mechanisms that adequately capture the standards. Hard standards typically involve mechanical counts or technology-enabled measurement of time or errors. Soft standards require perceptual measurements through the use of trailer surveys or employee monitoring. Employee monitoring is illustrated by the practice of supervisors listening in on employee calls. You may have experienced this practice when you called customer service numbers for many organizations and noticed that the voice prompts tell you that calls may be monitored for quality purposes. The purpose of this monitoring is to provide feedback on employee performance to the standards set by the organization to meet customer needs. One critical aspect of developing feedback mechanisms is ensuring that performance captures the process from the customer's view rather than the company's perspective. A supervisor monitoring an employee's handling of a customer service call, for example, should focus not so much on how quickly the employee gets the customer off the phone as with how adequately she handles the customer's request.

Step 6: Establish Measures and Target Levels

The next step requires that companies establish target levels for the standards. Without this step the company lacks a way to quantify whether the standards have been met. Figure 9.6 provided a good example of the approach used to set standards for timeliness in a service company. Each time a complaint was made to the company, and each time one was resolved, employees logged in the times. They also asked each customer his or her satisfaction with the performance in resolving the complaint. The company was then able to plot the information from each complaint on the chart to determine how well the company was performing as well as where the company wished to be in the future. The vertical axis in the figure shows the satisfaction levels of customers, and the horizontal axis shows the number of hours it took the company to resolve customer problems. This technique is but one of several for determining the target level.

Another technique is a simple perception–action correlation study. When the service consists of repetitive processes, companies can relate levels of customer satisfaction with actual performance of a behavior or task. Consider, for example, a study to determine the standard for customers' wait time in a line. The information needed includes customer perceptions of their wait in line (soft perceptual measure) and the amount of time they actually stand in line (hard operations measure). The joint collection of these data over many transactions provides evidence of the sensitivity of customers to different wait times.

An airline conducted precisely this study by having a flight attendant intercept customers as they approached the ticket counter. As each customer entered the line, the attendant stamped the entry time on a ticket (using a machine like those in parking lots) and handed the customer the stamped ticket. As the customer exited the line at the end of the transaction, the flight attendant restamped the ticket with the exit time and asked the customer three or four questions about perceptions of the wait in line and satisfaction with the transaction. Aggregating the individual customer data provided a graph that allowed the company to evaluate the impact on perceptions of various levels of line waits.

Step 7: Track Measures against Standards

Roger Milliken, former head of Milliken Industries, is reported to have said, "In God we trust, all others bring data." Successful service businesses, such as Federal Express and Walt Disney, have careful and comprehensive fact-based systems about their operations. One company that lives and thrives through management by fact is Granite Rock in Watsonville, California. The 90-year-old, family-run business (concrete, asphalt, and crushed stone) that won a Baldrige Award in the small business category has been described as a "huge mechanism for gathering, analyzing, and acting on information." Statistical process control and other types of charts are everywhere, tracking characteristics of its concrete and crushed stone and processes such as the time it takes customers to fill their trucks. Customer complaints are also tracked through what the company calls "product-service discrepancy reports" and root-cause analysis, and updates are distributed to all plants. The reports show how long it takes to resolve complaints and provide detailed quarterly analyses of trends. Plants can track their trends for four years running. As a result, the company has reduced its product liability costs to one-tenth the industry average. When it comes to product quality and customer service, Granite Rock leaves nothing to chance. According to Dave Franceschi, manager of quality support,

> We simply have to know how we're doing. And as soon as we see a dip in the numbers, we need to do some root-cause analysis. If something goes wrong, we have to figure out what happened and prevent it from happening again, so we can get back on that upward climb.[14]

Since the quality movement of the 1980s, many techniques have been developed to track measures against standards. W. Edwards Deming, one of the most influential leaders of the quality movement, developed an approach called the P-D-C-A cycle (Plan-Do-Check-Act) that is applied to processes to measure and continuously improve their performance. Joseph Juran, another founder of the quality movement, was one of the first to apply statistical methods to improvement, leading to the widespread use of statistical process control as a way to measure performance to standards.

Step 8: Provide Feedback about Performance to Employees

Federal Express communicates the performance on its service quality indicator daily so that everyone in the company knows how it is performing. When problems occur, they can be identified and corrected. The SQI measurement gives everyone in the company immediate feedback on activity that is strongly related to customer perceptions. In a general sense, data and facts need to be analyzed and distributed to support evaluation and decision making at multiple levels within the company. The data also must be deployed quickly enough that the people who need it to make decisions about service or processes can do so. Responsibility for meeting service requirements must also be communicated throughout the organization. All parts of the organization must be measuring their services to internal customers, and ultimately measuring how that performance relates to external customer requirements.[15]

Step 9: Periodically Update Target Levels and Measures

The final step involves revising the target levels, measures, and even customer requirements regularly enough to keep up with customer expectations.

SERVICE PERFORMANCE INDEXES

One outcome from following the process just described is a service performance index. *Service performance indexes* are comprehensive composites of the most critical performance standards. Development of an index begins by identifying the set of customer-defined standards that the company will use to drive behavior. Not all service performance indexes contain customer-defined standards, but the best ones, like FedEx's SQI, are based on them. Most companies build these indexes by (1) understanding the most important requirements of the customer, (2) linking these requirements to tangible and measurable aspects of service provision, and (3) using the feedback from these indexes to identify and improve service problems. The most progressive companies also use the feedback for reward and recognition systems within the company. Here are a few examples of the service performance indexes of U.S. companies.

Southern Pacific At one time Southern Pacific was rated lowest in its industry on customer satisfaction. Since then it has passed the competition in many areas because of a revised customer satisfaction measurement program and service performance index. It began by redesigning its survey around 19 key attributes that drove customer satisfaction. After gaining management commitment to these priorities, it linked these attributes to real operational measures and also to financial performance. It eliminated any operational measures that could not be directly linked to the 19 customer requirements. It now compares itself to the best railroad and trucking firms.

USAA's Family of Measures (FOM) The United Services Automobile Association tracks the quality of individual and unit performance to ensure that persons or groups are showing improvement in service delivery. The company focuses on continuous improvement—that people want an ongoing picture of how they're doing, that they want to be measured in accordance with standards they themselves have helped to set, and that they value the opportunity to improve performance without direct reference to compensation—and therefore it focuses on improvement over time, rather than on giving grades. Every month FOM tracks five areas: quality, quantity of work completed, service timeliness, resource utilization, and customer satisfaction. The FOM is a flexible evaluation process that is developed by a representative group of employees from a work unit. To develop their index, each group asks itself four questions: (1) Is the activity under our control? (2) Is it significant? (3) Does it involve some form of data that we can collect? (4) Can we easily analyze the results? The groups decide which measures to include and the relative weight of each measure in the system. Two measures—quality and quantity—are weighted for each unit.[16]

Airline Performance Index This index (developed by the National Institute for Aviation Research, Wichita State University) identifies a comprehensive set of factors that influence airline service perceptions and rates all U.S. airlines annually on the index. These factors include the following:

1. On-time flights
2. Number of accidents
3. Flight problems
4. Pilot errors
5. Overbookings
6. Mishandled baggage
7. Fare complaints
8. Frequent flier awards
9. Other complaints
10. Refund complaints
11. Service complaints
12. Ticket complaints[17]

Among the issues companies must tackle when developing service performance indexes are (1) the number of components to be contained, (2) what overall or summary measures will be included, (3) whether the index should be weighted or unweighted (to put greater emphasis on the performance of the attributes considered most important to customers), and (4) whether all parts of the business (departments, sectors, or business units) will be held to the same performance measures. One of the most important goals of an index is to simply and clearly communicate business performance in operational and perceptual terms. Companies must develop the rigor in these measurement areas that they have in financial performance.

Summary

This chapter discussed the discrepancy between company perceptions of customer expectations and the standards they set to deliver to these expectations. Among the major causes for provider gap 2 are inadequate standardization of service behaviors and actions, absence of formal processes for setting service quality goals, and lack of customer-defined standards. These problems were discussed and detailed, along with strategies to close the gap.

Customer-defined standards are at the heart of delivery of service that customers expect: they are the link between customer's expressed expectations and company actions to deliver to those expectations. Creating these service standards is not a common practice in U.S. firms. Doing so requires that companies' marketing and operations departments work together by using the marketing research as input for operations. Unless the operations standards are defined by customer priorities, they are not likely to have an impact on customer perceptions of service.

Discussion Questions

1. How does the service measurement that we describe in this chapter differ from the service measurement in Chapter 5? Which of the two types do you think is most important? Why?

2. In what types of service industries are standards most difficult to develop? Why? Recommend three standards that might be developed in one of the firms from the industries you specify. How would employees react to these standards? How could you gain buy-in for them?

3. Given the need for customer-defined service standards, do firms need company-defined standards at all? Could all standards in a company be customer defined? Why or why not? What functional departments in a firm would object to having all standards customer defined?

4. What is the difference between hard and soft standards? Which do you think would be more readily accepted by employees? By management? Why?

5. Consider the university or school you currently attend. What are examples of hard standards, soft standards, and one-time fixes that would address student requirements? Does the school currently use these standards for delivery of service to students? Why or why not? Do you think your reasons would apply to private-sector companies as well? To public or nonprofit companies?

6. Think about a service that you currently use, then map out the service encounter sequence for that service. What is your most important requirement in each interaction? Document these requirements, and make certain that they are expressed at the concrete level of behaviors and actions.

7. Which of the service performance indexes described at the end of this chapter is the most effective? Why? What distinguishes the one you selected from the others? How would you improve each of the others?

Exercises

1. Select a local service firm. Visit the firm and ascertain the service measurements the company tracks. What hard measures does it monitor? Soft measures? On the basis of what you find, develop a service performance index.

2. Choose one of the peripheral services (such as computer, library, placement) provided by your school. What hard standards would be useful to track to meet stu-

dent expectations? What soft standards? What one-time fixes would improve service?

3. Think about a service company you have worked for or know about. Using Figure 9.3, write in customer requirements at each of the levels. How far down in the chart can you describe requirements? Is that far enough?

4. Look at three websites from which you can order products (such as <u>amazon.com</u> or llbean.com). What are the companies' delivery promises? What types of standards might they set for these? Are these customer- or company-defined standards?

Notes

1. "Taking the Measure of Quality," *Service Savvy,* March 1992, p. 3.
2. Ibid.
3. Speech by Federal Express Manager in Baltimore, Maryland, June 1993.
4. T. Levitt, "Industrialization of Service," *Harvard Business Review,* September–October 1976, pp. 63–74.
5. B. S. Lunde and S. L. Marr, "Customer Satisfaction Measurement: Does It Pay Off?" (Indianapolis: Walker Customer Satisfaction Measurements, 1990).
6. D. Reed, "Hotels Penalize Late Arrivals, Early Departures," *The Wall Street Journal,* August 18, 1998, p. B1.
7. "Fast, Reliable Delivery Processes Are Cheered by Time-Sensitive Customers," *The Service Edge* 4, no. 3 (1993): 1.
8. F. Reichhold, "e-loyalty," *Harvard Business Review,* July–August 2000, pp. 105–13.
9. R. E. Kordupleski, R. T. Rust, and A. J. Zaharik, "Why Improving Quality Doesn't Improve Quality (or Whatever Happened to Marketing?)," *California Management Review* 35, no. 3 (Spring 1993), p. 89.
10. D. E. Hansen and P. J. Danaher, "Inconsistent Performance during the Service Encounter: What's a Good Start Worth?" *Journal of Service Research* 1, February 1999, pp. 227–35.
11. W. E. Crosby, "American Airlines—A Commitment to Excellence," in *Services Marketing in a Changing Environment* (Chicago: American Marketing Association, 1985), pp. 11–12.
12. "Taking the Measure of Quality," p. 3.
13. G. Russell, "Where the Customer Is Still King," *Time,* February 2, 1987.
14. "Managing by Fact: It's Exhaustive, Expensive, and Essential," *The Service Edge* 6, no. 5 (May 1993).
15. "Taking the Measure of Quality," p. 3.
16. T. Ehrenfeld, "Merit Evaluation and the Family of Measures," *Harvard Business Review,* September–October 1991, p. 122.
17. D. Carroll, "Expert: Being on Time Isn't Everything for Airlines," *USA Today,* March 5, 1992, p. 6B.

10

PHYSICAL EVIDENCE AND THE SERVICESCAPE

This chapter's objectives are to

1. Explain the impact on customer perceptions of physical evidence, particularly the servicescape.

2. Illustrate differences in types of servicescapes, the roles played by the servicescape, and the implications for strategy.

3. Explain why the servicescape affects employee and customer behavior, using a framework based in marketing, organizational behavior, and environmental psychology.

4. Analyze four different approaches for understanding the effects of physical evidence and servicescapes, namely environmental surveys, direct observation, experiments, and photographic blueprints.

5. Present elements of an effective physical evidence strategy.

Using Physical Evidence to Position a New Service

When Speedi-Lube opened its doors in Seattle, Washington, it was one of the first 10-minute oil and lubrication services ever introduced. Now there are thousands of such outlets, but then the concept was totally new. The idea was to offer an alternative to corner gas stations for basic car lubrication service, quickly (within 10 minutes), with no appointment necessary. Because the concept was unknown to consumers at the time, the owners of Speedi-Lube needed to communicate and position the service clearly so that consumers would form accurate expectations. And because car maintenance is highly intangible and consumers often don't understand what is actually done to their cars, the owners relied heavily on tangible physical evidence to communicate the concept before, during, and after the sale.

To communicate an image of fast, efficient service, Speedi-Lube relied on straightforward, to-the-point advertising using clean, crisp letters. For example, a large billboard read in large blue and white letters: SPEEDI-LUBE, 10-MINUTE OIL

CHANGE, NO APPOINTMENT, OPEN 7 DAYS, 9 TO 6. The very buildings where the service was performed communicated the efficiency theme clearly. In fact, the exteriors of some of the first Speedi-Lube facilities had the look of a fast-food restaurant, not inconsistent with the intended image of speed, efficiency, and predictability. Entrance and exit signs were clearly displayed so that customers coming to Speedi-Lube for the first time would know exactly where to drive their cars.

On driving into the service bay the customer was greeted with additional physical evidence that clearly differentiated Speedi-Lube from its competitors at that time. The service bay was very neat and brightly painted, with a professional-appearing service counter in the bay where the customer filled out paperwork to get the service. Service personnel in professional uniforms helped with the paperwork, and the customer was invited to wait in a clean and functional waiting area where coffee and magazines were provided. (Alternatively, customers were welcome to stay in the service area to observe the work on their cars.) On one of the waiting room walls was displayed a large schematic that showed the underside of an automobile and identified all of the lubrication points and exactly what was being done to the car (Figure 10.1). This form of evidence informed customers and gave them confidence in what was being done.

On completion, the customer was given a checklist itemizing the lubrication services provided. As a finishing touch, the employee would then lubricate the door locks on the car to indicate that nothing had been overlooked. Three months later Speedi-Lube would mail a reminder postcard suggesting that it was time for another oil change.

It is difficult to imagine a time when 10-minute oil and lubrication services didn't exist on every street corner. Yet when Speedi-Lube was established the quick oil change concept was totally unknown to consumers. Speedi-Lube was dealing with both a totally new concept and an industry in which services are generally high in credence attributes. The company used physical evidence very effectively to communicate the

FIGURE 10.1
Speedi-Lube spells out the service offering.

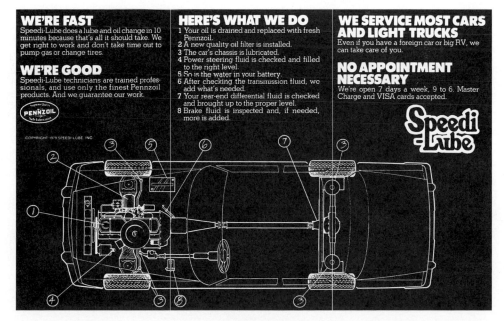

new concept and to make elements of the process itself very concrete. The schematic on the waiting room wall detailing what the service entailed, as well as the checklist showing exactly what had been done, were ways the company tried to make credence attributes more tangible.

In this chapter we explore the importance of physical evidence for communicating service quality attributes, setting customer expectations, and creating the service experience. As defined in Chapter 1 when we introduced the expanded marketing mix for services, *physical evidence is the environment in which the service is delivered and where the firm and the customer interact, and any tangible commodities that facilitate performance or communication of the service.* The first part of this definition encompasses the actual physical facility where the service is performed, delivered, and consumed; throughout this chapter the physical facility is referred to as the *servicescape.*[1]

Physical evidence is particularly important for communicating about credence services (such as auto repair), but it is also important for services such as hotels, hospitals, and theme parks that are dominated by experience attributes. Think of how effectively Disney uses the physical evidence of its service to excite its customers. The brightly colored displays, the music, the fantastic rides, and the costumed characters all reinforce the feelings of fun and excitement that Disney seeks to generate in its customers. Think also of how effective Disney is in portraying consistent physical evidence that is compatible with its goals. The physical evidence and servicescape, or the "stage" in Disney's terms, is always stimulating to the extreme, is always clean, is always in top repair, and never fails to deliver what it has promised to consumers, and more. In this chapter we see many examples of how physical evidence communicates with customers and how it can play a role in creating the service experience, in satisfying customers, and in enhancing customers' perceptions of quality.

PHYSICAL EVIDENCE—WHAT IS IT?

Because services are intangible, customers often rely on tangible cues, or physical evidence, to evaluate the service before its purchase and to assess their satisfaction with the service during and after consumption. Effective design of physical, tangible evidence is important for closing gap 2.

General elements of physical evidence are shown in Table 10.1. They include all aspects of the organization's physical facility (the servicescape) as well as other forms

TABLE 10.1
Elements of Physical Evidence

Servicescape	Other Tangibles
Facility exterior	Business cards
Exterior design	Stationery
Signage	Billing statements
Parking	Reports
Landscape	Employee dress
Surrounding environment	Uniforms
Facility interior	Brochures
Interior design	Web pages
Equipment	Virtual servicescape
Signage	
Layout	
Air quality/temperature	

Technology Spotlight
Virtual Servicescapes: Experiencing Services on the Internet

Web pages and virtual service tours allow customers to preview a service experience and see tangible evidence of the service. This medium offers firms tremendous potential to communicate experiential aspects of their service in ways that were previously very difficult, if not impossible.

For example, travelers can now preview destinations, view hotels and their rooms, and tour through entertainment venues before booking their trips or even deciding where to travel. In booking a trip to Great Britain, for example, websites that show hotels, bed and breakfast inns, and other lodging all over the country can be previewed. Exteriors of the facilities as well as actual rooms can be examined in selecting accommodations. Prior to the Internet, this kind of servicescape knowledge, across a wide range of choices and available at a moment's notice, would have been impossible. And a visit to British Airways' website provides the opportunity to view all aspects of its award-winning seat design and other aspects of its in-flight services. Thus a traveler to Great Britain who chooses to fly British Airways can view the aircraft, destination, and hotel room, all before experiencing the service.

In the retail context, customers can view merchandise and literally walk through a store in real time, viewing the merchandise and zooming in on things they would like to buy. Gallery Furniture in Houston, Texas, offers this service for its customers, allowing them to tour the company's showroom remotely. The owner tells the story of a woman from the Middle East whose husband was recently employed by a Texas oil company. While he was still in his home country, she was in Houston, purchasing furniture and setting up their new home. She was able to link her husband into the store's website, tour the store with him in real time via the store's live video cameras, and decide on furniture with him even though they were half a world apart.

In a different context, a Ford motor company body shop and repair facility allows its customers to view their automobile's progress as it moves through the repair process. Customers can sign onto the dealer's website, click on their vehicle's ID numbers, and be shown photos of their cars as they are being repaired. Repair of major damage to a vehicle can take several weeks, during which the customer would formerly have had no idea what was being done to the car; with the "virtual shop tour" the customer can see exactly what is being done to the vehicle. To implement this service, the dealer changed the servicescape substantially to make it more appealing and presentable to customers. The result is that a "mysterious" and sometimes time-consuming service is now more transparent to customers.

Internet technology clearly provides tremendous opportunities for firms to communicate about their services. But with these opportunities come some risks and responsibilities as well. It suddenly is apparent how important the tangible images on the Web can be and how important it is to show a true picture of the service. It is also apparent that the images and service tours presented via the Internet need to be consistent with the positioning of the service brand, and should be planned in conjunction with other marketing messages. Given the ease of putting photos and other tangible evidence on the Web, these precautions are not always adhered to, resulting in mixed (and even wrong) messages being sent out to customers.

of tangible communication. Elements of the servicescape that affect customers include both exterior attributes (such as signage, parking, and the landscape) and interior attributes (such as design, layout, equipment, and decor). Note that web pages and virtual servicescapes conveyed over the Internet are more recent forms of physical evidence that companies can use to communicate about the service experience, making services more tangible for customers both before and after purchase. These advances are illustrated in our Technology Spotlight.

Physical evidence examples from different service contexts are given in Table 10.2. It is apparent that some services (like hospitals, resorts, and child care) communicate heavily through physical evidence while others (insurance, express mail) provide

TABLE 10.2
Examples of Physical Evidence from the Customer's Point of View

| Service | Physical Evidence | |
	Servicescape	Other Tangibles
Insurance	Not applicable	Policy itself Billing statements Periodic updates Company brochure Letters/cards Website
Hospital	Building exterior Parking Signs Waiting areas Admissions office Patient care room Medical equipment Recovery room	Uniforms Reports/stationery Billing statements Website
Airline	Airline gate area Airplane exterior Airplane interior (decor, seats, air quality)	Tickets Food Uniforms Website
Express mail	Not applicable	Packaging Trucks Uniforms Computers Website
Sporting event	Parking Stadium exterior Ticketing area Entrance Seating Restrooms Concession areas Playing field	Signs Tickets Program Uniforms Website

limited physical evidence. All of the elements of evidence listed for each service communicate something about the service to consumers and/or facilitate performance of the service. Although we focus in this chapter primarily on the servicescape and its effects, keep in mind that what is said applies to the other forms of evidence as well.

Consumer researchers know that the design of the servicescape can influence customer choices, expectations, satisfaction, and other behaviors. For example, retailers know that customers are influenced by smell, decor, music, and store layout. On the basis of a totally separate area of research, we know that the design of work environments can affect employees' productivity, motivation, and satisfaction.[2] The challenge in many service settings is to design the physical space and evidence so that it can support the needs and preferences of both customers and employees simultaneously. For example, in a study of employee and customer preferences in a bank environment, customers tended to agree that "A bank should not look like too much money was spent on the decor," whereas employees tended not to agree.[3] Customers may perceive that they are paying for expensive decor. Employees, on the other hand, may perceive an investment in the environment as an indication of management's concern for their feelings of job satisfaction.

In this chapter we explain the roles played by the servicescape and how it affects employees and customers and their interactions. The chapter relies heavily on ideas and concepts from environmental psychology, a field that encompasses the study of human beings and their relationships with built (man-made), natural, and social environments.[4]

TYPES OF SERVICESCAPES

The physical setting may be more or less important in achieving the organization's marketing and other goals depending on certain factors. Table 10.3 is a framework for categorizing service organizations on two dimensions that capture some of the key differences that will impact the management of the servicescape. Organizations that share a cell in the matrix will face similar issues and decisions regarding their physical spaces.

Servicescape Use

First, organizations differ in terms of *whom* the servicescape will actually affect. That is, who actually comes into the service facility and thus is potentially influenced by its design—customers, employees, or both groups? The first column of Table 10.3 suggests three types of service organizations that differ on this dimension. At one extreme is the *self-service* environment, where the customer performs most of the activities and few if any employees are involved. Examples of self-service environments include ATMs, movie theaters, express mail drop-off facilities, self-service entertainment such

TABLE 10.3
Typology of Service Organizations Based on Variations in Form and Use of the Servicescape

	Complexity of the Servicescape	
Servicescape Usage	**Elaborate**	**Lean**
Self-service (customer only)	Golf Land Surf 'n Splash	ATM Shopping mall information kiosk Post office kiosk Internet services Express mail drop-off
Interpersonal services (both customer and employee)	Hotel Restaurant Health clinic Hospital Bank Airline School	Dry cleaner Hot dog stand Hair salon
Remote service (employee only)	Telephone company Insurance company Utility Many professional services	Telephone mail-order desk Automated voice messaging services

Source: From M. J. Bitner, "Servicescapes: The Impact of Physical Surroundings on Customers and Employees," *Journal of Marketing* 56 (April 1992), pp. 57–71. Reprinted with permission of the American Marketing Association.

as golf and theme parks, and online Internet services. In these primarily self-service environments the organization can plan the servicescape focusing exclusively on marketing goals such as attracting the right market segment and making the facility pleasing and easy to use.

At the other extreme of the use dimension is the *remote service,* where there is little or no customer involvement with the servicescape. Telecommunications, utilities, financial consultants, editorial, and mail-order services are examples of services that can be provided without the customer ever seeing the service facility. In fact, the facility may be in a different state or a different country. To illustrate, all of AT&T's customer service calls are handled out of a small number of call centers located throughout the United States. A person calling from New York in the middle of the night may talk to a service representative in Arizona. In these remote services, decisions about how the facility should be designed can focus almost exclusively on the employees' needs and preferences. The place can be set up to keep employees motivated and to facilitate productivity, teamwork, operational efficiency, or whatever organizational behavior goal is desired without any consideration of customers because they will never need to see the servicescape.

In Table 10.3, *interpersonal services* are placed between the two extremes and represent situations where both the customer and the employee must be present in the servicescape. Examples abound such as hotels, restaurants, hospitals, educational settings, and banks. In these cases the servicescape must be planned to attract, satisfy, and facilitate the activities of both customers and employees simultaneously. Special attention must also be given to how the servicescape affects the nature and quality of the social interactions between and among customers and employees. A cruise ship provides a good example of a service setting where the servicescape must support customers and the employees who work there and also facilitate interactions between the two groups.

Complexity of the Servicescape

The horizontal dimension of Table 10.3 suggests another factor that will influence servicescape management. Some service environments are very simple, with few elements, few spaces, and few pieces of equipment. Such environments are termed *lean.* Shopping mall information kiosks and FedEx drop-off facilities would be considered lean environments because both provide service from one simple structure. For lean servicescapes, design decisions are relatively straightforward, especially in self-service or remote service situations in which there is no interaction among employees and customers.

Other servicescapes are very complicated, with many elements and many forms. They are termed *elaborate* environments. An example is a hospital with its many floors and rooms, sophisticated equipment, and complex variability in functions performed within the physical facility. In such an elaborate environment, the full range of marketing and organizational objectives theoretically can be approached through careful management of the servicescape. For example, a patient's hospital room can be designed to enhance patient comfort and satisfaction while simultaneously facilitating employee productivity. Firms such as hospitals that are positioned in the elaborate interpersonal service cell face the most complex servicescape decisions. To illustrate, when the Mayo Clinic, probably the best-known name in U.S. health care, opened its hospital in Scottsdale, Arizona, in 1998, the organization painstakingly considered the interrelated goals, needs, and feelings of its employees, doctors, patients, and visitors in designing its distinctive servicescape (see Exhibit 10.2 later in this chapter).

Typology Implications

By locating itself in the appropriate cell of the typology, an organization can start to answer the following questions:

1. *Who should be consulted in making servicescape and other evidence decisions?* If a company finds itself in the self-service cell, it can focus on the needs and preferences of customers. If it is in the remote service cell, it can focus on employees. If, however, the organization finds itself in one of the interpersonal service cells, it will know that decisions about the servicescape can potentially affect both customers and employees, as well as their interactions. Thus both groups' needs and preferences should be considered, suggesting a more difficult decision process.

2. *What organizational goals might be targeted through servicescape design?* For self-service firms, the focus can be on marketing goals such as customer attraction and customer satisfaction. For remote service firms, priority can be given to work-group needs and employee motivation, productivity, and satisfaction in designing the service facility. For interpersonal services, both marketing and organizational goals could potentially be targeted, with the understanding that the solutions for one set of goals may not be compatible with the other set.

3. *How complex is the set of decisions regarding the servicescape?* Decisions will clearly be more complex for elaborate than for lean service environments. The more elaborate the servicescape in terms of spaces, equipment, and diversity of services delivered, the more complex will be decisions about its design. Added complexity will also require more resources in terms of time, money, and people involvement in design decisions. The most complex servicescape decisions will be in the elaborate, interpersonal services cell where multiple needs (employees, customers, and their interactions) will be considered as well.

ROLES OF THE SERVICESCAPE

Within the cells of the typology, the servicescape can play many roles simultaneously. An examination of the variety of roles and how they interact makes clear how strategically important it is to provide appropriate physical evidence of the service.

Package

Similar to a tangible product's package, the servicescape and other elements of physical evidence essentially "wrap" the service and convey an external image of what is "inside" to consumers. Product packages are designed to portray a particular image as well as to evoke a particular sensory or emotional reaction. The physical setting of a service does the same thing through the interaction of many complex stimuli. The servicescape is the outward appearance of the organization and thus can be critical in forming initial impressions or setting up customer expectations—it is a visual metaphor for the intangible service. This packaging role is particularly important in creating expectations for new customers and for newly established service organizations that are trying to build a particular image. The physical surroundings offer an organization the opportunity to convey an image in a way not unlike the way an individual chooses to "dress for success." The packaging role extends to the appearance of contact personnel through their uniforms or dress and other elements of their outward appearance.[5]

Interestingly, the same care and resource expenditures given to package design in product marketing are not generally provided for services, even though the service package serves a variety of important roles. There are many exceptions to this generality, however. Smart companies like Starbucks, FedEx, and Marriott spend a lot of time and money relating their servicescape design to their brand, providing their customers with strong visual metaphors and "service packaging" that conveys the brand positioning. FedEx, for example, embarked on a major overhaul of its image by rethinking and redesigning all of its tangibles—everything from its drop boxes to its service centers to the bags carried by its couriers.[6] The first step was to redesign the look of its 1,400 U.S. service centers through extensive customer and employee research and testing of a full-scale prototype built around the idea of three zones, or walls. The idea is to convey through the customer and agent zones a consistent look and feel of "things are simple here," and "here, give us your package; we'll take care of everything." At the same time the service centers reinforce the FedEx brand by telling a visual story about FedEx on the brand wall.

Facilitator

The servicescape can also serve as a facilitator in aiding the performances of persons in the environment. How the setting is designed can enhance or inhibit the efficient flow of activities in the service setting, making it easier or harder for customers and employees to accomplish their goals. A well-designed, functional facility can make the service a pleasure to experience from the customer's point of view and a pleasure to perform from the employee's. On the other hand, poor and inefficient design may frustrate both customers and employees. For example, an international air traveler who finds himself in a poorly designed airport with few signs, poor ventilation, and few places to sit or eat will find the experience quite dissatisfying, and employees who work there will probably be unmotivated as well. The same international traveler will appreciate seats on the airplane that are conducive to work and sleep. The seating itself, part of the physical surroundings of the service, has been improved over the years to better facilitate travelers' needs to sleep. In fact, the competition for better seat design continues as a major point of contention among the international airline carriers, and the results have translated into greater customer satisfaction for business travelers.[7] British Airways has even seen its market share increase on some routes as a direct result of its award-winning Club-World seat.[8] The seat, demonstrated on its website and featured in British Airways ads, turns into a six-foot, fully flat bed and benefits from an in-flight entertainment pod and movable privacy screen. All of these factors emphasize the facilitator role of the servicescape.

Socializer

The design of the servicescape aids in the socialization of both employees and customers in the sense that it helps to convey expected roles, behaviors, and relationships. For example, a new employee in a professional services firm would come to understand her position in the hierarchy partially through noting her office assignment, the quality of her office furnishings, and her location relative to others in the organization.

The design of the facility can also suggest to customers what their role is relative to employees, what parts of the servicescape they are welcome in and which are for employees only, how they should behave while in the environment, and what types of interactions are encouraged. For example, consider a Club Med vacation environment that is set up to facilitate customer–customer interactions as well as to facilitate guest interactions with Club Med staff. The organization also recognizes the need for privacy, providing areas that encourage solitary activities. To illustrate further, in some

Starbucks locations, the company is experimenting with shifting to more of a traditional coffeehouse environment where customers spend social time rather than coming in for a quick cup of coffee on the run. To encourage this type of socializing, these Starbucks locations have comfortable lounge chairs and tables set up to encourage interaction and staying longer.

Differentiator

The design of the physical facility can differentiate a firm from its competitors and signal the market segment the service is intended for. Given its power as a differentiator, changes in the physical environment can be used to reposition a firm and/or to attract new market segments. In shopping malls the signage, colors used in decor and displays, and type of music wafting from a store signal the intended market segment. In another context, Washington Mutual Bank clearly communicates through its servicescape its differentiation as a bank for consumers and families.[9] As you enter one of its branches, the first thing you see is a mural of children. Then you are greeted by an informal, khaki-clad concierge. There is an area for children to play as well as a retail store offering financial books, software, and piggy banks, clearly differentiating this bank from those whose focus is commercial accounts or private, upscale banking.

The design of a physical setting can also differentiate one area of a service organization from another. This is commonly the case in the hotel industry where one large hotel may have several levels of dining possibilities, each signaled by differences in design. Price differentiation is also often partially achieved through variations in physical setting. Bigger rooms with more physical amenities cost more, just as larger seats with more leg room (generally in first class) are more expensive on an airplane. A development in movie theaters is the addition of luxury screening rooms with club chairs and waiters.[10] Taking advantage of this alternative, customers who are willing to pay a higher price to see the same film can experience the service in an entirely different environment.

FRAMEWORK FOR UNDERSTANDING SERVICESCAPE EFFECTS ON BEHAVIOR

Although it is useful from a strategic point of view to think about the multiple roles of the servicescape and how they interact, making actual decisions about servicescape design requires an understanding of why the effects occur and how to manage them. The next sections of the chapter present a framework or model of environment and behavior relationships in service settings.

The Underlying Framework

The framework for understanding servicescape effects on behavior follows from basic *stimulus–organism–response* theory. In the framework the multidimensional environment is the *stimulus,* consumers and employees are the *organisms* that respond to the stimuli, and behaviors directed at the environment are the *responses.* The assumptions are that dimensions of the servicescape will impact customers and employees and they will behave in certain ways depending on their internal reactions to the servicescape.

Let's focus on a particular example. Assume there is a cookie cart that is parked outside the student union on campus. The cart is colorful and playful in design, and an aroma of baking cookies wafts from it. The design and the aroma are two elements of the servicescape that will impact customers in some way. Now assume you are a hungry student, just out of class, strolling across campus. The fun design of the cart attracts your attention, and simultaneously you smell baking cookies. The fun design and the delicious smell cause you to feel happy, relaxed, and hungry at the same time. You are attracted to the cart and decide to buy a cookie because you have another class to attend before lunch. The movement toward the cart and the purchase of a cookie are behaviors directed at the servicescape. Depending on how much time you have, you may even choose to converse with the vendor or other customers standing around munching cookies, other forms of behavior directed at the servicescape.

The framework shown in Figure 10.2 is detailed and developed in the next sections. It represents a comprehensive stimulus–organism–response model that recognizes complex dimensions of the environment, impacts on multiple parties (customers, employees, and their interactions), multiple types of internal responses (cognitive, emotional, and physiological), and a variety of individual and social behaviors that can result.

Our discussion of the framework will begin on the right side of the model with *behaviors*. Next we will explain and develop the *internal responses* portion of the model. Finally we will turn to the dimensions of the *environment* and the holistic perception of the environment.

FIGURE 10.2 **A Framework for Understanding Environment–User Relationships in Service Organizations**

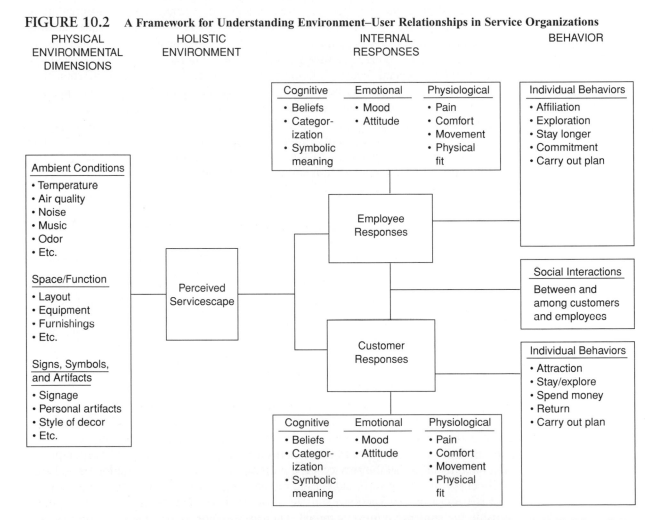

Source: Adapted from M. J. Bitner, "Servicescapes: The Impact of Physical Surroundings on Customers and Employees," *Journal of Marketing* 56 (April 1992), pp. 57–71. Reprinted with permission of the American Marketing Association.

Behaviors in the Servicescape

That human behavior is influenced by the physical setting in which it occurs is essentially a truism. Interestingly, however, until the 1960s psychologists largely ignored the effects of physical setting in their attempts to predict and explain behavior. Since that time, a large and steadily growing body of literature within the field of environmental psychology has addressed the relationships between human beings and their built environments.

Individual Behaviors

Environmental psychologists suggest that individuals react to places with two general, and opposite, forms of behavior: approach and avoidance. Approach behaviors include all positive behaviors that might be directed at a particular place, such as desire to stay, explore, work, and affiliate.[11] Avoidance behaviors reflect the opposite—a desire not to stay, to explore, to work, or to affiliate. In a study of consumers in retail environments, researchers found that approach behaviors (including shopping enjoyment, returning, attraction and friendliness toward others, spending money, time spent browsing, and exploration of the store) were influenced by perceptions of the environment.[12] At one 7-Eleven store the owners played "elevator music" to drive away the youthful market segment that was detracting from the store's image. And the cookie cart example just given is reminiscent of cinnamon roll bakeries in malls that attract patrons through the power of smell.

In addition to attracting or deterring entry, the servicescape can actually influence the degree of success consumers and employees experience in executing their plans once inside. Each individual comes to a particular service organization with a goal or purpose that may be aided or hindered by the setting. NBA basketball fans are aided in their enjoyment of the game by adequate, easy-access parking; clear signage directing them to their seats; efficient food service; and clean rest rooms. Figure 10.3 shows how Marriott Hotels clearly understands the role of the servicescape for its business travelers. The ability of employees to do their jobs effectively is also influenced by the servicescape. Adequate space, proper equipment, and comfortable temperature and air quality all contribute to an employee's comfort and job satisfaction, causing him or her to be more productive, stay longer, and affiliate positively with coworkers.

Social Interactions

In addition to its effects on their individual behaviors, the servicescape influences the nature and quality of customer and employee interactions, most directly in interpersonal services. It has been stated that "all social interaction is affected by the physical container in which it occurs."[13] The "physical container" can affect the nature of social interaction in terms of the duration of interaction and the actual progression of events. In many service situations, a firm may want to ensure a particular progression of events (a "standard script") and limit the duration of the service. Environmental variables such as physical proximity, seating arrangements, size, and flexibility can define the possibilities and limits of social episodes such as those occurring between customers and employees, or customers and other customers. The Carnival Cruise Line photo shown in Figure 10.4 illustrates how the design of the servicescape can help to define the social rules, conventions, and expectations in force in a given setting, thus serving to define the nature of social interaction.[14] The close physical proximity of passengers on the sunbathing deck will in and of itself prescribe certain patterns of

FIGURE 10.3

Marriott recognizes the important roles of the servicescape for its business customers.

behavior. This is not a vacation designed for a social recluse! Others have implied that recurring social behavior patterns are associated with particular physical settings and that when people encounter typical settings, their social behaviors can be predicted.[15]

Examples of how environments shape social interactions—and how these interactions in turn influence the environment—are abundant.[16] Even casual observation of the retail phenomenon "Nike Town Chicago" (Exhibit 10.1) shows how this form of "entertainment retail" shapes the behaviors of consumers but at the same time allows them to interpret and create their own realities and experiences.[17] In a river-rafting trip, the "wilderness servicescape" profoundly influences the behaviors, interactions, and total experiences of rafting consumers and their guides. In this case the natural, for the most part uncontrollable, environment is the setting for the service.[18]

Internal Responses to the Servicescape

Employees and customers respond to dimensions of their physical surroundings cognitively, emotionally, and physiologically, and those responses are what influence their behaviors in the environment as shown in the middle portion of Figure 10.2. In other words, the perceived servicescape does not directly *cause* people to behave in certain ways. Although the internal responses are discussed independently here, they are clearly interdependent: A person's beliefs about a place, a cognitive response, may well influence the person's emotional response, and vice versa. For example, patients who come into a dentist's office that is designed to calm and sooth their anxieties

FIGURE 10.4
Social interactions are defined partially by the configuration of the servicescape.

Source: Carnival Cruise Lines.

(emotional responses) may believe as a result that the dentist is caring and competent (cognitive responses).

Environment and Cognition

The perceived servicescape can have an effect on people's beliefs about a place and their beliefs about the people and products found in that place. In a sense the servicescape can be viewed as a form of nonverbal communication, imparting meaning through what is called "object language."[19] For example, particular environmental cues such as the type of office furniture and decor and the apparel worn by the lawyer may influence a potential client's beliefs about whether the lawyer is successful, expensive, and trustworthy. In a consumer study, variations in descriptions of store atmospheres were found to alter beliefs about a product (perfume) sold in the store.[20] Another study showed that a travel agent's office decor affected customer attributions and beliefs about the travel agent's behavior.[21] Travel agents whose facilities were more organized and professional were viewed more positively than were those whose facilities were disorganized and unprofessional.

In other cases, perceptions of the servicescape may simply help people to distinguish a firm by influencing how it is categorized. The overall perception of the servicescape enables the consumer or employee to categorize the firm mentally. Research shows that in the restaurant industry a particular configuration of environmental cues suggests "fast food," whereas another configuration suggests "elegant sit-down restaurant."[22] In such situations, environmental cues serve as a shortcut device enabling customers to categorize and distinguish among types of restaurants.

Environment and Emotion

In addition to influencing beliefs, the perceived servicescape can directly elicit emotional responses that, in turn, influence behaviors. Just being in a particular place can make us feel happy, lighthearted, and relaxed, whereas being in another place may

Nike Town Chicago is built as a theater, where our consumers are the audience participating in the production. Nike Town gives us the opportunity to explore and experiment with innovative ways to connect with our consumers.

Nike Town Chicago (NTC) is the embodiment of Nike's corporate tagline "Just Do It." NTC and other Nike Towns around the United States epitomize the role of service-scape design in building the brand, providing customers with a way to interact with the brand, and making Nike come alive. NTC represents the height of retail theater.

So what is so special about NTC? What sets it apart from other retail environments? First, NTC is a showcase for the full range of Nike products. A common reaction of consumers is that they had no idea Nike made and carried all of the products displayed. And every designed element of the servicescape encourages impulsive behavior, inviting instant gratification. But the prices are very high—higher

Nike Town Elicits Emotional Responses from Customers
Source: Courtesy of Nike, Inc.

make us feel sad, depressed, and gloomy. The colors, decor, music, and other elements of the atmosphere can have an unexplainable and sometimes very subconsciousness effect on the moods of people in the place. For some people, certain environmental stimuli (noises, smells) common in a dental office can bring on immediate feelings of fear and anxiety. In very different contexts, the marble interior and grandeur of the Supreme Court buildings in Washington, D.C., call up feelings of pride and awe and respect for many; lively music and bright decor in a local night spot may cause people to feel excited and happy. In all of these examples, the response from the consumer probably doesn't involve thinking, but rather is just an unexplained feeling. Consumers' responses to Nike Town Chicago (Exhibit 10.1) are in large part emotional.

Environmental psychologists have researched people's emotional responses to physical settings.[23] They have concluded that any environment, whether natural or engineered, will elicit emotions that can be captured by two basic dimensions: (1) pleasure/displeasure and (2) degree of arousal (amount of stimulation or excitement).[24] Servicescapes that are both pleasant and arousing would be termed *exciting*, whereas those that are pleasant and nonarousing, or sleepy, would be termed *relaxing*. Unpleasant servicescapes that are arousing would be called *distressing*, while unpleasant,

than prices on the same items in other stores. This is by design. Here the servicescape and the experience of NTC are meant to build the brand—not necessarily to sell the products and especially not to compete with other Nike stores and dealers.

When consumers enter NTC, they are struck by the extensive array of products. The first floor of the store has an open-air feel that gives the sense of a small-town shopping district, complete with cobblestone streets and manhole covers. Statues and framed photos of celebrities, large fish tanks, a video pond that projects the illusion of water and underwater scenes, and exhibit cases containing products and memorabilia greet the visiting customers. Visitors are also struck by the immensity of the store, which occupies three full stories.

As they enter through the vestibule, they are greeted by framed pictures of Nike sports celebrity endorsers and a unique display of athletic shoes with a banner over them proclaiming "There Is No Finish Line." The theme of "touching greatness" is echoed throughout the store in framed photos, statues of famous athletes, and background sounds of basketball and other sports.

The image of Michael Jordan weaves throughout the store, starting with his encased statue in the vestibule. On the second floor of the store, consumers are dwarfed by a multistory fantasy photograph of Michael Jordan, as he seems to soar through the clouds in his Jump Man pose. Also on the second floor is a half-court basketball unit, and the sounds of the Chicago Bull's team introduction music can be heard in the background. While other sports are featured as well (aerobics, tennis, golf) and appropriate displays and even soundscapes accompany them, the focus of the second floor is basketball, Michael Jordan, and other superstars. It is even possible to place one's hands and feet into the casts of the likes of Charles Barkley and Penny Hardaway.

On the third floor consumers are provided aerial views of the store and can view the Air Jordan Pavilion—a shrine to the Jump Man. Kids' pavilions are also on the third floor, as well as cased exhibits showing the history of the Nike brand.

From the detail of door handles and railing supports cast in the shape of the distinctive Nike swoosh logo to the expansiveness of the multistory photograph of Jordan, NTC embodies the Nike brand. The space is the brand—the customer creates his or her own relationship with it through experiencing the servicescape.

Source: J. F. Sherry, Jr., "The Soul of the Company Store: Nike Town Chicago and the Emplaced Brandscape," in *Servicescapes: The Concept of Place in Contemporary Markets*, ed. J. F. Sherry, Jr. (Chicago: NTC/Contemporary Publishing Company, 1998), pp. 109–46. Copyright © 1998 by NTC Business Books. Reprinted by permission of NTC Contemporary Books. The initial quotation is from "Nike Town Comes to Chicago," Nike press release, July 2, 1992, as quoted in ibid., p. 109.

sleepy servicescapes would be *gloomy*. These basic emotional responses to environments can be used to begin predicting the expected behaviors of consumers and employees who find themselves in a particular type of place.

Environment and Physiology

The perceived servicescape may also affect people in purely physiological ways. Noise that is too loud may cause physical discomfort, the temperature of a room may cause people to shiver or perspire, the air quality may make it difficult to breathe, and the glare of lighting may decrease ability to see and cause physical pain. All of these physical responses may, in turn, directly influence whether people stay in and enjoy a particular environment. It is well known that the comfort of seating in a restaurant influences how long people stay. The hard seats in a fast-food restaurant cause most people to leave within a predictable period of time. Similarly, environmental design and related physiological responses affect whether a person can perform his or her job function well.

A vast amount of research in engineering and design has addressed human physiological responses to ambient conditions as well as physiological responses to equipment design.[25] Such research fits under the rubric of *human factors design* or *ergonomics.* Human factors research systematically applies relevant information about human capabilities and limitations to the design of things and procedures people use. For example, Choice Hotels International, rated the number one lodging franchise company in 1998, has targeted empty-nester couples and senior citizens in the redesign of many of the rooms in its Rodeway and EconoLodge brands. A significant percentage of the rooms in these hotels have been converted to senior-friendly suites with brighter lighting, larger-button telephones and TV remotes, and grab bars in the showers.[26] Wall switches have lights so they can be found easily at night. To help people with arthritis, doors have lever handles instead of knobs so that every door and every drawer in the room can be opened with a fist rather than requiring hand and wrist dexterity.

Variations in Individual Responses

In general, people respond to the environment in the ways just described—cognitively, emotionally, physiologically—and their responses influence how they behave in the environment. However, the response will not be the same for every individual, every time. Personality differences as well as temporary conditions such as moods or the purpose for being there can cause variations in how people respond to the servicescape.[27]

One personality trait that has been shown to affect how people respond to environments is *arousal seeking.* Arousal seekers enjoy and look for high levels of stimulation, whereas arousal avoiders prefer lower levels of stimulation. Thus an arousal avoider in a loud, bright disco with flashing neon might show strong dislike for the environment, whereas an arousal seeker would be very happy. In a related vein, it has been suggested that some people are better *screeners* of environmental stimuli than others.[28] Screeners of stimuli would be able to experience a high level of stimulation but not be affected by it. Nonscreeners would be highly affected and might exhibit extreme responses even to low levels of stimulation.

The particular purpose for being in a servicescape can also affect a person's response to it. A person who is on an airplane for a one-hour flight will likely be less affected by the atmosphere on the plane than will the traveler who is embarking on a 10-hour overseas flight. Similarly, a day-surgery hospital patient will likely be less sensitive and demanding of her environment than would a patient who is spending two weeks in the hospital. And a person who is staying at a resort hotel for a business meeting will respond differently to the environment than a couple on their honeymoon.

Temporary mood states can also cause people to respond differently to environmental stimuli. A person who is feeling frustrated and fatigued after a long day at work is likely to be affected differently by a highly arousing restaurant than the person would be after a relaxing three-day weekend.

The important thing to remember is that not every person will always respond in the same way to the environment—individual moods, purposes, and expectations may influence the response. And common personality characteristics (arousal seeking, environment screening) may cause certain groups of people to respond in predictably similar ways.

Environmental Dimensions of the Servicescape

The preceding sections have described customer and employee behaviors in the servicescape and the three primary responses—cognitive, emotional, and physiological— that lead to those behaviors. In this section we turn to the complex mix of environmental features that influence these responses and behaviors (the left portion of Figure 10.2). Specifically, environmental dimensions of the physical surroundings can include all of the objective physical factors that can be controlled by the firm to enhance (or constrain) employee and customer actions. There is an endless list of possibilities—lighting, color, signage, textures, quality of materials, style of furnishings, layout, wall decor, temperature, and so on. In the figure and in the discussion that follows here, the hundreds of potential elements have been categorized into three composite dimensions: *ambient conditions; spatial layout and functionality;* and *signs, symbols, and artifacts.* Exhibit 10.2 illustrates how the Mayo Clinic took into consideration all of these dimensions in designing its hospital to accommodate patients, doctors, employees, and visitors.

Although the three dimensions will be discussed separately, we know from environmental psychology that people respond to their environments holistically. That is, although individuals perceive discrete stimuli (for example, they can perceive noise level, color, decor as distinct elements), it is the total configuration of stimuli that determines their reactions to a place. Hence, though the dimensions of the environment are defined independently below, it is important to recognize that they are perceived by employees and customers as a holistic pattern of interdependent stimuli. The holistic response is shown in Figure 10.2 as the "perceived servicescape."

Ambient Conditions

Ambient conditions include background characteristics of the environment such as temperature, lighting, noise, music, scent, and color. All of these factors can profoundly affect how people feel, think, and respond to a particular service establishment. For example, a number of studies have documented the effects of music on consumers' perceptions of products, their perceptions of how long they have waited for service, and the amount of money they spend.[29] When there is music, shoppers tend to perceive they spend less time shopping and in line than when there is no music. Slower music tempos at lower volumes tend to make shoppers more leisurely, and, in some cases, they spend more. In the Mayo Hospital lobby, piano music serves to reduce stress (see Exhibit 10.2). Shoppers also spend more time when the music "fits" the product or matches their musical tastes.

Other studies have similarly shown the effects of scent on consumer responses.[30] We know that scent in bakeries, coffee shops, and tobacco shops, for example, can be used to draw people in, and pleasant scents can increase lingering time. We also know that the presence of a scent can reduce perceptions of time spent and improve store evaluations. Scents that are congruent with the product type cause customers to spend more time thinking about their product decisions. A nursing home chain discovered that in its facilities "the best odor was no odor." Patients and their families believed that unpleasant odors signified an unclean facility, whereas the odor of cleaning solvents signified that unpleasant odors were being covered up.

As a general rule, ambient conditions affect the five senses. Sometimes such dimensions may be totally imperceptible (gases, chemicals, infrasound) yet have profound effects, particularly on employees who spend long hours in the environment.

The effects of ambient conditions are especially noticeable when they are extreme. For example, people attending a symphony in a hall where the air conditioning has failed and the air is hot and stuffy will be uncomfortable, and their discomfort will be reflected in how they feel about the concert. If the temperature and air quality were within a comfort tolerance zone, these ambient factors would probably go unnoticed. Ambient conditions also have a greater effect when the customer or employee spends considerable time in the servicescape. The impact of temperature, music, odors, and colors builds over time. Another instance in which ambient conditions will be particularly influential is when they conflict with what the customer or employee expects.

In 1998 Mayo opened the Mayo Clinic Hospital in Scottsdale, Arizona, the first hospital planned, designed, and built by Mayo Clinic. Located on a 210-acre site, the hospital houses 178 hospital rooms on five floors. Over 250 physicians; 950 nursing, technical, and support staff; and 300 volunteers work at the facility.

What is unique about this hospital facility is the tremendous care that was taken in its design to serve the needs of patients, doctors, staff, and visitors. The hospital is designed as a "healing environment" focused on patient needs, and focus groups were held with all constituents to determine how the hospital should be designed to facilitate this overall goal. A quotation from the Mayo brothers (founders of the clinic) captures the underlying belief that supported the design of the hospital: "The best interest of the patient is the only interest to be considered." This statement lies at the foundation of all Mayo does, even today, over 100 years after the Mayo brothers began their practice of medicine. To focus on the best interests of the patient also requires acknowledgment of the needs of the care providers and the patient's family and friend support system. All of these interests were clearly considered in the design of the hospital.

A Five-Story Atrium Low-Stress Entry   As patients and others enter the Mayo Hospital, they encounter a five-story enclosed atrium, reminiscent of a luxury hotel lobby. A grand piano sits in the lobby, and volunteers play beautiful, relaxing music throughout the day. An abundance of plants and glass gives the lobby a natural feel and provides a welcoming atmosphere. On entering, visitors see the elevator bank directly in front of them across the atrium, so there is no stress in figuring out where to go.

Mayo Hospital Lobby
Source: Photo courtesy of Mayo Clinic Scottsdale

Spatial Layout and Functionality

Because service environments generally exist to fulfill specific purposes or needs of customers, spatial layout and functionality of the physical surroundings are particularly important. *Spatial layout* refers to the ways in which machinery, equipment, and furnishings are arranged, the size and shape of those items, and the spatial relationships among them. *Functionality* refers to the ability of the same items to facilitate the accomplishment of customer and employee goals. Previous examples in this chapter illustrate the layout and functionality dimensions of the servicescape; for example the Carnival ad in Figure 10.4, and the design of the Mayo Hospital (Exhibit 10.2).

The spatial layout and functionality of the environment are particularly important for customers in self-service environments, where they must perform the service on their own and cannot rely on employees to assist them. Thus the functionality of an ATM machine and of self-serve restaurants, gasoline pumps, and Internet shopping are critical to success and customer satisfaction.

The importance of facility layout is particularly apparent in retail settings, where research shows it can influence customer satisfaction, store performance, and con-

All Patient and Visitor Services Are Together All services needed by patients and their families (information desk, cafeteria, chapel, patient admissions, gift shop) are located around the atrium, easily visible and accessible. There is a sense of peace and quiet in the lobby—all by deliberate design to reduce stress and promote a sense of caring and wellness. There is no confusion here, and very little that reminds one of a typical hospital entry.

Rooms Are Designed Around Patient Needs and Feelings On disembarking the elevators to go to patient rooms, people again sense relaxation and peace in the environment. As the doors open, patients and guests face a five-story wall of paned glass with views out to the desert and mountains that ring the hospital site. As one progresses left or right down well-marked corridors to the patient rooms, the atmosphere becomes even quieter. Rooms (all of them private) are arranged in 12-bed pods surrounding a nursing station. Nurses are within 20 steps of any patient room. Nurses and other attendants use cell phones—there is no paging system with constant announcements as in many hospitals.

The rooms themselves have interesting features, some designed by patients. For example, there is a multishelf display area on which patients can put cards, flowers, and other personal items. Fold-out, cushioned bed-chairs are in each room so family members can nap or even spend the night with their loved ones. Visitors are never told they must leave. The rooms are arranged considering what patients see from the beds, where they spend the most time. For example, special attention is paid to the ceilings, which patients view while flat on their backs; all rooms have windows; and a white board on the wall at the foot of each bed displays important information that patients want to know (like the name of the nurse on duty, the date, the room phone number, and other information).

Departments That Work Together Are Adjacent Another interesting design feature in this hospital is that departments that work together are housed very close to each other to facilitate communication and to reduce walking time between areas. This important feature allows caregivers to spend more time with patients and also lessens employee fatigue.

Maximize Nurses' Time with Patients It has been shown that a critical element in the recovery of patients is the quality of care they are given by nurses. Many of the Mayo Clinic Hospital design features facilitate the quality of nursing care. The pod design puts nurses close to their patients; the white boards in the rooms allow easy communication; and the accessible placement of supplies and relevant departments help to maximize the time nurses spend with patients.

It is clear that the design of the Mayo Hospital takes into account the critical importance of the servicescape in facilitating Mayo's primary goal: patient healing. All parties' voices were heard, and the place itself provides an environment that promotes well-being for patients, visitors, doctors, nurses, and other staff.

Sources: *Teamwork at Mayo: An Experiment in Cooperative Individualism* (Rochester, MN: Mayo Press, 1998); http://www.mayo.edu; author's personal tour of the Mayo Clinic Hospital in Scottsdale, 2001.

sumer search behavior.[31] Research conducted in two large department stores in Korea found that store facilities significantly affected consumers' emotional responses.[32] Layout accessibility, facility aesthetics, and seating comfort have all been shown to impact patrons' perceptions of quality in spectator sports and casino settings as well.[33]

Signs, Symbols, and Artifacts

Many items in the physical environment serve as explicit or implicit signals that communicate about the place to its users. Signs displayed on the exterior and interior of a structure are examples of explicit communicators. They can be used as labels (name of company, name of department, and so on), for directional purposes (entrances, exits), and to communicate rules of behavior (no smoking, children must be accompanied by an adult). Adequate signs have even been shown to reduce perceived crowding and stress.

Other environmental symbols and artifacts may communicate less directly than signs, giving implicit cues to users about the meaning of the place and norms and expectations for behavior in the place. Quality materials used in construction, artwork, presence of certificates and photographs on walls, floor coverings, and personal objects displayed in the environment can all communicate symbolic meaning and create an overall aesthetic impression. The meanings attached to environmental symbols and artifacts are culturally embedded, as illustrated in the Global Feature. Restaurant managers in the United States, for example, know that white tablecloths and subdued lighting symbolically convey full service and relatively high prices, whereas counter service, plastic furnishings, and bright lighting symbolize the opposite. In U.S. office environments, certain cues such as desk size and placement symbolize status and may be used to reinforce professional image.[34]

Signs, symbols, and artifacts are particularly important in forming first impressions and for communicating new service concepts. When customers are unfamiliar with a particular service establishment, they will look for environmental cues to help them categorize the place and begin to form their quality expectations. In a study of dentists' offices it was found that consumers use the environment, in particular its style of decoration and level of quality, as a cue to the competence and manner of the service provider.[35]

APPROACHES FOR UNDERSTANDING SERVICESCAPE EFFECTS

It is obvious from the framework, theories, and research results discussed thus far in this chapter that the servicescape can profoundly affect both customers and employees in service settings. To design environments that work from both marketing and organizational behavior perspectives, firms need to research environmental decisions and plan them strategically. The needs of ultimate users and the requirements of various functional units must be incorporated into environmental design decisions.

In this section we look at various means whereby an organization can learn about users' reactions to and preferences for different types of environments. We discuss these approaches here because often it is very challenging to capture the true importance of physical evidence. Each of the approaches has advantages and disadvantages.

Environment Surveys

An environment survey asks people (either customers or employees) to express their needs and preferences for different environmental configurations by answering predetermined questions in a questionnaire format.

This is the type of research conducted in a retail bank setting that was designed to measure the importance of different environmental dimensions and elicit user expectations about bank facilities.[36] The study surveyed 3,000 bank customers and 2,000 bank employees about 32 environmental variables organized into five categories: ambient conditions, aesthetics, privacy, efficiency/convenience, and social conditions. Across the categories, employees and customers often had different expectations for the bank facility. Although this study was conducted in one specific setting, more recent research has developed a general measurement scale to assess "perceived servicescape quality." The scale measures perceptions of three servicescape factors—ambience, design, and social conditions. The measure was developed using perceptions of 1,674 consumers across 10 different industries.[37]

The advantages of surveys are the ease of administration and interpretation of results. Usually the data are collected via standardized questions and the results can be entered into a computer and easily interpreted. Thousands of questionnaires can be sent out or administered over the phone, so sample sizes can be very large and many

Our reactions to elements of the physical environment and design are shaped to a large degree by culture and expectations we have formed through our life experiences, dominated by the culture we live in. Just think of one design element—color—and the variety of uses it has across cultures. Consider the commonly used earth tones in the decor of Japanese restaurants around the world compared with the glossy reds that are so evident in Chinese restaurants. Other cultural differences—personal space requirements, social distance preferences, sensitivity to crowding—can affect how consumers experience servicescapes around the world.

McDonald's Corporation recognizes these culturally defined expectations in allowing its franchisees around the world tremendous freedom in designing their service-scapes. In most McDonald's franchises a large percentage of the ownership is retained locally. Employees are nationals, and marketing strategies reflect local consumers' buying and preference patterns. In all cases, the restaurant is a "community institution," involved in social causes as well as local events.

It is McDonald's strategy to have its restaurants worldwide reflect the cultures and communities in which they are found—to mirror the communities they serve. At the same time it allows this creative energy to flourish in design and marketing strategies, McDonald's is extremely tight on its operating procedures and menu standards.

While the golden arches are always present, a brief tour around the globe shows the wide variation in McDonald's face to the community:

- Bologna, Italy: In this city, known as the "City of Arches" for hundreds of years, McDonald's has taken on the weathered, crafted look of the neighboring historic arches. Even the floor in the restaurant was done by hand, using old-world techniques. The restaurant used local architects and artists to bring the local architectural feel to the golden arches.

- Paris, France: Near the Sorbonne in Paris, the local McDonald's reflects its studious neighbor. The servicescape there has the look of a leather-bound library with books, statues, and heavy wood furniture.

- Salen, Sweden: On the slopes of Lindvallen Resort in Salen, Sweden, you can find the world's first "ski-thru" restaurant, named McSki, located next to the main ski lift. The building is different from any other McDonald's restaurant, built in a typical mountain style with

Source: Bill Bachmann/The Image Works, Inc.

wood panels and natural stone from the surroundings. Skiers can simply glide to the counter without taking off their skis, or they can be seated indoors or out.

- Beijing, China: McDonald's restaurants here have become a "place to hang out," very different from the truly "fast-food" role they play in the United States. They are part of the community, serving young and old, families and couples. Customers can be seen lingering for long periods of time, relaxing, chatting, reading, enjoying the music, or celebrating birthdays. Teenagers and young couples even find them to be very romantic environments. The emphasis on a Chinese-style family atmosphere is apparent from the interior walls of local restaurants that are covered by posters emphasizing family values.

- Tokyo, Japan: While some McDonald's restaurants in Japan are located in high real estate value areas such as the Ginza in Tokyo, many others are situated near major train stations or other high-traffic locations. The emphasis at these locations is on convenience and speed, not on comfort or socializing. Many of these locations have little frontage space and limited seating. Customers frequently stand while eating, or they may sit on stools at narrow counters. Even the elite Ginza location has few seats. Some locations have a small ordering and service area on the first floor, with limited seating (still primarily stools rather than tables and chairs) on the second floor. Young people—from teenagers to schoolchildren—are a common sight in Japanese McDonald's.

Sources: *Golden Arches East: McDonald's in East Asia,* ed. J. L. Watson (Stanford, CA: Stanford University Press, 1997); "A Unique Peak," *Franchise Times* 3, no. 4 (1997), p. 46; "McDonald's Turns Up the Heat on Fast Food," Video Case Series, accompanying C. L. Bovee, M. J. Houston, and J. V. Thill, *Marketing,* 2nd ed. (New York: McGraw-Hill, 1995).

environmental variables can be explored simultaneously. The primary disadvantage of an environmental survey is that sometimes the results may be less valid than results from other methods—that is, the answers to the survey questions may not truly reflect how people feel or how they will behave.

Direct Observation

Using observation methods, trained observers make detailed accounts of environmental conditions and dimensions, also observing and recording the reactions and behaviors of customers and employees in the servicescape. Essentially the observer attempts to fill in the boxes in the framework shown in Figure 10.2 with details for a specific setting by observing that setting over time. An example of such a study was done in a retail gift shop context. Through direct observation, depth interviews, and photography, researchers compared detailed accounts of gift giving as it was observed and experienced in two separate retail stores: The Mouse House and Baubles.[38] Over time and extended involvement with the stores, the researchers were able to explore settings, actors, events, processes, and objects related to gift giving.

The advantages of direct observation, when done by highly trained and skilled observers, are the depth of information acquired and its accuracy. The interrelationship of elements of the environment and the reactions and interactions of participants in the environment can be unobtrusively recorded, increasing the validity of the findings beyond what is typically found in a standardized survey. The findings could be very useful in redesigning the servicescape or in comparing different facilities. Direct observation can also be useful when there is a very specific servicescape question that needs answering—for example, "What are the foot traffic flow patterns in the mall during peak business hours, and are the new signs effective in directing people?"

The disadvantages of direct observation are primarily related to time and dollar costs. First, the researchers who observe the servicescape must be highly trained and skilled in ethnographic methods, which makes data collection expensive. Second, they must be allowed to observe for some period of time, and the interpretation of their detailed records can be very labor intensive. Unlike the survey method, the data cannot as a rule be entered into a computer and analyzed with nice, clean quantitative results.

Experiments

Experimental methods are among the best ways to assess specific customer and employee reactions to environmental changes or alternatives when it is important to know their true reactions and preferences. Experiments involve exposing groups of customers to different environmental configurations and measuring their reactions. For example, one experiment asked travelers to imagine that they had not received the cheapest air fare as requested from their travel agents.[39] Half of the travelers were shown a photo of an organized travel agency while the others saw a photo of a disorganized agency (see Figure 10.5). Results of the experiment showed that subjects exposed to the organized travel agency were more satisfied and more forgiving of the agent's error than were subjects exposed to the disorganized agency. In two other studies, background music type and tempo have been varied in grocery stores and restaurants and the effect on traffic pace, sales, and other variables has been measured.[40] In both cases, the type of music played had an effect on sales. Yet it is unlikely that shoppers would be conscious of this effect, nor would they be able to predict that they would buy more when a certain type of music is playing, if asked such a question on a survey.

The advantages of experiments lie primarily in the validity of the results; that is, if the experiment is carefully done, you can believe and rely on the results. Because environmental dimensions often affect people subconsciously and the multitude of dimensions interact to form a composite impression, it is difficult to get accurate responses to questions about the environment in the absence of actual experience.

As with direct observation methods, the disadvantages of experiments relate primarily to costs and time. Ideally, actual servicescape prototypes would be designed

FIGURE 10.6
Photos Used in Travel Agency Experiment: Organized versus Disorganized Environments

and various groups of consumers would respond to the alternatives. Marriott Hotels has used this approach in designing its hotel rooms. However, because of the expense involved in constructing actual servicescapes, some form of simulation (verbal descriptions, photos/slides, scale models, videos, computer simulations) will likely be used. Environmental psychologists and marketers have shown that simulated environments can work well in achieving results similar to what would be found in actual, constructed environments.[41] Our Technology Spotlight showed how advances in computer technology can be used to employ virtual reality techniques for effective environmental simulation.

Photographic Blueprints

In Chapter 8 we briefly introduced the idea of photographic blueprints in the general discussion of service blueprints. A photographic blueprint essentially provides a visualization of the service at each customer action step. The visual can be a slide, a photograph, or the entire service process as videotaped from the customer's point of view. By combining a service blueprint with photos, managers and other service employees can see the evidence of service from the customer's point of view. The photographic blueprint can provide a powerful analytic tool to begin assessing the service process. A photographic blueprint of the "Overnight Hotel Stay" in Chapter 8 would include the blueprint as shown in Figure 8.8 together with photos or videotape of all of the evidence shown across the top of the blueprint.

Photographic blueprints are extremely useful in providing clear and logical documentation of the physical evidence as it currently exists in a given service situation. Before changes can be made, the current state of physical evidence should be made apparent to all concerned. The photos and/or videotapes give more depth to the process blueprint, and the blueprint forces a certain logic on the analysis of the physical evidence. The photographic blueprint can give a vivid picture of how things are. The main disadvantage of a photographic blueprint is that it is just a starting point. In and of itself it doesn't answer any questions, but many questions can be asked of it. It doesn't give any clues as to customer and employee preferences and needs; it could, however, be used as a catalyst for gathering customer and employee opinions.

GUIDELINES FOR PHYSICAL EVIDENCE STRATEGY[42]

To this point in the chapter we have presented ideas, frameworks, psychological models, and research approaches for understanding the effects of physical evidence, and most specifically the effects of the physical facility or servicescape. In this section we suggest some general guidelines for an effective physical evidence strategy.

Recognize the Strategic Impact of Physical Evidence

Physical evidence can play a prominent role in determining service quality expectations and perceptions. For some organizations, just acknowledging the impact of physical evidence is a major first step. After this step they can take advantage of the potential of physical evidence and plan strategically.

For an evidence strategy to be effective, it must be linked clearly to the organization's overall goals and vision. Thus planners must know what those goals are and then determine how the evidence strategy can support them. At a minimum, the basic service concept must be defined, the target markets (both internal and external) identified, and the firm's broad vision of its future known. Because many evidence decisions are relatively permanent and costly (particularly servicescape decisions), they must be planned and executed deliberately.

Map the Physical Evidence of Service

The next step is to map the service. Everyone should be able to see the service process and the existing elements of physical evidence. An effective way to depict service evidence is through the service map, or blueprint. (Service blueprinting was presented in detail in Chapter 8.) While service maps clearly have multiple purposes, they can be particularly useful in visually capturing physical evidence opportunities. People, process, and physical evidence can be seen in the service map. From the map you can read the actions involved in service delivery, the complexity of the process, the points of human interaction that provide evidence opportunities, and the tangible representations present at each step. To make the map even more useful, photographs or videotape of the process can be added to develop a photographic blueprint, as described in the preceding section.

Clarify Roles of the Servicescape

Early in the chapter we discussed the varying roles played by the servicescape and how firms could locate themselves in the typology shown in Table 10.3 to begin to identify those roles in their particular cases. For example, a child care company would locate itself in the "elaborate, interpersonal" cell of the matrix and quickly see that its servicescape decisions would be relatively complex and that the servicescape strategy (1) would have to consider the needs of both the children and the service providers and (2) could impact marketing, organizational behavior, and consumer satisfaction goals.

Sometimes the servicescape may have no role in service delivery or marketing from the customer's point of view. This is essentially the case for telecommunications services or utilities. Clarifying the roles played by the servicescape in a particular situation will aid in identifying opportunities and deciding just who needs to be consulted in making facility design decisions.

Assess and Identify Physical Evidence Opportunities

Once the current forms of evidence and the roles of the servicescape are understood, possible changes and improvements can be identified. One question to ask is, Are there missed opportunities to provide service evidence? The service map of an insurance or utility service may show that little if any evidence of service is ever provided to the customer. A strategy might then be developed to provide more evidence of service to show customers exactly what they are paying for. Speedi-Lube, our opening example, effectively used this approach in providing multiple forms of evidence to make car maintenance service more tangible to the consumer.

Or it may be discovered that the evidence provided is sending messages that don't enhance the firm's image or goals or that don't match customer expectations. For example, a restaurant might find that its high-price cue is not consistent with the design of the restaurant, which suggests "family dining" to its intended market segment. Either the pricing or the facility design would need to be changed, depending on the restaurant's overall strategy.

Another set of questions to address concerns whether the current physical evidence of service suits the needs and preferences of the target market. To begin answering such questions, the framework for understanding environment–user relationships (Figure 10.2) and the research approaches suggested in this chapter could be employed. And finally, does the evidence strategy take into account the needs (sometimes incompatible) of both customers and employees? This question is particularly relevant in making decisions regarding the servicescape.

Be Prepared to Update and Modernize the Evidence

Some aspects of the evidence, particularly the servicescape, require frequent or at least periodic updating and modernizing. Even if the vision, goals, and objectives of the company don't change, time itself takes a toll on physical evidence, necessitating change and modernization. There is clearly an element of fashion involved, and over time different colors, designs, and styles may come to communicate different messages. Organizations obviously understand this when it comes to advertising strategy, but sometimes they overlook other elements of physical evidence.

Work Cross-Functionally

In presenting itself to the consumer, a service firm is concerned with communicating a desired image, with sending consistent and compatible messages through all forms of evidence, and with providing the type of service evidence the target customers want and can understand. Frequently, however, evidence decisions are made over time and by various functions within the organization. For example, decisions regarding employee uniforms may be made by the human resources area, servicescape design decisions may be made by the facilities management group, process design decisions are most frequently made by operations managers, and advertising and pricing decisions may be made by the marketing department. Thus it is not surprising that the physical evidence of service may at times be less than consistent. Service mapping, or blueprinting, can be a valuable tool for communicating within the firm, identifying existing service evidence, and providing a springboard for changing or providing new forms of physical evidence.

A multifunction team approach to physical evidence strategy is often necessary, particularly for making decisions about the servicescape. It has been said that "Facility planning and management . . . is a problem-solving activity that lies on the boundaries between architecture, interior space planning and product design, organizational [and consumer] behavior, planning and environmental psychology."[43]

Summary

In this chapter we explored the roles of physical evidence in forming customer and employee perceptions. Because services are intangible and because they are often produced and consumed at the same time, they can be difficult to comprehend or evaluate before their purchase. The physical evidence of the service thus serves as a primary cue for setting customer expectations before purchase. These tangible cues, particularly the servicescape, can also influence customers' responses as they experience the service. Because customers and employees often interact in the servicescape, the physical surroundings also influence employees and the nature of employee–customer interactions.

The chapter focused primarily on the servicescape—the physical surroundings or the physical facility where the service is produced, delivered, and consumed. A typology of servicescapes was presented that illustrated their range of complexity and usage. By locating itself in the appropriate cell of the typology, an organization can quickly see who needs to be consulted regarding servicescape decisions, what objectives might be achieved through careful design of the facility, and how complex the decisions are likely to be. General roles of the servicescape were also described. The servicescape can serve as a package (a "visual metaphor" for the service itself), a facilitator in aiding the accomplishment of customer and employee goals, a socializer in prescribing behaviors in the environment, and a differentiator to distinguish the organization from its competitors.

Given this grounding in the importance of physical evidence, in particular the servicescape, the chapter presented a general framework for understanding servicescape effects on employee and customer behaviors. The servicescape can affect the approach and avoidance behaviors of individual customers and employees as well as their social interactions. These behavioral responses come about because the physical environment influences (1) people's beliefs or cognitions about the service organization, (2) their feelings or emotions in response to the place, and (3) their actual physiological reactions while in the physical facility. The chapter also pointed out that individuals may respond differently to the servicescape depending on their personality traits, the mood they are in, or the goals they are trying to accomplish.

Three categories of environmental dimensions were presented to capture the complex nature of the servicescape: ambient conditions; spatial layout and functionality; and signs, symbols, and artifacts. These dimensions affect people's beliefs, emotions, and physical responses, causing them to behave in certain ways while in the servicescape.

Given the importance of physical evidence and its potentially powerful influence on both customers and employees, it is important for firms to think strategically about the management of the tangible evidence of service. This means that the impact of physical evidence and design decisions needs to be researched and planned as part of the marketing strategy.

The chapter concluded with a discussion of four different approaches for understanding servicescapes and specific guidelines for evidence strategy. If physical evidence is researched, planned, and implemented effectively, key problems leading to service quality shortcomings can be avoided. Through careful thinking about physical evidence decisions, an organization can avoid miscommunicating to customers via incompatible or inconsistent evidence or overpromising and raising customer expectations unrealistically. Beyond its role in helping to avoid these negative outcomes, an effective physical evidence strategy can play a critically important role in communicating to customers and in guiding them in understanding the firm's offerings and setting up accurate expectations. During the service experience, physical evidence can be part of an effective delivery strategy as well.

Discussion Questions

1. What is physical evidence, and why have we devoted a whole chapter to it in a marketing text?

2. Describe and give an example of how servicescapes play each of the following roles: package, facilitator, socializer, and differentiator.

3. Imagine that you own an independent copying and printing shop (similar to Kinko's). Where (in which cell) would you locate your business in the typology of servicescapes shown in Table 10.3? What are the implications for designing your physical facility?

4. How can an effective physical evidence strategy help to close provider gap 2? Explain.

5. Why are both customers and employees included in the framework for understanding servicescape effects on behavior (Figure 10.2)? What types of

behaviors are influenced by the servicescape according to the framework? Think of examples.

6. Using your own experiences, give examples of times when you have been affected cognitively, emotionally, and physiologically by elements of the servicescape (in any service context).

7. Why is everyone not affected in exactly the same way by the servicescape?

8. Describe the physical environment of your favorite restaurant in terms of the three categories of servicescape dimensions: ambient conditions; spatial layout and functionality; and signs, symbols, and artifacts.

9. Imagine that you are serving as a consultant to a local health club. How would you advise the health club to begin the process of developing an effective physical evidence strategy?

Exercises

1. Choose two very different firms (different market segments or service levels) in the same industry. Observe both establishments. Describe the service "package" in both cases. How does the package help to distinguish the two firms? Do you believe the package sets accurate expectations for what the firm delivers? Is either firm overpromising through the manner in which its servicescape (or other types of physical evidence) communicates with customers?

2. Think of a particular service organization (it can be your project company, the company you work for, or some other organization) where you believe physical evidence is particularly important in communicating with and satisfying customers. Prepare the text of a presentation you would give to the manager of that organization to convince him or her of the importance of physical evidence in the organization's marketing strategy.

3. Create a photographic blueprint for a service of your choice.

4. Choose a service organization and collect all forms of physical evidence that the organization uses to communicate with its customers. If customers see the firm's facility, also take a photo of the servicescape. Analyze the evidence in terms of compatibility, consistency, and whether it overpromises or underpromises what the firm can deliver.

5. Visit the websites of several service providers. Does the physical evidence of the website portray an image consistent with other forms of evidence provided by the organizations?

Notes

1. The term *servicescape* used throughout this chapter, and much of the content of this chapter, are based, with permission, on M. J. Bitner, "Servicescapes: The Impact of Physical Surroundings on Customers and Employees," *Journal of Marketing* 56 (April 1992), pp. 57–71. For recent contributions to this topic, see *Servicescapes: The Concept of Place in Contemporary Markets,* ed. J. F. Sherry, Jr. (Chicago: NTC/Contemporary Publishing Company, 1998); and M. J. Bitner, "The Servicescape," in *Handbook of Services Marketing and Management,* ed. T. A. Swartz and D. Iacobucci (Thousand Oaks, CA: Sage Publications, 2000), pp. 37–50.

2. See, for example, E. Sundstrom and I. Altman, "Physical Environments and Work-Group Effectiveness," *Research in Organizational Behavior* 11 (1989), pp. 175–209; or E. Sundstrom and M. G. Sundstrom, *Work Places* (Cambridge, MA: Cambridge University Press, 1986).

3. J. Baker, L. L. Berry, and A. Parasuraman, "The Marketing Impact of Branch Facility Design," *Journal of Retail Banking* 10, no. 2 (1988), pp. 33–42.

4. For reviews of environmental psychology, see D. Stokols and I. Altman, *Handbook of Environmental Psychology* (New York: John Wiley, 1987); S. Saegert and G. H. Winkel, "Environmental Psychology," *Annual Review of Psychology* 41 (1990), pp. 441–77; and E. Sundstrom, P. A. Bell, P. L. Busby, and C. Asmus, "Environmental Psychology 1989–1994," *Annual Review of Psychology* 47 (1996), pp. 485–512.

5. See M. R. Solomon, "Dressing for the Part: The Role of Costume in the Staging of the Servicescape," in *Servicescapes: The Concept of Space in Contemporary Markets,* ed. J. F. Sherry, Jr. (Chicago: NTC/Contemporary Publishing Company, 1998); and A. Rafaeli, "Dress and Behavior of Customer Contact Employees: A Framework for Analysis," in *Advances in Services Marketing and Management,* vol. 2, ed. T. A. Swartz, D. E. Bowen, and S. W. Brown (Greenwich, CT: JAI Press, 1993), pp. 175–212.

6. S. Casey, "Federal Expressive," *www.ecompany.com,* May 2001, pp. 45–48.

7. D. Michaels, "Business-Class Warfare: Rival Airlines Scramble to Beat BA's Reclining Bed Seats," *The Wall Street Journal,* March 16, 2001, p. B1.

8. Ibid.; and British Airways' website, www.britishairways.com.

9. E. Gately, "Washington Mutual Banking on Being Different," *Mesa Tribune,* March 25, 2001, p. B1.

10. "The New VIP Rooms," *The Wall Street Journal,* December 11, 1998, p. W1.

11. A. Mehrabian and J. A. Russell, *An Approach to Environmental Psychology* (Cambridge, MA: Massachusetts Institute of Technology, 1974).

12. R. Donovan and J. Rossiter, "Store Atmosphere: An Environmental Psychology Approach," *Journal of Retailing* 58 (Spring 1982), pp. 34–57.

13. D. J. Bennett and J. D. Bennett, "Making the Scene," in *Social Psychology through Symbolic Interactionism,* ed. G. Stone and H. Farberman (Waltham, MA: Ginn-Blaisdell, 1970), pp. 190–96.

14. J. P. Forgas, *Social Episodes* (London: Academic Press, 1979).

15. R. G. Barker, *Ecological Psychology* (Stanford, CA: Stanford University Press, 1968).

16. For a number of excellent papers on this topic spanning a range from toy stores, to bridal salons, to cybermarketspaces, to Japanese retail environments and others, see *Servicescapes: The Concept of Place in Contemporary Markets,* ed. J. F. Sherry, Jr. (Chicago: NTC/Contemporary Publishing Company, 1998).

17. J. F. Sherry, Jr., "The Soul of the Company Store: Nike Town Chicago and the Emplace Brandscape," in *Servicescapes: The Concept of Place in Contemporary Markets,* ed. J. F. Sherry, Jr. (Chicago: NTC/Contemporary Publishing Company, 1998), pp. 81–108.

18. E. J. Arnould, L. L. Price, and P. Tierney, "The Wilderness Servicescape: An Ironic Commercial Landscape," in *Servicescapes: The Concept of Place in Contemporary Markets,* ed. J. F. Sherry, Jr. (Chicago: NTC/Contemporary Publishing Company, 1998), pp. 403–38.

19. A. Rapoport, *The Meaning of the Built Environment* (Beverly Hills, CA: Sage Publications, 1982); R. G. Golledge, "Environmental Cognition," in *Handbook of Environmental Psychology,* vol. 1, ed. D. Stokols and I. Altman (New York: John Wiley, 1987), pp. 131–74.

20. M. P. Gardner and G. Siomkos, "Toward a Methodology for Assessing Effects of In-Store Atmospherics," in *Advances in Consumer Research,* vol. 13, ed. R. J. Lutz (Ann Arbor, MI: Association for Consumer Research, 1986), pp. 27–31.

21. M. J. Bitner, "Evaluating Service Encounters: The Effects of Physical Surroundings and Employee Responses," *Journal of Marketing* 54 (April 1990), pp. 69–82.

22. J. C. Ward, M. J. Bitner, and J. Barnes, "Measuring the Prototypicality and Meaning of Retail Environments," *Journal of Retailing* 69, no. 2 (1992), pp. 194–220.

23. See, for example, Mehrabian and Russell, *An Approach to Environmental Psychology;* J. A. Russell and U. F. Lanius, "Adaptation Level and the Affective Appraisal of Environments," *Journal of Environmental Psychology* 4, no. 2 (1984), pp. 199–235; J. A. Russell and G. Pratt, "A Description of the Affective Quality Attributed to Environments," *Journal of Personality and Social Psychology* 38, no. 2 (1980), pp. 311–22; and J. A. Russell and J. Snodgrass, "Emotion and the Environment," in *Handbook of Environmental Psychology,* vol. 1, ed. D. Stokols and I. Altman (New York: John Wiley, 1987), pp. 245–81.

24. J. A. Russell, L. M. Ward, and G. Pratt, "Affective Quality Attributed to Environments," *Environment and Behavior* 13, no. 3 (May 1981), pp. 259–88.

25. See, for example, M. S. Sanders and E. J. McCormick, *Human Factors in Engineering and Design* (New York: McGraw-Hill, 1987); and D. J. Osborne, *Ergonomics at Work,* 2nd ed. (New York: John Wiley, 1987).

26. *Entrepreneur* magazine, 1998; "Empty Nests, Full Pockets," *Brandweek,* September 23, 1996, pp. 36ff; and "Lodging Chain to Give Older Guests a Choice," *The Wall Street Journal,* February 19, 1993, p. B1.

27. Mehrabian and Russell, *An Approach to Environmental Psychology;* Russell and Snodgrass, "Emotion and the Environment."

28. A. Mehrabian, "Individual Differences in Stimulus Screening and Arousability," *Journal of Personality* 45, no. 2 (1977), pp. 237–50.

29. For recent research documenting the effects of music on consumers, see J. Baker, D. Grewal, and A. Parasuraman, "The Influence of Store Environment on Quality Inferences and Store Image," *Journal of the Academy of Marketing Science* 22 (1994), pp. 328–39; J. C. Chebat, C. Gelinas-Chebat, and P. Filliatrault, "Interactive Effects of Musical and Visual Cues on Time Perception: An Application to Waiting Lines in Banks," *Perceptual and Motor Skills* 77 (1993), pp. 995–1020; L. Dube, J. C. Chebat, and S. Morin, "The Effects of Background Music on Consumers' Desire to Affiliate in Buyer–Seller Interactions," *Psychology and Marketing* 12, no. 4 (1995), pp. 305–19; J. D. Herrington and L. M. Capella, "Effects of Music in Service Environments: A Field Study," *Journal of Services Marketing* 10, no. 2 (1996), pp. 26–41; J. D. Herrington and L. M. Capella, "Practical Applications of Music in Service Settings," *Journal of Services Marketing* 8, no. 3 (1994), pp. 50–65; M. K. Hui, L. Dube, and J. C. Chebat, "The Impact of Music on *Consumers'* Reactions to Waiting for Services," *Journal of Retailing* 73, no. 1 (1997), pp. 87–104; A. S. Matila and J. Wirtz, "Congruency of Scent and Music as a Driver of In-Store Evaluations and Behavior," *Journal of Retailing* 77, no. 2 (Summer 2001), pp. 273–89; L. Dube and S. Morin, "Background Music Pleasure and Store Evaluation: Intensity Effects and Psychological Mechanisms," *Journal of Business Research* 54, no. 2 (November 2001), pp. 107–13.

30. For recent research documenting the effects of scent on consumer responses, see D. J. Mitchell, B. E. Kahn, and S. C. Knasko, "There's Something in the Air: Effects of Congruent and Incongruent Ambient Odor on Consumer Decision Making," *Journal of Consumer Research* 22 (September 1995), pp. 229–38; and E. R. Spangenberg, A. E. Crowley, and P. W. Henderson, "Improving the Store Environment: Do Olfactory Cues Affect Evaluations and Behaviors?" *Journal of Marketing* 60 (April 1996), pp. 67–80.

31. See J. M. Sulek, M. R. Lind, and A. S. Marucheck, "The Impact of a Customer Service Intervention and Facility Design on Firm Performance," *Management*

Science 41, no. 11 (1995), pp. 1763–73; and P. A. Titus and P. B. Everett, "Consumer Wayfinding Tasks, Strategies, and Errors: An Exploratory Field Study," *Psychology and Marketing* 13, no. 3 (1996), pp. 265–90.

32. C. Yoo, J. Park, and D. J. MacInnis, "Effects of Store Characteristics and In-Store Emotional Experiences on Store Attitude," *Journal of Business Research* 42 (1998), pp. 253–63.

33. K. L. Wakefield and J. G. Blodgett, "The Effect of the Servicescape on Customers' Behavioral Intentions in Leisure Service Settings," *Journal of Services Marketing* 10, no. 6 (1996), pp. 45–61.

34. T. R. V. Davis, "The Influence of the Physical Environment in Offices," *Academy of Management Review* 9, no. 2 (1984), pp. 271–83.

35. J. C. Ward and J. P. Eaton, "Service Environments: The Effect of Quality and Decorative Style on Emotions, Expectations, and Attributions," in *Proceedings of the American Marketing Association Summer Educators' Conference,* eds. R. Achrol and A. Mitchell (Chicago: American Marketing Association 1994), pp. 333–34.

36. Baker, Berry, and Parasuraman, "Marketing Impact of Branch Facility Design."

37. J. J. Cronin, Jr., R. Hightower, Jr., and G. T. M. Hult, "PSSQ: Measuring Consumer Perceptions of the Servicescape," working paper, Florida State University, 1999.

38. J. F. Sherry, Jr., and M. A. McGrath, "Unpacking the Holiday Presence: A Comparative Ethnography of Two Gift Stores," in *Interpretive Consumer Research,* ed. E. C. Hirschman (Provo, UT: Association for Consumer Research, 1989), pp. 148–67.

39. Bitner, "Evaluating Service Encounters."

40. R. Milliman, "Using Background Music to Affect the Behavior of Supermarket Shoppers," *Journal of Marketing* 46 (Summer 1982), pp. 86–91; R. Milliman, "The Influence of Background Music on the Behavior of Restaurant Patrons," *Journal of Consumer Research* 13 (September 1986), pp. 286–89.

41. See J. E. G. Bateson and M. Hui, "The Ecological Validity of Photographic Slides and Videotapes in Simulating the Service Setting," *Journal of Consumer Research,* September 1992, pp. 271–81; and J. L. Nasar, "Perception, Cognition, and Evaluation of Urban Places," in *Public Places and Spaces,* ed. I. Altman and E. H. Zube (New York: Plenum Press, 1989), pp. 31–56.

42. This section is adapted from M. J. Bitner, "Managing the Evidence of Service," in *The Service Quality Handbook,* ed. E. E. Scheuing and W. F. Christopher (New York: AMACOM, 1993), pp. 358–70.

43. F. D. Becker, *Workspace* (New York: Praeger, 1981).

Part 4

DELIVERING AND PERFORMING SERVICE

In the gaps model of service quality, provider gap 3 is the discrepancy between development of customer-driven service standards and actual service delivery (see the accompanying figure). Even when guidelines exist for performing services well and treating customers correctly, high-quality service performance is not a certainty. Standards must be backed by appropriate resources (people, systems, and technology) and also must be supported to be effective; that is, employees must be trained, motivated, measured, and compensated on the basis of performance along those standards. Thus, even when standards accurately reflect customers' expectations, if the company fails to provide support for them—if it does not facilitate, encourage, and require their

Provider Gap 3

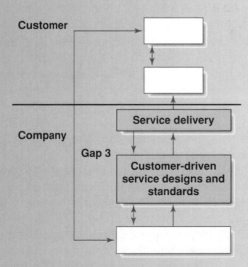

achievement—standards do no good. When the level of service delivery performance falls short of the standards (provider gap 3), it falls short of what customers expect as well. Narrowing gap 3, by ensuring that all the resources needed to achieve the standards are in place, reduces the gap.

Research and company experience have identified many of the critical inhibitors to delivering and performing service well. Those that relate to employees and their roles in service delivery are discussed in Chapter 11. Issues that are of particular concern include employees who do not clearly understand the roles they are to play in the company, employees who feel in conflict between customers and company management, the wrong employees, inadequate technology, inappropriate compensation and recognition, and lack of empowerment and teamwork. These factors all relate to the company's human resource function, involving internal practices such as recruiting, training, feedback, job design, motivation, and organizational structure. To close provider gap 3, the issues must be addressed across functions (for example, with both marketing and human resources) if they are to be effective.

Most companies have, in addition to external customers, a variety of *internal customers*—employees or departments that directly interact with customers and sell, advise, maintain, or troubleshoot for other departments or functions in the company. For example, company salespeople who interact directly with the external customer can be considered internal customers of many other departments and functions in the company (such as the market research function, the administrative staff, and the product development department). Salespeople depend on these other functions to perform effectively for them, the internal customer, so that they, in turn, can perform for the external customer. Unless the company acknowledges the importance of internal customers, these internal intermediaries may have different goals, incentives, and motives than the department developing the service.

As we have just discussed, part of the variability in provider gap 3 comes from employees that are involved with service delivery. Chapter 12 discusses another important variable, the customer. Even if contact employees and internal intermediaries are 100 percent consistent in their service delivery (an unlikely but highly desirable state!), the uncontrollable variable of the customer can introduce heterogeneity in service delivery. If customers do not perform their roles appropriately—if, for example, they fail to provide all the information necessary to the provider or neglect to read and follow instructions—service quality is jeopardized. An example of customer-induced variability is in nightclubs or dance clubs where some guests drink too much, are rowdy, and interfere with the service experiences of other guests. Perhaps a more vivid example is the behavior of airline passengers when a flight cancellation is announced. Both business and leisure customers, all intending to get to their destinations at a promised time and frustrated with their inability to do so, become "customers from hell," demanding and even abusive. Their behavior affects the performance of service providers and also may incite other passengers or, at a minimum, create uncomfortable confrontations and competition for seats on the next available plane.

Effective service organizations acknowledge the role of customer variability and develop strategies to teach customers to perform their roles appropriately. When customers do not perform their roles well—when they do not provide information needed or do not follow instructions—they rarely obtain full value from the service. For example, clients of consulting firms who don't provide necessary but sensitive information or who do not follow the advice given do not get what they pay for from the service. Some companies develop customer education or communication programs to teach customers to be good customers. Service companies can and do use strategies to improve their own productivity and effectiveness by enlisting the customer's cooperation. Chapter 12 discusses the issues associated with customer participation and the strategies companies use to address them.

Another difficulty associated with delivering service involves the challenge of incorporating intermediaries such as retailers, franchisees, agents, and brokers, discussed in Chapter 13. Because quality in service occurs in the human interaction between customers and service providers, control over the service encounter by the company is crucial, yet rarely is it fully possible. Most service (and many manufacturing) companies face an even more formidable task: attaining service excellence and consistency in the presence of intermediaries who represent them, interact with their customers, and yet are not under their direct control. Franchisers of services depend on their franchisees to execute service delivery as they have specified it. And it is in the execution by the franchisee that the customer evaluates the service quality of the company. When a McDonald's franchisee cooks the McNuggets too short a time, the customer's perception of the company—and of other McDonald's franchisees—is tarnished. When one Holiday Inn franchise has unsanitary conditions, it reflects on all others and on the company itself. With franchises and other types of intermediaries, someone other than the producer is critically important to the fulfillment of quality service. In a business-to-business context, subcontractors (such as software makers, network providers, and others involved in completing most projects in the information technology industry) become essential but potentially problematic. The service delivery process is complicated by outside parties that are likely to embrace goals and values that do not directly align with those of the service organization. For this reason a firm must develop ways to either control or motivate these intermediaries to meet company goals. These challenges and strategies are the focus of Chapter 13.

Every day more services are being developed and offered via electronic channels such as the Internet, online computer links, and phone-based technologies. In addition to presenting strategies for dealing with human intermediaries, Chapter 13 also addresses the issues, challenges, and strategies of delivering services through electronic intermediaries.

A final key issue in gap 3 is the need in service firms to synchronize demand and capacity. Because services are perishable and cannot be inventoried, service companies frequently face situations of over- or underdemand. Lacking inventories to handle overdemand, companies lose sales when capacity is inadequate to handle customer needs. On the other hand, capacity is frequently underutilized in slow periods. Most companies rely on operations strategies such as cross-training or varying the size of the employee pool to synchronize supply and demand. The use of marketing strategies in many companies is limited. Marketing strategies for managing demand, such as price changes, advertising, promotion, and alternative service offerings, can supplement approaches for managing supply. Chapter 14 discusses the challenges raised by fluctuations in demand and supply and describes the ways that companies cope with these challenges.

Chapter 11

EMPLOYEES' ROLES IN SERVICE DELIVERY

This chapter's objectives are to

1. Illustrate the critical importance of service employees in creating customer satisfaction and service quality.

2. Demonstrate the challenges inherent in boundary-spanning roles.

3. Provide examples of strategies for creating customer-oriented service delivery through hiring the right people, developing employees to deliver service quality, providing needed support systems, and retaining the best service employees.

4. Show how the strategies can support a service culture where providing excellent service to both internal and external customers is a way of life.

Employees Are the Service and the Brand

Noted service expert Leonard Berry has documented that investments in employee success are key drivers of sustained business success in companies as diverse as Charles Schwab, Midwest Express, USAA Insurance, Chick-fil-A, and Special Expeditions Travel.[1] Why is this true? Why do these companies choose to invest heavily in their employees?

For clues, consider the following true stories:

- On a long overseas Singapore Airlines flight, a restless toddler repeatedly dropped his pacifier. Every time the child would cry and someone (the mother, another passenger, or a flight attendant) would retrieve the pacifier. Finally, one of the attendants picked up the pacifier, attached it to a ribbon, and sewed it to the child's shirt. The child and mother were happy, and passengers seated nearby gave the attendant a standing ovation.[2]

- A phone associate at Universal Card Services received a call from a husband whose wife, suffering from Alzheimer's disease, had vanished. The husband hoped that he could find his wife through tracing her use of her Universal

Card. The phone associate placed a hold on the card and arranged to be called personally the moment there was any activity on the card. When it happened, about a week later, the associate contacted the husband, the doctor, and the police, who were then able to assist the missing woman and get her home.[3]

- At the Fairmont Hotel in San Francisco a computer programmer made a room reservation for a discounted price. On arrival he discovered that all rooms were filled. The front desk clerk responded by sending him to the Sheraton and picking up his room charge, which was over twice what he would have paid the Fairmont. He also paid for the guest's parking fee at the Fairmont and taxi fare to the new hotel, and threw in a free meal at the Fairmont as well.[4]

These stories illustrate the important roles played by service employees in creating satisfied customers and in building customer relationships. The front-line service providers in each example are enormously important to the success of the organizations they represent. They are responsible for understanding customer needs and for interpreting customer requirements in real time as suggested by Figure 11.1. Leonard Berry has documented that in case after case, companies that represent sustained service success all recognize the critical importance of their employees.[5]

In this chapter we focus on service employees and human resource practices that facilitate delivery of quality services. The assumption is that even when customer expectations are well understood (gap 1) and services have been designed and specified to conform to those expectations (gap 2), there may still be discontinuities in service quality when the service is not delivered as specified. These discontinuities are labeled gap 3—the service performance gap—in the service quality framework. Because employees frequently deliver or perform the service, human resource issues are a major cause of this gap. By focusing on the critical role of service employees, and by developing strategies that will lead to effective customer-oriented service, organizations can begin to close the service delivery gap.

The failure to deliver services as designed and specified can result from a number of employee and human performance factors: ineffective recruitment of service-oriented employees; role ambiguity and role conflict among contact employees; poor employee–technology–job fit; inappropriate evaluation and compensation systems; and lack of empowerment, perceived control, and teamwork. The chapter gives you an understanding of these factors and strategies for overcoming them.

FIGURE 11.1
Service employees directly impact customers' satisfaction.

Source: Ken Lax/Photo Researchers, Inc.

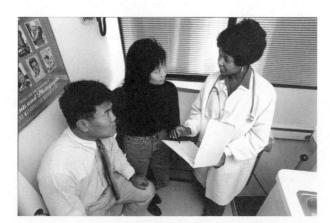

THE CRITICAL IMPORTANCE OF SERVICE EMPLOYEES

An often-heard quote about service organizations goes like this: "In a service organization, if you're not serving the customer, you'd better be serving someone who is."[6] People—front-line employees and those supporting them from behind the scenes—are critical to the success of any service organization. The importance of people in the marketing of services is captured in the *people* element of the services marketing mix, which we described in Chapter 1 *as all of the human actors who play a part in service delivery and thus influence the buyer's perceptions; namely, the firm's personnel, the customer, and other customers in the service environment.*

In this chapter we focus on service employees because

- They *are* the service.
- They *are* the organization in the customer's eyes.
- They *are* the brand.
- They *are* marketers.

In many cases, the contact employee is the service—there is nothing else. For example, in most personal and professional services (like haircutting, physical trainers, child care, cleaning/maintenance, limousine services, counseling, and legal services) the contact employee provides the entire service singlehandedly. The offering *is* the employee. Thus, investing in the employee to improve the service parallels making a direct investment in the improvement of a manufactured product.

Even if the contact employee doesn't perform the service entirely, he or she may still personify the firm in the customer's eyes. All of the employees of a law firm or health clinic—from the professionals who provide the service to the receptionists and office staff—represent the firm to the client, and everything these individuals do or say can influence perceptions of the organization. Even in a nonservice setting, Audi, an automobile manufacturer, recognizes the importance of its employees in representing and reinforcing the brand image of the company. As a result, Audi recruits staff at all levels whose psychological traits parallel and support the Audi brand image.[7] The brand image isn't just built and maintained by the cars themselves and advertising: it is a function of the people who work at Audi.

Even off-duty employees, such as flight attendants or restaurant employees on a break, reflect on the organizations they represent. If they are unprofessional or make rude remarks about or to customers, customers' perceptions of the organization will suffer even though the employee is not on duty. This is why the Disney Corporation insists that its employees maintain "onstage" attitudes and behaviors whenever they are in front of the public and that they relax these behaviors only when they are truly behind the scenes or "backstage" in underground tunnels where guests can't see them in their off-duty times.

Because contact employees represent the organization and can directly influence customer satisfaction, they perform the role of marketers. They physically embody the product and are walking billboards from a promotional standpoint. Some may also perform more traditional selling roles. For example, bank tellers are often called on to cross-sell bank products, a departure from the traditional teller role of operations function only.

Whether acknowledged or not, actively selling or not, service employees perform marketing functions. They can perform these functions well, to the organization's advantage, or poorly, to the organization's detriment. In this chapter we examine frameworks, tools, and strategies for ensuring that service employees perform their marketing functions well.

The Services Triangle

Services marketing is about promises—promises made and promises kept to customers. A strategic framework known as the *services triangle* (illustrated in Figure 11.2) visually reinforces the importance of people in the ability of firms to keep their promises and succeed in building customer relationships.[8] The triangle shows the three interlinked groups that work together to develop, promote, and deliver services. These key players are labeled on the points of the triangle: the *company* (or SBU or department or "management"); the *customers;* and the *providers.* Providers can be the firm's employees, subcontractors, or outsourced entities who actually deliver the company's services. Between these three points on the triangle, three types of marketing must be successfully carried out for a service to succeed: external marketing, interactive marketing, and internal marketing.

On the right side of the triangle are the *external marketing* efforts that the firm engages in to set up its customers' expectations and make promises to customers regarding what is to be delivered. Anything or anyone that communicates to the customer before service delivery can be viewed as part of this external marketing function. But external marketing is just the beginning for services marketers: promises made must be kept. On the bottom of the triangle is what has been termed *interactive marketing* or *real-time marketing*. Here is where promises are kept or broken by the firm's employees, subcontractors, or agents. People are critical at this juncture. If promises are not kept, customers become dissatisfied and eventually leave. The left side of the triangle suggests the critical role played by *internal marketing.* These are the activities that management engages in to aid the providers in their ability to deliver on the service promise: recruiting, training, motivating, rewarding, and providing equipment and technology. Unless service employees are able and willing to deliver on the promises made, the firm will not be successful, and the services triangle will collapse.

All three sides of the triangle are essential to complete the whole, and the sides of the triangle should be aligned. That is, what is promised through external marketing should be the same as what is delivered; and the enabling activities inside the organization should be aligned with what is expected of service providers. Strategies for

FIGURE 11.2
The Services Marketing Triangle

Source: Adapted from M. J. Bitner, "Building Service Relationships: It's All about Promises," *Journal of the Academy of Marketing Science* 23, 4 (1995), pp. 246–51; C. Gronroos, *Service Management and Marketing* (Lexington, MA: Lexington Books, 1990); and P. Kotler, *Marketing Management: Analysis, Planning, Implementation, and Control,* 8th ed. (Englewood Cliffs, NJ: Prentice Hall, 1994), p. 470.

Company

Internal Marketing
Enabling
promises

External Marketing
Making
promises

Providers

Customers

Interactive Marketing
Keeping promises

aligning the triangle, particularly the strategies associated with internal marketing, are the subject of this chapter.

Employee Satisfaction, Customer Satisfaction, and Profits

There is concrete evidence that satisfied employees make for satisfied customers (and satisfied customer can, in turn, reinforce employees' sense of satisfaction in their jobs). Some have even gone so far as to suggest that unless service employees are happy in their jobs, customer satisfaction will be difficult to achieve.[9]

Through their research with customers and employees in 28 different bank branches, Benjamin Schneider and David Bowen have shown that both a *climate for service* and a *climate for employee well-being* are highly correlated with overall customer perceptions of service quality.[10] That is, both service climate and human resource management experiences that *employees* have within their organizations are reflected in how *customers* experience the service. In a similar vein, Sears found customer satisfaction to be strongly related to employee turnover. In its stores with the highest customer satisfaction, employee turnover was 54 percent, whereas in stores with the lowest customer satisfaction, turnover was 83 percent.[11] Other research suggests that employees who feel they are treated fairly by their organizations will treat customers better, resulting in greater customer satisfaction.[12]

The underlying logic connecting employee satisfaction and loyalty to customer satisfaction and loyalty and ultimately profits is illustrated by the service profit chain shown in Figure 11.3.[13] In the earlier chapters we focused on customer satisfaction and retention; here we focus on employee issues. The service profit chain suggests that there are critical linkages among internal service quality; employee satisfaction/ productivity; the value of services provided to the customer; and ultimately customer satisfaction, retention, and profits.

Service profit chain researchers are careful to point out that the model does not suggest causality. That is, employee satisfaction does not *cause* customer satisfaction; rather the two are interrelated and feed off each other. The model does imply that companies that exhibit high levels of success on the elements of the model will be more successful and profitable than those that do not. This is borne out in other research. Jeffrey Pfeffer of the Stanford Graduate School of Business reports that companies that manage people right will outperform companies that don't by 30 to 40 percent.[14] *Fortune* magazine also determined that the publicly traded companies making their list of the "100 Best Companies to Work for in America" delivered higher average annual

FIGURE 11.3 **The Service Profit Chain**

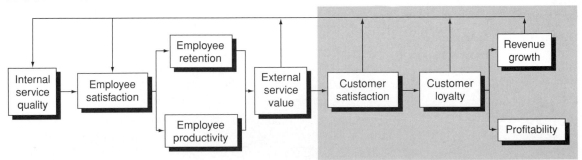

returns to shareholders than did companies making up the Russell 3000, a general index of companies similar to the *Fortune* sample.[15]

Service Quality Dimensions Are Driven by Employee Behaviors

Customers' perceptions of service quality will be impacted by the customer-oriented behaviors of employees.[16] In fact, all of the five dimensions of service quality (reliability, responsiveness, assurance, empathy, and tangibles) can be influenced directly by service employees.

Delivering the service as promised—*reliability*—is often totally within the control of front-line employees. Even in the case of automated services (such as ATMs, automated ticketing machines, or self-serve and pay gasoline pumps), behind-the-scenes employees are critical for making sure all of the systems are working properly. When services fail or errors are made, employees are essential for setting things right and using their judgment to determine the best course of action for service recovery.

Front-line employees directly influence customer perceptions of *responsiveness* through their personal willingness to help and their promptness in serving customers. Consider the range of responses you receive from different retail store clerks when you need help finding a particular item of clothing. One employee may ignore your presence, whereas another offers to help you search and calls other stores to locate the item. One may help you immediately and efficiently, whereas another may move slowly in accommodating even the simplest request.

The *assurance* dimension of service quality is highly dependent on employees' ability to communicate their credibility and to inspire trust and confidence. The reputation of the organization will help, but in the end, individual employees with whom the customer interacts confirm and build trust in the organization or detract from its reputation and ultimately destroy trust. For startup or relatively unknown organizations, credibility, trust, and confidence will be tied totally to employee actions.

It is difficult to imagine how an organization would deliver "caring, individualized attention" to customers independent of its employees. *Empathy* implies that employees will pay attention, listen, adapt, and be flexible in delivering what individual customers need.[17] For example, research documents that when employees are customer-oriented, have good rapport with customers, and exhibit perceptive and attentive listening skills, customers will evaluate the service more highly and be more likely to return.[18] Employee appearance and dress are important aspects of the *tangibles* dimension of quality, along with many other factors that are independent of service employees (the service facility, decor, brochures, signage, and so on).

BOUNDARY-SPANNING ROLES

Our focus in this chapter is on front-line service employees who interact directly with customers, although much of what is described and recommended can be applied to internal service employees as well. The front-line service employees are referred to as *boundary spanners* because they operate at the organization's boundary. As indicated in Figure 11.4, boundary spanners provide a link between the external customer and environment and the internal operations of the organization. They serve a critical function in understanding, filtering, and interpreting information and resources to and from the organization and its external constituencies.

Who are these boundary spanners? What types of people and positions comprise

FIGURE 11.4
Boundary spanners interact with and provide information to both internal and external constituents.

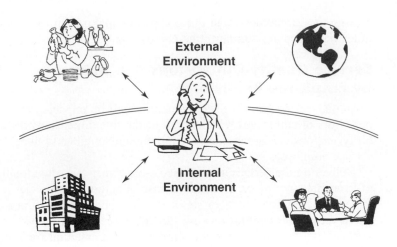

critical boundary-spanning roles? Their skills and experience cover the full spectrum of jobs and careers. In industries such as fast food, hotels, telecommunication, and retail, the boundary spanners are the least skilled, lowest-paid employees in the organization. They are order takers, front-desk employees, telephone operators, store clerks, truck drivers, and delivery people. In other industries, boundary spanners are well-paid, highly educated professionals—for example, doctors, lawyers, accountants, consultants, architects, and teachers.

No matter what the level of skill or pay, boundary-spanning positions are often high-stress jobs. In addition to mental and physical skills, these positions require extraordinary levels of emotional labor, frequently demand an ability to handle interpersonal and interorganizational conflict, and call on the employee to make real-time trade-offs between quality and productivity on the job. These stresses and trade-offs can result in failure to deliver services as specified, which widens gap 3.

Emotional Labor

The term *emotional labor* was coined by Arlie Hochschild to refer to the labor that goes beyond the physical or mental skills needed to deliver quality service.[19] It means delivering smiles, making eye contact, showing sincere interest, and engaging in friendly conversation with people who are essentially strangers and who may or may not ever be seen again. Friendliness, courtesy, empathy, and responsiveness directed toward customers all require huge amounts of emotional labor from the front-line employees who shoulder this responsibility for the organization. Emotional labor draws on people's feelings (often requiring them to suppress their true feelings) to be effective in their jobs. A front-line service employee who is having a bad day or isn't feeling just right is still expected to put on the face of the organization when dealing with customers. One of the clearest examples of emotional labor is the story (probably apocryphal) of the flight attendant who was approached by a businessman who said, "Let's have a smile." "Okay," she replied, "I'll tell you what, first you smile and then I'll smile, okay?" He smiled. "Good," she said. "Now hold that for 15 hours," and walked away.[20]

Many of the strategies we'll discuss later in the chapter can help organizations and employees deal with the realities of emotional labor on the job. For the organization such strategies include carefully selecting people who can handle emotional stress, training them in needed skills (like listening and problem solving), and teaching or giving them coping abilities and strategies (via job rotation, scheduled breaks, teamwork, or other techniques). Delta Airlines puts prospective employees through simulated customer contact exercises to see the kind of friendliness and warmth they naturally communicate.[21] Other companies train employees in how *not* to absorb a customer's bad mood, by having them spend hours role playing to suppress the natural reaction to return an insult with an insult. Providing good physical working conditions and allowing employees to take scheduled breaks, to rely on each other for support, and to rotate positions among the most demanding front-line jobs also help to reduce the stress of excessive emotional labor.

Sources of Conflict

Front-line employees often face interpersonal and interorganizational conflicts on the job. Their frustration and confusion can, if left unattended, lead to stress, job dissatisfaction, a diminished ability to serve customers, and burnout.[22] Because they represent the customer to the organization and often need to manage a number of customers simultaneously, front liners inevitably have to deal with conflicts, including person/role conflicts, organization/client conflicts, and interclient conflicts as suggested by Figure 11.5 and discussed in the next paragraphs.[23]

Person/Role Conflicts

In some situations, boundary spanners feel conflicts between what they are asked to do and their own personalities, orientations, or values. In a society such as the United States, where equality and individualism are highly valued, service workers may feel role conflict when they are required to subordinate their feelings or beliefs, as when they are asked to live by the motto "The customer is always right—even when he is wrong." Sometimes there is a conflict between role requirements and the self-image or self-esteem of the employee. An Israeli service expert tells an example from that culture:

> In Israel, for instance, most buses are operated by one man, the driver, who is also responsible for selling tickets. No trays are installed in buses for the transferring of bus fare from passenger to driver, and the money is transferred directly. Bus drivers often complain about the humiliating experience of having to stretch out their hands like beggars in order to collect the fare. Another typical case in Israeli buses is when money changes hands and a coin falls down accidentally onto the bus floor. The question, who will bend down to lift the coin, the driver or the passenger, clearly reflects the driver's role conflict.[24]

Whoever stoops to pick up the coin is indicating subservient status.

FIGURE 11.5
Sources of Conflict for Boundary-Spanning Workers

• Person versus role
• Organization versus client
• Client versus client
• Quality versus productivity

Person/role conflict also arises when employees are required to wear specific clothing or change some aspect of their appearance to conform to the job requirements. A young lawyer, just out of school, may feel an internal conflict with his new role when his employer requires him to cut his long hair and trade his casual clothes for a three-piece suit.

Organization/Client Conflict

A more common type of conflict for front-line service employees is the conflict between their two bosses, the organization and the individual customer. Service employees are typically rewarded for following certain standards, rules, and procedures. Ideally these rules and standards are customer based, as described in Chapter 9. When they are not, or when a customer makes excessive demands, the employee has to choose whether to follow the rules or satisfy the demands. The conflict is greatest when the employee believes the organization is wrong in its policies and must decide whether to accommodate the client and risk losing her job or follow the policies. These conflicts are especially severe when service employees depend directly on the customer for income. For example, employees who depend on tips or commissions are likely to face greater levels of organization/client conflict because they have even greater incentives to identify with the customer.

Interclient Conflict

Sometimes conflict occurs for boundary spanners when there are incompatible expectations and requirements from two or more customers. This occurs most often when the service provider is serving customers in turn (a bank teller, a ticketing agent, a doctor) or is serving many customers simultaneously (teachers, entertainers).

In the case of serving customers in turn, the provider may satisfy one customer by spending additional time, customizing the service, and being very flexible in meeting the customer's needs. Meanwhile, waiting customers are becoming dissatisfied because their needs are not being met in a timely way. Beyond the timing issue, different clients may prefer different modes of service delivery. Having to serve one client who prefers personal recognition and a degree of familiarity in the presence of another client who is all business and would prefer little interpersonal interaction can also create conflict for the employee.

In the case of serving many customers at the same time, it is often difficult or impossible to serve the full range of needs of a group of heterogeneous customers simultaneously. This type of conflict is readily apparent in any college classroom where the instructor must meet a multitude of expectations and different preferences for formats and style.

Quality/Productivity Trade-Offs

Front-line service workers are asked to be both effective and efficient: they are expected to deliver satisfying service to customers and at the same time to be cost-effective and productive in what they do. A physician in an HMO, for example, is expected to deliver caring, quality, individualized service to her patients but at the same time to serve a certain number of patients within a specified time frame. A checker at a grocery store is expected to know his customers and to be polite and courteous, yet also to process the groceries accurately and move people through the line quickly. An architectural draftsperson is expected to create quality drawings, yet to produce a required quantity of drawings in a given period of time. These essential trade-offs between quality and quantity, and between maximum effectiveness and efficiency, place real-time demands and pressures on service employees.

Peter Drucker suggests that productive performance in all service jobs will combine both quality and quantity objectives.[25] For some jobs, such as that of a research scientist, quality is really all that matters—the number of results, or quantity, is quite secondary. If a scientist can develop one new drug with the potential of saving millions of lives and generating substantial revenues for a company, that one quality result is invaluable. At the other extreme, there are service jobs that are almost totally quantity dominated—for example, filing papers, processing claims, cleaning rooms, serving fast food. Most service jobs fall somewhere between that of the research scientist and that of the claims processor. Most require a balance of quality and quantity, and often the worker is faced with making the trade-off.

Research suggests that these trade-offs are more difficult for service businesses than for manufacturing and packaged goods businesses and that pursuing goals of customer satisfaction and productivity simultaneously is particularly challenging in situations in which service employees are required to customize service offerings to meet customer needs.[26]

Jagdip Singh, a noted services researcher, has studied productivity and quality as two types of performance inherent in front line service jobs.[27] He explains the difficult tradeoffs that employees face and has developed ways to measure these two types of performance together with a theoretical model to predict the causes and consequences of these tradeoffs. He finds that quality of job performance is particularly susceptible to burnout and job stress. He also finds that internal support from understanding managers and control over the job tasks can help employees in making quality and productivity tradeoffs, avoiding burnout, and maintaining their performance. Technology is being used to an ever-greater degree to balance the quality/quantity trade-off to increase productivity of service workers and at the same time free them to provide higher-quality service for the customer, as is discussed in the Technology Spotlight.

STRATEGIES FOR CLOSING GAP 3

A complex combination of strategies is needed to ensure that service employees are willing and able to deliver quality services and that they stay motivated to perform in customer-oriented, service-minded ways. These strategies for enabling service promises are often referred to as *internal marketing,* as shown on the left side of Figure 11.2.[28] Even during slow economic times, the importance of attracting, developing, and retaining good people in knowledge- and service-based industries cannot be overemphasized. Paraphrasing from a recent issue of *Fast Company* magazine provides a contemporary view:

> When it comes to building great companies, the most urgent business challenge is finding and keeping great people. Sure a Web strategy is important, and the stock market is scary, but still the best companies know that people are the foundation of greatness.[29]

By approaching human resource decisions and strategies from the point of view that the primary goal is to motivate and enable employees to deliver customer-oriented promises successfully, an organization will move toward closing gap 3. The strategies presented here are organized around four basic themes. To build a customer-oriented, service-minded workforce, an organization must (1) hire the right people, (2) develop

Technology Spotlight
Quality versus Productivity—How CRM Systems Help Employees

Providing quality service to individual customers while at the same time being productive and efficient is an ongoing challenge for sales and service providers—the front line of the organization. These are the people that produce revenue and build customer relationships for the company. In many leading companies these employees are challenged daily to satisfy increasing numbers of customers more effectively and efficiently.

In recent years, sophisticated "customer relationship management" software has helped make quality service achievable and efficient. Also known as "front-office automation," this type of software represents the fastest-growing segment of the software industry. The large players include the industry leader, Siebel Systems Inc., and PeopleSoft, Oracle, SAP, and Nortel Networks. These big companies bought some of the early leaders in this industry—for instance, Vantive was bought by People-Soft and Clarify by Nortel. Smaller companies also serving this niche including E.Piphany, Interact Commerce, Kana, Onyx, and Vignette. All of these competitors focus on providing software tools for increasing employee productivity in sales, service, and customer management.

How exactly do these CRM systems support sales and service people to make them more productive? AT&T's customer sales and service centers provide one example. Through software applications, calls coming into AT&T's centers are identified (by phone number and market segment) and routed to the right customer segment personnel even before the calls are answered. Employees get the calls that they are trained for and best able to handle. The software also allows the employee to view the entire account history of the caller, and this information is available on the employee's computer screen simultaneously with the incoming call. Employees have at their fingertips information on the wide variety of calling plans and other options available to customers. The person who answers the call is empowered to make decisions, answer questions, and encourage sales in ways that were totally impractical prior to this technology. As AT&T's "front door," the employees in the customer sales and service centers are equipped to build customer relationships and ultimately increase revenues for the company. Once viewed as an expense, these employees are now viewed as a key to the company's growth, thanks to front-office automation. The technology also allows employees to take the time to customize service and satisfy individual customers, while at the same time being productive.

CRM is also revolutionizing the sales function. By giving detailed customer histories and integrated service

people to deliver service quality, (3) provide the needed support systems, and (4) retain the best people. Within each of these basic strategies are a number of specific sub-strategies for accomplishing the goal, as shown in Figure 11.6.

Specific approaches for hiring and energizing front-line workers take on a different look and feel across companies based on the organizations' values, culture, history, and vision.[30] For example, "developing people to deliver service quality" is accomplished quite differently at Southwest Airlines when compared with Disney. At Disney the orientation and training process is highly structured, scripted, and standardized. At Southwest, the emphasis is more on developing needed skills but then empowering employees to be spontaneous and nonscripted in their approach to customers. Although the style and culture of the two organizations are different, both pay special attention to all four of the basic themes shown in Figure 11.6. Both have made significant investments in their people, recognizing the critical roles they play.

Hire the Right People

One of the best ways to close gap 3 is to start with the right service delivery people from the beginning. This implies that considerable attention should be focused on hiring and recruiting service personnel. Such attention is contrary to traditional practices

and pricing information, these tools allow the salesperson to be much more consultative and to add more value than in the past. IBM, for example, is implementing the most comprehensive integrated customer relationship management software system in the world for its sales and service people worldwide. Using Siebel's eBusiness Applications, the goal is to integrate the whole company around its customers so that anyone in the company can respond to the customer in a consistent manner with the same basic account information. This is no small task in a company with over 80,000 internal system users, 30,000 business partners, and millions of customers.

Although front-office CRM systems hold great promise and have provided tremendous bottom-line benefits for companies already, they come with their own, often significant, challenges. They can require major monetary and human investments. They often mandate integration of incompatible information systems, significant internal training costs, and incentives to be sure they are used effectively. Frequently they fail, at least on the initial try, for a variety of reasons. Some companies don't anticipate the amount of work involved, and many don't realize how resistant their employees will be to making the necessary changes. CRM projects also fail when they don't have the support of top management.

Even giant Microsoft faced significant challenges when it attempted to integrate all of its 36 distinct customer information applications worldwide. Microsoft underestimated the internal demands of such a large deployment and cut back on end user training at the wrong time. It learned that training (of both employees and even customers sometimes) is critical to the success of the technology. Despite some bumps in the road, however, the system soon began to pay for itself, allowing Microsoft service staff and salespeople to make decisions better and in a more timely fashion, satisfying customers and building the business.

Many companies now see implementation of front-office CRM software as not only a potential competitive advantage, but in some cases, a requirement for survival. As customers encounter world-class service from companies like AT&T, FedEx, IBM, or Cisco, they come to expect it from others—even in different industries.

Sources: M. Boslet, "CRM: The Promise, The Peril, The Eye-Popping Price," *The Industry Standard,* August 6–13, 2001, pp. 61–65; L. M. Fisher, "Here Comes Front-Office Automation," *Strategy and Business* 13 (4th quarter 1998), pp. 53–65; "Inside Big Blue's CRM Transformation," *The Siebel Journal: Best Practices,* www.siebel.com, 2002.

in many service industries, where service personnel are the lowest on the corporate ladder and work for minimum wage. But even in these industries, managers are beginning to focus on more effective recruitment practices. At the other end of the spectrum, in the professional services, the most important recruiting criteria are typically technical training, certifications, and expertise. However, here too many organizations are looking above and beyond the technical qualifications of applicants to assess their customer and service orientation as well. Figure 11.6 shows a number of ways to improve service employee recruitment efforts to get the right people from the beginning.

Compete for the Best People

To get the best people, an organization needs to identify them and compete with other organizations to hire them. Leonard Berry and A. Parasuraman refer to this as "competing for talent market share."[31] They suggest that firms act as marketers in their pursuit of the best employees, just as they use their marketing expertise to compete for customers. Thinking of recruiting as a marketing activity results in addressing issues of market (employee) segmentation, product (job) design, and promotion of job availability in ways that attract potential long-term employees. For firms like Washington Mutual, Cox Communication, the Limited, Inc., AOL Time Warner, and others, thinking of

FIGURE 11.6
Human Resource Strategies for Closing Gap 3

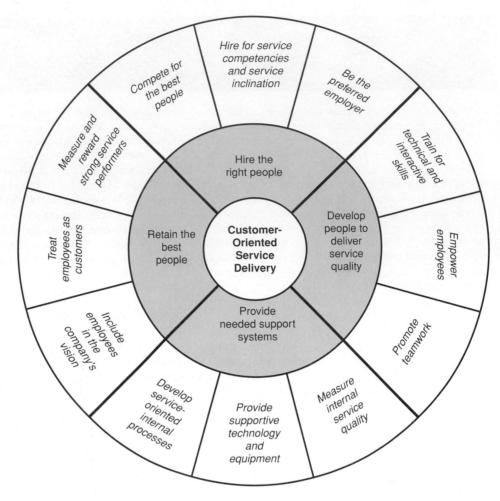

recruiting in this way has resulted in changing the title of the head recruiting person to vice president of talent acquisition. Doing so recognizes the importance of the function and helps to elevate the role to the strategic importance it deserves.[32]

A complementary strategy is to interview multiple employees for every position. At Southwest Airlines, the People Department (the name Southwest has given to what others call the human resource, or personnel, department) is relentless in its pursuit of talented employees. A quote from Southwest's long-time president, Herb Kelleher, illustrates the point: "The People Department came to me one day and said, 'We've interviewed 34 people for this ramp agent's position, and we're getting a little worried about the time and effort and cost that's going into it.' And I said if you have to interview 154 people to get the right person, do it."[33]

Another way to compete for the best people is to raise what might be unnecessarily low standards in order to identify more qualified employees. Sometimes these potential recruits may be found in unlikely places, and among nontraditional populations. Women and minorities are increasingly represented in the labor pool in the United States, as are senior citizens, recent immigrants, and disabled persons. Many of the potentially best employees are likely to be represented in these groups, and firms that ignore them are missing real opportunities. Developing a diverse employee base can have an added benefit of complementing the increasingly diverse customer base that most service organizations are experiencing.

Hire for Service Competencies and Service Inclination

Once potential employees have been identified, organizations need to be conscientious in interviewing and screening to truly identify the best people from the pool of candidates. It has been suggested that service employees need two complementary capacities: they need both *service competencies* and *service inclination*.[34]

Service competencies are the skills and knowledge necessary to do the job. In many cases, competencies are validated by achieving particular degrees and certifications, such as attaining a doctor of law (JD) degree and passing the relevant state bar examination for lawyers. Similar rites of passage are required of doctors, airline pilots, university professors, teachers, and many other job seekers before they are ever interviewed for service jobs in their fields. In other cases, service competencies may not be degree related, but may instead relate to basic intelligence or physical requirements. A retail clerk, for example, must possess basic math skills and the potential to operate a cash register.

Given the multidimensional nature of service quality, service employees should be screened for more than their service competencies. They must also be screened for *service inclination*—their interest in doing service-related work—which is reflected in their attitudes toward service and orientation toward serving customers and others on the job. Self-selection suggests that most service jobs will draw applicants with some level of service inclination, and that most employees in service organizations are inclined toward service. However, some employees clearly have a greater service inclination than others. Research has shown that service effectiveness is correlated with having service-oriented personality characteristics such as helpfulness, thoughtfulness, and sociability.[35] An ideal selection process for service employees assesses both service competencies and service inclination, resulting in employee hires who are high on both dimensions.[36]

In addition to traditional employment interviews, many firms use innovative approaches to assessing service inclination and other personal characteristics that fit the organization's needs. Southwest Airlines looks for people who are compassionate and who have common sense, a sense of humor, a "can do" attitude, and an egalitarian sense of themselves (they think in terms of "we" rather than "me"). One way the company assesses these service inclinations is by interviewing potential flight attendants in groups to see how they interact with each other. Pilots are also interviewed in groups to assess their teamwork skills, a critical factor above and beyond the essential technical skills they are required to possess.

In many cases a component of the selection process will include a form of work simulation that allows employees to demonstrate how they would actually perform on the job. A simulation may take the form of role playing or a series of exercises that parallel the demands of the actual job. In hiring future managers, Ford Motor Company uses a full-day assessment center for evaluating potential hires. Applicants come to Detroit and are given an "office," a desk, and an in-box. They are asked to perform as they would on a typical day—interacting with customers, auto dealers, and supervisors and dealing with paperwork and calendar issues. Through the process they are being observed not so much for technical job skills, but for their approach to customers, attitude, problem-solving skills, and ability to prioritize and pay attention to what is most important. In addition to being a good way to assess potential employee abilities, simulations can give the potential hire a better view of what the job is actually like. Those who don't like what they experience can back out of the applicant pool before being hired and finding out the job isn't what they had expected.

Be the Preferred Employer

One way to attract the best people is to be known as the preferred employer in a particular industry or in a particular location. Rosenbluth International, headquartered in Philadelphia, is a company that enjoys a reputation as a preferred employer. With close to 600 offices in 48 states, London, and Tokyo, Rosenbluth is the fourth largest travel agency in the United States. The company's president, Hal Rosenbluth, has gone so far as to say, "We don't believe that the customer can come first unless our people come first. If our people don't come first, then they're not free to focus on our clients; they're worrying about other kinds of things."[37]

Other strategies that support a goal of being the preferred employer include providing extensive training, career and advancement opportunities, excellent internal support, and attractive incentives, and offering quality goods and services that employees are proud to be associated with. Exhibit 11.1 illustrates why SAS Institute is a preferred employer in the statistical software industry. Employees who work for SAS are, for the most part, professional or technical and well paid. In a very different industry, dominated by lower-paid workers, Marriott International has a stated company goal of being the "preferred employer" in its industry. Marriott uses employee stock options, a social services referral network, day care, welfare-to-work training classes, and English and reading classes as some of its ways of being the preferred employer in the highly competitive hospitality industry.[38] SAS Institute and Marriott International were numbers 2 and 90, respectively, on the list of most admired companies to work for in America in 2001.[39]

Develop People to Deliver Service Quality

To grow and maintain a workforce that is customer oriented and focused on delivering quality, an organization must develop its employees to deliver service quality. That is, once it has hired the right employees, the organization must train and work with these individuals to ensure service performance.

Train for Technical and Interactive Skills

To provide quality service, employees need ongoing training in the necessary technical skills and knowledge and in process or interactive skills.[40] Examples of technical skills and knowledge are working with accounting systems in hotels, cash machine procedures in a retail store, underwriting procedures in an insurance company, and any operational rules the company has for running its business. Most service organizations are quite conscious of and relatively effective at training employees in technical skills. These skills may be taught through formal education, as is the case at McDonald's "Hamburger University," which trains McDonald's managers from all over the world. Additionally, technical skills are often taught through on-the-job training, as when education majors work with experienced teachers in internship programs, or when telephone service trainees listen in on the conversations of experienced employees. Recently companies are increasing their use of information technology to train employees in the technical skills and knowledge needed on the job.

Service employees also need training in interactive skills that allow them to provide courteous, caring, responsive, and empathetic service. Exhibit 11.2 explains how the Tokyo Imperial Hotel in Japan effectively combines service employee training in both the technical and interactive skills needed to provide quality service.

11.1 SAS Institute Is a Preferred Employer in Its Industry

SAS Institute is the world's largest privately held software company, with revenue growing by double-digit percentages for the past 24 years. The hugely profitable company is known for its statistical software products that allow its more than 37,000 customers in over 111 countries to analyze huge amounts of data, searching for categories, patterns, and trends. Among its customers are the U.S. Census Bureau. Ninety percent of the *Fortune* 500 are SAS customers.

Although relatively unknown, SAS ranked number 3 in *Fortune*'s list of the 100 best companies to work for in America. SAS has also been on *Working Mothers* magazine's list of 100 best companies for which to work for 12 years, and it has earned numerous other awards for quality and excellence. Employee turnover is approximately 4 percent in an industry that averages more than 20 percent. SAS receives hundreds of applications for each job opening despite the current highly competitive environment where most companies are scrambling to find qualified technical people. Here are some of the reasons employees love working for this company, and why it can be considered a preferred employer in its industry.

Founder, chairman, and majority owner of the company James H. Goodnight "likes happy people," and he believes strongly that happy employees are more productive, produce better quality for customers, and ultimately stay in their jobs longer, thus producing long-term benefits for the company.

A quote from the company's website captures SAS's philosophy about its people: "If you treat employees as if they make a difference to the company, they will make a difference to the company." The company invests heavily in its people, and the best performers at SAS seldom leave to work for competitors.

The wooded 200-acre campus outside of Raleigh, North Carolina, is first of all a beautiful setting to work in. Every employee has a private office, and much attention is given to flexible, family-oriented policies. A 35-hour schedule is promoted, flexible hours are available, and the company provides two top-quality day care centers with very reasonable prices on site. Employees get an extra week of paid vacation between Christmas and New Year's. Break rooms are stocked with free sodas, fresh fruit, candies, and pastries. Employees receive discounts on properties they purchase near SAS as well as discounts on country club memberships and tuition breaks at Cary Academy, a private school. Year-end bonuses and profit sharing are also valued perks.

While SAS provides all of these amenities, other types of perks are deliberately excluded. For example, stock options, common in the high-technology industry, are not offered at SAS; nor are tuition reimbursements or sales commissions. Mr. Goodnight's belief is that these types of benefits encourage autonomy, competition, and high-pressure tactics that are not compatible with the organization's culture. Neither are salaries notably high. Despite these absences, professional and technical people are clamoring to work for SAS because of the unique benefits and family-oriented culture it perpetuates.

Jeffrey Pfeffer, Stanford University business professor, says that his research on SAS leads him to conclude the company has found an enormously effective business model. He figures that the approximately $50 million a year the company saves in low turnover pays for the family-friendly practices and corporate amenities.

Sources: T. D. Schellhardt, "An Idyllic Workplace under a Tycoon's Thumb," *The Wall Street Journal,* November 23, 1998, p. B1; R. Levering and M. Moskowitz, "The 100 Best Companies to Work For," *Fortune,* January 8, 2001, pp. 148–68; www.sasinstitute.com, 2002.

Successful companies invest heavily in training and make sure that the training fits their business goals and strategies. For example, at Midwest Express, the company that takes pride in offering "the best care in the air," all employees (pilots, baggage handlers, aircraft groomers) take part in a two-day orientation program. The focus revolves around the company values and customer service. In Zagat's 1997 international airline survey, Midwest Express was the only U.S. airline to rank in the top 10.[41] At the Ritz-Carlton, all employees go through extensive initial training and carry the organization's credo card with them. The credo card specifies the three steps of service as well as Ritz-Carlton's well-known motto, "We are Ladies and Gentlemen Serving Ladies and Gentlemen," along with the credo. All employees are given pocket-sized,

Tokyo's Imperial Hotel provides an excellent example of training for both knowledge and skills as well as interactive service quality. The hotel's "Capability Development Program" consists of training in "occupational abilities and knowledge" (technical skills) as well as "service manners training" (interactive skills). The first type of training involves on-the-job apprenticing, rotations through all of the major departments within the hotel, visitations and inspection tours of comparable hotels in other countries, and focused study tours (for example, Imperial Hotel's senior waiters and sommeliers might tour famous wineries in California and France every three years). In addition, employees get specialized skills training through independent educational organizations on needed topics ranging from management strategy decision making to food hygiene to presentation know-how.

The "service manners training" focuses on the etiquette and psychology of guest contact and attitudes of service. Proper etiquette is taught via role playing and videotaping (to critique appearance, mannerisms, and personal idiosyncrasies). The way the staff should appear to hotel guests is stressed and demonstrated, with emphasis placed on cleanliness, a sense of understated elegance, and good taste. Guest psychology is discussed, emphasizing the following main points:

1. Imperial Hotel patrons, given the rank and reputation of the hotel, expect that you will consider them your most important priority, the center of your attention.

2. Guests do not want to suffer losses of any kind while in the hotel.

3. Guests expect to be received in a warm, welcoming fashion.

4. A guest does not want to be extended a level of treatment that is in any way inferior to that provided to other guests of the hotel.

5. Guests wish to experience an appropriate feeling of prestige or superiority, purely by virtue of their using what is commonly evaluated as a deluxe enterprise.

6. Guests enjoy feeling possessive about the hotel's facilities and services, and expect exclusive attention.

Finally, the basic principles of nonverbal communication and body language are discussed. Demonstrations and detailed explanations of appropriate behaviors are given, covering such points as facial expressions, appearance, and posture when standing; pleasing, attractive ways of talking and carriage; proper posture; and courtesy when escorting guests within the hotel premises. Because the bow is used regardless of the national origin of the guest, considerable time is spent on the intricacies of proper bowing. A bow of welcome involves a 15-degree angle, a bow of gratitude is 30 degrees, and a bow of apology is a full 45 degrees from the normal straight standing position. The remainder of the service manners training concentrates on the complexities of the Japanese language and the appropriate applications for hotel service. Trainees are instructed in some 25 common daily expressions, learning their politest forms as well as the English equivalents.

Ongoing training and service improvement programs at all levels are part of the hotel's total operations strategy.

Source: Reprinted from M. I. Cronin, 3rd, "Staff Training Delivers Quality Service at Tokyo's Imperial Hotel," in *The Service Quality Handbook*, eds. E. E. Scheuing and W. F. Christopher. Copyright © 1993 AMACOM, a division of the American Management Association International, New York, NY. All rights reserved. http://www.amanet.org.

laminated credo cards to carry in their wallets. Further, employees in every hotel stop for a brief standing staff meeting each day to review one of Ritz-Carlton's "Gold Standards: The 20 Basics" to continually reinforce earlier training.

It isn't just front-line service personnel who need this combination of service skills and interactive training. Support staff, supervisors, and managers need service training as well. Unless contact employees experience the same values and behaviors from their supervisors, they are unlikely to deliver high-quality service to customers. Scandinavian Airline Systems, a highly regarded international carrier, applied this logic in its dramatic turnaround in 1981 and again in a move to "reinvent" the company in the 1990s. Both times it started with service training for top management and then worked through the organization to supervisors and contact employees, giving everyone a shared vision and perspective on service.

Empower Employees

Many organizations have discovered that to be truly responsive to customer needs, front-line providers need to be empowered to accommodate customer requests and to recover on the spot when things go wrong. *Empowerment* means giving employees the desire, skills, tools, and authority to serve the customer. While the key to empowerment is giving employees authority to make decisions on the customer's behalf, authority alone is not enough. Employees need the knowledge and tools to be able to make these decisions, and they need incentives that encourage them to make the right decisions. Organizations do not succeed in empowering their employees if they simply tell them, "You now have the authority to do whatever it takes to satisfy the customer." First, employees often don't believe this, particularly if the organization has functioned hierarchically or bureaucratically in the past. Second, employees often don't know what it means to "do whatever it takes" if they have not received training, guidelines, and the tools needed to make such decisions.

Research suggests that there may indeed be positive benefits to empowering front-line service workers. Some of these benefits include reduction in job-related stress, improved job satisfaction, greater adaptability, and better outcomes for customers.[42] But such success does not come easily. In fact, some experts have concluded that few organizations have truly taken advantage of, or properly implemented, successful empowerment strategies.[43] Nor is empowerment the answer for all organizations. Exhibit 11.3 enumerates both the costs and benefits of empowerment as documented by David Bowen and Edward Lawler, experts on this subject.[44] These authors suggest that firms should employ a contingency view of empowerment, meaning that while empowerment has many benefits, it may be more or less appropriate under certain circumstances. They contrast an *empowerment approach* with a *production line approach* for managing services. An empowered organization is characterized by flexibility, quick decisions, and authority given to front-line people, whereas a production line organization is characterized by standardization and little decision-making latitude or authority given to front-line employees.[45]

Both models can be successful under certain circumstances. Bowen and Lawler suggest that organizations well suited to empowerment strategies are ones in which (1) the business strategy is one of differentiation and customization, (2) customers are long-term relationship customers, (3) technology is nonroutine or complex, (4) the business environment is unpredictable, and (5) managers and employees have high growth and social needs and strong interpersonal skills. Service organizations that have the opposite characteristics will favor the production line approach.

Promote Teamwork

The nature of many service jobs suggests that customer satisfaction will be enhanced when employees work as teams. Because service jobs are frequently frustrating, demanding, and challenging, a teamwork environment will help to alleviate some of the stresses and strains. Employees who feel supported and that they have a team backing them up will be better able to maintain their enthusiasm and provide quality service. "An interactive community of coworkers who help each other, commiserate, and achieve together is a powerful antidote to service burnout,"[46] and, we would add, an important ingredient for service quality. By promoting teamwork an organization can enhance the employees' *abilities* to deliver excellent service while the camaraderie and support enhance their *inclination* to be excellent service providers.

11.3 POTENTIAL COSTS AND BENEFITS OF EMPOWERMENT

BENEFITS

Quicker online responses to customer needs during service delivery. Employees who are allowed to make decisions on behalf of the customer can make decisions more quickly, bypassing what in the past might have meant a long chain of command, or at least a discussion with an immediate supervisor.

Quicker online responses to dissatisfied customers during service recovery. When there are failures in the delivery system, customers hope for an immediate recovery effort on the part of the organization. Empowered employees can recover on the spot, and a dissatisfied customer can potentially be turned into a satisfied, even loyal one.

Employees feel better about their jobs and themselves. Giving employees control and authority to make decisions makes them feel responsible and gives them ownership for the customer's satisfaction. Decades of job design research suggest that when employees have a sense of control and of doing meaningful work, they are more satisfied. The result is lower turnover and less absenteeism.

Employees will interact with customers with more warmth and enthusiasm. Because they feel better about themselves and their work, these feelings will spill over into their feelings about customers and will be reflected in their interactions.

Empowered employees are a great source of service ideas. When employees are empowered, they feel responsible for the service outcome and they will be excellent sources of ideas about new services or how to improve current offerings.

Great word-of-mouth advertising from customers. Empowered employees do special and unique things that customers will remember and tell their friends, family, and associates about.

COSTS

A potentially greater dollar investment in selection and training. To find employees who will work well in an empowered environment requires creative, potentially more costly selection procedures. Training will also be more expensive in general since employees need more knowledge about the company, its products, and how to work in flexible ways with customers.

Higher labor costs. The organization may not be able to use as many part-time or seasonal employees, and it may need to pay more for asking employees to assume responsibility.

Potentially slower or inconsistent service delivery. If empowered employees spend more time with all, or even some, customers, then service overall may take longer. This may annoy customers who are waiting. Empowerment also means that customers will get what they need or request. When decisions regarding customer satisfaction are left to the discretion of employees, there may be inconsistency in the level of service delivered.

May violate customers' perceptions of fair play. Customers may perceive that sticking to procedures with every customer is fair. Thus, if they see that customers are receiving different levels of service or that employees are cutting special deals with some customers, they may believe that the organization is not fair.

Employees may "give away the store" or make bad decisions. Many people fear that empowered employees will make costly decisions that the organization cannot afford. While this can happen, good training and appropriate guidelines will help.

Source: Reprinted from D. E. Bowen and E. E. Lawler III, "The Empowerment of Service Workers: What, Why, How, and When," *Sloan Management Review*, Spring 1992, pp. 31–39, by permission of the publisher. Copyright 1992 by the Sloan Management Review Association. All rights reserved.

One way of promoting teamwork is to encourage the attitude that "everyone has a customer." That is, even when employees are not directly responsible for or in direct interaction with the final customer, they need to know whom they serve directly and how the role they play in the total service picture is essential to the final delivery of quality service. If each employee can see how he or she is somehow integral in delivering quality to the final customer, and if each employee knows whom to support to make service quality a reality, teamwork will be enhanced. Service blueprints, described in Chapter 8, can serve as useful tools to illustrate for employees their integral roles in delivering service quality to the ultimate customer.

Team goals and rewards also promote teamwork. When teams of individuals are given rewards, rather than all rewards being based on individual achievements and performance, team efforts and team spirit are encouraged.

The effective promotion of teamwork may require restructuring around market-based groupings rather than along traditional functional lines. This means that all people who impact the customer (or a particular customer segment) will work together as a team to coordinate their efforts, regardless of their functional affiliations. On the other hand, when functionalism dominates in an organization, the operations, marketing, and human resource groups may work at cross-purposes almost unknowingly, and as a result inhibit teamwork directed at satisfying the customer. Creating teams and supporting effective teamwork, especially across functions, is no small task, and there are many barriers and obstacles to overcome in implementing such strategies in most traditional organizational structures. When done well, however, the benefits for both customers and employees can be tremendous.[47]

Provide Needed Support Systems

To be efficient and effective in their jobs, service workers require internal support systems that are aligned with their need to be customer focused. This point cannot be overemphasized. In fact, without customer-focused internal support and customer-oriented systems, it is nearly impossible for employees to deliver quality service no matter how much they want to. For example, a bank teller who is rewarded for customer satisfaction as well as for accuracy in bank transactions needs easy access to up-to-date customer records, a well-staffed branch (so that he isn't constantly facing a long line of impatient customers), and supportive customer-oriented supervisors and back-office staff. In examining customer service outcomes in Australian call centers, researchers found that internal support from supervisors, teammates, and other departments as well as evaluations of technology used on the job were all strongly related to employee satisfaction and ability to serve customers.[48] The following sections suggest strategies for ensuring customer-oriented internal support.

Measure Internal Service Quality

One way to encourage supportive internal service relationships is to measure and reward internal service. By first acknowledging that everyone in the organization has a customer and then measuring customer perceptions of internal service quality, an organization can begin to develop an internal quality culture. Internal customer service audits and internal service guarantees are two strategies used to implement a culture of internal service quality. Through the audit, internal organizations identify their customers, determine their needs, measure how well they are doing, and make improvements. The process parallels market research practices used for external customers. Exhibit 11.4 outlines the steps in an internal service audit.

Internal service guarantees can augment the measurement of internal service quality. For example, at GTE's corporate education center—the Management Development Center (MDC)—a 100 percent satisfaction guarantee helped the organization to ensure it was delivering the level of quality education its internal customers required. Instructors and administrators took pride in the guarantee, and course participants took

11.4 STEPS IN CONDUCTING AN INTERNAL CUSTOMER SERVICE AUDIT

1. *Define your customer.*
   a. List all the people or departments in the organization who need help from you or your department in any way. This may include specific departments, particular staff people, the CEO, certain executives, or the board of directors.
   b. Prioritize the names on the list, placing the people or departments that rely on you the most at the top.
2. *Identify your contribution.*
   a. For each of these customers, specify the primary need you think they have to which you can contribute. Talk to your internal customers about what problems they are trying to solve and think about how you can help.
3. *Define service quality.*
   a. What are the critical moments of truth that really define the department–internal customer interface from your customer's point of view? Map the process, and list the moments of truth.
   b. For each major internal customer, design a customer report card (based on customer input) and a set of evaluation criteria for your department's service package, as seen through the eyes of that customer. The criteria might include such dimensions as timeliness, reliability, and cost.
4. *Validate your criteria.*
   a. Talk to your customers. Allow them to revise, as necessary, how you saw their needs and the criteria they used in assessing your performance. This dialogue itself can go a long way toward building internal service teamwork.
5. *Measure service quality.*
   a. Evaluate your service (using internal measures and/or customer surveys) against the quality criteria you established in talking to your customers. See how you score. Identify opportunities for improvement. Set up a process and timetable for following through.
6. *Develop a mission statement based on what you contribute.*
   a. Consider drafting a brief, meaningful service mission statement for your operation. Be certain to frame it in terms of the value you *contribute,* not what you *do.* For example, the mission of the HR department should not be "to deliver training" (the action); it would be "to create competent people" (the contribution).

Source: Reprinted from K. Albrecht, *At America's Service* (Homewood, IL: Dow-Jones-Irwin, 1988), pp. 139–42, as discussed in B. Schneider and D. E. Bowen, *Winning at the Service Game* (Boston: The Harvard Business School Press, 1995), pp. 231–32. © 1988 by Dow-Jones-Irwin. Reprinted by permission of The McGraw-Hill Companies.

pride in the implied importance of their opinions. The information gained from customers who invoked the guarantee was invaluable in making improvements and enhancing internal service quality.[49]

A Cautionary Note One risk of measuring and focusing on internal service quality and internal customers is that people can sometimes get so wrapped up in meeting the needs of internal customers that they forget they are in business to serve the ultimate, external customers.[50] In measuring internal service quality, therefore, it is important to constantly draw the linkages between what is being delivered internally and how it supports the delivery of the final service to customers. Service blueprinting, introduced in Chapter 8, can help to illustrate these critical linkages.

Provide Supportive Technology and Equipment

When employees don't have the right equipment, or their equipment fails them, they can be easily frustrated in their desire to deliver quality service. To do their jobs effectively and efficiently, service employees need the right equipment and technology.

Our Technology Spotlight in this chapter highlights the role of front-office automation in providing technology support for employees.

Having the right technology and equipment can extend into strategies regarding workplace and workstation design. For example, in designing their corporate headquarters offices, Scandinavian Airline Systems identified particular service-oriented goals that it wished to achieve, among them teamwork and open, frequent communication among managers. An office environment was designed with open spaces (to encourage meetings) and internal windows in offices (to encourage frequent interactions). In this way the work space facilitated the internal service orientation.

Develop Service-Oriented Internal Processes

To best support service personnel in their delivery of quality service on the front line, an organization's internal processes should be designed with customer value and customer satisfaction in mind. In other words, internal procedures must support quality service performance. In many companies internal processes are driven by bureaucratic rules, tradition, cost efficiencies, or the needs of internal employees. Providing service- and customer-oriented internal processes can therefore imply a need for total redesign of systems. This kind of wholesale redesign of systems and processes has become known as "process reengineering." Although developing service-oriented internal processes through reengineering sounds sensible, it is probably one of the most difficult strategies to implement, especially in organizations that are steeped in tradition. Refocusing internal processes and introducing large amounts of new, supportive technology were among the changes made by Yellow Freight Systems in its transition from a traditional, operations-driven company to a customer-focused one (see Exhibit 11.5).[51]

Retain the Best People

An organization that hires the right people, trains and develops them to deliver service quality, and provides the needed support must also work to retain the best ones. Employee turnover, especially when the best service employees are the ones leaving, can be very detrimental to customer satisfaction, employee morale, and overall service quality. And, just as they do with customers, some firms spend a lot of time attracting employees but then tend to take them for granted (or even worse), causing these good employees to search for job alternatives. Although all of the strategies noted in the internal marketing wheel (Figure 11.6) will support the retention of the best employees, here we will focus on some strategies that are particularly aimed at this goal.

Include Employees in the Company's Vision

For employees to remain motivated and interested in sticking with the organization and supporting its goals, they need to share an understanding of the organization's vision. People who deliver service day in and day out need to understand how their work fits into the big picture of the organization and its goals. They will be motivated to some extent by their paychecks and other benefits, but the best employees will be attracted away to other opportunities if they aren't committed to the vision of the organization. And they can't be committed to the vision if that vision is kept secret from them. What this means in practice is that the vision is communicated to employees frequently, and that it is communicated by top managers, often by the CEO.[52] Respected CEOs such as Herb Kelleher of Southwest Airlines, Howard Schulz of Starbucks, Fred Smith of FedEx, Bill Marriott of Marriott International, and Charles

Yellow Transportation (formerly Yellow Freight) is one of the largest and oldest transportation companies in the United States. Over a period of approximately six years, Yellow has been transformed from a traditional, operations-driven trucking company to a service and transportation company with a customer-focused culture and innovative services. The transformation required a new vision for the company, listening to customers and employees, investments in technology, and hundreds of small, detailed actions. Here is a summary of some of what took place over the six years.

In 1996 Bill Zollars, a respected and experienced executive, was recruited to serve as president of Yellow Transportation. At the time the company was recovering from its worst financial year in its over 70-year history and was still feeling the effects of a long Teamsters strike two years earlier. Zollars's challenge was to help the company start over and turn the negative trends around. His goal was to transform the tradition-bound, formerly regulated company into one that offered multiple services and unprecedented customer service—a customer-centered service business rather than an operations-driven trucking company.

Sharing the Vision   The first thing Zollars did was share his vision of the new company with all company employees. He did this not through memos or videos, but rather by visiting in person, over about a year and a half, almost every one of the company's U.S. terminals. He talked personally with dockworkers, office people, sales staff, and customers—sharing the same consistent message with each group. The company was going to change, and to do so required the involvement of all employees and feedback and ideas from customers.

Top management education was also an integral piece of the transformation. Zollars brought his two dozen top

Yellow's success depends on employees being motivated and having the tools to succeed.

Source: Courtesy of yellow freight

managers—across all functions of the company—to Arizona State University to build their team and to learn cutting edge concepts of services marketing and management. He attended the program with them, and in future

Schwab of Schwab are known for communicating their visions clearly and often to employees. Bill Zollars, CEO of Yellow Corporation, exemplifies this type of behavior, which was a critical ingredient to his success in turning the company around (see Exhibit 11.5).

Tom Siebel of Siebel Systems, the industry leader in CRM software applications, is another good example. He communicates clearly, through words and actions, that the company's mission is "customer first," no matter what the situation. He believes in putting customers ahead of technology and discipline ahead of inspiration; and he upholds these strong messages through his own actions—at every fork in the road, the decision rule is "customer first." In fact, he has several times turned down potentially lucrative business accounts if he felt that they would take away from current customer needs or that the company wasn't ready to provide 100 percent satisfaction to the potential customers. This type of action sends a strong message to employees, reinforc-

years sent smaller groups of new and continuing executives back for refreshers and continuing team building.

Investments in Technology Support To become customer-focused, Yellow invested in state-of-the-art technology, not for technology's sake, but rather to allow every aspect of its business to focus on satisfying customer needs efficiently. Since 1994, about $80 million a year has been spent on technology infusion, affecting how orders get processed, how dispatchers assign drivers for pickups and deliveries, and how dockworkers load and unload the trucks. Each dockworker has a wireless mobile data terminal that speeds up the loading and unloading process. Employees who operate the customer service center (1-800-GO-YELLOW) have instant access to calling customers' account profiles, including customer location, type of loading dock, history of previous shipments, destinations, and delivery signatures. Investments in customer-facing technology allow customers to interact with the firm in whatever way they please—via phone, fax, e-mail, interactive voice response, or the Internet. The company is now considered a technology leader in its industry.

Listening to Customers By initiating customer feedback processes, the company learned of new service needs of its customers, and of service issues it needed to address. A major issue, addressed early on, was reliability. The most important thing for customers in the freight-handling business is that their shipments get picked up on time and delivered on time and that nothing is damaged. These are simple rules of service reliability that Yellow and many of its competitors were not performing well six years ago. Now Yellow has fixed these basic issues through the infusion of technology and lots of employee communication, training,

motivation, and incentive programs. Major investments in service recovery processes were also part of the solution.

Through the customer feedback process, Yellow also identified opportunities for new, innovative services that have taken it way beyond its roots in less-than-truckload freight distribution. One of its most innovative, popular, and profitable forays into the future is Exact Express—an expedited, time-definite, guaranteed service for large shipments. The service allows customers to specify exactly when they want their shipments picked up and delivered, and Yellow is on the mark 98 percent of the time. This new service has resulted in Yellow getting some unique jobs, such as shipping 10,000 pounds of air freshener to ground zero after the World Trade Center attack and carrying 40,000 flashlights from Los Angeles to Washington, D.C., for the 2001 presidential inauguration.

Results During the transformation, employees and customers alike have responded with enthusiasm to the changes at Yellow. Financial results have been impressive; and even during the downturn in 2001, Yellow continued to grow its newest services and receive recognition and awards. It has won awards for its innovative business practices, for its website, and for quality based on industry surveys. Nowhere is the excitement more apparent than at the company's annual employee and customer conference in Las Vegas (called "Transformation"), where each year 1,000 employees and 500 customers attend workshops and sessions together on change. Although much has been accomplished in six years, this transformation will surely continue for a long time into the future.

Sources: C. Salter, "On the Road Again," *Fast Company*, January 2002, pp. 50–58; www.yellowcorp.com, 2002; author's observations.

---

ing the company vision.[53] When the vision and direction are clear and motivating, employees are more likely to remain with the company through the inevitable rough spots along the path to the vision.

Treat Employees as Customers

If employees feel valued and their needs are taken care of, they are more likely to stay with the organization. Tom Siebel, for example, sees the CEO's primary job as cultivating a corporate culture that benefits all employees and customers. "If you build a company and a product or service that delivers high levels of customer satisfaction, and if you spend responsibly and manage your human capital assets well, the other external manifestations of success, like market valuation and revenue growth, will follow."[54] An extreme example of this view is provided by a quotation from Hal Rosenbluth, CEO of Rosenbluth Travel:

As I watched people knocking themselves out for Rosenbluth Travel, I suddenly realized that it was my responsibility to make their lives more pleasant. In simple terms, that meant giving people the right working environment, the right tools, and the right leadership. It meant eliminating fear, frustration, bureaucracy, and politics. Of course, it meant decent compensation—and bonuses when the company did well—but it also meant helping people develop as human beings.[55]

Many companies have adopted the idea that employees are also customers of the organization, and that basic marketing strategies can be directed at them.[56] The products that the organization has to offer its employees are a job (with assorted benefits) and quality of work life. To determine whether the job and work-life needs of employees are being met, organizations conduct periodic internal marketing research to assess employee satisfaction and needs. For example, within American Express Travel Related Services, the Travelers Check Group (TCG) had a goal of "Becoming the Best Place to Work" by doing the following:[57]

- Treating employees as customers.

- Using employee input and a fact-based approach for decision making in the design and implementation of human resources policies, programs, and processes.

- Measuring employee satisfaction and trying to continuously improve the workplace environment.

- Benchmarking and incorporating best practices.

On the basis of the research, TCG launched a number of initiatives to benefit employees including an expanded employee assistance program; child care resource and referral service; adoption assistance; health care and dependent care reimbursement plans; family leave; family sick days; flexible returns; sabbaticals; improved part-time employee benefits; flexible benefits; and workplace flexibility initiatives including job-sharing, flexplace, and flextime scheduling. What American Express and many other companies are finding is that to ensure employee satisfaction, productivity, and retention they are getting more and more involved in the private lives and family support of their workers.[58]

In addition to basic internal research, organizations can apply other marketing strategies to their management of employees. For example, segmentation of the employee population is apparent in many of the flexible benefit plans and career path choices now available to employees. Organizations that are set up to meet the needs of specific segments and to adjust as people proceed through their lives will benefit from increased employee loyalty. Advertising and other forms of communication directed at employees can also increase their sense of value and enhance their commitment to the organization.[59]

Measure and Reward Strong Service Performers

If a company wants the strongest service performers to stay with the organization, it must reward and promote them. This may seem obvious, but often the reward systems in organizations are not set up to reward service excellence. Reward systems may value productivity, sales, or some other dimension that can potentially work *against* good service. Even those service workers who are intrinsically motivated to deliver high service quality will become discouraged at some point and start looking elsewhere if their efforts are not recognized and rewarded.

Reward systems need to be linked to the organization's vision and to outcomes that are truly important. For instance, if customer satisfaction and retention are viewed as critical outcomes, service behaviors that increase those outcomes need to be recognized and rewarded. At Siebel Systems all employees—the salespeople, the service people, the engineers, the product marketers, and everyone else—receive incentive compensation based on the company's customer satisfaction scores. For salespeople the bulk of their incentive compensation is paid only *after* the company knows the level of customer satisfaction—four quarters after the sales contract is signed.[60] At Intel, the "Vender of Choice" (VOC) customer retention measure is incorporated into all employees' incentives systems. For example, in January 2002 when VOC was 96 percent across the entire company, all employees received an extra day of pay, costing the company millions of dollars. The VOC score is calculated from customers' statements as to whether Intel is their first-choice vendor for a particular product or service. The measure itself, along with all of the analyses and service improvement initiatives that are behind it, is intended to align employee behavior around retaining customers.

In companies where customer satisfaction in every service encounter is a goal, there is often a need to adjust the criteria by which employee performance is judged. In some cases this means shifting from a total emphasis on productivity data and hard numbers to other means of assessment. At AT&T's customer sales and service centers, part of the reward system for individual associates is based on customer satisfaction measured at the level of the employee. Ongoing "true moments" surveys are used, whereby customers are called and asked to assess the level of service they received from the particular employee they interacted with over the phone. These measurements (multiple customers for each employee each quarter) are then integrated into the employee's performance evaluation and rewarded. Such measurement systems are challenging to effectively implement. The measures must be appropriate, the sampling of customers must be performed fairly, and the employees must buy in to the validity of the results. AT&T has been perfecting its process, with employee involvement, for many years.

Aligning reward systems with customer outcomes can be challenging. Reward systems are usually well entrenched, and employees have learned over time how they need to perform within the old structures. Change is difficult both for the managers who may have created and still may believe in the old systems and for employees who are not sure what they need to do to succeed under the new rules. In many organizations, however, reward and incentives systems are still not matched with customer satisfaction and loyalty goals.[61]

In developing new systems and structures to recognize customer focus and customer satisfaction, organizations have turned to a variety of types of rewards. Traditional approaches such as higher pay, promotions, and one-time monetary awards or prizes can be linked to service performance. In some organizations employees are encouraged to recognize each other by personally giving a "peer award" to an employee they believe has excelled in providing service to the customer. Other types of rewards include special organizational and team celebrations for achieving improved customer satisfaction or for attaining customer retention goals. In most service organizations it is not only the major accomplishments but the daily perseverance and attention to detail that move the organization forward, so recognition of the "small wins" is also important.

SERVICE CULTURE

Most of this chapter has focused on strategies for enabling customer-oriented service delivery. Looking at the bigger picture, beyond the specific strategies, it is apparent that the behavior of employees in an organization will be heavily influenced by the culture of the organization, or the pervasive norms and values that shape individual and group behavior. *Corporate culture* has been defined as "the pattern of shared values and beliefs that give the members of an organization meaning, and provide them with the rules for behavior in the organization."[62] *Culture* has been defined more informally as "what we do around here," or "organizational glue," or "central themes."

Piglet in *Winnie the Pooh* might refer to culture as one of those things we sense "in an underneath sort of way." To understand at a personal level what corporate culture is, think of different places you've worked or organizations you've been a member of such as churches, fraternities, schools, or associations. Your behavior and the behaviors of others were no doubt influenced by the underlying values, norms, and culture of the organization. Even when you first interview for a new job, you can begin to get a sense of the culture through talking to a number of employees and observing behavior. Once on the job your formal training as well as informal observation of behavior will work together to give you a better picture of the organization's culture.

Experts have suggested that a customer-oriented, service-oriented organization will have at its heart a *service culture,* defined as "a culture where an appreciation for good service exists, and where giving good service to internal as well as ultimate, external customers is considered a natural way of life and one of the most important norms by everyone."[63] This is a very rich definition with many implications for employee behaviors. First, a service culture exists if there is an "appreciation for good service." This doesn't mean that the company has an advertising campaign that stresses the importance of service, but "in that underneath sort of way" people know that good service is appreciated and valued. A second important point in this definition is that good service is given to internal as well as external customers. It is not enough to promise excellent service to final customers; all people within the organization deserve the same kind of service. Finally, in a service culture good service is "a way of life" and it comes naturally because it is an important norm of the organization.

Developing a Service Culture

The last point just made suggests why a service culture cannot be developed quickly and why there is no magic, easy answer for how to sustain a service culture. The human resource and internal marketing practices illustrated by the strategies wheel in Figure 11.6 will support the development of a service culture over time. If, however, an organization has a culture that is rooted in government regulation–, product-, or operations-oriented traditions, no single strategy will change it overnight. Hundreds of little (but significant) things, not just one or two big things, are required to build and sustain a service culture.[64] Successful companies such as AT&T, Yellow Transportation, and IBM Global Services, to name just a few examples, have all found that it takes years of consistent, concerted effort to build a service culture and to shift the organization from its old patterns to new ways of doing business. Even for companies such as FedEx, Charles Schwab, Disney, and the Ritz-Carlton that started out with a strong service and customer focus, sustaining their established service cultures still takes constant attention to hundreds of details.

Transporting a Service Culture

As you might imagine, transporting a service culture through international business expansion is also very challenging. While there are tremendous opportunities in the global marketplace, the many legal, cultural, and language barriers become particularly evident for services that depend on human interaction. Our Global Feature highlights some of the issues and experiences of several companies as they attempt to transport their service cultures.

Although there are tremendous opportunities for growth in international markets, many companies find significant challenges when they attempt to transport their services to other countries. As you have learned in this chapter, services depend on people, are often delivered by people, and involve the interaction between employees and customers. Differences in values, norms of behavior, language, and even the definition of service become evident quickly and have implications for training, hiring, and incentives that can ultimately affect the success of the international expansion. Companies with strong service cultures are faced with the question of whether to try to replicate their culture and values in other countries or to adapt significantly. A few examples illustrate different approaches.

MCDONALD'S APPROACH

McDonald's has been very successful in its international expansion. In some ways it has remained very "American" in everything it does—people around the world want an American experience when they go to McDonald's. However, the company is sensitive to cultural differences as well. This subtle blending of the "McDonald's" way with adaptions to cultural nuances has resulted in great success. One way that McDonald's maintains its standards is through its Hamburger University, which is required training for *all* McDonald's employees worldwide before they can become managers. Each year approximately 3,000 employees from nearly 100 countries enroll and attend the Advanced Operations Course at HU, located in Oak Brook, Illinois. The curriculum is 80 percent devoted to communications and human relations skills. The result is that all managers in all countries have the same "ketchup in their veins," and the restaurant's basic human resources and operating philosophies remain fairly stable from operation to operation. Certain adaptations in decor, menu, and other areas of cultural differences are then allowed (see the Global Feature in Chapter 10 for some specific examples).

UPS'S EXPERIENCE

UPS has a strong culture built on employee productivity, highly standardized service delivery processes, and structured training. Their brown trucks and uniforms are instantly recognizable in the United States. As it expanded into countries across Europe, UPS was surprised by some of the challenges of managing a global workforce. Here are some of the surprises: indignation in France, when drivers were told they couldn't have wine with lunch; protests in Britain, when drivers' dogs were banned from delivery trucks; and dismay in Spain, when it was found the brown UPS trucks resembled the local hearses.

DISNEY IN EUROPE

When Disney first expanded into Europe by opening EuroDisney near Paris, it also faced challenges and surprises. The highly structured, scripted, and customer-oriented approach that Disney used in the United States was not easily duplicated with European employees. In particular, the smiling, friendly, always customer-focused behaviors of Disney's U.S. workforce did not suit the experience and values of young French employees. In attempting to transport the Disney culture and experience to Europe, the company confronted clashing values and norms of behavior in the workplace that made the expansion difficult. Customers also needed to be "trained" in the Disney way—not all cultures are comfortable with waiting in long lines, for example. And not all cultures treat their children the same. For example, in the United States, families will spend lots of money at Disneyland on food, toys, and other things that their children "must" have. Some European cultures view this behavior as highly indulgent, so families will visit the park without buying much beyond the ticket for admission.

A U.S. LAW FIRM GOES TO THE UNITED KINGDOM

The professions such as law and medicine have well-established and quite unique practices across cultures. Pay rates, work styles, and business models can be quite different. So what happens when a law firm seeks to expand its services to another country? Unlike many U.S. law firms that tend to populate their international offices with American lawyers, Weil, Gotshal and Manges, a New York firm, opened its offices in London by hiring primarily British solicitors who would function as a "firm within a firm." One of the biggest challenges was how to blend the very different American and British legal cultures. First, the U.S. lawyers at Weil, Gotshal and Manges tend to be workaholics—commonly billing 2,500 hours a year, while in London a partner would bill a respectable 1,500 hours. Pay differences were also obvious—$650,000 on average for London partners, $900,000 for Americans. Conflict, rather than synergy, sometimes resulted from the deeply rooted cultural differences. Despite the challenges, Weil, Gotshal says that its London operation broke even in 1998, its second year of operations, and predicted a profit in 1999.

Sources: G. Flynn, "Can't Get This Big without HR Deluxe," *Personnel Journal* 75, no. 12 (December 1996), pp. 46–53; D. Milbank, "Can Europe Deliver?" *The Wall Street Journal,* September 30, 1994, pp. R15, R23; and P. M. Barrett, "Joining the Stampede to Europe, Law Firm Suffers a Few Bruises," *The Wall Street Journal,* April 27, 1999, p. A1.

Summary

Because many services are delivered by people to people in real time, closing the service performance gap is heavily dependent on human resource strategies. Often service employees are the service, and in all cases they represent the organization in customers' eyes. They affect service quality perceptions to a large degree through their influence on the five dimensions of service quality: reliability, responsiveness, empathy, assurance, and tangibles. It is essential to match what the customer wants and needs with service employees' abilities to deliver.

In this chapter we focused on service employees to provide understanding of the critical nature of their roles and appreciation of the inherent stresses and conflicts they face. You learned that front-line service jobs demand significant investments of emotional labor and that employees confront a variety of on-the-job conflicts. Sometimes service employees are personally uncomfortable with the roles they are asked to play; other times the requirements of the organization may conflict with client expectations and employees must resolve the dilemma on the spot. Sometimes there are conflicting needs among customers who are being served in turn (such as in a bank teller line) or among customers being served simultaneously (as in a college classroom). At other times a front-line employee may be faced with a decision regarding satisfying a customer versus meeting productivity targets (such as an HMO physician who is required to see a certain number of patients in a defined period of time).

Grounded in this understanding of the importance of service employees and the nature of their roles in the organization, the chapter focused on strategies for integrating appropriate human resource practices into service firms. The strategies are aimed at allowing employees to be effective in satisfying customers as well as efficient and productive in their jobs. The strategies were organized around four major human resource goals in service organizations: to hire the right people, to develop people to deliver service quality, to provide needed support systems, and to retain the best people.

By focusing on these goals and developing practices to support them, an organization can move toward a true service culture where "an appreciation for good service exists, and where giving good service to internal as well as ultimate, external customers is considered a natural way of life and one of the most important norms by everyone."[65] A company that works toward implementing the strategies is certain to diminish gap 3 as well.

Discussion Questions

1. Why are service employees critical to the success of any service organization? Why do we include an entire chapter on service employees in a marketing course?

2. What is emotional labor? How can it be differentiated from physical or mental labor?

3. Reflect on your own role as a front-line service provider, whether in a current job or in any full- or part-time service job you've had in the past. Did you experience the kinds of conflicts described in the boundary-spanning roles section of the chapter? Be prepared with some concrete examples for class discussion.

4. Select a service provider (your dentist, doctor, lawyer, hair stylist) with whom you are familiar and discuss ways this person could positively influence the five dimensions of service quality in the context of delivering his or her services. Do the same for yourself (if you are currently a service provider).

5. Describe the four basic human resource strategy themes and why each plays an important role in building a customer-oriented organization.

6. What is the difference between technical and interactive service skills? Provide examples (preferably from your own work context, or from another context with which you are familiar). Why do service employees need training in both?

7. Is empowerment always the best approach for effective service delivery? Why is employee empowerment so controversial?

8. Define *service culture*. Can a manufacturing firm have a service culture? Why or why not?

Exercises

1. Review the section of the chapter on boundary-spanning roles. Interview at least two front-line service personnel regarding the stresses they experience in their jobs. How do the examples they provide relate to the sources of conflict and trade-offs described in the text?

2. Assume that you are the manager of a crew of front-line customer-service employees in a credit card company. Assume that these employees work over the phone and that they deal primarily with customer requests, questions, and complaints. In this specific context

   a. Define what is meant by "boundary-spanning roles," and discuss the basic purposes or functions that participants in these roles perform.

   b. Discuss two of the potential conflicts that your employees may face on the basis of their roles as boundary spanners.

   c. Discuss how you, as their supervisor, might deal with these conflicts based on what you have learned.

3. Choose one or more of the human resource strategy themes (hire the right people, develop people to deliver service quality, provide needed support systems, retain the best people). Interview a manager in a service organization of your choice regarding his or her current practices within the theme you have chosen. Describe the current practices and recommend any appropriate changes for improving them.

4. Visit the websites of two companies with known world-class service cultures (such as Ritz-Carlton, FedEx, or Starbucks). How does the information conveyed on the website reinforce the company's service culture?

Notes

1. L. L. Berry, *Discovering the Soul of Service* (New York: The Free Press, 1999).
2. Interview with Singapore Airlines senior vice president of marketing services, included in "How May I Help You?" *Fast Company,* March 2000, pp. 93–126.
3. P. Gallagher, "Getting It Right from the Start," *Journal of Retail Banking* 15, no. 1 (Spring 1993), pp. 39–41.
4. J. S. Hirsch, "Now Hotel Clerks Provide More than Keys," *The Wall Street Journal,* March 5, 1993, p. B1.
5. Berry, *Discovering the Soul of Service.*
6. This quote is most frequently attributed to J. Carlzon of Scandinavian Airline Systems.
7. J. Garrett, "The Human Side of Brand: Why Audi Hires Workers with the Same Traits as Its Luxury Cars," *Gallup Management Journal,* Summer 2001, pp. 4–5.
8. The conceptualization of the services triangle presented in Figure 11.2 and the related text discussion are based on M. J. Bitner, "Building Service Relationships: It's All about Promises," *Journal of the Academy of Marketing Science* 23, no. 4 (1995), pp. 246–51; P. Kotler, *Marketing Management: Analysis, Planning, Implementation, and Control,* 8th ed. (Englewood Cliffs, NJ: Prentice Hall, 1994); and C. Gronroos, *Service Management and Marketing* (Lexington, MA: Lexington Books, 1990).
9. See, for example, H. Rosenbluth, "Tales from a Nonconformist Company," *Harvard Business Review,* July–August 1991, pp. 26–36; and L. A. Schlesinger and J. L. Heskett, "The Service-Driven Service Company," *Harvard Business Review,* September–October 1991, pp. 71–81.
10. B. Schneider and D. E. Bowen, "The Service Organization: Human Resources Management Is Crucial," *Organizational Dynamics,* Spring 1993, pp. 39–52.
11. Ibid.
12. D. E. Bowen, S. W. Gilliland, and R. Folger, "How Being Fair with Employees Spills Over to Customers," *Organizational Dynamics* (New York: American Management Association, Winter 1999).

13. See J. L. Heskett, T. O. Jones, G. W. Loveman, W. E. Sasser, Jr., and L. A. Schlesinger, "Putting the Service–Profit Chain to Work," *Harvard Business Review,* March–April 1994, pp. 164–74; G. W. Loveman, "Employee Satisfaction, Customer Loyalty, and Financial Performance," *Journal of Service Research* 1, no. 1 (August 1998), pp. 18–31; A. Rucci, S. P. Kirn, and R. T. Quinn, "The Employee–Customer Profit Chain at Sears," *Harvard Business Review,* January–February 1998, pp. 82–97; and R. Hallowell and L. L. Schlesinger, "The Service-Profit Chain," in *The Handbook for Services Marketing and Management,* T. A. Swartz and D. Iacobucci (Thousand Oaks, CA: Sage Publications, 2000), pp. 203–22.

14. J. Pfeffer, *The Human Equation* (Boston: Harvard Business School Press, 1998); and A. M. Webber, "Danger: Toxic Company," *Fast Company,* November 1998, pp. 152–62.

15. S. Branch, "The 100 Best Companies to Work for in America," *Fortune,* January 11, 1999, pp. 118–44.

16. M. K. Brady and J. J. Cronin, Jr., "Customer Orientation: Effects on Customer Service Perceptions and Outcome Behaviors," *Journal of Service Research* 3, no. 3 (February 2001), pp. 241–51.

17. L. A. Bettencourt and K. Gwinner, "Customization of the Service Experience: The Role of the Frontline Employee," *International Journal of Service Industry Management* 7, no. 2 (1996), pp. 3–20.

18. For research on the influence of front line employee behaviors on customers see D. D. Gremler and K. P. Gwinner, "Customer–Employee Rapport in Service Relationships," *Journal of Service Research* 3, no. 1 (August 2000), pp. 82–104; K. de Ruyter and M. G. M. Wetzels, "The Impact of Perceived Listening Behavior in Voice-to-Voice Service Encounters," *Journal of Service Research* 2, no. 3 (February 2000), pp. 276–84; Tom J. Brown, John C. Mowen, D. Todd Donavan and Jane W. Licata, "The Customer Orientation of Service Workers: Personality Trait Effects of Self- and Supervisor Performance Ratings," *Journal of Marketing Research,* Vol. XXXIX (February 2002), pp. 110–19.

19. A. Hochschild, *The Managed Heart, Commercialization of Human Feeling* (Berkeley: University of California Press, 1983).

20. A. Hochschild, "Emotional Labor in the Friendly Skies," *Psychology Today,* June 1982, pp. 13–15.

21. J. Solomon, "Trying to Be Nice Is No Labor of Love," *The Wall Street Journal,* November 29, 1990, p. B1.

22. M. D. Hartline and O. C. Ferrell, "The Management of Customer-Contact Service Employees: An Empirical Investigation," *Journal of Marketing* 60 (October 1996), pp. 52–70; J. Singh, J. R. Goolsby, and G. K. Rhoads, "Burnout and Customer Service Representatives," *Journal of Marketing Research* 31 (November 1994), pp. 558–69.

23. B. Shamir, "Between Service and Servility: Role Conflict in Subordinate Service Roles," *Human Relations* 33, no. 10 (1980), pp. 741–56.

24. Ibid., pp. 744–45.

25. P. F. Drucker, "The New Productivity Challenge," *Harvard Business Review,* November–December 1991, pp. 69–79.

26. E. W. Anderson, C. Fornell, and R. T. Rust, "Customer Satisfaction, Productivity and Profitability: Differences between Goods and Services," *Marketing Science* 16, no. 2 (1997), pp. 129–45.

27. J. Singh, "Performance Productivity and Quality of Frontline Employees in Service Organizations," *Journal of Marketing* 64 (April 2000), pp. 15–34.

28. For discussions of internal marketing, see L. L. Berry and A. Parasuraman, "Marketing to Employees," chap. 9 in *Marketing Services* (New York: The Free Press, 1991); C. Gronroos, "Managing Internal Marketing—A Prerequisite for Successful External Marketing," chap. 10 in *Service Management and Marketing* (Lexington, MA: Lexington Books, 1990).

29. B. Breen and A. Muoio, "PeoplePalooza 2001," *Fast Company,* January 2001, cover and feature article.

30. J. R. Katzenbach and J. A. Santamaria, "Firing Up the Front Line," *Harvard Business Review,* May–June 1999, pp. 107–17.

31. Berry and Parasuraman, "Marketing to Employees," p. 153.

32. K. J. Dunham, "The Jungle: Focus on Recruitment, Pay, and Getting Ahead," *The Wall Street Journal,* April 10, 2001, p. B14.

33. T. W. Ferguson, "Airline Asks Government for Room to Keep Rising," *The Wall Street Journal,* March 9, 1993, p. A17.

34. This section on hiring for service competencies and service inclination draws from work by B. Schneider and colleagues, specifically, B. Schneider and D. Schechter, "Development of a Personnel Selection System for Service Jobs," in *Service Quality, Multidisciplinary and Multinational Perspectives,* ed. S. W. Brown, E. Gummesson, B. Edvardsson, and B. Gustavsson (Lexington, MA: Lexington Books, 1991), pp. 217–36.

35. J. Hogan, R. Hogan, and C. M. Busch, "How to Measure Service Orientation," *Journal of Applied Psychology* 69, no. 1 (1984), pp. 167–73. See also Brown et al., "The Customer Orientation of Service Workers."

36. For a detailed description of a model selection system for telephone sales and service people see Schneider and Schechter, "Development of a Personnel Selection System."

37. R. Levering and M. Moskowitz, *100 Best Companies to Work for in America* (New York: Penguin Group, 1994), p. 457.

38. "Low Wage Lessons: How Marriott Keeps Good Help Even at $7.40 an Hour," *Business Week,* cover story, November 11, 1996, pp. 108–16.

39. R. Levering and M. Moskowitz, "The 100 Best Companies to Work For," *Fortune,* January 8, 2001, pp. 148–168.

40. R. Normann, "Getting People to Grow," *Service Management* (New York: John Wiley, 1984), pp. 44–50.

41. Berry, *Discovering the Soul of Service.*

42. J. C. Chebat and P. Kollias, "The Impact of Empowerment on Customer Contact Employees' Roles in Service Organizations," *Journal of Service Research* 3, no. 1 (August 2000), pp. 66–81.

43. C. Argyris, "Empowerment: The Emperor's New Clothes," *Harvard Business Review* 76, no. 8 (May–June 1998), pp. 98–105.

44. D. E. Bowen and E. E. Lawler III, "The Empowerment of Service Workers: What, Why, How, and When," *Sloan Management Review,* Spring 1992, pp. 31–39.

45. D. E. Bowen and E. E. Lawler III, "Empowering Service Workers," *Sloan Management Review,* Summer 1995, pp. 73–84.

46. Berry and Parasuraman, "Marketing to Employees," p. 162.

47. C. R. Emery and L. D. Fredendall, "The Effect of Teams on Firm Profitability and Customer Satisfaction," *Journal of Service Research* 4, no. 3 (February 2002), pp. 217–29.

48. A. Sergeant and S. Frenkel, "When Do Customers Contact Employees Satisfy Customers?" *Journal of Service Research* 3, no. 1 (August 2000), pp. 18–34.

49. C. W. L. Hart, "The Power of Internal Guarantees," *Harvard Business Review,* January–February 1995, pp. 64–73.

50. B. Scheider and D. E. Bowen, *Winning the Service Game* (Boston: The Harvard Business School Press, 1995), pp. 230–34.

51. C. Salter, "On The Road Again," *Fast Company,* January 2002, pp. 50–58.

52. O. Gadiesh and J. L. Gilbert, "Transforming Corner-Office Strategy into Front-line Action," *Harvard Business Review,* May 2001, pp. 73–79.

53. B. Fryer, "High Tech the Old Fashioned Way," *Harvard Business Review,* March 2001, pp. 119–25; C. Hawn, "The Man Who Sees around Corners," *Forbes,* January 21, 2002, pp. 72–78.

54. B. Fryer, "High Tech the Old-Fashioned Way."

55. H. Rosenbluth, "Tales from a Nonconformist Company," *Harvard Business Review,* July–August 1991, p. 33.

56. L. L. Berry, "The Employee as Customer," *Journal of Retail Banking* 3, no. 1 (March 1981), pp. 33–40.

57. C. Hegge-Kleiser, "American Express Travel Related Services: A Human Resources Approach to Managing Quality," in *Managing Quality in America's Most Admired Companies,* ed. J. W. Spechler (San Francisco: Berrett-Koehler Publishers, 1993), pp. 205–12.

58. "Balancing Work and Family," *Business Week,* cover story, September 16, 1996, pp. 74–84.

59. M. C. Gilly and M. Wolfinbarger, "Advertising's Internal Audience," *Journal of Marketing* 62, no. 1 (January 1998), pp. 69–88.

60. B. Fryer, "High Tech the Old-Fashioned Way."

61. See Schneider and Bowen, *Winning the Service Game,* chap. 6, for an excellent discussion of the complexities and issues involved in creating effective reward systems for service employees.

62. S. M. Davis, *Managing Corporate Culture* (Cambridge, MA: Ballinger, 1985).

63. Gronroos, *Service Management and Marketing,* p. 244.

64. For an excellent discussion of the complexities involved in creating and sustaining a service culture, see Schneider and Bowen, *Winning the Service Game,* chap. 9. See also Michael D. Hartline, James G. Maxham III, and Daryl O. McKee, "Corridors of Influence in the Dissemination of Customer-Oriented Strategy to Customer-Contact Service Employees," *Journal of Marketing* 64 (April 2000), pp. 35–50.

65. Gronroos, *Service Management and Marketing,* p. 244.

12

CUSTOMERS' ROLES IN SERVICE DELIVERY

This chapter's objectives are to

1. Illustrate the importance of customers in successful service delivery.

2. Enumerate the variety of roles that service customers play: productive resources for the organization; contributors to quality and satisfaction; competitors.

3. Explain strategies for involving service customers effectively to increase both quality and productivity.

iPrint = Self-Service Printing Online

In the current environment of online and Internet-based services, customers can produce services for themselves with little or no interpersonal interaction with the provider. One company, iPrint, is changing the way home office and small business customers interact with commercial printers. iPrint.com, a Web-based custom printing service, bills itself as the "most complete, fully automated, self-service online creation, ordering, and commercial printing environment that the industry has ever seen."[1]

iPrint opened its Internet storefront in January 1997 and successfully survived the dramatic downturn in Internet-based businesses in 2000, earning many industry awards for e-commerce innovation, website design, and customer service in the last several years. Much of the company's success can be attributed to its business model, which provides customers an easy, continually accessible way to independently create and order customized print jobs, sometimes at half the cost of traditional commercial printers. A quote from a satisfied customer is indicative: "Not only is it fun to design everything myself, but the quality is fabulous! You're my favorite company on the Internet!"

Customers of iPrint create their own value through participation in the production of customized printing services. Customers with little or no knowledge of graphic design can easily, quickly, and from the convenience of their own homes or offices create their own designs on a wide range of products. iPrint offers business cards, notepads, stationery, various gift items, and promotional products.

New products such as photo calendars and additional business forms are continually being added, many at the request of loyal customers.

Although creating graphic designs is a highly complex process with hundreds of variables to consider, iPrint created a simple step-by-step process to create personalized products. Customers adapt existing designs to meet their specifications and then view the finished products, selecting from a wide range of options such as paper, font, size, and color as well as clip art or business logos.

Completed designs can be purchased over the Internet and are typically received in a few days. Designs are also automatically saved to allow for easy reordering. Although iPrint notifies customers via e-mail when the order is placed and when it has been printed, customers are also able to actively participate after the order has been placed by tracking the order throughout processing, printing, and shipping.

In addition to extensive customer education through detailed step-by-step instructions, iPrint provides easy access to frequently asked questions, and contact with service providers is available through e-mail, phone, or fax if necessary. Customers participating in the design of their own products are rewarded with prices significantly lower than what they would normally pay.

iPrint has successfully transformed a people-intensive, manual service business into an electronically automated, self-service function where customers are empowered to create their own value and satisfaction. Because they do so much of the work, customers essentially become "coproducers" of the service, enhancing iPrint's productivity, which allows the company to charge lower prices. Everyone wins. The company merged in 2001 with Wood Associates, creating iPrint Technologies, Inc. The merger combines Wood's strength as a leading supplier of promotional and marketing materials to *Fortune* 1,000 businesses with iPrint's focus on home office and small business customers.

So does that mean traditional providers of commercial printing services will be driven out of business by companies like iPrint? Probably not. Some customers will always want personal advice and the direct involvement of professional designers. However, there are segments of customers in the marketplace who will respond to new choices and who are willing to co-produce services, creating value and satisfaction for themselves.

In this chapter we examine the unique roles played by customers in service delivery situations. Service customers are often present in the "factory" (the place the service is produced and/or consumed), interacting with employees and with other customers. For example, in a classroom or training situation, students (the customers) are sitting in the factory interacting with the instructor and other students as they consume the educational services. Because they are present during service production, customers can contribute to or detract from the successful delivery of the service and to their own satisfaction. These roles are unique to service situations. In a manufacturing context, rarely does the production facility contend with customer presence on the factory floor, nor does it rely on the customer's immediate real-time input to manufacture the product. As the example in the opening paragraphs of the chapter illustrates, service customers can actually produce the service themselves and to some extent are responsible for their own satisfaction. Using iPrint's online services, customers create value for themselves and in the process also reduce the prices they pay for printing services.

Because customers are participants in service production and delivery, they can potentially contribute to the widening of gap 3. That is, customers themselves can influence whether the delivered service meets customer-defined specifications.

Sometimes customers contribute to gap 3 because they lack understanding of their roles and exactly what they should do in a given situation. This is particularly true in cases where the customer may be confronting a service concept for the first time. For example, customers using the services of iPrint for the first time need detailed, but simple, instructions to help them understand how to use the service effectively and get the greatest value.

At other times customers may understand their roles but be unwilling or unable to perform for some reason. In a health club context, members may understand that to get into good physical shape they must follow the workout guidelines set up by the trainers. If work schedule or illness keeps the members from living up to their part of the guidelines, the service will not be successful because of customer inaction. In a different situation, customers may choose not to perform the roles defined for them because they are not rewarded in any way for contributing their effort. When service customers are enticed through price reductions, greater convenience, or some other tangible benefit, they are more likely to perform their roles willingly, as in the case of our opening vignette about iPrint.

Finally, gap 3 may be widened not through actions or inactions on the part of the customer, but because of what *other* customers do. Other customers who are in the service factory either receiving the service simultaneously (passengers on an airplane flight) or waiting their turn to receive the service sequentially (bank customers waiting in line, Disneyland customers waiting for one of the rides) can influence whether the service is effectively and efficiently delivered.

This chapter focuses on the roles of customers in service delivery and strategies to effectively manage customers in the production process to enhance productivity, quality, and customer satisfaction.

THE IMPORTANCE OF CUSTOMERS IN SERVICE DELIVERY

Customer participation at some level is inevitable in service delivery. Services are actions or performances, typically produced and consumed simultaneously. In many situations employees, customers, and even others in the service environment interact to produce the ultimate service outcome. Because they participate, customers are indispensable to the production process of service organizations, and they can actually control or contribute to their own satisfaction.[2]

The importance of customers in successful service delivery is obvious if one thinks of service performances as a form of drama. The drama metaphor for services (discussed in Chapter 2) suggests the reciprocal, interactive roles of employees (actors) and customers (audience) in creating the service experience. The service actors and audience are surrounded by the service setting or the servicescape (discussed in Chapter 10). The drama metaphor argues that the development and maintenance of an interaction (a service experience) relies on the audience's input as well as the actors' presentation. Through this metaphor, service performances or service delivery situations are viewed as tenuous, fragile processes that can be influenced by behaviors of customers as well as by employees.[3] Service performance results from actions and interactions among individuals in both groups.

Consider the services provided by a cruise ship company. The actors (ship's personnel) provide the service through interactions with their audience (the passengers) and among each other. The audience also produces elements of the service through interactions with the actors and other audience members. Both actors and audience are surrounded by an elaborate setting (the cruise ship itself) that provides a context to facilitate the service performance. The drama metaphor provides a compelling frame of reference for recognizing the interdependent roles of actors and audience in service delivery.[4]

Recognition of the role of customers is also reflected in the definition of the *people* element of the services marketing mix given in Chapter 1: *all human actors who play a part in service delivery and thus influence the buyer's perceptions; namely, the firm's personnel, the customer, and other customers in the service environment.* Chapter 11 thoroughly examined the role of the firm's employees in delivering service quality. In this chapter we focus on the customer receiving the service and on other customers in the service environment—that is, the "service audience."

Customer Receiving the Service

Because the customer receiving the service participates in the delivery process, he or she can contribute to gap 3 through appropriate or inappropriate, effective or ineffective, productive or unproductive behaviors. Even in a relatively simple service such as retail mail order, customers' actions and preparation can have an effect on service delivery.[5] Customers who are unprepared in terms of what they want to order can soak up the customer service representative's time as they seek advice. Similarly, shoppers who are not prepared with their credit card numbers can "put the representative on hold" while they search for their cards or go to another room or even out to their cars to get them. Meanwhile, other customers and calls are left unattended, causing longer wait times and potential dissatisfaction.

The level of customer participation—low, medium, high—varies across services, as shown in Table 12.1. In some cases, all that is required is the customer's physical presence (*low level of participation*), with the employees of the firm doing all of the

TABLE 12.1 **Levels of Customer Participation across Different Services**

Low: Consumer Presence Required during Service Delivery	*Moderate:* Consumer Inputs Required for Service Creation	*High:* Customer Cocreates the Service Product
Products are standardized.	Client inputs customize a standard service.	Active client participation guides the customized service.
Service is provided regardless of any individual purchase.	Provision of service requires customer purchase.	Service cannot be created apart from the customer's purchase and active participation.
Payment may be the only required customer input.	Customer inputs (information, materials) are necessary for an adequate outcome, but the service firm provides the service.	Customer inputs are mandatory and cocreate the outcome.
End Consumer Examples		
Airline travel Motel stay Fast-food restaurant	Haircut Annual physical exam Full-service restaurant	Marriage counseling Personal training Weight reduction program Major illness or surgery
Business-to-Business Customer Examples		
Uniform cleaning service Pest control Interior greenery maintenance service	Agency-created advertising campaign Payroll service Freight transportation	Management consulting Executive management seminar Installation of computer network

Source: Adapted from A. R. Hubbert, "Customer Co-Creation of Service Outcomes: Effects of Locus of Causality Attributions," doctoral dissertation, Arizona State University, Tempe, Arizona, 1995.

service production work, as in the case of a symphony concert. Symphony-goers must be present to receive the entertainment service, but little else is required once they are seated. In other cases, consumer inputs are required to aid the service organization in creating the service (*moderate level of participation*). Inputs can include *information, effort,* or *physical possessions.* All three of these are required for a CPA to prepare a client's tax return effectively: information in the form of tax history, marital status, and number of dependents; effort in putting the information together in a useful fashion; and physical possessions such as receipts and past tax returns. In some situations, customers can actually be involved in cocreating the service (*high level of participation*). For these services customers have mandatory production roles that, if not fulfilled, will affect the nature of the service outcome. This is the case for complex or long-term business-to-business consulting engagements, where the client can be involved in activities such as identification of issues, shared problem solving, ongoing communication, provision of equipment and work space, and implementation of solutions.[6] Facilitating this type of positive customer participation can help ensure a successful outcome, as suggested by the Integrated Information Systems (IIS) example described in Exhibit 12.1.

Table 12.1 provides several examples of each level of participation for both consumer and business-to-business services. The effectiveness of customer involvement at all of the levels will impact organizational productivity and, ultimately, quality and customer satisfaction.

Other Customers

In many service contexts, customers receive the service simultaneously with other customers or must wait their turn while other customers are being served. In both cases, "other customers" are present in the service environment and can affect the nature of the service outcome or process. Other customers can either *enhance* or *detract* from customer satisfaction and perceptions of quality.[7]

Some of the ways other customers can negatively affect the service experience are by exhibiting disruptive behaviors, causing delays, overusing, excessively crowding, and manifesting incompatible needs. In restaurants, hotels, airplanes, and other environments where customers are cheek to jowl as they receive the service, crying babies, smoking patrons, and loud, unruly groups can be disruptive and detract from the experiences of their fellow customers. The customer is disappointed through no direct fault of the provider. In other cases, overly demanding customers (even customers with legitimate problems) can cause a delay for others while their needs are met. This is a common occurrence in banks, post offices, and customer service counters in retail stores. Excessive crowding or overuse of a service can also affect the nature of the customer's experience. Visiting Sea World in San Diego on the Fourth of July is a very different experience from visiting the same park midweek in February. Similarly, the quality of telecommunication services can suffer on special holidays such as Christmas and Mother's Day when large numbers of customers all try to use the service at once.

Finally, customers who are being served simultaneously but who have incompatible needs can negatively affect each other. This can occur in restaurants, college classrooms, hospitals, and any service establishment where multiple segments are served simultaneously. In a study of critical service encounters occurring in tourist attractions across central Florida, researchers found that customers negatively affected each other when they failed to follow either explicit or implicit "rules of conduct." Customers re-

12.1 IIS—CUSTOMER PARTICIPATION IN BUSINESS-TO-BUSINESS RELATIONSHIPS

Integrated Information Systems is an international technology and business consultancy based in Tempe, Arizona. IIS works with clients on defining, designing, building, integrating, and managing complex information systems. Because it is critical that IIS work closely with its clients during projects, IIS often utilizes a collaborative work group approach to understand a client's business, continuously align expectations, and optimize project success.

Clients often engage IIS to conduct an IIS NextDimension workshop. In this workshop, IIS and client project team members participate in various visual and interactive exercises, which facilitate the rapid translation of business ideas into usable technology solutions. The workshop provides a unique opportunity for all stakeholders to align disparate expectations and reach consensus on compelling business needs.

IIS also conducts a project kick-off meeting with each client. In this meeting, IIS and client project team members participate in interactive team-building exercises and review the entire project process. Team members get project binders that include materials describing each phase of the project, a project responsibility matrix outlining IIS and client responsibilities, and samples of the documentation and deliverables that will be created during the project. The primary objectives of the project kick-off session are to:

- Ensure that everyone involved with the project understands the project process.

- Ensure that everyone on the project team understands the respective roles and responsibilities.

- Build a cohesive team of employees from both organizations.

The business plan resulting from the collaborative work group sets the stage for action. This resulting comprehensive understanding of a client's business is then combined with IIS' process knowledge and technical skills to define an effective action plan, and subsequently a project plan that encompasses scope, schedule, and cost.

IIS uses this highly collaborative approach to align customer expectations about the strategic direction of the project, the project process, and the roles and responsibilities of the parties. Clients thus become valuable coproducers of the service and achieve better quality outcomes. IIS also benefits by having clients that clearly understand their roles and contribute positively to the project outcome. Ultimately this translates into greater productivity for IIS and increased client satisfaction and loyalty.

Sources: Personal interviews and IIS annual report, 2000 (www.iis.com).

---

ported such negative behaviors as pushing, shoving, smoking, drinking alcohol, being verbally abusive, or cutting in line. Other times, dissatisfaction resulted when other customers were impersonal, rude, unfriendly, or even spiteful.[8]

There are just as many examples of other customers enhancing satisfaction and quality for their fellow customers as detracting from them. Sometimes the mere presence of other customers enhances the experience. This is true at sporting events, in movie theaters, and in other entertainment venues. The presence of other patrons is essential for true enjoyment of the experience. In other cases, other customers provide a positive social dimension to the service experience. At health clubs, churches, and resorts such as Club Med, other customers provide opportunities to socialize and build friendships as suggested in Figure 12.1. Long-time, established customers may also socialize new customers by teaching them about the service and how to use it effectively.

In some situations, customers may actually help each other to achieve service goals and outcomes. The success of the Weight Watchers organization, for example, depends significantly on the camaraderie and support that group members provide each other during weight loss. In the study of central Florida tourist attractions mentioned earlier, it was found that customers increased the satisfaction of others by having friendly conversations while waiting in line, taking photos, assisting with children, and returning dropped or lost items.[9]

FIGURE 12.1

Social interactions with others can influence health club members' satisfaction with the service.

Source: David Madison/Getty Images

Customers helping each other is not limited to consumer service contexts. An interesting example occurs at networking giant Cisco. By giving business customers open access to its information and systems through its online self-service, Cisco enables customers to engage in dialogue with each other, helping themselves and other customers who may be experiencing similar challenges. PeopleSoft, the enterprise software provider, assists its customers in helping each other through its annual user meetings, where customers share their experiences using PeopleSoft products.

CUSTOMERS' ROLES

The following sections examine in more detail three major roles played by customers in service delivery: customers as productive resources; customers as contributors to quality and satisfaction; and customers as competitors (Figure 12.2).

Customers as Productive Resources

Service customers have been referred to as "partial employees" of the organization—human resources who contribute to the organization's productive capacity.[10] Some management experts have suggested that the organization's boundaries be expanded to consider the customer as part of the service system. In other words, if customers contribute effort, time, or other resources to the service production process, they should be considered as part of the organization. (Later in the chapter we devote a section to defining customers' jobs and strategies for managing them effectively.)

Customer inputs can affect the organization's productivity through both the quality of what they contribute and the resulting quality and quantity of output generated. For example, research suggests that in an IT consulting context, clients who clearly articulate the solution they desire, provide needed information in a timely manner, communicate openly, gain the commitment of key internal stakeholders, and raise issues during the process before it is too late will get better service.[11] In turn the consulting firm will spend less time redoing the service or waiting for information, allowing it to be more productive overall. The contributions of the client thus enhance the overall productivity of the firm in both quality and quantity of service. In a very different context, Southwest Airlines depends on customers to perform critical service roles for themselves, thus increasing the overall productivity of the airline. Passengers are asked to carry their own bags when transferring to other airlines, get their own food, and seat themselves.

Customer participation in service production raises a number of issues for organizations. Because customers can influence both the quality and quantity of production, some experts believe the delivery system should be isolated as much as possible from customer inputs in order to reduce the uncertainty they can bring into the production process. This view sees customers as a major source of uncertainty—the timing of their demands, and the uncontrollability of their attitudes and actions. The logical conclusion is that any service activities that do not require customer contact or involvement should be performed away from customers: the less direct contact there is between the customer and the service production system, the greater the potential for the system to operate at peak efficiency.[12]

Other experts believe that services can be delivered most efficiently if customers are truly viewed as partial employees and their participative roles are designed to maximize their contributions to the service creation process. The logic in this case is that organizational productivity can be increased if customers learn to perform service-related activities they currently are not doing or are educated to perform more effectively the tasks they are already doing.[13]

For example, when self-service gasoline stations first came into being, customers were asked to pump their own gas. With customers performing this task, fewer employees were needed and the overall productivity of gas stations improved. Now many gas stations offer customers the option of paying for their gas at the pump by popping their credit cards into a slot on the pump, or using a wireless device, and leaving the station without dealing directly with a cashier. Similarly, the introduction of many automated airline services such as baggage self–check-in and self-ticketing are intended to speed up the process for customers while freeing employees for other tasks.[14] This increases organizational productivity by using customers as a resource in performing tasks they have never done before. In both business-to-business and business-to-consumer contexts, organizations are turning to automated and online customer service, as we noted in our Technology Spotlight in Chapter 1. One prominent goal with online customer service is to increase organizational productivity by using the customer as a partial employee, performing his or her own service.

FIGURE 12.2
Customer Roles in Service Delivery

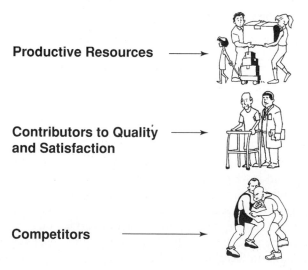

Productive Resources ⟶

Contributors to Quality and Satisfaction ⟶

Competitors ⟶

Customers as Contributors to Service Quality and Satisfaction

Another role customers can play in services delivery is that of contributor to their own satisfaction and the ultimate quality of the services they receive. Customers may care little that they have increased the productivity of the organization through their participation, but they likely care a great deal about whether their needs are fulfilled. Effective customer participation can increase the likelihood that needs are met and that the benefits the customer seeks are actually attained. Think about services such as health care, education, personal fitness, and weight loss, where the service outcome is highly dependent on customer participation. In these cases, unless the customers perform their roles effectively, the desired service outcomes are not possible.

Research has shown that in education, active participation by students—as opposed to passive listening—increases learning (the desired service outcome) significantly.[15] The same is true in health care, where patient compliance in terms of taking prescribed medications or changing diet or other habits can be critical to whether patients regain their health (the desired service outcome).[16] In both of these examples, the customers contribute directly to the quality of the outcome and to their own satisfaction with the service. In a business-to-business context, Yellow Transportation and others in the industry have found that in many situations customers cause their own *dissatisfaction* with the service by failing to pack shipments appropriately, resulting in breakage or delays when things need to be repacked.

Research suggests that customers who believe they have done their part to be effective in service interactions are more satisfied with the service. In a study of the banking industry, bank customers were asked to rate themselves (on a scale from "strongly agree" to "strongly disagree") on questions related to their contributions to service delivery, as follows:

What They Did—Technical Quality of Customer Inputs

I clearly explained what I wanted the bank employee to do.

I gave the bank employee proper information.

I tried to cooperate with the bank employee.

I understand the procedures associated with this service.

How They Did It—Functional Quality of Customer Inputs

I was friendly to the bank employee.

I have a good relationship with the bank employee.

I was courteous to the bank employee.

Receiving this service was a pleasant experience.

Results of the study indicated that the customers' perceptions of both what they did and how they did it were significantly related to customers' satisfaction with the service they received from the bank.[17] That is, those customers who responded more positively to the questions were also more satisfied with the bank. Research in another context showed that customers' perceptions of service quality increased with greater levels of participation. Specifically, customers (in this case members of a YMCA) who participated more in the club gave the club higher ratings on aspects of service quality than those who participated less.[18]

12.2 Which Customer (A or B) Will Be Most Satisfied?

For each scenario, ask "Which customer (A or B) will be most satisfied and receive the greatest quality and value, and why?"

Scenario 1: A Major International Hotel Guest A called the desk right after check-in to report that his TV was not working and that the light over the bed was burned out; both problems were fixed immediately. The hotel staff exchanged his TV for one that worked and fixed the light bulb. Later they brought him a fruit plate to make up for the inconvenience. Guest B did not communicate to management until checkout time that his TV did not work and he could not read in his bed. His complaints were overheard by guests checking in, who wondered whether they had chosen the right place to stay.

Scenario 2: Office of a Professional Tax Preparer Client A has organized into categories the information necessary to do her taxes and has provided all documents requested by the accountant. Client B has a box full of papers and receipts, many of which are not relevant to her taxes but which she brought along "just in case."

Scenario 3: An Airline Flight from London to New York Passenger A arrives for the flight with a portable tape player and reading material and wearing warm clothes; passenger A also called ahead to order a special meal. Passenger B, who arrives empty-handed, becomes annoyed when the crew runs out of blankets, complains about the magazine selection and the meal, and starts fidgeting after the movie.

Scenario 4: Architectural Consultation for Remodeling an Office Building Client A has invited the architects to meet with its remodeling and design committee made up of managers, staff, and customers in order to lay the groundwork for a major remodeling job that will affect everyone who works in the building as well as customers. The committee has already formulated initial ideas and surveyed staff and customers for input. Client B has invited architects in following a decision the week previously to remodel the building; the design committee is two managers who are preoccupied with other more immediate tasks and have little idea what they need or what customers and staff would prefer in terms of a redesign of the office space.

Customers contribute to quality service delivery when they ask questions, take responsibility for their own satisfaction, and complain when there is a service failure. Consider the service scenarios shown in Exhibit 12.2.[19] The four scenarios illustrate the wide variations in customer participation that can result in equally wide variations in service quality and customer satisfaction. Customers who take responsibility, and providers who encourage their customers to become their partners in identifying and satisfying their own needs, will together produce higher levels of service quality. Our Global Feature shows how Sweden's IKEA, the world's largest retailer of home furnishings, has creatively engaged its customers in a new role: "IKEA wants its customers to understand that their role is not to *consume* value but to *create* it."[20]

In addition to contributing to their own satisfaction by improving the quality of service delivered to them, some customers simply enjoy participating in service delivery. These customers find the act of participating to be intrinsically attractive.[21] They enjoy using the Internet to attain airline tickets, or they may like to do all of their banking via ATMs and automated phone systems, or to pump their own gas. Often customers who like self-service in one setting are predisposed to serving themselves in other settings as well.

Interestingly, because service customers must participate in service delivery, they frequently blame themselves (at least partially) when things go wrong. Why did it take so long to reach an accurate diagnosis of my health problem? Why was the service contract for our company's cafeteria food full of errors? Why was the room we reserved for our meeting unavailable when we arrived? If customers believe they are partially (or totally) to blame for the failure, they may be less dissatisfied with the service provider than when they believe the provider is responsible.[22]

IKEA of Sweden has managed to transform itself from a small mail-order furniture company in the 1950s into the world's largest retailer of home furnishings. In 2001 its 150 stores in 29 countries around the world generated more than $11 billion in revenues. The company sells simple Scandinavian design furnishings, charging 25 to 50 percent less than its competitors. Approximately 67 percent of sales come from Europe, 4 percent from North America, and 29 percent from Asia. The first IKEA store in mainland China opened in 1998, and the first in Russia opened in 2000. A key to IKEA's successful global expansion has been the company's policy of allowing each store to tailor its mix according to local market needs and budgets.

Another fascinating key to IKEA's success is the company's relationship with its customers. IKEA has drawn the customer into its production system: "If customers agree to take on certain key tasks traditionally done by manufacturers and retailers—the assembly of products and their delivery to customers' homes—then IKEA promises to deliver well-designed products at substantially lower prices." In effect IKEA's customers become essential contributors to value—they create value for themselves through participating in the manufacturing and delivery process.

IKEA has made being part of the value creation process an easy, fun, and pleasant experience for customers. The company's stores are a pleasure to shop in. Free strollers and supervised child care are provided, as well as wheelchairs for those who need them. When customers enter the store they are given catalogs, tape measures, pens, and notepaper to use as they shop, allowing the customer to perform functions commonly done by sales and service staff. After payment, customers take their purchases to their cars on carts; if necessary they can rent or buy a roof rack to carry larger purchases. Thus customers also provide furniture loading and delivery services for themselves.

At home, the IKEA customer then takes on the role of manufacturer in assembling the new furnishings following carefully written, simple, and direct instructions. IKEA prints catalogs in 17 different languages, making its products and instructions for their use accessible worldwide.

IKEA's success is attributable in part to recognizing that customers can be part of the business system, performing roles they have never performed before. The company's implementation of this idea through clearly defining customers' new roles and making it fun to perform these roles is the genius of its strategy. Through the process, customers create and contribute to their own satisfaction.

Sources: http://www.ikea.com; R. Normann and R. Ramirez, "From Value Chain to Value Constellation: Designing Interactive Strategy," *Harvard Business Review,* July–August 1993, pp. 65–77; "IKEA Ranked First among Retailers in Terms of Being Most Global," *Global Finance* 12, no. 10 (October 1998), p. 50, www.ikea.com, 2002.

Customers as Competitors

A final role played by service customers is that of potential competitor. If self-service customers can be viewed as resources of the firm, or as "partial employees," self-service customers could in some cases partially perform the service or perform the entire service for themselves and not need the provider at all. Customers thus in a sense are competitors of the companies that supply the service. Whether to produce a service for themselves (*internal exchange*)—for example, child care, home maintenance, car repair—or have someone else provide the service for them (*external exchange*) is a common dilemma for consumers.[23]

Similar internal versus external exchange decisions are made by organizations. Firms frequently choose to outsource service activities such as payroll, data processing, research, accounting, maintenance, and facilities management. They find that it is advantageous to focus on their core businesses and leave these essential support services to others with greater expertise. Alternatively, a firm may decide to stop purchasing services externally and bring the service production process in-house.

Whether a household or a firm chooses to produce a particular service for itself or contract externally for the service depends on a variety of factors. A proposed model of internal/external exchange suggests that such decisions depend on the following:[24]

Expertise capacity: The likelihood of producing the service internally is increased if the household or firm possesses the specific skills and knowledge needed to produce it. Having the expertise will not necessarily result in internal service production, however, because other factors (available resources and time) will also influence the decision. (For firms, making the decision to outsource is often based on recognizing that although they may have the expertise, someone else can do it better.)

Resource capacity: To decide to produce a service internally, the household or firm must have the needed resources including people, space, money, and materials. If the resources are not available internally, external exchange is more likely.

Time capacity: Time is a critical factor in internal/external exchange decisions. Households and firms with adequate time capacity are more likely to produce services internally than are groups with time constraints.

Economic rewards: The economic advantages or disadvantages of a particular exchange decision will be influential in choosing between internal and external options. The actual monetary costs of the two options will sway the decision.

Psychic rewards: Rewards of a noneconomic nature have a potentially strong influence on exchange decisions. Psychic rewards include the degree of satisfaction, enjoyment, gratification, or happiness that is associated with the external or internal exchange.

Trust: In this context *trust* means the degree of confidence or certainty the household or firm has in the various exchange options. The decision will depend to some extent on the level of self-trust versus trust of others in the particular context.

Control: The household or firm's desire for control over the process and outcome of the exchange will also influence the internal/external choice. Entities that desire and can implement a high degree of control over the task are more likely to engage in internal exchange.

The important thing to remember from this section is that in many service scenarios customers can and do choose to fully or partially produce the service themselves. Thus, in addition to recognizing that customers can be productive resources and cocreators of quality and value, organizations also need to recognize the customer's role as a potential competitor.

SELF-SERVICE TECHNOLOGIES—THE ULTIMATE IN CUSTOMER PARTICIPATION

Self-service technologies are services produced entirely by the customer without any direct involvement or interaction with the firm's employees. As such they represent the ultimate form of customer participation along a continuum from services that are produced entirely by the firm to those that are produced entirely by the customer. This continuum is depicted in Figure 12.3, using the example of retail gasoline service to illustrate the various ways the same service could be delivered along all points on the continuum. At the far right end of the continuum, the gas station attendant does everything from pumping the gas to taking payment. On the other end of the spectrum, the customer does everything; in between are various forms and levels of customer participation. Many service delivery options, across industries, could be laid out on this type of continuum from total customer production through total firm production.

A Proliferation of New SSTs

Advances in technology, particularly the Internet, have allowed the introduction of a wide range of self-service technologies that occupy the far left end of the customer participation continuum in Figure 12.3. These technologies have proliferated as companies see the potential cost savings and efficiencies that can be achieved, potential sales growth, increased customer satisfaction, and competitive advantage. A partial list of some of the self-service technologies available to consumers includes

- ATMs.
- Pay at the pump.
- Airline check-in.
- Hotel check-in and checkout.
- Automated car rental.
- Automated filing of legal claims.
- Online driver's license testing.
- Automated betting machines.
- Electronic blood pressure machines.
- Various vending services.
- Tax preparation software.
- Self-scanning at retail stores.

- Internet banking.
- Vehicle registration online.
- Online auctions.
- Home and car buying online.
- Automated investment transactions.
- Insurance online.
- Package tracking.
- Internet shopping.
- Internet information search.
- Interactive voice response phone systems.
- Distance education.

Customer Usage of SSTs

Some of the SSTs just listed—ATMs, pay-at-the-pump gas, Internet information search—have been very successful, embraced by customers for the benefits they provide in terms of convenience, accessibility, and ease of use.[25] Benefits to firms in terms of cost savings and revenue growth can also result for those that succeed. Others—airline ticket kiosks, online hotel bookings, grocery self-scanning—have been less successful.

Failure results when customers see no benefit for them in the new technology or

FIGURE 12.3
Services Production Continuum

Source: Adapted from M. L. Meuter and M. J. Bitner, "Self-Service Technologies: Extending Service Frameworks and Identifying Issues for Research," in *Marketing Theory and Applications,* ed. D. Grewal and C. Pechmann (American Marketing Association Winter Educators' Conference, 1998), pp. 12–19.

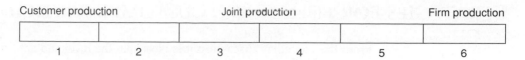

Customer production		Joint production		Firm production	
1	2	3	4	5	6

Gas station illustration
1. Customer pumps gas and pays at the pump with automation.
2. Customer pumps gas and goes inside to pay attendant.
3. Customer pumps gas and attendant takes payment at the pump.
4. Attendant pumps gas and customer pays at the pump with automation.
5. Attendant pumps gas and customer goes inside to pay attendant.
6. Attendant pumps gas and takes payment from customer at the pump.

when they don't have the ability to use it or know what they are supposed to do. Often adopting a new SST requires customers to change their traditional behaviors significantly, and many are reluctant to make those changes. Research looking at customer adoption of SSTs found that "customer readiness" was a major factor in determining whether customers would even try a new self-service option.[26] Customer readiness results from a combination of personal motivation (What's in it for me?), ability (Do have the ability to use this SST?), and role clarity (Do I understand what I'm supposed to do?). Other times customers see no value in using the technology when compared to the alternative interpersonal mode of delivery; or the SSTs may be so poorly designed that customers may prefer not to use them, as noted earlier in the Technology Spotlight in Chapter 2.[27]

Success with SSTs

Throughout the text we have highlighted some of the most successful self-service technologies in the marketplace today: Cisco Systems (Chapter 7), Wells Fargo (Chapter 8), Amazon.com (Chapter 4), and iPrint (the opening vignette in this chapter). These have been successful because they offer clear benefits to customers, the benefits are well understood and appreciated compared to the alternative delivery modes, and the technology is user-friendly and reliable. In addition, customers understand their roles and have the capability to use the technology.

From a strategic perspective, research suggests that as firms move into SSTs as a mode of delivery, these questions are important to ask:[28]

- What is our strategy? What do we hope to achieve through the SST (cost savings, revenue growth, competitive advantage)?

- What are the benefits to customers of producing the service on their own through the SST? Do they know and understand these benefits?

- How can customers be motivated to try the SST? Do they understand their role? Do they have the capability to perform this role?

- How "technology ready" are our customers?[29] Are some segments of customers more ready to use the technology than others?

- How can customers be involved in the design of the service technology system and processes so that they will be more likely to adopt and use the SST?

- What forms of customer education will be needed to encourage adoption? Will other incentives be needed?

STRATEGIES FOR ENHANCING CUSTOMER PARTICIPATION

From the preceding discussion it is clear that the level and nature of customer participation in the service process are strategic decisions that can impact an organization's productivity, its positioning relative to competitors, its service quality, and its customers' satisfaction. In the following sections we'll examine the strategies captured in Figure 12.4 for involving customers effectively in the service delivery process. The overall goals of a customer participation strategy will typically be to increase productivity and customer satisfaction while simultaneously decreasing uncertainty due to unpredictable customer actions.

Define Customers' Jobs

In developing strategies for addressing customer involvement in service delivery, the organization first determines what type of participation it wants from customers, thus beginning to define the customer's "job." Identifying the current level of customer participation can serve as a starting point. Customers' roles may be partially predetermined by the nature of the service, as suggested earlier in Table 12.1. The service may require only the customer's presence (a concert, airline travel), or it may require moderate levels of input from the customer in the form of effort or information (a haircut, tax preparation), or it may require the customer to actually cocreate the service outcome (fitness training, consulting self-service offerings).

The organization may decide that it is satisfied with the existing level of participation it requires from customers but wants to make the participation more effective. For example, Charles Schwab has always positioned itself as a company whose customers are highly involved in their personal investment decisions. Over time this position has been implemented in different ways. Advances in technology have allowed Charles Schwab to solidify its position as a leading investment company for independent investors.

Alternatively, the organization may choose to increase the level of customer participation, which may reposition the service in the customer's eyes. Experts have suggested that higher levels of customer participation are strategically advisable when service production and delivery are inseparable; marketing benefits (cross-selling,

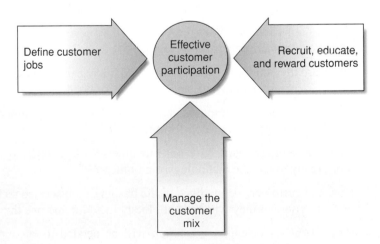

FIGURE 12.4
Strategies for Enhancing Customer Participation

building loyalty) can be enhanced by on-site contact with the customer; and customers can supplement for the labor and information provided by employees.[30]

In health care, researchers and providers are working on ways to gain more active customer participation in treatment decisions. The Internet and other technology advances have helped to propel customers into this role in taking responsibility for their own health and well-being, as illustrated in our Technology Spotlight.

Finally, the organization may decide it wants to reduce customer participation due to all the uncertainties it causes. In such situations the strategy may be to isolate all but the essential tasks, keeping customers away from the service facility and employees as much as possible.[31] Mail order is an extreme example of this form of service. Customers are in contact with the organization via telephone or the Internet, never see the organization's facility, and have limited employee interactions. The customer's role is thus extremely limited and can interfere very little with the service delivery process.

Once the desired level of participation is clear, the organization can define more specifically what the customer's "job" entails.[32] The customer's "job description" will vary with the type of service and the organization's desired position within its industry. The job might entail helping oneself, helping others, or promoting the company.

Helping Oneself

In many cases the organization may decide to increase the level of customer involvement in service delivery through active participation, as shown in Figure 12.5. In such situations the customer becomes a productive resource, performing aspects of the service heretofore performed by employees or others. Many of the examples presented in this chapter are illustrations of customers "helping themselves" (IKEA of Sweden, Charles Schwab, the Technology Spotlight). The result may be increased productivity for the firm and/or increased value, quality, and satisfaction for the customer.

Helping Others

Sometimes the customer may be called on to help others who are experiencing the service. A child at a day care center might be appointed "buddy of the day" to help a new

FIGURE 12.5
Customers help produce the service for themselves through scanning their own groceries.

Source: NCR FastLane™ self checkout from NCR Corporation

Technology Spotlight
Technology Facilitates Customer Participation in Health Care

Customer participation is facilitated by technology in many industries. For example, in education, technology allows students to interact with each other and their professors via e-mail and discussion boards. In real estate, technology allows buyers to preview homes and develop lists of places they would like to visit without having to rely totally on a real estate agent to find all available properties. And in high-technology industries, business customers often interact with each other on the Web, helping each other solve problems, answering each other's questions, and so forth. All of these are examples of how technology—particularly the Internet—has facilitated customer participation and, as in the cases just described, increased customer satisfaction.

Nowhere is this more apparent than in health care. There is probably no greater, higher-participation service context than health care, where the customer must participate and where the provider and customer clearly co-create the service. Patient participation is required at multiple levels. To achieve optimal health outcomes, patients must

- Provide accurate information about symptoms and health background.

- Answer detailed questions.

- Help to decide on a course of treatment.

- Carry out the prescribed regimen leading to recovery.

Technology is clearly influencing how customers perform these roles and shifting in some senses the power of information into the hands of consumers. Two recent studies by the Pew Internet and American Life Project, funded by the Pew Charitable Trusts, illuminate the trends in online health care as well as some of the challenging issues. This research showed that as of September 2001, 61 percent of U.S. Internet users, or over 65 million people, had gone online in search of health information. Of these "health seekers," a majority go online for health care information at least once per month, and about half say the advice found there helped improve the way they take care of themselves. They seek information about specific diseases, mental health, nutrition and fitness, drugs and drug interactions, and specific doctors and hospitals. Over 40 percent were seeking information for themselves and their own medical conditions, and over 50 percent sought information on behalf of a friend or family member. People like getting health information this way because of the convenience, the wealth of information that is available, and the fact that research can be done anonymously.

Thousands of Internet sites provide some type of health-related information. Some belong to health care providers like Mayo Clinic (www.mayo.edu) or pharmacy benefits providers like Advance PCS (www.advanceparadigm.com). Others are operated totally online—like WebMD (www.webmd.com), or Drugstore.com (www.drugstore.com)—without affiliation to a spe-

---

child acclimate into the environment. Long-time residents of retirement communities often assume comparable roles to welcome new residents. Many universities have established mentoring programs, particularly for students from minority groups, in which experienced students with similar backgrounds help newcomers adjust and learn the system. Many membership organizations (like health clubs, churches, and social organizations) also rely heavily, although often informally, on current members to help orient new members and make them feel welcome. In performing these types of roles, customers are again performing productive functions for the organization, increasing customer satisfaction and retention. Acting as a mentor or facilitator can have very positive effects on the person performing the role and is likely to increase his or her loyalty as well.

Promoting the Company

In some cases the customer's job may include a sales or promotional element. As you know from previous chapters, service customers rely heavily on word-of-mouth en-

cific health care provider. Yet others are information sites for specific health conditions such as AIDS, depression, diabetes, breast cancer, and the like. Although some of the purely online health information sites did not survive the dot-com downturn, many are still thriving and very popular with customers.

All of this readily available medical information has the potential to change the role of the health care consumer to one of active participant in diagnosing illnesses, assessing treatment options, and determining overall well-being. Armed with information, patients gain confidence in asking questions and seeking appropriate diagnoses. In some cases they can e-mail questions to their doctors or other providers or find support in chat groups, bulletin boards, and e-mail lists on the Internet.

Despite this growth and popularity, there are a number of concerns that patients and doctors share regarding health information online. The two primary concerns are privacy of patient data and reliability of health information provided online. The Pew study of Internet health care usage found that 63 percent of those who sought health information on the Internet felt that putting their own private medical records and information on the Web would be a bad idea; 89 percent were concerned that their information could be sold to a third party; 85 percent were concerned their insurance company might raise their rates or deny coverage based on sites they visited; and 52 percent were concerned about employers finding out which sites they visited. Many (86

percent) were also concerned about the reliability of the information they found on the Web.

Although health laws being implemented in the United States are intended to protect patient information privacy, it appears that many websites may fall between the cracks in terms of being required to follow the new laws unless they are owned or operated by a health care provider, a health plan, or a health care clearinghouse. Thus consumers will continue to be wary of putting their personal health information on the Web.

As for information reliability, many sites are now making very apparent the sources of their information. For example, Intelihealth (www.Intelihealth.com) is now closely linked with Harvard's medical school. National and international associations are also developing standards and "seal of approval" programs to address privacy, security, and quality of information on the Internet.

Despite the concerns and issues, the usage of health care information on the Web continues to increase and will forever change the way patients participate in health care.

Sources: "The Online Health Care Revolution: How the Web Helps Americans Take Better Care of Themselves," The Pew Internet and American Life Project, November 2000, www.pewinternet.org; "Exposed Online: Why the New Federal Health Privacy Regulation Doesn't Offer Much Protection to Internet Users," The Pew Internet and American Life Project, November 2001, www.pewinternet.org.

dorsements in deciding which providers to try. They are more comfortable getting a recommendation from someone who has actually experienced the service than from advertising alone. A positive recommendation from a friend, relative, colleague, or even an acquaintance can pave the way for a positive service experience. Many service organizations have been very imaginative in getting their current customers to work as promoters or salespeople, as shown in Exhibit 12.3.

Individual Differences: Not Everyone Wants to Participate

In defining customers' jobs it is important to remember that not everyone will want to participate.[33] Some customer segments enjoy self-service, whereas others prefer to have the service performed entirely for them. Companies that provide education and training services to organizations know that some customers want to be involved in designing the training and perhaps in delivering it to their employees. Other companies want to hand over the entire training design and delivery to the consulting organization, staying at arms length with little of their own time and energy invested in the

12.3 CUSTOMERS AS SERVICE PROMOTERS

Organizations often encourage their customers to help promote their services through word of mouth. Here we share a variety of examples from different industry contexts:

A dental practice encourages referrals by sending flowers, candy, or tickets to a local sports event to its patients whose names appear frequently in their "who referred you?" database.

A bowling alley holds a drawing for its regular patrons. The person whose name is drawn is given a party at the bowling alley to which he or she can invite friends for free bowling. This effectively creates a "word-of-mouth champion" who brings new people into the establishment.

A chiropractor gives a free next exam to people who refer new patients. Patients who make referrals have their names listed on a board in the office waiting area.

To increase membership, a credit union published a member referral coupon in its newsletter. Those who referred new members were then given $5.

A credit card, which gives customers frequent flyer points every time they use their credit cards, offers 10,000 free miles to those who can solicit a new credit card customer.

A nightclub holds regular drawings (using business cards left by its patrons). Those whose names are drawn get a free party (no entry charge) for as many of their friends as they want to invite.

An express contact lens company asks patrons to list friends' names on a card. For each friend who buys, the original patron gets $15 or a free pair of disposable contacts.

---

service. In health care, it is clear that some patients want lots of information and want to be involved in their own diagnosis and treatment decisions. Others simply want the doctor to tell them what to do. Despite all of the customer service and purchase options now available via the Internet, many customers still prefer human, high-contact service delivery rather than self-service. Research has shown, for example, that customers with a high "need for human interaction" are less likely to try new self-service options offered via the Internet and automated phone systems.[34] Because of these differences in preferences, most companies find they need to provide service delivery choices for different market segments.

Often an organization can customize its services to fit the needs of these different segments—those who want to participate and those who prefer little involvement. Banks typically do this by offering both automated self-service options and high-touch, human delivery options. At other times, as in the case of Charles Schwab or IKEA (see the Global Feature), the organization can effectively position itself to specifically serve only segments of customers who want to participate.

Recruit, Educate, and Reward Customers

Once the customer's role is clearly defined, the organization can think in terms of facilitating that role. In a sense, the customer becomes a "partial employee" of the organization at some level, and strategies for managing customer behavior in service production and delivery can mimic to some degree the efforts aimed at service employees discussed in Chapter 11. As with employees, customer participation in service production and delivery will be facilitated when (1) customers understand their roles and how they are expected to perform, (2) customers are able to perform as expected, and (3) there are valued rewards for performing as expected.[35] Through these means, the organization will also reduce the inherent uncertainty associated with the unpredictable quality and timing of customer participation.

Recruit the Right Customers

Before the company begins the process of educating and socializing customers for their roles, it must attract the right customers to fill those roles. The organization should seek to attract customers who will be comfortable with the roles. To do this, it should clearly communicate the expected roles and responsibilities in advertising, personal selling, and other company messages. By previewing their roles and what is required of them in the service process, customers can self-select into (or out of) the relationship. Self-selection should result in enhanced perceptions of service quality from the customer's point of view and reduced uncertainty for the organization.

To illustrate, a child care center that requires parent participation on the site at least one-half day per week needs to communicate that expectation before it enrolls any child in its program. For some families, this level of participation will not be possible or desirable, thus precluding them from enrolling in the center. Another center could choose to have a variety of options available for families ranging from no on-site participation to daily participation. Whatever the case, the expected level of participation needs to be communicated clearly in order to attract customers who are ready and willing to perform their roles. In a sense this is similar to a manufacturing firm exercising control over the quality of inputs into the production process.[36]

Educate and Train Customers to Perform Effectively

Customers need to be educated or in essence "socialized" so that they can perform their roles effectively. Through the socialization process, it is possible for service customers to gain an appreciation of specific organizational values, develop the abilities necessary to function within a specific context, understand what is expected of them, and acquire the skills and knowledge to interact with employees and other customers.[37] Earlier, in Exhibit 12.1, an example of customer orientation and socialization workshops in IT business-to-business consulting was described. Customer education programs can take the form of formal orientation programs, written literature provided to customers, directional cues and signage in the service environment, and learning from employees and other customers. These forms of education are discussed further in the following paragraphs.

Many services offer "customer orientation" programs to assist customers in understanding their roles and what to expect from the process before experiencing it. Universities offer orientation programs for new students, and often for their parents as well, to preview the culture, university procedures, and expectations of students. Similarly, health clubs use formal training programs to educate customers on how to use the facilities and equipment. When customers begin the Weight Watchers program, their first group meeting includes a thorough orientation to the program and their responsibilities, as described in Exhibit 12.4. In a mammography screening context, research has found that orientation and formal education of customers can relieve customer fears and perceptions of risk and ultimately increase customer satisfaction (see Exhibit 12.5).

Customer education can also be partially accomplished through written literature and customer "handbooks" that describe customers' roles and responsibilities. Many hospitals have developed patient handbooks, very similar in appearance to employee handbooks, to describe what the patient should do in preparation for arrival at the hospital, what will happen when he or she arrives, and policies regarding visiting hours and billing procedures. The handbook may even describe the roles and responsibilities of family members.

When new members first join Weight Watchers, one of the largest and most successful commercial weight loss organizations in the world, they are thoroughly educated regarding the program and their responsibilities. For example, when a new member attends her first meeting at a local chapter of Weight Watchers of Arizona, she watches a video that tells about the program and reviews how the food plan works. New members are also given a booklet called "Welcome to Weight Watchers" that covers various introductory topics.

In addition to the video, the booklet, and a discussion of all topics led by the group leader, the new member also receives a "Program Planner and Tracker." This form is used by the member to record daily food selections and physical activity. Weight Watchers knows that its business can succeed only if members do their part in following the weight loss plan. Through the orientation, the booklets, and the food and activity forms, the organization clearly defines the member's responsibilities and makes the plan as easy as possible to follow.

Although formal training and written information are usually provided in advance of the service experience, other strategies can continue customer socialization during the experience itself. On site, customers require two kinds of orientation: *place orientation* (Where am I? How do I get from here to there?) and *function orientation* (How does this organization work? What am I supposed to do?).[38] Signage, the layout of the service facility, and other orientation aids can help customers answer these questions, allowing them to perform their roles more effectively. Orientation aids can also take the form of rules that define customer behavior for safety (airlines, health clubs), appropriate dress (restaurants, entertainment venues), and noise levels (hotels, classrooms, theaters). Before showing a movie, many theaters now flash a sign on the screen that says "Please, no talking, or crying babies." In a similar vein, while riding in a taxi in Australia the authors encountered a poster called "The Taxi User's Charter of Rights." The prominent poster explicitly laid out the responsibilities of the taxi passenger: wear a seat belt; do not eat, drink, or smoke; do not swear or be offensive; pay the correct fare; and so on.

Customers are also socialized to their expected roles through information provided by employees and by observing other customers. It has been said that when McDonald's first went to England, the British customers were not accustomed to busing their own trays. They quickly learned, however, by observing the customers McDonald's had hired to "demonstrate" appropriate busing behavior. These customers were paid to sit in the restaurants and at predictable intervals carry a dirty tray over to the trash can and dispose of it.

Reward Customers for Their Contributions

Customers are more likely to perform their roles effectively, or to participate actively, if they are rewarded for doing so. Rewards are likely to come in the form of increased control over the delivery process, time savings, monetary savings, and psychological or physical benefits. For instance, some CPA firms have clients complete extensive forms before they meet with their accountants. If the forms are completed, the CPAs will have less work to do and the clients will be rewarded with fewer billable hours. Those clients who choose not to perform the requested role will pay a higher price for the service. ATM customers who perform banking services for themselves are also rewarded through greater access to the bank, in terms of both locations and times. In health care contexts, patients who perform their roles effectively are likely to be re-

12.5 REALISTIC SERVICE PREVIEWS REDUCE CUSTOMER ANXIETY AND IMPROVE SATISFACTION

Research in a mammography screening context found that if potential patients are oriented through a realistic preview of the process, patient anxiety is reduced and ultimate satisfaction increased. An experiment was conducted that involved 134 women who had never experienced a mammogram and who had little knowledge about the procedure. Half of the women were given a realistic preview of the process, while the others received no preview. The preview consisted of written information about mammography, including sections on how the procedure works, instructions to follow before mammography, what happens during mammography, after the examination, the role of mammography, and some common misconceptions. The realistic preview also included a seven-minute videotape illustrating the entire procedure. The written materials and the videotape helped to both dispel overly pessimistic expectations and guard against overly positive ideas the potential patients may have had.

After the preview (or no preview), women in the experiment answered questions that assessed the accuracy of their expectations, their sense of control, and their level of anxiety relative to mammography. The women then read one of three versions of an actual mammography experience and were asked to imagine themselves as the woman in the story. One version of the story followed the realistic preview exactly; another version included several blunders on the part of the fictitious provider; and the final version enhanced the service experience, making it even better than the realistic preview. After reading the story and imagining that the events had actually happened to them, the women responded to questions regarding their satisfaction with the mammography screening process.

Results of the study showed that those women who had been oriented through the realistic preview did indeed have more realistic and accurate expectations for the mammography experience than those who had no preview. Second, the women who saw the preview reported significantly less anxiety and significantly greater perceptions of control over the process than women who had no preview. Finally, across all of the different scenarios, women who received the preview were more satisfied with the actual service experience. The realistic preview thus affected potential mammography patients' preservice feelings (anxiety and control) as well as their satisfaction with the service.

Source: W. T. Faranda, "Customer Participation in Service Production: An Empirical Assessment of the Influence of Realistic Service Previews," doctoral dissertation, Arizona State University, Tempe, Arizona, 1994.

---

warded with better health or quicker recovery. For a long time airlines offered price discounts for passengers who ordered tickets online, providing a monetary incentive for customer participation.

Customers may not realize the benefits or rewards of effective participation unless the organization makes the benefits apparent to them. In other words, the organization needs to clarify the performance-contingent benefits that can accrue to customers just as it defines these types of benefits to employees. The organization also should recognize that not all customers are motivated by the same types of rewards. Some may value the increased access and time savings they can gain by performing their service roles effectively. Others may value the monetary savings. Still others may be looking for greater personal control over the service outcome.

Avoid Negative Outcomes of Inappropriate Customer Participation

If customers are not effectively socialized, the organization runs the risk that inappropriate customer behaviors will result in negative outcomes:[39]

1. Customers who do not understand the service system or the process of delivery may slow down the service process and negatively affect their own as well as other customers' outcomes. In a rental car context, customers who do not understand the

reservation process, the information needed from them, insurance coverage issues, and the pick-up and drop-off procedures can slow the flow for employees and other customers, lowering both productivity and quality of service.

2. If customers don't perform their roles effectively, it may not be possible for employees to provide the levels of technical and process quality promised by the organization. For example, in a management consulting practice, clients who do not provide the information and cooperation needed by the consultants will likely receive inferior service in terms of both the usefulness of the management report and the timeliness of the delivery.

3. If customers are frustrated because of their own inadequacies and incompetencies, employees are likely to suffer emotionally and be less able to deliver quality service. For example, if customers routinely enter the service delivery process with little knowledge of how the system works and their role in it, they are likely to take out their frustrations on front-line employees. This negative impact on individual employees can take its toll on the organization in the form of turnover and decreased motivation to serve.

Manage the Customer Mix

Because customers frequently interact with each other in the process of service delivery and consumption, another important strategic objective is the effective management of the mix of customers who simultaneously experience the service. If a restaurant chooses to serve two segments during the dinner hour that are incompatible with each other—for example, single college students who want to party and families with small children who want quiet—it may find that the two groups do not merge well. Of course it is possible to manage these segments so that they do not interact with each other by seating them in separate sections or by attracting the two segments at different times of day. Major tourism attractions around the world face the challenge of accommodating visitors who differ in the languages they speak, the foods they want to eat, their values, and their perceptions of appropriate behaviors. Sometimes these visitors can clash when they do not understand and appreciate each other.

The process of managing multiple and sometimes conflicting segments is known as *compatibility management,* broadly defined as "a process of first attracting homogeneous consumers to the service environment, then actively managing both the physical environment and customer-to-customer encounters in such a way as to enhance satisfying encounters and minimize dissatisfying encounters."[40] Compatibility management will be critically important for some businesses (such as health clubs, public transportation, and hospitals) and less important for others. Table 12.2 lists seven interrelated characteristics of service businesses that will increase the importance of compatibility management.

To manage multiple (and sometimes conflicting) segments, organizations rely on a variety of strategies. Attracting maximally homogeneous groups of customers through careful positioning and segmentation strategies is one approach. This is the strategy used by the Ritz-Carlton Hotel Company, for which upscale travelers are the primary target segment. The Ritz-Carlton is positioned to communicate that message to the marketplace, and customers self-select into the hotel. However, even in that context there are potential conflicts—for example, when the hotel is simultaneously hosting a large business convention and serving individual business travelers. A second strategy is often used in such cases. Compatible customers are grouped together physically so that the segments are less likely to interact directly with each other. The Ritz-Carlton

TABLE 12.2   **Characteristics of Service that Increase the Importance of Compatible Segments**

Characteristic	Explanation	Examples
Customers are in close physical proximity to each other.	Customers will more often notice each other and be influenced by each other's behavior when they are in close physical proximity.	Airplane flights Entertainment events Sports events
There is verbal interaction among customers.	Conversation (or lack thereof) can be a component of both satisfying and dissatisfying encounters with fellow patrons.	Full-service restaurants Cocktail lounges Educational settings
Customers are engaged in numerous and varied activities.	When a service facility supports varied activities all going on at the same time, the activities themselves may not be compatible.	Libraries Health clubs Resort hotels
The service environment attracts a heterogeneous customer mix.	Many service environments, particularly those open to the public, will attract a variety of customer segments.	Public parks Public transportation Open-enrollment colleges
The core service is compatibility.	The core service is to arrange and nurture compatible relationships between customers.	Big Brothers/Big Sisters Weight loss group programs Mental health support groups
Customers must occasionally wait for the service.	Waiting in line for service can be monotonous or anxiety producing. The boredom or stress can be magnified or lessened by other customers, depending on their compatibility.	Medical clinics Tourist attractions Restaurants
Customers are expected to share time, space, or service utensils with each other.	The need to share space, time, and other service factors is common in many services, but may become a problem if segments are not comfortable with sharing or with each other or when the need to share is intensified due to capacity constraints.	Golf courses Hospitals Retirement communities Airplanes

Source: Adapted from C. I. Martin and C. A. Pranter, "Compatibility Management: Customer-to-Customer Relationships in Service Environments," *Journal of Services Marketing* 3, no. 3 (Summer 1989), pp. 5–15. Reprinted with the permission of MCB University Press.

keeps meetings and large group events separated from the areas of the hotel used by individual businesspeople.

Other strategies for enhancing customer compatibility include customer "codes of conduct" such as the regulation of smoking behavior and dress codes. Clearly such codes of conduct may vary from one service establishment to another. Finally, training employees to observe customer-to-customer interactions and to be sensitive to potential conflicts is another strategy for increasing compatibility among segments. Employees can also be trained to recognize opportunities to foster positive encounters among customers in certain types of service environments.

Summary

This chapter focused on the role of customers in service delivery. The customer receiving the service and the other customers in the service environment can all potentially cause a widening of gap 3 if they fail to perform their roles effectively. A number of reasons why customers may widen the service delivery gap were suggested: customers lack understanding of their roles; customers are unwilling or unable to perform their roles; customers are not rewarded for good performance; other customers interfere; or market segments are incompatible.

The challenge of managing customers in the process of service delivery is unique to service firms. Whereas manufacturers are not concerned with customer participation in the manufacturing process, service managers constantly face this issue because their customers are often present and active partners in service production. As participants in service production and delivery, customers can perform three primary roles, discussed and illustrated in the chapter: *productive resources* for the organization, *contributors* to service quality and satisfaction, and *competitors* in performing the service for themselves.

Through understanding the importance of customers in service delivery and identifying the roles played by the customer in a particular context, managers can develop strategies to enhance customer participation. Strategies discussed in the text include defining the customers' roles and jobs, recruiting customers who match the customer profile in terms of desired level of participation, educating customers so they can perform their roles effectively, rewarding customers for their contributions, and managing the customer mix to enhance the experiences of all segments. By implementing these strategies, organizations should see a reduction in gap 3 due to effective, efficient customer contributions to service delivery.

Discussion Questions

1. Discuss the general importance of customers in the successful delivery of service using your own personal examples.

2. Why might customer actions and attitudes cause gap 3 to occur? Use your own examples to illustrate your understanding.

3. Using Table 12.1, think of specific services you have experienced that fall within each of the three levels of customer participation: low, medium, high. Describe specifically what you did as a customer in each case. How did your involvement vary across the three types of service situations?

4. Describe a time when your satisfaction in a particular situation was *increased* because of something another customer did. Could (or does) the organization do anything to ensure that this happens routinely? What does it do? Should it try to make this a routine occurrence?

5. Describe a time when your satisfaction in a particular situation was *decreased* because of something another customer did. Could the organization have done anything to manage this situation more effectively? What?

6. Discuss the customer's role as a *productive resource* for the firm. Describe a time when you played this role. What did you do and how did you feel? Did the firm help you to perform your role effectively? How?

7. Discuss the customer's role as a *contributor to service quality and satisfaction*. Describe a time when you played this role. What did you do and how did you feel? Did the firm help you to perform your role effectively? How?

8. Discuss the customer's role as a potential *competitor*. Describe a time when you chose to provide a service for yourself rather than pay someone to provide the service for you. Why did you decide to perform the service yourself? What could

have changed your mind, causing you to contract with someone else to provide the service?

Exercises

1. Visit a service establishment where customers can influence each other (such as a theme park, entertainment establishment, resort, shopping mall, restaurant, airline, school, or hospital). Observe (or interview) customers and record cases of positive and negative customer influence. Discuss how you would manage the situation to increase overall customer satisfaction.

2. Interview someone regarding his or her decision to outsource a service—for example, legal services, payroll, or maintenance in a company; or cleaning, child care, or pet care in a household. Use the criteria for internal versus external exchange described in the text to analyze the decision to outsource.

3. Think of a service where a high level of customer participation is necessary for the service to be successful (health club, weight loss, educational setting, health care, golf lessons, or the like). Interview a service provider in such an organization to find out what strategies the provider uses to encourage effective customer participation.

4. Visit a service setting where multiple types of customer segments use the service at the same time (such as a theater, golf course, resort, or theme park). Observe (or interview the manager about) the organization's strategies to manage these segments effectively. Would you do anything differently if you were in charge?

5. Visit iPrint's website (http://www.iPrint.com). Compare its printing service process to similar onsite services offered by Kinko's. Compare and contrast the customer's role in each situation.

Notes

1. P. B. Seybold, *Customers.com: How to Create a Profitable Business Strategy for the Internet and Beyond* (New York: Random House, 1998), pp. 235–44; www.iPrint.com, 2002.

2. See B. Schneider and D. E. Bowen, *Winning the Service Game* (Boston: Harvard Business School Press, 1995), chap. 4; L. A. Bettencourt, "Customer Voluntary Performance: Customers as Partners in Service Delivery, *Journal of Retailing* 73, no. 3 (1997), pp. 383–406; P. K. Mills and J. H. Morris, "Clients as 'Partial' Employees: Role Development in Client Participation," *Academy of Management Review* 11, no. 4 (1986), pp. 726–35; C. H. Lovelock and R. F. Young, "Look to Customers to Increase Productivity," *Harvard Business Review,* Summer 1979, pp. 9–20; A. R. Rodie and S. S. Kleine, "Customer Participation in Services Production and Delivery," in *Handbook of Services Marketing and Management,* ed. T. A. Swartz and D. Iacobucci (Thousand Oaks, CA: Sage Publications, 2000), pp. 111–26; and C. K. Prahalad and V. Ramaswamy, "Co-opting Customer Competence," *Harvard Business Review,* January–February 2000, p. 7.

3. S. J. Grove, R. P. Fisk, and M. J. Bitner, "Dramatizing the Service Experience: A Managerial Approach," in *Advances in Services Marketing and Management,* ed. T. A. Swartz, D. E. Bowen, and S. W. Brown, vol. 1 (Greenwich, CT: JAI Press, 1992), pp. 91–122.

4. For an interesting view of work and business as theater, see B. Joseph Pine II and J. H. Gilmore, *The Experience Economy: Work Is Theatre and Every Business a Stage* (Boston: Harvard Business School Press, 1999).

5. R. Berner, "Attention Mail-Order Shoppers: Please Be Nicer to That Salesperson," *The Wall Street Journal,* December 22, 1998, p. B1.

6. L. A. Bettencourt, S. W. Brown, A. L. Ostrom, and R. I. Roundtree, "Client Co-Production in Knowledge-Intensive Business Services," working paper, Indiana University, 2002.

7. See S. J. Grove and R. P. Fisk, "The Impact of Other Customers on Service Experiences: A Critical Incident Examination of 'Getting Along,'" *Journal of Retailing* 73, no. 1 (1997), pp. 63–85; C. I. Martin and C. A. Pranter, "Compatibility Management: Customer-to-Customer Relationships in Service Environments," *Journal of Services Marketing* 3, no. 3 (Summer 1989), pp. 5–15.

8. S. J. Grove and R. P. Fisk, "The Impact of Other Customers on Service Experiences: A Critical Incident Examination of 'Getting Along,'" *Journal of Retailing* 73, no. 1 (1997), pp. 63–85.

9. Ibid.

10. See P. K. Mills, R. B. Chase, and N. Margulies, "Motivating the Client/Employee System as a Service Production Strategy," *Academy of Management Review* 8, no. 2 (1983), pp. 301–10; D. E. Bowen, "Managing Customers as Human Resources in Service Organizations," *Human Resource Management* 25, no. 3 (1986), pp. 371–83; and Mills and Morris, "Clients as 'Partial' Employees."

11. Bettencourt et al, "Client Co-Production in Knowledge-Intensive Business Services."

12. R. B. Chase, "Where Does the Customer Fit in a Service Operation?" *Harvard Business Review,* November–December 1978, pp. 137–42.

13. Mills, Chase, and Margulies, "Motivating the Client/Employee System."

14. Marilyn Adams, "Tech Takes Bigger Role in Air Services," *USA Today,* July 18, 2001, p. 1.

15. See D. W. Johnson, R. T. Johnson, and K. A. Smith, *Active Learning: Cooperation in the College Classroom* (Edina, MN: Interaction Book Company, 1991).

16. S. Dellande and M. C. Gilly, "Gaining Customer Compliance in Services," in *Advances in Services Marketing and Management,* ed. T. A. Swartz, D. E. Bowen, and S. W. Brown, pp. 265–92.

17. S. W. Kelley, S. J. Skinner, and J. H. Donnelly, Jr., "Organizational Socialization of Service Customers," *Journal of Business Research* 25 (1992), pp. 197–214.

18. C. Claycomb, C. A. Lengnick-Hall, and L. W. Inks, "The Customer As a Productive Resource: A Pilot Study and Strategic Implications," *Journal of Business Strategies* 18, no. 1 (Spring 2001), pp. 47–69.

19. Several of the scenarios are adapted from C. Goodwin, "'I Can Do It Myself': Training the Service Consumer to Contribute to Service Productivity," *Journal of Services Marketing* 2, no. 4 (Fall 1988), pp. 71–78.

20. R. Normann and R. Ramirez, "From Value Chain to Value Constellation: Designing Interactive Strategy," *Harvard Business Review,* July–August 1993, pp. 65–77; www.ikea.com, 2002.

21. J. E. G. Bateson, "The Self-Service Customer—Empirical Findings," in *Emerging Perspectives in Services Marketing,* eds. L. L. Berry, G. L. Shostack, and G. D. Upah (Chicago: American Marketing Association, 1983), pp. 50–53.

22. V. S. Folkes, "Recent Attribution Research in Consumer Behavior: A Review and New Directions," *Journal of Consumer Research* 14 (March 1988), pp. 548–65; and M. J. Bitner, "Evaluating Service Encounters: The Effects of Physical Surroundings and Employee Responses," *Journal of Marketing* 54 (April 1990), pp. 69–82.

23. R. F. Lusch, S. W. Brown, and G. J. Brunswick, "A General Framework for Explaining Internal vs. External Exchange," *Journal of the Academy of Marketing Science* 10, no. 2 (Spring 1992), pp. 119–34.

24. Lusch, Brown, and Brunswick, "A General Framework."

25. See P. Dabholkar, "Consumer Evaluations of New Technology-Based Self-Service Options: An Investigation of Alternative Models of Service Quality," *International Journal of Research in Marketing* 13 (1), pp. 29–51; F. Davis, "User Acceptance of Information Technology: System Characteristics, User Perceptions and Behavioral Impact," *International Journal of Man-Machine Studies* 38 (1993), pp. 475–87; L. M. Bobbitt and P. A. Dabholkar, "Integrating Attitudinal Theories to Understand and Predict Use of Technology-Based Self-Service," *International Journal of Service Industry Management* 12, no. 5 (2001), pp. 423–50.

26. M. L. Meuter, M. J. Bitner, A. L. Ostrom, and S. W. Brown, "Customer Adoption of Self-Service Technologies: An Investigation of Key Mediating Variables," working paper, California State University at Chico, 2002.

27. M. L. Meuter, A. L. Ostrom, R. I. Roundtree, and M. J. Bitner, "Self-Service Technologies: Understanding Customer Satisfaction with Technology-Based Service Encounters," *Journal of Marketing* 64, no. 3 (July 2000), pp. 50–64.

28. Meuter et al., "Customer Adoption of Self-Service Technologies"; see also Y. Moon and F. X. Frei, "Exploding the Self-Service Myth," *Harvard Business Review,* May–June 2000.

29. A. Parasuraman and C. L. Colby, *Techno-Ready Marketing: How and Why Your Customers Adopt Technology* (New York: The Free Press, 2001).

30. Bowen, "Managing Customers as Human Resources."

31. Chase, "Where Does the Customer Fit in a Service Operation?"

32. See Schneider and Bowen, *Winning the Service Game,* chap. 4. The four job descriptions in this section are adapted from M. R. Bowers, C. L. Martin, and A. Luker, "Trading Places, Employees as Customers, Customers as Employees," *Journal of Services Marketing* 4 (Spring 1990), pp. 56–69.

33. Bateson, "The Self-Service Customer."

34. Meuter et al., "Customer Adoption of Self-Service Technologies."

35. Bowen, "Managing Customers as Human Resources"; and Schneider and Bowen, *Winning the Service Game,* chap. 4; Meuter et al., "Customer Adoption of Self-Service Technologies."

36. C. Goodwin and R. Radford, "Models of Service Delivery: An Integrative Perspective," in *Advances in Services Marketing and Management,* ed. T. A. Swartz, D. E. Bowen, and S. W. Brown, pp. 231–52.

37. S. W. Kelley, J. H. Donnelly, Jr., and S. J. Skinner, "Customer Participation in Service Production and Delivery," *Journal of Retailing* 66, no. 3 (Fall 1990), pp. 315–35; and Schneider and Bowen, *Winning the Service Game,* chap. 4.

38. Bowen, "Managing Customers as Human Resources."

39. Ibid.

40. Martin and Pranter, "Compatibility Management," pp. 5–15.

13

DELIVERING SERVICE THROUGH INTERMEDIARIES AND ELECTRONIC CHANNELS

This chapter's objectives are to

1. Identify the primary channels through which services are delivered to end customers.

2. Provide examples of each of the key service intermediaries.

3. View delivery of service from two perspectives—the service provider and the service deliverer.

4. Identify the benefits and challenges of each method of service delivery.

5. Outline the strategies that are used to manage service delivery through intermediaries.

Distance Learning Is Scorching Hot![1]

Distance learning is education that is accessible at a time, place, location, and pace that is convenient to the user. It can come in many forms: over phone lines, on CD-ROM, over the Internet, or through a video camera. It can be an instructor in Omaha videoconferencing with managers in Mobile, Lexington, and Minneapolis on the fundamentals of risk analysis. It can be an engineer taking a motor repair certification course online at home. It can be a lineman on a laptop during his lunch break brushing up on the latest pole maintenance techniques via CD-ROM. It can be a customer learning about the features of a product online before making a purchase. Distance learning

Source: Dick Blume/The Image Works

breaks down the boundaries of the classroom and makes education more accessible than ever.[2]

Perhaps the widest application of distance learning is on-the-job training. But did you realize that more than three-quarters of all U.S. colleges and universities now offer "virtual" courses—delivered electronically at a distance—and many offer or are developing complete degrees that a student can earn without ever setting foot on a campus? While total college enrollments are rising 1–2 percent a year, distance education enrollments are increasing 30 percent annually.[3] Even though you may never earn a degree electronically, you are almost certainly going to take at least one distance learning course in your life—if not in college, then at work. In the future, the number one vehicle for company training will be distance education: training delivered where it is needed, when it is needed, and to whom it is needed.

Although not new, the concept of distance learning has evolved in technology and scope. At its best, distance learning involves a rich interactive environment with multimedia including slides, video, text, e-mail, chat rooms, and two-way communication. The most effective environments also involve some ability to interact with the professor. In fact, an expert in distance learning found that successful programs had in common one factor: a minimum of 30 percent airtime dedicated to student interaction in which the learner is actively asking questions, talking with experts in the field, working in small groups, or putting answers into the keypad.[4]

At both Arizona State University and the University of North Carolina, where the authors of this book are professors, business courses and degree programs are now offered online via the Internet to serve a wider market. ASU's online MBA is customized and offered to individual companies like John Deere and Lucent

Technologies, who contract with the university to educate selected groups of employees. The coursework is a combination of onsite, in-person instruction; online self-paced modules; and active learning assignments. Technology makes it possible for students to take courses when and where they wish, frequently time zones and continents away from other students and their professors.

While most universities, and specifically business schools, are involved in distance education in various forms (see the Internet site www.edsurf.net/edshack/virtualu.htm for the full list and www.lifelonglearning.com for an evaluation of different programs), one stands out as a unique entrant into this marketplace. UNext's Cardean University is a high-profile, private online university designed to deliver business and professional education and training at the MBA level. Launched in 2000, UNext has partnered with leading universities including Columbia Business School, Stanford University, University of Chicago, Carnegie Mellon, and London School of Economics. Three Nobel laureates are on Cardean's faculty, and its president, Geoffrey Cox, left Stanford University to join UNext, believing in its value and potential. The goal of UNext is to provide high-quality education to students around the globe who can't afford either the expense or the time to attend top institutions, or who already have degrees but desire ongoing education and lifelong learning opportunities. The courses offered by UNext are problem-focused and provide the students with activity-based assignments through the Internet that form the core of the educational experience. Technology allows the students to access courses when and where they wish, an attractive feature for students and companies alike. This is what recently attracted GM to contract with UNext to offer business courses to 88,000 white-collar workers in its company. Estimates suggest that the distance education sector is worth over $6 billion annually.[5]

Distance learning has its critics, among them the director of accreditation at the American Assembly of Collegiate Schools of Business, who said, "It's kind of like McEducation. I can't imagine that they could convince one of our committees that their faculty have the appropriate qualifications."[6] Despite this cynicism, in March 1999 Jones International University near Denver became the first U.S. university operating entirely online to earn regional accreditation from the North Central Association of Colleges and Schools.

Here are some of the most frequently asked questions about distance learning and the answers we have to date:

Who are the biggest consumers of distance learning? High-tech companies use more distance learning than any other industry because of the fast pace of product change. Higher education statistics show that 90 percent of all higher education institutions with more than 10,000 students and 85 percent of those with enrollments of 3,000 to 10,000 offer distance education courses.[7]

How effective is distance learning? "Some skeptics overlook the fact that learning is not a place; it's a process," claims Vicky Phillips, author of *The Best Distance Learning Graduate Schools*. Current research is sketchy, but one study supports her point. A researcher analyzed studies from 248 separate sources on the effectiveness of online degree programs and concluded that people learn just as well with a personal computer as they do by spending hours sitting in lecture halls.[8] Much remains to be learned about the effectiveness of distance learning as a whole as well as the types of distance learning that are most successful. People who read a lot adapt best, as they consider distance learning the same as a book but with more interaction and hands-on activity.[9]

How effective is distance learning in other cultures and countries? Thomas Cooper, an expert on mass communications, emphasizes that trust is a critical component of communications. Trust in many cultures involves either touch or direct vision, something that is not achieved with technology. The United States is one of the few cultures in which most consumers trust technologies such as ATMs. Videoconferencing seems to be culturally insensitive if not inappropriate for cultures where surrogate or substitute people are either offensive or not acceptable. Also, there are some cultures that accept distance learning but still feel "reduced, trivialized, muzzled, or as in the work, distanced from the educational process."[10] One success story in distance education is the 50-year-old, 30-campus ITESM (Technological Institute of Monterrey) in Mexico, which has online MBA courses, computer programs for the blind, online doctorates taught by top experts from Carnegie-Mellon University, and seminars for Latin American journalists. One of the most innovative was a professional-level course for 150 mayors and municipal officers on how to run honest and open governments.[11]

How does a distance learning degree measure up to a traditional degree? *Business Week* recently reported that while enrollment in virtual MBA programs will jump from 5,000 students in 2000 to more than 50,000 in 2002, graduates face a disadvantage in getting the jobs they want. A survey of corporate recruiters found that an overwhelming majority had not even considered applicants who earned their MBAs online.[12] For-profit universities that have neither a track record nor a recognizable brand name offer many MBA programs, and the quality of faculty varies. However, some firms are open to considering candidates with dot-com credentials, notably established tech companies such as IBM and Xerox.

Only time will tell how far the distance learning revolution will go, but many prognosticators expect it to completely alter the way learning is achieved. According to one expert:

> Education will change from a place-centered enterprise to "education where you need it." A decade from now, it wouldn't surprise me if the majority of education took place in people's homes, in people's offices, on the production line, wherever it is needed.[13]

Although experts tend to agree that great value exists in an on-campus educational experience, the truth is that for much of the world's population that isn't a realistic alternative.

Except for situations such as distance learning, where electronic channels can distribute services, providers and consumers come into direct contact in service provision. Because of the inseparability of production and consumption in service, providers must either be present themselves when customers receive service or find ways to involve others in distribution. Involving others can be problematic because quality in service occurs in the service encounter between company and customer. Unless the service distributor is willing and able to perform in the service encounter as the service principal would, the value of the offering decreases and the reputation of the original service may be damaged. Chapter 11 pointed out the challenges of controlling encounters within service organizations themselves, but most service (and many manufacturing) companies face an even more formidable task: attaining service excellence and consistency when intermediaries represent them to customers. This chapter discusses both the challenges of delivering service through intermediaries and approaches that engender alignment with the goals of the service provider.

Two services marketers are involved in delivering service through intermediaries: the *service principal,* or originator, and the *service deliverer,* or intermediary. The service principal is the entity that creates the service concept (whose counterpart is the manufacturer of physical goods), and the service deliverer is the entity that interacts with the customer in the actual execution of the service (whose counterpart is the distributor or wholesaler of physical goods). Because both the service supplier and the service deliverer are potential roles that you may play in your career, we examine the issues surrounding distribution of services from both perspectives.

SERVICE INTERMEDIARIES

Service intermediaries perform many important functions for the service principal. First, they often coproduce the service, fulfilling service principals' promises to customers. Franchise services such as haircutting, key making, and dry cleaning are produced by the intermediary (the franchisee) using a process developed by the service principal (hence the phrase "coproducer"). Service intermediaries also make services locally available, providing time and place convenience for the customer. Because they represent multiple service principals, such intermediaries as travel and insurance agents provide a retailing function for customers, gathering together in one place a variety of choices. And in many financial or professional services, intermediaries function as the glue between the brand or company name and the customer by building the trusting relationship required in these complex and expert offerings.

In contrast to channels for products, channels for services are almost always direct, if not to the customer then to the intermediary that sells to the customer. Because services cannot be owned, there are no titles or rights to most services that can be passed along a delivery channel. Because services are intangible and perishable, inventories cannot exist, making warehousing a dispensable function. In general, because services can't be produced, warehoused, and then retailed as goods can, many channels available to goods producers are not feasible for service firms. Many of the primary functions distribution channels serve—inventorying, securing, and taking title to goods— have no meaning in services. The focus in service distribution is on identifying ways to bring the customer and principal or its representative together. The options for doing so are limited to franchisees, agents, brokers, and electronic channels.

We do not include retailers in our short list of service intermediaries because most retailers—from department stores to discount stores—are channels for delivering physical goods rather than services. Retailers that sell only services (movie theaters, film-processing kiosks, restaurants) or retail services that support physical products (automobile dealers, gas stations) can also be described as dealers or franchises. For our purposes in this chapter, they are grouped into the franchise category because they possess the same characteristics, strengths, and weaknesses as franchises.

Goods retailers, by the way, are service organizations themselves, making them intermediaries for goods if not services. Manufacturing companies depend on retailers to represent, explain, promote, and ensure their products—all presale services. They also need retailers to return, exchange, support, and service products—all postsale services. These roles are increasingly critical as products become more complex, technical, and expensive. For example, camera and computer firms rely on retailers carrying their products to understand and communicate highly technical information so that customers choose products that fit their needs. A retailer that leads the customer to the wrong product choice or that inadequately instructs on how to use it creates service problems that strongly influence the manufacturer's reputation.

Service principals depend on their intermediaries to deliver service to their specifications. Service intermediaries determine how the customer evaluates the quality of the company. When a McDonald's franchisee cooks the McNuggets too short a time, the customer's perception of the company—and of other McDonald's franchisees—is tarnished. When one Holiday Inn franchisee has unsanitary conditions, it reflects on all others and on the Holiday Inn brand itself. Unless service providers ensure that the intermediary's goals, incentives, and motives are consistent with their own, they lose control over the service encounters between the customer and the intermediary. When someone other than the service principal is critical to the fulfillment of quality service, a firm must develop ways to either control or motivate these intermediaries to meet company goals and standards. This chapter describes the types and roles of service intermediaries.

DIRECT OR COMPANY-OWNED CHANNELS

Although we call this chapter "Delivering Service through Intermediaries and Electronic Channels," it is important to acknowledge that many services are distributed directly from provider to customer. Some of these are local services—doctors, dry cleaners, and hairstylists—whose area of distribution is limited. Others are national chains with multiple outlets but are considered direct channels because the provider owns all the outlets. Starbucks, the popular chain of coffee shops, is an example of a service provider with all company-owned outlets. Its 4,000 U.S.-based coffee shops are completely run and managed by the company. Exhibit 13.1, which describes some of the reasons for the success of the chain, illustrates the general benefits of company-owned outlets: control, consistency, and maintenance of image.

Perhaps the major benefit of distributing through company-owned channels is that the company has complete control over the outlets. One of the most critical implications of this type of control is that the owner can maintain consistency in service provision. Standards can be established and will be carried out as planned because the company itself monitors and rewards proper execution of the service. Control over hiring, firing, and motivating employees is also a benefit of company-owned channels. As demonstrated in Exhibit 13.1, one of the keys to Starbucks' success is hiring the right baristas or coffee makers, something the company is far more likely to do than a franchisee. Using company-owned channels also allows the company to expand or contract sites without being bound by contractual agreements with other entities. A final benefit is that the company owns the customer relationship.

In service industries where skilled or professional workers have individual relationships with customers, a major concern is whether the loyalty the customer feels is for the company or for the individual service employee. It is well known, for example, that most people are loyal to individual hairstylists and will follow them from one place of business to another. Therefore, one of the important issues in service delivery is who owns the customer relationship—the store or the employee. With company-owned channels, the company owns both the store and the employee and therefore has complete control over the customer relationship.

However, several disadvantages exist with company-owned channels. First, and probably the largest impediment to most service chains, the company must bear all the

One of the biggest marketing success stories of the last decade is Starbucks Coffee Company, although it has been in business for almost 30 years. Twenty years ago, its owner began to think of coffee not as something to retail in a store but instead as something to experience in a coffeehouse. At that point, he created the Starbucks that we know today, the Starbucks that "successfully replicates a perfectly creamy café latte in stores from Seattle to St. Paul." Consistency of service and product are two of the most important reasons that Starbucks has grown to more than 4,000 U.S.-based outlets and expanded internationally, and that it annually reports profit growth of more than 50 percent a year. (Even a world-class service provider such as Starbucks can have a "bad day," as we saw in Chapter 7!) Because Starbucks owns every domestic outlet, it maintains control over all that takes place in them, and here are some of the efforts it undertakes to ensure that the Starbucks experience is always the same, always positive.

Employee Training: Learning to Be a Barista

All employees are called partners, and those who prepare coffee are called "baristas," the Italian name for one who prepares and serves coffee. As many as 400 to 500 employees per month nationally are carefully trained to "call" ("triple-tall nonfat mocha"), make drinks, clean espresso machines, and deliver quality customer service. Baristas are taught "coffee knowledge," so that among other things they know how everything tastes, and "customer service," so that they can explain the Italian drink names to customers.

Ensuring Product Quality

"Retail skills" are another portion of the training, which teaches such specifics as how to wipe oil from the coffee bin, open a giant bag of beans, and clean the milk wand on the espresso machine, all of this to ensure that the coffee

Source: Reprinted with permission of Starbucks Coffee Company

financial risk. When expanding, the firm must find all the capital, sometimes using it for store proliferation rather than for other uses (such as advertising, service quality, or new service development) that would be more profitable. Second, large companies are rarely experts in local markets—they know their businesses but not all markets. When adjustments are needed in business formats for different markets, they may be unaware of what these adjustments should be. This is especially true when companies expand into other cultures and other countries. Partnering or joint venturing is almost always preferred to company-owned channels in these situations.

When two or more service companies want to offer a service and neither has the full financial capability or expertise, they often undertake service partnerships. These operate very much like company-owned channels except that they involve multiple owners. The benefit is that risk and effort are shared, but the disadvantage is that control and returns are also distributed among the partners. Several areas in which partnerships are common are telecommunications, high-technology services, Internet-based services, and entrepreneurial services. Service partnerships also proliferate

drinks taste just right. Another part, "brewing the perfect cup at home," helps baristas teach customers how to use the espresso machines and coffee they buy at Starbucks to replicate the product they get in the coffeehouse.

Service Standards

No pot of Starbucks coffee sits on a burner for more than 20 minutes. An espresso machine with unused coffee must be purged regularly. And no one goes home at night unless everything is completed, cleaned, and polished according to the service standards in the manual. Using such standards ensures that both service and quality are maintained.

Star Skills

To hire, keep, and motivate the very best employees, Starbucks has three guidelines for on-the-job interpersonal relations: (1) maintain and enhance self-esteem, (2) listen and acknowledge, and (3) ask for help. These and other human resource practices, including higher-than-average pay, health insurance, and stock options, lower barista turnover to 60 percent compared with 140 percent for hourly workers in the fast-food business in general.

Starbucks and the Internet

Starbucks had high hopes for the Internet, given that its shops attract young, affluent, tech-savvy customers, 70 percent of whom are Internet users. It appears to have overestimated its ability to transition success offline to the Internet environment, stumbling in several high-profile online initiatives including Starbucks X, a quasi-separate division built around the Internet, and minority investments in online furniture retailing and chat services. The company finally settled on a successful Internet store that sells coffee beans, mugs, and brewing machines, supporting its offline core business. Starbucks refused to offer Internet connections in the coffee shops themselves, not wanting to create dimly lit cybercafés with people hunched over machines. The firm recently decided how to bring the Internet onsite without scaring away other customers: the company now provides high-speed wireless Internet connections in 70 percent of its stores.

If you have any doubt about whether all these steps pay off in terms of quality product and service, check out Starbucks at airports or on the turnpike. You'll notice a difference. While the company doesn't franchise domestically, it does license sites to companies with contracts from public agencies to run those facilities. No highly trained baristas work at these outlets, and no service quality standards are enforced in them. The result is a less consistent, less pleasant, and less flavorful experience. And, if you need further evidence, compare a coffee shop cup of Starbucks coffee to one offered on any United Airlines flight. It's the same coffee, but a harried flight attendant with 65 passengers needing meals and drinks just can't provide the same consistency and attention to every cup.

Sources: J. Reese, "Starbucks: Inside the Coffee Cult," *Fortune,* December 9, 1996, pp. 190–200; G. Anders, "Starbucks Brews a New Strategy," *Fast Company,* August 2001, pp. 144–46; "Starbucks Keeps Pace," *Beverage Industry,* October 2001, p. 11.

when companies expand beyond their country boundaries—typically one partner provides the business format and the other provides knowledge of the local market.

COMMON ISSUES INVOLVING INTERMEDIARIES

Key problems with intermediaries include conflict over objectives and performance, conflict over costs and rewards, difficulty controlling quality and consistency across outlets, tension between empowerment and control, and channel ambiguity.

Channel Conflict over Objectives and Performance

The parties involved in delivering services do not always agree about how the channel should operate. Channel conflict can occur between the service provider and the service intermediary, among intermediaries in a given area, and between different types of channels used by a service provider (such as when a service principal has its own outlets as well as franchised outlets). The conflict most often centers on the parties having different goals, competing roles and rights, and conflicting views of the way the channel is performing. Sometimes the conflict occurs because the service principal and its intermediaries are too dependent on each other.

Channel Conflict over Costs and Rewards

The monetary arrangement between those who create the service and those who deliver it is a pivotal issue of contention. Nowhere was this type of conflict better demonstrated than when major airlines surprised their major distribution channel (travel agencies) with caps on fees. Instead of the traditional 10 percent commission on total airfare, Delta pioneered a $50-or-less fee per ticket, unilaterally and dramatically altering the compensation arrangement. The manner in which the airlines made the change so infuriated travel agencies that they struck back against the airlines through such strategies as teaching consumers how to buy cheap tickets without staying over a Saturday night, purchasing wholesale tickets, and recommending small, discount carriers.

Difficulty Controlling Quality and Consistency across Outlets

One of the biggest difficulties for both principals and their intermediaries involves the inconsistency and lack of uniform quality that result when multiple outlets deliver services. When shoddy performance occurs, even at a single outlet, the service principal suffers because the entire brand and reputation are jeopardized, and other intermediaries endure negative attributions to their outlets. The problem is particularly acute in highly specialized services such as management consulting or architecture, where execution of the complex offering may be difficult to deliver to the standards of the principal.

Tension between Empowerment and Control

McDonald's and other successful service businesses were founded on the principle of performance consistency. Both they and their intermediaries attained profits and longevity by the company's controlling virtually every aspect of their intermediaries' businesses. McDonald's, for example, is famous for its demanding and rigid service standards (such as "turn, never flip, hamburgers on the grill"), carefully specified supplies, and performance monitoring. The strategy makes sense: unless an intermediary delivers service exactly the same way the successful company outlets provide it, the service may not be as desirable to customers. From the principal's point of view, its name and reputation are on the line in each outlet, making careful control a necessity.

Control, however, can have negative ramifications within intermediaries. Many service franchisees, for example, are entrepreneurial by nature and select service franchising because they can own and operate their own businesses. If they are to deliver according to consistent standards, their independent ideas must be integrated into and often subsumed by the practices and policies of the service principal. In these situations they often feel like automatons with less freedom than they had in corporate jobs.

Channel Ambiguity

When empowerment is the chosen strategy, doubt exists about the roles of the company and the intermediary. Who will undertake market research to identify customer requirements, the company or an intermediary? Who owns the results and in what way are they to be used? Who determines the standards for service delivery, the franchiser or the franchisee? Who should train a dealer's customer service representatives, the company or the dealer? In these and other situations, the roles of the principal and its intermediaries are unclear, leading to confusion and conflict.

KEY INTERMEDIARIES FOR SERVICE DELIVERY

One way to organize the discussion of delivering service through intermediaries is to describe the primary channels of service distribution. Services can be distributed to the end customer through franchisees, agents, brokers, and electronic channels. *Franchisees* are service outlets licensed by a principal to deliver a unique service concept it has created or popularized. Examples include fast-food chains (McDonald's, Burger King), video stores (Blockbuster), automobile repair services (Jiffy Lube), and hotels (Holiday Inn). *Agents* and *brokers* are representatives who distribute and sell the services of one or more service suppliers. Examples include insurance (Paul Revere Insurance Company), financial services (Oppenheimer mutual funds), and travel services (American Express). *Electronic channels* include all forms of service provision through television, telephone, interactive multimedia, and computers. Many financial and information services are currently distributed through electronic media: banking, bill paying, education.

Exhibit 13.2 reviews basic principles about distribution.

Franchising

Franchising is the most common type of distribution in services, with more than 2,500 U.S. franchisers licensing their brand names, business processes or formats, unique products, services, or reputations in return for fees and royalties. Franchising works well with services that can be standardized and duplicated through the delivery process, service policies, warranties, guarantees, promotion, and branding. Jiffy Lube, H&R Block tax services, McDonald's, and Red Roof Inns are examples of companies that are ideal for franchise operations. At its best, franchising is a relationship or partnership in which the service provider—the franchiser—develops and optimizes a service format that it licenses for delivery by other parties—the franchisees. There are benefits and disadvantages for both the franchiser and the franchisee in this relationship (see Table 13.1).

The Franchiser's Perspective

A franchiser typically begins by developing a business concept that is unique in some way. Perhaps it is a fast-food concept (such as McDonald's) with unique cooking or delivery processes. Perhaps it is a health and fitness center (such as Gold's Gym) with established formats for marketing to customers, pricing, and hiring employees. Or maybe it is a video store (such as Blockbuster) with unique store environments, employee training, purchasing, and computer systems. A franchiser typically expands business through this method because it expects the following benefits:

- *A leveraged business format for greater expansion and revenues.* Most franchisers want wider distribution—and increased revenues, market share, brand name recognition, and economies of scale—for their concepts and practices than they can support in company outlets.

- *Consistency in outlets.* When franchisers have strong contracts and unique formats, they can require that service be delivered according to their specifications. This

Rather than reiterate topics covered in your marketing principles course and textbook, here we list and briefly summarize the basics about distribution. Knowing these basics allows you to step right into our chapter's discussion of service intermediaries.

Basic Channel Functions

Decreasing the cost of delivering products and services to customers: Because the channel allows specialization, all parties can concentrate on what they do best, thereby lowering cost.

Regrouping activities: Intermediaries are charged with sorting out, accumulating, allocating, and assorting products and services.

Standardizing transactions: Intermediaries deliver products or services in consistent form, based on the needs of the buyer and the supply of the seller.

Matching buyers and sellers: Intermediaries spend time in the market, learning about customers and about what sellers have to offer them.

Providing customer service and support: Intermediaries provide various services including technical support, delivery, transportation, and education.

Types of Intermediaries

Retailers: Intermediaries who sell directly to end customers. They may be retail stores, mail order, door-to-door, even vending machines.

Wholesalers: Organizations that buy from producers and sell to retailers and organizational customers.

Number of Intermediaries

Three strategies are available for distribution of products and services:

Intensive distribution: Locating the offering in numerous outlets.

Selective distribution: Use of more than one but fewer than all intermediaries who are willing.

Exclusive distribution: Limiting the number of intermediaries to one per given area.

Criteria for Evaluating the Channel Alternatives

Economic criteria: The sales expected and costs associated with the channel.

Control criteria: The degree to which the service provider can expect to have its policies and procedures adhered to in the relationship.

Adaptive criteria: The extent to which the type of channel is able to change and be flexible when desired by the service provider.

"Push" versus "Pull" Strategies

"Push" strategy involves companies aggressively promoting their products to intermediaries through personal selling, trade advertising, and trade incentives.

"Pull" strategy consists of building a reputation with customers through direct advertising and branding, creating a desire for the manufacturer's brand which is then pulled through the channel of distribution.

chapter's Global Feature, for example, shows how Starbucks is maintaining consistency across cultures and countries through franchising.

- *Knowledge of local markets.* National chains are unlikely to understand local markets as well as the businesspeople that live in the geographic areas. With franchising, the company obtains a connection to the local market.

- *Shared financial risk and more working capital.* Franchisees must contribute their own capital for equipment and personnel, thereby bearing part of the risk of doing business.

Franchising is not without its challenges, however. Most franchisers encounter the following disadvantages:

TABLE 13.1
Benefits and Challenges in Franchising

Benefits	Challenges
For Franchisers	
Leveraged business format for greater expansion and revenues	Difficulty in maintaining and motivating franchisees
Consistency in outlets	Highly publicized disputes and conflict
Knowledge of local markets	Inconsistent quality
Shared financial risk and more working capital	Control of customer relationship by intermediary
For Franchisees	
An established business format	Encroachment
National or regional brand marketing	Disappointing profits and revenues
Minimized risk of starting a business	Lack of perceived control over operations
	High fees

- *Difficulty in maintaining and motivating franchisees.* Motivating independent operators to price, promote, deliver, and hire according to standards the principal establishes is a difficult job, particularly when business is down.

- *Highly publicized disputes between franchisees and franchisers.* Franchisees are organizing and hiring lobbyists and lawyers to gain more economic clout. Many states and even the federal government have implemented legislation boosting franchisee rights.

- *Inconsistent quality.* Some franchisees perform worse than others, which can undermine the company's name and reputation.

- *Customer relationships controlled by the franchisee rather than the franchiser.* The closer a company is to the customer, the better able it is to listen to that customer's concerns and ideas. When franchisees are involved, a relationship forms between the customer and the franchise rather than between the customer and the franchiser. All customer information, including demographics, purchase history, and preferences, is in the hands of the intermediary rather than the principal.

The Franchisee's Perspective

Because you might become a franchisee at some point in your career, we will review the benefits and disadvantages from that perspective as well. One of the main benefits is obtaining an established business format on which to base a business, something one expert has defined as an "entrepreneur in a prepackaged box, a super-efficient distributor of services and goods through a decentralized web."[14] A second benefit is receiving national or regional brand marketing. Franchisees obtain advertising and other marketing expertise as well as an established reputation. Finally, franchising minimizes the risks of starting a business. The U.S. Small Business Administration estimates that whereas 63 percent of new businesses fail within six years, only 5 percent of new franchises fail.[15] Some of the most successful franchises in the world are profiled in Exhibit 13.3.

Disadvantages for franchisees also exist. One of the most problematic is *encroachment*—the opening of new units near existing ones without compensation to the

Even in [China's] Forbidden City—where emperors and empresses, concubines and eunuchs, palanquins and peons roamed for five centuries—there could not have been a more striking contraposition in the only store I found in the palace interior: a Starbucks!

—Michael Shermer in *Scientific American*

Earlier in this chapter we talked about Starbucks coffeehouses as an example of a very successful company-owned service organization with 4,000 outlets in the United States. The company now has more than 1,000 outlets abroad in places as close as Canada and as far as China. When the company chose to go international, management realized that its best route was not to own but instead to franchise or form other types of alliances with organizations within each country. This approach would allow Starbucks to understand the individual markets better and would limit the capital investment necessary to expand. In an unusual twist, the company began its expansion in Asia rather than in Europe. In each country it met different scenarios and challenges, as illustrated by its experiences in Japan, China, and Canada.

JAPAN

Joining with Sazaby, Inc., a Japanese retailer and restaurateur, Starbucks opened more than a dozen stores in Japan beginning in 1997. The company chose Japan as its first expansion outside North America because it is the third largest coffee-consuming country in the world (6.1 million bags per year compared with 18.1 million bags in the United States). Possibly the most compelling result of the announcement of the entry of Starbucks was intense fear on the part of existing coffee-bar owners in Japan. Even though Starbucks was introducing a mere dozen outlets, the owners of the mega-chains were filled with anxiety. A manager of Doutor Coffee Company, Japan's number one coffee-bar chain (453 shops), exclaimed, "They're a big threat and could take customers away from us." Many coffee bars imitated Starbucks in design and started offering "Seattle coffee." Executives such as Seiji Homma, president of Pronto Corporation (94 stores), traveled to the United States to gather intelligence from more than 20 Starbucks locations on the West Coast. He, like others, worried that the Japanese outlets lacked the sophistication of Starbucks, the ability to "(package) the store: (mesh) such elements as store design, package design, and other merchandising techniques into a compelling entity." Starbucks had so successfully created and distributed its service in the United States that the Japanese were afraid they could not compete. But as Starbucks opens more stores (it plans hundreds in the next five years), the Japanese will be ready. Rather than entering quietly and gaining a toehold before having to compete, Starbucks was targeted before it opened its first Japanese store.

CHINA

After selling Starbucks coffee to Beijing hotels for four years, the company decided to open franchise outlets there in 1998. Challenges abounded. "There (was) of course, the challenge of persuading members of a tea-drinking nation to switch to java. But more immediate has been the challenge of establishing local managers to run shops that can convey the spirit of Seattle in Beijing." The problem was hiring, motivating, and training both baristas who could deliver the consistent service and coffee drinks that made the chain so successful in the United States and managers who would uphold the high standards of the company. The company approached the hiring problem for managers by targeting young people who had experience running successful American-style restaurants such as the Hard Rock Café. They recruited baristas through job fairs and ads and focused on aspects such as career and personal development as well as the "cool" factor of being associated with the pop-culture scene in Seattle. Starbucks dealt with the motivation issue by sending the best manager recruits to Seattle for three months to absorb the culture and lifestyle of Starbucks and the West Coast. The structured training, as it turns out, helped motivate and keep employees because they felt confident in the company. The informality and culture of listening at Starbucks also help because they inculcate trust in employees and thereby generate loyalty.

Starbucks' first outlet in China opened in January 1999 at the China World Trade Centre in Beijing. It now has more than 35 shops, mainly in Beijing and Shanghai. According to David Sun, president of Beijing Mei Da Coffee Company, which owns the Starbucks franchise for northern China, expansion is going well: "When we first started, people didn't know who we were and it was rough finding sites. Now landlords are coming to us."

Cultural opposition occasionally occurs, such as when Starbucks touched a nationalist nerve by opening a small outlet in a souvenir shop in Beijing's Forbidden City, a symbol of Chinese pride. Although more than 45,000 people replying to an online survey opposed the outlet, it is still serving coffee, and there are no plans to close it. "The management of the Forbidden City is 100 percent with us," says Mr. Sun, who hoped to open five more outlets by the end of 2001.

CANADA

When Starbucks considered opening stores in Canada, the firm realized it was dealing with an area unique enough to require firsthand knowledge. Rather than open its own shops, the company decided to license Interaction Restaurants, Inc., to lead the firm into Montreal. Interaction Restaurants plans to expand the handful of Starbucks stores to 50 to 70 outlets in Quebec, most of them in the Montreal area.

Moving the firm into the Montreal culture while maintaining the Starbucks identity was a concern. Starbucks wanted to maintain the essence of its image, so it was very careful about the company it chose to become its ambassador. Starbucks had dealt with different cultures—such as the U.S. Hispanic community, Japan, and China—but there were important differences in Quebec. One involves the language, which is mandated by government and is a very emotional issue. In 2000, three coffee shops belonging to Second Cup Ltd., a rival of Starbucks, were bombed by an anti-English group because the company retained its English name. To prevent such problems yet remain consistent, Starbucks agreed to be called Café Starbucks Coffee, which combines French and English. Notably, this is the only place in the world where Starbucks has a different company name!

Perhaps a larger issue was that Montreal residents had a firmly entrenched, sophisticated coffee culture with a history of small coffee shops and Van Houtte (the dominant firm in the market) serving dark, rich coffee. Unlike in the United States, where Starbucks popularized the latte and the coffee tradition that went with it, "[t]here already is a café paradigm there, so Starbucks [didn't] have quite the free rein to invent café culture in Quebec." Fortunately, Starbucks' darkly roasted taste was consistent with the preferences in Montreal. Even so, the firm created a special blend called Melange Mont-Royal to recognize the new market and acknowledge that it was special.

The Canadian outlets are also different in that they contain a kitchen for preparing sandwiches and simple meals and an oven for breads and muffins. Freshly prepared food is not typical of Starbucks, and it will be an interesting experiment to see if the outlets can operate the kitchens as efficiently as they do their coffee machines.

Sources: N. Shirouzu, "Japan's Staid Coffee Bars Wake Up and Smell the Starbucks," *The Wall Street Journal,* July 25, 1996, pp. B1ff; J. Lee-Young, "Starbucks' Expansion in China Is Slated; Coffee-Shop Managers Face Cultural Challenges," *The Wall Street Journal,* October 5, 1998, pp. A27Lff; "Business: Coffee with Your Tea? Starbucks in China," *The Economist,* October 6, 2001, p. 62; Z. Olijnyk, "Latte, s'il Vous Plait," *Canadian Business,* September 3, 2001, pp. 50–52. M. Shermer, "Starbucks in the Forbidden City," *Scientific American,* July 2001, pp. 34–35.

---

existing franchisee. When encroachment occurs, potential revenues are diminished and competition is increased. Another frequent disadvantage involves disappointing profits and revenues: "Most people think of franchising as some kind of bonanza . . . the reality is you get a solid operation, work damn hard, and if you're making $40,000 a year after four years, that's good."[16] Other disadvantages include lack of perceived control over operations and high fees. Many of these problems are due to overpromising by the franchiser, but others are caused by unrealistic expectations about what will be achieved in a franchise agreement.

Agents and Brokers

In common terminology, an *agent* is an intermediary who acts on behalf of a service principal (such as a brokerage firm or a popular sports figure) and is authorized to make agreements between customers and the principal. Agents and brokers do not take title to services but instead deliver the rights to them. They have legal authority to market services as well as to perform other marketing functions on behalf of producers. The two forms of intermediaries perform many of the same functions but are distinct from each other in some ways.

Agents

Agents generally work for principals continuously, rather than for a single deal.

Selling agents have contractual authority to sell a service principal's output (which can be anything from an athlete's time to travel, insurance, or financial services), usually because the principal is not interested, feels unqualified, or lacks the resources to do so. Athletes use selling agents because they want to focus on their sports instead of negotiations, promotion, and contracts. Three major sports marketing firms—International Management Group, Octagon Marketing & Athlete Representation, and SFX Entertainment—dominate the field in representing athletes. But others, such as Impact Sports Marketing, are selling agents in specialty areas such as baseball. Impact represents New York Yankee Bernie Williams, whom the company paired with Coca-Cola

13.3   What Makes a Franchise or Retail Store a Star?

A *Wall Street Journal* reporter answered this question by locating the biggest U.S. outlet for 20 big brands, among them many service businesses. He concluded that location, luck, and service determine the winners. Here are several of the star franchisees that won. Although this list comes from 1993, it still presents the best examples of franchise winners that exist today.

HERTZ RENT A CAR
PARENT COMPANY: Hertz Corp.
BIGGEST OUTLET: Los Angeles International Airport
SIZE INDICATOR: Most rentals a day
EXPLANATION: Nine counters in seven terminals serve customers around the clock at the West Coast's busiest airport. Daily rentals average 2,000. In the first half of 1992, the facility grossed $37 million. Hertz parking lots, maintenance facilities, and offices cover 36 acres. The operation pumps more than 1 million gallons of gasoline a year. Seventeen buses shuttle customers to and from vehicles. Most popular car: Ford Taurus. Five percent of airport rentals are convertibles. Hertz's staff at the airport numbers 300. The size of the operation multiplies problems, such as a flight-delaying fog. "If we make a mistake we can upset several hundred customers at a time," says Charles Shafer, division vice president.

FTD FLORAL DELIVERY
PARENT COMPANY: Florists' Transworld Delivery Association
BIGGEST OUTLET: McShan Florist Inc., Dallas
SIZE INDICATOR: Most flowers-by-wire orders in U.S.
EXPLANATION: Serving Dallas but not neighboring Fort Worth, the florist typically fills 1,100 FTD orders a week; an arrangement averages $38. McShan employs 150 and has more than two dozen phone lines, a 27,000-square-foot store, and 50 delivery trucks, but no greenhouse. Neiman Marcus is a major local customer. Obituary-page ads read, "We don't sell flowers, we sell love." Dallas literally grew up to McShan's door. Once surrounded by cotton fields, the store now is ringed by homes, many of which it landscaped. The business hasn't branched out because, says president Bruce McShan, "We prefer to have one big headache instead of a lot of little ones."

MCDONALD'S
PARENT COMPANY: McDonald's Corp.
BIGGEST OUTLET: On turnpike near Darien, Conn.
SIZE INDICATOR: Most McDonald's customers served in U.S.
EXPLANATION: Near the New York–Connecticut border on Interstate 95, this round-the-clock McDonald's serves nearly 3 million travelers a year. On average, the franchise sells 8,000 meals daily. Everything about the store is mammoth: 19 cash registers, including portables for overflow crowds, a 12-foot fry grill, 32 telephones. Employees work in teams. One directs traffic; another operates a yogurt bar. Retirees pass out maps in a tourist center equipped with an automatic teller machine. Owner–operator George Michell says the busiest days of the year are on Thanksgiving weekend.

FEDERAL EXPRESS
PARENT COMPANY: Federal Express Corp.
BIGGEST OUTLET: Center at 525 Seventh Ave., New York City
SIZE INDICATOR: Handles most packages and documents daily.
EXPLANATION: Located in the heart of New York City's Garment Center, between 38th and 39th streets. This is the busiest of Federal Express's 434 U.S. service centers; its daily volume of 1,000 items is three times the average. Proximity to Penn Station is a traffic booster. Major customers include dressmakers and fashion design houses as well as neighborhood department stores. "Many parcels are boxes you couldn't carry home," says manager Valerie Blanchard. The center also handles a heavy volume of tickets for travel agents. Seven full-time employees staff the facility, which is open until 9:30 P.M. weekdays and 7 P.M. on Saturdays.

H&R BLOCK
PARENT COMPANY: H&R Block Inc.
BIGGEST OUTLET: Downtown Stamford, Conn.
SIZE INDICATOR: Most clients served
Explanation: The office handled more than 8,000 returns last year—almost twice the next-busiest office. Why? "It's a mystery to me," says district manager Jack Marvill. The volume was so large that two more Stamford outlets recently opened. The downtown office doesn't offer unusual services, and its clientele is described as a typical mixture of commercial and individual taxpayers. The facility has 19 tax preparation stations and employs about 50.

HILTON HOTELS
PARENT COMPANY: Hilton Hotels Corp.
BIGGEST OUTLET: Flamingo Hotel, Las Vegas
SIZE INDICATOR: Most rooms
EXPLANATION: This 3,530-room hotel, built by gangster Bugsy Siegel in the 1940s, is popular with tourists; the nearby 3,200-room Las Vegas Hilton caters to high rollers and conventioneers. With single rooms priced at under $50, the Flamingo averages a 90 percent occupancy rate and is Hilton's most profitable, says vice president Marc Grossman. Located at one of the busiest "Strip" intersections, the hotel is staffed by nearly 4,000 employees. Its 27 stories include a casino, two grand ballrooms, eight restaurants, three lounges, 55 elevators, parking for 2,830, and a furrier. A $100 million expansion will add a tower and waterfalls.

Source: R. Gibson, "Location, Luck, Service Can Make a Store Top Star," *The Wall Street Journal,* February 1, 1993, p. B1. Published by permission of Dow Jones, Inc. via Copyright Clearance Center, Inc., © 1993 Dow Jones and Conpany, Inc. All Rights Reserved Worldwide.

Co., Foot Locker, Kraft Foods, and Sprint PCS, and more than 100 other ballplayers in deals with Outback Steakhouse, Progressive Corp., and the U.S. Army. Selling agents act as a sales force with a difference: because they know the market better than the service principal, they are typically entrusted with influence over prices, terms, and conditions of sale. Unlike a sales force, the selling agent normally has no territorial limits but represents the service principal in all areas.

Purchasing agents also have long-term relationships with buyers, evaluating and making purchases for them. They are knowledgeable and provide helpful market information to clients as well as obtaining the best services and prices available. Purchasing agents are frequently hired by companies and individuals to find art, antiques, and rare jewelry.

Facilitating agents help with the marketing process by adding expertise or support such as financial services, risk taking, or transportation.

Brokers

Brokers bring buyers and sellers together while assisting in negotiation. They are paid by the party who hired them, rarely become involved in financing or assuming risk, and are not long-term representatives of buyers or sellers. The most familiar examples are real estate brokers, insurance brokers, and security brokers.

Benefits and challenges in using agents and brokers are summarized in Table 13.2.

Benefits of Agents and Brokers

The travel industry provides an example of both agents and brokers. Three main categories of travel intermediaries exist: tour packagers, retail travel agents, and specialty channelers (including incentive travel firms, meeting and convention planners, hotel representatives, association executives, and corporate travel offices). You are likely to be most familiar with traditional retail travel agents. Industry convention terms the travel companies as brokers and the individuals who work for them as travel agents or sales associates. We will illustrate some of the benefits and challenges of agents and brokers using this industry. We note that this traditional industry is changing rapidly due to electronic channels, and will illustrate these new entrants and their impact later in the chapter.

Reduced Selling and Distribution Costs If an airline or resort hotel needed to contact every potential traveler to promote its offerings, costs would be exorbitant. Because most travel services are transactional rather than long-term, travelers would need to expend tremendous effort to find services that meet their needs. Travel agents and brokers accomplish the intermediary role by assembling information from travel suppliers and offering it to travelers.

TABLE 13.2
Benefits and Challenges in Distributing Services through Agents and Brokers

Benefits	Challenges
Reduced selling and distribution costs	Loss of control over pricing and other aspects of marketing
Intermediary's possession of special skills and knowledge	Representation of multiple service principals
Wide representation	
Knowledge of local markets	
Customer choice	

Possession of Special Skills and Knowledge   The three intermediaries have special knowledge and skills in their areas. Retail travel agents know the industry well and know how to access the information they do not possess, often through reference materials and online services. Tour packagers have a more specialized role—they assemble, promote, and price bundles of travel services from travel suppliers, then offer these bundles either to travelers themselves or to retail travel agents. Specialty channelers (which we could put in the category of facilitating agents) have even more specialized roles. Some work in corporate travel offices to lend their skills to an entire corporation; others are business meeting and convention planners who act almost as tour packagers for whole companies or associations; and some are incentive travel firms that focus on travel recognition programs in corporations or associations.

Wide Representation   Because agents and brokers are paid by commission rather than by salary, there is little risk or disadvantage in extending the service offerings to a wide geography. Thus companies have representatives in many places, far more places than the company would place them if fixed costs such as buildings, equipment, and salaries were required.

Knowledge of Local Markets   Another key benefit of agents and brokers is that they become experts in the markets they serve. They know or learn the unique needs of different markets, including international markets. They understand what their clients' preferences are and how to adapt the principal's services to match the needs of clients. This benefit is particularly needed and appreciated when clients are dispersed internationally. Knowing the culture and taboos of a country is critical for successful selling. Most companies find that obtaining local representation by experts with this knowledge is necessary.

Customer Choice   Travel and insurance agents provide a retailing service for customers—they represent the services of multiple suppliers. If a traveler needed to visit six or eight different travel agencies, each of which carried the services of a single supplier, imagine the effort a customer would need to make to plan a trip! Independent insurance agents have the right to sell a wide variety of insurance, which allows them to offer customers a choice. These types of agents also are able to compare prices across suppliers and get the best prices for their clients.

Challenges of Delivering Service through Agents and Brokers

Loss of Control over Pricing and Other Aspects of Marketing   As representatives of service principals and experts on customer markets, agents and brokers are typically empowered to negotiate price, configure services, and otherwise alter the marketing of a principal's service. This issue could be particularly important—and possibly detrimental—when a service provider depends on a particular (high) price to convey a level of service quality. If the price can be changed, it might drop to a level that undermines the quality image. In addition, the agent has the flexibility to give different prices to different customers. As long as the customers are geographically dispersed, this will not create a problem for the service principal; however, if buyers compare prices and realize they are being given different prices, they may perceive the service principal as unfair or unethical.

Representation of Multiple Service Principals   As we already discussed, when independent agents represent multiple suppliers they offer customer choice. From the perspective of the service principal, however, customer choice means that the agent represents—and in many cases advocates—a competitive service offering. This is the same challenge a manufacturer confronts when distributing products in a retail store. Only in rare cases are its products the only ones in a given category on the retail floor. In a service context, consider the use of independent insurance agents. These agents carry a range of insurance products from different companies, serving as a surrogate service retail store for customers. When they find a customer who needs insurance, they sell from their portfolio the offerings that best match customers' requirements.

Electronic Channels

Electronic channels are the only service distributors that do not require direct human interaction. What they do require is some predesigned service (almost always information, education, or entertainment) and an electronic vehicle to deliver it. We are all familiar with telephone and television channels and the Internet and Web and may be aware of the other electronic vehicles that are currently under development. The consumer and business services that are made possible through these vehicles include movies on demand, interactive news and music, banking and financial services, multimedia libraries and databases, distance learning, desktop videoconferencing, remote health services, and interactive, network-based games.

The more a service relies on technology and/or equipment for service production and the less it relies on face-to-face contact with service providers, the less the service is characterized by inseparability and nonstandardization. As you will see in the following section using electronic channels overcomes some of the problems associated with service inseparability and allows a form of standardization not previously possible in most services. Table 13.3 summarizes the benefits and challenges of electronic distribution.

Benefits of Electronic Channels

Consistent Delivery for Standardized Services Electronic channels such as television and telecommunication do not alter the service, as channels with human interaction tend to do. Unlike delivery from a personal provider, electronic delivery does not interpret the service and execute it according to that interpretation. Its delivery is likely to be the same in all transmissions.

Distribution of television programming from networks through affiliate television

TABLE 13.3 **Benefits and Challenges in Electronic Distribution of Services**	**Benefits**	**Challenges**
	Consistent delivery for standardized services	Customers are active, not passive
	Low cost	Lack of control of the electronic environment
	Customer convenience	Price competition
	Wide distribution	Inability to customize with highly standardized services
	Customer choice and ability to customize	Lack of consistency due to customer involvement
	Quick customer feedback	Requires changes in consumer behavior
		Security concerns
		Competition from widening geographies

and radio stations illustrates standardized electronic distribution. Networks create and finance programming including shows, news, and sports and distribute them through local stations in return for fees and advertising dollars. In most cases, the local stations deliver what is fed to them through the networks. Local stations can elect not to carry a particular show because of low ratings or lack of fit with the local market. They can also refuse to carry advertising spots that are judged in bad taste or too controversial. Except for these situations, which are not common, what is distributed through electronic channels is what the service creator sends.

Low Cost   Electronic media offer more efficient means of delivery than does interpersonal distribution. For example, the cost of reaching buyers using a direct sales force has been estimated to exceed $150 per interaction, whereas the use of electronic media such as television or radio often costs less than $30 per *thousand* interactions. Critics could rightly claim that the personal sales interaction is more powerful and effective, but with interactive media service advertisers will be able to gain some of the credibility benefits (being able to answer individual questions or tailor the service for individuals) of personal interaction.

Customer Convenience   With electronic channels, customers are able to access a firm's services when and where they want. "Retailers still tell customers, You have to come to us. But online consumers are saying, No way—*you* have to come to *us*. My place, my time is the new mantra of consumers everywhere."[17] Just as catalog shopping freed working women from the perceived drudgeries of having to go to the mall—and fattened the purses of forward-thinking companies that recognized an underserved market—e-commerce is changing the way people shop. Many mail-order companies still limit their hours of availability, a real mistake if they are going to match the customer convenience of being able to order online 24 hours a day, seven days a week. For the marketer, electronic channels allow access to a large group of customers who would otherwise be unavailable to them because of busy schedules that do not allow them to shop in other ways. One has only to witness the incredible success of amazon.com to realize this customer benefit and to see its potential for profitability for companies.

Wide Distribution   Electronic channels do more than allow the service provider to interact with a large number of end users. They also allow the service provider to interact (often simultaneously) with a large number of intermediaries. The costs and effort to inform, select, and motivate nonelectronic channels are higher than the costs to accomplish the same activities with electronic channels. Many franchisers are now finding that prospecting through the Internet provides better-qualified franchisees than the traditional methods of mainstream advertising and trade shows. Seattle-based World Inspection Network, a franchiser of home inspection operators, increased its franchisee pool fivefold using evaluation and prequalification on the Internet.[18]

Customer Choice and Ability to Customize   Consider the options that will be available in movies and videos to customers who use video-on-demand services. Just as Dell Computer, a physical product, allows customers to configure entire products to their own particular needs and desires, the Internet will allow many companies to design services from the beginning. Suppose you want to renovate your kitchen, for example. It is now possible to go to many Internet sites, specify your requirements, and order what you wish. Whether a large retailer such as Home Depot or a small start-up company is the supplier, you get exactly what you want.

Quick Customer Feedback   Rapid customer feedback is without doubt one of the major strengths of e-commerce. Companies can find out immediately what customers think of services and of their transactions and can gain far higher participation from customers in surveys. With quick customer feedback, changes can be made rapidly to service assortments, problems can be addressed immediately, and the learning cycles of companies can speed up dramatically.

Challenges in Distributing Services through Electronic Channels

Customers Are Active, Not Passive, and Must Be Enticed   Traditional advertising media such as magazines and television consider the customer a passive receiver of their messages. A customer reading an article or watching a television program will most likely see the advertisement. We know that not all customers stay in the room for a television advertisement, but most of us see hundreds of ads a day and accept this as an inevitable by-product of consuming entertainment and informational media. The user of the Web, however, is different:

> It's not that Web users aren't interested in learning about new products and services or getting a great buy on an old standby, but they want to learn on their own terms. They want the choice to click or not, to view or not, and anything more than the gentlest form of persuasion from an advertiser is likely to be construed as an intrusion.[19]

The idea of presenting to Web users the advertising information the service provider wants is not acceptable. "The Web is not about push; it's about suck: Online consumers can suck out of cyberspace whatever interests them and leave behind whatever doesn't."[20] What does this mean to online service marketers? The advertising must educate, entertain, and draw the customer in. There must be clear benefits for the customer to read the marketer's information. One of the most promising approaches, called "permission-based marketing," is a method of enticing customers to visit websites for the payback they receive. The company designs games, offers prizes, creates contests, and in other ways sends customers to websites to help advertisers build relationships with customers.

Lack of Control of the Electronic Environment   It did not take long for the Internet to face the challenges of unregulated media. As soon as the network became popular, pornographic and other controversial material started to appear. When a service's advertising or information appears in proximity to such material, the result can be a negative spillover effect. It is similar to the challenge advertisers face in using print media such as *TV Guide*—the advertiser has to be careful to separate its advertising for banking from the ever-present ads for balding concealment devices and quick weight loss programs. With the *TV Guide,* however, the advertiser could request or pay for the right positioning, something not possible on the Internet at this time.

Price Competition   One of the traditional differences between goods and services has been the difficulty of directly comparing features and prices of services with each other. Whereas goods can typically be compared in retail settings, few retail settings exist that offer services from multiple sources. The Internet has changed all that. Services such as travelocity.com and Priceline.com make it simple for customers to compare prices for a wide variety of services. Priceline.com allows customers to name their price for a service such as an airline ticket, wait until Priceline.com finds an airline willing to accept it, then purchase the ticket. Never has the customer had such ability to bid on prices for services. In Chapter 16 we describe another type of price competition spawned by the Internet: the Internet auction as presented by such companies as eBay, which sells millions of products and services in more than 1,000 categories.

Inability to Customize with Highly Standardized Electronic Services Some of you have experienced learning college basics through large, video-transmitted courses. If you consider what you missed in learning that way compared with learning directly from a professor, you will understand this challenge. In mass sections, you cannot interact directly with the professor, ask questions, raise points for clarification, or experience the connection that you receive in person. In electronic classes—as in videoconferences that are springing up in many businesses—the quality of the service can also be impeded by the way the audience reacts (or doesn't react) in those situations. People talk among themselves, leave, laugh, and criticize, among other behaviors.

Customization can be increased in these channels. In college courses such as those described at the beginning of this chapter, small groups of students can be led by teaching assistants to discuss the electronic lecture. Call-in questions can simulate direct interaction. Two-way video can control the behavior of receivers.

Lack of Consistency because of Customer Involvement While electronic channels are very effective in minimizing the inconsistency from employees or providers of service, customer variability still presents a problem. Many times the customer produces the service himself using the technology, leading to errors or frustration unless the technology is highly user-friendly. Maneuvering online can sometimes be overwhelming, and not all websites are easy to use. Furthermore, a large percentage of customers do not have computers and, even if they do, may be reluctant to try or continue using the medium.

Requires Changes in Consumer Behavior A consumer purchasing a service through electronic channels engages in very different behavior from a consumer entering a retail store and talking to a salesperson. Considerable changes—in the willingness to search for information, in the willingness to perform some aspects of the services themselves, in the acceptance of different levels of service—are necessary when customers use electronic channels. Behavior change is difficult, even for a consumer wanting to make a change; therefore marketers wishing to motivate consumers to alter long-established patterns will be challenged.

Security Concerns One issue confronting marketers using electronic channels is the lack of security of information, particularly health and financial information. Many customers are still hesitant about giving credit-card numbers on the Web and Internet (see the Technology Spotlight). These problems can undermine consumers' trust in the Internet as a safe place to do business. Companies have devised ways to keep hackers out and thereby protect the systems, but many of these are temporary solutions. Among the specific problems are penetration, vandalism, eavesdropping, and impersonation.[21] With penetration, intruders steal passwords and exploit unprotected modems and connections, actually taking over the sites. With vandalism, hackers crash corporate and other computers. To combat these problems, firewalls and other software scan for unusual activity. With eavesdropping, hackers snoop on information as it passes through multiple computers to the Internet. The typical solution is encryption software that scrambles electronic mail and other data to make it unintelligible to eavesdroppers. Finally, with impersonation criminals could use phony identities

Technology Spotlight
Nine Reasons to Worry about Privacy in Electronic Channels

Studies indicate that as many as 94 percent of people are concerned about privacy on the Internet. According to Adam Cohen of *Time* magazine, they have reasons to worry. Recently he outlined the nine areas that privacy advocates and law enforcement are emphasizing in their fight for privacy.

1. *Someone might steal your identity.* More than 500,000 Americans have their identities stolen each year. In one high-profile 2001 case, Abraham Abdallah was caught with the Social Security numbers, bank account information, and mothers' maiden names of some of the 400 richest people in the world, including Steven Spielberg, Oprah Winfrey, and Martha Stewart.

2. *You may reveal information about yourself in cyberspace.* The "cookie" files that collect data about you on the Internet—including your name, e-mail addresses, and address—can be captured and combined with other information on the sites you visit. For example, Eli Lilly started an e-mail campaign reminding more than 600 users of its depression, bulimia, and obsessive-compulsive disorder medications to take their dosages. When the company decided to discontinue the service, it notified subscribers via e-mail. But due to a technical problem, every person who received the message was able to see the entire list of e-mail addresses! Sometimes the cookies keep information that you may not want known, such as what prescriptions you take or what videos you watch.

3. *Personal information you give to a website might be sold or stolen.* E-commerce sites routinely share or sell your information. Macys.com, for example, was found to be giving away information from its bridal registry to business partners, and amazon.com considers customer data an asset it may sell or transfer. Further, if a site goes bankrupt, it could be legally required to sell your data to the highest bidder. Although the defunct site E-Tours had a privacy policy that explicitly promised that its information

would not be sold to third parties, Jeeves Inc.—the company that purchased its assets—considered its customer demographic database highly valuable. And theft is also possible: Egghead.com disclosed in 2000 that hackers had broken into its system and accessed millions of credit card numbers.

4. *You may enter your credit card number on a fake website.* Russian hackers created a counterfeit website mimicking the real home page of PayPal, the online fund transfer service. They e-mailed PayPal users and got them to click on a hyperlink with the spoof site's domain name, www.paypai.com.

5. *The government may give out your home address, Social Security number, and other personal information online.* In Ohio, anyone who types your name into a county database can learn your address and how much your house is worth. In Wisconsin, arrest and court records, including traffic violations, are available online. And federal courts have put many of their records of Social Security numbers, financial assets, and names of minor children online through a system called Public Access to Court Electronic Records.

6. *Companies and people who don't like you may broadcast your private information on the Internet.* Data brokers provide background information to employers, creditors, and others who use it legitimately. But many sell Social Security numbers and private information to anyone willing to pay, including thieves and stalkers.

7. *Someone you know may use your computer to spy on you.* Companies have the legal right to monitor their employees' Web surfing, e-mail, and instant messaging. Employers, including the *New York Times* and Dow Chemical, have fired workers for sending inappropriate e-mail. But the fastest-growing area for Internet spying is the home. SpectorSoft, a manufacturer of spyware, targets its products to spouses and romantic partners who want to check what

to buy goods and services or create bogus businesses. A form of encryption technology is used to deal with this problem and special service companies confirm signature holders.[22]

their partners are doing online. "In just one day of running Spector on my home PC, I was able to identify my fiancé's true personality," a testimonial on the company website says; "I found all 17 of his girlfriends."

8. *A stranger may use your computer to spy on you.* Hackers can get into your computer and look through everything on it, particularly if it is connected through cable or DSL connections. Viruses are also a threat. Remember the "I Love You" virus? It retrieved passwords from victims' computers to send back to its creator.

9. *You may have a cyberstalker.* Working Halt Online Abuse says it receives reports of nearly 100 cases of cyberstalking a week. The stalkers meet their victims via e-mail, chat groups, newsgroups, and instant messaging.

A recent study by Harris Interactive designed to understand consumer perceptions of online privacy found

- Consumers worry that their information will be used for purposes other than those stated in a company's privacy policy.

- Privacy seals (such as those shown in this spotlight) increase consumer confidence, with almost half (49 percent) of those who have seen them saying they are more willing to provide personal information as a result.

- Only 15 percent of consumers are using existing tools and technologies to protect their privacy.

- Consumers have mixed opinions about the benefits of personalization, saying that they give up privacy for personalization.

What is being done to deal with these privacy concerns? Although the Constitution is silent on the matter of privacy—and the courts have never found a general right to privacy—over 250 pieces of privacy legislation have been presented to Congress. Some states have Internet

privacy policies. New federal regulations for companies in health care (Heath Insurance Portability and Accountability Act) and financial services (Gramm–Leach–Bliley Act) require Internet companies to post clear, highly visible privacy policies on the Web and to remind users that they can opt out of marketing initiatives that may violate their privacy. The Children's Online Privacy Protection Act limits the collection of information from children under the age of 13, and the FTC plans to increase by 50 percent the resources it dedicates to privacy protection.

Sources: A. Cohen, "Internet Insecurity," *Time,* July 2, 2001, pp. 44–51; G. Anders, "Can You Keep a Secret?" *Fast Company,* June 2001, pp. 186–89; "Study Examines Trust Gap between Consumers and Businesses," *Direct Marketing,* June 2001, pp. 26–27; L. Dobrow, "Tread Carefully on Privacy," *Advertising Age,* October 29, 2001, p. S6; J. C. Montana, "Data Mining: A Slippery Slope," *Information Management Journal,* October 2001, pp. 50–54.

Competition from Widening Geographies Many services were somewhat protected from competition because customers had limited choice among the providers they could physically drive to. Banks, for example, supplied all local customers with checking accounts, savings accounts, and mortgages. In fact, it used to be said that since services could not be transported they were limited in their scope. Not any longer—and not with electronic channels. Virtually all financial services can be purchased from institutions far from the local area.

Electronic Channels in Action

The possibilities for selling and servicing on the Internet and other electronic channels are virtually limitless. Some baseball teams let you see the view of the field from any seat before you buy your ticket. At Lands' End you can create a model onscreen with your figure, then try all the clothes on the model to find out how they will look on you. Progressive real estate firms let you tour homes as if you were walking through them. Some of the most interesting and innovative applications of the Web, Internet, and other electronic channels are illustrated next.

Interactive Television Interactive television is an electronic channel that has been developed or proposed in many different forms, but essentially consists of television where the viewer participates actively rather than passively receiving the information. One might wonder why anything beyond the 500+ channels now available from some cable companies is necessary, but the possibilities are compelling. Perhaps the simplest form is video-on-demand, a more sophisticated version of Spectravision, the service offered in hotel rooms. With video-on-demand, provided by companies such as OnSet in the Northeast, a customer can choose from 150 movie titles on the cable system and watch as if using a VCR—pause, rewind, and stop as desired. It's like a video rental store right in the cable system for which customers pay a monthly fee of around $7 and a per-movie cost of approximately $4. Another, more interactive version of the technology is offered. While a customer watches TV, a small icon will appear in the corner of the screen on various channels. When the customer clicks the remote, a menu of information will show. For example, on ESPN, sports scores will be available with one option; with another, viewers can participate in a poll; with another, a fan can purchase a new sports video. The technology is free to customers and involves the insertion of a software application in the cable box. The network and cable companies then pass along tiny "applets" containing the information. Companies sign up to offer their services or information for a fee in return for customer orders and data (such as how many consumers clicked to get more information about their product).[23] Even more exciting are the possibilities of choosing different camera angles for sports events; listening to 30 channels of prerecorded, commercial-free music; banking; and playing video games with customers in other households.

Super ATMs Move over, standard banking ATMs. Enter multipurpose ATMs: ATMs that allow you to purchase discount lift tickets and ski lessons for Lake Tahoe resorts at no fee (Wells Fargo ATMs); ATMs that show movie clips and commercials while you wait for your money (EDS ATMs in San Diego); ATMs that convert currencies on international flights using satellites to send card information to your bank (Inflight ATI in Irvine, CA); ATMs that let you book flights and print tickets for any airline for $4 to $7 (Docunet in San Francisco). Other companies are experimenting with machines that sell stamps and are customizing ATM screens to make your electronic banking even easier than it now is.[24]

Online Travel Online travel has been one of the biggest success stories in electronic channels. One of the few industries to produce profitable companies, the industry had more than $18 billion in travel revenues completed online in 2001. The Internet has been an extremely effective channel for travel for three key reasons:

1. Prices are more competitive than offline prices, and the technology can conjure up literally thousands of providers in an instant.

2. Online travel companies have no inventory costs and therefore low cost of goods sold.

3. Sites obtain significant advertising revenue due to focused clientele, with advertisers knowing that all users are potential buyers of their travel services.[25]

Expedia.com and priceline.com are notable, but the most successful, profitable online travel site is Travelocity.com. Like other online travel sites, it sells airline tickets, hotel rooms, and car rentals directly to consumers, avoiding travel agents. It has held the number one spot in online travel sites since its inception in 1996 by Sabre Holdings, Inc. In 2001 it had record revenues (up 76 percent from the previous year), 29 million members, and a profit of $55.5 million. The site earned the loyalty of its users by being very customer-focused in an industry that is all too often technology focused. Based on focus groups and surveys to assess site design and ease of use, the company created excellent customer service, carefully detailed explanations, and guarantees of its credit card security and privacy policies (see Figure 13.1 for Travelocity's U.K. website). The company has a special help desk that focuses on taking credit card numbers over the telephone for those afraid to input them online. The site also offers instantaneous price quotes and the ability to track prices to cities customers plan to visit.

A unique strength of Travelocity has been its ability to nurture an online community of travelers who post online reviews for travel services around the world. Many users e-mail each other directly, further cementing their loyalty to the site. The average customer—a 41-year-old female with a household income of $84,169—spends almost 25 minutes on the site and looks at 23.5 pages while she's there.[26]

Investing Online   Prior to the downturn in 2001, online trading had become one of the most successful examples of electronic service distribution, and the most effective company in implementing online trading has been Charles Schwab. Schwab was one of the first no-frills discount brokers who opted to target customers who didn't want service and advice as much as they wanted lower prices. Schwab offers personalized information to the customer—real-time quotes, news, historical financial data, and sophisticated software tools—and allows customers to set up their own personal accounts and asset allocation models. Schwab went outside the company to an expert in Web design called Razorfish, who provided a consistent look to the site as well as made it easy to navigate. The company now shows investors the total returns on the securities in their portfolios and offers graphically rich e-mails to alert them when their portfolios are not in balance with their asset allocation models.

Be Your Own Shoemaker   Companies that mass-market consumer items such as packaged goods have been challenged to use the Internet as a channel to increase loyalty and create customer excitement. Nike.com found success when the company launched an Internet service allowing shoppers using its website to create personalized shoes. Users can select shoes, color them to fit their tastes, and then emblazon their own names on the shoes. This costs just $10 more than off-the-rack shoes in the stores, and customers now buy thousands of such custom pairs per day. The initiative was just

FIGURE 13.1
Travelocity's U.K.
Website

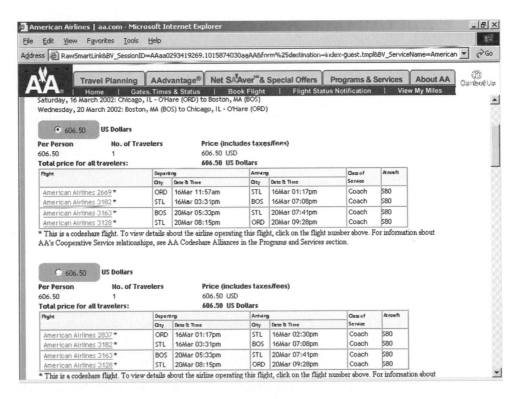

one step toward far greater custom services on the Web, including using the Internet to size their feet and custom fit shoes to unique foot sizes.

STRATEGIES FOR EFFECTIVE SERVICE DELIVERY THROUGH INTERMEDIARIES

Service principals, of course, want to manage their service intermediaries to improve service performance, solidify their images, and increase profits and revenues. The principal has a variety of choices, which range from strict contractual and measurement control to partnering with intermediaries in a joint effort to improve service to the customer. One of the biggest issues a principal faces is whether to view intermediaries as extensions of its company, as customers, or as partners. We discuss three categories of intermediary management strategies: control strategies, empowerment strategies, and partnering strategies.

Control Strategies

In this category, the service principal believes that intermediaries will perform best when it creates standards both for revenues and service performance, measures results, and compensates or rewards on the basis of performance level. To use these strategies the principal must be the most powerful participant in the channel, possessing unique services with strong consumer demand or loyalty, or other forms of economic power.

Measurement

Some franchisers maintain control of the service quality delivered by their franchisees by ongoing measurement programs that feed data back to the principal. Virtually all automobile dealers' sales and service performance is monitored regularly by the manufacturer, which creates the measurement program, administers it, and maintains control of the information. The company surveys customers at key points in the service encounter sequence: after sale, 30 days out, 90 days out, and after a year. The manufacturer designs the survey instruments (some of them with the assistance of dealer councils) and obtains the customer feedback directly. On the basis of this information, the manufacturer rewards and recognizes both individuals and dealerships that perform well and can potentially punish those that perform poorly. The obvious advantage to this approach is that the manufacturer retains control; however, the trust and goodwill between manufacturers and dealers can easily be eroded if dealers feel that the measurement is used to control and punish.

Review

Some franchisers control through terminations, nonrenewals, quotas, and restrictive supplier sources. Expansion and encroachment are two of the tactics being used today. Another means by which franchisers exert control over franchisees is through quotas and sales goals, typically by offering price breaks after a certain volume is attained.

Empowerment Strategies

Empowerment strategies, where the service principal allows greater flexibility to intermediaries based on the belief that their talents are best revealed in participation rather than acquiescence, are useful when the service principal is new or lacks sufficient power to govern the channel using control strategies. In empowerment strategies, the principal provides information, research, or processes to help intermediaries perform well in service.

Help the Intermediary Develop Customer-Oriented Service Processes

Individual intermediaries rarely have the funds to sponsor their own customer research studies or training programs. One way for a company to improve intermediary performance is to conduct research or standard-setting studies relating to service performance, then provide them as a service to intermediaries. As an example, H&R Block amassed its customer information and codified it in a set of 10 "Ultimate Client Service" standards, which are displayed in each office. The standards include the following:

- No client will wait more than 30 minutes in the waiting area.

- Phone calls will be answered by the fourth ring, and no caller will be on hold for more than one minute.

- Every tax preparation client will receive a thorough interview to determine the client's lowest legal tax liability.

- Accurately prepared and checked returns will be delivered in four days or fewer.

Rather than administer this customer program from the home office, which could lead it to be perceived as a measurement "hammer," the company asks each franchisee to devise a way to measure the standards in its own offices, then report this information to H&R Block.

Provide Needed Support Systems

After Ford Motor Company conducted customer research and identified six sales standards and six service standards that address the most important customer expectations, it found that dealers and service centers did not know how to implement, measure, and improve service with them. For example, one sales standard specified that customers be approached within the first minute they enter the dealership and be offered help when and if the customer needs it. While dealers could see that this standard was desirable, they did not immediately know how to make it happen. Ford stepped in and provided the research and process support to help the dealers. As another form of support, the company created national advertising featuring dealers discussing the quality care standards.

In airlines and hotels, as well as other travel and ticketing services, the service principal's reservation system is an important support system. Holiday Inn has a franchise service delivery system that adds value to the Holiday Inn franchise and differentiates it from competitors.

Develop Intermediaries to Deliver Service Quality

In this strategy, the service originator invests in training or other forms of development to improve the skills and knowledge of intermediaries and their employees. Prudential Real Estate Associates, a national franchiser of real estate brokers, recently engaged in a companywide program of service excellence. To teach sales associates (real estate agents) about what buyers and sellers expect, the company first conducted focus group interviews with end customers, then created a half-day training program to communicate what the research revealed. To teach brokers (the companies that employ the sales associates), the company created a highly successful operations review that examined the operational and financial aspects of the brokers, assessed their levels of effectiveness, then communicated individually with each broker about the specific issues that needed to be addressed and the approaches that would be successful in improving performance.

Change to a Cooperative Management Structure

Companies such as Taco Bell use the technique of empowerment to manage and motivate franchisees. They develop worker teams in their outlets to hire, discipline, and handle financial tasks such as deposits and audits. Taco Bell deliberately reduced levels of management (regional managers used to oversee 5 stores; now they oversee 50 stores) and reports improvements in revenue, employee morale, and profits.

Partnering Strategies

The group of strategies with the highest potential for effectiveness involves partnering with intermediaries to learn together about end customers, set specifications, improve delivery, and communicate honestly. This approach capitalizes on the skills and strengths of both principal and intermediary and engenders a sense of trust that improves the relationship.

Alignment of Goals

One of the most successful approaches to partnering involves aligning company and intermediary goals early in the process. Both the service principal and the intermediary have individual goals that they strive to achieve. If channel members can see that they benefit the ultimate consumer of services and in the process optimize their own revenues and profit, they begin the relationship with a target in mind. Sonic Corp, a drive-in hamburger chain, is attempting to retain open relationships with its franchisees, continually adapting to changing customer needs and franchisee suggestions.

Consultation and Cooperation

This strategy is not as dramatic as setting joint goals, but it does result in intermediaries participating in decisions. In this approach, which could involve virtually any topic, from compensation to service quality to the service environment, the principal makes a point of consulting intermediaries and asking for their opinions and views before establishing policy. Alpha-Graphics, a franchiser of rapid printing services based in Tucson, Arizona, habitually consults its franchisees to hear how they think the operation should be run. When the franchiser found that the outlets needed greater support in promotion, the company began to make customer mailings for franchisees. When the franchiser found that many franchisees were dissatisfied with the one-sided contracts they received, the principal revised contracts to make it easier for them to leave the system, changed fees to reflect a sliding scale linked to volume, and allowed franchisees to select the ways they use their royalty fees. This approach makes the franchisees feel that they have some control over the way they do business and also generates a steady stream of improvement ideas. Taco John's, the second-largest Mexican fast-food chain, has torn up its old contracts to forge a new state-of-the-art, cooperative relationship with franchisees.

Summary

This chapter discussed the benefits and challenges of delivering service through intermediaries. Service intermediaries perform many important functions for the service principal—coproducing the service, making services locally available, and functioning as the bond between the principal and the customer. The focus in service distribution is on identifying ways to bring the customer and principal or its representatives together.

In contrast to channels for products, channels for services are almost always direct, if not to the customer then to the intermediary that sells to the customer. Many of the primary functions distribution channels serve—inventorying, securing, and taking title to goods—have no meaning in services because of services' intangibility. Because services cannot be owned, most have no titles or rights that can be passed along a delivery channel. Because services are intangible and perishable, inventories cannot exist, making warehousing dispensable. In general, because services can't be produced, warehoused, and then retailed as goods can, many channels available to goods producers are not feasible for service firms.

Four forms of distribution in service were described in the chapter: franchisees, agents/brokers, and direct and electronic channels. The benefits and challenges of each type of intermediary were discussed, and examples of firms successful in delivering services through each type were detailed. Discussion centered on strategies that could be used by service principals to improve management of intermediaries.

Discussion Questions

1. In what specific ways does the distribution of services differ from the distribution of goods?

2. Which of the reasons for channel conflict described at the beginning of this chapter is the most problematic? Why? Based on the chapter, and in particular the strategies discussed at the end of the chapter, what can be done to address the problem you selected? Rank the possible strategies from most effective to least effective.

3. Identify other service firms that are company owned and see whether the services they provide are more consistent than ones provided by the franchisees mentioned in this chapter.

4. List five services that could be distributed on the Internet that are not mentioned in this chapter. Why are these particular services appropriate for electronic distribution? Choose two that you particularly advocate. How would you address the challenges to electronic media discussed in this chapter?

5. List services that are sold through selling agents. Why is the use of agents the chosen method of distribution for these services? Could any be distributed in the other ways described in this chapter?

6. What are the main differences between agents and brokers?

7. What types of services are bought through purchasing agents? What qualifies a purchasing agent to represent a buyer in these transactions? Why does the buyer not engage in the purchase herself, rather than hiring someone to do so?

8. Which of the three categories of strategies for effective service delivery through intermediaries do you believe is most successful? Why? Why are the other two categories less successful?

Exercises

1. Develop a brief franchising plan for a service concept or idea that you believe could be successful.

2. Visit a franchisee and discuss the pros and cons of the arrangement from his or her perspective. How closely does this list of benefits and challenges fit the one

provided in this chapter? What would you add to the chapter's list to reflect the experience of the franchisee you interviewed?

3. Select a service industry with which you are familiar. How do service principals in that industry distribute their services? Develop possible approaches to manage intermediaries using the three categories of strategies in the last section of this chapter. Which approach do you believe would be most effective? Why? Which approaches are currently used by service principals in the industry?

4. On the Internet, locate three services that you believe are interesting. What benefits does buying on the Internet have over buying those services elsewhere?

Notes

1. L. Bertagnoli, "Education Reservation," *Marketing News,* February 12, 2001, p. 4.
2. P. Mangan, "What Is Distance Learning?" *Management Quarterly,* Fall, 2001 pp. 30–35.
3. Bertagnoli, "Education Reservation."
4. A. E. Hancock, "The Evolving Terrain of Distance Learning," *Satellite Communications,* March 1999, pp. 24ff.
5. J. McCormick, "The New School," *Newsweek,* April 24, 2000; www.unext.com.
6. S. Stecklow, "At Phoenix University, Class Can Be Anywhere—Even in Cyberspace," *The Wall Street Journal,* September 12, 1994, p. A1.
7. Hancock, "The Evolving Terrain of Distance Learning," p. 24.
8. A. Fisher, "Getting a BA Online," *Fortune,* February 1, 1999, p. 144.
9. L. J. Goff, "E-Learning Evangelists," *Computerworld,* September 10, 2001, pp. 40–41.
10. Hancock, "The Evolving Terrain of Distance Learning," p. 25.
11. A. Senzek, "Surfing for Credit," *Business Mexico,* July 2001, pp. 46–47.
12. E. Dash, "The Virtual MBA: A Work in Progress," *Business Week,* October 2, 2000, p. 96.
13. R. Cwiklik, "Pieces of the Puzzle—a Different Course: For Many People, College Will No Longer Be a Specific Place, or a Specific Time," *The Wall Street Journal,* November 6, 1998, p. R31.
14. A. E. Serwer, "Trouble in Franchise Nation," *Fortune,* March 6, 1995, pp. 115–18.
15. L. Bongiorno, "Franchise Fracas," *Business Week,* March 22, 1993, pp. 115–18.
16. Serwer, "Trouble in Franchise Nation," p. 116.
17. G. Hamel and J. Sampler, "The e-Corporation," *Fortune,* December 7, 1998, pp. 80–92.
18. C. A. Laurie, "Franchisers Meet Challenges of Growth, Change," *Franchising World,* March/April 1999, pp. 11–14.
19. Hamel and Sampler, "The e-Corporation," p. 82.
20. Ibid., p. 82.
21. D. Clark, "Safety First," *The Wall Street Journal,* December 7, 1998, p. R14.
22. Ibid.
23. M. Gunther, "Interactive TV: It's Baaack," *Fortune,* July 20, 1998, pp. 136–37.
24. K. K. Choquette, "Super ATMs Sell Lift Tickets, Exchange Currencies," *USA Today,* January 19, 1998, p. B1.
25. D. Coleman, "Internet Success Stories: Travelocity," australia.internet.com, November 12, 2001, p. 1.
26. C. Rosen, "Great Sites: Travelocity," informationweek.com, August 27, 2001.

14

MANAGING DEMAND AND CAPACITY

This chapter's objectives are to

1. Explain the underlying issue for capacity-constrained services: lack of inventory capability.

2. Present the implications of time, labor, equipment, and facilities constraints combined with variations in demand patterns.

3. Lay out strategies for matching supply and demand through (a) shifting demand to match capacity or (b) flexing capacity to meet demand.

4. Demonstrate the benefits and risks of yield management strategies in forging a balance among capacity utilization, pricing, market segmentation, and financial return.

5. Provide strategies for managing waiting lines for times when capacity and demand cannot be aligned.

How to Fill 281 Rooms 365 Days of the Year

The Ritz-Carlton Hotel in Phoenix, Arizona, is an upscale hotel in the center of a metropolitan area of over 2 million people. It ranked 17th in the 2001 *Travel and Leisure* ratings of the top 100 hotels in the United States.[1] The hotel has 281 luxury rooms, two restaurants, beautiful pools, and spacious meeting and conference facilities. These restaurants and meeting facilities are available to guests 365 days and nights of the year. Yet natural demand for them varies tremendously. During the tourist season from November through mid-April, demand for rooms is high, often exceeding available space. From mid-May through September, however, when temperatures regularly exceed 100 degrees Fahrenheit, demand for rooms drops considerably. Because the hotel caters to business travelers and business meetings, demand has a weekly cycle in addition to the seasonal fluctuations. Business travelers don't stay over weekends. Thus demand for rooms from the hotel's primary market segment drops on Friday and Saturday nights.

To smooth the peaks and valleys of demand for its facilities, the Ritz-Carlton in Phoenix has employed a variety of strategies. Group business (primarily business conferences) is pursued throughout the year to fill the lower demand periods from Thursday through Sunday. The timing works well for many groups who can also take advantage of the lower air fares available for staying over Saturday night. During the hot summer months the hotel encourages local Phoenix and nearby Tucson residents to experience the luxury of the hotel on weekends. One creative package included an attractively priced Friday or Saturday night stay at the hotel combined with a "progressive dinner" at nearby restaurants. The progressive dinner started with a reception in the hotel, a walk to one restaurant for appetizers, followed by dinner at a second restaurant. The evening finished with champagne and dessert in the guests' room. By encouraging local people to use the hotel, the hotel increases its weekend occupancy while residents of the community get a chance to enjoy an experience they probably wouldn't be able to afford during the high season.

Most downtown hotels face the same weekly demand fluctuations that the Phoenix Ritz-Carlton deals with, and many have found a partial solution by catering to families and children on the weekends.[2] For many dual-career couples, weekend getaways are a primary form of relaxation and vacation. And with discounted air fares for Saturday night stays, many families can afford to travel on weekends. The downtown hotels cater to these couples and families by offering discounted room rates, child-oriented activities and amenities, and an environment where families feel comfortable. For example, at the Costa Mesa Marriott Suites in Orange County, California, employees dress casually on the weekend and toasters are put on the breakfast buffet, just for kids. The Hyatt Regency Reston in Reston, Virginia, rented its 21 executive suites for kids' slumber parties on the weekend. The Chicago Hilton initiated a "Vacation Station" program that included gifts and games for kids, plenty of cribs in inventory, and gummi bears in the minibars. The result for the Chicago Hilton is that Saturday nights are usually sold out and Friday nights' average occupancy is frequently higher than its weekday occupancy level.

For the Ritz-Carlton Hotel in Phoenix and the other hotels just mentioned, managing demand and utilizing the hotel's fixed capacity of rooms, restaurants, and meeting facilities can be a seasonal, weekly, and even daily challenge. While the hotel industry epitomizes the challenges of demand and capacity management, many service providers face similar problems. For example, tax accountants and air-conditioning maintenance services face seasonal demand fluctuations, whereas services such as commuter trains and restaurants face weekly and even hourly variations in customer demand. For some, demand is predictable, as for a tax accountant. For others, such as management or technology consultants, demand may be less predictable, fluctuating based on customer needs and business cycles. Sometimes there is too much demand for the existing capacity and sometimes capacity sits idle.

Overuse or underuse of a service can directly contribute to gap 3—failure to deliver what was designed and specified. For example, when demand for services exceeds maximum capacity, the quality of service may drop because staff and facilities are overtaxed. And some customers may be turned away, not receiving the service at all. During periods of slow demand it may be necessary to reduce prices or cut service amenities, changing the makeup of the clientele and the nature of the service and thus running the risk of not delivering what customers expect. At the Chicago Hilton mentioned in the vignette, older travelers or business groups who are in the hotel on a weekend may resent the invasion of families and children because it changes the nature of the service they expected. At the pool, for example, collisions can occur between adults trying to swim laps and children playing water games.[3]

In this chapter we focus on the challenges of matching supply and demand in capacity-constrained services. Gap 3 can occur when organizations fail to smooth the peaks and valleys of demand, overuse their capacities, attract an inappropriate customer mix in their efforts to build demand, or rely too much on price in smoothing demand. The chapter gives you an understanding of these issues and strategies for addressing them. The effective use of capacity is frequently a key success factor for service organizations.

THE UNDERLYING ISSUE: LACK OF INVENTORY CAPABILITY

The fundamental issue underlying supply and demand management in services is the lack of inventory capability. Unlike manufacturing firms, service firms cannot build up inventories during periods of slow demand to use later when demand increases. This lack of inventory capability is due to the perishability of services and their simultaneous production and consumption. An airline seat that is not sold on a given flight cannot be resold the following day: the productive capacity of that seat has perished. Similarly, an hour of a lawyer's billable time cannot be saved from one day to the next. Services also cannot be transported from one place to another or transferred from person to person. Thus the Ritz-Carlton's services cannot be moved to an alternative location in the summer months—say, to the Pacific Coast where summers are ideal for tourists and demand for hotel rooms is high.

The lack of inventory capability combined with fluctuating demand leads to a variety of potential outcomes, as illustrated in Figure 14.1.[4] The horizontal lines in Figure 14.1 indicate service capacity, and the curved line indicates customer demand for the service. In many services, capacity is fixed; thus capacity can be designated by a flat

FIGURE 14.1 **Variations in Demand Relative to Capacity**

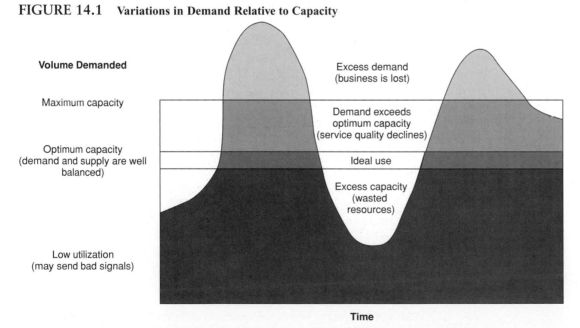

Source: Reprinted from C. Lovelock, "Getting the Most Out of Your Productive Capacity," in *Product Plus* (Boston: McGraw Hill, 1994), chap. 16, p. 241. © 1994 by The McGraw-Hill Companies, Inc. Reprinted by permission of The McGraw-Hill Companies.

horizontal line over a certain time period. Demand for service frequently fluctuates, however, as indicated by the curved line. The topmost horizontal line in Figure 14.1 represents maximum capacity. For example, in our opening vignette, the horizontal line would represent the Ritz-Carlton's 281 rooms, or it could represent the approximately 70,000 seats in a large university football stadium. The rooms and the seats remain constant while demand for them fluctuates. The band between the second and third horizontal lines represents optimum capacity—the best use of the capacity from the perspective of both customers and the company (optimal versus maximal capacity utilization is discussed later in the chapter). The areas in the middle of Figure 14.1 are labeled to represent four basic scenarios that can result from different combinations of capacity and demand:

1. *Excess demand.* The level of demand exceeds maximum capacity. In this situation some customers will be turned away, resulting in lost business opportunities. For the customers who do receive the service, its quality may not match what was promised because of crowding or overtaxing of staff and facilities.

2. *Demand exceeds optimum capacity.* No one is being turned away, but the quality of service may still suffer because of overuse, crowding, or staff being pushed beyond their abilities to deliver consistent quality.

3. *Demand and supply are balanced at the level of optimum capacity.* Staff and facilities are occupied at an ideal level. No one is overworked, facilities can be maintained, and customers are receiving quality service without undesirable delays.

4. *Excess capacity.* Demand is below optimum capacity. Productive resources in the form of labor, equipment, and facilities are underutilized, resulting in lost productivity and lower profits. Customers may receive excellent quality on an individual level because they have the full use of the facilities, no waiting, and complete attention from the staff. If, however, service quality depends on the presence of other customers, customers may be disappointed or may worry that they have chosen an inferior service provider.

Not all firms will be challenged equally in terms of managing supply and demand. The seriousness of the problem will depend on the *extent of demand fluctuations over time,* and the *extent to which supply is constrained* (Table 14.1).[5] Some types of organizations will experience wide fluctuations in demand (telecommunications, hospitals, transportation, restaurants), whereas others will have narrower fluctuations (insurance, laundry, banking). For some, peak demand can usually be met even when demand fluctuates (electricity, telephone), but for others peak demand may frequently exceed capacity (hospital emergency rooms, restaurants, hotels). Those firms with wide variations in demand (cells 1 and 4 in Table 14.1), and particularly those with wide fluctuations and demand that regularly exceeds capacity (cell 4), will find the issues and strategies in this chapter particularly important to their success. Those firms that find themselves in cell 3 need a "one-time-fix" to expand their capacity to match regular patterns of excessive demand. The example industries in Table 14.1 are provided to illustrate where *most* firms in those industries would likely be classified. In reality, an individual firm from any industry could find itself in any of the four cells, depending on its immediate circumstances.

To identify effective strategies for managing supply and demand fluctuations, an organization needs a clear understanding of the constraints on its capacity and the underlying demand patterns.

TABLE 14.1
Demand versus Supply

Extent to Which Supply Is Constrained	Extent of Demand Fluctuations over Time	
	Wide	Narrow
	1	2
Peak demand can usually be met without a major delay.	Electricity Natural gas Telephone Hospital maternity unit Police and fire emergencies	Insurance Legal services Banking Laundry and dry cleaning
	4	3
Peak demand regularly exceeds capacity.	Accounting and tax preparation Passenger transportation Hotels Restaurants Hospital emergency rooms	Services similar to those in 2 that have insufficient capacity for their base level of business

Source: C. H. Lovelock, "Classifying Services to Gain Strategic Marketing Insights," *Journal of Marketing* 47, no. 3 (Summer 1983): 17. Reprinted by permission from the American Marketing Association.

UNDERSTANDING CAPACITY CONSTRAINTS

As we see later in the chapter, there are some creative ways to expand and contract capacity in the short and long term, but at a given point in time we can assume service capacity is fixed. Depending on the type of service, critical fixed-capacity factors can be time, labor, equipment, facilities, or (in many cases) a combination of these.

Time, Labor, Equipment, Facilities

For some service businesses, the primary constraint on service production is *time*. For example, a lawyer, a consultant, a hairdresser, and a psychological counselor all primarily sell their time. If their time is not used productively, profits are lost. If there is excess demand, time cannot be created to satisfy it. From the point of view of the individual service provider, time is the constraint.

From the point of view of a firm that employs a large number of service providers, *labor* or staffing levels can be the primary capacity constraint. A law firm, a university department, a consulting firm, a tax accounting firm, and a repair and maintenance contractor may all face the reality that at certain times demand for their organizations' services cannot be met because the staff is already operating at peak capacity. However, it doesn't always make sense (nor may it be possible in a competitive labor market) to hire additional service providers if low demand is a reality at other times.

In other cases, *equipment* may be the critical constraint. For trucking or air-freight delivery services, the trucks or airplanes needed to service demand may be the capacity limitation. During the Christmas holidays, UPS, Federal Express, and other delivery service providers face this issue. Health clubs also deal with this limitation, particularly at certain times of the day (before work, during lunch hours, after work) and in certain months of the year. Telecommunications companies face equipment constraints when everyone wants to communicate during prime hours on holidays. For network service providers, bandwidth, servers, and switches represent their perishable capacity.

Finally, many firms face restrictions brought about by their limited *facilities*. Hotels have only a certain number of rooms to sell, airlines are limited by the number of seats on the aircraft, educational institutions are constrained by the number of rooms and

TABLE 14.2
Constraints on Capacity

Nature of the Constraint	Type of Service*
Time	Legal
	Consulting
	Accounting
	Medical
Labor	Law firm
	Accounting firm
	Consulting firm
	Health clinic
Equipment	Delivery services
	Telecommunications
	Network services
	Utilities
	Health club
Facilities	Hotels
	Restaurants
	Hospitals
	Airlines
	Schools
	Theaters
	Churches

*The examples illustrate the most common capacity constraint for each type of service. In reality, any of the service organizations listed can be operating under multiple constraints. For example, a law firm may be operating under constrained labor capacity (too few attorneys) and facilities constraints (not enough office space) at the same time.

the number of seats in each classroom, and restaurant capacity is restricted to the number of tables and seats available.

Understanding the primary capacity constraint, or the combination of factors that restricts capacity, is a first step in designing strategies to deal with supply and demand issues (Table 14.2).

Optimal versus Maximal Use of Capacity

To fully understand capacity issues, it is important to know the difference between optimal and maximal use of capacity. As suggested earlier in Figure 14.1, optimum and maximum capacity may not be the same. Using capacity at an optimum level means that resources are fully employed but not overused and that customers are receiving quality service in a timely manner. Maximum capacity, on the other hand, represents the absolute limit of service availability. In the case of a football game, optimum and maximum capacity may be the same. The entertainment value of the game is enhanced for customers when every single seat is filled, and obviously the profitability for the team is greatest under these circumstances (Figure 14.2). On the other hand, in a university classroom it is usually not desirable for students or faculty to have every seat filled. In this case, optimal use of capacity is less than the maximum. In some cases, maximum use of capacity may result in excessive waiting by customers, as in a popular restaurant. From the perspective of customer satisfaction, optimum use of the restaurant's capacity will again be less than maximum use.

In the case of equipment or facilities constraints, the maximum capacity at any given time is obvious. There are only a certain number of weight machines in the health club, a certain number of seats in the airplane, and a limited amount of space in a cargo carrier. In the case of a bottling plant, when maximum capacity on the assembly line is exceeded, bottles begin to break and the system shuts down. Thus it is relatively easy to observe the effects of exceeding maximum equipment capacity.

FIGURE 14.2
For sports and other entertainment venues, maximal and optimal capacity use are close to the same.

Source: Robert Brenner/PhotoEdit

When the limitation is people's time or labor, maximum capacity is harder to specify because people are in a sense more flexible than facilities and equipment. When an individual service provider's maximum capacity has been exceeded, the result is likely to be decreased quality, customer dissatisfaction, and employee burnout and turnover, but these outcomes may not be immediately observable even to the employee herself. It is often easy for a consulting firm to take on one more assignment, taxing its employees beyond their maximum capacity, or for an HMO clinic to schedule a few more appointments in a day, stretching its staff and physicians beyond their maximum capacity. Given the potential costs in terms of reduced quality and customer and employee dissatisfaction, it is critical for the firm to understand optimum and maximum human capacity limits.

Professional services and consulting firms face this dilemma all the time—whether to stretch their human capacity beyond what might be optimal for employees and for customers. An interview with Tom Siebel of Siebel Systems provides an excellent example of the difficulty in making these types of trade-offs when human capacity and firm resources are constrained.

> We had an opportunity (in 1994) to sell MCI a call center system. I had a contract on my desk for $250,000 with the opportunity to expand the system to 11,000 users, which could have turned into millions in revenue for us—an unimaginable amount of money to us back then. . . . We could have signed the contract and received the revenue. But we did not have the resources at that time to make MCI happy *and* keep our other customers happy. So I sent their contract back. . . . This was a strategic decision. It communicated the values and culture for our company to key people at both MCI and Siebel Systems—and it was the right thing to do. Today, MCI-WorldCom is one of our largest and happiest customers.[6]

UNDERSTANDING DEMAND PATTERNS[7]

To manage fluctuating demand in a service business, it is necessary to have a clear understanding of demand patterns, why they vary, and the market segments that comprise demand at different points in time. A number of questions need to be answered regarding the predictability and underlying causes of demand.

Charting Demand Patterns

First, the organization needs to chart the level of demand over relevant time periods. Organizations that have good computerized customer information systems can do this very accurately. Others may need to chart demand patterns more informally. Daily, weekly, and monthly demand levels should be followed, and if seasonality is a suspected problem, graphing should be done for data from at least the past year. In some services, such as restaurants or health care, hourly fluctuations within a day may also be relevant. Sometimes demand patterns are intuitively obvious; in other cases patterns may not reveal themselves until the data are charted.

Predictable Cycles

In looking at the graphic representation of demand levels, is there a predictable cycle daily (variations occur by hours), weekly (variations occur by day), monthly (variations occur by day or week), and/or yearly (variations occur according to months or seasons)? In some cases, predictable patterns may occur at all periods. For example, in the restaurant industry, especially in seasonal tourist settings, demand can vary by month, by week, by day, and by hour.

If there is a predictable cycle, what are the underlying causes? The Ritz-Carlton in Phoenix knows that demand cycles are based on seasonal weather patterns and that weekly variations are based on the workweek (business travelers don't stay at the hotel over the weekend). Tax accountants can predict demand based on when taxes are due, quarterly and annually. Services catering to children and families respond to variations in school hours and vacations. Retail and telecommunications services have peak periods at certain holidays and times of the week and day. When predictable patterns exist, generally one or more causes can be identified.

Random Demand Fluctuations

Sometimes the patterns of demand appear to be random—there is no apparent predictable cycle. Yet even in this case, causes can often be identified. For example, day-to-day changes in the weather may affect use of recreational, shopping, or entertainment facilities. Although the weather cannot be predicted far in advance, it may be possible to anticipate demand a day or two ahead. Health-related events also cannot be predicted. Accidents, heart attacks, and births all increase demand for hospital services, but the level of demand cannot generally be determined in advance. Natural disasters such as floods, fires, and hurricanes can dramatically increase the need for such services as insurance, telecommunications, and health care. Acts of war and terrorism such as that experienced in the United States on September 11, 2001, generate instantaneous need for services that can't be predicted.

AT&T was faced with a sudden increase in demand for services to the military during the Gulf War. During this period, 500,000 U.S. troops were deployed to the Middle East, many without advance warning. Before their deployment these men and women had little time to attend to personal business, and all of them left behind concerned family and friends. With mail delivery between the United States and the Middle East taking more than six weeks, troops needed a quick way to communicate with their families and to handle personal business. Communications with home were determined by the military to be essential to troop morale. AT&T's ingenuity, responsiveness, and capacities were challenged to meet this unanticipated communication need. During and after the Gulf War crisis more than 2.5 million calls were placed over temporary public phone installations, and AT&T sent more than 1.2 million free faxes to family and friends of service men and women.[8]

Our Global Feature illustrates how one company with seemingly random and chaotic demand for its services was able to change its business to serve customers.

Imagine a business in which customers' orders are unpredictable, where more than half of all customer orders are changed, often repeatedly and at the last minute, and where the product being delivered is never more than 90 minutes from spoiling. Welcome to the concrete delivery business. Cemex, based in Monterrey, Mexico, founded in 1906, is a highly successful player in this industry, with annual revenues of more than $3.7 billion.

Yet, when two internal consultants examined the business several years ago, they were amazed at the chaos that ruled the industry. Wild weather, unpredictable traffic, spontaneous labor disruptions, and sporadic government inspections of construction sites all combined with ever-changing customer orders to create a sense of chaos and uncontrollability in the business. Combine this with 8,000 grades of concrete available through a half-dozen regional mixing plants, and you have an extremely complex system to manage.

Historically, Cemex had attempted to run the business through controlling its customers to stick with their orders and by imposing fines for changed orders. Efficiency ruled, not customers—all this to conquer the natural randomness of demand and the customers' needs to change orders at the last minute.

The company began searching for new ways to do business. It turned to FedEx and to the 911 emergency dispatch center in Houston, Texas, for ideas. What it found were organizations that, instead of trying to control demand for their services, had developed people and technology to be flexible in meeting customers' seemingly random demand patterns. Instead of penalizing customers for changing their orders, FedEx does not restrict its customers and, in fact, guarantees delivery at a certain time to any and all locations. This ability to serve customers is made possible by sophisticated information systems that track demand and schedule pickups and deliveries, customer-focused front-line employees, and a customer-centric corporate culture that supports it all. From the 911 center in Houston Cemex learned that even seemingly random occurrences such as emergency health needs and accidents occur in

Demand Patterns by Market Segment

If an organization has detailed records on customer transactions, it may be able to disaggregate demand by market segment, revealing patterns within patterns. Or the analysis may reveal that demand from one segment is predictable while demand from another segment is relatively random. For example, for a bank, the visits from its commercial accounts may occur daily at a predictable time, whereas personal account holders may visit the bank at seemingly random intervals. Health clinics often notice that walk-in or "care needed today" patients tend to concentrate their arrivals on Monday, with fewer numbers needing immediate attention on other days of the week. Knowing that this pattern exists, some clinics schedule more future appointments (which they can control) for later days of the week, leaving more of Monday available for same-day appointments and walk-ins.

STRATEGIES FOR MATCHING CAPACITY AND DEMAND

When an organization has a clear grasp of its capacity constraints and an understanding of demand patterns, it is in a good position to develop strategies for matching sup-

sufficient number to allow patterns of demand to be discerned and planned for. Referring to Figure 14.1 in this chapter, what FedEx and the 911 emergency center did was adjust their capacity to meet the peaks and valleys of customer demand rather than insisting the customers adjust their demand to fit the company's constrained capacity.

The experiences at FedEx and in Houston at the 911 center were a revelation to Cemex's team. The company went back, determined to embrace the complexity of its marketplace and to do business on the customers' terms. The company launched a project called Sincronizacion Dinamica de Operaciones: the dynamic synchronization of operations. It unleashed trucks from previous zone assignments, allowing them to roam the city. It outfitted the trucks with transmitters and receivers connected to a GPS system so that locations, direction, and speed of every vehicle could be tracked. It enrolled its drivers in secondary education classes over a period of two years so they would be more service oriented and able to deal with customers.

Impressed with FedEx's guaranteed service, Cemex worked toward being able to offer "same-day service, with free, unlimited order changes." Now, if a load fails to arrive within 20 minutes of its scheduled delivery time, the buyer gets back 20 pesos per cubic meter—"guarantia 20 × 20"—amounting to roughly 5 percent of the total cost.

Cemex embraced the chaos of its industry instead of trying to adjust and change it. By using technology, people, and systems, it was able to match its capacity constraints with its customers' wildly fluctuating demands. And the company came out a winner. Cemex can afford to offer its 20 × 20 guarantee now that its reliability exceeds 98 percent!

Sources: T. Petzinger, Jr., "This Promise Is Set in Concrete," *Fast Company,* April 1999, pp. 216–18; see also T. Petzinger, Jr., *The New Pioneers* (New York: Simon & Schuster, Inc., 1999), pp. 91–93. Reprinted with the permission of Simon & Schuster, Inc. Copyright © 1999 by Thomas Petzinger, Jr.

ply and demand. There are two general approaches for accomplishing this match. The first is to smooth the demand fluctuations themselves by shifting demand to match existing supply. This implies that the peaks and valleys of the demand curve (Figure 14.1) will be flattened to match as closely as possible the horizontal optimum capacity line. The second general strategy is to adjust capacity to match fluctuations in demand. This implies moving the horizontal capacity lines shown in Figure 14.1 to match the ups and downs of the demand curve. Each of these two basic strategies is described next with specific examples.

Shifting Demand to Match Capacity

With this strategy an organization seeks to shift customers away from periods in which demand exceeds capacity, perhaps by convincing them to use the service during periods of slow demand. This may be possible for some customers but not for others. For example, many business travelers are not able to shift their needs for airline, car rental, and hotel services; pleasure travelers, on the other hand, can often shift the timing of their trips. Those who can't shift and can't be accommodated will represent lost business for the firm.

FIGURE 14.3 **Strategies for Shifting Demand to Match Capacity**

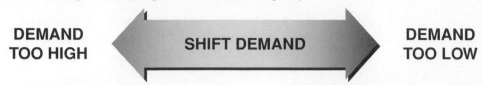

DEMAND TOO HIGH	DEMAND TOO LOW

- Use signage to communicate busy days and times.
- Offer incentives to customers for usage during nonpeak times.
- Take care of loyal or "regular" customers first.
- Advertise peak usage times and benefits of nonpeak use.
- Charge full price for the service—no discounts.

- Use sales and advertising to increase business from current market segments.
- Modify the service offering to appeal to new market segments.
- Offer discounts or price reductions.
- Modify hours of operation.
- Bring the service to the customer.

During periods of slow demand, the organization seeks to attract more and/or different customers to utilize its productive capacity. A variety of approaches, detailed in the following sections, can be used to shift or increase demand to match capacity. Frequently a firm uses a combination of approaches. Ideas for how to shift demand during both slow and peak periods are shown in Figure 14.3.

Vary the Service Offering

One approach is to change the nature of the service offering, depending on the season of the year, day of the week, or time of day. For example, Whistler Mountain, a ski resort in Vancouver, Canada, offers its facilities for executive development and training programs during the summer when snow skiing is not possible. A hospital in the Los Angeles area rents use of its facilities to film production crews who need realistic hospital settings for movies or TV shows. Accounting firms focus on tax preparation late in the year and until April 15, when federal taxes are due in the United States. During other times of the year they can focus on audits and general consulting activities. Airlines even change the configuration of their plane seating to match the demand from different market segments. In some planes there may be no first-class section at all. On routes with a large demand for first-class seating, a significant proportion of seats may be placed in first class. Our opening example featured ways in which downtown hotels have changed their offerings to appeal to the family market segment on weekends. In all of these examples, the service offering and associated benefits are changed to smooth customer demand for the organization's resources.

Care should be exercised in implementing strategies to change the service offering, because such changes may easily imply and require alterations in other marketing mix variables—such as promotion, pricing, and staffing—to match the new offering. Unless these additional mix variables are altered effectively to support the offering, the strategy may not work. Even when done well, the downside of such changes can be a confusion in the organization's image from the customers' perspective, or a loss of strategic focus for the organization and its employees.

Communicate with Customers

Another approach for shifting demand is to communicate with customers, letting them know the times of peak demand so they can choose to use the service at alternative times and avoid crowding or delays. For example, signs in banks and post offices that let customers know their busiest hours and busiest days of the week can serve as a warning, allowing customers to shift their demand to another time if possible. Forewarning customers about busy times and possible waits can have added benefits. Many customer service phone lines provide a similar warning by informing waiting customers of approximately how long it will be until they are served. Those who don't want to wait may choose to call back later when the lines are less busy. Research in a bank context found that customers who were forewarned about the bank's busiest hours were more satisfied even when they had to wait than were customers who were not forewarned.[9]

In addition to signage communicating peak demand times to customers, advertising and other forms of promotion can emphasize different service benefits during peak and slow periods. Advertising and sales messages can also remind customers about peak demand times.

Modify Timing and Location of Service Delivery

Some firms adjust their hours and days of service delivery to more directly reflect customer demand. Historically, U.S. banks were open only during "bankers' hours" from 10 A.M. to 3 P.M. every weekday. Obviously these hours did not match the times when most people preferred to do their personal banking. Now U.S. banks open early, stay open until 6 P.M. many days, and are open on Saturdays, better reflecting customer demand patterns. Theaters also accommodate customer schedules by offering matinees on weekends and holidays when people are free during the day for entertainment. Movie theaters are sometimes rented during weekdays by business groups—an example of varying the service offering during a period of low demand.

Differentiate on Price

A common response during slow demand is to discount the price of the service. This strategy relies on basic economics of supply and demand. To be effective, however, a price differentiation strategy depends on solid understanding of customer price sensitivity and demand curves. For example, business travelers are far less price sensitive than are families traveling for pleasure. For the Ritz-Carlton in Phoenix (our opening example), lowering prices during the slow summer months is not likely to increase bookings from business travelers dramatically. However, the lower summer prices attract considerable numbers of families and local guests who want an opportunity to experience a luxury hotel but are not able to afford the rooms during peak season.

For any hotel, airline, restaurant, or other service establishment, all of the capacity could be filled with customers if the price were low enough. But the goal is always to ensure the highest level of capacity utilization without sacrificing profits. We explore this complex relationship among price, market segments, capacity utilization, and profitability later in the chapter in the section on yield management.

Heavy use of price differentiation to smooth demand can be a risky strategy. Overreliance on price can result in price wars in an industry where eventually all competitors suffer. Price wars are well known in the airline industry, where total industry profits suffered as a result of airlines simultaneously trying to attract customers through price discounting. Another risk of relying on price is that customers grow accustomed to the lower price and expect to get the same deal the next time they use the service. If communications with customers are unclear, customers may not understand the reasons for the discounts and will expect to pay the same during peak demand periods. Overuse or exclusive use of price as a strategy for smoothing demand is also risky due to the potential impact on the organization's image and the possibility of attracting undesired market segments.

FIGURE 14.4 **Strategies for Flexing Capacity to Match Demand**

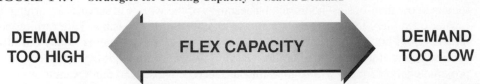

DEMAND TOO HIGH	DEMAND TOO LOW

- Stretch time, labor, facilities, and equipment.
- Cross-train employees.
- Hire part-time employees.
- Request overtime work from employees.
- Rent or share facilities.
- Rent or share equipment.
- Subcontract or outsource activities.

- Perform maintenance, renovations.
- Schedule vacations.
- Schedule employee training.
- Lay off employees.

Flexing Capacity to Meet Demand

A second strategic approach to matching supply and demand focuses on adjusting or flexing capacity. The fundamental idea here is to adjust, stretch, and align capacity to match customer demand (rather than working on shifting demand to match capacity as just described). During periods of peak demand the organization seeks to stretch or expand its capacity as much as possible. During periods of slow demand it tries to shrink capacity so as not to waste resources. General strategies for flexing the four primary service resources (time, people, equipment, and facilities) are discussed next. Specific ideas for adjusting capacity during periods of peak and slow demand are summarized in Figure 14.4. Often a number of different strategies are used simultaneously.

Stretch Existing Capacity

The existing capacity of service resources can often be expanded temporarily to match demand. In such cases no new resources are added; rather people, facilities, and equipment are asked to work harder and longer to meet demand.

Stretch Time   It may be possible to extend the hours of service temporarily to accommodate demand. A health clinic might stay open longer during flu season, retailers are open longer hours during the Christmas shopping season, and accountants have extended appointment hours (evenings and Saturdays) before tax deadlines.

Stretch Labor   In many service organizations, employees are asked to work longer and harder during periods of peak demand. For example, consulting organizations face extensive peaks and valleys with respect to demand for their services. During peak demand, associates are asked to take on additional projects and work longer hours. And front-line service personnel in banks, tourist attractions, restaurants, and telecommunications companies are asked to serve more customers per hour during busy times than during hours or days when demand is low.

Stretch Facilities   Theaters, restaurants, meeting facilities, and classrooms can sometimes be expanded temporarily by the addition of tables, chairs, or other equipment needed by customers. Or, as in the case of a commuter train, a car can hold a number of people seated comfortably or can "expand" by accommodating standing passengers.

Stretch Equipment   Computers, telephone lines, and maintenance equipment can often be stretched beyond what would be considered the maximum capacity for short periods to accommodate peak demand.

In using these types of "stretch" strategies, the organization needs to recognize the wear and tear on resources and the potential for inferior quality of service that may go with the use. These strategies should thus be used for relatively short periods in order to allow for later maintenance of the facilities and equipment and refreshment of the people who are asked to exceed their usual capacity. As noted earlier, sometimes it is difficult to know in advance, particularly in the case of human resources, when capacity has been stretched too far.

Align Capacity with Demand Fluctuations

This basic strategy is sometimes known as a "chase demand" strategy. By adjusting service resources creatively, organizations can in effect chase the demand curves to match capacity with customer demand patterns. Time, labor, facilities, and equipment are again the focus, this time with an eye toward adjusting the basic mix and use of these resources. Specific actions might include the following.[10]

Use Part-Time Employees   In this case the organization's labor resource is being aligned with demand. Retailers hire part-time employees during the holiday rush, tax accountants engage temporary help during tax season, tourist resorts bring in extra workers during peak season. Restaurants often ask employees to work split shifts (work the lunch shift, leave for a few hours, and come back for the dinner rush) during peak mealtime hours.

Outsourcing   Firms that find they have a temporary peak in demand for a service that they cannot perform themselves may choose to outsource the entire service. For example, in recent years, many firms have found they don't have the capacity to fulfill their own needs for technology support, Web design, and software-related services. Rather than try to hire and train additional employees, these companies look to firms that specialize in outsourcing these types of functions as a temporary (or sometimes long-term) solution. Companies like NeoIT perform this function, handling entire technology service projects or assisting firms in hiring individual contractors to provide the needed technology skills. NeoIT has offices in both the United States and India and in fact finds many of its highly skilled technology contractors in India, matching them with project needs and suppliers from over 50 countries.[11]

Rent or Share Facilities or Equipment   For some organizations it is best to rent additional equipment or facilities during periods of peak demand. For example, express mail delivery services rent or lease trucks during the peak holiday delivery season. It would not make sense to buy trucks that would sit idle during the rest of the year. Sometimes organizations with complementary demand patterns can share facilities. An example is a church that shares its facilities during the week with a Montessori preschool. The school needs the facilities Monday through Friday during the day; the church needs the facilities evenings and on the weekend.

Schedule Downtime during Periods of Low Demand   If people, equipment, and facilities are being used at maximum capacity during peak periods, then it is imperative to schedule repair, maintenance, and renovations during off-peak periods. This ensures that the resources are in top condition when they are most needed. With regard to employees, this means that vacations and training are also scheduled during slow demand periods.

Cross-Train Employees   If employees are cross-trained, they can shift among tasks, filling in where they are most needed. This increases the efficiency of the whole system and avoids underutilizing employees in some areas while others are being overtaxed. Many airlines cross-train their employees to move from ticketing to working the gate counters to assisting with baggage if needed. In some fast-food restaurants, employees specialize in one task (like making french fries) during busy hours, and the team of specialists may number 10 people. During slow hours the team may shrink to three, with each person performing a variety of functions. Grocery stores also use this strategy, with most employees able to move as needed from cashiering to stocking shelves to bagging groceries.

Modify or Move Facilities and Equipment   Sometimes it is possible to adjust, move, or creatively modify existing capacity to meet demand fluctuations. Hotels accomplish this by reconfiguring rooms—two rooms with a locked door between can be rented to two different parties in high demand times or turned into a suite during slow demand. The airline industry offers dramatic examples of this type of strategy. Using an approach known as "demand-driven dispatch," airlines have begun to experiment with methods that assign airplanes to flight schedules on the basis of fluctuating market needs.[12] The method depends on accurate knowledge of demand and the ability to quickly move airplanes with different seating capacities to flight assignments that match their capacity. The Boeing 777 aircraft is so flexible that it can be reconfigured within hours to vary the number of seats allocated to one, two, or three classes.[13] The plane can thus be quickly modified to match demand from different market segments, essentially molding capacity to fit demand.

Another strategy may involve moving the service to a new location to meet customer demand or even bringing the service to customers. Mobile training facilities, libraries, and blood donation facilities are examples of services that physically follow customers. Exhibit 14.1 illustrates how this strategy is used in the banking industry.

YIELD MANAGEMENT: BALANCING CAPACITY UTILIZATION, PRICING, MARKET SEGMENTATION, AND FINANCIAL RETURN

Yield management is a term that has become attached to a variety of methods, some very sophisticated, matching demand and supply in capacity-constrained services. Using yield management models, organizations find the best balance at a particular point in time among the prices charged, the segments sold to, and the capacity used. The goal of yield management is to produce the best possible financial return from a limited available capacity. Specifically, yield management has been defined as "the process of allocating the right type of capacity to the right kind of customer at the right price so as to maximize revenue or yield."[14]

Although the implementation of yield management can involve complex mathematical models and computer programs, the underlying effectiveness measure is the ratio of actual revenue to potential revenue for a particular measurement period:

$$\text{Yield} = \frac{\text{Actual revenue}}{\text{Potential revenue}}$$

One way to meet customers' fluctuating demand for service is to move the service to where the customers are. At least 50 different financial institutions—from the small to the very large—have started doing this in recent years.

As discussed in Chapter 8, Wells Fargo (the fifth largest U.S. bank) actually built its entire strategy around alternative delivery modes that meet customers' natural demand patterns better than traditional banks with 9-to-5 banking hours. Focusing on convenience and being available when and where its customers want financial services, Wells Fargo provides more and more of its services through mini-branches in grocery stores and through online and phone banking. In essence it is adapting its capacity to fit its customers' natural demand patterns. To educate its customers on Internet and online brokerage services, Wells equipped a bus that travels around the western U.S. demonstrating and allowing customers to try out these new services.

Other banks also use "rolling bank branches" to capture demand for financial services. NationsBank sends a portable ATM around Florida to dispense cash at parades and other events that draw large crowds. The portable ATM can also be mobilized during a natural disaster such as a hurricane.

U.S. Bank operates a bankmobile to cover areas of western Pennsylvania where residents are spread too thin to justify construction of a permanent bank branch. Mobile banking units are also useful for reaching the elderly and disabled populations who can't physically travel to the bank themselves. For U.S. Bank the $300,000 cost of the customized van is far less than the cost of an actual bank facility. Monthly costs of operation are also much less than a traditional branch.

Sources: M. Murray, "On the Road with a Rolling Bank Branch," *The Wall Street Journal,* November 6, 1997, p. B1; www.wellsfargo.com, 2002.

where

$$\text{Actual revenue} = \text{actual capacity used} \times \text{average actual price}$$
$$\text{Potential revenue} = \text{total capacity} \times \text{maximum price}$$

The equations indicate that yield is a function of price and capacity used. Recall that capacity constraints can be in the form of time, labor, equipment, or facilities. Yield is essentially a measure of the extent to which an organization's resources (or capacities) are achieving their full revenue-generating potential. Assuming that total capacity and maximum price cannot be changed, yield approaches 1 as actual capacity utilization increases or when a higher actual price can be charged for a given capacity used. For example, in an airline context, a manager could focus on increasing yield by finding ways to bring in more passengers to fill the capacity, or by finding higher-paying passengers to fill a more limited capacity. In reality, expert yield managers will work on capacity and pricing issues simultaneously to maximize revenue across different customer segments.

Yield Management Examples

Take, for example, a hotel that has 200 rooms that it can rent at a rate of $100 per night (potential revenue of $20,000). One night it rents all of the rooms at a reduced rate of $50 per night, yielding a revenue of $10,000. Although capacity was used to the maximum level that night, yield was only 50 percent ($10,000/$20,000). If, on the other hand, the hotel had charged its full rate it might have sold only 40 percent of its rooms because of customer price sensitivity. The yield under these circumstances would have been 40 percent ($8,000/$20,000). At the $100 rate the hotel may thus be maximizing the per-room price but not the potential yield—or revenue generation—for the entire hotel. Perhaps a combination of the two room rates would be the best solution. If the hotel could fill 40 percent of the rooms at $100 per night and the other 60 percent at $50, the revenue would be $14,000, resulting in a yield of 70 percent ($14,000/$20,000), clearly better than the other two alternatives.

Technology Spotlight
Information and Technology Drive Yield Management Systems

Yield management is not a new concept. In fact, the basic idea behind yield management—achieving maximum profits through the most effective use of capacity—has been around forever. It is easy to find examples of capacity-constrained businesses using price to shift demand: theaters that charge different prices for matinees versus evening performances, intercity trains with different prices on weekdays than on weekends, ski resorts with cheaper prices for night skiing, and restaurants with "twilight" dinner specials. All of these strategies illustrate attempts to smooth the peaks and valleys of demand using price as the primary motivator.

The difference in these basic pricing strategies and more sophisticated yield management approaches currently in use by airlines, hotels, shippers, and others is the reliance of these latter strategies on massive databases, sophisticated mathematical algorithms, and complex analyses. These forms of yield management consider not only price but also market segments, price sensitivity among segments, timing of demand, and potential profitability of customer segments—all simultaneously. What makes new forms of yield management possible are the technology and systems underlying them. Here we provide a few examples of what some companies and industries are doing.

American Airlines
American Airlines is the original pioneer and still the king of yield management. Beginning with Super Saver Fares in the mid-1970s, American depends on systems developed by Sabre (the oldest and leading provider of tech-

nology for the travel industry) to support an exceedingly complex system of fares. Using a system of models containing algorithms that optimize prices, manage wait lists, and handle traffic management, American allocates seats on every one of its flights. The number of seats sold on each of American's flights is continuously compared with a sales forecast for that flight. Blocks of seats are moved from higher to lower fares if sales are below projections. If sales are at or above the forecast, no changes are made. The objective is to "sell the right seats to the right customers at the right price." To do this requires massive amounts of data! The typical yield management database for a large airline can exceed 300 gigabytes of data, equivalent to a 6,350-meter stack of paper. A person scanning this data would need to work 43 years, 40 hours per week, and spend only five seconds per page.

Austrian Airlines
Austrian Airlines has been one of the most consistently profitable airlines in Europe. Prior to deregulation of airlines in Europe, Austrian foresaw the need to develop a competitive advantage that would carry it into the deregulated future. The airline invested in a revenue management decision support computer system to build a two-year historical database of booking data that would monitor flights up to 250 days into the future. Using the system, Austrian saw significant improvements in both number of passengers carried and revenue. By being more selective in its discounting practices than were its competitors, Austrian has achieved excellent results.

In a different context, a law firm could determine the best mix of business for using its labor capacity to yield the highest returns. For example, if one attorney has 40 potential billable hours in a given week and her rate is $200 per hour for private corporate clients, then maximum revenue generation by that attorney in a week is $8,000. Assume her rate for public and nonprofit clients is $100 per hour. As in the preceding hotel example, if the attorney could bill out all of her hours in a week to public clients at the $100 rate, yield would be 50 percent. If she were to hold out for private corporate clients, she might be able to sell only 30 percent of her available time (12 hours), resulting in a yield of 30 percent ($2,400/$8,000). By combining the two strategies the attorney could possibly sell 30 percent of her time at $200 per hour to private corporate clients and the remaining 70 percent to public clients for $100 per hour, resulting in a yield of 65 percent ($5,200/$8,000), clearly better than the other two alternatives.

Yield management attempts to manage demand to meet capacity (fixed number of

Marriott Hotels

The hotel industry has also begun to embrace the concepts of yield management, and Marriott Hotels has been the leader. One example of what the systems at Marriott do is to maximize profits for a hotel across full weeks rather than by day. In their hotels that target business travelers, Marriott has peak days during the middle of the week. Rather than simply sell the hotel out on those nights on a first-come, first-served basis with no discounts, the revenue management system (which is reviewed and revised daily) now projects guest demand both by price and length of stay, providing discounts in some cases to guests who will stay longer, even on a peak demand night. One early test of the system was at the Munich Marriott during Oktoberfest. Typically no discounts would be offered during this peak period. However, the yield management system recommended that the hotel offer some rooms at a discount, but only for those guests who stayed an extended period before or after the peak days. Although the average daily rate was down 11.7 percent for the period, occupancy was up over 20 percent, and overall revenues were up 12.3 percent. Using this and other yield management practices, Marriott Hotels estimates that yield management results in an additional $400 million per year in revenue.

Yellow Transportation

Pricing in the freight industry still seems to be stuck in a regulated mind-set where costs dominate and discounts from class rates are determined by complex formulas. However, companies such as Yellow Transportation (formerly Yellow Freight) are moving toward market-driven models that price services consistent with the value as perceived by the customer. New pricing structures recognize the customers' and freight providers' desires for simplification while combining this with sophisticated use of yield management models that take into account the most profitable use of resources. Yield management systems encourage more rational scheduling of trucks and drivers by considering such subtle factors as equipment type and skills of a particular driver. The systems can match hundreds of drivers with loads in fractions of seconds to make the best dispatch and driver decisions. By analyzing its services, prices, and demand patterns in this way, Yellow was able to project the success of its new time-definite delivery service—Exact Express. This service targets a particular segment of customers who are willing to pay for guaranteed, time-definite delivery.

Sources: The primary source for this Technology Spotlight is R. G. Cross, *Revenue Management* (New York: Broadway Books, 1997). Other sources include "Dynamic Pricing at American Airlines," *Business Quarterly* 61, no. 1 (Autumn 1996), p. 45; N. Templin, "Your Room Costs $250 . . . No! $200 . . . No," *The Wall Street Journal,* May 5, 1999, p. B1; H. Richardson, "Simplify! Simplify! Simplify!," *Transportation and Distribution* 39, no. 10 (October 1998), pp. 111–17; and C. Salter "On the Road Again," *Fast Company,* January 2002, pp. 50–58.

rooms or fixed number of hours in these examples) by deciding what amount of capacity to offer at what price to what market segments in order to maximize revenues over a particular period. It forces recognition of the trade-offs inherent in serving a lower-paying market segment to fill capacity when there may be some demand from higher-paying clientele.

Implementing a Yield Management System

Our Technology Spotlight illustrates several examples of how information technology supports effective yield management applications. To implement a yield management system, an organization needs detailed data on past demand patterns by market segment as well as methods of projecting current market demand. The data can be combined through mathematical programming models, threshold analysis, or use of expert systems to project the best allocation of limited capacity at a particular point in time.[15]

Allocations of capacity for specific market segments can then be communicated to sales representatives or reservations staff as targets for selling rooms, seats, time, or other limited resources. Sometimes the allocations, once determined, remain fixed. At other times allocations change weekly or even daily or hourly in response to new information.

Passenger airlines are the most sophisticated and long-time users of technology-assisted yield management systems. Probably the most experienced is American Airlines, which has been using the techniques since the 1980s to juggle the timing and allotment of discount tickets with potential sales from higher-paying travelers. Decisions are made continuously on how many seats to allocate to discount travelers, how many to groups, and how many to hold for last-minute full-fare customers. The percentage of seats that should be overbooked to handle "no shows" is also factored into the decisions.

Recent research indicates traditional yield management approaches are most profitable when (1) a service provider faces different market segments that arrive or make their reservations at different times and (2) those who arrive or reserve early are more price sensitive than those who arrive or reserve late.[16] This is exactly the situation for airlines and many hotels—industries that have effectively and extensively used yield management techniques to allocate capacity. In other services (entertainment, sports, fashion), those customers willing to pay the higher prices are the ones who buy early rather than late. People who really want to see a particular performance reserve their seats at the earliest possible moment. Discounting for early purchases in these situations would reduce profits. In these situations, the price generally starts out high and is reduced later to fill capacity if needed.

Interestingly, some airlines now use both of these strategies effectively. They start with discounted seats for those who are willing to buy early, usually leisure and discretionary travelers. They charge a higher fare for those who want a seat at the last minute, typically the less price-sensitive business travelers whose destinations and schedules are inflexible. However, in some cases a bargain fare can be found at the last minute as well, commonly via Internet sales to fill seats that would otherwise go unoccupied. Online auctions and services offered by companies like Internet-based priceline.com serve a purpose in filling capacity at the last minute, often charging much lower fares. (See the Technology Spotlight in Chapter 16 for more on priceline.com and other examples of dynamic pricing via the Internet.)

Challenges and Risks in Using Yield Management

There is evidence that yield management programs can significantly improve revenues. However, while yield management may appear to be an ideal solution to the problem of matching supply and demand, it is not without risks. By becoming focused on maximizing financial returns through differential capacity allocation and pricing, an organization may encounter these problems:[17]

- *Loss of competitive focus.* Yield management may result in overfocusing on profit maximization and inadvertent neglect of aspects of the service that provide long-term competitive success.

- *Customer alienation.* If customers learn that they are paying a higher price for service than someone else, they may perceive the pricing as unfair, particularly if they don't understand the reasons. Customer education is thus essential in an effective yield management program. Customers can be further alienated if they fall victim (and are not compensated adequately) to overbooking practices that are often necessary to make yield management systems work effectively.

- *Employee morale problems.* Yield management systems take much guesswork and judgment away from sales and reservations people. Although some employees may appreciate the guidance, others may resent the rules and restrictions on their own discretion.

- *Incompatible incentive and reward systems.* Employees may resent yield management systems if these don't match incentive structures. For example, many managers are rewarded on the basis of capacity utilization *or* average rate charged, whereas yield management balances the two factors.

- *Lack of employee training.* Extensive training is required to make a yield management system work. Employees need to understand its purpose, how it works, how they should make decisions, and how the system will affect their jobs.

- *Inappropriate organization of the yield management function.* To be most effective with yield management, an organization must have centralized reservations. While airlines and some large hotel chains and shipping companies do have such centralization, other smaller organizations may have decentralized reservations systems and thus find it difficult to operate a yield management system effectively.

WAITING LINE STRATEGIES: WHEN DEMAND AND CAPACITY CANNOT BE ALIGNED

Sometimes it is not possible to manage capacity to match demand, or vice versa. It may be too costly—for example, for most health clinics it would not be economically feasible to add additional facilities or physicians to handle peaks in demand during the winter flu season; patients usually simply have to wait to be seen. Or demand may be very unpredictable and the service capacity very inflexible (it can't be easily stretched to match unpredictable peaks in demand). Sometimes waits may occur when demand backs up because of the variability in length of time for service. For example, even though patients are scheduled by appointments in a physician's office, frequently there is a wait because some patients take longer to serve than the time allotted to them. According to many sources, the misalignment in capacity and demand has reached crisis proportions in the emergency health care context, as is described in Exhibit 14.2.

For most service organizations, waiting customers are a fact of life at some point. Waiting can occur on the telephone (customers put on hold when they call in to ask for information, order something, or make a complaint) and in person (customers waiting in line at the bank, post office, Disneyland, or a physician's office). Waiting can occur even with service transactions through the mail—delays in mail-order delivery, or backlogs of correspondence on a manager's desk.

In today's fast-paced society, waiting is not something most people tolerate well. As people work longer hours, individuals have less leisure, and families have fewer hours together, the pressure on people's time is greater than ever. In this environment, customers are looking for efficient, quick service with no wait. Organizations that make customers wait take the chance that they will lose business or at the very least that customers will be dissatisfied.[18]

Nowhere is there a more vivid example of demand and capacity issues than in the nearly 5,000 emergency departments in hospitals across the United States ("emergency department" is the preferred term within the medical community for what has traditionally been called the ER). In a typical ED, rooms are filled, the corridors may be clogged with waiting patients, wait time may be anywhere from 15 minutes to 8 or 10 hours, and ambulances are routinely turned away to seek other hospitals on what is called "reroute" or "diversion." Many experts have referred to these issues as a national crisis in health care. The emergency department is the front door of hospitals and is also the treatment of last resort for many. Why has this overcrowding issue reached national proportions? Many factors come into play, including increased demand and severe capacity constraints.

Increased Demand for Services

Emergency departments are to some extent victims of their own success. Decades of public health campaigns urging people to call 911 in case of medical emergency have been successful in educating people to do just that—and they end up in the ED. Many do indeed have life-threatening emergencies that belong in the ED. Others waiting in the ED are uninsured—43 million people in the United States. The ED is their only option, and legally the ED must care for them. But it is not only the uninsured and those with life-threatening emergencies that crowd the ED. It is also insured patients who can't get appointments with their doctors in a timely manner, or who learn that it may be their fastest entry into a hospital bed. Patients and their doctors are becoming aware that they can get sophisticated care in the ED relatively quickly. Thus the demand for ED services has increased.

Capacity Constraints

It is not just an increase in demand that is causing the overcrowding. It is also a shrinkage of critical capacity at the same time. Doctors are overbooked in private practices, so patients who don't want to wait turn to the ED. There is also a shortage of specialists who are willing to take patients on call from the ED. This results in increased waiting times because these patients waiting for specialized care occupy beds in the ED longer than necessary. Another very critical capacity constraint is the number of beds in hospitals. Over the years many hospitals across the country have closed for financial reasons, reducing the number of beds available. So ED patients often cannot get beds right away even if they need one, again increasing waiting time for themselves and others. There is a critical shortage of nurses as well, and a hospital bed requires a nurse to attend it before it can be occupied. In the 1990s enrollment in nursing programs slumped as people turned to more lucrative careers, and the average age of a registered nurse is now 45. Many hospitals have 20 percent of their nursing slots empty. Staffing shortages in housekeeping also play a roll. A bed may be empty, but until it is cleaned and remade, it is not available for a waiting patient.

Here are a few things that are being done or considered to address this complex set of issues:

Technology and Systems Improvements A partial solution is to turn to technology to smooth the process of admitting patients into the ED and to track the availability of hospital

To deal effectively with the inevitability of waits, organizations employ a variety of strategies, described next and illustrated in Figure 14.5.

Employ Operational Logic

If customer waits are common, a first step is to analyze the operational processes to remove any inefficiencies. It may be possible to redesign the system to move customers along more quickly. Modifications in the operational system were part of the solution employed by the First National Bank of Chicago in its efforts to reduce customer waiting and improve service. The bank developed a computer-based customer information system to allow tellers to answer questions more quickly, implemented an electronic queuing system, hired "peak time" tellers, expanded its hours, and provided

beds. Some Web-based systems are used to reroute ambulances to hospitals that have capacity. Other systems help EDs track the availability of rooms in their own hospitals in terms of knowing exactly when a bed is vacant and when it has been cleaned and is available—similar to what hotels have done for decades. Wireless systems for registering patients at bedside and "radar screens" that track everything going on in the ED are other partial solutions. These screens can track patients, staff, carts, and equipment, making the service delivery process more efficient and quicker.

Other hospitals have segmented their patients and have developed parallel "fast track" processes for dealing with minor emergency patients that can account for 30–50 percent of total visits. This process can be separated from the major-emergency situations that may require more time and special equipment. Quicker admitting processes, sometimes done on wireless devices, are also being implemented. Instead of having a patient fill out long forms with detailed questions, the quicker process asks just three to four questions initially, saving the longer admitting forms for after treatment.

Yet another innovation is to have staff administer routine tests while the patient is waiting so that when a doctor finally sees the patient he or she has information at hand. This also satisfies the patient's need for "something to happen" during the waiting time. Giving patients pagers so they can do something else while waiting is another way that EDs are helping patients cope with the long waits.

Increasing Capacity   Another set of partial solutions relates directly to hospital and staff capacity issues. Some hospitals have already begun adding rooms and other facilities. More urgent care centers are being built to take some of the pressure off EDs. For patients who need to be admitted to the hospital, however, this is not a total solution. The nursing shortage, one of the most critical problems, is very difficult to solve. Individual hospital systems have gotten creative in their efforts to steal nurses away from other hospitals, even recruiting heavily overseas. However, in the long term the solution rests more in making the occupation attractive in salaries and working conditions, thus increasing the number of people entering nursing programs.

Insuring the Uninsured   A major political and social issue is how to handle the growing numbers of uninsured in the United States. Finding a way to provide coverage to these millions of Americans—many of whom are employed, but whose employers do not provide health insurance—has been a focus of political debate for decades.

It is obvious that this classic dilemma of matching supply and demand in a service context has multiple, deeply rooted causes when examined in the context of emergency care. The solutions to the issues are also multifaceted—some can be undertaken by individual hospitals, whereas others need to be addressed by the entire health care industry. Some, however, are societal issues with only long-term solutions. Yet all of these issues play out daily in the very immediate environment of hospital emergency departments.

Sources: L. Landro, "ERs Now Turn to Technology to Help Deal with Overcapacity," *The Wall Street Journal,* July 13, 2001, p. B1; J. Snyder, "Curing the ER," *The Arizona Republic,* December 9, 2001, p. D1+; N. Shute and M. B. Marcus, "Crisis in the ER," *US News & World Report,* September 10, 2001.

customers with alternative delivery channels. Collectively these efforts reduced customer wait time, increasing productivity and improving customer satisfaction.[19]

In introducing its express check-in, Marriott Hotels used an operations-based modification to eliminate much of the waiting previously experienced by its guests. Guests who use a credit card and preregister can avoid waiting in line at the hotel front desk altogether. The guest can make it from the curb outside the hotel to his or her room in as little as three minutes when escorted by a "guest service associate" who checks the guest into the hotel, picks up keys and paperwork from a rack in the lobby, and then escorts the guest directly to the room.[20]

When queues are inevitable, the organization faces the operational decision of what kind of queuing system to use, or how to configure the queue. Queue configuration

FIGURE 14.5
**Waiting Line
Strategies**

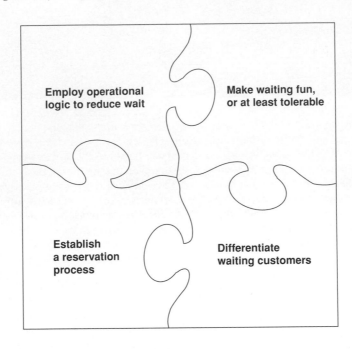

Employ operational
logic to reduce wait

Make waiting fun,
or at least tolerable

Establish
a reservation
process

Differentiate
waiting customers

refers to the number of queues, their locations, their spatial requirement, and their effect on customer behavior.[21] Several possibilities exist, as shown in Figure 14.6. In the multiple-queue alternative, the customer arrives at the service facility and must decide which queue to join and whether to switch later if the wait appears to be shorter in another line. In the single-queue alternative, fairness of waiting time is ensured in that the first-come, first-served rule applies to everyone; the system can also reduce the average time customers spend waiting overall. However, customers may leave if they perceive the line is too long or if there is no opportunity to select a particular service provider. The last option shown in Figure 14.6 is the take-a-number option, where arriving customers take a number to indicate line position. Advantages are similar to the single-queue alternative with the additional benefit that customers are able to mill about, browse, and talk to each other. The disadvantage is that customers must be on the alert to hear their numbers when they are called. Many service businesses have become experts at handling queues effectively in terms of minimizing customer dissatisfaction. Some of the benchmarks include Disney, Marriott, and FedEx. In fact, in its effort to plan and implement an effective, efficient, service-oriented security process at U.S. airports, the U.S. government consulted these benchmark companies for advice.[22]

Establish a Reservation Process

When waiting cannot be avoided, a reservation system can help to spread demand. Restaurants, transportation companies, theaters, physicians, and many other service providers use reservation systems to alleviate long waits. The idea behind a reservation system is to guarantee that the service will be available when the customer arrives. Beyond simply reducing waiting time, a reservation system has the added benefit of potentially shifting demand to less desirable time periods. A challenge inherent in reservation systems, however, is what to do about "no shows." Inevitably there will be customers who reserve a time but do not show up. Some organizations deal with this

FIGURE 14.6
Waiting Line Configurations

Source: J. A. Fitzsimmons and M. J. Fitzsimmons, *Service Management,* 3rd ed. (New York: Irwin/McGraw-Hill, 2000), chap. 11, p. 304. © 2000 by The McGraw-Hill Companies, Inc. Reprinted by permission of The McGraw-Hill Companies.

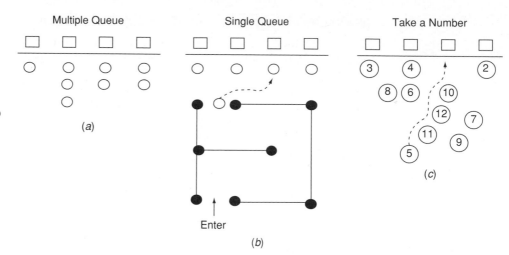

by overbooking their service capacity on the basis of past records of no-show percentages. If the predictions are accurate, overbooking is a good solution. When predictions are inaccurate, however, customers may still have to wait and sometimes may not be served at all, as when airlines overbook the number of seats available on a flight. Victims of overbooking may be compensated for their inconvenience in such cases. To minimize the no-show problem, some organizations (such as hotels, airlines, conferences/training programs, and theaters) charge customers who fail to show up or cancel their reservations within a certain time frame.

Differentiate Waiting Customers

Not all customers necessarily need to wait the same length of time for service. On the basis of need or customer priority, some organizations differentiate among customers, allowing some to experience shorter waits for service than others. Known as "queue discipline," such differentiation reflects management policies regarding whom to select next for service.[23] The most popular discipline is first-come, first-served. However, other rules may apply. Differentiation can be based on factors such as[24]

- *Importance of the customer.* Frequent customers or customers who spend large amounts with the organization can be given priority in service by providing them with a special waiting area or segregated lines.

- *Urgency of the job.* Those customers with the most urgent need may be served first. This is the strategy used in emergency health care. It is also the strategy used by maintenance services such as air-conditioning repair that give priority to customers whose air conditioning is not functioning over those who call for routine maintenance.

- *Duration of the service transaction.* In many situations, shorter service jobs get priority through "express lanes." At other times, when a service provider sees that a transaction is going to require extra time, the customer is referred to a designated provider who deals only with these special-needs customers.

- *Payment of a premium price.* Customers who pay extra (first class on an airline, for example) are often given priority via separate check-in lines or express systems.

Make Waiting Fun, or at Least Tolerable

Even when they have to wait, customers can be more or less satisfied depending on how the wait is handled by the organization. Of course the actual length of the wait will affect how customers feel about their service experience. But it isn't just the actual time spent waiting that has an impact on customer satisfaction—it's how customers feel about the wait and their perceptions during it. The type of wait (for example, a standard queue versus a wait due to a delay of service) can also influence how customers will react.[25] In a classic article entitled "The Psychology of Waiting Lines," David Maister proposes several principles regarding waiting, each of which has implications for how organizations can make waiting more pleasurable, or at least tolerable.[26]

Unoccupied Time Feels Longer Than Occupied Time   When customers are unoccupied they will likely be bored and will notice the passage of time more than when they have something to do. Providing something for waiting customers to do, particularly if the activity offers a benefit in and of itself or is related in some way to the service, can improve the customer's experience and may benefit the organization as well.[27] Examples include giving customers menus to look at while waiting in a restaurant, providing interesting information to read in a dentist's office, or playing entertaining programs over the phone while customers are on hold. At Macy's in New York, children waiting to see Santa Claus wend their way through displays of dancing teddy bears, elves, and electric trains that become part of the total service adventure.[28]

Preprocess Waits Feel Longer Than In-Process Waits   If wait time is occupied with activities that relate to the upcoming service, customers may perceive that the service has started and they are no longer actually waiting. This in-process activity will make the length of the wait seem shorter and will also benefit the service provider by making the customer better prepared when the service actually does begin. Filling out medical information while waiting to see the physician, reading a menu while waiting to be seated in a restaurant, and watching a videotape of the upcoming service event are all activities that can at the same time educate the customer and reduce perceptions of waiting.

Research in a restaurant context found that customers reacted less negatively to in-process waits than to either preprocess or postprocess waits.[29] Other researchers have found the same for waits due to routine slowness of the process. However, if the wait is due to a service failure, then the in-process wait is viewed more negatively than the preprocess wait.[30] Thus it seems that how customers perceive preprocess, in-process, and postprocess waits may depend on the cause of the wait to some extent.

Anxiety Makes Waits Seem Longer   When customers fear that they have been forgotten or don't know how long they'll have to wait, they become anxious, and this anxiety can increase the negative impact of waiting. Anxiety also results when customers are forced to choose in a multiple-line situation and they discover they have chosen the "wrong line." To combat waiting line anxiety, organizations can provide information on the length of the wait. This is what Disney does at its theme parks: it uses signs at intervals along the line that let customers know how long the wait will be from that point on. Using a single line also alleviates customer anxiety over having chosen the wrong line. Explanations and reassurances that no one has forgotten them alleviate customer anxiety by taking away their cause for worry. At the Omni Park Central Hotel in New York, when the line exceeds a certain length assistant managers bring orange and grapefruit juice to serve those waiting.[31] The customers know they have not been forgotten.

Uncertain Waits Are Longer Than Known, Finite Waits   Anxiety is intensified when customers don't know how long they'll have to wait. Health care providers combat this by letting customers know when they check in how far behind the physician is that day. Some patients resolve this uncertainty themselves by calling ahead to ask. Maister provides an interesting example of the role of uncertainty, which he terms the "appointment syndrome." Customers who arrive early for an appointment will wait patiently until the scheduled time, even if they arrive very early. However, once the expected appointment time has passed, customers grow increasingly anxious. Before the appointment time the wait time is known; after that, the length of the wait is not known.

Research in an airline context has suggested that as uncertainty about the wait increases, customers become more angry, and their anger in turn results in greater dissatisfaction.[32] Research also shows that giving customers information on the length of the anticipated wait and/or their relative position in the queue can result in more positive feelings and acceptance of the wait and ultimately more positive evaluation of the service.[33]

Unexplained Waits Are Longer Than Explained Waits   When people understand the causes for waiting, they frequently have greater patience and are less anxious, particularly when the wait is justifiable. An explanation can reduce customer uncertainty and may help customers estimate how long they'll be delayed. Customers who don't know the reason for a wait begin to feel powerless and irritated.

Unfair Waits Are Longer Than Equitable Waits   When customers perceive that they are waiting while others who arrived after them have already been served, the apparent inequity will make the wait seem even longer. This can easily occur when there is no apparent order in the waiting area and many customers are trying to be served. Queuing systems that work on a first-come, first-served rule are best at combatting perceived unfairness. However, as pointed out earlier, there may be reasons for the use of other approaches in determining whom will be served next. For example, in an emergency medical care situation, the most seriously ill or injured patients would be seen first. When customers understand the priorities and the rules are clearly communicated and enforced, fairness of waiting time should not be an issue.

The More Valuable the Service, the Longer the Customer Will Wait   Customers who have substantial purchases or who are waiting for a high-value service will be more tolerant of long wait times and may even expect to wait longer. For example, in a supermarket, customers who have a full cart of groceries will generally wait longer than customers who have only a few items and expect to be checked through quickly. And we expect to wait longer for service in an expensive restaurant than we do when eating at a "greasy spoon."

Solo Waits Feel Longer Than Group Waits   People will wait longer when they are in a group than when they are alone due to the distractions provided by other members of the group. There is also comfort in waiting with a group rather than alone.[34] In some group waiting situations, such as at Disneyland or when patrons are waiting in long lines to purchase concert tickets, customers who are strangers begin to talk to each other and the waiting experience can actually become fun and a part of the total service experience.

Summary

Because service organizations lack the ability to inventory their products, the effective use of capacity can be critical to success. Idle capacity in the form of unused time, labor, facilities, or equipment represents a direct drain on bottom-line profitability. When the capacity represents a major investment (for example, airplanes, expensive medical imaging equipment, or lawyers and physicians paid on a salary), the losses associated with underuse of capacity are even more accentuated. Overused capacity is also a problem. People, facilities, and equipment can become worn out over time when used beyond optimum capacity constraints. People can quit, facilities become run down, and equipment can break. From the customer's perspective, service quality also deteriorates. For organizations focused on delivering quality service, therefore, there is a natural drive to balance capacity utilization and demand at an optimum level in order to meet customer expectations.

This chapter has provided you with an understanding of the underlying issues of managing supply and demand in capacity-constrained services by exploring the lack of inventory capability, the nature of service constraints (time, labor, equipment, facilities), the differences in optimal versus maximal use of capacity, and the causes of fluctuating demand.

Based on grounding in the fundamental issues, the chapter presented a variety of strategies for matching supply and demand. The basic strategies fall under two headings: *demand strategies* (shifting demand to match capacity) and *supply strategies* (flexing capacity to meet demand). Demand strategies seek to flatten the peaks and valleys of demand to match the flat capacity constraint, whereas supply strategies seek to align, flex, or stretch the fixed capacity to match the peaks and valleys of demand. Organizations frequently employ several strategies simultaneously to solve the complex problem of balancing supply and demand.

Yield management was presented as a sophisticated form of supply and demand management that balances capacity utilization, pricing, market segmentation, and financial return. Long practiced by the passenger airline industry, this strategy is growing in use by hotel, shipping, car rental, and other capacity-constrained industries where bookings are made in advance. Essentially, yield management allows organizations to decide on a monthly, weekly, daily, or even hourly basis to whom they want to sell their service capacity at what price.

All strategies for aligning capacity and demand need to be approached with caution. Any one of the strategies is likely to imply changes in multiple marketing mix elements to support the strategy. Whenever such changes are made, even if done well, there is a risk of the firm losing focus or inadvertently altering its image in pursuit of increased revenues. While this is not necessarily bad, the potential strategic impact on the total organization should definitely be considered.

The last section of the chapter discussed situations where it is not possible to align supply and demand. In these unresolved capacity utilization situations, the inevitable result is customer waiting. Strategies for effectively managing waiting lines were described such as employing operational logic, establishing a reservation process, differentiating waiting customers, and making waiting fun or at least tolerable.

Discussion Questions

1. Why do service organizations lack the capability to inventory their services? Compare a car repair and maintenance service with an automobile manufacturer/dealer in terms of inventory capability.

2. Discuss the four scenarios presented in Figure 14.1 and presented in the text (excess demand, demand exceeds optimum capacity, demand and supply are balanced, excess capacity) in the context of a basketball team selling seats for its games. What are the challenges for management under each scenario?

3. Discuss the four common types of constraints (time, labor, equipment, facilities) facing service businesses and give an example of each (real or hypothetical).

4. How does optimal capacity utilization differ from maximal capacity utilization? Give an example of a case where the two might be the same and an example of where they are different.

5. Choose a local restaurant or some other type of service with fluctuating demand. What is the likely underlying pattern of demand? What causes the pattern? Is it predictable or random?

6. Describe the two basic strategies for matching supply and demand, and give at least two specific examples of each.

7. What is yield management? Discuss the risks in adopting a yield management strategy.

8. How might yield management apply in the management of the following: a Broadway theater? A consulting firm? A commuter train?

9. Describe the four basic waiting line strategies, and give an example of each one, preferably based on your own experiences as a consumer.

Exercises

1. Choose a local service organization that is challenged by fixed capacity and fluctuating demand. Interview the marketing manager (or other knowledgeable person) to learn (*a*) in what ways capacity is constrained, (*b*) the basic patterns of demand, and (*c*) strategies the organization has used to align supply and demand. Write up the answers to these questions, and make your own recommendations regarding other strategies the organization might use.

2. Assume you manage a winter ski resort in Colorado or Banff, Canada. (a) Explain the underlying pattern of demand fluctuation that is likely to occur at your resort and the challenges it would present to you as a manager. Is the pattern of demand predictable or random? (b) Explain and give examples of how you might use both demand-oriented and supply-oriented strategies to smooth the peaks and valleys of demand during peak and slow periods.

3. Choose a local organization where you know people have to wait in line for service. Design a waiting line strategy for the organization.

4. Visit the website of Wells Fargo Bank (www.wellsfargo.com), a leader in online banking. What online services does the bank currently offer? How do these online services help Wells Fargo manage the peaks and valleys of customer demand? How do its strategies to use more ATMs, in-store bank branches, and other alternative delivery strategies (see Exhibit 14.1) complement the online strategies?

Notes

1. www.ritzcarlton.com, 2002.
2   J. S. Hirsch, "Vacationing Families Head Downtown to Welcoming Arms of Business Hotels," *The Wall Street Journal,* June 13, 1994, p. B1.
3. Ibid.
4. C. Lovelock, "Getting the Most Out of Your Productive Capacity," in *Product Plus* (Boston: McGraw-Hill, 1994), chap. 16.

5. C. H. Lovelock, "Classifying Services to Gain Strategic Marketing Insights," *Journal of Marketing* 47, no. 3 (Summer 1983), pp. 9–20.

6. B. Fryer, "High Tech the Old-Fashioned Way: An Interview with Tom Siebel of Siebel Systems," *Harvard Business Review,* March 2001, p. 123.

7. Portions of this section are based on C. H. Lovelock, "Strategies for Managing Capacity-Constrained Service Organizations," in *Managing Services: Marketing, Operations, and Human Resources,* 2nd ed. (Englewood Cliffs, NJ: Prentice Hall, 1992), pp. 154–68.

8. D. Kenny, H. McGrath, T. J. Olsen, B. Sullivan, M. R. Tutton, and S. Yusko, "Service Quality under Crisis . . . AT&T Serving the Service—a Case Study," in *Advances in Services Marketing and Management,* vol. 1, ed. T. A. Swartz, D. E. Bowen, and S. W. Brown (Greenwich, CT: JAI Press, 1992), pp. 229–46.

9. E. C. Clemmer and B. Schneider, "Toward Understanding and Controlling Customer Dissatisfaction with Waiting during Peak Demand Times," in *Designing a Winning Service Strategy,* ed. M. J. Bitner and L. A. Crosby (Chicago: American Marketing Association, 1989), pp. 87–91.

10. Lovelock, "Getting the Most Out of Your Productive Capacity."

11. www.NeoIt.com, 2002.

12. M. E. Berge and C. A. Hopperstad, "Demand Driven Dispatch: A Method for Dynamic Aircraft Capacity Assignment, Models and Algorithms," *Operations Research* 41, no. 1 (January–February 1993), pp. 153–68.

13. Lovelock, "Getting the Most Out of Your Productive Capacity."

14. See S. E. Kimes, "Yield Management: A Tool for Capacity-Constrained Service Firms," *Journal of Operations Management* 8, no. 4 (October 1989), pp. 348–63; and S. E. Kimes and R. B. Chase, "The Strategic Levers of Yield Management," *Journal of Service Research* 1, no. 2 (November 1998), pp. 156–66.

15. Kimes, "Yield Management."

16. R. Desiraji and S. M. Shugan, "Strategic Service Pricing and Yield Management," *Journal of Marketing* 63, no. 1 (January 1999), pp. 44–56.

17. Kimes, "Yield Management."

18. For research supporting the relationship between longer waits and decreased satisfaction and quality evaluations see Clemmer and Schneider, "Toward Understanding and Controlling Customer Dissatisfaction"; A. Th. H. Pruyn and A. Smidts, "Customer Evaluation of Queues: Three Exploratory Studies," *European Advances in Consumer Research* 1 (1993), pp. 371–82; S. Taylor, "Waiting for Service: The Relationship between Delays and Evaluations of Service," *Journal of Marketing* 58 (April 1994), pp. 56–69; K. L. Katz, B. M. Larson, and R. C. Larson, "Prescription for the Waiting-in-Line Blues: Entertain, Enlighten, and Engage," *Sloan Management Review,* Winter 1991, pp. 44–53; and S. Taylor and J. D. Claxton, "Delays and the Dynamics of Service Evaluations," *Journal of the Academy of Marketing Science* 22, no. 3 (1994), pp. 254–64.

19. L. L. Berry and L. R. Cooper, "Competing with Time-Saving Service," *Business,* April–June 1990, pp. 3–7.

20. R. Henkoff, "Finding, Training and Keeping the Best Service Workers," *Fortune,* October 3, 1994, pp. 110–22.

21. J. A. Fitzsimmons and M. J. Fitzsimmons, *Service Management,* 3rd ed. (New York: Irwin/McGraw-Hill, 2000), chap. 11.

22. S. Power, "Mickey Mouse, Nike Give Advice on Air Security," *The Wall Street Journal,* January 24, 2002, p. B1.

23. Fitzsimmons and Fitzsimmons, *Service Management,* chap. 11.

24. Lovelock, "Getting the Most Out of Your Productive Capacity."

25. For an excellent review of the literature on customer perceptions of and reactions to various aspects of waiting time, see S. Taylor and G. Fullerton, "Waiting for Services: Perceptions Management of the Wait Experience," in *Handbook of Services Marketing and Management,* eds. T. A. Swartz and D. Iacobucci (Thousands Oaks, CA: Sage Publications), 2000, pp. 171–89.

26. D. A. Maister, "The Psychology of Waiting Lines," in *The Service Encounter,* ed. J. A. Czepiel, M. R. Solomon, and C. F. Surprenant (Lexington, MA: Lexington Books, 1985), pp. 113–23.

27. S. Taylor, "The Effects of Filled Waiting Time and Service Provider Control over the Delay on Evaluations of Service," *Journal of the Academy of Marketing Science* 23, no. 1 (1995), pp. 38–48.

28. A. Bennett, "Their Business Is on the Line," *The Wall Street Journal,* December 7, 1990, p. B1.

29. L. Dube-Rioux, B. H. Schmitt, and F. Leclerc, "Consumer's Reactions to Waiting: When Delays Affect the Perception of Service Quality," in *Advances in Consumer Research,* vol. 16, ed. T. Srull (Provo, UT: Association for Consumer Research, 1988), pp. 59–63.

30. M. K. Hui, M. V. Thakor, and R. Gill, "The Effect of Delay Type and Service Stage on Consumers' Reactions to Waiting," *Journal of Consumer Research* 24 (March 1998), pp. 469–79.

31. Dube-Rioux, Schmitt, and Leclerc, "Consumer's Reactions to Waiting."

32. Taylor, "Waiting for Service."

33. M. K. Hui and D. K. Tse, "What to Tell Consumers in Waits of Different Lengths: An Integrative Model of Service Evaluation," *Journal of Marketing* 60 (April 1996), pp. 81–90.

34. J. Baker and M. Cameron, "The Effects of the Service Environment on Affect and Consumer Perception of Waiting Time: An Integrative Review and Research Propositions," *Journal of the Academy of Marketing Science* 24(4), 1996, pp. 338–49.

Part 5

MANAGING SERVICE PROMISES

The fourth provider gap, shown in the accompanying figure, illustrates the difference between service delivery and the service provider's external communications. Promises made by a service company through its media advertising, sales force, and other communications may potentially raise customer expectations that serve as the standard against which customers assess service quality. The discrepancy between actual and promised service therefore broadens the customer gap. Broken promises can occur for many reasons: ineffective marketing communications, overpromising in advertising or personal selling, inadequate coordination between operations and marketing, and differences in policies and procedures across service outlets. As an example, when a bank participating in a study conducted by one of the authors introduced a new student loan program, the marketing arm of the bank sold too many of the loans too

Provider Gap 4

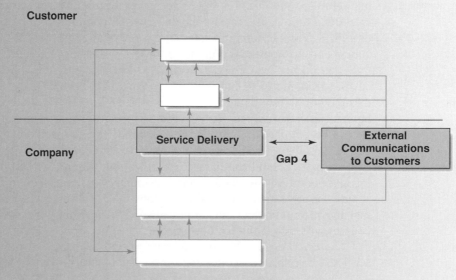

fast without verifying in advance whether the operations group was geared up to mail out the loan checks as promised. As you may imagine, broken promises and irate customers were the result. During the month following the introduction of the loan service the bank received more than 500 complaint letters from frustrated customers asking, "Where's my check?"

In addition to unduly elevating expectations through exaggerated claims, there are other, less obvious ways in which external communications influence customers' service quality assessments. Customers' service perceptions may be enhanced if the company educates them to be better users of the service. As one bank executive observed, "We don't teach our customers how to use us well and why we do the things we do." Customers may also be more satisfied if companies manage their expectations, teaching them what is to come in the service rather than allowing them to form their own (often too lofty) expectations of what is to come. Part of managing expectations involves not deliberately overpromising, but another part involves simply being realistic and concrete about what a customer can anticipate occurring in the service.

Inadequate management of promises reflects a breakdown in coordination between employees responsible for delivering the service and employees in charge of describing and/or promoting the service to customers. When employees who promote the service do not fully understand the reality of service delivery, they are likely to make exaggerated promises or fail to communicate to customers aspects of the service intended to serve them well. For instance, a securities brokerage company that participated in a study done by one of the authors had a "48-hour rule" prohibiting its account executives from buying or selling securities for their personal accounts for the first 48 hours after information about the securities was supplied by the company. The brokers could advise clients and buy or sell on their behalf right away, but they themselves had to wait 48 hours before buying or selling for their own accounts. The company did not communicate this information to its customers, contributing to a perception that "all the good deals are probably made by the brokers for themselves." The result was poor service quality perceptions. Effectively coordinating actual service delivery with external communications, therefore, narrows provider gap 4 and favorably affects the customer gap as well.

In service companies, a fit between communications about service and actual service delivery is necessary. Chapter 15 is devoted to the topic of integrated services marketing communications—careful integration and organization of all of a service marketing organization's external and internal communications channels. The chapter describes why this communication is necessary and how companies can do it well. Accurate and appropriate communications—advertising, personal selling, and publicity—that do not overpromise or misrepresent are essential in delivering services that customers perceive as high in quality. One of the major difficulties associated with these types of communications is that they involve issues that cross disciplinary boundaries. Because service advertising promises what _people_ do, and because what people do cannot be controlled in the same way as machines that produce physical goods, this type of communication involves functions other than the marketing department. Successful company communications are the responsibility of both marketing and operations: marketing must accurately but beguilingly reflect what happens in actual service encounters, and operations must deliver what is promised in advertising. If communications set up unrealistic expectations for customers, the actual encounter will disappoint the customer.

Chapter 16 deals with another issue related to managing promises, the pricing of services. In packaged goods (and even in durable goods), many customers possess enough price knowledge before purchase to be able to judge whether a price is fair or in line with competition. For example, even though variability in prices exists, the majority of customers knows what a six-pack of Coke, a pair of Gap khakis, or a toothbrush costs. With services, customers often have no internal reference point for prices before purchase and consumption. Pricing strategies such as discounting, "everyday prices," and couponing obviously need to be different with services in cases where the customer has no sense of the price to start with! Techniques for developing prices for services are more complicated than those for pricing tangible goods, and all of the approaches for setting prices must be adapted for the special characteristics of services.

In summary, external communications—whether from marketing communications or pricing—can create a larger customer gap by raising expectations about service delivery. In addition to improving service delivery, companies must also manage all communications to customers so that inflated promises do not lead to higher expectations. Companies must also manage the messages conveyed by pricing so that customer expectations are in line with what they perceive they receive.

15

INTEGRATED SERVICES MARKETING COMMUNICATIONS

This chapter's objectives are to

1. Introduce the concept of integrated services marketing communications, and discuss the key reasons for service communication problems.

2. Present four key ways to integrate marketing communications in service organizations.

3. Present specific strategies for managing promises, managing customer expectations, educating customers, and managing internal communications.

4. Provide perspective on the popular service objective of exceeding customer expectations.

Mail Boxes, Etc. Integrates Marketing Communications

If you are one of the estimated 140 million people who annually watch the Super Bowl, you may have noticed in the past few years a somewhat unusual 30-second commercial among the Budweiser lizards and the Toyota trucks. Rather than being for a mammoth global firm, these commercials feature the "little guys" of business—businesses, in fact, with fewer than 20 employees—businesses such as Jeremy's MicroBatch Ice Creams, a company run from the apartment of its 22-year-old founder Jeremy Kraus, or tiny Pump Products, which makes a handheld basketball-inflating pocket pump. According to owners Robert Lange and Chuck Davey, the Super Bowl ad for Pump Products "resulted in tens of thousands of dollars in sales. We're still catching our breath."[1]

How can these small companies afford the roughly $1.6 million per commercial cost for such advertising? The answer lies in one of the most ingenious services marketing communication campaigns of the last decade. The campaign was sponsored by the San Diego–based service franchise organization Mail Boxes, Etc., the world's largest nonfood franchise operation with more than 4,000 centers in 58 countries. In addition to mailboxes, Mail Boxes, Etc. (MBE) offers all forms of mailing (FedEx, UPS, U.S. Postal Service), communication (voice mail, secretarial and answering services, fax, Internet, Western Union), packaging, and other office services (color copying, office supplies, design and printing of cards and stationery). The Super Bowl ad was part of MBE's overall program to reach and convince its primary target market: small businesses.

The company created the idea of a contest for a 15-second commercial slot inside MBE's 30-second commercial on the Super Bowl to extend its investment in advertising by generating publicity and word of mouth. To be eligible for the contest, small businesses were required to submit both an application and an essay of 100 or fewer words about why they deserve to be featured. On-site mailings and promotions to franchisees built interest in the campaign. According to the agency handling the promotion, the contest "takes a commercial and turns it into an event," garnering publicity and extensive word of mouth.[2] An important side benefit of the contest was that the company was able to build an electronic database of its franchisees' customers from the entries, which then became the foundation for subsequent direct mailings.

The contest began as part of MBE's $4 million "Making Business Easier Worldwide" campaign, designed to emphasize the chain's ability to provide full-service solutions for small business. The initial mass advertising campaign aired on television news and sports broadcasts, prime-time network TV programming, and national cable outlets. Radio and point-of-purchase advertising, including in-store materials and entry forms, were also disseminated. To further extend and coordinate the communication program, entries could be submitted on the Web, which contained more details and more advertising.[3]

In the first year of the campaign, the company received more than 3,500 entries. The total cost of the promotion was $3 million, including the Super Bowl commercial. An advertising critic from the trade paper *Advertising Age* pointed out that the contest and Super Bowl feature "not only taps [sic] vicarious excitement for the lucky entrepreneurs, it underscores MBE's dedication to small business." In his words, it was "the best idea on the Super Bowl."[4]

MBE's external advertising campaign is not the only element of its communication program that deserves mention. The company's website (www.mbe.com), shown in Figure 15.1, encapsulates the integrated services communications approach: customers can view a television ad, open a franchise, find out about next year's Super Bowl promotion, read current publicity, send an e-mail to the customer service department, and even find a job. As you will see in this chapter, servicescapes (discussed in Chapter 10) are part of a service firm's communication program. MBE, along with USA Technologies, recently deployed MBE Business Express, a new service in the form of kiosks in Marriott and Best Western hotels that allow 24-hour access to office equipment (PC, laser printer, fax, photocopier, laptop hookup, and high-speed Internet connections) when travelers are away from the office in a hotel. And to facilitate internal communications—another critical part of the services marketing communications mix—MBE has established Internet communications within its system and for providing services to its franchisees and their customers. Among the internal communications implemented using the Internet are a "chat room" on the firm's Internet site that enables franchisees to discuss their problems and help one another; direct communications from corporate headquarters, including the monthly publication *Notes and News* with articles of interest to franchisees; and the capability to tailor an individual

FIGURE 15.1 **The website for MBE demonstrates the company's successful efforts to integrate services marketing communications. (Courtesy Mail Boxes, Etc.)**

store's home page to show the special services it offers that other MBE franchisees do not.[5]

Mail Boxes, Etc., has used many elements of the services marketing communications mix effectively, particularly by coordinating external communication, by generating effective internal communication between the company and its franchisees and among franchisees, and by creating appropriate tangibles. All of its communication mix elements are designed to convey the same message about the company—that MBE provides service solutions and makes doing business easier.

A major cause of poorly perceived service is the difference between what a firm promises about a service and what it actually delivers. Customer expectations are shaped by both uncontrollable and company-controlled factors. Word-of-mouth communication, customer experiences with other service providers, and customer needs are key factors that influence customer expectations but are rarely controllable by the firm. However, controllable factors such as company advertising, personal selling, and the promises made by service personnel also influence the expectations that customers hold for a service. In this chapter we focus on these controllable factors. Accurate, coordinated, and appropriate company communication—advertising, personal selling, and online and other messages that do not overpromise or misrepresent—is essential to delivering services that customers perceive as high in quality.

Because company communications about services promise what people do, and because people's behavior cannot be standardized like physical goods produced by machines, the potential for a mismatch between customer expectations and perceptions of service delivery (provider gap 4) is high. By regulating and coordinating communication within and outside the organization, companies can minimize the size of this gap.

THE NEED FOR COORDINATION IN MARKETING COMMUNICATION

Marketing communication is not what it used to be. In the past, customers received information about goods and services from a limited number of sources, often mass marketing sources such as television and newspapers. In this type of environment, it was not difficult for a marketer to convey a uniform brand image and to coordinate promises. However, today's consumers of both goods and services receive communications from a far richer variety of sources—targeted magazines, online sources, coupons, and a host of sales promotion tools. And consumers of services receive even more communications from sources such as servicescapes, customer service departments, and everyday service encounter interactions with employees. These vehicles add to the variety and volume of information about a particular brand or company, but also to the complexity of that information. If the messages conflict, confused company images and promises can result, leading to a difference between what customers expect based on the messages and what they receive in service delivery. (See Exhibit 15.1)

Any company that disseminates information through different channels needs to be concerned with integrating them so that the customer receives unified messages and promises about its offerings. Service companies must add to the traditional communications or promotion mix a concern about the ways that customers receive information about services through interactive marketing, or marketing between employees and customers. Figure 15.2 shows an enhanced version of the marketing triangle we presented in Chapter 11, demonstrating that the customer of services is the target of two types of marketing communication. First, external marketing communication extends from the company to the customer and includes such traditional communication channels as advertising, sales promotion, and public relations. Exhibit 15.2 provides a review of basic

FIGURE 15.2
Communications and the Services Marketing Triangle

Source: Adapted by permission of Prentice Hall, Englewood Cliffs, NJ, based on P. Kotler, *Marketing Management: Analysis, Planning, Implementation, and Control,* 8th ed. (1994), p. 470.

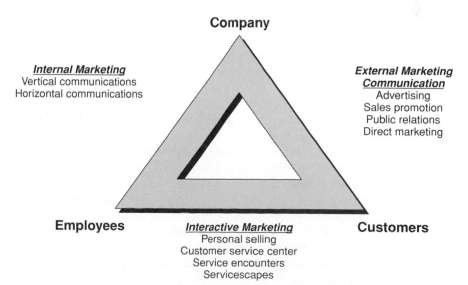

Company

Internal Marketing
Vertical communications
Horizontal communications

External Marketing Communication
Advertising
Sales promotion
Public relations
Direct marketing

Employees

Interactive Marketing
Personal selling
Customer service center
Service encounters
Servicescapes

Customers

15.1 INTEGRATED BUSINESS-TO-BUSINESS MARKETING CAMPAIGNS

In addition to the business-to-consumer Mail Boxes, Etc., example in the chapter opener, three companies illustrate effective integrated external marketing campaigns, all of them in the business-to-business arena. These include Cisco, Accenture, and Metropolitan Insurance Company. Cisco created a "Cisco Internet Generation" campaign that effectively portrays the themes of reliability, precision, and innovation through broadcast, print, and Internet advertising. Because it is a network equipment manufacturer that provides hardware designed for seamless communication, its marketing needs to communicate this seamless communication. It does so by using a signature tag line, "Empowering the Internet generation," throughout all the advertising and by consistently linking print and broadcast with an Internet presence. For example, one print ad features people walking through a rice paddy with an airplane reflected in the water. The text simply states, "Last year your customers spent $172 billion on business travel" with a Web address pointing to Cisco's videoconferencing technology that can save money. Similarly, all ads are targeted to particular levels in a company—whether business strategist or technical expert—and each points to a website tuned to the target's level of technical expertise and interest. This allows each ad to link to a call for action on the website, bringing customers closer to buying product. The ads have been very effective, raising unaided brand awareness 80 percent, outpacing competitors Lucent Technologies and Nortel Networks. In a study designed to examine the impact of the campaign, Cisco's reputation as an Internet expert was 250 percent higher than Microsoft and 500 percent higher than IBM.

In 2001 Accenture won the Annual Sawyer Award for the best integrated marketing campaign for business-to-business advertising. The company had an unusual challenge: it was ordered by a court to change its name from Andersen Consulting with less than four months to launch its new name and position. Accenture and its agency created a $175 million rebranding campaign including TV, print, and outdoor ads showing a ripped-through signature of its former name with the date 01-01-01 as its "rebirth" and the tag line "Now it gets interesting." To support the advertising, the company also sponsored a pro golf tournament and unusual, creative tactics such as putting its name on hang gliders. Because the company was repositioning itself as a consultant not just for business but also in technology, it used images of virtual surgery and bacteria in computer chip technology. In the words of the judges, "The campaign is stellar work, encompassing original ideas, beautiful photography and clear messaging." After six months, it clearly had succeeded: it achieved an increase of 75–100 percent awareness.

The runner-up in the Sawyer ad contest for integrated campaign, Metropolitan Insurance Company, was acknowledged for its ability to tie together online and offline advertising components. The print ads and direct mail pieces drive customers to an online calculator that helps a company's employees determine the right amount of insurance they need.

Sources: J. E. Frook, "Cisco Scores with Its Latest Generation of Empowering Ads," *B to B*, August 20, 2001, p. 20; K. Maddox, "Sawyer Awards," *B to B*, December 10, 2001, pp. 19–21.

principles of external marketing communication. Second, interactive marketing communication involves the messages that employees give to customers through such channels as personal selling, customer service interactions, service encounter interactions, and servicescapes (discussed in Chapter 10). While personal selling is a traditional communication vehicle and interactions with customer service departments of companies occur with goods as well as services, the other two forms of communication are unique to services. A service company must be sure that these interactive messages are consistent both among themselves and with those sent through external communications. To do so, the third side of the triangle, internal marketing communications, must be managed so that communications from the company to employees are accurate, complete, and consistent with what the customer is hearing or seeing.

Consider an example from your own experience that may illustrate what happens when services marketing communications are not integrated. Have you ever seen an advertisement for a service, such as a new sandwich from McDonald's, then gone to

15.2 REVIEW OF MARKETING PRINCIPLES ABOUT COMMUNICATIONS

Some of the basics about communication are the same for goods as for services. We will not cover all the basics again in this chapter; instead, we will discuss the aspects of communication that are different for services and will illustrate communications in a service context. To give you a quick review of the basics that you learned in your marketing principles class, a brief summary is provided here. For more information, return to your marketing principles textbook.

Marketing Communications Mix

The traditional components of the marketing communications mix communicate information to customers about products and services:

- *Advertising:* any paid form of nonpersonal presentation and promotion of a company's offerings by an identified sponsor.

- *Sales promotion:* short-term incentives such as coupons, premiums, or discounts that stimulate customer purchases.

- *Public relations:* building a favorable company image with a firm's publics though publicity, relations with the news media, and community events.

- *Direct marketing:* the use of mail, telephone, fax, e-mail, and other nonpersonal tools to communicate directly with specific consumers to obtain a direct response.

- *Personal selling:* personal presentation by a representative from the firm to make sales and build customer relationships.

Steps in Developing Effective Communication

1. *Select the target audience,* including potential buyers, current users, and possibly others who influence the buying decision.

2. *Determine the communication objectives,* typically involving such goals as awareness, knowledge, liking, preference, conviction, and purchase.

3. *Decide on a budget,* including how much to spend on the total campaign as well as what to allocate to various promotion types.

4. *Create a message,* capturing what to say, how to say it, and who will deliver the message.

5. *Choose media,* among them personal communication channels such as personal selling or nonpersonal communication channels such as television and newspapers. We also distinguish between mass media (such as television) and targeted media (such as specialized magazines and direct mail).

6. *Collect feedback,* which includes researching how effective the communications were in meeting the objectives.

Whether services or goods, the steps involved in designing an external communication mix are the same. Each of these steps involves many substeps and a variety of decisions, all of which are described in the source from which we obtained this overview. These steps, however, do not cover the internal communication and coordination that needs to be achieved in a service organization. These issues are treated in the text of this chapter.

your local McDonald's and not found it available? Did the employee behind the counter offer a reason the sandwich was not available? Did he or she even realize that it was advertised and for sale elsewhere? One of the authors consulted for a bank on the West Coast where both customers and employees constantly faced this situation. Bank advertising was changed frequently and quickly to meet competitive offerings, but the bank tellers' training in the new offerings did not keep pace with the changes in advertising. As a result, customers came in expecting new accounts and rates to be available, and employees were embarrassed because they hadn't been informed.

This example hints at one of the main reasons that integrated marketing communications have not been the norm in many companies. All too often, various parts of the company are responsible for different aspects of communication. The sales department develops and executes sales communication. The marketing department prepares and disseminates advertising. A public relations firm may be responsible for publicity.

Functional specialists handle sales promotions, direct marketing, and company websites. The human resources department trains front-line employees for service interactions, and still another area is responsible for the customer service department. Rarely is one person responsible for the overall communications strategy in a company.

Today, however, more companies are adopting the concept of *integrated marketing communications (IMC),* where the company carefully integrates and organizes all of its external communications channels. As a marketing executive explained it,

> Integrated marketing communications build a strong brand identity in the marketplace by tying together and reinforcing all your images and messages. IMC means that all your corporate messages, positioning and images, and identity are coordinated across all venues. It means that your PR materials say the same things as your direct mail campaign, and your advertising has the same 'look and feel' as your website.[6]

In this chapter we propose that a more complex type of integrated marketing communication is needed for services than for goods. Not only must external communications channels be coordinated, as they need to be with physical goods; but with services, both external communications and interactive communication channels must be organized and communicated to produce the service promise. To do that, internal marketing communications channels must be managed so that employees and the company are in agreement about what is communicated to the customer. As Figure 15.2 shows, this requires both vertical communications—typically called *internal marketing communications*—and horizontal communications across departments and areas of the firm. We call this more complicated version of IMC *integrated services marketing communications (ISMC).* ISMC requires that everyone involved with communication clearly understand both the company's marketing strategy and its promises to consumers.

KEY REASONS FOR SERVICE COMMUNICATION PROBLEMS

Discrepancies between service delivery and external communications, in the form of exaggerated promises and/or the absence of information about service delivery aspects intended to serve customers well, can powerfully affect consumer perceptions of service quality. The factors that contribute to these communication problems include (1) inadequate management of service promises, (2) elevated customer expectations, (3) insufficient customer education, and (4) inadequate internal communications. In this chapter, we first describe the problems stemming from these factors and then detail strategies that firms have found useful in dealing with them.

Inadequate Management of Service Promises

A discrepancy between service delivery and promises occurs when companies fail to manage service promises—the vows made by salespeople, advertising, and service personnel. One of the primary reasons for this discrepancy is that the company lacks the information and integration needed to make fulfillable promises. Salespeople often sell services, particularly new business services, before their actual availability and without having an exact date when they will be ready for market. Demand and supply variations also contribute to problems in fulfilling service promises. They make service provision possible at some times, improbable at others, and difficult to predict. The traditional functional structure in many companies obscures the end-to-end processes that allow the company to project when work will be accomplished or whether the service to be delivered will match what is promised.

Inadequate Management of Customer Expectations

Appropriate and accurate communication about services is the responsibility of both marketing and operations. Marketing must accurately (if compellingly) reflect what happens in actual service encounters; operations must deliver what is promised in communications. For example, when a management consulting firm introduces a new offering such as return-on-quality analysis, the marketing and sales departments must make the offering appealing enough to be viewed as superior to competing services. In promoting and differentiating the service, however, the company cannot afford to raise expectations above the level at which its consultants can consistently perform. If advertising, personal selling, or any other external communication sets up unrealistic expectations, actual encounters will disappoint customers.

Because of increasing deregulation and intensifying competition in the services sector, many service firms feel more pressure than ever before to acquire new business and to meet or beat competition. To accomplish these ends, service firms often over-promise in selling, advertising, and other company communications. In the airline industry, advertising is a constant battlefield of competing offers and price reductions to gain the patronage of customers. The greater the extent to which a service firm feels pressured to generate new customers, and perceives that the industry norm is to over-promise ("everyone else in our industry overpromises"), the greater is the firm's propensity to overpromise.

If advertising shows a smiling young worker at the counter in a McDonald's commercial, the customer expects that, at least most of the time, there will be a smiling young worker in the local McDonald's. If advertising claims that a customer's wake-up call will always be on time at a Ramada Inn, the customer expects no mistakes. Raising expectations to unrealistic levels may lead to more initial business but invariably fosters customer disappointment and discourages repeat business.

Inadequate Customer Education

Differences between service delivery and promises also occur when companies do not sufficiently educate their customers. If customers are unclear about how the service will be provided, what their role in delivery involves, and how to evaluate services they have never used before, they will be disappointed and often hold the service company, not themselves, responsible. Research by TARP, a service research firm, reveals that one-third of all customer complaints are related to problems caused by customers themselves. These errors or problems in service—even when they are "caused" by the customer—still lead customers to defect. For this reason the firm must assume responsibility for educating customers.

Inexperienced customers, by definition, may not understand how to use services correctly. As an example, burgeoning online services have high visibility and publicity; hardly a day goes by without a story about a new service on the Internet. Because this service industry is ever-changing, the services are beyond the understanding of many customers, and the churn rate (defection of customers) is high because customers are not accurately informed.

For services high in credence properties—expert services that are difficult for customers to evaluate even after they have received the services—many customers do not know the criteria by which they should judge the service.

For high-involvement services, such as long-term medical treatment or purchase of a first home, customers are also unlikely to comprehend and anticipate the service process. First-time home buyers rarely understand the complex set of services (inspection, title services, insurance) and processes (securing a mortgage, offers and counteroffers, escrow) that will be involved in their purchases. Professionals and other providers of high-involvement services often forget that customers are novices who must be educated about each step in the process. They assume that an overview at the beginning of the service, or a manual or set of instructions, will equip the customer. Unfortunately this is rarely sufficient, and customers defect because they can neither understand the process nor appreciate the value received from the service.

A final condition under which customer education can be beneficial involves services where demand and supply are not synchronized as discussed in Chapter 14. If the customer is not informed about peaks and valleys in demand, service overloads and failures, not to mention underutilized capacity, are likely to result.

Inadequate Internal Marketing Communications

Another major difficulty associated with providing service that matches promises is that multiple functions in the organization, such as marketing and operations, must be coordinated to achieve the goal of service provision. Because service advertising and personal selling promise what *people* do, frequent and effective communication across functions—horizontal communication—is critical. If internal communication is poor, perceived service quality is at risk. If company advertising and other promises are developed without input from operations, contact personnel may not be able to deliver service that matches the image portrayed in marketing efforts.

Not all service organizations advertise, but all need coordination or integration across departments or functions to be able to deliver quality service. All need internal communication between the sales force and service providers. Horizontal communication also must occur between the human resource and marketing departments. To deliver excellent customer service, firms must be certain to inform and motivate employees to deliver what their customers expect. If those who understand customer expectations (marketing and sales personnel) do not communicate this information to contact employees, their lack of knowledge will affect the quality of service that employees deliver.

A final form of internal coordination central to providing service quality is consistency in policies and procedures across departments and branches. If a service organization operates many outlets under the same name, whether franchised or company owned, customers expect similar performance across those outlets. If managers of individual branches or outlets have significant autonomy in procedures and policies, customers may not receive the same level of service quality across the branches.

FOUR CATEGORIES OF STRATEGIES TO MATCH SERVICE PROMISES WITH DELIVERY

Figure 15.3 shows four categories of strategies to match service delivery with promises: (1) manage service promises, (2) manage customer expectations, (3) improve customer education, and (4) manage internal marketing communication. Managing service promises involves coordinating the vows made by all external and interactive marketing sources to ensure that they are consistent and feasible. Managing customer expectations incorporates strategies that tell customers the firm cannot or may not always provide the level of service they expect. Educating customers means providing them with information about the service process or evaluative criteria about important aspects of the service. Finally, managing internal marketing communication means transmitting information across organizational boundaries— upward, downward, and

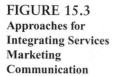

FIGURE 15.3
Approaches for
Integrating Services
Marketing
Communication

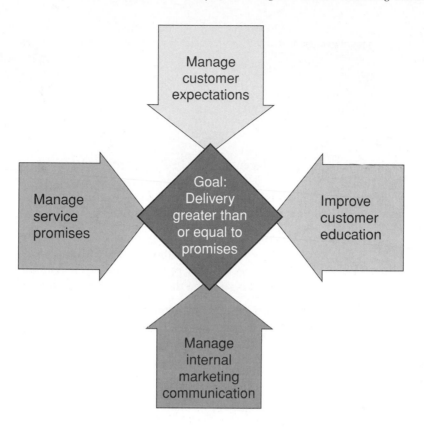

across—to align all functions with customer expectations. Strategies in each of these categories are discussed in detail in the following sections.

Manage Service Promises

In manufacturing physical goods, the departments that make promises and those that deliver them can operate independently. Goods can be fully designed and produced and then turned over to marketing for promotion and sale. In services, however, the sales and marketing departments make promises about what other employees in the organization will fulfill. Because what employees do cannot be standardized like physical goods produced mechanically, greater coordination and management of promises are required. Successful services advertising and personal selling become the responsibility of both marketing and operations.

Figure 15.4 shows specific strategies that are effective in managing promises.

Create Effective Services Advertising

One of the most critical ways that services promises are communicated is through advertising. Intangibility makes services advertising different from product advertising and difficult for marketers. The intangible nature of services creates problems for consumers both before and after purchase. Before buying services, consumers have difficulty understanding them and coming up with evoked sets of services to consider.[7] After buying services, consumers have trouble evaluating their service experiences. Various authors have suggested strategies to overcome these problems, but before we turn to them, we will discuss intangibility in greater depth.

FIGURE 15.4
Approaches for Managing Service Promises

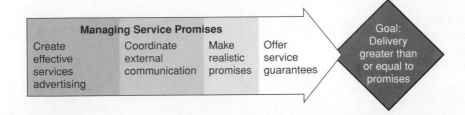

Banwari Mittal recently described the particular difficulties associated with intangibility by dividing it into five properties, each of which has implications for services advertising. In his view, intangibility involves incorporeal existence, abstractness, generality, nonsearchability, and mental impalpability:[8]

- *Incorporeal existence.* The service product is neither made out of physical matter nor occupies physical space. Although the delivery mechanism (such as a Jiffy Lube outlet) may occupy space, the service itself (car servicing and oil change) does not. This makes showing the service difficult compared to a product.

- *Abstractness.* Services are considered apart from any particular instances or material objects.[9] Service benefits such as financial security, fun, or health do not correspond directly with objects, making them difficult to visualize and understand. The Ad Council and the U.S. State Department are currently working together to create a media campaign to promote American goodwill at home and abroad and to help fight the war against terrorism. This abstract concept will be challenging to portray, and at this writing the Ad Council has not arrived at a sufficiently concrete and effective approach.[10]

- *Generality versus specificity. Generality* refers to a class of things, persons, events, or properties, whereas *specificity* refers to particular objects, people, or events. Many services and service promises are described in generalities (wonderful experience, superior education, completely satisfied customers), making them difficult to differentiate from those of competitors.

- *Nonsearchability.* Because service is a performance, it often cannot be previewed or inspected in advance of purchase. As we discussed in Chapter 2, this is particularly true of services that are classified as either experience or credence services.

- *Mental impalpability.* Services are often too complex, multidimensional, and difficult to grasp mentally. Impalpability is the absence of prior exposure, familiarity, or knowledge, which makes services difficult to interpret.

According to Mittal, only incorporeal existence is an inevitable property of services. The other four often tend to be present but are not intrinsic to intangibility. By following the strategies shown in Table 15.1, service advertising can overcome these challenging properties. The abstract can be made concrete, the general can be made specific, the nonsearchable can be made searchable, and the mentally impalpable can be made palpable.

Service marketers have created guidelines for service advertising effectiveness. These guidelines include the following:

- *Use narratives to demonstrate the service experience.* Many services are experiential, and a uniquely effective approach to communicating them involves story-based appeals. Research conducted by Mattila concluded that consumers with relatively

TABLE 15.1
Services Advertising Strategies Matched with Properties of Intangibility

Source: Adapted from B. Mittal, "The Advertising of Services: Meeting the Challenge of Intangibility," *Journal of Service Research* 2, no. 1, August 1999, pp. 98–116.

Property of Intangibility	Advertising Strategy	Description
Incorporeal existence	Physical representation	Show physical components of service that are unique, indicate high quality, and create the right association.
Generality	*Make the message claim specific by*	
	• System documentation.	Objectively document physical system capacity by showing facts and figures.
	• Performance documentation.	Document and cite past positive performance statistics.
	• Service performance episode.	Present a vivid story of an actual service delivery incident that relates to the important service attribute.
Abstractness	Service consumption episode	Capture and display typical customers benefiting from the service, evoking particular incidents.
Nonsearchability	Performance documentation	Cite independently audited performance.
	Consumption documentation	Obtain and present customer testimonials.
Impalpability	Service process episode	Present a vivid documentary on the step-by-step service process.
	Case history episode	Present an actual case history of what the firm did for a specific client.

low familiarity with a service category prefer appeals based on stories to appeals based on lists of service attributes. Furthermore, the relative advantage of the story is intensified when the novice consumer is in a happy mood rather than a sad one.[11] An award-winning IBM television ad called "Heist" aptly illustrates this narrative approach. It opens with police cars pulling up to a building, sirens blaring, and a harried business executive greeting the investigators and taking them into an apparently empty room. While the executive tells them that all the computers were stolen—and with them the payroll, research and development, and customer records—a geeky-looking techie casually walks through. When told that all the servers have been stolen, he calmly points to a small, black IBM server standing against the wall, saying that he has moved all the data onto it. The tag line: "Good infrastructure. It can save you a bundle."

- *Present vivid information.* Advertisers should use information that creates a strong or clear impression on the senses and produces a distinct mental picture. One way to use vivid information is to evoke strong emotion, such as in AT&T's successful "Reach Out and Touch Someone" campaign. Vividness can also be achieved by concrete language and dramatization. One of the most effective examples of vividness is an Ad Council advertisement called "I am an American," created after the September 11, 2001, attacks. The spot features people of different races and cultures who are all American citizens. The ad is simple and powerful, and TV stations picked it up immediately. Using vivid information cues is particularly desirable when services are highly intangible and complex.

- *Use interactive imagery.* One type of vividness involves what is called *interactive imagery.*[12] Imagery (defined as a mental event that involves the visualization of a concept or relationship) can enhance recall of names and facts about service. Interactive imagery integrates two or more items in some mutual action, resulting in improved recall. Some service companies effectively integrate their logos or symbols with an expression of what they do, such as the Prudential rock—the image of the rock is solid, and that impression is designed to carry over to the services company. Figure 15.5 shows a print advertisement for the U.S. Postal Service that makes use of interactive imagery. It was created to restore faith in its services after the anthrax scares during the post–September 11 period and uses various stamps to spell out the word "Peace," illustrating the varied holidays celebrated, from Christmas to Kwanzaa to Hanukkah.

- *Focus on the tangibles.*[13] Another way that advertisers can increase the effectiveness of services communications is to feature the tangibles associated with the service, such as showing a bank's marble columns or gold credit card. Because services are abstract, they are often difficult to communicate clearly. Showing the tangibles provides clues about the nature and quality of the service. Figure 15.6, an advertisement for the Sierra Club, features the tangible benefits of the club in saving the gray wolf from extinction. Showing the wolf itself communicates the benefits of the organization emphatically, far more clearly than if words alone were used.

  Berry and Clark propose four strategies of tangibilization: association, physical representation, documentation, and visualization.[14] *Association* means linking the service to a tangible person, place, or object, such as "being in good hands with Allstate." A recent campaign for Allstate's sponsorship of the 2002 Olympics takes its approach one step further in its "The right hands make all the difference" campaign by depicting the hands of Olympic athletes such as speed skaters Dan Jansen and Bonnie Blair and figure skater Brian Boitano. The athletes' hands are shown together and individually, with text showing how their personal stories relate to Allstate. *Physical representation,* the second technique, means showing tangibles that are directly or indirectly part of the service, such as employees, buildings, or equipment. *Documentation* means featuring objective data and factual information. *Visualization* is a vivid mental picture of a service's benefits or qualities, such as showing people on vacation having fun.

- *Feature service employees in communication.* Customer contact personnel are an important second audience for services advertising.[15] Featuring actual employees doing their jobs or explaining their services in advertising is effective for both the primary audience (customers) and the secondary audience (employees) because it communicates to employees that they are important. Furthermore, when employees who perform a service well are featured in advertising, they become standards for other employees' behaviors.

- *Promise what is possible.*[16] In line with the strategies we discuss in the next section, all service communications should promise only what is possible and not attempt to make services more attractive than they actually are. Many companies hope to create good service by leading with good advertising, but this strategy can backfire when the actual service does not live up to the promises in advertising.

- *Encourage word-of-mouth communication.* Because services are often high in experience and credence properties, people frequently turn to others for information rather than to traditional marketing channels. As we showed in the opening vignette

FIGURE 15.5   **A U.S. Postal Service Ad**

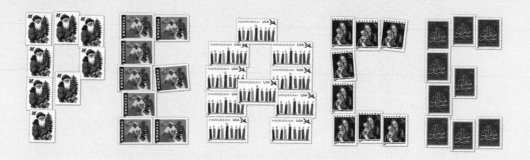

BACK BY POPULAR DEMAND.

It took a public outcry and an act of Congress to save the gray wolf from literally vanishing off the face of the earth. But we did it. Today, a lot of other creatures face similar extinction. And unless we step up our efforts to protect their habitats, they may not be so lucky. At the Sierra Club, we've mounted a major campaign to defend the Endangered Species Act and preserve threatened habitats before their inhabitants are gone forever. Please, contact us to find out how you can help protect threatened and endangered animals. Because no amount of popular demand can bring an extinct species back to life.

Protect America's Environment: For Our Families, For Our Future.

85 Second Street, San Francisco, CA 94105 • (415) 977-5653
Or visit our website at: www.sierraclub.org
Email us at: information@sierraclub.org

about Mail Boxes, Etc., services advertising and other external messages can generate word of mouth that extends the investment in paid communication and improves the credibility of the messages. Advertising that generates talk because it is humorous, compelling, or unique can be particularly effective.

- *Feature service customers.* As the Mail Boxes, Etc., vignette showed, one way to generate positive word of mouth is to feature satisfied customers in the communications. Advertising testimonials featuring actual service customers simulate personal communications between people and are thereby a credible way to communicate the benefits of service. Referrals from satisfied customers have long been used in personal selling to convey the trust needed for a new customer to purchase a service that may appear risky.

- *Use transformational advertising.*[17] Transformational advertising is image advertising that changes the experience of buying and consuming the product. Most advertising for vacation destinations is transformational: it invites the consumer to escape into a world that is necessarily subjective and perceptual. This approach involves making the ad vivid or rich in detail, realistic, and rewarding.

The Technology Spotlight describes how one form of advertising, banner advertising on the Internet, is faring today.

Coordinate External Communication

For any organization, one of the most important yet challenging aspects of managing brand equity involves coordinating all the external communication vehicles that send information to consumers. This includes advertising, public relations, personal selling, direct mail, and the Internet. But with services, the interactions with all other points of contact with the customer—customer service, service encounters, and telecommunications—must also be consistent to ensure not just brand equity but also that service promises are managed. As the executive vice president of global advertising at American Express clearly states,

> Service brands are not created solely in advertising. In fact, much of a brand's equity stems from the direct consumer experiences with the brand. We partner with Bronner [Bronner, Slosberg Humphrey, a relationship marketing company] to help us manage consumer experiences with our brand across all products and services—Card, Travel, Financial Services, and Relationship Services—via all direct channels, including phone, Internet, and mail.[18]

Michael Bronner, the founder of the relationship marketing company that American Express uses, emphasizes the need for coordinating external and interactive marketing communications: "The client [such as American Express] may spend millions on network advertising but lose when the customer is working his way through layer upon layer of voice response options on the customer service line."[19]

Make Realistic Promises

The expectations customers bring to the service affect their evaluations of its quality: the higher the expectation, the higher the delivered service must be to be perceived as high quality. Therefore, promising reliability in advertising is appropriate only when reliability is actually delivered. Promising no surprises at a hotel, as Holiday Inn did, is disastrous if what actually happens in the delivery process includes many surprises. It is essential for the marketing or sales department to understand the actual levels of service delivery (percentage of times the service is provided correctly, percentage and number of problems that arise) before making promises about reliability. To be appropriate and effective, communications about service quality must accurately reflect what customers will actually receive in service encounters.

Offer Service Guarantees

As discussed in Chapter 7, service guarantees are formal promises made to customers about aspects of the service they will receive. While many services carry implicit service satisfaction guarantees, the true benefits from them—an increase in the likelihood

Technology Spotlight
Does the Banner Still Wave in Internet Advertising?

Since 1994, when the first Internet banner ad went online, advertisers have spent billions of dollars to catch the attention of online users. Today Web ads are a $2 billion per year business, yet banner ad effectiveness as a marketing tool is being seriously questioned. At issue is the fact that click-through rates, the most common measure of effectiveness, have dropped from 10 percent to .025 percent over the years.

The Opportunity
The idea of flashing full-color images of products and services to a growing number of sophisticated users on the Web offered two big possibilities: (1) stimulate users to click and instantly surf to the vendor's site and (2) build brand recognition. As both banner ads and surfers proliferated, the click-through rate was as high as 10 percent. One of the biggest attractions was that the click-through rate gave advertisers the immediate ability to measure how "successful" their ads were. Seeking ever-higher click-through rates, marketers assigned more of their budgets to the Internet.

The Disappointment
Between 1998 and 1999, online ad spending increased dramatically. Instead of increasing, however, click-through percentages plummeted to their current low of .025 percent. Analysts have suggested the following reasons for the drops:

- *Banner clutter.* As spending increased, so did the number of ads, reducing the novelty and creating sites filled with banners that often led to no value. Just as with other advertising clutter, users learned to stop paying attention.

- *Boring banners.* Although the potential to create fun and interactive banner ads existed, many advertisers simply created me-too banners that were low on content and creativity.

- *Annoying banners.* Once advertisers started using animation and other colorful attention-getting devices, the ads became intrusive, interfering with the users' "surfing stream" and with the time they spent on sites. Some ads took so long to download that they delayed and derailed user's interactions on the Web.

Advertisers had to face the fact that their hopes for banner ads were not being fulfilled, at least as measured simply by click-through rates. According to Mary Mitchell, managing director of the FCB Interactive agency, "The click-through simply doesn't say a lot . . . What happens when people click and spend 12 minutes with your brand? How do you compare a 30-second spot to 12 minutes of time with your brand?"

When advertisers turn to the value of Internet advertising for brand building, however, they remain unsure of how to measure success. Recent research is providing some evidence: size does matter in online ads. Larger, more prominent banner ads were found by five research companies (Jupiter Media Metrix, the IAB, DoubleClick, CNet, and MSN) to result in as much as 40 percent increases in brand awareness. Skyscrapers, very tall ads, and large, rectangular ads can improve brand awareness up to 27 percent and boost message association as much as 73 percent.

Guidelines for Success
Two professional websites were developed to assist advertisers in making Internet advertising more successful: (1) the site for the Interactive Advertising Bureau (IAB), which is http://www.iab.neV and (2) a site called How Banner Ads Work, which is http://howstuffworks.com/

of a customer choosing or remaining with the company—come only when the customer knows that guarantees exist and trusts that the company will stand behind them. Among the most well-known service guarantees are those from Domino's Pizza (30-minute delivery), L.L. Bean (100 percent customer satisfaction), Bennigan's (15-minute service), and Hampton Inn (100 percent customer satisfaction).

Manage Customer Expectations

Many service companies find themselves in the position of having to tell customers that service previously provided will be discontinued or available only at a higher price. In the 1990s, service from large computer companies such as IBM typically in-

banner-ads.htm. These sources report that the best banner ads follow these guidelines:

- *Captivating, interesting, and tempting.* The best ads have animation but don't take long to load. They are specific and relevant and give the viewer a reason to click.

- *Targeted.* Successful ads use a segmented strategy and place the ads where prequalified users will see them.

- *Varied.* Just as the most effective television advertising features variety in the commercials aired, the best Internet advertisers avoid "banner burnout" by cycling different banners.

- *Innovative.* Ads must stand out. Streaming media units and rich-media interstitials are promising. At the time of this writing, several other compelling ideas have been developed. Point roll is a promising approach that enables advertisers to simultaneously deliver multiple ad messages within a single banner ad when users point and roll their mice across the banner. LiquidImage ads allow a user to reveal hidden layers of editorial content, including streaming audio and video, advertising information, and e-commerce capabilities.

A Winning Banner Case: ClassMates.com

"Looking for old friends?" is a tag line you've seen if you've been anywhere near the Internet in the last few years. The tag line belongs to ClassMates.com, a subscription service that allows users to find yearbook photographs of U.S. high school graduates. More than 22 million subscribers pay up to $19.95 to access these photographs of their old friends. The site is an Internet advertising success story: all of its subscribers were generated through Web advertising or word of mouth generated through the Web.

The company considered virtually everyone on the Web to be in its target market, and it uses banners and keywords on a wide variety of sites. The firm experimented with different ads and formats, their CEO stating, "We've learned that the only way to make this work is to test everything you have, from the creative to the placement." Classmates.com is the number two or number three online advertiser (after amazon.com) in reach and frequency.

The Future

James DePonte, a partner at PricewaterhouseCoopers, claims, "Everyone is focusing on the short-term bubble that we were in. But they're missing the big picture. The Internet is the best ad platform that exists today." The Internet now reaches more than 57 percent of U.S. households at home, with a deeper penetration at work. Internet access is increasing, with expectations of 70.5 million households going online by 2005. Forrester Research says online spending will double within the next three years to a total of $63 billion. One self-described direct marketing veteran claims that online advertising is just experiencing growing pains: "People believed this was a panacea, but the reality is that it's just one more incredibly rich, and new, communications channel."

Sources: R. Bayani, "Banner Ads—Still Working after All These Years?" *Link-up,* November–December 2001, pp. 2, 6; S. J. Heim, "Online Ads, Part Two," *Brandweek,* September 24, 2001, p. SR36; H. Fattah, "Banners May Yet Wave," *Adweek Magazines, Technology Marketing,* September 2001, pp. 24–28.

---

cluded salespeople who interacted with customers in person. This level of service attention was deemed necessary (because without it customers comprehended neither the options nor their needs adequately) and worthwhile (because almost all customers were perceived to be potentially large customers for computers). When demand for computers shifted from mainframes to PCs, the personal attention provided by direct salespeople was no longer necessary or cost-effective. Instead of the traditional face-to-face service, the companies shifted to telephone interaction alone, a distinct—and for many customers disappointing—departure from the past. Credit card companies that offered multiple value-added services when interest rates were high also found they needed to withdraw these services when interest rates dropped.

FIGURE 15.7
Approaches for Managing Customer Expectations

Offer choices

Create tiered-value offerings

Communicate criteria for service effectiveness

Negotiate unrealistic expectations

Goal: Delivery greater than or equal to promises

Service delivery has been cut back in many service industries, but few as dramatically as in the health care industry. Hospital patients now experience far shorter stays and fewer diagnostic procedures. Patients requiring psychotherapy are limited to six visits unless their doctors can substantiate in writing the need for more. Alcohol treatment is handled on an outpatient rather than inpatient basis.

How can a company gracefully give the customer news that service will not be as expected? Figure 15.7 summarizes four possible strategies.

Offer Choices

One way to reset expectations is to give the customer options for any aspects of service that are meaningful, such as time and cost. A clinical psychologist charging $100 per hour, for example, might offer clients the choice between a price increase of $10 per hour or a reduction in the number of minutes comprising the hour (such as 50 minutes). With the choice, clients can select the aspect of the trade-off (time or money) that is most meaningful to them. Making the choice solidifies the client's expectations of service.

This strategy is effective in business-to-business situations, particularly in terms of speed versus quality. Customers who are time conscious often want reports, proposals, or other written documents quickly. When asked to provide a 10-page proposal for a project within three days, an architectural firm responded that it could provide either a 2-page proposal in three days *or* a 10-page proposal in a week. Its customer selected the latter option, recognizing that the deadline could be extended. In most business-to-business services, speed is often essential but threatens performance. If customers understand this trade-off and are asked to make a choice, they are likely to be more satisfied because their service expectations for each option become more realistic.

Create Tiered-Value Service Offerings

Product companies are accustomed to offering different versions of their products with prices commensurate with the value customers perceive. Automobiles with different configurations of features carry price tags that match not their cost but instead their perceived value to the customer. This same type of formal bundling and pricing can be accomplished in services, with the extra benefit of managing expectations.

Credit card companies offer tiered-value offerings. American Express has multiple levels based on the type of service provided: the traditional green card offers basic service features, the gold card additional benefits, and the platinum card still more. Two advantages to the firm of tiered offerings are (1) the practice puts the burden of choosing the service level on the customer, thereby familiarizing the customer with specific service expectations and (2) the company can identify quite simply which customers are willing to pay higher prices for higher service levels.

The opportunity to set expectations accurately is present when the customer makes the decision up front and can be reminded of the terms of the agreement when support is requested that is above the level in the contract.

Communicate the Criteria and Levels of Service Effectiveness

At times companies can establish the criteria by which customers assess service. Consider a business customer who is purchasing market research services for the first time. Because market research is an expert service, it is high in credence properties that are hard for customers to judge. Moreover, the effectiveness of this type of service differs depending on the objectives the client brings to the service. In this situation, a service provider can teach the customer the criteria by which to evaluate the service. The provider that teaches the customer in a credible manner will have an advantage in shaping the evaluation process.

As an example, consider research company A, which communicates the following criteria to the customer: (1) a low price signals low quality, (2) reputation of the firm is critical, and (3) person-to-person interviews are the only type of customer feedback that will provide accurate information. A customer who accepts these criteria will evaluate all other suppliers using them. If research company B had talked to the customer first, consider these (very different!) criteria and their impact on the buyer: (1) market research companies with good reputations are charging for their reputation, not their skill, (2) telephone interviews have been found to work as well as person-to-person interviews, and (3) price does not indicate quality level.

The same approach can be used with service *levels* rather than evaluative criteria. If research company B tells the customer that it can provide four-day turnaround on the results of the data analysis, this sets the customer's expectation level for all other suppliers.

Negotiate Unrealistic Expectations

Sometimes customers express service requests as they would their lowest bid at a garage sale. The service they request for the price they are willing to pay is unrealistic; they know it and the firm knows it. It is, in effect, a starting point for discussion, not the expected end point. In these situations (common in business-to-business services when the purchasing agent, who is promoted and compensated on the basis of the low prices he or she negotiates, is the buyer), service providers must learn to present their offerings in terms of value and not price alone. They also must be aware of these practices and be prepared to negotiate more realistic expectations. If they do not, they may find themselves losing money in serving the client.

Improve Customer Education

As discussed in Chapter 12, customers must perform their roles properly for many services to be effective. If the customer forgets to perform this role, or performs it improperly, disappointment may result. For this reason, communication to customers can take the form of customer education. Figure 15.8 shows several types of customer education approaches that can help match promises with delivery.

FIGURE 15.8
Approaches for Improving Customer Education

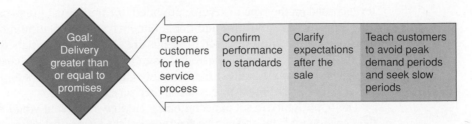

Goal: Delivery greater than or equal to promises

| Prepare customers for the service process | Confirm performance to standards | Clarify expectations after the sale | Teach customers to avoid peak demand periods and seek slow periods |

Prepare Customers for the Service Process

One of us, on a return trip from Singapore on Singapore Airlines, neglected to heed the airline's warning that return flights to the United States must be confirmed 24 hours in advance. On her arrival at the airport to return home, her seat had been given to another customer (who had conformed to the airline's request for confirmation). Depending on the perspective taken, one could argue that either the company or the customer was right in this situation. Whose responsibility is it to make sure that the customer performs her role properly?

Companies can avoid this situation by preparing customers for the service process. And they may need to prepare the customer often, even every step of the way, for the subsequent actions the customer needs to take. A business-to-business example will help illustrate this strategy.

Customers of management consulting services purchase intangible benefits: marketing effectiveness, motivated workforces, culture change. The very fact that companies purchase these services usually indicates that they do not know how to perform them alone. Many customers will also not know what to look for along the way to judge progress. In management consulting and other complex service situations, the provider must prepare the customer for the service process and may even need to create structure for the customer. At the beginning of the "engagement," the management consulting firm often establishes "checkpoints" throughout the process, at which times progress will be evaluated, and also leads the customer to establish objectives for project completion. Because customers do not know what that progress will look like, the consulting firm takes the lead in setting goals or criteria to be examined at those times.

A similar approach is sometimes necessary and effective with individual service customers. Do you remember registration at the beginning of your first college semester or quarter? How aware were you of the steps in the process and where to go after each step? It is unlikely that directions, even in great detail, made you feel confident and competent in the new service experience. You may have required step-by-step—"next call this telephone number or go to page B"—guidance.

As these and other examples show, any time a customer is inexperienced or a service process is new or unique, education about what to expect is essential.

Confirm Performance to Standards and Expectations

Service providers sometimes provide service, even explicitly requested service, yet fail to communicate to the customer that it has been accomplished. Providers sometimes stop short of getting credit for their actions when they do not reinforce their actions with appropriate communication about their fulfillment of the request. This may happen under one or more of the following conditions:

- The customer cannot evaluate the effectiveness of a service.

- The decision maker in the service purchase is a person different from the users of the service.

- The service is invisible.

- The provider depends on others to perform some of the actions to fulfill customer expectations.

When the customer cannot evaluate service effectiveness, usually because he or she is inexperienced or the service is technical, the provider may fail to communicate specific actions that address client concerns because the actions seem too complex for the customer to comprehend. In this situation the service provider needs to be able to translate the actions into customer-friendly terms. A personal injury lawyer who executes activities to aid a client with the medical and financial implications of an accident needs to be able to tell the client that these activities have been performed, in language the customer can understand.

When the decision maker in service purchases is a person different from the users of the service, the provider has insufficient contact with the decision maker and frequent contact with users. It is not unusual in these (typically) business-to-business situations for a wide discrepancy in satisfaction to exist between decision makers and users. An example is in the purchase of information technology products and services in a company. The decision maker—the manager of information technology or someone in a similar position—makes purchase decisions but interacts with the service provider only during the decision process and rarely during usage. Providers must make a special effort to keep these customers informed about performance to expectations.

Customers are not always aware of everything done behind the scenes to serve them well. Most services have invisible support processes. For instance, physicians frequently request diagnostic tests to rule out possible causes for illness. When these tests come back negative, the doctors may neglect to inform patients. Many hairstyling firms have guarantees that ensure customer satisfaction with haircuts, permanents, and color treatments. However, only a few of them actively communicate these guarantees in advertising because they assume customers know about them. The firm that explicitly communicates the guarantee may be selected over others by a customer who is uncertain about the quality of the service. Even though many competitors provide the same service, the firm that communicates it to customers will be the one chosen for that attribute. Making customers aware of standards or efforts to improve service that are not readily apparent can improve service quality perceptions.

Clarify Expectations after the Sale

When service involves a hand-off between sales and operations, as it does in most companies, clarifying expectations helps the service delivery arm of the company to align with customer expectations. Salespeople are motivated and compensated to raise customer expectations—at least to the point of making the sale—rather than to communicate realistically what the company can provide. In these situations, service providers can avoid future disappointment by clarifying what was promised as soon as the hand-off is made.

Teach Customers to Avoid Peak Demand Periods and Seek Slow Demand Periods

Few customers want to face lines or delays in receiving services. In the words of two researchers, "At best, waiting takes their time, and at worst, they may experience a range of unpleasant reactions—feeling trapped, tired, bored, angry, or demeaned."[20] In a bank setting, researchers tested three strategies for dealing with customer waits: (1) giving customers prior notice of busy times, (2) having employees apologize for the delays, and (3) assigning all visible employees to serving customers. Only the first strategy focuses on educating customers; the other two involve managing employees. Researchers expected—and confirmed—that customers warned of a wait in line tended to minimize the negative effects of waiting to justify their decision to seek service at peak times. In general, customers given a card listing the branch's busiest and slowest times were more satisfied with the banking service. The other two strategies, apology and all-tellers-serving, showed no effects on satisfaction.[21] Educating customers to avoid peak times benefits both customers (through faster service) and companies (by easing the problem of overdemand).

Manage Internal Marketing Communication

The fourth major category of strategies necessary to ensure that service delivery is greater than or equal to promises involves managing internal marketing communications (see Figure 15.9). Internal marketing communications can be both vertical and horizontal. *Vertical communications* are either downward, from management to employees, or upward, from employees to management. *Horizontal communications* are those across functional boundaries in an organization.

Create Effective Vertical Communications

Companies must give customer contact employees the information, tools, and skills to perform successful interactive marketing. Some of these skills come through training and other human resource efforts discussed in Chapter 11, but some are provided through downward communication. Among the most important forms of downward communication are company newsletters and magazines, corporate television networks, e-mail, briefings, videotapes and internal promotional campaigns, and recognition programs. One of the keys to successful downward communication is to keep employees informed of everything that is being conveyed to customers through external marketing. Employees should see company advertising before it is aired or published and should be familiar with the website, mailings, and direct selling approaches

FIGURE 15.9
Approaches for Managing Internal Marketing Communications

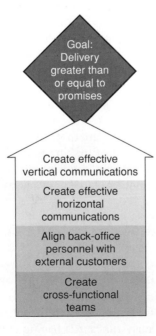

used. If these vertical communications are not present, both customers and employees suffer—customers will not receive the same messages from employees that they hear in company external marketing, and employees will feel uninformed and not be aware of what their company is doing. Customers come to them asking for services that have been marketed externally but not internally, making the employees feel uninformed, left out, and helpless.[22]

Upward communication is also necessary in closing the gap between service promises and service delivery. Employees are at the front line of service, and they know—more than anyone else in the organization—what can and cannot be delivered. They know when service breakdowns are occurring and, very often, why they are happening. Having open communication channels from employees to management can prevent service problems before they occur and minimize them when they do take place.

Create Effective Horizontal Communications

Horizontal communication—communication across functional boundaries in an organization—must be facilitated to coordinate efforts for service delivery. This is a difficult task because functions typically differ in goals, philosophies, outlook, and view of the customer, but the payoff is high. Coordination between marketing and operations can result in communication that accurately reflects service delivery, thus reducing the gap between customer expectations and actual service delivery. Integration of effort between marketing and human resources can improve the ability of each employee to become a better marketer. Coordination between finance and marketing can create prices that accurately reflect the customer's evaluation of a service. In service firms, all these functions need to be integrated to produce consistent messages and to narrow the service gaps.

One important strategy for effective horizontal communications is to open channels of communication between the marketing department and operations personnel. For example, when a company creates advertising that depicts the service encounter, it is essential that the advertising accurately reflect what customers will experience in actual service encounters. Puffery or exaggeration puts service quality perceptions at risk, especially when the firm is consistently unable to deliver to the level of service portrayed in the advertising. Coordination and communication between advertising and service providers are pivotal in delivering service that meets expectations.

Featuring actual employees doing their jobs or explaining the services they provide, a strategy we mentioned earlier in this chapter, is one way to coordinate advertising portrayals and the reality of the service encounter. To create this type of advertising, the advertising department or agency must interact directly with service employees, facilitating horizontal communications. Similar benefits can be achieved if employees are included in the advertising process in other ways, such as by being shown advertising in its pretest forms.

Another important strategy for horizontal communications involves opening channels of communication between sales and operations. Mechanisms for achieving this goal can be formal or informal and can include annual planning meetings, retreats, team meetings, or workshops where departments interact to clarify service issues. In these sessions, the departments can interact to understand the goals, capabilities, and constraints of the other. Some companies hold "gap workshops" at which employees from both functions meet for a day or two to try to understand the difficulties in matching promises made through selling with delivery accomplished by operations personnel.[23]

Involving the operations staff in face-to-face meetings with external customers is also a strategy that allows operations personnel to more readily understand the salesperson's role and the needs and desires of customers. Rather than filtering customers' needs through the sales force, operations employees can witness firsthand the pressures and demands of customers. A frequent and desirable result is better service to the internal customer—the salesperson—from the operations staff as they become aware of their own roles in satisfying both external and internal customers.

Align Back-Office and Support Personnel with External Customers through Interaction or Measurement

As companies become increasingly customer focused, front-line personnel develop improved skills in discerning what customers require. As they become more knowledgeable about and empathetic toward external customers, they also experience intrinsic rewards for satisfying customers. Back-office or support personnel, who typically do not interact directly with external customers, miss out on this bonding and, as a consequence, fail to gain the skills and rewards associated with it.

Interaction   Companies are creating ways to facilitate the interaction between back-office and support personnel and external customers. Xerox, for example, created a program called "Adopt a District" to allow employees to meet and build relationships with particular customers. Weyerhaeuser sends hourly employees to customers' plants to better understand their needs. When actual interaction is difficult or impossible, some companies have videotaped customers in their service facilities during the purchase and consumption process to vividly portray needs and requirements of customers and to show personnel the support front-line people need to deliver to those expectations.

Measurement   When company measurement systems are established, internal employees are sometimes judged on the basis of how they perform for the next internal customer in the chain. Although this approach provides feedback in terms of how well the employees are serving the internal customer, it lacks the motivation and reward that come from seeing their efforts affect the end customer. Federal Express is one company that has aligned internal personnel with the external customer using measurement. As we discussed in Chapter 9, FedEx's service quality indicator (SQI) computes daily the number of companywide service failures. To clearly communicate customer fail points to internal employees, the company created linking measures to trace the causes to each internal department. For example, the company's information technology department affects 8 of the 12 SQI measurements and therefore has submeasures that provide feedback on how the department's work is affecting the SQI.

Service guarantees, a technique discussed in an earlier section, can also be used to create alignment of back-office and support people.

Create Cross-Functional Teams

Another approach to improving horizontal communications to better serve customers is to involve employees in cross-functional teams to align their jobs with end customer requirements. For example, if a team of telecommunications service representatives was working to improve interaction with customers, back-office people such as computer technicians or training personnel could become part of the team. The team could learn requirements and set goals for achieving them together, an approach that directly creates communications across the functions.

An advertising agency is a context in which the cross-functional team approach can be understood. The individual in an advertising agency who typically interacts directly with the client is the account executive (often called a "suit" by the creative staff). In the traditional agency, the account executive visits the client, elicits client expectations, and then interacts with the various departments in the agency (art, copywriting, production, traffic, and media buying) that will perform the work. All functions are specialized and, in the extreme case, get direction for their portion of the work right from the account executive. A cross-functional team approach would involve having representatives from all of the areas meet with the account executive, even the client, and collectively discuss the account and approaches to address client needs. Each brings his or her function's perspectives and opens communication. All members can then understand the constraints and schedules of the other groups.

EXCEEDING CUSTOMER EXPECTATIONS: CAVEATS AND STRATEGIES

Throughout this chapter, we have focused on *meeting* customer expectations by closing the gap (provider gap 4) between customer perceptions and expectations. Our discussion demonstrated the difficulty in meeting expectations because of all the factors that must be coordinated to deliver on the firm's service promises. However, an increasingly popular service maxim urges companies to "exceed customer expectations"—to delight, excite, surprise, and otherwise amaze. According to this credo, which we briefly discussed in Chapter 3, merely *meeting* customer expectations is not enough; a company must *exceed* them to retain customers. This is an appealing slogan as well as one that sets a high performance standard for employees, but it holds the potential to overpromise to both customers and employees. In attempting to exceed customer expectations, a company must understand (1) what type of expectations can and should be exceeded, (2) what customer group or segment is to be targeted, and (3) the impact exceeding expectations has on future expectations of customers.

Understand Types of Expectations

In Chapter 3 we distinguished between types of service expectations including *desired service*, the level the customer hopes to receive, and *adequate service*, the minimum acceptable level of service. When service research has viewed expectations as desired service, perceptions of performance rarely meet customer expectations, and almost always produce a negative gap between expectations and perceptions. When focusing on desired service, it appears extremely difficult to exceed expectations. On the other hand, adequate service is not only feasible but also required for a company to remain viable. In research that included both desired and adequate service, three of four companies' services were perceived as being higher than the adequate service level, whereas they almost never met or exceeded desired service level.[24]

These results suggest that a company's ability to exceed expectations depends on the type of customer expectation: surpassing the desired service level on an ongoing basis may be infeasible, but exceeding the adequate service level is possible yet unimpressive. In essence, the goal of exceeding desired service may be too high and that of performing higher than adequate service may be too low. Setting a goal of exceeding desired service may frustrate employees and set the company up for overpromising. But exceeding adequate expectations is unlikely to produce "delight" in customers.

Know Which Customers' Expectations to Exceed

Another important issue involves actively deciding whether all customers' expectations should be exceeded or only those of certain segments of customers. Exceeding the expectations of poor relationship customers (from Chapter 6), those a firm is not making money from or who are difficult to do business with, will only exacerbate the negative impact of these customers. There are many cases when sound business decisions need to be made about the desirability of some customer segments. Another issue of customer selection involves the customer groups within companies that business-to-business service providers focus on, among them decision makers, users, and influencers. To exceed the expectations of all of these groups simultaneously would be overwhelming to employees and financially prohibitive.

Know the Future Impact of Exceeding Expectations Today

Another intriguing question about customer delight is whether delight is possible on a consistent basis. By most definitions, delight occurs when the customer is pleasantly surprised by an unexpected level of service provision. L.L. Bean accepts the return of a boot purchased 10 years ago, Nordstrom salespeople dash from the store to accessorize a customer's wardrobe from competing retailers, Hampton Inn housekeepers refund money because guest room temperature is too high or too low—all of these pleasantly surprise customers. A company's best chances to delight are when expected service is low to mediocre. But after the customer is delighted the first time, do his or her expectations rise, thereby making it ever more difficult to exceed them in the future? Are higher and higher levels of service required to continue the delight?

No matter how much a company might intend to meet customer needs, it may be unwilling or unable to do so at times. Customers sometimes expect more and higher levels of service than can be effectively or efficiently delivered by the firm. The customer may want a repairperson to come fix a broken appliance within an hour of the telephone call requesting service. A business telecommunications customer may want to cut the budget but increase service levels because the company is focusing on value while downsizing. A software firm may plan the introduction of a new product two months after a large customer needs the software. A gynecologist may have no free appointments for the next six months. In all of these cases, despite good intentions the company will not be able to exceed or even meet expectations.

The argument is that companies can aim for delight where and when it is appropriate and possible. Strategies for bypassing the pitfalls discussed here and reaching service goals include demonstrating understanding of customer expectations, leveraging the delivery dimensions, exceeding expectations of selected customers, underpromising and overdelivering, and positioning unusual service as unique.

Demonstrate Understanding of Customer Expectations

At the foundation of all strategies for meeting and exceeding customer expectations is the need to know and communicate back to the customer what his or her expectations are. Sometimes just the simple act of trying to understand expectations exceeds them—customers familiar with uncaring, indifferent service workers can be very impressed when someone actually listens to them. The action itself, at least in the short term, delights customers.

There is another, more basic, reason to understand and demonstrate understanding of customer expectations. Unless a company grasps what the customer expects, meeting requirements is random and unfocused. Company effort is wasted on service issues that are unimportant to the customer, and critical requirements may be overlooked altogether. A humorous illustration of this problem is shown in the Global Feature in this chapter.

Language is an obvious difference between cultures and one that is critical in communications. Service marketers must communicate in the language of the market if they are to be successful. Because of this, adaptation is often needed in advertising, personal selling, and all other forms of service marketing communication. When service provider and service customer are of different cultural backgrounds, sensitivity is especially needed to ensure clear and accurate communication.

Many business blunders result from simple errors in translation. Consider the following international misinterpretations of service messages:

- In a Bucharest hotel lobby: The lift is being fixed for the next day. During that time we regret that you will be unbearable.

- In a Yugoslavian hotel: The flattening of underwear with pleasure is the job of the chambermaid.

- In an advertisement by a Hong Kong dentist: Teeth extracted by the latest Methodists.

- In an Eastern European tourist agency: Take one of our horse-driven city tours—we guarantee no miscarriages.

- In a Copenhagen airline ticket office: We take your bags and send them in all directions.

- On the door of a Moscow hotel room: If this is your first visit to the USSR, you are welcome to it.

- From a brochure of a car rental firm in Tokyo: When passenger of foot heave in sight, tootle the horn. Trumpet him melodiously at first, but if he still obstacles your passage then tootle him with vigor.

- At a Budapest zoo: Please do not feed the animals. If you have any suitable food, give it to the guard on duty.

- In an Acapulco hotel: The manager has personally passed all the water served here.

The role of language has influence beyond that of message content. SPRINT Canada ran into difficulties using spokeswoman Candice Bergen in its advertising campaign. Response to commercials for discount long-distance services in Quebec lagged far behind that of English-speaking Canada. Ms. Bergen, who speaks French, filmed ads in the language. However, the actress' popular show "Murphy Brown" was dubbed into French before it was aired in Quebec, and therefore the voice that viewers associated with Candice Bergen was not her real voice. Further, the colloquialisms used in the ad copy, such as "Tigidou, mon minou" ("OK, my pussycat") were not the type of expressions used by the Quebecois.

Language can create problems in internal and interactional marketing communications as well. Kmart upset its clerks in Prague when it required them to wear name tags stating, "I am here for you." The salesclerks insisted that the tags be changed to read, "We are here for you," which is a sentiment more consistent with familiar Communist-era practices.

Sources: S. DeSantis, " 'Murphy Brown Goes to Canada,' or 'Parlez-vous Long Distance?' " *The Wall Street Journal,* November 25, 1994, p. B1; and D. E. Murphy, "New East Europe Retailers Told to Put on a Happy Face," *Los Angeles Times,* November 26, 1994, pp. A1, A18.

Leverage the Delivery Dimensions

Customers judge four of the service quality dimensions (responsiveness, assurance, empathy, and tangibles) primarily during the service delivery process. These four dimensions could aptly be called *delivery* or *process dimensions*. Reliability, which is judged for the most part following the service, could be called an *outcome dimension*. Although reliability is the most important dimension in meeting customers' service expectations, companies are supposed to be reliable—to provide the service they promise to deliver. Thus, it is difficult for firms to exceed customers' expectations by being reliable. The delivery dimensions—especially assurance, responsiveness, and empathy—are pivotal in exceeding them.[25]

The best opportunity for surprising customers is when service providers and customers interact during delivery. It is during delivery, when customers directly experience providers' service skills and "tone," that firms are best able to augment the service core of reliability in ways that differentiate. These delivery dimensions play a role different from the outcome dimension of reliability. Companies must be reliable simply to compete. If they also do well on the process dimensions, they have a chance to dominate the competition.[26]

Underpromise and Overdeliver

One proposal for delighting customers on a continuing basis is to deliberately underpromise the service to increase the likelihood of exceeding customer expectations. The strategy is to underpromise and overdeliver. If every service promise is less than what will eventually happen, customers can be delighted frequently. Although this reasoning sounds logical, a firm should weigh two potential problems before using this strategy.

First, customers with whom a company interacts regularly are likely to notice the underpromising and adjust their expectations accordingly, negating the desired benefit of delight. Customers will recognize the pattern of underpromising when time after time a firm promises one delivery time (we can't get that to you before 5 P.M. tomorrow) yet constantly exceeds it (by delivering at noon).

Second, underpromising in a sales situation potentially reduces the competitive appeal of an offering and must be tempered by what competition is offering. When competitive pressures are high, presenting a cohesive and honest portrayal of the service both explicitly (through advertising and personal selling) and implicitly (such as through the appearance of service facilities and the price of the service) may be wiser. Controlling the firm's promises, making them consistent with the deliverable service, may be a better approach.

Position Unusual Service as Unique, Not the Standard

At times the escalation of expectations as a result of improved service leads some companies to question the wisdom of exceeding customer expectations. They reason that exceeding customer expectations today will lead to higher expectations tomorrow, making the job of satisfying customers that much harder in the future. If they perform a miracle today, won't customers expect more miracles tomorrow and the next day?

One way to avoid this escalation while still surprising customers is to position unusual service as unique rather than the standard. On a flight between Raleigh-Durham and Charlotte, North Carolina, one of us experienced an example of this strategy. The flight is extremely short, less than half an hour, and typically too brief for beverage service. On the night in question, a crew member announced over the intercom that an unusually ambitious crew wanted to try to serve beverages anyway. He warned passengers that the crew may not get to all of them, and positioned the service as unique by imploring passengers not to expect beverage service on other flights. In this scenario, passengers seemed delighted but their expectations for regular service were not heightened by the action. (To this day, we have never received beverage service on that route, but are really not expecting it!).

Summary

Discrepancies between service delivery and external communications have a strong effect on customer perceptions of service quality. In this chapter we discussed the role of and need for integrated services marketing communications in minimizing these discrepancies. We described external, interactive, and internal marketing communications using the service triangle and emphasized the need to coordinate all three forms to deliver service that meets customer expectations. We also discussed the factors that lead to problems in marketing communications and four sets of strategies to deal with them. These strategies include (1) managing service promises, (2) managing customer expectations, (3) improving customer education, and (4) managing internal marketing communications. We closed by discussing the difficulty of exceeding customer expectations on a consistent basis and recommended ways that companies can avoid problems in promising to delight customers.

Discussion Questions

1. Think of another services company that provides integrated services marketing communications. Is it as comprehensive as Mail Boxes, Etc., as described in the opening vignette? Why or why not?

2. Which of the key reasons for provider gap 4 discussed in the beginning of this chapter is the easiest to address in a company? Which is the hardest to address? Why?

3. Review the four general strategies for achieving integrated services marketing communications. Would all of these be relevant in goods firms? Which would be most critical in goods firms? Which would be most critical in services firms? Are there any differences between those most critical in goods firms and those most critical in services firms?

4. What services do you know that advertise on the Internet? What are the most effective Internet advertisements you have seen? Why are they effective?

5. Review Exhibit 15.2 on basic marketing communication principles. Are there any other differences (beyond those we discussed in the chapter) between the way these work with goods and services?

6. Using the section on managing customer expectations, put yourself in the position of your professor, who must reduce the amount of "service" provided to the students in your class. Give an example of each strategy in this context. Which of the strategies would work best with you (the student) in managing your expectations? Why?

7. Why is internal marketing communication so important in service firms? Is it important in product firms?

8. Which form of internal marketing communication—vertical or horizontal—would you invest in if you had to select between them as an organization's CEO? Why?

9. What other strategies can you add to the four offered in the section on customer education? What types of education do you expect from service firms? Give an example of a firm from which you have received adequate education. What firm has not provided you with adequate education?

Exercises

1. Go to the Mail Boxes, Etc. (MBE) website at www.mbe.com. Explore each area of the site, and make a list of the types of information you can find based on the three categories of marketing communication (external, interactive, internal) discussed in this chapter. What additional information would you find useful on the site?

2. Find five effective service advertisements in newspapers and magazines. According to the criteria given in this chapter, identify why they are effective. Critique them using the list of criteria, and discuss ways they could be improved.

3. Debate the issue of exceeding customer expectations with another person or group in the class. One of the groups or individuals should be *for* establishing a company goal of exceeding customer expectations and one should be *against* establishing such a goal. What company evidence can you provide for your side of the argument?

Notes

1. R. Briggs, "Founder of Company Wins Free Ad in Super Bowl," *Greensboro News Record,* January 31, 1999, p. E8.
2. A. Z. Cuneo, "Promotion Prize: Super Bowl Ad," *Advertising Age,* September 1, 1997, p. 29.
3. Ibid., p. 29.
4. B. Garfield, "Bud Lizards Electrify Super Bowl Ads," *Advertising Age,* January 26, 1998, pp. 1, 53.
5. T. Love, "High Tech Meets Franchising," *Nation's Business,* June 1998, pp. 77–82.
6. P. G. Lindell, "You Need Integrated Attitude to Develop IMC," *Marketing News,* May 26, 1997, p. 5.
7. D. Legg and J. Baker, "Advertising Strategies for Service Firms," in *Add Value to Your Service,* ed. C. Suprenant (Chicago: American Marketing Association, 1987), pp. 163–68.
8. B. Mittal, "The Advertising of Services: Meeting the Challenge of Intangibility," *Journal of Service Research* 2, no. 1, August 1999, pp. 98–116.
9. E. Breivik and S. V. Troye, "Dimensions of Intangibility and Their Impact on Product Evaluations," *Developments in Marketing Science* 19, ed. E. Wilson and J. Hair (Miami, FL: Academy of Marketing Science, 1996), pp. 56–59.
10. P. Albiniak, "Promoting the United States," *Broadcasting and Cable,* October 29, 2001, p. 26.
11. A. S. Mattila, "The Role of Narratives in the Advertising of Experiential Services," *Journal of Service Research* 3, no. 1, August 2000, pp. 35–45.
12. K. L. Alesandri, "Strategies That Influence Memory for Advertising Communications," in *Information Processing Research in Advertising,* ed. R. J. Harris (Hillsdale, NJ: Erlbaum, 1983).
13. L. L. Berry and T. Clark, "Four Ways to Make Services More Tangible," *Business,* October–December 1986, pp. 53–54.
14. L. Berry and T. Clark, "Four Ways to Make Services More Tangible."

15. W. R. George and L. L. Berry, "Guidelines for the Advertising of Services," *Business Horizons,* May–June 1981, pp. 52–56.

16. Ibid.

17. B. Mittal, "The Advertising of Services."

18. D. E. Bell and D. M. Leavitt, "Bronner Slosberg Humphrey," *Harvard Business School Case 9-598-136,* 1998, p. 5.

19. Ibid., p. 4.

20. E. C. Clemmer and B. Schneider, "Managing Customer Dissatisfaction with Waiting: Applying Social-Psychological Theory in a Service Setting," in *Advances in Services Marketing and Management,* vol. 2, ed. T. Schwartz, D. E. Bowen, and S. W. Brown (Greenwich, CT: JAI Press, 1993), pp. 213–29.

21. Ibid.

22. L. L. Berry, V. A. Zeithaml, and A. Parasuraman, "Quality Counts in Services, Too," *Business Horizons,* May–June 1985, pp. 44–52.

23. V. A. Zeithaml, A. Parasuraman, and L. L. Berry, *Delivering Quality Service: Balancing Customer Perceptions and Expectations* (New York: The Free Press, 1990), p. 120.

24. P. Parasuraman, V. A. Zeithaml, and L. L. Berry, "Alternative Scales for Measuring Service Quality: A Comparative Assessment Based on Psychometric and Diagnostic Criteria," *Journal of Retailing* (1994) 70, no. 3, pp. 193–99.

25. L. L. Berry, A. Parasuraman, and V. A. Zeithaml, "Improving Service Quality in America: Lessons Learned," *Academy of Management Executive* 8, no. 2 (1994), pp. 32–48.

26. A. Parasuraman, L. L. Berry, and V. A. Zeithaml, "Understanding Customer Expectations of Service," *Sloan Management Review* 32, no. 3 (Spring 1991), pp. 39–48.

Chapter 16

PRICING OF SERVICES

This chapter's objectives are to

1. Discuss three major ways that service prices differ from goods prices for customers.

2. Demonstrate what value means to customers and the role that price plays in value.

3. Articulate the key ways that pricing of services differs from pricing of goods.

4. Delineate strategies that companies use to price services.

5. Give examples of pricing strategy in action.

What Will Consumers Pay for Music Online?

Welcome to the post-Napster era of rent-a-tune when music is leased instead of bought, and when every recording, from electric guitars to chamber ensembles, comes with strings attached.[1]

In their heyday, free online music exchange services such as Napster, FastTrack, and the Dutch firm KaZaA allowed more than 60 million Internet fans to download music free with virtually unrestricted availability of artists and selections. These companies were legally stopped from doing business by the major record companies and their artists, and so-called pay-for-play services are now emerging. These new services, offered by the entertainment and music companies, raise compelling issues about services pricing. Napster defined customer expectations for online music services—any time, anywhere, for free. So what happens now? What will consumers pay for online music (if they will pay at all)? At what point does the value of online service become too costly compared to CDs themselves? And are there any other costs besides money that must be taken into account in obtaining music online?

The offerings available at the time of this writing are shown in the accompanying chart.[2] Prices range from free to $25, but the pricing structure is much more complicated than it looks. All of the companies have major content gaps, and the price of the service is not straightforward or consistent with the usage on Napster. On Pressplay, jointly owned by Sony and Universal Music groups, a user can for $9.95 purchase a limited number of streaming audios and downloads. However, none of this music can be ripped or burned unless a $24.95 "platinum" membership is purchased, and then only 20 tracks a month—no more than two from a single artist—are allowed. If a user discontinues a subscription, the downloaded library is wiped out, so the service is more similar to renting or leasing than owning. And CDs can be burned to play only on home, car, or portable stereos rather than a portable MP3 player. Rhapsody offers unlimited streaming but no downloads for $7.99 per month, but has a limited choice of music. RealOne Music costs $9.95 per month for 100 streams and 100 downloads, but the downloads stay in your system for just 30 days. FullAudio allows unlimited access to its line of other, mostly independent, recordings for $15 per month, but prohibits downloading and instead permits songs to be streamed only while online.

These offerings illustrate an important issue about pricing that will be made clear in this chapter: price is not only monetary cost. Price also involves time, convenience, and psychological payments. In each of these offerings from online music companies, the consumer is being constrained in what she receives. How valuable is music if you must sit in front of your computer to hear it? How much is it worth to be able to burn a CD or transfer online music to an MP3 player? Is it enough to rent or license music, or will users want to own it as they have in the past?

At the time of this writing, with the new plans being criticized for their constraints, music executives at for-pay online services are promising that these are only the first attempts and that their systems will become more sophisticated over

INTERNET MUSIC SERVICES:
WHAT YOU GET, HOW MUCH IT COSTS

	MONTHLY COST	HIGH POINT	LOW POINT	AVAILABLE ARTISTS INCLUDE	ARTISTS NOT AVAILABLE
PRESSPLAY	$10–$25	Premium service allows some burning of songs to CD	Downloads expire if subscription lapses	Limp Bizkit, U2, Nirvana, Sting	Dave Matthews, Britney Spears
REALONE	$10–$20	Large selection of music	Downloads expire if subscription lapses	Kid Rock, Missy Elliott	System of a Down, Bruce Springsteen, Destiny's Child
FULL AUDIO	$5–$15	Lower price; enhanced Internet-radio options	Downloads expire if subscription lapses	Jay-Z, U2, Mariah Carey, Sum 41	Kid Rock, Pearl Jam, 'NSync, Alicia Keys
RHAPSODY	$6–$8	Offbeat music library; unlimited streaming	Streaming only	Scattered tracks from Bob Dylan, Beck, Madonna and many others	Alanis Morissette, Limp Bizkit (except on video)
FAST TRACK (KAZAA, GROKSTER, MORPHEUS)	Free	Unlimited downloads; huge selection; unlimited burning; free	Artists don't get paid	Just about everybody	Very few

time. Companies are trying to add value to their offerings by making it easy to organize tunes into playlists, offering fast and reliable downloads, and giving biographical notes on artists. These may compensate for some of the costs of online music. We predict that, as you read this, some of the questions in this chapter opener about services pricing will have been resolved, but that many others will still remain.

According to one of the leading experts on pricing, most service organizations use a "naive and unsophisticated approach to pricing without regard to underlying shifts in demand, the rate that supply can be expanded, prices of available substitutes, consideration of the price–volume relationship, or the availability of future substitutes."[3] What makes the pricing of services more difficult than pricing of goods? What approaches work well in the context of services?

This chapter builds on three key differences between customer evaluation of pricing for services and goods: (1) customers often have inaccurate or limited reference prices for services, (2) price is a key signal of quality in services, and (3) monetary price is not the only price relevant to service customers. As we demonstrate, these three differences can have profound impact on the strategies companies use to set and administer prices for services.

The chapter also discusses common pricing structures including (1) cost based, (2) competition based, and (3) demand based. One of the most important aspects of demand-based pricing is perceived value, which must be understood by service providers so that they price in line with offerings and customer expectations. For that reason we also describe how customers define value and discuss pricing strategies in the context of value.

THREE KEY WAYS SERVICE PRICES ARE DIFFERENT FOR CONSUMERS

What role does price play in consumer decisions about services? How important is price to potential buyers compared with other factors and service features? Service companies must understand how pricing works, but first they must understand how customers perceive prices and price changes. The three sections that follow describe what we know about the ways customers perceive services, and each is central to effective pricing.

Customer Knowledge of Service Prices

To what extent do customers use price as a criterion in selecting services? How much do consumers know about the costs of services? Before you answer these questions, take the services quiz in Exhibit 16.1. Were you able to fill in a price for each of the services listed? If you were able to answer the questions on the basis of memory, you have internal *reference prices* for the services. A reference price is *a price point in memory for a good or a service,* and can consist of the price last paid, the price most frequently paid, or the average of all prices customers have paid for similar offerings.[4]

To see how accurate your reference prices for services are, you can compare them with the actual price of these services from the providers in your hometown. If you are like many consumers, you feel quite uncertain about your knowledge of the prices of services, and the reference prices you hold in memory for services are not as accurate as those you hold for goods. There are many reasons for this difference.

1. What do the following services cost in your home-town?

    Dental checkup   _____

    General medical checkup   _____

    Legal help with a DWI (driving while intoxicated) charge   _____

    Dental braces   _____

    Rental of a videocassette for one night   _____

    One hour of housecleaning   _____

    Room at the Hilton   _____

    Haircut   _____

    Oil change and lube   _____

2. Which of the following would you select if you needed a filling replaced in a tooth?
    a. Dentist A—cost is $35, located 15 miles from your home, wait is three weeks for an appointment and 1.5 hours in waiting room
    b. Dentist B—cost is $50, located 15 miles from your home, wait is one week for appointment and 0.5 hour in waiting room
    c. Dentist C—cost is $105, located 3 miles from your job, wait is one week for appointment and no time in waiting room
    d. Dentist D—cost is $120, located 3 miles from your job, wait is one week for appointment and no time in waiting room; nitrous oxide used so no pain is involved

• *Service heterogeneity limits knowledge.* Because services are intangible and are not created on a factory assembly line, service firms have great flexibility in the configurations of services they offer. Firms can conceivably offer an infinite variety of combinations and permutations, leading to complex and complicated pricing structures. As an example, consider how difficult it is to get comparable price quotes when buying life insurance. With the multitude of types (such as whole life versus term), features (different deductibles), variations associated with customers (age, health risk, smoking or nonsmoking), few insurance companies offer exactly the same features and the same prices. Only an expert customer, one who knows enough about insurance to completely specify the options across providers, is likely to find prices that are directly comparable.

How did you answer the questions about prices for a medical checkup? If you are like most consumers, you probably wanted more information before you offered a reference price. You probably wanted to know what type of checkup the physician is providing. Does it include X rays and other diagnostic tests? What types of tests? How long does it take? What is its purpose? If the checkup is undertaken simply to get a signature on a health form or a marriage certificate, the doctor may take a brief medical history, listen for a heartbeat, and measure blood pressure. If, however, the checkup is to monitor a chronic ailment such as diabetes or high blood pressure, the doctor may be more thorough. The point we want to illustrate here is that a high degree of variability often exists across providers of services. Not every physician defines a checkup the same way. You may have found it easier to estimate dental services than medical services. Dental checkups are likely to be more standardized than medical services, consisting of two basic types: with X rays and without.

• *Providers are unwilling to estimate prices.* Another reason customers lack accurate reference prices for services is that many providers are unable or unwilling to estimate price in advance. Consider most medical or legal services. Rarely are legal or medical service providers willing—or even able—to estimate a price in advance. The fundamental reason in many cases is that they do not know themselves what the services will involve until they have fully examined the patient or the client's situation or until the process of service delivery (such as an operation in a hospital or a trial) unfolds. In a business-to-business context, companies will obtain bids or estimates for complex services such as consulting or construction, but this type of price estimation is typically not undertaken with end consumers; therefore, they often buy without advance knowledge about the final price of the service.

• *Individual customer needs vary.* Another factor that results in the inaccuracy of reference prices is that individual customer needs vary. Some hairstylists' service prices vary across customers on the basis of length of hair, type of haircut, and whether a conditioning treatment and style are included. Therefore, if you were to ask a friend what a cut costs from a particular stylist, chances are that your cut from the same stylist may be a different price. In a similar vein, a service as simple as a hotel room will have prices that vary greatly: by size of room, time of year, type of room availability, and individual versus group rate. These two examples are for very simple services. Now consider a service purchase as idiosyncratic as braces from a dentist or help from a lawyer. In these and many other services, customer differences in need will play a strong role in the price of the service.

• *Price information is overwhelming in services.* Still another reason customers lack accurate reference prices for services is that customers feel overwhelmed with the information they need to gather. With most goods, retail stores display the products by category to allow customers to compare and contrast the prices of different brands and sizes. Rarely is there a similar display of services in a single outlet. If customers want to compare prices (such as for dry cleaning), they must drive to or call individual outlets.

Earlier in this textbook we discussed several novel services being offered to help the time-deficient customer cope. See if you have reference prices for the unusual services of these providers: wedding adviser, pet nutritionist and therapist, baby-proofing expert, and executive organizer. We expect that your reference prices—if you can even come up with some—are even more uncertain and less accurate than for the services in the price quiz in Exhibit 16.1. Here are estimates from actual consultants: $3,500 for a wedding adviser's attention to all details, $75 to $125 a visit for depressed pets, $200 to $300 to protect a house for and from a baby, and $1,000 for four hours of executive organization.[5]

Here's one final test about reference pricing. Suppose you were having a birthday party and wanted a famous musician—say, Chris Isaak or Reba McEntire or Sheryl Crow—to perform. According to Chris Burke, cohead of corporate entertainment at the William Morris (talent) Agency, artists are willing to do so for the right price. How much would you expect to pay? Here are a few private performance prices:

Chris Isaak	$100,000
Reba McEntire	$250,000
Sheryl Crow	$150,000
Clint Black	$250,000

The fact that consumers often possess inaccurate reference prices for services has several important managerial implications. First, promotional pricing (as in couponing or special pricing) may be less meaningful for services, for which price anchors do not exist, than for goods, for which they do. Perhaps that is why price is not featured in service advertising as much as it is featured in advertising for goods. Promotional pricing may also create problems if the promotional price (such as a $50 permanent special from a salon) is the only one customers see in advertising, for it could become the customer's anchor price, making the regular price of $75 for a future purchase seem high by comparison.

The absence of accurate reference prices also suggests that advertising actual prices for services the customer is not used to purchasing may reduce uncertainty and overcome a customer's inflated price expectations for some services. For example, a marketing research firm's advertising citing the price for a simple study (such as $10,000) would be informative to business customers who are not familiar with the costs of research studies and therefore would be guessing at the cost. By featuring price in advertising, the company overcomes the fear of high cost by giving readers a price anchor.

• *Prices are not visible.* One requirement for the existence of customer reference prices is *price visibility*—the price cannot be hidden or implicit. In many services, particularly financial services, most customers know about only the rate of return and not the costs they pay in the form of fund and insurance fees. IDS Financial Services recently discovered how little customers know about prices of the company's services.[6] After being told by the independent agents who sell their services to customers that IDS was priced too high, the company did research to find out how much customers know about what they pay for financial services and how much price factors into customer value assessments.

The study surprised the company by revealing that customers knew even less than expected: not only did they not understand *what* they were paying for many of their services, very few consumers understood *how* they pay for financial services in general. Only for financial products where price was visible—such as with securities and term life insurance—were customers aware of fees. When price was invisible, such as in certificates, whole-life insurance, and annuities (which have rear-load charges), customers didn't know how they were charged and what they paid. Further, when customers were asked to indicate how important 10 factors (including price) were, price ranked seventh. Finally, the company found that shopping behavior in the category of financial services was extremely limited. Between 50 and 60 percent of customers bought financial products from the very first person they talked to.

For all of the reasons just listed, many customers don't see the price at all until *after* they receive certain services. Of course in situations of urgency, such as in accident or illness, customers must make the decision to purchase without respect to cost at all. And if cost is not known to the customer before purchase, it cannot be used as a key criterion for purchase as it often is for goods. Price is likely to be an important criterion in *repurchase,* however. Furthermore, in repurchase monetary price may be an even more important criterion than in initial purchase.

The Role of Nonmonetary Costs

In recent years economists have recognized that monetary price is not the only sacrifice consumers make to obtain products and services. Demand, therefore, is not just a function of monetary price but is influenced by other costs as well. Nonmonetary costs represent other sources of sacrifice perceived by consumers when buying and using a service. Time costs, search costs, and psychological costs often enter into the evaluation of whether to buy or rebuy a service, and may at times be more important

FIGURE 16.1
Customers will trade
money for other
service costs.

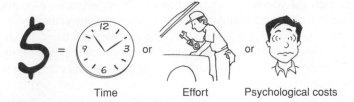

Time   Effort   Psychological costs

concerns than monetary price. Customers will trade money for these other costs, as shown in Figure 16.1.

• *Time costs.* Most services require direct participation of the consumer and thus consume real time: time waiting as well as time when the customer interacts with the service provider. Consider the investment you make to exercise, see a physician, or get through the crowds to watch a concert or baseball game. Not only are you paying money to receive these services; you're also expending time. Time becomes a sacrifice made to receive service in multiple ways. First, because service providers cannot completely control the number of customers or the length of time it will take for each customer to be served, customers are likely to expend time waiting to receive the service. The average waiting time in physicians' offices is 20.6 minutes, according to the American Medical Association, with 22 minutes for family practice doctors and 23 minutes for pediatricians, orthopedic surgeons, and gynecologists.[7] Waiting time for a service is virtually always longer and less predictable than waiting time to buy goods. Second, customers often wait for an available appointment from a service provider (in the price quiz, dentist A required a three-week wait while dentist D required only one week). Virtually all of us have expended waiting time to receive services.

• *Search costs.* Search costs—the effort invested to identify and select among services you desire—are also higher for services than for physical goods. Prices for

Customers will trade money for time savings. Customers who purchase lawn care, housekeeping, and other services often do so because the value of their time is higher than the value of money.

services are rarely displayed on shelves of service establishments for customers to examine as they shop, so these prices are often known only when a customer has decided to experience the service. As an example, how well did you estimate the costs of an hour of housecleaning in the price quiz? As a student, it is unlikely that you regularly purchase housecleaning, and you probably have not seen the price of an hour displayed in any retail store. Another factor that increases search costs is that each service establishment typically offers only one "brand" of a service (with the exception of brokers in insurance or financial services), so a customer must initiate contact with several different companies to get information across sellers.

• *Convenience costs.* There are also convenience (or perhaps more accurately inconvenience) costs of services. If customers have to travel to a service, they incur a cost, and the cost becomes greater when travel is difficult, as it is for elderly persons. Further, if service hours do not coincide with the customers' available time, they must arrange their schedules to correspond to the company's schedule. And if consumers have to expend effort and time to prepare to receive a service (such as removing all food from kitchen cabinets in preparation for an exterminator's spraying), they make additional sacrifices.

• *Psychological costs.* Often the most painful nonmonetary costs are the psychological costs incurred in receiving some services. Fear of not understanding (insurance), fear of rejection (bank loans), fear of uncertainty (including fear of high cost)— all of these constitute psychological costs that customers experience as sacrifices when purchasing and using services. All change, even positive change, brings about psychological costs that consumers factor into the purchase of services. When banks first introduced ATMs, customer resistance was significant, particularly to the idea of putting money into a machine: customers felt uncomfortable with the idea of letting go of their checks and bank cards. Direct deposit, a clear improvement in banking service for the elderly with limited mobility, was looked on with suspicion until the level of comfort improved. And consider how many customers rejected voice mail when it was first developed.

Nonmonetary Cost Priorities

You can assess your own priorities on these nonmonetary cost components—time, effort, search, psychological—by thinking about your answer to question 2 in the price quiz. If you chose dentist A, you are probably most concerned about monetary costs— you are willing to wait for an appointment and in the waiting room of the dentist's office. If you chose dentist B over dentist A, your time and convenience costs are slightly more important than your monetary costs, because you are willing to pay $15 more to reduce the waiting time. If you chose dentist C, you are much more sensitive to time and convenience costs, including travel time, than to monetary costs—you are willing to pay three times what you would pay for dentist A to avoid the other nonmonetary costs. And if you chose dentist D, you are someone who wants to minimize psychological costs as well, in this case fear and pain.

Reducing Nonmonetary Costs

The managerial implications of these other sources of sacrifice are compelling. First, a service firm may be able to increase monetary price by reducing time and other costs. For example, a services marketer can reduce the perceptions of time and convenience costs when use of the service is embedded in other activities (such as when a convenience store cashes checks, sells stamps, and serves coffee along with selling products). Second, customers may be willing to pay to avoid the other costs. Many customers willingly pay extra to have items delivered to their home—including restaurant meals—rather than transporting the services and products themselves. Some customers also pay a premium for fast check-in and checkout (as in joining the Hertz #1 club), for reduced waiting time in a professional's office (as in so-called executive appointments where, for a premium price, a busy executive comes early in the morning and does not have to wait), and to avoid doing the work themselves (such as paying one and one-half times the price per gallon to avoid having to put gas in a rental car before returning it). If time or other costs are pivotal for a given service, the company's advertising could effectively emphasize these savings rather than monetary savings.

Many other services save time, thus actually allowing the customer to "buy" time. Household cleaning services, lawn care, babysitting, interactive cable shopping, personal shopper service, home banking, home delivery of groceries, painting, and carpet cleaning—all of these represent net gains in the discretionary time of consumers and could effectively be marketed that way. Services that allow the customer to buy time are likely to have monetary value for busy consumers.

Price as an Indicator of Service Quality

One of the intriguing aspects of pricing is that buyers are likely to use price as an indicator of both service costs and service quality—price is at once an attraction variable and a repellent.[8] Customers' use of price as an indicator of quality depends on several factors, one of which is the other information available to them. When service cues to quality are readily accessible, when brand names provide evidence of a company's reputation, or when level of advertising communicates the company's belief in the brand, customers may prefer to use those cues instead of price. In other situations, however, such as when quality is hard to detect or when quality or price varies a great deal within a class of services, consumers may believe that price is the best indicator of quality. Many of these conditions typify situations that face consumers when purchasing services.[9] Another factor that increases the dependence on price as a quality indicator is the risk associated with the service purchase. In high-risk situations, many of which involve credence services such as medical treatment or management consulting, the customer will look to price as a surrogate for quality.

Because customers depend on price as a cue to quality and because price sets expectations of quality, service prices must be determined carefully. In addition to being chosen to cover costs or match competitors, prices must be chosen to convey the appropriate quality signal. Pricing too low can lead to inaccurate inferences about the quality of the service. Pricing too high can set expectations that may be difficult to match in service delivery.

Because goods are dominated by search properties, price is not used to judge quality as often as it is in services, where experience and credence properties dominate. Any services marketer must be aware of the signals that price conveys about its offerings.

APPROACHES TO PRICING SERVICES

Exhibit 16.2 briefly reviews some key concepts about pricing that apply equally to goods and services. Rather than repeat what you learned about pricing in your marketing principles class, we want to emphasize in this chapter the way that services prices and pricing differ from both the customer's and the company's perspective. We discuss these differences in the context of the three pricing structures typically used to

16.2 REVIEW OF MARKETING PRINCIPLES ABOUT PRICING

Many of the aspects of pricing of services are the same as pricing of goods. A very brief summary of the basics is provided here. For more details, return to your basic marketing textbook or to *Marketing Management: The Millennium Edition* by Philip Kotler, the text from which we excerpted these fundamental points about pricing.

1. The firm must consider many factors in setting its pricing policy: selecting the pricing objective, determining demand, estimating costs, analyzing competitors' prices and offers, selecting a pricing method, and selecting the final price.

2. Companies do not always seek to maximize profits through pricing. Other objectives they may have include survival, maximizing current revenue, maximizing sales growth, maximizing market skimming, and product/quality leadership.

3. Marketers need to understand how responsive demand would be to a change in price. To evaluate this important criterion of price sensitivity, marketers can calculate the price elasticity of demand, which is expressed as

$$\text{Elasticity} = \frac{\text{Percentage change in quantity purchased}}{\text{Percentage change in price}}$$

4. Various types of costs must be considered in setting prices, including direct and indirect costs, fixed and variable costs, indirect traceable costs, and allocated costs. If a product or service is to be profitable for a company, price must cover all costs and include a markup as well.

5. Competitors' prices will affect the desirability of a company's offerings and must be considered in establishing prices.

6. A variety of pricing methods exist including markup, target return, perceived-value, going-rate, sealed-bid, and psychological.

7. After setting a price structure, companies adapt prices using geographic pricing, price discounts and allowances, promotional pricing, discriminatory pricing, and product-mix pricing.

Source: P. Kotler, "Designing Pricing Strategies and Programs," in *Marketing Management: The Millennium Edition* (New York: Prentice Hall, 2000). Reprinted by permission of Prentice Hall, Inc., Upper Saddle River, NJ.

set prices: (1) cost-based, (2) competition-based, and (3) demand-based. These categories, as shown in Figure 16.2, are the same bases on which goods prices are set, but adaptations must be made in services. The figure shows the three structures interrelating, because companies need to consider each of the three to some extent in setting prices. In the following sections we describe in general each basis for pricing and discuss differences that occur when the approach is used in services pricing. Figure 16.2 summarizes those differences.

Cost-Based Pricing

In cost-based pricing, a company determines expenses from raw materials and labor, adds amounts or percentages for overhead and profit, and thereby arrives at the price. This method is widely used by industries such as utilities, contracting, wholesaling, and advertising. The basic formula for cost-based pricing is

$$\text{Price} = \text{Direct costs} + \text{Overhead costs} + \text{Profit margin}$$

Direct costs involve materials and labor that are associated with the service, overhead costs are a share of fixed costs, and the profit margin is a percentage of full costs (direct + overhead).

FIGURE 16.2
Three Basic Marketing Price Structures and Difficulties Associated with Their Use for Services

Problems:
1. Small firms may charge too little to be viable.
2. Heterogeneity of services limits comparability.
3. Prices may not reflect customer value.

Problems:
1. Costs are difficult to trace.
2. Labor is more difficult to price than materials.
3. Costs may not equal value.

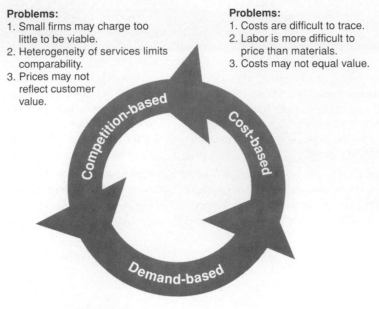

Problems:
1. Monetary price must be adjusted to reflect the value of nonmonetary costs.
2. Information on service costs is less available to customers, hence price may not be a central factor.

Special Problems in Cost-Based Pricing for Services

One of the major difficulties in cost-based pricing involves defining the units in which a service is purchased. Thus the price per unit—a well-understood concept in pricing of manufactured goods—is a vague entity. For this reason many services are sold in terms of input units rather than units of measured output. For example, most professional services (such as consulting, engineering, architecture, psychotherapy, and tutoring) are sold by the hour.

What is unique about services when using cost-based approaches to pricing? First, costs are difficult to trace or calculate in services businesses, particularly where multiple services are provided by the firm.[10] Consider how difficult it must be for a bank to allocate teller time accurately across its checking, savings, and money market accounts in order to decide what to charge for the services. Second, a major component of cost is employee time rather than materials, and the value of people's time, particularly nonprofessional time, is not easy to calculate or estimate.

An added difficulty is that actual service costs may underrepresent the value of the service to the customer. A tailor located in the hometown of one of the authors charges $10 for taking in a seam on a $350 ladies' suit jacket and an equal $10 for taking in a seam on a pair of $14 sweat shorts. The tailor's rationale is that both jobs require the same amount of time. What she neglects to see is that the customer would pay a higher price—and might even be happier about the alterations—for the expensive suit jacket, and that $10 is too high a price for the sweat shorts.

Examples of Cost-Based Pricing Strategies Used in Services

Cost-plus pricing is a commonly used approach in which component costs are calculated and a markup added. In product pricing this approach is quite simple; in service industries, however, it is complicated because the tracking and identification of costs are difficult. The approach is typically used in industries where cost must be estimated in advance, such as construction, engineering, and advertising. In construction or engineering, bids are solicited by clients on the basis of the description of the service desired. Using their knowledge of the costs of the components of the service (including the raw materials such as masonry and lumber), labor (including both professional and unskilled), and margin, the company estimates and presents to the client a price for the finished service. A contingency amount—to cover the possibility that costs may be higher than estimated—is also stated because in large projects specifications can change as the service is provided.

Fee for service is the pricing strategy used by professionals; it represents the cost of the time involved in providing the service. Consultants, psychologists, accountants, and lawyers, among other professionals, charge for their services on an hourly basis. Virtually all psychologists and social workers have a set hourly rate they charge to their clients, and most structure their time in increments of an hour.

In the early 1900s, lawyers typically billed clients a certain fee for services rendered regardless of the amount of time they spent delivering them. Then in the 1970s, law firms began to bill on an hourly rate, in part because the system offered accountability to clients and an internal budgeting system for the firm. One of the most difficult aspects of this approach is that recordkeeping is tedious for professionals. Lawyers and accountants must keep track of the time they spend for a given client, often down to 10-minute increments. For this reason the method has been criticized because it does not promote efficiency and sometimes ignores the expertise of the lawyers (those who are very experienced can accomplish much more than novices in a given time period, yet billings do not always reflect this). Clients also feared padding of their legal bills, and began to audit them. Despite these concerns, the hourly bill dominates the industry, with 77 percent of revenues billed this way.[11]

Competition-Based Pricing

This approach focuses on the prices charged by other firms in the same industry or market. Competition-based pricing does not always imply charging the identical rate others charge but rather using others' prices as an anchor for the firm's price. This approach is used predominantly in two situations: (1) when services are standard across providers, such as in the dry cleaning industry, and (2) in oligopolies where there are a few large service providers, such as in the airline or rental car industry. Difficulties involved in provision of services sometimes make competition-based pricing less simple than it is in goods industries.

Special Problems in Competition-Based Pricing for Services

Small firms may charge too little and not make margins high enough to remain in business. Many mom-and-pop service establishments—dry cleaning, retail, and tax accounting, among others—cannot deliver services at the low prices charged by chain stores.

Further, the heterogeneity of services across and within providers makes this approach complicated. Bank services illustrate the wide disparity in service prices. Customers buying checking accounts, money orders, or foreign currency, to name a few services, find prices are rarely similar across providers. For example, at one point NationsBank charged $5 for a money order when the Postal Service charged $0.75 and 7-Eleven stores charged $1.09.[12] Compare these prices for having a check drawn on foreign currency: Bank of America, $20; Thomas Cook, Inc., $7; and Citibank, $15. And fees for cashier's checks ranged from $10 to no charge, with a nationwide

Tipping

A Cornell University study recently revealed an interesting fact about tipping: The custom of tipping is more prevalent in countries where citizens value status and prestige more highly than in countries where they do not. Michael Lynn, an associate professor of consumer behavior and marketing at Cornell, found that the number of service professionals tipped is relatively small in countries where citizens value recognition and esteem less. "Tipping is really a form of conspicuous consumption. We tip more people in this country because we value status. Americans value recognition and esteem, and we receive that when we tip these service professionals."

One measure of the differences in tipping is the number of service professions who are given tips in different countries. The United States leads the list with about 35 different professions. Other countries that place a high value on recognition and esteem also tip a large number of professionals. These include Spain (29), Canada (25), India (25), and Italy (24). In contrast, in Denmark and Sweden, the number of tipped professionals is under 10, reflecting the lower value placed on recognition and esteem in these countries.

Service Fees

Rather than tips in Europe, Asia, and Latin America, fixed services charges are added to customers' bills in restaurants. Except for large parties, this had been an unusual practice in U.S. restaurants, perhaps for the reason cited in the previous paragraph. However, some U.S. establishments—such as the Chateaulin and Monet restaurants in Ashland, Oregon—are exchanging tips for service charges in spite of the preference of guests to choose what to tip. The reason is that the IRS has been leaning on restaurants to have their waiters and waitresses report tips. If reported tip income is less than 8 percent of gross receipts, the IRS

average of $2.69.[13] Banks claim that they set fees high enough to cover the costs of these services; the wide disparity in prices probably reflects the bank's difficulty in determining prices as well as their belief that financial customers find it difficult to shop around and discern the differences (if any) among offerings from different providers. A banking expert makes the point that "It's not like buying a quart of milk. . . . Prices aren't standardized."[14] Only in very standardized services (such as dry cleaning) are prices likely to be remembered and compared.

Examples of Competition-Based Pricing in Services Industries

Price signaling occurs in markets with a high concentration of sellers. In this type of market, any price offered by one company will be matched by competitors to avoid giving a low-cost seller a distinct advantage. The airline industry exemplifies price signaling in services. When any competitor drops the price of routes, others match the lowered price almost immediately.

Going-rate pricing involves charging the most prevalent price in the market. Rental car pricing is an illustration of this technique (and also an illustration of price signaling, because the rental car market is dominated by a small number of large companies). For years, the prices set by one company (Hertz) have been followed by the other

has now made restaurant owners liable for back taxes on unreported income unless they participate in a program to track their employee's tips. Service personnel don't like the change, partly because they make less money (the restaurant shares the service fee with kitchen personnel) and partly because they don't receive the instant gratification that tips provide. Guests are typically unfavorable as well: "We surveyed our guests and they seem to feel that they have a constitutional right to reward and punish waiters."

Priceless

A London restaurant called Just Around the Corner has an extraordinary demand-oriented pricing policy: it lets customers pay whatever they think the meal is worth. The policy has been extremely successful since it was started in 1986, with most customers paying more for their meals than the restaurant would charge if it set the prices. Customers average 25 pounds ($41) for a three-course dinner, but some are especially careful to pay enough. "One night, four American government officials handed over nearly $1,000 for a meal worth less than $200. They asked if they had left enough." The owner, Michael Vasos, claims, "I make more money from this restaurant than from any of my other [four] establishments." He thinks his customers' generosity accounts for the success of the restaurant and its pricing policies, although others state that the fear of embarrassment common to the English prevents patrons from paying too little.

Sources: "Study Examines Tipping," *Hotel and Motel Management,* March 17, 1997, p. 14; B. Ortega, "No Tips, Please—Just Pay the Service Fee," *The Wall Street Journal,* September 4, 1998, p. B1; "Priceless," *People,* February 15, 1999, p. 114; and I. Wall, "It May Be a Dog-Eat-Dog World, But This Restaurant Won't Prove It," *The Wall Street Journal,* December 11, 1998, p. B1.

companies. When Hertz instituted a new pricing plan that involved "no mileage charges, ever," other rental car companies imitated the policy, constraining themselves to depending on other variables for their prices. Those variables include base rates, size and type of car, daily or weekly rates, and drop-off charges. Prices in different geographic markets, even cities, depend on the going rate in that location, and customers often pay different rates in contiguous cities in the same state. The newsletter *Consumer Reports Travel Letter* advises customers that the national toll-free reservation lines offer better rates than are obtained calling local rental car companies in cities, perhaps because those rates are less influenced by the going rates in a particular area.[15]

The Global Feature in this chapter illustrates some of the practices in pricing, especially cost-based pricing, that differ across countries.

Demand-Based Pricing

The two approaches to pricing just described are based on the company and its competitors rather than on customers. Neither approach takes into consideration that customers may lack reference prices, may be sensitive to nonmonetary prices, and may judge quality on the basis of price. All of these factors can and should be accounted for in a company's pricing decisions. The third major approach to pricing, *demand-*

based pricing, involves setting prices consistent with customer perceptions of value: prices are based on what customers will pay for the services provided.

Special Problems in Demand-Based Pricing for Services

One of the major ways that pricing of services differs from pricing of goods in demand-based pricing is that nonmonetary costs and benefits must be factored into the calculation of perceived value to the customer. When services require time, inconvenience, and psychological and search costs, the monetary price must be adjusted to compensate. And when services save time, inconvenience, and psychological and search costs, the customer is likely to be willing to pay a higher monetary price. The challenge is to determine the value to customers of each of the nonmonetary aspects involved.

Another way services and goods differ with respect to this form of pricing is that information on service costs may be less available to customers, making monetary price not as large or salient a factor in initial service selection as it is in goods purchasing.

Four Meanings of Perceived Value

One of the most appropriate ways that companies price their services is basing the price on the perceived value of the service to customers. Among the questions a services marketer needs to ask are the following: What do consumers mean by *value?* How can we quantify perceived value in dollars so that we can set appropriate prices for our services? Is the meaning of value similar across consumers and services? How can value perceptions be influenced? To fully understand demand-based pricing approaches, we must fully understand what value means to customers.

This is not a simple task. When consumers discuss value, they use the term in many different ways and talk about myriad attributes or components. What constitutes value, even in a single service category, appears to be highly personal and idiosyncratic. Customers define value in four ways: (1) Value is low price. (2) Value is whatever I want in a product or service. (3) Value is the quality I get for the price I pay. (4) Value is what I get for what I give (Figure 16.3).[16] Let's take a look at each of these definitions more carefully.

Value Is Low Price Some consumers equate value with low price, indicating that what they have to give up in terms of money is most salient in their perceptions of value, as typified in these representative comments from customers:

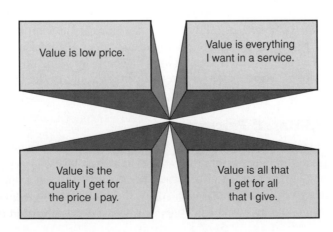

FIGURE 16.3
Four Customer Definitions of Value

Value is low price.

Value is everything I want in a service.

Value is the quality I get for the price I pay.

Value is all that I get for all that I give.

For dry cleaning: "Value means the lowest price."

For carpet steam cleaning: "Value is price—which one is on sale."

For a fast-food restaurant: "When I can use coupons, I feel that the service is a value."

For airline travel: "Value is when airline tickets are discounted."[17]

Value Is Whatever I Want in a Product or Service Rather than focusing on the money given up, some consumers emphasize the benefits they receive from a service or product as the most important component of value. In this value definition, price is far less important than the quality or features that match what the consumer wants. In the telephone industry, for example, business customers strongly value the reliability of the systems, and are very willing to pay for the safety and confidentiality of the telephone lines. Service customers describe this definition of value as follows:

For an MBA degree: "Value is the very best education I can get."

For medical services: "Value is high quality."

For a social club: "Value is what makes me look good to my friends and family."

For a rock or country music concert: "Value is the best performance."

Value Is the Quality I Get for the Price I Pay Other consumers see value as a trade-off between the money they give up and the quality they receive.

For a hotel for vacation: "Value is price first and quality second."

For a hotel for business travel: "Value is the lowest price for a quality brand."

For a computer services contract: "Value is the same as quality. No—value is affordable quality."

Value Is What I Get for What I Give Finally, some consumers consider all the benefits they receive as well as all sacrifice components (money, time, effort) when describing value.

For a housekeeping service: "Value is how many rooms I can get cleaned for what the price is."

For a hairstylist: "Value is what I pay in cost and time for the look I get."

For executive education: "Value is getting a good educational experience in the shortest time possible."

The four consumer expressions of value can be captured in one overall definition consistent with the concept of utility in economics: *Perceived value is the consumer's overall assessment of the utility of a service based on perceptions of what is received and what is given.* While what is received varies across consumers (some may want volume, others high quality, still others convenience), as does what is given (some are concerned only with money expended, others with time and effort), value represents a trade-off of the give and get components. Customers will make a purchase decision on the basis of perceived value, not solely to minimize the price paid. These definitions are the first step in identifying the elements that must be quantified in setting prices for services. We provide in the following a set of steps for breaking the give and get components of value into manageable pieces that can be useful in quantifying value.

Incorporating Perceived Value into Service Pricing

It is the buyers' perception of total value that prompts the willingness to pay a particular price for a service. To translate the customer's value perceptions into an appropriate price for a specific service offering, the marketer must answer a number of questions. What benefits does the service provide? How important is each of these benefits to the others? How much is it worth to the customer to receive a particular benefit in a service? At what price will the service be economically acceptable to potential buyers? In what context is the customer purchasing the service?

The most important thing a company must do—and often a difficult thing—is to estimate the value to customers of the company's services. Value may be perceived differently by consumers because of idiosyncratic tastes, knowledge about the service, buying power, and ability to pay. In this type of pricing, what the consumers value—not what they pay—forms the basis for pricing. Therefore its effectiveness rests solely on accurately determining what the market perceives the service to be worth. To do so, the following steps must take place:

1. Elicit customer definitions of value in their own words and terms, allowing for the full range of components.

2. Help customers articulate their expressions of value by identifying their value definition, key abstract benefits sought, and abstract dimensions of quality that are relevant to them.

3. Capture requirements information at the concrete level—linking them with the key benefits they indicate—so that the definition becomes actionable.

4. Quantify the monetary and nonmonetary value to customers.

5. Establish a price based on the value of the service to customers.

When the services are for the end consumer, most often service providers will decide that they cannot afford to give each individual exactly the bundle of attributes he or she values. They will, however, attempt to find one or more bundles that address segments of the market. On the other hand, when services are sold to businesses (or to end customers in the case of high-end services), the company can understand and deliver different bundles to each customer.

An interesting manifestation of demand-oriented pricing is shown in the Technology Spotlight.

One of the most complex and difficult tasks of services marketers is setting prices internationally. If services marketers price on the basis of perceived value, and if perceived value and willingness to pay differ across countries (which they do for the most part), then services marketers may provide essentially the same service but charge different prices in different countries. Here, as in pricing domestically, the challenge is to determine the perceived value not just to different customers but to different customers in different parts of the world. Pricing in Europe provides one of the most compelling examples of the pricing challenges marketers face internationally.

Historically, Europe was considered to be a loosely aligned group of more than 12 separate countries, and a services marketer could have as many different pricing approaches as it had countries in which it offered the services. While pricing was complex to administer, the marketer had full flexibility in pricing and could seek the profit-maximizing price in each country. Prices across countries tended to vary widely, both in services and in products: "In most markets, [there are] still enormous

Technology Spotlight
With Dynamic Pricing, the Internet Allows Price Adjustments Based on Supply and Demand

When shopping for an airline ticket on the Internet, have you ever found a low-priced ticket that you didn't purchase immediately, then returned four hours later to find the same ticket had increased $100 in price? This is dynamic pricing in action—the ability to shift prices quickly in response to supply of and demand for the offering. In the case of your airline ticket, chances are that other travelers had purchased tickets at the original low price, reducing the airlines' inventory and allowing the airline to gamble on getting customers to buy the remaining seats at higher prices.

Dynamic pricing accounted for 15 percent of the total $81 billion in e-commerce in 1999, but is forecast to be 40 percent of $1.4 trillion in total online transactions by 2004. The approach—often incorporating auctions and other forms of online bidding—is typically used at the end of the supply chain to eliminate surplus inventory or perishable service capacity, as with airline seats. Dynamic pricing has allowed companies to generate significant revenue from excess supply or discontinued products, which they used to turn over to intermediaries. In the past, liquidators would receive leftover products, getting five cents on the dollar in liquidation fees in addition to whatever they could get from reselling the products. Not only did the manufacturer not receive revenue from the sale of the products, but it also would have to pay for liquidation services.

Auctions: eBay, uBid The auction craze was started by eBay, but now is popular in every category. Whereas eBay focuses on consumer-to-consumer transactions, uBid.com acts as a consignment house for manufacturers selling directly to consumers. Forecast to more than double in revenues by 2004, auctions truly represent dynamic pricing because customers pay what they are willing and compete with each other for the goods they desire. Auctions are fun for consumers, with their extra appeal in the competition with other shoppers that no other mode of online shopping can match. With the rise in popularity of antiques and collectibles, eBay created the first truly global buying and selling venue. With more than 90 percent of the person-to-person auction marketing, over $5 billion of merchandise was sold on eBay alone in 2000.

Dutch Auctions: Klik-Klok.com, WRHambrecht.com Dutch auctions, which originated in the Netherlands for selling perishable items like tulips, reverse the typical auction in that the prices go down as the auction progresses. Also unlike typical auctions, where one of a particular type of product is sold, in Dutch auctions multiple—albeit limited—quantities of the same product are sold at the same time. The duration of the auction is very short and the price drops rapidly. At any given time (or price point), a bidder can stop the clock by bidding at the instantaneous price. The bid with time, price, and quantity is then recorded. This continues until all bids have been received. At that point all winning bidders pay the same price, which is the lowest "successful" bid. The catch here is that there is a limited supply of each product. As the clock progresses and the remaining available inventory decreases, the nonbidders (those waiting for the lowest selling price) risk not getting their desired quantities.

Reverse Auctions: Hotwire.com and priceline.com Reverse auctions allow buyers to see the lowest bid but do not identify the buyer or the seller. The brand or identity of the seller is revealed only if the seller decides to accept the bid. An advantage for buyers is that they do not need to guess at the price and can receive the same products and services offered elsewhere with static prices at significant discounts. A disadvantage is that while buyers see a rating of the seller, they cannot be sure who the seller is and what the service outcome will be. The brand is eliminated as a communicator of quality. Furthermore, the buyer has to sacrifice control over some aspects of the service that is being consumed. For instance, on priceline.com, the buyer cannot select flight time.

Group Buying: Clust.com, TogetherWeSave.com Group buying sites aggregate demand for sellers. The concept behind this form of dynamic pricing is that the more people who want to buy products, the lower the price will be for everyone. Sellers generally bucket the prices of the product being sold based on number of buyers: for example, for 0–10 buyers, the price for each buyer is $100; for 11–20 buyers, the price for each buyer is $95; and so on. Word of mouth is critical, so interested buyers are encouraged to enlist their friends and relatives to get a cheaper price for the whole group. Sellers motivate this action by placing an "Invite Your Friend" icon right next to the product or price information. Advantages of

Technology Spotlight
With Dynamic Pricing, the Internet Allows Price Adjustments Based on Supply and Demand—continued

this form of dynamic pricing are that the price decreases as more people bid, and the exact product and its specifications are known to buyers when bidding; also, most products sold through group buying have been new (surplus, not collectibles).

Others Variants: buy.com buy.com's slogan is "lowest prices on Earth." The Internet allows consumers to do quick price comparisons, and buy.com wants to make sure its products come up with the lowest prices in everyone's search. To deliver on its promises, buy.com uses software to monitor price changes for products on competing sites. When these prices change, the software then recommends price adjustments at buy.com. The process is automated, but the decision to change prices is made by a manager, usually once a day rather than moment to moment. buy.com relies on this strategy in highly competitive online categories such as consumer electronics and computer hardware and software. Prices tend to fall more often than they go up. buy.com has encountered its own financial hardships. Revenue for the second quarter of 2001 was $94.9 million, less than half of what it was a year earlier—resulting in significant downsizing and delisting from NASDAQ.

Sources: G. Dalton, "Going, Going, Gone!" *Informationweek,* October 4, 1999; D. Drucker, "Exchanges Learn to Negotiate—Ariba, CommerceOne Boost Marketplace Platforms with Dynamic Pricing, Other Variables," *Internetweek,* September 18, 2000; C. T. Heun, "Dynamic Pricing Boosts Bottom Line," *Informationweek,* October 29, 2001; R. D. Hof, "Will Auction Frenzy Cool?" *BusinessWeek,* September 18, 2000; M. Vizard, "With So Very Few Internet Players, Is Dynamic Pricing Good for Our Economy?" *InfoWorld,* March 26, 2001; M. Vizard, E. Scannel, and D. Neel, "Suppliers Toy with Dynamic Pricing," *InfoWorld,* May 14, 2001.

price differentials between countries. For identical consumer products, prices show typical deviations ranging between 30 and 150 percent—for example 115 percent for chocolate, 65 percent for tomato ketchup, and up to 155 percent for beer in Europe."[18] The European Community created a single internal market, holding the potential to simplify marketing in the area but also creating grave concerns about pricing. The largest concern is that marketers will be required to offer all services at a single European price—the lowest price offered in any European country—which could dramatically reduce revenues and profits.

PRICING STRATEGIES THAT LINK TO THE FOUR VALUE DEFINITIONS

In the next section we describe the approaches to services pricing that are particularly suited to each of the four value definitions. Exhibit 16.3 presents research approaches to setting prices.

Pricing Strategies When the Customer Means "Value Is Low Price"

When monetary price is the most important determinant of value to a customer, the company focuses mainly on price. This does not mean that the quality level and intrinsic attributes are always irrelevant, just that monetary price dominates in im-

16.3 PRICING RESEARCH FOR DECISION MAKING

In addition to the methods and strategies of pricing that are discussed in this chapter, there are other research approaches that marketers can use to help set prices and understand the impact of those prices. Four basic research methods exist for setting prices, each with its strengths and its limitations. They include purchase simulation, historical data modeling, trade-off analysis, and controlled market test.

Purchase simulation is a controlled simulated test where the researcher systematically varies aspects of pricing in order to study their impact on sales and revenue. Marketers select respondents who represent the ultimate customers of the product or service being studied, bring them to an interview location with different service or product displays, and give them 10 poker chips to place in front of the display to represent their next 10 service purchases. Respondents repeat the chip allocation exercise with different pricing approaches. The marketer then compares the purchasing behavior in the different price approaches. *Strengths:* inexpensive, quick, realistic, provides information about market segments, easy to understand/communicate, applicable to new products, appropriate for simple, low-risk questions. *Limitations:* artificial consumer behavior tasks, does not identify optimal price points (because it does not examine all possible prices), does not measure the impact of price change on demand for other products and services.

In the *historical data modeling* approach, researchers look at past buying patterns using a statistical approach such as regression analysis. The impact of different market-ing variables, including price, is examined for trends in past data. *Strengths:* enables "what-if" scenarios, uses real consumer data, finds optimal historical price points, is supported by personal software, and is based on well-developed statistical tools. *Limitations:* rarely identifies price points for different market segments, is limited to data within historical data ranges, requires researcher expertise, is not applicable to new products, and is the most cumbersome method.

Trade-off analysis includes two approaches: conjoint measurement and discrete choice modeling. Conjoint measurement asks respondents to choose what they prefer in a series of price/service combinations (groups of specific services with prices). Discrete choice modeling derives measures of importance that reflect the market's value system of preferences. *Strengths:* allows playing "what-if" games, achieves all pricing research objectives, is the most flexible method, analyzes market segments, is supported by PC software, measures interaction effects, is applicable to new products, and is the least costly method when studying multiple issues. *Limitations:* is based on simulated consumer tasks, is the most complex task for respondents, few researchers have expertise, and assumes "all else equal."

In the *controlled market test* approach, marketers select sample locations that are then divided into two groups: a control group and a test group. In the control group, prices do not change. In the test group, there is first a period with prices the same as in the control group and then a period

A Selected Comparison of When to Use Various Pricing Research Methods

Criteria	Purchase Simulation*	Historical Data Modeling	Trade-off Analysis	Controlled Market Test
Decision issue:	2	3	4	5
• Pricing strategies for existing product mix	1	4	5	3
• Price gap analysis	1	3	5	1
• Optimal pricing points	2	0	5	4
• Pricing new products	3	2	4	5
• Product switching patterns	0	0	5	0
• Value for product attributes	1	5	4	1
• Price promotion assessment	3	4	4	5
Cost	2	5	4	3
Statistical expertise required	2	4	4	5
Accuracy	2	4	5	3
Difficulty of understanding/interpreting results	1–4 weeks	1–4 weeks	1–2 months	1–2 months
Time horizon for implementation				

*Ratings: 0 = lowest; 5 = highest.

with test pricing. Sales activity and profitability are monitored in both the control and test groups. Identifying changes in the test group compared with the control group gives the marketer a measure of the impact of the new pricing approach. *Strengths:* examines behavior in the real marketplace, tests specific price strategies, is appropriate for new products, and is the best approach for high-risk questions. *Limitations:* is unable to examine many alternative price scenarios, is expensive, other variables in the market are hard to control, takes the longest to conduct, alerts competitors to what is being planned, does not measure cross-price elasticities, and is difficult to secure sample location cooperation.

Which approach is best to use? That depends on the decision issue, cost, statistical expertise required, accuracy, difficulty of understanding results, and time horizon for implementation. The table on the previous page rates each of the four pricing research methods on these criteria from 0 (lowest) to 5 (highest).

Source: From N. C. Mohn, "Pricing Research for Decision Making," *Marketing Research: A Magazine of Management and Applications* 7, no. 1 (Winter 1995), pp. 10–19. Reprinted with permission of the American Marketing Association.

portance. To establish a service price in this definition of value, the marketer must understand to what extent customers know the objective prices of services in this category, how they interpret various prices, and how much is too much of a perceived sacrifice. These are best understood when the service provider also knows the relative dollar size of the purchase, the frequency of past price changes, and the range of acceptable prices for the service. Some of the specific pricing approaches appropriate when customers define value as low price include discounting, odd pricing, synchro-pricing, and penetration pricing (Figure 16.4).

Discounting

Service providers offer discounts or price cuts to communicate to price-sensitive buyers that they are receiving value. Colleges are now providing many forms of discounting to attract students. Lehigh University allows top students to get a fifth year of undergraduate or graduate education free, and also offers scholarships based on criteria other than financial need. The business school also cut tuition 22 percent for its master's program and allows graduates to take two-thirds off the regular tuition price.[19] Discount pricing has become a creative art at other educational institutions. The University of Rochester offered a $5,000 grant to all New York State residents enrolling as freshmen.

FIGURE 16.4
Pricing Strategies When the Customer Defines Value as Low Price

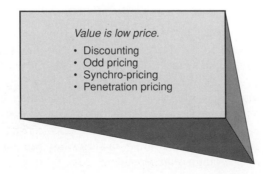

Value is low price.
- Discounting
- Odd pricing
- Synchro-pricing
- Penetration pricing

Odd Pricing

This is the practice of pricing services just below the exact dollar amount to make buyers perceive that they are getting a lower price. Dry cleaners charge $2.98 for a shirt rather than $3.00, health clubs have dues priced at $33.90 per month rather than $34, and haircuts are $9.50 rather than $10.00. Odd prices suggest discounting and bargains and are appealing to customers for whom value means low price.

Synchro-Pricing

Synchro-pricing is the use of price to manage demand for a service by using customer sensitivity to prices. Certain services, such as tax preparation, passenger transportation, long-distance telephone, hotels, and theaters have demand that fluctuates over time as well as constrained supply at peak times. For companies in these and other industries, setting a price that provides a profit over time can be difficult. Pricing can, however, play a role in smoothing demand and synchronizing demand and supply. Time, place, quantity, and incentive differentials have all been used effectively by service firms, as discussed in Chapter 14.

Place differentials are used for services where customers have a sensitivity to location. The front row at concerts, the 50-yard line in football, center court in tennis or basketball, ocean-side rooms in resort hotels—all these represent place differentials that are meaningful to customers and that therefore command higher prices.

Time differentials involve price variations that depend on when the service is consumed. Telephone service after 11 P.M., hospital rooms on weekends, airline tickets that include a Saturday night stay, and health spas in the off-season are time differentials that reflect slow periods of service. By offering lower prices for underused time periods, a service company can smooth demand and also gain incremental revenue.

Quantity differentials are usually price decreases given for volume purchasing. This pricing structure allows a service company to predict future demand for its services. Customers who buy a booklet of coupons for a tanning salon or facial, a quantity of tokens for public bridges, or packages of advertising spots on radio or television are all responding to price incentives achieved by committing to future services. Corporate discounts for airlines, hotels, and rental cars exemplify quantity discounts in the business context; by offering lower prices, the service provider locks in future business.

Differentials as incentives are lower prices for new or existing clients in the hope of encouraging them to be regular users or more frequent users. Some professionals—lawyers, dentists, electrologists, and even some physicians—offer free consultations at the front end, usually to overcome fear and uncertainty about high service prices. Other companies stimulate use by offering regular customers discounts or premiums during slow periods.

Penetration Pricing

Penetration pricing is a strategy in which new services are introduced at low prices to stimulate trial and widespread use. The strategy is appropriate when (1) sales volume of the service is very sensitive to price, even in the early stages of introduction; (2) it is possible to achieve economies in unit costs by operating at large volumes; (3) a service faces threats of strong potential competition very soon after introduction; and (4) there is no class of buyers willing to pay a higher price to obtain the service.[20] This form of pricing can lead to problems when companies then select a "regular" increased price. Care must be taken not to penetrate with so low a price that customers feel the regular price is outside the range of acceptable prices.

FIGURE 16.5
Pricing Strategies When the Customer Defines Value as Everything Wanted in a Service

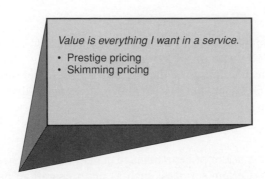

Value is everything I want in a service.
- Prestige pricing
- Skimming pricing

Pricing Strategies When the Customer Means "Value Is Everything I Want in a Service"

When the customer is concerned principally with the "get" components of a service, monetary price is not of primary concern. The more desirable intrinsic attributes a given service possesses, the more highly valued the service is likely to be and the higher the price the marketer can set. Figure 16.5 shows appropriate pricing strategies.

Prestige Pricing

This is a special form of demand-based pricing by service marketers who offer high-quality or status services. For certain services—restaurants, health clubs, airlines, and hotels—a higher price is charged for the luxury end of the business. Some customers of service companies who use this approach may actually value the high price because it represents prestige or a quality image. Others prefer purchasing at the high end because they are given preference in seating or accommodations and are entitled to other special benefits. In prestige pricing, demand may actually increase as price increases because the costlier service has more value in reflecting quality or prestige.

Skimming Pricing

This is a strategy in which new services are introduced at high prices with large promotional expenditures. It is an effective approach when services are major improvements over past services. In this situation many customers are more concerned about obtaining the service than about the cost of the service, allowing service providers to skim the customers most willing to pay the highest prices.

Pricing Strategies When the Customer Means "Value Is the Quality I Get for the Price I Pay"

In this definition, the customer primarily considers quality and monetary price. The task of the marketer is to understand what *quality* means to the customer (or segments of customers) and then to match quality level with price level. Specific strategies are shown in Figure 16.6.

"Value Pricing"

This widely used term has come to mean "giving more for less." In current usage it involves assembling a bundle of services that are desirable to a wide group of customers and then pricing them lower than they would cost alone. Taco Bell pioneered value pricing in 1988 with a $0.59 Value Menu. After sales at the chain rose 50 percent in two years to $2.4 billion, McDonald's and Burger King adopted the value pricing practice.

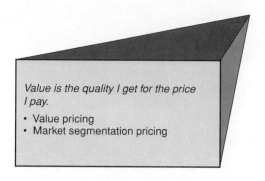

FIGURE 16.6
Pricing Strategies When the Customer Defines Value as Quality for the Price Paid

Value is the quality I get for the price I pay.

• Value pricing
• Market segmentation pricing

The menu at Taco Bell has since been reconfigured to emphasize plain tacos and burritos (which are easier and faster for the chain to make) for less than a dollar. Southwest Airlines also offers value pricing in its airline service: a low cost for a bundle of desirable service attributes such as frequent departures, friendly and funny employees, and on-time arrival. The airline offers consistently low fares with bare-bones service.

Market Segmentation Pricing

In this form of pricing, a service marketer charges different prices to groups of customers for what are perceived to be different quality levels of service, even though there may not be corresponding differences in the costs of providing the service to each of these groups. This pricing is based on the premise that different segments show different price elasticities of demand and desire different quality levels.

Some services marketers price by *client category,* based on the recognition that some groups find it difficult to pay a recommended price. Health clubs located in college communities will typically offer student memberships, recognizing that this segment of customers has limited ability to pay full price. Accompanying the lower price, student memberships may also carry with them reduced hours of use, particularly in peak use times. The same line of reasoning leads to memberships for "seniors," who are less able to pay full price and also are willing to patronize the clubs during daytime hours when most full-price members are working.

Companies also use market segmentation by *service version,* recognizing that not all segments want the basic level of service at the lowest price. When they can identify a bundle of attributes that are desirable enough for another segment of customers, they can charge a higher price for that bundle. Companies can configure service bundles that reflect price and service points appealing to different groups in the market. Hotels, for example, offer standard rooms at a basic rate but then combine amenities and tangibles related to the room to attract customers willing to pay more for the concierge level, jacuzzis, additional beds, and sitting areas.

Pricing Strategies When the Customer Means "Value Is All That I Get for All That I Give"

Figure 16.7 illustrates the pricing strategies described here.

Price Framing

Because many customers do not possess accurate reference prices for services, services marketers are more likely than product marketers to organize the price information for customers so they know how to view it. Customers naturally look for price

FIGURE 16.7
Pricing Strategies When the Customer Defines Value as All That Is Received for All That Is Given

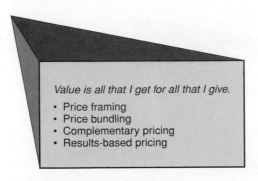

Value is all that I get for all that I give.

- Price framing
- Price bundling
- Complementary pricing
- Results-based pricing

anchors, as well as familiar services against which to judge focal services. If they accept the anchors, they view the price and service package favorably. Gerald Smith, a professor at Boston College, provided an enlightening example of the way price framing could have improved sales of the 1994 Olympic TripleCast, minute-by-minute coverage of different Olympic arenas that was a well-documented failure because few customers were willing to pay the price of $130. He suggested that if CBS had segmented the market, isolated meaningful packages of sports, and framed them in a way that was familiar to customers, the service might have been successful. He proposed a boxing package for $24.95, a skating package for $24.95, and equestrian and wrestling packages for $19.95. In each case the service could be framed in an appropriate price context. For example, boxing at $24.95 is priced somewhere between attending a boxing match and watching it on pay-per-view. Boxing aficionados would recognize the price for the full package of matches as a value.[21]

Price Bundling

Some services are consumed more effectively in conjunction with other services; other services accompany the products they support (such as extended service warranties, training, and expedited delivery). When customers find value in a package of services that are interrelated, price bundling is an appropriate strategy. Bundling, which means pricing and selling services as a group rather than individually, has benefits to both customers and service companies. Customers find that bundling simplifies their purchase and payment, and companies find that the approach stimulates demand for the firm's service line, thereby achieving cost economies for the operations as a whole while increasing net contributions.[22] Bundling also allows the customer to pay less than in purchasing each of the services individually, which contributes to perceptions of value.

The effectiveness of price bundling depends on how well the service firm understands the bundles of value that customers or segments perceive, and on the complementarity of demand for these services. Effectiveness also depends on the right choice of services from the firm's point of view. Since the firm's objective is to increase overall sales, the services selected for bundling should be those with a relatively small sales volume without the bundling to minimize revenue loss from discounting a service that already has a high sales volume.

Approaches to bundling include mixed bundling, mixed-leader bundling, and mixed-joint bundling.[23] In *mixed bundling,* the customer can purchase the services individually or as a package, but a price incentive is offered for purchasing the package. As an example, a health club customer may be able to contract for aerobics classes at $10 per month, weight machines at $15, and pool privileges at $15—or the group of three services for $27 (a price incentive of $8 per month).[24] In *mixed-leader bundling,* the price of one service is discounted if the first service is purchased at full price. For example, if cable TV customers buy one premium channel at full price, they can acquire a second premium channel at a reduced monthly rate. The objective is to reduce the price of the higher-volume service to generate an increase in its volume that "pulls" an increase in demand for a lower-volume but higher–contribution margin service. In *mixed-joint bundling,* a single price is formed for the combined set of services to increase demand for both services by packaging them together.

Complementary Pricing

This pricing includes three related strategies—captive pricing, two-part pricing, and loss leadership.[25] Services that are highly interrelated can be leveraged by using one of these forms of pricing. In *captive pricing* the firm offers a base service or product and then provides the supplies or peripheral services needed to continue using the service. In this situation the company could off-load some part of the price for the basic service to the peripherals. For example, cable services often drop the price for installation to a very low level, then compensate by charging enough for the peripheral services to make up for the loss in revenue. With service firms, this strategy is often called *two-part pricing* because the service price is broken into a fixed fee plus variable usage fees (also found in telephone services, health clubs, and commercial services such as rentals). *Loss leadership* is the term typically used in retail stores when providers place a familiar service on special largely to draw the customer to the store and then reveal other levels of service available at higher prices.

Results-Based Pricing

In service industries in which outcome is very important but uncertainty is high, the most relevant aspect of value is the *result* of the service. In personal injury law suits, for example, clients value the settlement they receive at the conclusion of the service. From tax accountants, clients value cost savings. From trade schools, students most value getting a job upon graduation. From Hollywood stars, production companies value high grosses. In these and other situations, an appropriate value-based pricing strategy is to price on the basis of results or outcome of the service.

Two simple examples, one for a consumer service and one for a business-to-business service, illustrate how results-based pricing reduces risk for customers. Boens-Aloisi, a small advertising agency in Pennsylvania, used this approach by drawing up contracts with its clients to receive the full fee if sales rise 10 percent, half fee if sales rise only 5 percent, and no fee if sales rise less than 5 percent. Obviously, the service provider must feel confident that its services will provide high value to customers: its sales and margins depend on it.

Contingency Pricing   The most commonly known form of results-based pricing is a practice called *contingency pricing* used by lawyers. Contingency pricing is the major way that personal injury and certain consumer cases are billed; it accounts for 12 percent of commercial law billings.[26] In this approach, lawyers do not receive fees or payment until the case is settled, when they are paid a percentage of the money that the client receives. Therefore, only an outcome in the client's favor is compensated. From the client's point of view, the pricing makes sense in part because most clients in these cases are unfamiliar with and possibly intimidated by law firms. Their biggest fears are high fees for a case that may take years to settle. By using contingency pricing, clients are assured that they pay no fees until they receive a settlement.

In these and other instances of contingency pricing, the economic value of the service is hard to determine before the service, and providers develop a price that allows them to share the risks and rewards of delivering value to the buyer. Partial contingency pricing, now being used in commercial law cases, is a version in which the client pays a lower fee than usual but offers a bonus if the settlement exceeds a certain level. Bickel and Brewer, a commercial law firm, agreed to cap fees for legal work at $800,000 but to split with its client, Prentiss Properties Ltd. any judgment over $10 million. When the federal judge awarded Prentiss $100 million in settlement, the law firm walked away with $45 million more in payment for taking the risk.

Sealed Bid Contingency Pricing   Companies wishing to gain the most value from their services purchases are increasingly turning to a form of results-based pricing that involves sealed bids guaranteeing results. Consider the challenge of a school district with energy bills (including heating oil, gas, and electricity) so high that money was diverted from its primary mission of educating students. In its most recent year, costs for energy were $775,000, and the proposed budget for the coming year was $810,000. The school board wanted a long-term solution to the problem, desiring to expend less of their budget on energy and more on direct education expenses. The EMS Company, an engineering firm providing services to control and reduce energy use in large buildings, was one of three companies submitting bids to the school district. EMS proposed a computer-controlled system that monitored energy use and operated on/off valves for all energy-using systems. The proposal specified a five-year contract with a fixed price of $254,500 per year, with the additional guarantee that the school district would save at least that amount of money each year or EMS would refund the difference. Included in the proposal was a plan to take into account energy prices, hours the buildings were in use, and degree days so as to provide a basis of calculating the actual savings occurring. After five years the school district would own the system with the option of purchasing a management operating service for an annual fee of $50,000.[27]

Although two other firms submitted lower multiyear bids of $190,000 and $215,000 annually, neither bid provided any guarantee for energy savings. The school board was intrigued by the EMS approach, because at worst the cost of the service was zero. EMS was awarded the bid. During the first year, actual calculated savings exceeded $300,000. A cost-plus bid by EMS would have been priced at $130,000 per year. The use of contingency pricing by EMS removed the risk from the school board's decision and added profits at EMS.[28]

Money-Back Guarantees   Vocational colleges offer one major promise: to get students jobs upon graduation. So many schools commit to this promise—often blatantly in television advertising—that prospective students have come to distrust all promises from these colleges. To give substance to its promise, Brown-MacKenzie College, a for-profit vocational college, offered a tuition-back guarantee to any graduate who, after due effort, failed to obtain a suitable position within 90 days of program completion. While other educational institutions cannot do this, largely because the results desired do not often arrive within a 90-day period, other results-based plans are taking shape. A future-income-dependent payment plan has been considered by many schools. Under such a plan, a student would receive a full scholarship and, after graduation, pay a fixed percentage of salary for a set period—for example, 5 percent of salary for 20 years. Under this plan, the more "value added" by education and the more money-oriented the student, the more the student and the institution would benefit financially.[29]

Commission   Many services providers—including real estate agents and advertising agencies—earn their fees through commissions based on a percentage of the selling price. In these and other industries, the convention is for commission to be paid by the supplier rather than the buyer. Advertising agencies are paid 15 percent commission by the print and broadcast media (newspaper, radio, TV, magazines) for the amount they place with them, not by their clients.

The commission approach to services pricing is compelling in that agents are compensated most when they find the highest rates and fares. It would seem that agents have an underlying motivation to avoid the lowest fares and rates for their clients.

Summary

This chapter began with three key differences between customer evaluation of pricing for services and goods: (1) customers often have inaccurate or limited reference prices for services, (2) price is a key signal to quality in services, and (3) monetary price is not the only relevant price to service customers. These three differences can have profound impact on the strategies companies use to set and administer prices for services. The chapter also discussed common pricing structures including (1) cost based, (2) competition based, and (3) demand based. Central to the discussion were the specific difficulties in each of these structures and the services pricing techniques that have emerged in practice.

The chapter also defined customer perceptions of value and suggested appropriate pricing strategies that match each customer definition. Figure 16.8 summarizes these definitions and strategies. The four value definitions include (1) value is low price, (2) value is whatever I want in a product or service, (3) value is the quality I get for the price I pay, and (4) value is all that I get for all that I give. Examples of specific pricing strategies that relate to these value definitions include discounting (for value is low price) and market segmentation pricing (for value is what I get for the price I pay).

FIGURE 16.8
Summary of Service Pricing Strategies for Four Customer Definitions of Value

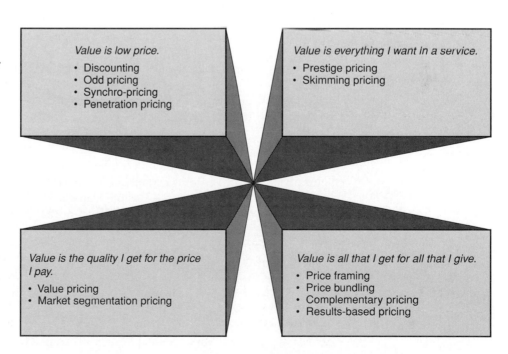

Value is low price.
- Discounting
- Odd pricing
- Synchro-pricing
- Penetration pricing

Value is everything I want in a service.
- Prestige pricing
- Skimming pricing

Value is the quality I get for the price I pay.
- Value pricing
- Market segmentation pricing

Value is all that I get for all that I give.
- Price framing
- Price bundling
- Complementary pricing
- Results-based pricing

Discussion Questions

1. Which approach to pricing (cost based, competition based, or demand based) is the most fair to customers? Why?

2. Is it possible to use all three approaches simultaneously when pricing services? If you answer yes, describe a service that is priced this way.

3. For what consumer services do you have reference prices? What makes these services different from others for which you lack reference prices?

4. Name three services you purchase in which price is a signal to quality. Do you believe that there are true differences across services that are priced high and those that are priced low? Why or why not?

5. Describe the nonmonetary costs involved in the following services: getting an automobile loan, belonging to a health club, having allergies diagnosed and treated, attending an executive education class, and getting braces.

6. Consider the specific pricing strategies for each of the four customer value definitions. Which of these strategies could be adapted and used with another value definition?

Exercises

1. List five services for which you have no reference price. Now put yourself in the role of the service providers for two of those services and develop pricing strategies. Be sure to include in your description which of the value definitions you believe customers will possess and what types of strategies would be appropriate given those definitions.

2. In the next week, find three price lists for services (such as from a restaurant, dry cleaner, or hairstylist). Identify the pricing base and the strategy used in each of them. How effective is each?

3. Consider that you are the owner of a new private college and can prepare a value/price package that is appealing to students. Describe your approach. How does it differ from existing offerings?

4. Go to the priceline.com Internet site and become familiar with the way it works.

Notes

1. P. Lewis, "Pay to Play," *Fortune,* January 7, 2002, pp. 115–17.
2. F. Goodman, "Will Fans Pay for Music Online?" *Rolling Stone,* January 31, 2002, pp. 17–18.
3. K. Monroe, "The Pricing of Services," *Handbook of Services Marketing,* ed. C. A. Congram and M. L. Friedman (New York: AMACOM, 1989), pp. 20–31.
4. Ibid.
5. "Pet Depressed? Call Us," *Newsweek,* May 22, 1989, p. 60.
6. M. A. Ernst, "Price Visibility and Its Implications for Financial Services," presentation at the Effective Pricing Strategies for Service Providers Conference, Institute for International Research, Boston, October 1994.
7. M. Chase, "Whose Time Is Worth More: Yours or the Doctor's," *The Wall Street Journal,* October 24, 1994, p. B1.
8. Monroe, "The Pricing of Services."
9. V. A. Zeithaml, "The Acquisition, Meaning, and Use of Price Information by Consumers of Professional Services," in *Marketing Theory: Philosophy of Science Perspectives,* ed. R. Bush and S. Hunt (Chicago: American Marketing Association, 1982), pp. 237–41.
10. C. H. Lovelock, "Understanding Costs and Developing Pricing Strategies," *Services Marketing* (New York: Prentice Hall, 1991), pp. 236–46.

11. A. Stevens, "Firms Try More Lucrative Ways of Charging for Legal Services," *The Wall Street Journal,* November 25, 1994, pp. B1ff.
12. K. H. Bacon, "Banks' Services Grow Costlier for Consumers," *The Wall Street Journal,* November 18, 1993, p. B1.
13. Ibid.
14. J. L. Fix, "Consumers Are Snarling over Charges," *USA Today,* August 2, 1994, pp. B1–B2.
15. C. L. Grossman, "The Driving Forces behind Rental Car Costs," *USA Today,* October 25, 1994, p. 50.
16. V. A. Zeithaml, "Consumer Perceptions of Price, Quality, and Value: A Means-End Model and Synthesis of Evidence," *Journal of Marketing* 52 (July 1988), pp. 2–22.
17. All comments from these four sections are based on those from ibid., pp. 13–14.
18. H. Simon, "If the Price Isn't Right," *World Link,* September–October 1994.
19. "Colleges Get Creative in Price-cutting," *St. Petersburg Times,* December 27, 1994, pp. B1, B6.
20. Monroe, "The Pricing of Services."
21. G. E. Smith, "Framing and Customers' Perceptions of Price and Value in Service-Oriented Businesses," presentation at the Effective Pricing Strategies for Service Providers Conference, Institute for International Research, Boston, October 1994.
22. Monroe, "The Pricing of Services."
23. Ibid.
24. J. P. Guiltinan, "The Price Bundling of Services: A Normative Framework," *Journal of Marketing* 51 (April 1987): 74–85.
25. G. J. Tellis, "Beyond the Many Faces of Price: An Integration of Pricing Strategies," *Journal of Marketing* 50 (October 1986): 146–60.
26. A. Stevens, "Clients Second-Guess Legal Fees," *The Wall Street Journal,* January 6, 1995, pp. B1, B6.
27. Example adapted from P. J. LaPlaca, "Pricing That Is Contingent on Value Delivered," given at the First Annual Pricing Conference, The Pricing Institute, New York, December 3, 4, 1987, and described in Monroe, "The Pricing of Services," p. 23.
28. Ibid.
29. K. Fox, *Service Marketing Newsletter* (Chicago: American Marketing Association, 1984), pp. 1–2.

Part 6

THE BIG PICTURE— CLOSING ALL THE GAPS

Chapter 17   The Financial and Economic Effect of Service

Chapter 18   The Integrated Gaps Model of Service Quality

In this final section of the text, we integrate the other chapters and sections in two different ways.

First, in Chapter 17 we discuss one of the most important questions about service that managers have been debating over the past 20 years: Are services and excellent service profitable to an organization? We pull together research and company experience, virtually all of it from the past decade and most from the past five years, to understand the answer to this question. We present our own model of how the relationship works and show you alternative models that have been used in companies such as Sears. We close Chapter 17 with a performance measurement model called the balanced performance scorecard that is being implemented or considered in many *Fortune* 500 firms. In addition to financial performance, the balanced performance scorecard allows a company to measure performance from the customers' perspective (in ways we discussed in Chapters 4 and 5), an operations perspective (from Chapter 9), the employees' perspective (from Chapter 11), and an innovation and new service perspective (from Chapter 8). Thus, in Chapter 17 we integrate the measurement issues that underly the provision of service and offer a way for companies to demonstrate that service is accountable financially. The balanced scorecard and similar models allow companies of the future to know much more accurately what their investments in service excellence bring to them.

Chapter 18 integrates the text using the full gaps model of service quality that has provided structure throughout the sections in the book. Although you saw this model briefly in Part 1, we elaborate on the gaps in this chapter and show how they fit together. Just as we began the text with the customer gap and followed with ways to close that gap by closing the provider gaps, Chapter 18 begins with the customer gap, then discusses the four provider gaps. By way of summary, we present the key factors responsible for each of the four provider gaps, then refer you back to the individual chapters that address these key factors. The gaps model, and this final chapter, can be used as a way to summarize the book and course, and also as a framework for organizing the issues a services company must face in meeting or exceeding customer expectations.

17

THE FINANCIAL AND ECONOMIC EFFECT OF SERVICE

This chapter's objectives are to

1. Examine the direct effects of service on profits.

2. Consider the effect of service on getting new customers.

3. Evaluate the role of service in keeping customers.

4. Examine the link between perceptions of service and purchase intentions.

5. Discuss what is known about the key service drivers of overall service quality, customer retention, and profitability.

6. Present a model called the balanced performance scorecard that allows for strategic focus on measurements other than financials.

"What return can I expect on service quality improvements?" —A typical CEO

Both authors of this text work with companies to improve their service quality and better meet their customers' expectations. The two most frequent questions asked by executives of these companies are

"How do I know that service quality improvements will be a good investment?"

"Where in the company do I invest money to achieve the highest return?"

For example, a restaurant chain, after conducting consumer research, found that service quality perceptions averaged 85 percent across the chain. The specific items receiving the lowest scores on the survey were appearance of the restaurant's exterior (70 percent), wait time for service (78 percent), and limited menu (76 percent). The company's CEO wanted to know, first of all, whether making improvements in overall service quality or to any of the specific areas would result in revenues that exceeded their costs. Moreover, he wanted guidance as to which of the service aspects to tackle. He could determine how much each of the initiatives would cost to change, but that was as far as his financial estimates would take him. Clearly, the restaurant's exterior was most in need of change because it was rated lowest; but wouldn't it also be by far the most expensive to change? What could he expect in return for each? Would adjustments in the other two factors be better investments? Which of the three service initiatives would generate noticeable improvements to raise the overall customer perceptions of the restaurant?

Ten years ago, these questions had to be answered on the basis of executive intuition. Today, fortunately, more analytical and rigorous approaches exist to help managers make these decisions about service quality investments. The best known and most widely respected approach is called return on service quality (ROQ) and was developed by Roland Rust, Anthony Zahorik, and Tim Keiningham, a team of researchers and consultants.[1] The ROQ approach is based on the following assumptions:

1. Quality is an investment.

2. Quality efforts must be financially accountable.

3. It is possible to spend too much on quality.

4. Not all quality expenditures are equally valid.

Their approach looks at investments in services as a chain of effects of the following form:

1. A service improvement effort will produce an increased level of customer satisfaction at the process or attribute level. For example, expending money to refurbish the exterior of the restaurants will likely increase customers' satisfaction level from the current low rating of 70 percent.

2. Increased customer satisfaction at the process or attribute level will lead to increased overall customer satisfaction. If satisfaction with the restaurant's exterior goes from 70 to 80 percent, overall service quality ratings may increase from 85 to 90 percent. (Both of these percentage changes could be accurately measured the next time surveys are conducted and could even be projected in advance using the ROQ model.)

3. Higher overall service quality or customer satisfaction will lead to increased behavioral intentions, such as greater repurchase intention and intention to increase usage. Customers who have not yet eaten at the restaurant will be drawn to do so, and many who currently eat there once a month will consider increasing their patronage.

4. Increased behavioral intentions will lead to behavioral impact, including repurchase or customer retention, positive word of mouth, and increased usage. Intentions about patronizing the restaurant will become reality, resulting in higher revenues and more positive word-of-mouth communications.

5. Behavioral effects will then lead to improved profitability and other financial outcomes. Higher revenues will lead to higher profits for the restaurant, assuming that the original investment in refurbishing the exterior is covered.

> The ROQ methodology can help distinguish among all the company strategies, processes, approaches, and tactics that can be altered. The ROQ approach is informative because it can be applied in companies to direct their individual strategies. Software has been developed to accompany the approach, and consulting firms work with companies to apply it. No longer do firms like the restaurant discussed here have to depend on intuition alone to guide them in their service quality investments.

In the current era of accountability and streamlining, virtually all companies hunger for evidence and tools to ascertain and monitor the payoff and payback of new investments in service. Many managers still see service and service quality as costs rather than as contributors to profits, partly because of the difficulty involved in tracing the link between service and financial returns. Determining the financial effect of service parallels the age-old search for the connection between advertising and sales. Service quality's results—like advertising's results—are cumulative, and therefore, evidence of the link may not come immediately or even quickly after investments. And, like advertising, service quality is one of many variables—among them pricing, advertising, efficiency, and image—that simultaneously influence profits. Furthermore, spending on service per se does not guarantee results because strategy and execution must both also be considered.

In recent years, however, researchers and company executives have sought to understand the relationship between service and profits and have found strong evidence to support the relationship. They are also realizing that the link between service and profits is neither straightforward nor simple. Service quality affects many economic factors in a company, some of them leading to profits through variables not traditionally in the domain of marketing. For example, the traditional total quality management approach expresses the financial effect of service quality in lowered costs or increased productivity. These relationships involve operational issues that concern marketing only in the sense that marketing research is used to identify service improvements that customers notice and value.

More recently, other types of evidence have become available on which to examine the relationship between service and profitability. The overall goal of this chapter is to synthesize that recent evidence and to identify relationships between service and profits. This chapter is divided into six sections, paralleling the chapter's objectives. In each section we assess the evidence and identify what is currently known about the topics. The chapter is organized using a conceptual framework linking all the variables in the topics.

SERVICE AND PROFITABILITY: THE DIRECT RELATIONSHIP

Figure 17.1 shows the underlying question at the heart of this chapter. Managers were first interested in this question in the 1980s when service quality emerged as a pivotal competitive strategy. The executives of leading service companies such as Federal Express and Disney were willing to trust their intuitive sense that better service would lead to improved financial success. Without formal documentation of the financial

FIGURE 17.1
The Direct Relationship between Service and Profits

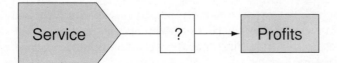

payoff, they committed resources to improving service and were richly rewarded for their leaps of faith. In the 1990s, the strategy of using service for competitive advantage and profits was embraced by forward-thinking manufacturing and information technology companies such as General Electric and IBM. However, executives in other companies withheld judgment about investing in service, waiting for solid evidence of its financial soundness.

Because tools such as return on quality analysis did not exist at the time, individual firms turned for insight to a group of early 1990s studies that explored total quality management (TQM) effects across a broad sample of manufacturing and service firms. The news was not encouraging. McKinsey and Company found that nearly two-thirds of quality programs examined had either stalled or fallen short of delivering real improvements.[2] In two other studies, A. T. Kearney found that 80 percent of British firms reported no significant impact as a result of TQM, and Arthur D. Little claimed that almost two-thirds of 500 U.S. companies saw "zero competitive gain" from TQM.[3]

Partially in response to early versions of these studies, the U.S. General Accounting Office (GAO) in 1991 sought grounds for belief in the financial effect of quality in companies that had been finalists or winners of the Malcolm Baldrige National Quality Award. The GAO found that these elite quality firms had benefited in terms of market share, sales per employee, return on sales, and return on assets. Based on responses from 22 companies who won or were finalists in 1988 and 1989, the GAO found that 34 of 40 financial variables measured in the years the companies won (or were finalists for) the award showed positive performance improvements while only six measurements were negative or neutral.[4]

In later years, evidence from more rigorous research showed the positive effect of service. One study showed the favorable financial effect of complaint recovery systems.[5] Another found a significant and positive relationship between patient satisfaction and hospital profitability. In this study, specific dimensions of hospital service quality, such as billing and discharge processes, explained 17 to 27 percent of hospital earnings, net revenues, and return on assets.[6] Extending the definition of financial performance to include stock returns, another study found a significant positive link between changes in customer quality perceptions and stock return while holding constant the effects of advertising expenditures and return on investment.[7]

Exhibit 17.1 shows how some of these relationships have been examined at Sears in the context of what is called the "employee–customer–profit chain." While some companies continued to approach the relationship at a broad level, others began to focus more specifically on particular elements of the relationship. For example, executives and researchers soon recognized that service quality played a different role in getting new customers than it did in retaining existing customers.

OFFENSIVE MARKETING EFFECTS OF SERVICE: ATTRACTING MORE AND BETTER CUSTOMERS

Service quality can help companies attract more and better customers to the business through *offensive marketing*.[8] Offensive effects (shown in Figure 17.2) involve market capture, market share, reputation, and price premiums. When service is good, a company gains a positive reputation and through that reputation a higher market share and the ability to charge more than its competitors for services. These benefits have been documented in a multiyear, multicompany study called PIMS (profit impact of marketing strategy). The PIMS research shows that companies offering superior service achieve higher-than-normal market share growth and that the mechanisms by

One way to view the relationship between service and profit has been developed by a group of Harvard professors and is called the "service-profit chain." The professors who created it argue many of the same points made in this chapter—that the longer customers stay with companies, the lower the costs to serve them, the higher the volume of purchases they make, the higher the price premium they tolerate, and the greater the positive word-of-mouth communication they engage in. They have provided evidence from in-depth studies in multiple companies such as Sears, Intuit, and Taco Bell to document these relationships. We take one of these companies, Sears, and illustrate the approach used both to examine the relationships among employees, customers, and profits as well as to improve the overall financial performance of the organization using these relationships.

The year 1992 was the worst in the history of Sears, with a net loss of $3.9 billion on sales of $52.3 billion. Between 1993 and 1998, however, Sears transformed itself into a company built around its customers. Using an ongoing process of data collection and analysis, the company created a set of total performance indicator (TPI) measures that show how well it is doing with customers, employees, and investors. Because of the extensive analysis the company undertook, it understood the influence of each of these measures on the others and ran the business on the basis of the indicators.

Early on, Sears recognized that everyone—managers and employees—must feel a sense of ownership in the program. After extensive work in teams, managers were aligned because they created the model around which the system was built—called the 3 Cs and 3 Ps. The 3 Cs were known as the three "compellings": make Sears into a "compelling place to work, shop, and invest." The 3 Ps were the company's three shared values—"passion for the customer, our people add value, and performance leadership."

As the accompanying figure shows, sets of specific objectives and measures captured the 3 Cs so that the company could be managed according to them. These objectives include many of the priorities we discuss in this chapter and text, including customer loyalty and excellent service. Believing that these objectives could be obtained only if employees were committed and involved, parallel goals and measures were established for that group of internal customers. Sears management spent a great deal of time and effort in communication and education to store-level personnel about their value and the worth of the customer. In 1998, the company declared the model successful:

We use the TPI at every level of the company, in every store and facility; and nearly every manager has some portion of his or her compensation at risk on the basis of nonfinancial measures. . . . [I]n the course of the last 12 months, employee satisfaction

which service quality influences profits include increased market share and premium prices as well as lowered costs and less rework.[9] An example of one finding relating to marketing is that businesses rated in the top fifth of competitors on relative service quality average an 8 percent price premium versus their competitors.[10]

FIGURE 17.2
Offensive Marketing Effects of Service on Profits

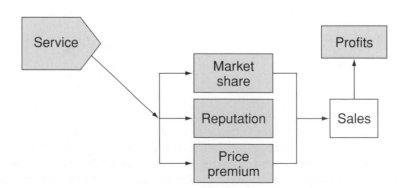

THE INITIAL MODEL:
FROM OBJECTIVES TO MEASURES

The first step in creating an employee–customer–profit model was to devise a set of measures
based on our objectives in our three categories: a compelling place to work, to shop, and to invest.

	A COMPELLING PLACE TO WORK	A COMPELLING PLACE TO SHOP	A COMPELLING PLACE TO INVEST
OBJECTIVE	• Environment for personal growth and development • Support for ideas and innovation • Empowered and involved teams and individuals	• Great merchandise at great values • Excellent customer service from the best people • Fun place to shop • Customer loyalty	• Revenue growth • Superior operating income growth • Efficient asset management • Productivity gains
MEASURES	• Personal growth and development • Empowered teams	• Customer needs met • Customer satisfaction • Customer retention	• Revenue growth • Sales per square foot • Inventory turnover • Operating income margin • Return on assets

on the Sears TPI has risen by almost 4% and customer satisfaction by 4% . . . if our model is correct—and its predictive record is extremely good—that 4% improvement in customer satisfaction translates into more than $200 million in additional revenues in the past 12 months.

Sources: J. L. Heskett, W. E. Sasser, Jr., and L. A. Schlesinger, *The Service Profit Chain* (New York: The Free Press, 1997). An exhibit from A. J. Rucci, S. P. Kirn, and R. T. Quinn, "The Employee-Customer-Profit Chain at Sears," *Harvard Business Review,* January–February 1998, pp. 83–97. Copyright © 1998 by the President and Fellows of Harvard College, all rights reserved. Reprinted by permission of *Harvard Business Review.*

To document the impact of service on market share, a group of researchers described their version of the path between quality and market share, claiming that satisfied customers spread positive word of mouth, which leads to the attraction of new customers and then to higher market share. They claim that advertising service excellence without sufficient quality to back up the communications will not increase market share. Further, they confirm that there are time lags in market share effects, making the relationship between quality and market share difficult to discern in the short term.[11]

DEFENSIVE MARKETING EFFECTS OF SERVICE: CUSTOMER RETENTION

When it comes to keeping the customers a firm already has, an approach called *defensive marketing,*[12] researchers and consulting firms have in the last 10 years documented and quantified the financial impact of existing customers. In Chapter 6 we explained that customer defection or "customer churn" is widespread in service

FIGURE 17.3
Defensive Marketing Effects of Service on Profits

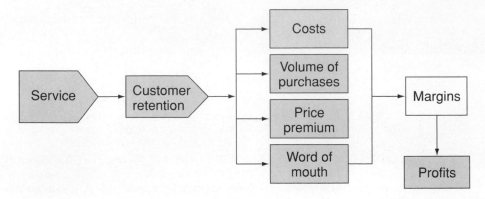

businesses. This is costly to companies because new customers must replace lost customers, and replacement comes at a high cost. Getting new customers is expensive; it involves advertising, promotion, and sales costs as well as start-up operating expenses. New customers are often unprofitable for a period of time after acquisition. In the insurance industry, for example, the insurer does not typically recover selling costs until the third or fourth year of the relationship. Capturing customers from other companies is also an expensive proposition: a greater degree of service improvement is necessary to make a customer switch from a competitor than to retain a current customer. Selling costs for existing customers are much lower (on average 20 percent lower) than selling to new ones.[13]

In general, the longer a customer remains with the company, the more profitable the relationship is for the organization:

> Served correctly, customers generate increasingly more profits each year they stay with a company. Across a wide range of businesses, the pattern is the same: the longer a company keeps a customer, the more money it stands to make.[14]

The money a company makes from retention comes from four sources (shown in Figure 17.3): costs, volume of purchases, price premium, and word-of-mouth communication. This section provides research evidence for many of the sources.

Lower Costs

It has been found that attracting a new customer is five times as costly as retaining an existing one. Consultants who have focused on these relationships assert that customer defections have a stronger effect on a company's profits than market share, scale, unit costs, and many other factors usually associated with competitive advantage.[15] They also claim that, depending on the industry, companies can increase profits from 25 to 85 percent by retaining just 5 percent more of their customers. The General Accounting Office study of semifinalists in the Malcolm Baldrige competition (described earlier in this chapter) found that quality reduced costs: order processing time decreased on average by 12 percent per year, errors and defects fell by 10 percent per year, inventory shrank by 7.2 percent, and cost of quality declined by 9 percent per year.

Consider the following facts about the role of service quality in lowering costs:

- "Our highest quality day was our lowest cost of operations day" (Fred Smith, Federal Express).

- "Our costs of not doing things right the first time were from 25 to 30 percent of our revenue" (David F. Colicchio, regional quality manager, Hewlett-Packard Company).[16]

- Profit on services purchased by a 10-year customer is on average three times greater than for a 5-year customer.[17]

- Bain & Company, a consulting organization specializing in retention research, estimates that in the life insurance business, a 5 percent annual increase in customer retention lowers a company's costs per policy by 18 percent.

Volume of Purchases

Customers who are satisfied with a company's services are likely to increase the amount of money they spend with that company or the types of services offered. A customer satisfied with a broker's services, for example, will likely invest more money when it becomes available. Similarly, a customer satisfied with a bank's checking services is likely to open a savings account with the same bank and to use the bank's loan services as well.

Price Premium

Evidence suggests that a customer who notices and values the services provided by a company will pay a price premium for those services. Graniterock, a winner of the Baldrige Award, has been able to command prices up to 30 percent higher than competitors for its rock (a product that many would claim is a commodity!) because it offers off-hour delivery and 24-hour self-service. In fact, most of the service quality leaders in industry command higher prices than their competitors: Federal Express collects more for overnight delivery than the U.S. Postal Service, Hertz rental cars cost more than Avis cars, and staying at the Ritz-Carlton is a more expensive undertaking than staying at the Hyatt.

Word-of-Mouth Communication

In Chapter 2 of this text, we described the valuable role of word-of-mouth communications in purchasing service. Because word-of-mouth communication is considered to be more credible than other sources of information, the best type of promotion for a service may well come from other customers who advocate the services provided by the company. Word-of-mouth communication brings new customers to the firm, and the financial value of this form of advocacy can be calibrated by the company in terms of the promotional costs it saves as well as the streams of revenues from new customers.

Many questions remain about defensive marketing, among them the ones shown in Exhibit 17.2. While we have come a long way in the last decade, researchers and companies must continue working on these questions for a more complete understanding of the impact of service on defensive marketing.

CUSTOMER PERCEPTIONS OF SERVICE AND PURCHASE INTENTIONS

In Chapter 4 we highlighted the links among customer satisfaction, service quality, and increased purchases. Here we provide more research and empirical evidence supporting these relationships. For example, researchers at Xerox offered a compelling insight about the relationship between satisfaction and purchase intentions during the company's early years of customer satisfaction research. Initially, the company focused on satisfied customers, which they identified as those checking either a "4" or a "5" on a five-point satisfaction scale. Careful analysis of the data showed that customers giving Xerox 5's were six times more likely to indicate they would repurchase Xerox

Managers of service firms are only beginning to understand the topics discussed in this chapter. For each of the sections on the service quality/profitability relationship in this chapter, an inventory of questions that managers and researchers most want to know is listed in Table 17.1. To give you an idea of the specific kinds of questions that managers are asking, we present them here for the topic of defensive marketing.

1. *What is a loyal customer?* Customer loyalty can be viewed as the way customers feel or as the way they act. A simple definition is possible with some products and services: customers are loyal as long as they continue to use a good or service. For washing machines or long-distance telephone service, customers are deemed loyal if they continue to use the machine or telephone service. Defining customer loyalty for other products and services is more problematic. What is the definition of loyalty to a restaurant: always eat there, eat there more times than at other restaurants, or eat there at least once during a given period? These questions highlight the growing popularity of the concept of "share of wallet" that company managers are very interested in. "Share of wallet" means what percentage of the spending in a particular service category is made on a given service provider. The other way to define loyalty is in terms of the customer's sense of be-

longing or commitment to the product. Some companies have been noted for their "apostles," customers who care so much about the company that they stay in contact to provide suggestions for improvement and constantly preach to others the benefits of the company. Is this the best way to define loyalty?

2. *What is the role of service in defensive marketing?* Quality products at appropriate prices are important elements in the retention equation, but both of these marketing variables can be imitated. Service plays a critical role—if not the critical role—in retaining customers. Providing consistently good service is not as easy to duplicate and therefore is likely to be the cementing force in customer relationships. Exactly how important is service in defensive marketing? How does service compare in effectiveness to other retention strategies such as price? To date no studies have incorporated all or most factors to examine their relative importance in keeping customers. Many companies actually have survey data that could answer this question but either have not analyzed the data for this purpose or have not reported their findings.

3. *What levels of service provision are needed to retain customers?* How much spending on service quality is enough to retain customers? Initial investigations into

equipment than those giving 4's. This relationship encouraged the company to focus on increasing the 5's, rather than the 4's and 5's, because of the strong implied sales and profitability implications.[18] The shaded boxes in Figure 17.4 show this relationship.

FIGURE 17.4
Perceptions of Service, Behavioral Intentions, and Profits

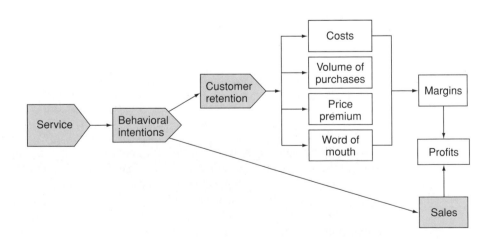

this question have been argued but have not been confirmed. One consultant, for example, proposed that when satisfaction rose above a certain threshold, repurchase loyalty would climb rapidly. When satisfaction fell below a different threshold, customer loyalty would decline equally rapidly. Between these thresholds, he believed that loyalty was relatively flat. The material discussed in Chapter 3 of this text offered a different prediction. The zone of tolerance in that chapter captured the range within which a company is meeting expectations. This framework suggests that firms operating within the zone of tolerance should continue to improve service, even to the point of reaching the desired service level. This hypothesis implies an upward-sloping (rather than flat) relationship with the zone of tolerance.

4. *What aspects of service are most important for customer retention?* The only studies that have examined specific aspects of service and their impact on customer retention have been early studies looking at customer complaint management. A decade ago this was appropriate as service was often equated with customer service, the after-sale function that dealt with dissatisfied customers. But today, most companies realize that service is multifaceted and want to identify the specific aspects of service provision that will lead to keeping customers.

5. *How can defection-prone customers be identified?* Companies find it difficult to create and execute strategies responsive enough to detect customer defections. Systems must be developed to isolate potential defecting customers, evaluate them, and retain them if it is in the best interest of the company. One author and consultant advises that companies focus on three groups of customers who may be candidates for defection: (a) customers who close their accounts and shift business to a competitor, (b) customers who shift some of their business to another firm, and (c) customers who actually buy more but whose purchases represent a smaller share of their total expenditures. The first of these groups is easiest to identify, and the third group is the most difficult. Among the other customers who would be vulnerable are any customer with a negative service experience, new customers, and customers of companies in very competitive markets. Developing early warning systems of such customers is a pivotal requirement for companies.

Source: Reprinted with permission from V. A. Zeithaml, "Service Quality, Profitability and the Economic Worth of Customers," *Journal of the Academy of Marketing Science,* January 2000, © 2000 by the Academy of Marketing Science.

Evidence also shows that customer satisfaction and service quality perceptions affect consumer intentions to behave in other positive ways—praising the firm, preferring the company over others, increasing volume of purchases, or agreeably paying a price premium. Most of the early evidence looked only at overall benefits in terms of purchase intention rather than examining specific types of behavioral intentions. One study, for example, found a significant association between overall patient satisfaction and intent to choose a hospital again.[19] Another, using information from a Swedish customer satisfaction barometer, found that stated repurchase intention is strongly related to stated satisfaction across virtually all product categories.[20]

More recently, studies have found relationships between service quality and more specific behavioral intentions. In one study involving university students, strong links between service quality and other behavioral intentions of strategic importance to a university were found, including saying positive things about the school, planning to contribute money to the class pledge upon graduation, and planning to recommend the school to employers as a place from which to recruit.[21] Another comprehensive study examined a battery comprised of 13 specific behavioral intentions likely to result from perceived service quality. The overall measure was significantly correlated with customer perceptions of service quality.[22]

TABLE 17.1   **Service Quality and the Economic Worth of Customers: We Still Need to Know More**

Topic	Key Research Questions
Service quality and profitability: the direct relationship	1. What methodologies need to be developed to allow us to capture the effect of service quality on profit? 2. What measures are necessary to examine the relationship in a consistent, valid, and reliable manner? 3. Does the relationship between service quality and profitability vary by industry, country, category of business (e.g., in services companies versus goods companies, in industrial versus packaged goods companies), or other variables? 4. What are the moderating factors of the relationship between service quality and profitability? 5. What is the optimal spending level on service in order to affect profitability?
Offensive effects of service quality	1. What is the optimal amount of spending on service quality to obtain offensive effects on reputation? 2. To obtain offensive effect, are expenditures on advertising or service quality itself more effective? 3. In what ways can companies signal high service quality to customers to obtain offensive effects?
Defensive effects of service quality	1. What is a loyal customer? 2. What is the role of service in defensive marketing? 3. How does service compare in effectiveness to other retention strategies such as price? 4. What levels of service provision are needed to retain customers? 5. How can word-of-mouth communication from retained customers be quantified? 6. What aspects of service are most important for customer retention? 7. How can defection-prone customers be identified?
Perceptions of service quality, behavioral intentions, and profits	1. What is the relationship between customer purchase intentions and initial purchase behavior in services? 2. What is the relationship between behavioral intentions and repurchase in services? 3. Does the degree of association between service quality and behavior change at different quality levels?
Identifying the key drivers of service quality, customer retention, and profits	1. What service encounters are most responsible for perceptions of service quality? 2. What are the key drivers in each service encounter? 3. Where should investments be made to affect service quality, purchase, retention, and profits? 4. Are key drivers of service quality the same as key drivers of behavioral intentions, customer retention, and profits?

Individual companies have also monitored the impact of service quality on selected behavioral intentions. Toyota found that intent to repurchase a Toyota automobile increased from a base of 37 to 45 percent with a positive sales experience, from 37 to 79 percent with a positive service experience, and from 37 to 91 percent with both positive sales and service experiences.[23] A similar study quantitatively assessed the relationship between level of service quality and willingness to purchase at AT&T. Of AT&T's customers who rated the company's overall quality as excellent, more than 90 percent expressed willingness to purchase from AT&T again. For customers rating the service as good, fair, or poor, the percentages decreased to 60, 17, and 0 percent, respectively. According to these data, willingness to repurchase increased at a steeper rate (by 43 percent) as the service quality rating improved from fair to good than when it went from poor to fair (17 percent) or from good to excellent (30 percent).[24]

Table 17.1 shows a list of the questions that we still need to know more about on this topic and the others in this chapter.

THE KEY DRIVERS OF SERVICE QUALITY, CUSTOMER RETENTION, AND PROFITS

Understanding the relationship between overall service quality and profitability is important, but it is perhaps more useful to managers to identify specific drivers of service quality that most relate to profitability (shown in Figure 17.5). Doing so will help firms understand what aspects of service quality to change to influence the relationship, and therefore where to invest resources.

Most evidence for this issue has come from examining the aspects of service (such as empathy, responsiveness, and tangibles) on overall service quality, customer satisfaction, and purchase intentions rather than on financial outcomes such as retention or profitability. As we have discovered in this text, service is multifaceted, consisting of a wide variety of customer-perceived dimensions including reliability, responsiveness, and empathy and resulting from innumerable company strategies such as technology and process improvement. In research exploring the relative importance of service dimensions on overall service quality or customer satisfaction, the bulk of the support confirms that reliability is most critical; but others have demonstrated the importance of customization and other factors. Because the dimensions and attributes are delivered in many cases with totally different internal strategies, resources must be allocated where they are most needed, and study in this topic could provide direction. The Global Feature shows a research approach in the United Kingdom to identify where to place the emphasis and resources.

Some companies and researchers have viewed the effect of specific service encounters on overall service quality or customer satisfaction and the effect of specific behaviors within service encounters. As we discussed more fully in Chapters 4 and 7, Marriott Hotels conducted extensive customer research to determine what service elements contribute most to customer loyalty. They found that four of the top five factors came into play in the first 10 minutes of the guest's stay—those that involved the early encounters of arriving, checking in, and entering the hotel rooms. Other companies have found that mistakes or problems that occur in early service encounters are particularly critical, because a failure at early points results in greater risk for dissatisfaction in each ensuing encounter. Both AT&T and IBM found that the sales encounter was the most critical of all, in large part because salespeople establish expectations for the remaining service encounters.

FIGURE 17.5
The Key Drivers of Service Quality, Customer Retention, and Profits

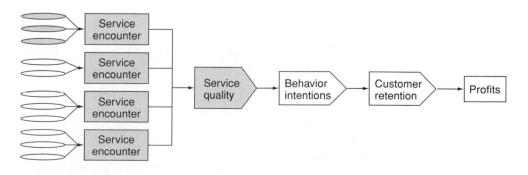

Banking in the United Kingdom is dominated by a small number of large banks providing retail and corporate services both nationally and internationally. The small business segment generates the greatest profit and revenue opportunities but has been one that has been difficult to target and serve well. Small business customers want close relationships with banks that understand them well, yet this has been a weakness of U.K. banks as well as those in Germany and France. Some banks have tried to correct this deficiency by approaches such as introducing small business account managers, but the effectiveness of these attempts has not been evaluated.

One recent study attempted to carefully examine the aspects of service that had the most potential to keep small business customers from defecting from U.K. banks. The study is an ideal illustration of the attempt to identify key drivers of service quality and purchase intention: it was comprehensive in identifying the factors that a bank could vary in attempting to improve service and increase customer loyalty. The large number of variables identified as potentially important demonstrated how difficult it is for banks to decide how to allocate their money—so many attributes are desired, and yet managers have little guidance on where to invest.

Loyal customers were defined as those who had not considered changing their banks in the previous year and accounted for 52 percent of the sample that responded to the survey. Three broad categories of drivers of retention were identified, as were specific attributes in these categories, as follows:

- *Specific product features,* including overdraft funding, rate of interest, collateral ratios, and overdraft limit.

- *Overall service quality,* including questions about a range of aspects of bank services falling into three underlying dimensions—knowledge and the advice offered, personalization in the service delivery process, and general product characteristics.

Another way of looking at the problem, based largely in the operations and management literature, has investigated the effect of service programs and managerial approaches within an organization on financial measures such as profitability. A new customer-focused approach to metrics is described in Exhibit 17.3. For example, one study estimated the effect of continuous improvement programs on profits in 280 automotive suppliers and found a 17 percent increase in profits over a two- to three-year period.[25] Another revealed that delegated teams were particularly effective at improving people and that statistical process control was most effective in improving processes in TQM programs.[26]

COMPANY PERFORMANCE MEASUREMENT: THE BALANCED PERFORMANCE SCORECARD

Traditionally, organizations have measured their performance almost completely on the basis of financial indicators such as profit, sales, and return on investment. This

- *Overall banking relationship,* including the extent to which respondents felt that the policies of the bank constrained the performance of their business plus 11 aspects of the relationship between the business and the bank manager, including trust and approachability.

These drivers as well as customer characteristics were measured on a questionnaire sent to approximately 16,000 members of the Forum of Private Business in the United Kingdom. The survey received a high response rate of 37.5 percent.

The findings indicated that the factor with the greatest effect on potential for defection was lack of trust in the banking relationship. Other important factors leading to potential defection were the degree to which managers believed their business to be constrained and the lack of approachability the customer felt toward the bank manager. The service quality variables were next in importance, showing that improved service quality—particularly knowledge and advice offered—reduced the potential for defection.

The findings are very useful to managers in the United Kingdom because they point out what factors drive customer retention. Because more than half of the respondents in the study indicated that they considered leaving their banks, it would seem critical for U.K. bank managers to identify these key drivers and then set out to improve their performances to address them. This study suggests that in the United Kingdom, this means forging more trusting relationships between bank customers and managers.

Sources: Reprinted with permission of Blackwell Publishers from C. T. Ennew and M. R. Binks, "The Impact of Service Quality and Service Characteristics on Customer Retention: Small Businesses and Their Banks in the UK," *British Journal of Management 7* (1996), pp. 219–30; and M. R. Binks, C. T. Ennew, and G. V. Reed, "Information Asymmetries and the Provision of Finance to Small Firms," *International Journal of Small Business* 11, no. 1 (1992), pp. 35–46.

short-term approach leads companies to emphasize financials to the exclusion of other performance indicators. Today's corporate strategists recognize the limitations of evaluating corporate performance on financials alone, contending that these income-based financial figures measure yesterday's decisions rather than indicate future performance. This recognition came when many companies' strong financial records deteriorated because of unnoticed declines in operational processes, quality, or customer satisfaction.[27] In the words of one observer of corporate strategy:

> Financial measures emphasize profitability of inert assets over any other mission of the company. They do not recognize the emerging leverage of the soft stuff—skilled people and employment of information—as the new keys to high performance and near-perfect customer satisfaction. . . . If the only mission a measurement system conveys is financial discipline, an organization is directionless.[28]

For this reason, companies began to recognize that *balanced performance scorecards*—strategic measurement systems that captured other areas of performance—were needed. The developers of balanced performance scorecards defined them as follows:

17.3 CUSTOMER LIFETIME VALUE AND CUSTOMER EQUITY: METRICS TO MATCH A CUSTOMER-CENTERED VIEW OF MARKETING

Although the marketing concept has articulated a customer-centered viewpoint since the 1960s, marketing theory and practice have become incrementally customer-centered over the last 40 years. For example, marketing has only recently decreased its emphasis on short-term transactions and increased its focus on long-term customer relationships. Much of this stems from the changing nature of the world's leading economies, which have undergone a dramatic shift from the goods sector to the service sector, reflecting a century-long trend.

Because service tends often to be more relationship based, this structural shift in the economy has resulted in more attention to relationships and therefore more attention to customers. This customer-centered viewpoint is starting to be reflected in the concepts and metrics that drive marketing management, including such metrics as customer value and voice of the customer measures. For example, the concept of brand equity, a fundamentally product-centered concept, is now being challenged by the customer-centered concept of *customer equity,* which can be defined as the total of the discounted lifetime values summed over all of the firm's customers.

In other words, customer equity is obtained by summing up the customer lifetime values of the firm's customers. In fast-moving and dynamic industries that involve customer relationships, products come and go, but customers remain. This suggests that customers and customer equity may be more central to many firms than brands and brand equity, although current management practices and metrics do not yet fully reflect this shift. The shift from product-centered thinking to customer-centered thinking implies the need for an accompanying shift from product-based metrics to customer-based metrics.

Customer Equity and Lifetime Value

As just defined, customer equity is the total of the discounted lifetime values summed over all of the firm's customers. Thus, to accurately evaluate a firm's customer equity, the firm must do a good job of evaluating the lifetime value of its customers.

Customer lifetime value first received serious consideration in direct marketing, but the concept has gained increasing attention throughout marketing. Traditional approaches to customer lifetime value consider a customer's contribution to profit (which may or may not change over time), the likelihood that the customer is retained from period to period, and the firm's discount rate. There are different approaches and levels of sophistication of customer lifetime value calculation, depending on the nature of the business and the amount of customer level data. Even without a detailed customer-level database, it is possible to make some approximate calculations. The minimum information includes annual revenues per customer, cost of goods or profit margin, retention rate, time horizon for

. . . a set of measures that gives top managers a fast but comprehensive view of the business . . . [that] complements the financial measures with operational measures of customer satisfaction, internal processes, and the organization's innovation and improvement activities—operational measures that are the drivers of future financial performance.[29]

Having a firm handle on what had been viewed as "soft" measures became the way to help organizations identify customer problems, improve processes, and achieve company objectives.

Balanced performance scorecards have become extremely popular. One recent report indicates that as many as 60 percent of the *Fortune* 1,000 companies surveyed by Renaissance Worldwide, Inc., have or are experimenting with balanced performance scorecards.[30] Another recent study by the Institute of Management Accountants showed that 64 percent of U.S. companies are anticipating using a new performance measurement system. Furthermore, according to a report called "Measures That Matter" from Ernst & Young's Center for Business Innovation, investors give nonfinancial measures an average of one-third the weight when making a decision to buy or sell any

planning, and the discount rate. There have been considerable improvements in the assessment of customer lifetime value in recent years due to the increasing prevalence of customer databases and the increasing recognition of the value of customer relationships. Determining customer contribution to profit is itself a complicated and difficult problem, but considerable progress has been made in recent years.

Using Customer Equity in a Strategic Framework

Consider the issues facing a typical marketing manager or marketing-oriented CEO. How do I manage my brand? How will my customers react to changes in service and service quality? Should I raise price? What is the best way to enhance the relationships with my current customers? Where should I focus my efforts? Determining customer lifetime value or customer equity is the first step, but the more important step is to evaluate and test ideas and strategies using lifetime value as the measuring stick. At a very basic level, strategies for building customer relationships can affect five things: retention rate, referrals, increased sales, reduced direct costs, and reduced marketing costs.

Rust, Zeithaml, and Lemon have developed an approach based on customer equity that can help a business executive answer these questions. In this context, customer equity is a new approach to marketing and corporate strategy that finally puts the customer—and, more importantly,

strategies that grow the value of the customer—at the heart of the organization. They identify the drivers of customer equity—value equity, brand equity, and relationship equity—and explain how these drivers work, independently and together, to grow customer equity. Service strategies are prominent in both value equity and relationship equity. Within each of these drivers are specific, incisive actions ("levers") the firm can take to enhance the firm's overall customer equity.

Why Is Customer Equity Important?

For most firms, customer equity is certain to be the most important determinant of the long-term value of the firm. Although customer equity is not responsible for the entire value of the firm (consider, for example, physical assets, intellectual property, research and development competencies, and so on), the firm's current customers provide the most reliable source of future revenues and profits—and provide a focal point for marketing strategy.

Although it may seem obvious that customer equity is key to long-term success, understanding how to grow and manage customer equity is much more complex. How to grow customer equity is of utmost importance, and doing it well can lead to significant competitive advantage.

Source: R. Rust, V. Zeithaml, and K. Lemon, *Driving Customer Equity* (New York: The Free Press, 2000).

given stock,[31] strongly demonstrating to companies that investors recognize the value of the new forms of measurement.

As shown in Figure 17.6, the balanced performance scorecard captures three perspectives in addition to the financial perspective: customer, operational, and learning. The balanced scorecard brings together, in a single management report, many of the previously separated elements of a company's competitive agenda and forces senior managers to consider all the important measures together. The scorecard has been facilitated by recent developments in enterprisewide software (discussed in the Technology Spotlight) that allow companies to create, automate, and integrate measurements from all parts of the company.

Methods for measuring financial performance are the most developed and established in corporations, having been created more than 400 years ago. In contrast, efforts to measure market share, quality, innovation, human resources, and customer satisfaction have only recently been created. Companies can improve their performance by developing this discipline in their measurement of all four categories.

FIGURE 17.6 **Sample Measurements for the Balanced Scorecard**

Financial Measures

Price premium
Volume increases
Value of customer referrals
Value of cross sales
Long-term value of customer

Customer Perspective

Service perceptions
Service expectations
Perceived value
Behavioral intentions:
  Percentage of loyalty
  Percentage of intent to
    switch
  Number of customer
    referrals
  Number of cross sales
  Number of defections

Operation Perspective

Right first time (percentage of
  hits)
Right on time (percentage of
  hits)
Responsiveness (percentage
  on time)
Transaction time (hours, days)
Throughput time
Reduction in waste
Process quality

Innovation and Learning Perspective

Number of new products
Return on innovation
Employee skills
Time to market
Time spent talking to customers

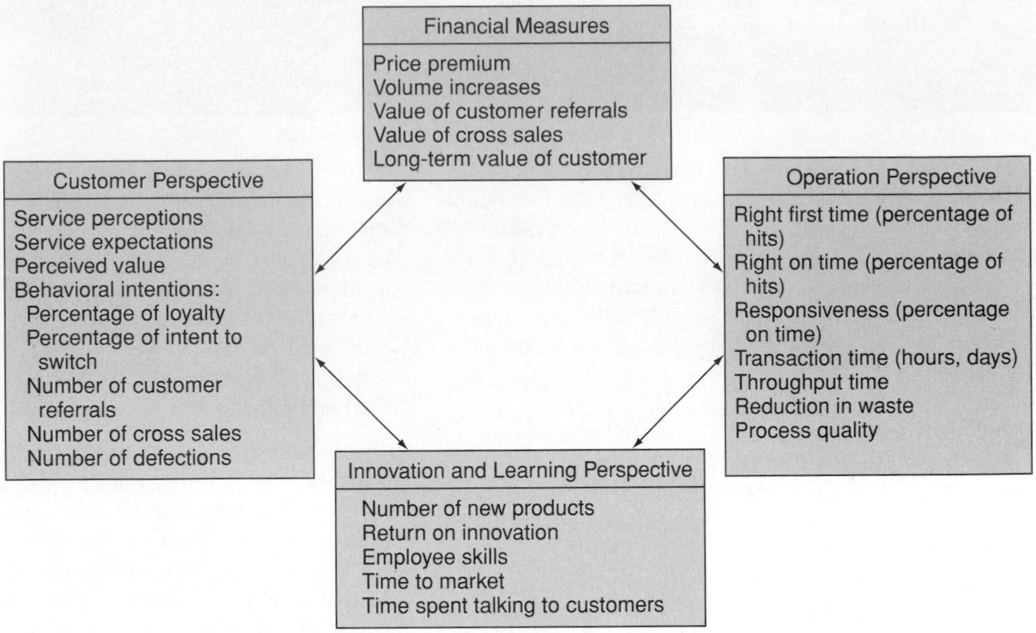

Source: An exhibit from R. S. Kaplan and D. P. Norton, "The Balanced Scorecard—Measures That Drive Performance," *Harvard Business Review,* January–February 1992. Copyright © 1992 by the President and Fellows of Harvard College, all rights reserved. Adapted by permission of *Harvard Business Review.*

Changes to Financial Measurement

One way service leaders are changing financial measurement involves calibrating the defensive effect of retaining and losing customers. The monetary value of retaining customers can be projected based on average revenues over the lifetimes of customers. The number of customer defections can then be translated into lost revenue to the firm and become a critical company performance standard:

> Ultimately, defections should be a key performance measure for senior management and a fundamental component of incentive systems. Managers should know the company's defection rate, what happens to profits when the rate moves up or down and why defections occur.[32]

Companies can also measure actual increases or decreases in revenue from retention or defection of customers by capturing the value of a loyal customer, including expected cash flows over a customer's lifetime or lifetime customer value (as described in Chapter 6). Other possible financial measures (as shown in Figure 17.6) include (1) the value of price premiums, (2) volume increases, (3) value of customer referrals, (4) cross sales, and (5) long-term value of customers.

Customer Perceptual Measures

Customer perceptual measures are leading indicators of financial performance. As we discussed in this chapter, customers who are not happy with the company will defect and will tell others about their dissatisfaction. As we also discussed, perceptual

Technology Spotlight
Enterprise Software Allows Companies to Link All Internal Databases to Make Strategic Decisions

We started this chapter by stating that documenting the financial worth of service quality is possible if companies have data (such as costs, revenues, profits, customer service attributes, sales) and the ability to link these data together. Ten years ago these two requirements were virtually impossible to attain—most companies had information systems that were created for purely functional reasons and were therefore highly incompatible with each other. What was needed was an information systems technology to provide an overall structure for collecting information about various parts of a business that was compatible across functions.

Enter Enterprise Software
Enterprise software, the biggest revolution in corporate information systems, offers companies a way to automate virtually all their functions and to link the data generated from the functions together. The heart of enterprise software is the enterprise resource planning (ERP) business, where several large companies (notably J. D. Edwards, Baan Oracle, PeopleSoft, and industry leader SAP) sell products to automate finance, manufacturing, and human resource processes. Scores of new vendors, nearly 500 in total, are working around the edges to create software packages that automate other functions (like marketing, sales, and customer service) and to allow them to be integrated into the basic ERP databases.

The Industry Leader: SAP SAP, headquartered in Walldorf, Germany, is the leading global provider of enterprise software, which is now available in 14 languages. Five former IBM employees founded the company in 1972. The 10 U.S. companies with the highest market value use SAP software, as do 8 of the 10 largest U.S. corporations and 8 of the 10 highest-profit U.S. companies. The firm has more than 7,500 customers in over 90 countries and revenues of $6 billion.

An Example: PeopleSoft Enterprise Performance Management Although PeopleSoft's market share is not as high as that of SAP, the company has created a system that perfectly illustrates the ability to combine important measurements across the company. In particular, the software helps a company measure and understand four key areas that affect future growth of its organiza-

tion: workforce, internal business processes, customer relationships, and finance and strategy.

- *Workforce analytics* help companies manage the composition of their workforce by understanding the skills inventory, hiring and retention effectiveness, employee goals, and compensation packages.

- *Internal process management* gives companies the tools to analyze the efficiency of their current business processes and evaluate the effectiveness of proposed changes.

- *Customer relationship management* offers tools for analyzing and managing customer profitability, customer behavior, marketing effectiveness, and sales and service relationships.

- *Financial and strategic management* delivers detailed financial measures, including ones based on advance costing techniques.

Each of these sections is considered a "solution" with various components that a company can customize. A company can obtain a high-level, top-down, exceptions-based performance overview using a version of the balanced scorecard discussed in the chapter, with measures in all four categories. Then PeopleSoft "workbenches" show the organization specific real-time measurements using targeted applications.

Putting It All Together
The notion of being able to integrate information with usage data and profits is critical to this chapter. Each of the five basic sections that have been discussed so far contain what is known about the link between service quality and profitability. Most of these were developed without the richness of information that is now available thanks to enterprise software. The return on quality model that we presented in the chapter opener can be traced using the information from the software. The information systems play an important part in allowing managers to go beneath the summary-level balanced scorecard measures. The software signals unusual measurements and allows managers to access underlying data to investigate the causes of problems or analyze trends and correlation. The information systems from the top vendors incorporate the following key features:

Technology Spotlight
Enterprise Software Allows Companies to Link All Internal Databases to Make Strategic Decisions—continued

- At-a-glance exception alerting.

- Rapid access to summarized data.

- Successive levels of detail.

- Reporting of impacts of underlying objectives on scorecard measures.

- Graphical creation and modification of objectives, measures, and relationships.

- Integration of existing corporate data sources.

The benefits of using enterprise software and developing an integrated measurement system can be financially dramatic. The impact of adopting a balanced approach to measurement—as implemented through enterprise software—has been estimated at 15–30 percent in profitability.

Sources: D. Coon, "Enterprise Performance Management Delivers Forward-Looking Insights," *PeopleTalk Online Magazine,* February 2000; D. Kirkpatrick, "The E-ware War: Competition Comes to Enterprise Software," *Fortune,* December 7, 1998, pp. 102–12; the SAP Fan Club, www.sapfans.com.

measures reflect customer beliefs and feelings about the company and its products and services and can predict how the customer will behave in the future. Overall forms of the measurements we discussed in Chapters 4 and 5 (shown in the customer perspective box of Figure 17.6) are the types of measures that can be included in this category. Among the measures that are valuable to track are overall service perceptions and expectations, customer satisfaction, perceptual measures of value, and behavioral intention measures such as loyalty and intent to switch. It is easy to see that a company noticing a decline in these numbers should be concerned that the decline will translate into lost dollars for the company.

Operational Measures

These measures involve the translation of customer perceptual measures into the standards or actions that must be set internally to meet customers' expectations. While virtually all companies count or calculate operational measures in some form, the balanced scorecard requires that these measures stem from the business processes that have the greatest effect on customer satisfaction. In other words, these measures are not independent of customer perceptual measures but instead are intricately linked with them. In Chapter 9 we called these customer-linked operational measures *customer-defined standards*—operational standards determined through customer expectations and calibrated the way the customer views and expresses them.

Innovation and Learning

This final area of measurement involves a company's ability to innovate, improve, and learn—by launching new products, creating more value for customers, and improving operating efficiencies. This is the measurement area that is most difficult to capture quantitatively but can be accomplished using performance-to-goal percentages. For example, a company can set a goal of launching 10 new products a year, then measure what percentage of that goal it achieves in a year. If four new products are launched, its percentage for the year is 40 percent, which can then be compared with subsequent years.

The Balanced Scorecard in Practice at Analog Devices and the City of Charlotte, North Carolina

We illustrate the use of the balanced performance scorecard with two very different types of organizations, one a for-profit company called Analog Devices and another the city government in Charlotte, North Carolina.

Analog Devices, located about 20 minutes outside of Boston, makes computer chips used in communications, military, aviation, and cellular phone applications. After performing poorly in the 1980s, the company started to survey customers and engage in benchmarking studies that showed that customers cared about delivery time and improved quality:

> Overall, there were about 15 nonfinancial measures that we identified as critical to the company's performance. . . . These were things like the rate of on-time deliveries, product development cycle times, number of new products, and so on.[33]

The model the company now uses links these measurements to financial indicators. For example, it can measure the percentage of sales resulting from new product introductions as well as gross margins on new products. It has developed key ratios as scorecard items that managers watch closely for any variance, which must then be explained. A manager with a low "new product ratio," for example, must show that she is spending research and development dollars effectively. A low product ratio indicates a lag in new product development, which would have gone unnoticed without the scorecard item.

Analog Devices has fared well with the measurement system, doubling revenue in one year, increasing operating profits from 3 to 19 percent in a single year, and quadrupling its stock price.[34]

Charlotte, North Carolina, was the first government organization to apply the balanced scorecard concept to the public sector. Frustrated with its traditional approach of setting objectives and tracking performance against them, Charlotte's governmental body decided to stop focusing on the past and set strategic direction for the future. In the early 1990s the Charlotte City Council chose five areas—community safety, transportation, economic development, neighborhoods, and restructuring government—on which to focus its strategic plan. Table 17.2 shows Charlotte's scorecard, which emphasizes strategic processes that the city must improve to meet its goals.

In 1996 Charlotte's overall "corporate" scorecard process was repeated by the planning, transportation, engineering and property management, and police departments. Each department created objectives that matched council-level objectives to be sure that the city would achieve its highest priorities. The program has been a success for the city: "With the council's support and the participation of the departments, the city has been able to clarify its critical objectives, identify the processes necessary to meet them, and produce a concise model to assist officials in tracking the city's progress."[35]

The balanced performance scorecard gives managers and their companies four different strategic perspectives from which to choose measures. It goes beyond traditional financial indicators by also calibrating customer perceptions and expectations, operational processes, and innovation and improvement activities. By reducing the measures to those that are absolutely essential in each of the perspectives, the scorecard becomes

TABLE 17.2   **Charlotte's Corporate Scorecard**

Customer Perspective	Financial Accountability Perspective	Internal Process Perspective	Learning and Growth Perspective
Reduce crime		Increase positive contacts	
Increase perception of safety	Maximize benefit/cost	Promote community-based problem solving	Enhance knowledge management capabilities
Strengthen neighborhoods	Expand noncity funding	Secure funding/service partners	Close the skills gap
Improve service quality	Grow the tax base	Improve productivity	Achieve positive employee climate
Provide safe, convenient transportation	Maintain AAA rating	Streamline customer interactions	
Maintain competitive tax rates		Increase infrastructure capacity	

Source: P. Syfert, N. Elliott, and L. Schumacher, "Charlotte Adapts the 'Balanced Scorecard,' " *The American City and County* (Pittsfield, NC, October 1998). Reprinted by permission of the City of Charlotte, North Carolina, Budget and Evaluation Department.

an extension of the company's strategic vision. Companies can customize their scorecards to fit their missions, strategies, technology, and culture.

Summary

This chapter is divided into six sections, five of which assess the evidence and identify what is currently known about the relationship between service and profitability. The chapter used a conceptual framework to link all the variables in these topics: (1) the direct relationship between service and profits; (2) offensive effects of service quality; (3) defensive effects of service quality; (4) the relationship between service quality and purchase intentions; (5) key drivers of service quality, customer retention, and profits. While considerable progress has been made in the last 10 years in investigating service quality, profitability, and the economic worth of customers, many questions remain unanswered that would allow managers to make informed decisions about service quality investments. The chapter concluded with a discussion of the balanced performance scorecard approach to measuring corporate performance, which offers a strategic approach for measuring all aspects of a company's performance.

Discussion Questions

1. Why has it been difficult for executives to understand the relationship between service improvements and profitability in their companies?
2. What is the ROQ model, and what is its significance to corporate America?
3. To this day, many companies believe that service is a cost rather than a revenue producer. Why might they hold this view? How would you argue the opposite view?
4. What is the difference between offensive and defensive marketing? How does service affect each of these?
5. What are the main sources of profit in defensive marketing?
6. What are the main sources of profit in offensive marketing?

7. How will the balanced performance scorecard help us understand and document the information presented in this chapter? Which of the five sections that discuss different aspects of the relationship between service quality and profits can it illuminate?

8. How can enterprise software help companies implement the balanced performance scorecard?

9. What is your evaluation of the balanced performance scorecard that Charlotte, North Carolina, developed to help it set strategic direction?

Exercises

1. On the Internet, use a search engine to locate three companies that make enterprise software. Include SAP, the industry leader, as one of the companies. What are the software companies' current offerings? How can the software firms help individual companies understand the concepts and relationships discussed in this chapter? Which of the three companies would you select based on the information you locate?

2. Interview a local firm and see what it knows about its key drivers of financial performance. What are the key service drivers of the firm? Does the company know whether these relate to profit?

3. Select a service industry (such as fast food) or a company (such as McDonald's) you are familiar with, either as a customer or employee, and create a balanced scorecard. Describe the operational, customer, financial, and learning measures that could be used to capture performance.

Notes

1. R. T. Rust, A. J. Zahorik, and T. L. Keiningham, *Return on Quality* (Chicago: Probus, 1994).

2. J. Matthews and P. Katel, "The Cost of Quality: Faced with Hard Times, Business Sours on Total Quality Management," *Newsweek,* September 7, 1992, pp. 48–49.

3. "The Cracks in Quality," *The Economist* 18 (April 1992), pp. 67–68.

4. *Management Practice, U.S. Companies Improve Performance through Quality Efforts,* Report No. GAO/NSIAD-91-190 (Washington, DC: U.S. General Accounting Office, 1992).

5. R. Rust, B. Subramanian, and M. Wells, "Making Complaints a Management Tool," *Marketing Management* 3 (1993), pp. 40–45.

6. E. Nelson, R. T. Rust, A. Zahorik, R. L. Rose, P. Batalden, and B. Siemanski, "Do Patient Perceptions of Quality Relate to Hospital Financial Performance?" *Journal of Healthcare Marketing,* December 1992, pp. 1–13.

7. D. A. Aaker and R. Jacobson, "The Financial Information Content of Perceived Quality," *Journal of Marketing* 58 (May 1994), pp. 191–201.

8. C. Fornell and B. Wernerfelt, "Defensive Marketing Strategy by Customer Complaint Management: A Theoretical Analysis," *Journal of Marketing Research* 24 (November 1987), pp. 337–46; see also C. Fornell and B. Wernerfelt, "A Model for Customer Complaint Management," *Marketing Science* 7 (Summer 1988), pp. 271–86.

9. B. Gale, "Monitoring Customer Satisfaction and Market-Perceived Quality," *American Marketing Association Worth Repeating Series,* no. 922CS01 (Chicago: American Marketing Association, 1992).

10. Ibid.

11. R. E. Kordupleski, R. T. Rust, and A. J. Zahorik, "Why Improving Quality

Doesn't Improve Quality (or Whatever Happened to Marketing?)," *California Management Review* 35, no. 3 (1993), pp. 82–95.

12. Fornell and Wernerfelt, "Defensive Marketing Strategy by Customer Complaint Management," also Fornell and Wernerfelt, "A Model for Customer Complaint Management."

13. T. J. Peters, *Thriving on Chaos* (New York: Alfred A. Knopf, 1988).

14. F. Reichheld and E. Sasser, "Zero Defections: Quality Comes to Services," *Harvard Business Review,* September–October 1990, p. 106.

15. Ibid., p. 105.

16. D. F. Colicchio, regional quality manager, Hewlett-Packard Company, personal communication.

17. S. Rose, "The Coming Revolution in Credit Cards," *Journal of Retail Banking,* Summer 1990, pp. 17–19.

18. J. L. Heskett, W. E. Sasser, Jr., and L. A. Schlesinger, *The Service Profit Chain* (New York: The Free Press, 1997).

19. A. Woodside, L. Frey, and R. Daly, "Linking Service Quality, Customer Satisfaction and Behavioral Intentions," *Journal of Health Care Marketing* 9 (December 1989), pp. 5–17.

20. E. W. Anderson and M. Sullivan, "The Antecedents and Consequences of Customer Satisfaction for Firms," *Marketing Science* 12 (Spring 1992), pp. 125–43.

21. W. Boulding, R. Staelin, A. Kalra, and V. A. Zeithaml, "Conceptualizing and Testing a Dynamic Process Model of Service Quality," report no. 92-121, Marketing Science Institute, 1992.

22. V. A. Zeithaml, L. L. Berry, and A. Parasuraman, "The Behavioral Consequences of Service Quality," *Journal of Marketing* 60 (April 1996), pp. 31–46.

23. J. P. McLaughlin, "Ensuring Customer Satisfaction Is a Strategic Issue, Not Just an Operational One," presentation at the AIC Customer Satisfaction Measurement Conference, Chicago, December 6–7, 1993.

24. Gale, "Monitoring Customer Satisfaction."

25. C. Fitzerald and T. Erdmann, *Actionline,* American Automotive Industry Action Group, October 1992.

26. R. Mann and D. Kehoe, "An Evaluation of the Effects of Quality Improvement Activities on Business Performance," *International Journal of Quality and Reliability Management* 11, no. 4 (1994), pp. 29–45.

27. R. S. Kaplan and D. P. Norton, "The Balanced Scorecard—Measures That Drive Performance," *Harvard Business Review,* January–February 1992.

28. D. Zielinski, "A Sole Focus on Finances Can Trouble the Heart of Business," *Total Quality Newsletter,* July 1994, p. 3.

29. Kaplan and Norton, "The Balanced Scorecard."

30. S. Silk, "Automating the Balance Scorecard," *Management Accounting,* May 1998, pp. 38–42.

31. D. A. Light, "Performance Measurement: Investors' Balance Scorecards," *Harvard Business Review,* November–December 1998, pp. 17–20.

32. Reichheld and Sasser, "Zero Defections," p. 111.

33. J. Kurtzman, "Is Your Company Off Course? Now You Can Find Out Why," *Fortune,* February 17, 1997, pp. 128–30.

34. Ibid., p. 129.

35. P. Syfert, N. Elliott, and L. Schumacher, "Charlotte Adapts the 'Balanced Scorecard,'" *The American City and County* (Pittsfield, NC, October 1998).

Chapter 18

THE INTEGRATED GAPS MODEL OF SERVICE QUALITY

As you have observed throughout this text, effective services marketing is a complex undertaking involving many different skills and tasks. Executives of services organizations have long been confused about how to approach this complicated topic in an organized manner. This text was designed around one approach: viewing services in a structured, integrated way called *the gaps model of service quality.* It was used to frame the entire text and to organize Chapters 2 through 16. Each of the first five part openers in the text focused on specific aspects of the model that were covered in the chapters following it. In this chapter we draw all of that material together in one place, reinforcing the general ideas and structure of the gaps model and thereby summarizing the text and course.

The gaps model positions the key concepts, strategies, and decisions in services marketing in a manner that begins with the customer and builds the organization's tasks around what is needed to close the gap between customer expectations and perceptions. The integrated gaps model of service quality, which was first overviewed in the Part 1 opener, is shown in Figure 18.1.[1]

The central focus of the gaps model is the *customer gap,* the difference between customer expectations and perceptions. Firms need to close this gap—between what customers expect and receive—in order to satisfy their customers and build long-term relationships with them. To close this all-important customer gap, the model suggests that four other gaps—the *provider gaps*—need to be closed.

The following four provider gaps, shown below the horizontal line in Figure 18.1, are the underlying causes behind the customer gap:

Gap 1: Not knowing what customers expect.

Gap 2: Not selecting the right service designs and standards.

Gap 3: Not delivering to service standards.

Gap 4: Not matching performance to promises.

FIGURE 18.1

Gaps Model of Service Quality

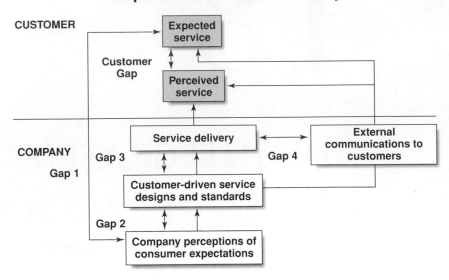

CLOSING THE CUSTOMER GAP

Above the center horizontal line in Figure 18.1 are the two boxes that correspond to *customer expectations* and *customer perceptions.* Customer perceptions are subjective assessments of actual service experiences; customer expectations are the standards of, or reference points for, performance against which service experiences are compared. The sources of customer expectations consist of marketer-controlled factors, such as advertising, as well as factors that the marketer has limited ability to affect, such as innate personal needs. Ideally, expectations and perceptions are identical: customers perceive that they get what they think they will and should. In practice, a customer gap typically exists. Services marketing bridges this distance, and we devoted virtually the entire text to describing strategies and practices designed to close this customer gap.

In this text, we attempted to show that the unique characteristics of services discussed in Chapter 1—intangibility, heterogeneity, inseparability of production and consumption, and perishability—necessitated different consumer evaluation processes from those used in assessing goods.

The key factors leading to the customer gap are shown in Figure 18.2. Each of these factors was discussed in Chapters 2, 3, and 4, and strategies used to address them were offered in those same chapters.

PROVIDER GAP 1: NOT KNOWING WHAT CUSTOMERS EXPECT

Provider gap 1 is the difference between customer expectations of service and company understanding of those expectations. Many reasons exist for managers not being aware of what customers expect: they may not interact directly with customers, be unwilling to ask about expectations, or be unprepared to address them. When people with the authority and responsibility for setting priorities do not fully understand customers' service expectations, they may trigger a chain of bad decisions and suboptimal resource allocations that result in perceptions of poor service quality. In this text,

FIGURE 18.2
Key Factors Leading to the Customer Gap

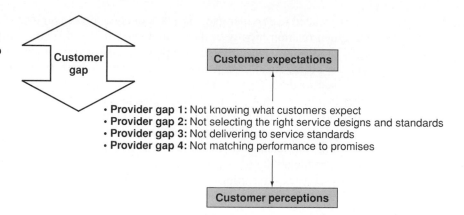

- **Provider gap 1:** Not knowing what customers expect
- **Provider gap 2:** Not selecting the right service designs and standards
- **Provider gap 3:** Not delivering to service standards
- **Provider gap 4:** Not matching performance to promises

we broadened the responsibility for the first provider gap from managers alone to any employee in the organization with the authority to change or influence service policies and procedures. In today's changing organizations, the authority to make adjustments in service delivery is delegated to empowered teams and front-line people.

Figure 18.3 shows the key factors responsible for provider gap 1. An inadequate marketing research orientation is one of the critical factors. When management or empowered employees do not acquire accurate information about customers' expectations, provider gap 1 is large. Formal and informal methods to capture information about customer expectations must be developed through market research. Techniques involving a variety of traditional research approaches must be used to stay close to the customer, among them customer visits, survey research, complaint systems, and customer panels. More innovative techniques—such as quality function deployment, structured brainstorming, and service quality gap analysis—are often needed.

Another key factor that is related to provider gap 1 is lack of upward communication. Front-line employees often know a great deal about customers; if management is not in contact with front-line employees and does not understand what they know, the gap widens.

FIGURE 18.3
Key Factors Leading to Provider Gap 1

- ***Inadequate marketing research orientation***
  Insufficient marketing research
  Research not focused on service quality
  Inadequate use of market research
- ***Lack of upward communication***
  Lack of interaction between management and customers
  Insufficient communication between contact employees and managers
  Too many layers between contact personnel and top management
- ***Insufficient relationship focus***
  Lack of market segmentation
  Focus on transactions rather than relationships
  Focus on new customers rather than relationship customers
- ***Inadequate service recovery***

Also related to provider gap 1 is a lack of company strategies to retain customers and strengthen relationships with them, an approach called *relationship marketing.* When organizations have strong relationships with existing customers, provider gap 1 is less likely to occur. Relationship marketing is distinct from *transactional marketing,* the term used to describe the more conventional emphasis on acquiring new customers rather than on retaining them. When companies focus too much on attracting new customers, they may fail to understand the changing needs and expectations of their current customers. One of the major marketing factors that is leveraged in relationship marketing, particularly in manufacturing companies, is service. Technology affords companies the ability to acquire and integrate vast quantities of data on customers that can be used to build relationships. Frequent flyer travel programs conducted by airlines, car rental companies, and hotels are among the most familiar programs of this type.

The final key factor associated with provider gap 1 is lack of service recovery. Even the best companies, with the best of intentions and clear understanding of their customers' expectations, sometimes fail. It is critical for an organization to understand the importance of service recovery—why people complain, what they expect when they complain, and how to develop effective service recovery strategies for dealing with inevitable service failures. This might involve a well-defined complaint-handling procedure and empowering employees to react on the spot, in real time, to fix the failure; other times it involves a service guarantee or ways to compensate the customer for the unfulfilled promise.

To address the factors in provider gap 1, this text covered topics that included how to understand customers through multiple research strategies (Chapter 5), how to build strong relationships and understand customer needs over time (Chapter 6), and how to implement recovery strategies when things go wrong (Chapter 7). Through these strategies, provider gap 1—the customer expectations gap—can be minimized.

PROVIDER GAP 2: NOT HAVING THE RIGHT SERVICE QUALITY DESIGNS AND STANDARDS

A recurring theme in service companies is the difficulty experienced in translating customers' expectations into service quality specifications. These problems are reflected in *provider gap 2,* the difference between company understanding of customer expectations and development of customer-driven service designs and standards. Figure 18.4 shows the key factors leading to this gap. Customer-driven standards are different from the conventional performance standards that most services companies establish in that they are based on pivotal customer requirements that are visible to and measured by customers. They are operations standards set to correspond to customer expectations and priorities rather than to company concerns such as productivity or efficiency.

Provider gap 2 exists in service organizations for a variety of reasons. Those responsible for setting standards, typically management, sometimes believe that customer expectations are unreasonable or unrealistic. They may also believe that the degree of variability inherent in service defies standardization and therefore that setting standards will not achieve the desired goal. However, the quality of service delivered by customer contact personnel is critically influenced by the standards against which they are evaluated and compensated. Standards signal to contact personnel what management priorities are and which types of performance really count. When service standards are absent or when the standards in place do not reflect customers' expecta-

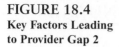

FIGURE 18.4
Key Factors Leading
to Provider Gap 2

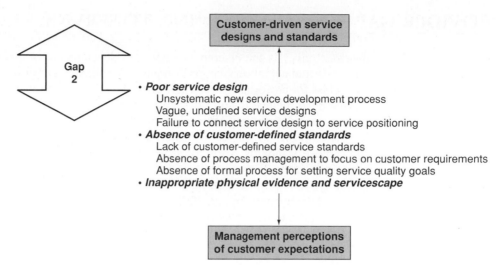

tions, quality of service as perceived by customers is likely to suffer. In contrast, when there are standards reflecting what customers expect, the quality of service they receive is likely to be enhanced. Therefore, closing provider gap 2—by setting customer-defined performance standards—has a powerful positive effect on closing the customer gap.

Because services are intangible, they are difficult to describe and communicate. This is particularly true when new services are being developed. It is critical that all people involved (managers, front-line employees, and behind-the-scenes support staff) be working with the same concepts of the new service, based on customer needs and expectations. For a service that already exists, any attempt to improve it will also suffer unless everyone has the same vision of the service and associated issues. One of the most important ways to avoid gap 2 is to design services clearly without oversimplification, incompleteness, subjectivity, or bias. To do this, tools are needed to ensure that new and existing services are developed and improved in as careful a manner as possible.

Another factor involved in provider gap 2 is *physical evidence*—the tangibles surrounding the service, including everything from business cards to reports, signage, Internet presence, equipment, and facilities used to deliver the service. The *servicescape,* the physical setting where the service is delivered, must be appropriate. Think of a restaurant, a hotel, a theme park, a health club, a hospital, or a school. The servicescape—the physical facility—is critical in these industries in terms of communicating about the service and making the entire experience pleasurable. Service organizations must explore the importance of physical evidence, the variety of roles it plays, and strategies for effectively designing physical evidence and the servicescape to meet customer expectations.

In this text, you learned to develop effective strategies for new services and to use service blueprinting as an implementation tool (Chapter 8), to develop customer-defined (as opposed to company-defined) service standards (Chapter 9), and to effectively design physical evidence and the servicescape to meet customer expectations (Chapter 10). Through these strategies, provider gap 2—the service design and standards gap—can be minimized.

PROVIDER GAP 3: NOT DELIVERING TO SERVICE STANDARDS

Provider gap 3 is the discrepancy between development of customer-driven service standards and actual service performance by company employees. Even when guidelines exist for performing services well and treating customers correctly, high-quality service performance is not a certainty. Standards must be backed by appropriate resources (people, systems, and technology) and also must be enforced to be effective—that is, employees must be measured and compensated on the basis of performance along those standards. Thus, even when standards accurately reflect customers' expectations, if the company fails to provide support for them—if it does not facilitate, encourage, and require their achievement—standards do no good. When the level of service delivery performance falls short of the standards, it falls short of what customers expect as well. Narrowing gap 3—by ensuring that all the resources needed to achieve the standards are in place—reduces the customer gap.

Research and company experience have identified many of the critical inhibitors to closing gap 3 (see Figure 18.5). These include employees who do not clearly understand the roles they are to play in the company, employees who see conflict between customers and company management, the wrong employees, inadequate technology, inappropriate compensation and recognition, and lack of empowerment and teamwork. These factors all relate to the company's human resource function, involving internal practices such as recruitment, training, feedback, job design, motivation, and organizational structure. To deliver better service performance, these issues must be addressed across functions (such as with both marketing and human resources) if they are to be effective.

One of the difficulties associated with gap 3 involves the challenge in delivering

FIGURE 18.5
Key Reasons Leading to Provider Gap 3

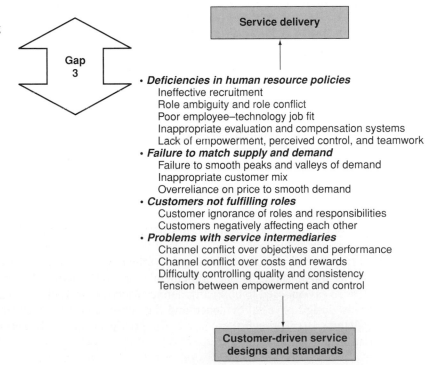

service through such intermediaries as retailers, franchisees, agents, and brokers. Because quality in service occurs in the human interaction between customers and service providers, control over the service encounter by the company is crucial, yet it rarely is fully possible. Most service (and many manufacturing) companies face an even more formidable task: attaining service excellence and consistency in the presence of intermediaries who represent them, interact with their customers, yet are not under their direct control. Among the intermediaries that play a central role in service delivery are retailers, franchisees, and dealers.

Franchisers of services depend on their franchisees to execute service delivery as they have specified it. And it is in the execution by the franchisee that the customer evaluates the service quality of the company. With franchises and other types of intermediaries, someone other than the producer is critically important to the fulfillment of quality service. The service delivery process is complicated by outside parties who are likely to embrace goals and values that do not directly align with those of the service organization. For this reason, a firm must develop ways to either control or motivate these intermediaries to meet company goals.

As we have just discussed, part of the variability in provider gap 3 comes from employees and intermediaries who are involved with service delivery. The other important variable is the customer. Even if contact employees and intermediaries are 100 percent consistent in their service delivery, the uncontrollable variable of the customer can introduce heterogeneity in service delivery. If customers do not perform their roles appropriately—if, for example, they fail to provide all the information necessary to the provider or neglect to read and follow instructions—service quality is jeopardized.

Another issue in gap 3 is the need in service firms to synchronize demand and capacity. Because services are perishable and cannot be inventoried, service companies frequently face situations of over- or underdemand. Lacking inventories to handle overdemand, companies lose sales when capacity is inadequate to handle customer needs. On the other hand, capacity is frequently underutilized in slow periods. Most companies rely on operations strategies such as cross-training or varying the size of the employee pool to synchronize supply and demand. The use of marketing strategies in many companies is limited. Marketing strategies for managing demand—such as price changes, advertising, promotion, and alternative service offerings—can supplement approaches for managing supply.

We discussed strategies to deal with the roles of employees in Chapter 11, customers in Chapter 12, intermediaries in Chapter 13, and demand and capacity in Chapter 14.

PROVIDER GAP 4: WHEN PROMISES DO NOT MATCH PERFORMANCE

Provider gap 4 illustrates the difference between service delivery and the service provider's external communications. Promises made by a service company through its media advertising, sales force, and other communications may potentially raise customer expectations that serve as the standard against which customers assess service quality. The discrepancy between actual and promised service therefore has an adverse effect on the customer gap. Broken promises can occur for many reasons: overpromising in advertising or personal selling, inadequate coordination between operations and marketing, and differences in policies and procedures across service outlets. Figure 18.6 shows the key factors that lead to provider gap 4.

FIGURE 18.6
Key Reasons for
Provider Gap 4

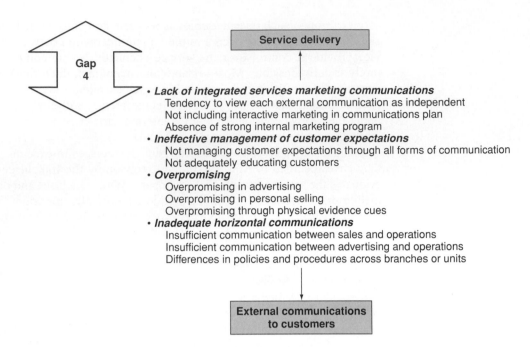

In addition to unduly elevating expectations through exaggerated claims, there are other, less obvious ways in which external communications influence customers' service quality assessments. Service companies frequently fail to capitalize on opportunities to educate customers to use services appropriately. They also frequently fail to manage customer expectations of what they will receive in service transactions and relationships.

One of the major difficulties associated with provider gap 4 is that communications to consumers involve issues that cross disciplinary boundaries. Because service advertising promises what people do, and because what *people* do cannot be controlled in the way that machines that produce physical goods can be controlled, this type of communication involves functions other than the marketing department. This is what we called *interactive marketing*—the marketing between contact people and customers—and it must be coordinated with the conventional types of *external marketing* used in product and service firms. When employees who promote the service do not fully understand the reality of service delivery, they are likely to make exaggerated promises or fail to communicate to customers aspects of the service intended to serve them well. The result is poor service quality perceptions. Effectively coordinating actual service delivery with external communications, therefore, narrows provider gap 4 and favorably affects the customer gap as well.

Another issue related to gap 4 is associated with the pricing of services. In packaged goods (and even in durable goods), many customers possess enough price knowledge before purchase to be able to judge whether a price is fair or in line with competition. With services, customers often have no internal reference point for prices before purchase and consumption. Pricing strategies such as discounting, "everyday prices," and couponing obviously need to be different with services in cases where the customer has no sense of the price to start with. Techniques for developing prices for services are more complicated than those for pricing of tangible goods.

In summary, external communications—whether from marketing communications or pricing—can create a larger customer gap by raising expectations about service delivery. In addition to improving service delivery, companies must also manage all communications to customers so that inflated promises do not lead to higher expectations. Chapters 15 (which discussed integrated services marketing communications) and 16 (which covered pricing) of this text described methods to accomplish these objectives.

PUTTING IT ALL TOGETHER: CLOSING THE GAPS

The full conceptual model shown in Figure 18.1 conveys a clear message to managers wishing to improve the quality of service: the key to closing the customer gap is to close provider gaps 1 through 4 and keep them closed. To the extent that one or more of provider gaps 1 through 4 exist, customers perceive service quality shortfalls. The model, called the gaps model of service quality, serves as a framework for service organizations attempting to improve quality service and services marketing.

This model begins where the process of improving service quality begins: by gaining an understanding of the nature and extent of the customer gap. Given the strong focus on the customer and the need to use knowledge about the customer to drive business strategy, we believe this foundation of emphasis is warranted.

Summary

The chapter presented the integrated gaps model of service quality (shown in Figure 18.1), a framework for understanding and improving service delivery. The entire text was organized around this model of service quality, which focuses on five pivotal gaps in delivering and marketing services:

The customer gap: Difference between customer expectations and perceptions.

Provider gap 1: Not knowing what customers expect.

Provider gap 2: Not selecting the right service designs and standards.

Provider gap 3: Not delivering to service standards.

Provider gap 4: Not matching performance to promises.

The gaps model positions the key concepts, strategies, and decisions in services marketing in a manner that begins with the customer and builds the organization's tasks around what is needed to close the gap between customer expectations and perceptions.

Discussion Questions

1. If you were the manager of a service organization and wanted to apply the gaps model to improve service, which gap would you start with? Why? In what order would you proceed to close the gaps?
2. Can provider gap 4 be closed prior to closing any of the other three provider gaps? How?
3. Which of the four provider gaps do you believe is hardest to close? Why?
4. Using Figure 18.3, return to Chapters 5, 6, and 7 and make a chart that lists the strategies that address each of the key factors.

5. Using Figure 18.4, return to Chapters 8, 9, and 10 and make a chart that lists the strategies that address each of the key factors.

6. Using Figure 18.5, return to Chapters 11 through 14 and make a chart that lists the strategies that address each of the key factors.

7. Using Figure 18.6, return to Chapters 15 and 16 and make a chart that lists the strategies that address each of the key factors.

Exercises

1. Choose an organization to interview, and use the integrated gaps model of service quality as a framework. Ask the manager whether the organization suffers from any of the factors listed in the figures in this chapter. Which factor in each of Figures 18.3 through 18.6 does the manager consider the most troublesome? What does the company do to try to address these problems?

2. Use the Internet to locate the website of Walt Disney, Marriott, Ritz-Carlton, or any other well-known, high-quality service organization. Which of the provider gaps does it appear the company has closed? How can you tell?

3. Interview a nonprofit or public sector organization in your area (it could be some part of your school if it is a state school). Find out if the integrated gaps model of service quality framework makes sense in the context of its organization.

Note

1. V. A. Zeithaml, A. Parasuraman, and L. L. Berry, *Delivering Quality Service: Balancing Customer Perceptions and Expectations* (New York: The Free Press, 1990).

1

VIRGIN ATLANTIC AIRWAYS— TEN YEARS AFTER

June 1994. Virgin Atlantic Airways celebrated the 10th anniversary of its inaugural flight to New York. Richard Branson, the airline's chairman and founder, reminisced about its tremendous growth. In 10 short years, he had established Virgin Atlantic as Britain's second largest long-haul airline, with a reputation for quality and innovative product development. Richard Branson turned his thoughts to the challenges that lay ahead.

THE ORIGINS OF THE VIRGIN GROUP

"Branson, I predict you will either go to prison, or become a millionaire." These were the last words that the 17-year-old Richard Branson heard from his headmaster as he left school. Twenty-five years later, Richard Branson ruled over a business empire whose 1993 sales exceeded £1.5 billion.[1] He had started his first entrepreneurial business at the age of 12, selling Christmas trees. Soon after leaving school, he set up *Student,* a national magazine, as "a platform for all shades of opinion, all beliefs and ideas . . . a vehicle for intelligent comment and protest." The magazine, whose editorial staff had an average age of 16, featured interviews by Richard Branson with celebrities and articles on controversial issues.

In 1970, Richard Branson founded a mail-order record business—called Virgin to emphasize his own commercial innocence. The first Virgin record shop was opened in London's Oxford Street in 1971, soon followed by a recording studio and a label which produced records for performers such as Phil Collins, Genesis, and Boy George. The

This case was prepared by Pantéa Denoyelle, research associate, under the supervision of Jean-Claude Larréché, Alfred H. Heineken professor of marketing at INSEAD. It is intended to be used as a basis for class discussion rather than to illustrate either effective or ineffective handling of an administrative situation. Copyright © 1995 INSEAD, Fontainebleau, France.

[1] In June 1994, one pound sterling (£) = 1.51 US dollar ($).

EXHIBIT 1   **The Virgin Group of Companies**

Virgin consists of three wholly owned separate holding companies involved in distinct business areas from media and publishing to retail, travel, and leisure. There are over 100 operating companies across the three holding companies in 12 countries worldwide.

Virgin Retail Group	Virgin Communication	Voyager Investments		
		Virgin Group	**Voyager Group**	**Virgin Travel Group**
Operates a chain of megastores in the U.K., Continental Europe, Australia, and the Pacific selling music, video, and other entertainment products. Operates game stores in the U.K. Wholesale record exports and imports. *Note:* Marui of Japan own 50% of Virgin Megastores Japan. WH Smith own 50% of Virgin Retail U.K.	Publishing of computer entertainment software Management of investments in broadcasting including Music Box. Investments in related publishing and entertainment activities, television postproduction services Book publishing Virgin Radio, Britain's first national commercial contemporary music station	Investments: joint ventures Property developments Magnetic media distribution Management and corporate finance services to the Virgin organization	Clubs and hotels Airship and balloon operations Storm model agency	U.K.'s second largest long-haul international airline: Virgin Atlantic Airways Freight handling and packaging Inclusive tour operations: Virgin Holidays

Source: Virgin Atlantic.

Venue nightclub opened in 1978. In 1980, Virgin Records began expanding overseas, initially on a licensing basis; it later set up its own subsidiaries. Virgin Vision was created in 1983, followed by Virgin Atlantic Airways and Virgin Cargo in 1984, and Virgin Holidays in 1985.

In November 1986, the Virgin Group, which included the Music, Communication, and Retail divisions, was floated on the London stock exchange. The airline, clubs, and holidays activities remained part of the privately owned Voyager Group Ltd. In its first public year, Virgin Group Plc. had a profit of £13 million on £250 million turnover—far beyond expectations. Its public status, however, was short-lived: Richard Branson believed he could not be an entrepreneur while chairing a public company. In October 1988, he regained full control by buying back all outstanding shares. The constraints that he had struggled with during the company's public life were replaced by an overwhelming sense of relief and freedom. A partnership with Seibu Saison International, one of Japan's largest retail and travel groups, was equally brief. In 1990, Richard Branson sold 10 percent of the equity of Voyager Travel Holdings, the holding company for Virgin Atlantic, to the Japanese group in return for an injection of £36 million of equity and convertible loan capital—only to buy out his Japanese partner for £45 million in 1991.

In 1992, Richard Branson sold Virgin Music (by then the world's sixth largest record company) to Thorn EMI for £560 million. By 1994, the Virgin Group consisted of three holding companies: Virgin Retail Group, Virgin Communication, and Virgin Investments, which controlled over 100 entities in 12 countries. Exhibit 1 summarizes the group's activities.

THE CREATION OF VIRGIN ATLANTIC AIRWAYS

In 1984, Richard Branson was approached by Randolph Fields, a 31-year-old lawyer who wanted to start a transatlantic airline. Fields's plan was to operate a business class–only B747 service to New York. Richard Branson quickly made up his mind. He announced that the new airline, to be named Virgin Atlantic Airways, would be operational within three months. Needless to say, his decision struck Virgin's senior management as completely insane.

Richard Branson, who knew nothing about the airline business, set out to learn from the downfall of Laker Air, an airline launched in 1970 by Freddie Laker with six planes and 120 employees. Laker Air was originally designed as a low-risk business, flying under contract for package-holiday firms; in 1971, however, it introduced a low-budget, no-frills service between London and New York. Laker's overconfidence led to several mistakes, including purchasing three DC-10s before the U.S. government had approved his London–New York line, and generally ordering more aircraft than he could afford. He accumulated a £350 million debt while the big transatlantic carriers slashed prices. This eventually led to Laker Airways' demise in 1981.

Richard Branson hired two former Laker executives, Roy Gardner (who later became Virgin Atlantic's co-managing director) and David Tait. Branson decided that his new airline should not be all business class, but combine an economy section with a first class section at business class prices. His goal was clear: "To provide all classes of travelers with the highest quality travel at the lowest cost." Richard Branson also leased a secondhand 747. The contract he negotiated with Boeing had a sell-back option at the end of the first, second, or third year; a clause protected Virgin against currency fluctuations. Another priority was to recruit air crew. Fortunately, British Airways had recently lowered the optional retirement age for its crew, creating a pool of experienced pilots from which Virgin could draw; this gave it the most experienced crew of any British airline.

Obtaining permission to fly to New York from American regulatory bodies was not easy; authorization to land at Newark was granted only three days before Virgin's first flight was scheduled. Forbidden to advertise in the United States until the approval, Virgin decided to launch a teaser campaign. Skywriters festooned the Manhattan sky with the words "WAIT FOR THE ENGLISH VIRGI . . ."

Virgin Atlantic's inaugural flight took off from London on June 22, 1984, packed with friends, celebrities, reporters, and Richard Branson wearing a World War I leather flight helmet. Once the plane had taken off, passengers were surprised to see on the video screen the cockpit, where the crew—Richard Branson and two famous cricket players—greeted them. Although this was obviously a recording, it was a memorable moment for passengers.

Early Years (1984–89)

Virgin Atlantic's early years were slightly chaotic. "I love the challenge," Richard Branson said. "I suspect that before I went into the airline business, a lot of people thought I would never be able to make a go of it. It made it even more challenging to prove them wrong." Richard Branson's determination and enthusiasm, as well as the experienced management team that he assembled, made up for the initial amateurism.

Virgin Atlantic extended its operations progressively. Its early routes, all from London, were to New York (Newark since 1984 and John F. Kennedy airport since 1988),

Miami (1986), Boston (1987), and Orlando (1988). Flights to Tokyo and Los Angeles were added in 1989 and 1990. In 1987, Virgin celebrated its one millionth transatlantic passenger. Until 1991, all Virgin flights left from London's Gatwick airport, which was much smaller than Heathrow. Virgin countered this commercial disadvantage with a free limousine service for Upper Class passengers and a Gatwick Upper Class lounge, inaugurated in 1990.

While Richard Branson had always befriended rock stars, he had otherwise kept a low profile. This changed when he launched the airline: "I knew that the only way of competing with British Airways and the others was to get out there and use myself to promote it," he explained. Richard made a point of being accessible to reporters and never missed an opportunity to cause a sensation, wearing a stewardess's uniform or a bikini on board, or letting himself be photographed in his bath. What really caught the public's attention were his Atlantic crossings. In 1986, his "Virgin Atlantic Challenger II" speedboat recorded the fastest time ever across the Atlantic with Richard Branson on board. Even more spectacular was the 1987 crossing of the "Virgin Atlantic Flyer"—the largest hot-air balloon ever flown and the first to cross the Atlantic. Three years later Richard Branson crossed the Pacific in another balloon from Japan to Arctic Canada, a distance of 6,700 miles, breaking all existing records with speeds of up to 245 miles per hour.

The Years of Professionalization (1989–94)

The professionalization of Virgin Atlantic's management began in 1989. Until then Virgin Atlantic had had a flat structure, with 27 people reporting to Richard Branson directly. As the airline expanded, it had outgrown its entrepreneurial ways, and needed to become customer-driven.

Richard Branson asked Syd Pennington, a veteran Marks & Spencer retailer, to look into the airline's duty-free business in addition to his other responsibilities at Virgin Megastores. Some time later, Pennington, coming back from a trip, learned that he had been promoted to co-managing director of the airline. When Pennington expressed his surprise, Richard explained, "It's easier to find good retail people than good airline people." Syd Pennington saw that Virgin Atlantic lacked controls and procedures, and he devoted himself to professionalizing its management. His objective was to infuse the business with Richard Branson's charisma and energy while also making it effective enough to succeed. Exhibit 2 has a five-year summary of Virgin Atlantic's financial performance and labor force. Exhibit 3 shows the three-year evolution of passengers carried and market shares.

After years of campaigning, Virgin Atlantic was granted the right to fly out of Heathrow in 1991. Heathrow, Britain's busiest airport, handled 100,000 passengers a day—a total of 40 million in 1990, compared with 1.7 million at Gatwick. Virgin Atlantic was assigned to Heathrow's Terminal 3, where it competed with 30 other airlines serving over 75 destinations on five continents. In Richard Branson's eyes, gaining access to Heathrow was a "historic moment and the culmination of years of struggle." His dream to compete with other long-haul carriers on an equal footing had come true. A new era began for Virgin. Flying from Heathrow enabled it to have high load factors all year and to attract more business and full-fare economy passengers. It could also carry more interline flyers and more cargo, since Heathrow was the U.K.'s main air freight center. On the morning of the airline's first flight from Heathrow, a Virgin "hit squad" encircled the model British Airways Concorde at the airport's entrance and pasted it over with Virgin's logo. Richard Branson, dressed up as a pirate, was pho-

EXHIBIT 2
Financial Results and Labor Force of Virgin Atlantic Airways

Source: Virgin Atlantic.

Financial Year	Turnover (£m)	Profit (Loss) before Tax (£m)
1988/89	106.7	8.4
1989/90	208.8	8.5
1990/91	382.9	6.1
1991/92	356.9	(14.5)
1992/93	404.7	0.4

Note: The reporting year ends on 31 July until 1990, and on 31 October as of 1991. The 1990/91 period covers 15 months.

Year	Number of Employees*
1988	440
1989	678
1990	1,104
1991	1,591
1992	1,638
1993	1,627
1994	2,602

*As of 31 December (31 May for 1994).

tographed in front of the Concorde before security forces could reach the site. A huge party marked the end of the day.

In April 1993, Virgin ordered four A340s from Airbus Industries, the European consortium in which British Aerospace had a 20 percent share. The order, worth over £300m, reflected the airline's commitment to new destinations. "We are proud to buy an aircraft which is in large part British-built, and on which so many jobs in the U.K. depend," said Richard Branson. The A340, the longest-range aircraft in the world, accommodated 292 passengers in three cabins, and had key advantages such as low fuel consumption and maintenance costs. When the first A340 was delivered in December, Virgin became the first U.K. carrier to fly A340s. Virgin also ordered two Boeing 747-400s and took options on two others. It also placed a $19 million order for the most advanced in-flight entertainment system available, featuring 16 channels of video, which it planned to install in all three sections. In keeping with the airline's customization efforts, the new aircraft's cabin was redesigned. Upper Class passengers would find electronically operated 54-inch seats with a 55-degree recline and an on-board bar. There was a rest area for flight and cabin crew.

In June 1993, Virgin scheduled a second daily flight from Heathrow to JFK. "We've

EXHIBIT 3
Market Shares of Virgin Atlantic Airways (Revenue Passengers)

Source: Virgin Atlantic.

Route	1993	1992	1991
New York (JFK & Newark)	19.6%	17.2%	18.0%
Florida (Miami & Orlando)	33.2%	30.6%	25.2%
Los Angeles	23.6%	21.8%	25.8%
Tokyo	18.4%	15.5%	16.0%
Boston	22.2%	20.0%	15.3%
Total passengers carried	1,459,044	1,244,990	1,063,677

Note: Flights from Gatwick and LHR.

given travelers a wider choice on their time of travel," said Richard Branson. "The early evening departure is timed to minimize disruption to the working day, a welcome bonus to both busy executives and leisure travelers." In March 1994, Virgin put an end to British Airways' and Cathay Pacific's long-standing duopoly on the London–Hong Kong route, launching its own A340 service.

Virgin's first Boeing 747-400 was delivered in May 1994. Only days later, Virgin opened its San Francisco line (until then a British Airways–United duopoly). In press releases, Virgin emphasized the continuation of its expansion plans, the renewal of its fleet, and the "better alternative" that it offered customers on both sides of the Atlantic. During the inaugural flight 150 guests—and some fare-paying flyers who had been warned that it would not be a quiet flight—were entertained with a fashion show and a jazz band. In San Francisco the aircraft stopped near a giant taximeter. The door opened, Richard Branson appeared, and inserted a huge coin in the taximeter, out of which popped the Virgin flag. Airport authorities offered Richard Branson a giant cake decorated with a miniature Golden Gate Bridge. Guests were entertained for a whirl-wind five days, which included a tour of the Napa Valley and a visit to Alcatraz prison where Richard Branson was jailed in a stunt prepared by his team. Virgin also took advantage of the launch to unveil a recycling and environmental program. A stewardess dressed in green—rather than the usual red Virgin uniform—gave passengers information on the program, which had delivered savings of £500,000 since it was launched in late 1993.

At the time of Virgin's 10th anniversary, its fleet comprised eight B747-200s, a B747-400, and three A340s. The airline awaited delivery of its second B747-400 and fourth A340 and also planned to retire two older B747-200s by the end of 1994. By then, half of its fleet would be brand new. By comparison, the average age of British Airways' fleet was eight years.[2] Richard Branson planned to expand his fleet to 18 planes, which would serve 12 or 15 destinations by 1995. Proposed new routes included Washington, D.C., Chicago, Auckland, Singapore, Sydney, and Johannesburg. The London–Johannesburg license, granted in 1992, had been a major victory for Virgin: when exploited, it will end a 50-year duopoly enjoyed by British Airways and South African Airways.

All Virgin Atlantic planes were decorated with a Vargas painting of a red-headed, scantily dressed woman holding a scarf. The names of most Virgin aircraft evoked the "Vargas Lady" theme, starting with its first aircraft, "Maiden Voyager." (Exhibit 4 lists the aircraft's names.) The first A340, inaugurated by the Princess of Wales, was christened "The Lady in Red."

VIRGIN CLASSES

Richard Branson originally proposed to call Virgin's business and economy classes Upper Class and Riff Raff respectively; in the latter case, however, he bowed to the judgment of his managers, who urged him to desist. Virgin Atlantic strove to offer the highest-quality travel to all classes of passengers at the lowest cost, and to be flexible enough to respond rapidly to their changing needs. For instance, Virgin catered to the needs of children and infants with special meals, a children's channel, pioneering safety seats, changing facilities, and baby food.

"Offering a First Class service at less than First Class fares" had become a slogan

---

[2] BA's fleet had 240 aircraft, including some 180 Boeings, 7 Concordes, 10 A320s, 15 BAe ATPs, and 7 DC-10s.

EXHIBIT 4
Virgin Atlantic Fleet

Source: Courtesy of Virgin
Atlantic Airways.

Aircraft	Type	Name	Into service
G-VIRG	B747-287B	Maiden Voyager	1984
G-VGIN	B747-243B	Scarlet Lady	1986
G-TKYO	B747-212B	Maiden Japan	1989
G-VRGN	B747-212B	Maid of Honour	28/08/89
G-VMIA	B747-123	Spirit of Sir Freddy	09/05/90
G-VOYG	B747-283B	Shady Lady	10/03/90
G-VJFK	B747-238B	Boston Belle	06/03/91
G-VLAX	B747-238B	California Girl	28/05/91
G-VBUS	A340-311	Lady in Red	16/12/93
G-VAEL	A340-311	Maiden Toulouse	01/01/94
G-VSKY	A340-311	China Girl	21/03/94
G-VFAB	B747-4Q8	Lady Penelope	19/05/94
G-VHOT	B747-4Q8		delivery 10/94
G-VFLY	A340-311		delivery 10/94

for Virgin Atlantic. Marketed as a first class service at business class prices, Upper Class competed both with other carriers' first class and business class. Since its 1984 launch, this product had won every major travel industry award.

The Economy Class promised the best value for money, targeting price-sensitive leisure travelers who nevertheless sought comfort. It included three meal options, free drinks, seat-back video screens, and ice cream during movies on flights from London.

After years of operating only two classes, business and economy, Virgin had introduced its Mid Class in 1992 after realizing that 23 percent of Economy passengers traveled for business. Mid Class was aimed at cost-conscious business travelers who required enough space to work and relax. This full-fare economy class offered flyers a level of service usually found only in business class, with separate check-in and cabin, priority meal service, armrest or seat-back TVs, and the latest in audio and video entertainment. Exhibit 5 shows Virgin's three sections: Upper Class, Mid Class, and Economy.

Virgin's B747 configuration on the Heathrow/JFK route consisted of 50 seats in Upper Class, 38 in Mid Class, and 271 in Economy. The typical British Airways B747 configuration on the same route was 18 First Class seats, 70 seats in Club World, and 282 in World Traveler Class.[3]

SERVICE THE VIRGIN WAY

Virgin Atlantic wanted to provide the best possible service while remaining original, spontaneous, and informal. Its goal was to turn flying into a unique experience, not to move passengers from one point to another. It saw itself not only in the airline business but also in entertainment and leisure. According to a staff brochure:

> We must be memorable, we are not a bus service. The journeys made by our customers are romantic and exciting, and we should do everything we can to make them feel just that. That way they will talk about the most memorable moments long after they leave the airport.

Virgin Atlantic saw that as it became increasingly successful, it risked also becoming complacent. The challenge was to keep up customers' interest by keeping service at the forefront of activities. Virgin was often distinguished for the quality and consistency of its service, winning over 70 awards from travel magazines and associations between 1986 and 1994. It won the Executive Travel Airline of the Year award for an unprecedented three consecutive years. Service delivery, in other words "getting it right the first time," was of key importance. The airline was also perceived to excel in the art of service recovery, where it aimed to be proactive, not defensive. It handled complaints from Upper Class passengers within 24 hours, those from Economy Class flyers within a week. If a flight was delayed, passengers received a personalized fax of apology from Richard Branson or a bottle of champagne. Passengers who had complained were occasionally upgraded to Upper Class.

Innovation

Virgin's management, who wanted passengers never to feel bored, introduced video entertainment in 1989. They chose the quickest solution: handing out Sony Watchmans on board. Virgin later pioneered individual video screens for every seat, an idea that competitors quickly imitated. In 1994, Virgin's onboard entertainment offered up to 20 audio channels and 16 video channels including a shopping channel and a game channel. A gambling channel would be introduced at year-end. In the summer, a "Stop Smoking Program" video was shown on all flights—Virgin's contribution to a controversy over whether smoking should be permitted on aircraft.

The presence of a beauty therapist or a tailor was an occasional treat to passengers. The beautician offered massages and manicures. On some flights to Hong Kong, the

[3] As of April 1994, the Club World and World Traveler—Euro Traveler for flights within Europe—were the names given to British Airways' former Business and Economy Classes respectively.

EXHIBIT 5
Virgin Atlantic's Three Classes

Source: Courtesy of Virgin Atlantic Airways.

Upper Class

- Reclining sleeper seat with 15" more legroom than other airlines
- Latest seat arm video/audio entertainment
- Unique Clubhouse lounge at Heathrow featuring health spa (includes hair salon, library, music room, games room, study, and brasserie)
- Virgin Arrival Clubhouse with shower, sauna, swimming pool, and gym
- Inflight beauty therapist on most flights
- Onboard lounges and stand-up bars
- "Snoozzone" dedicated sleeping section with sleeper seat, duvet, and sleep suit
- Complimentary airport transfers including chauffeur-driven limousine or motorcycle to and from airport
- Free confirmable Economy ticket for round trip to US/Tokyo

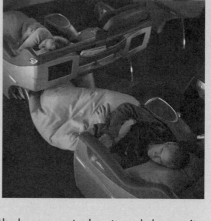

Mid Class

- Separate check-in and cabin
- Most comfortable economy seat in the world with 38" seat pitch (equivalent to many airlines' business class seat)
- Complimentary pre-takeoff drinks and amenity kits
- Frequent Flyer program
- Priority meal service
- Priority baggage reclaim
- Armrest/seatback TVs and latest audio/video entertainment

Economy Class

- Contoured, space-saving seats, maximizing legroom, seat pitch up to 34"
- Three meal option service (including vegetarian) and wide selection of free alcoholic and soft drinks
- Seatback TVs and 16 channels of the latest inflight entertainment
- Pillow and blankets
- Advance seat selection
- Complimentary amenity kit and ice cream (during movies on flights from London)

tailor faxed passengers' measurements so that suits could be ready on arrival. In 1990, Virgin became the only airline to offer automatic defibrillators on board and to train staff to assist cardiac arrest victims. A three-person Special Facilities unit was set up in 1991 to deal with medical requests. Its brief was extended to handle arrangements for unaccompanied minors or unusual requests such as birthday cakes, champagne for newlyweds, public announcements, or mid-flight marriage proposals. The unit also informed passengers of flight delays or cancellations, and telephoned clients whose options on tickets had expired without their having confirmed their intention to travel. Another service innovation was motorcycle rides to Heathrow for Upper Class passengers. The chauffeur service used Honda PC800s with heated leather seats. Passengers wore waterproof coveralls and a helmet with a built-in headset for a cellular phone.

In February 1993, Britain's Secretary of State for Transport inaugurated a new Upper Class lounge at Heathrow: the Virgin Clubhouse. The £1 million Clubhouse had an unusual range of facilities: Victorian-style wood-paneled washrooms with showers and a grooming salon offering massages, aromatherapy, and haircuts; a 5,000-volume library with antique leather armchairs; a game room with the latest computer technology; a music room with a CD library; and a study with the most recent office equipment. Many of the furnishings came from Richard Branson's own home: a giant model railway, the Challenger II Trophy, a three-meter galleon model. A two-ton, five-meter table, made in Vienna from an old vessel, had to be installed with a crane. Upon the opening of the Hong Kong route, a blackjack table was added at which visitors received "Virgin bills" that the dealer exchanged for tokens. There was also a shoe shine service. Passengers seemed to enjoy the lounge. One remarked in the visitors' book: "If you have to be delayed more than two hours, it could not happen in a more pleasant environment."

Customer Orientation, Virgin Style

Virgin tried to understand passengers' needs and go beyond their expectations. While it described itself as a "niche airline for those seeking value-for-money travel," its standards and reputation could appeal to a broad spectrum of customers. It managed to serve both sophisticated, demanding executives and easy-going, price-sensitive leisure travelers in the same aircraft. According to Marketing Director Steve Ridgeway, Virgin attracted a broader range of customers than its competitors because it managed this coexistence between passenger groups better. This had enabled the airline to reach high load factors soon after opening new lines, as shown in Exhibit 6.

Virgin Atlantic initially had marketed itself as an economical airline for young people who bought Virgin records and shopped at Virgin stores, but gradually its target shifted. The danger, which Richard Branson saw clearly, was that people would perceive it as a "cheap and cheerful" airline, a copy of the defunct Laker Airways. Richard Branson knew that his airline's survival depended on high-yield business travelers.

EXHIBIT 6
Load Factors of Virgin Atlantic Airways

Source: Virgin Atlantic promotional materials. This information is no longer made public since 1991.

Year	Newark	Miami	Tokyo	JFK	Los Angeles	Boston
1990–1991	82.0%	89.5%	65.9%	76.9%	84.5%	83.3%
1989–1990	83.3%	92.1%	68.3%	74.2%	79.8%	
1988–1989	82.8%	86.7%	52.4%			
1987–1988	77.1%	85.0%				
1986–1987	74.4%	76.4%				
1985–1986	72.9%					
1984–1985	72.0%					

After establishing a strong base in leisure traffic, Virgin turned to the corporate segment and strove to establish itself as a sophisticated, business class airline that concentrated on long-haul routes. The idea of fun and entertainment, however, was not abandoned. Upper Class was upgraded and incentives were added to attract the business traveler. By 1991, 10 percent of the airline's passengers and 35 to 40 percent of its income came from the business segment. Virgin's competitive advantage was reinforced through the combination of corporate travel buyers' price consciousness and the rising service expectations of travelers. Richard Branson actively wooed business customers by regularly inviting corporate buyers to have lunch at his house and seeking their comments.

As part of Virgin's drive to meet customers' standards, on each flight 30 passengers were asked to fill out a questionnaire. Their answers formed the basis of widely distributed quarterly reports. Virgin's senior managers flew regularly, interviewing passengers informally, making critical comments on the delivery of service and circulating their reports among top management. Richard Branson himself, who welcomed every opportunity to obtain feedback from customers, took time to shake hands and chat with passengers. The preoccupation with service was so strong that staff were often more exacting in their evaluation of each other than the customers were.

Business executives, unlike younger leisure travelers, did not readily relate to other aspects of the Virgin world: the records, the Megastores, the daredevil chairman. Their good feelings about Virgin stemmed mainly from their positive experiences with the airline. These tough and demanding customers appreciated Virgin's style, service, innovations, and prices. Some were enthusiastic enough to rearrange their schedules in order to fly Virgin despite punctuality problems. Aside from complaints about flight delays, their only serious criticism was that Virgin did not serve enough destinations.

Virgin's People

Virgin Atlantic attracted quality staff despite the relatively low salaries it paid. In management's eyes, the ideal employee was "informal but caring": young, vibrant, interested, courteous, and willing to go out of his or her way to help customers. Richard Branson explained:

> We aren't interested in having just happy employees. We want employees who feel involved and prepared to express dissatisfaction when necessary. In fact, we think that the constructively dissatisfied employee is an asset we should encourage and we need an organization that allows us to do this—and that encourages employees to take responsibility, since I don't believe it is enough for us simply to give it.

Richard Branson believed that involving management and staff was the key to superior results: "I want employees in the airline to feel that it is *they* who can make the difference, and influence what passengers get," he said. He wrote to employees regularly to seek their ideas and to ensure that relevant news was communicated to them. His home phone number was given to all staff, who could call him at any time with suggestions or complaints.

Virgin Atlantic's philosophy was to stimulate the individual. Its dynamic business culture encouraged staff to take initiatives and gave them the means to implement them. Staff often provided insights into what customers wanted or needed—sometimes anticipating their expectations better than the customers themselves. Virgin Atlantic had a formal staff suggestion scheme and encouraged innovation from employees, both in project teams and in their daily work. Employees' suggestions were given serious consideration; many were implemented, such as the idea of serving ice cream as a snack, although formal marketing research had never shown the need for such a service.

Richard Branson himself was open to suggestions and innovations. He talked to everyone and was a good listener, inquisitive and curious about all aspects of the business. He spent time with passengers, and visited the lounge without any advance notice. While he personified a "hands-on" approach to management, he never appeared controlling or threatening. His constant presence was a sign of involvement and a source of motivation for staff, who felt a lot of affection for him. It was not unusual to hear crew discuss his recent decisions or activities, mentioning "Mr. Branson" or "Richard" with admiration and respect.

In the difficult environment of the late 1980s and early 1990s, most airline employees were anxious to keep their jobs. With most operating costs—fuel prices, aircraft prices, insurance, landing, and air traffic control fees—beyond management's control, labor costs were the main target of cutbacks. In 1993, the world's top 20 airlines cut 31,600 jobs, or 3.6 percent of their workforce, while the next 80 airlines added nearly 14,000, or 2.4 percent. That same year, Virgin Atlantic maintained its labor force, and was in the process of recruiting at the end of the year. In June 1994, Virgin Atlantic had 2,602 employees and recruited 880 cabin crew members. Opening a single long-haul line required hiring about 400 people.

THE AIRLINE INDUSTRY

Deregulation of the U.S. air transport industry in 1978 had reduced the government's role and removed protective rules, thereby increasing competition among American airlines. A decade later, deregulation hit Europe. The liberalization movement began in an effort to end monopolies and bring down prices. In fact, European carriers had been engaged in moderate competition in transatlantic travel while the domestic scheduled market remained heavily protected through bilateral agreements. European airlines were mostly state-owned, in a regulated market where access was denied to new entrants. In April 1986, the European Court of Justice ruled that the Treaty of Rome's competition rules also applied to air transportation. Deregulation took place in three phases between 1987—when price controls were relaxed and market access was opened—and 1992, when airlines were allowed to set their own prices, subject to some controls.

In this atmosphere of deregulation and falling prices, traffic revenue grew briskly until 1990, when a global recession and the Gulf War plunged airlines in their worst crisis since World War II. The 22-member association of European airlines saw the number of passengers plummet by 7 million in 1991. Traffic recovered in 1992, when the world's 100 largest airlines saw their total revenue, measured in terms of tonnage or passengers, increase by just over 10 percent. However, the airlines recorded a net loss of $8 billion in 1992, after losses of $1.84 billion in 1991 and $2.66 billion in 1990. Some experts believed that the industry would ultimately be dominated by a handful of players, with a larger number of midsize carriers struggling to close the gap. Exhibits 7 and 8 show financial and passenger load data for some international airlines.

VIRGIN'S COMPETITORS

Virgin's direct competitor was British Airways (BA). Both carriers were fighting each other intensely on the most attractive routes out of London. BA, the number one British airline, was 15 times the size of second-placed Virgin. Exhibit 9 compares Virgin's and British Airways' flights and fares.

EXHIBIT 7   Financial Results of Selected International Airlines

Airline Company	Ranking 92	Ranking 91	Sales US$ Million 1992	Sales US$ Million % Change	Operating Results US$ Million	Net Results US$ Million 1992	Net Results US$ Million 1991	Net Margin % 1992	Jet and Turbo Fleet	Total Employees	Productivity Sales/ Employee $000
American	1	1	14,396	11.7	(25.0)	(935.0)	(239.9)	-6.5	672	102,400	140
United	2	2	12,889	10.5	(537.8)	(956.8)	(331.9)	-7.4	536	84,000	153
Delta	3	4	11,639	15.7	(825.5)	(564.8)	(239.6)	-4.9	554	79,157	147
Lufthansa	4	5	11,036	7.1	(198.5)	(250.4)	(257.7)	-2.3	302	63,645	173
Air France	5	3	10,769	-1.1	(285.0)	(617.0)	(12.1)	-5.7	220	63,933	168
British Airways	6	6	9,307	6.5	518.4	297.7	687.3	3.2	241	48,960	190
Swissair	16	16	4,438	7.0	152.8	80.7	57.9	1.8	60	19,025	233
TWA Inc	18	18	3,634	-0.7	(404.6)	(317.7)	34.6	-8.7	178	29,958	121
Singapore	19	19	3,443	5.4	548.0	518.5	558.4	15.1	57	22,857	150
Qantas	20	20	3,099	2.9	79.1	105.7	34.6	3.4	46	14,936	207
Cathay Pacific	21	21	2,988	11.3	464.0	385.0	378.0	12.9	49	13,240	225
Southwest	34	41	1,685	28.3	182.6	103.5	26.9	6.1	141	11,397	148
Virgin Atlantic	62	62	626	7.3	(22.0)	Not reported	3.8	Not reported	8	2,394	261

Source: *Airline Business*, September 1993, "Much Pain, No Gain." Productivity computed for this exhibit.

EXHIBIT 8 Passenger Load Factors of Selected International Airlines

Airline Company	1992 Revenue Tonne km Million				1992 Revenue Passenger km		1992 Passengers		Passenger Load Factor			1992
	Passenger	Freight	Total	% Change	Million	% Change	Million	% Change	1992 %	1991 %	Year-End	Rank
American	14,223	2,176	16,399	19.7	156,786	18.3	86.01	13.3	63.7	61.7	Dec. 92	1
United	13,489	2,522	16,010	12.0	149,166	12.6	67.00	8.1	67.4	66.3	Dec. 92	2
Delta	11,761	1,765	13,525	20.2	129,632	19.6	82.97	11.8	61.3	60.3	Dec. 92	3
Lufthansa	5,882	4,676	10,725	14.4	61,274	17.1	33.70	14.2	65.0	64.0	Dec. 92	4
Air France	5,238	3,970	9,208	5.3	55,504	4.0	32.71	3.4	67.4	66.8	Dec. 92	5
British Airways	7,622	2,691	10,313	13.2	80,473	15.6	28.10	10.5	70.8	70.2	Mar. 93	6
Swissair	1,573	1,063	2,684	9.1	16,221	7.0	8.01	0.4	60.3	61.6	Dec. 92	16
TWA Inc	4,258	734	4,992	1.4	46,935	1.8	22.54	8.5	64.7	64.7	Dec. 92	18
Singapore Air	3,675	2,412	6,086	14.2	37,861	8.5	8.64	6.3	71.3	73.5	Mar. 93	19
Qantas	2,684	1,220	3,904	4.9	28,836	7.2	4.53	9.4	66.2	66.0	Jun. 92	20
Cathay Pacific	2,695	1,671	4,366	13.3	27,527	12.7	8.36	13.1	73.5	73.6	Dec. 92	21
Southwest Air	2,032	49	2,082	23.4	22,187	22.0	27.84	22.6	64.5	61.1	Dec. 92	34
Virgin Atlantic	984	285	1,269	27.4	9,001	8.7	1.23	5.6	76.1	81.6	Oct. 92	62

Source: *Airline Business*, September 1993, "Much Pain, No Gain."

EXHIBIT 9 Virgin Atlantic and British Airways Fares (£)

Route	Virgin Atlantic			British Airways			
	Upper Class ①	Mid Class ①	Economy 21 day Apex ②	First Class ①	Club ①	Economy	21 day Apex ③
New York	1,195	473	489	1,935	1,061	620	538
San Francisco	1,627	595	538 ④	2,179	1,627	920	638
Los Angeles	1,627	604	538	2,179	1,627	920	638
Tokyo	1,806	783	993	2,751	1,806	1,580	993
Hong Kong	979	600	741	3,280	2,075	1,808	741
Boston	1,082	473	439	1,935	1,061	620	538
Miami	1,144	529	498	2,085	1,144	780	598
Orlando	1,144	529	498	2,085	1,144	780	598

Note:
① One-way weekend peak-time fares in pounds sterling (£).
② Economy fare for Virgin is "Economy 21 day Apex" (reservation no later than 21 days prior to departure).
③ 21 day Apex round-trip ticket.
④ Between May 17 and June 30, 1994, a special launch fare round-trip ticket was sold at £299.

British Airways became the state-owned British airline in 1972 as the result of a merger between British European Airways and British Overseas Airways Corporation. In the early 1980s, it was the clear leader in the highly lucrative and regulated transatlantic route, where operating margins were approximately 15 percent of sales. However, its overall profitability was shaky when Lord King became chairman in 1981. He transformed BA into a healthy organization and prepared it for its successful privatization in 1987. Since this time, BA has remarkably outperformed its European rivals.

British Airways traditionally benefited from a strong position at Heathrow, but competition toughened in 1991 when TWA and Pan Am sold their slots to American and United Airlines for $290 million and $445 million, respectively. In the same year, Virgin also received slots at Heathrow. These slot attributions so infuriated Lord King that he scrapped its annual £40,000 donation to Britain's ruling Conservative Party. At the time of the Heathrow transfer, BA scheduled 278 flights a week across the Atlantic from London, with 83,000 seats, while American had 168 flights with 35,000 seats and United 122 with 30,000. Virgin had 84 flights with 30,000 seats.

Despite these competitive pressures and the recent airline recession, British Airways remained one of the world's most profitable airlines. The largest carrier of international passengers, serving 150 destinations in 69 countries, it was making continuous progress in terms of cost efficiency, service quality, and marketing. BA recruited marketing experts from consumer goods companies who implemented a brand approach to the airline's classes. Some of the actions undertaken by BA in the early 1990s included the relaunching of its European business class Club Europe with £17.5 million and spending £10 million on new lounges (with a traditional British feel), check-in facilities, and ground staff at Heathrow. It was also rumored that BA was preparing to spend nearly £70 million on an advanced in-flight entertainment and information system for its long-haul fleet before the end of 1994.

British Airways and Virgin had fiercely competed against one another from the onset. One major incident that marked their rivalry was what became known as the "Dirty Tricks Campaign." In 1992, Virgin Atlantic filed a lawsuit against BA, accusing it of entering Virgin's computer system and spreading false rumors. In January 1993, Virgin won its libel suit against BA in London. The wide press coverage caused much embarrassment to British Airways. Later that year, Virgin filed a $325 million lawsuit in the Federal Court of New York, accusing BA of using its monopoly power to distort competition on North American routes.

In addition to British Airways, Virgin competed with at least one major carrier on each of its destinations. For instance, it was up against United Airlines to Los Angeles, American Airlines to New York, and Cathay Pacific to Hong Kong. Most of its competitors surpassed Virgin many times in terms of turnover, staff, and number of aircraft. Yet, Virgin was not intimidated by the size of its competitors; it saw its modest size as an advantage that enabled it to react quickly and remain innovative.

VIRGIN ATLANTIC'S MANAGEMENT STRUCTURE

Virgin Atlantic's headquarters were in Crawley, a suburb near Gatwick. The airline had a loose organization combined with a high level of dialogue and involvement, as well as strong controls. A senior manager explained, "Our business is about independence, entrepreneurial flair, and people having autonomy to make decisions; yet we pay a great deal of attention to overhead and cost levels." Members of the management team came from other airlines, other industries, or other divisions of the Virgin Group. The three top executives—co-managing directors Roy Gardner and Syd Pennington and finance director Nigel Primrose—reported directly to Richard Branson.

Gardner had joined Virgin Airways as technical director in 1984 after working at Laker Airways and British Caledonian Airways. He was responsible for the technical aspects of operations: quality, supplies, maintenance, emergency procedures. Pennington oversaw commercial operations, marketing, sales, and flight operations. Primrose, a chartered accountant with 20 years of international experience, had been part of the senior team that set up Air Europe in 1978 and Air UK in 1983 before joining Virgin Atlantic in 1986. He was Virgin Atlantic's company secretary with responsibility for route feasibility, financial planning, financial accounts, treasury, and legal affairs.

Steve Ridgeway headed the marketing department. After assisting Richard Branson in several projects, including the Transatlantic Boat Challenge, he had joined the airline in 1989 to develop its frequent traveler program, becoming head of marketing in 1992. Paul Griffiths, who had 14 years of commercial aviation experience, became Virgin Atlantic's Director of Commercial Operations after spending two years designing and implementing its information management system. Personnel Director Nick Potts, a business studies graduate, had been recruited in 1991 from Warner Music UK where he was the head of the personnel department.

MARKETING ACTIVITIES

Steve Ridgeway's marketing department covered a variety of activities. Some traditional marketing disciplines, such as advertising, promotions, planning, and the Freeway frequent flyer program, reported to Ruth Blakemore, Head of Marketing. Catering, retail operations (for example, duty-free sales), product development, and public relations reported directly to Steve Ridgeway.

Virgin Atlantic spent 2 percent of turnover on advertising, well below the 5 to 7 percent industry norm. Virgin's advertising had featured a series of short campaigns handled by various agencies. The winning of a quality award was often a campaign opportunity, as was the opening of a new line. On one April Fool's Day, Virgin announced that it had developed a new bubble-free champagne. It also launched ad hoc campaigns in response to competitors' activities, as in Exhibit 10. The survey in Exhibit 11 shows

EXHIBIT 10
Virgin Atlantic Advertising (Spring 1994) Response to a British Airways Campaign

The world's favourite airline?
Not in our book.

BEATS THE PANTS OFF BA! VERY GOOD SERVICE.

JAMES ARMSTRONG
B. S. LIMITED

Excellent. Keep BA on the run!

JEREMY HATTON
NORWICH CRUISE CENTRE

The best service from the best airline in the World! Absolutely Fabulous - !!

VINCE CRAWLEY
COUNTRY CASUALS LTD

With a deal like this, who the hell wants to fly BA anyway!!

BOB BROWN
FILMCO EUROFORM

A previously dedicated and loyal British Airways customer, now a dedicated and loyal Virgin customer!

ROBERT CASSON
PFIZER INC

Best Business Class price service in the air.

GEOFF TOVEY
SMITHKLINE BEECHAM

Such a refreshing change from BA! Great entertainment & service! - Looking forward to another flight!

ANDREW TURNER
REED TRAVEL GROUP

I am your biggest fan - I promise never to fly another airline if I can help it. It is always a pleasure on Virgin!

KATHY BRADY
BANKERS TRUST

As ever, Virgin leads the field.

PAUL JACKSON
CARLTON TV

My first time too on Virgin Atlantic and it's unquestionably better than the equivalent BA. The service, for example, was first class.

SHERBAN CANTACUZINO
ROYAL FINE ART COMMISSION

Virgin Atlantic's Upper Class costs the same as BA Club Class. And it's not just the comments in our visitors' book that are better. Hope to see you soon.

 Upper Class   Virgin atlantic

EXHIBIT 11   **Brand Equity Survey**

	British Airways	Virgin Atlantic	American	United
Perceived strongest brand name in transatlantic travel (% of respondents)	70	24	2	1
Spontaneous awareness (%)	96	74	49	22
Usage (%)	93	48	44	23
Rating of brand names (0–100 scale)	85	80	61	58

Source: Business Marketing Services Limited (BMSL). Based on 141 interviews of executives from the U.K.'s top 500 organizations.

that Virgin Atlantic enjoyed a strong brand equity, as well as a high level of spontaneous awareness and a good image in the United Kingdom. In order to increase the trial rate, its advertising had evolved from a conceptual approach to more emphasis on specific product features.

In 1990, the airline launched its Virgin Freeway frequent travelers' program in Britain (it started in the U.S. in 1992). While Virgin Freeway was an independent division of the Virgin Travel Group, it operated within the airline's marketing department. Freeway miles were offered to members who flew Mid Class or Upper Class or who used the services of international companies such as American Express, Inter-Continental Hotels, British Midland, SAS, and others. Miles could be exchanged for free flights to Europe, North America, and Japan, as well as a wide range of activities: hot-air ballooning, polo lessons, rally driving, luxury country getaways for two, five days' skiing in the U.S. As part of the Freeway Program, Virgin offered a free standby ticket for every Upper Class ticket purchased.

The Virgin Freeway was run in partnership with SAS and other international groups which, according to Ruth Blakemore, enabled it to compete with British Airways. Virgin also had ties with SAS through another Freeway partner, British Midland, wholly owned by Airlines of Britain in which SAS had a 35 percent stake. Virgin delivered significant interline traffic to British Midland, and Blakemore believed that there was a useful common ground for all three to join forces against British Airways.

In May 1993, Virgin Atlantic unveiled a promotional campaign targeted at BA passengers who had never tried Virgin. Members of BA's Executive Club USA program who had accumulated 50,000 miles or more qualified for a free Upper Class Companion ticket on Virgin; those with 10,000 to 49,999 miles qualified for a free Mid Class ticket. The campaign was launched with a radio commercial in which Richard Branson said, "In recent years, Virgin has done about everything we can think of to get those remaining British Airways' passengers to try Virgin Atlantic."

The marketing department handled the franchising of the Virgin Atlantic brand, which included two routes. London–Athens, launched from Gatwick in March 1992 in partnership with South East European Airlines of Greece, was transferred to Heathrow seven months later. London City Airport–Dublin, with City Jet, was launched in January 1994. In both cases, the aircraft and crew bore Virgin's name and colors, but Virgin's partner was the operator and paid royalties to Virgin for the use of its brand, marketing, and sales support, and for assistance in the recruitment and training of flight staff.

In April 1994, Virgin announced a partnership with Delta Air Lines—its first alliance with a major international airline. Delta would purchase a set percentage of seats on Virgin flights between London and Los Angeles, New York (Newark and

JFK), Miami, San Francisco, Orlando, and Boston which it would price and sell independently. The alliance, which increased Virgin's annual revenue by $150 million and gave Delta access to Heathrow, had received the blessing of the British government and was awaiting U.S. approval.

Virgin Atlantic's public relations department, known as "the press office" and led by James Murray, played an important role. "We are not here just to react to press inquiries," explained Murray. "We also try to gain publicity for the airline's products and services and to show how much better we are than the competition." Virgin Atlantic enjoyed excellent relations with the media—not the rule in the airline industry—because of a combination of factors: Richard Branson's persona, the airline's openness in dealing with the press, its "David vs. Goliath" quality, the news value of its innovations, and a good management of media relationships.

For instance, Virgin had readily accepted an invitation to participate in BBC television's prime time *Secret Service* series, in which investigators posing as customers test service at well-known firms. Failures in service delivery were exposed and discussed. British Airways, which the BBC had approached first, had declined. While the program did identify some shortcomings in Virgin's operations, including delays in meal service (due to oven problems) and in answering passenger calls, it gave a lively demonstration of the quality of service in Upper Class and of Virgin's willingness to take corrective action.

The Public Relations department comprised three people in Crawley and two in the group press office, where James Murray spent two days a week. Originally set up in Richard Branson's own house, the group press office had to move next door as the amount of work increased. Staff were on call round-the-clock, sometimes taking calls from journalists in the middle of the night. During a one-hour car ride with James Murray, the casewriters watched him handle a constant flow of requests ranging from invitations to the inaugural San Francisco flight to questions on Virgin's position on privatizing the Civil Aviation Agency or the possible banning of peanuts on flights after reports of allergy risks—all on the car phone.

A five-member Product Development department evaluated and developed innovations. It handled a broad range of new product activities—a new identity program for the aircraft, selection of seat design and internal decoration, the catering system, or new lounges—and coordinated the input from other departments. Typically, the marketing, engineering, commercial, and sales departments also participated in developing new products. For example, Airport Services played a crucial role in setting up the Clubhouse lounge.

By June 1994, Virgin had taken steps to correct its main weaknesses: the age of its fleet and its punctuality problems. More than half the fleet would be renewed by the end of the year, and Virgin was undertaking an "On-Time Initiative" in which cabin crew were to shut doors exactly 10 minutes before departure time, even if late passengers had not boarded—even Richard Branson, who was notorious for being late. Virgin was also implementing a new corporate identity program. In addition to the Virgin logo and the "Vargas Lady," all aircraft would bear the words **virgin atlantic** in large gray letters.

CHALLENGES FOR THE FUTURE

During its first decade Virgin Atlantic had confronted great challenges and survived the worst recession in the history of air transportation. Amidst rumors over the airline's financial health, Richard Branson had always stressed his personal commitment. "I would put everything I had into making sure that Virgin Atlantic was here in 20 years time," he said.

Virgin Atlantic had demonstrated its capacity to innovate, to satisfy customers, and to be financially viable in difficult times. As the world economy began to recover, the airline was poised for a quantum leap in the scale of its operations. When Richard Branson had founded it in 1984, his ambition had been to build an airline unlike any other. Ten years later, what set Virgin apart was its reputation for giving customers what they wanted at prices they could afford, pioneering new concepts in service and entertainment, and restoring a sense of pleasure and excitement to long-distance travel.

The main challenge the airline faced as it celebrated its 10th anniversary was to foster this difference throughout the 1990s. What sort of airline should it be? How could it achieve that goal? How could it remain profitable? How could it retain its competitive edge in innovations? Was it possible to grow while retaining the organizational advantages of a small entrepreneurial company? How could it keep employees motivated and enthusiastic? How would it keep the momentum of its success? These were some of the questions that went through Richard Branson's mind as his 400 guests and himself watched a Virgin 747 Jumbo fly over the Thames and Westminster to mark Virgin's first decade.

Case 2

CUSTOM RESEARCH INC. (A)

INTRODUCTION

Custom Research Inc. (CRI) had just passed its 16th birthday, but without much to celebrate. Profitability as a percentage of sales had been declining for several years and revenue growth had been flat recently. CRI partners Jeff Pope and Judy Corson had reached a turning point. They had just completed an extensive financial analysis and found that a large majority of their clients were clients who only did a few projects a year and while profitable, the small client project revenue did not add up to a big part of their total company revenue. They had started the company with, and continued to espouse, a "take all comers" philosophy as to prospective clients. "We've been operating under the presumption that there's no such thing as a 'bad' client. They all pay our bills," said Jeff Pope, "but we are now beginning to question this assumption." Should they stop working with these smaller clients? What would happen if they did? Could the company survive if they did not?

Furthermore, there were serious questions as to CRI's organizational structure. For example, staff members responsible for selling projects were also responsible for implementing project design, interviewing, and analysis. Did this structure make sense moving into the future? These were just a few of the questions senior staff were raising during a series of off-site meetings with Sam Marcus, currently Managing Partner—Brecker & Merryman, Inc., a New York management consulting firm.

BACKGROUND

Judith Corson, fresh from completing a liberal arts degree at the University of Minnesota in 1964, decided she didn't want to be a "nurse or a teacher like everyone else." Through her sorority network, she was contacted by Norma Friedrichs, the manager of project administration in commercial research at The Pillsbury Company. Corson was promptly hired as one of three project directors in charge of project implementation of marketing research for Pillsbury.

Pillsbury, unlike a number of its competitors at this time, had a comprehensive internal research department. Marketing research analysts would request a study and Pillsbury's own internal research department would then implement the entire process from designing the methodology to composing the questionnaire to hiring interviewing services to tabulating results. Most other consumer products companies only had a group of in-house marketing research analysts who would contract their studies out to an independent research firm.

Corson led Pillsbury's new-product marketing research implementation effort on and off for a period of 10 years (she had a stint in marketing research at Scott Paper in Philadelphia from 1967 to 1969 before returning to Pillsbury). In the late 1960s, Pillsbury established a central telephone interviewing capability in-house. Soon it became obvious that the peaks and valleys in Pillsbury's marketing research work volume made it impossible to staff this telephone facility. Operating as a stand-alone profit center funded by charging its time to various departments that needed its services, the marketing research department's problem of having a "single client" made it difficult to generate enough studies for the telephone center staff and therefore difficult to retain personnel.

In 1968, two marketing research analysts left Pillsbury to work for Johnson Wax. Without any internal marketing research department to turn to at their new firm, the analysts called Judy Corson to ask if she could continue to do studies for them. Her boss, Dudley Ruch, gave her permission to do so (and to seek other outside clients). Judy's outside research client business was soon profitable (enjoying 15 to 20 percent profit margins while the company as a whole averaged approximately 4 to 5 percent). This outside research group was able to supplement funding for developing new commercial research techniques.

After a few years, it became necessary to structure the outside research group's relationship to the company in a more formal way. Management demanded that the outside research group become a separate free-standing business—in essence, a line organization, paying corporate taxes to the firm. Seeing this as unfair (marketing research did their own accounting, HR, etc.), Corson became increasingly frustrated with the status of her department. "We were paying corporate taxes, but we weren't getting any services in return!"

Furthermore, industry diversification was giving rise to a number of potential conflicts of interest that prevented Corson from accepting more outside business from other consumer research companies. For example, after Pillsbury bought Burger King, Corson was forced to turn down lucrative marketing research work from McDonald's. This prevented her from growing the outside research business as quickly as she wished.

In January 1974, when Dudley Ruch left Pillsbury to work for Quaker Oats and Corson had no one to report to, she decided it was finally time for a change. She approached Norma Friedrichs, her original boss, to ask her if she would like to go into business together. At that time, Norma was responsible for project implementation of all Pillsbury marketing research. They, in turn, asked Jeff Pope, a Pillsbury product manager who, prior to joining Pillsbury, had also done marketing research for an independent research company and KPMG, to join the team. Custom Research Inc. was founded in August 1974.

Immediately upon beginning the firm, the trio hired a lawyer to implement a buy-sell agreement which proved to be a wise first step—two years later, Norma Friedrichs left the company and Judy Corson and Jeff Pope exercised the agreement, buying out Friedrichs and becoming 50/50 partners in CRI.

THE INDUSTRY

While the marketing research industry began as an in-house function of the larger consumer goods companies, CRI's experience was typical of the trend in the late 1960s and 1970s as companies began to contract with independent research firms. During this period, the industry was very fragmented, with a multitude of small, one- or two-person firms and a few well-established larger organizations.

In the recent decade, however, the trend was toward consolidation, with a few larger firms at the top able to complete all aspects of the research process from data collection to analysis and literally thousands of very small firms competing for data collection and tabulation business only. Furthermore, in a 1987 study of Council of American Survey Research Organizations (CASRO) member firms, a large majority expected custom research spending to grow slowly or remain the same over the next few years. (See Exhibit 1 for industry breakdown.)

THE MARKETING RESEARCH STUDY

A marketing research study typically includes the following steps:

1. *Study design:* Establishes client's research and information needs, determines the limitations of available research tools and methods, and draws up plans for implementing the study. Includes development of detailed client questionnaire.

2. *Proposal:* Explains study design to client, offers cost and timing estimate within 10 percent of final cost to client.

3. *Data collection:* Uses questionnaire to gather data necessary to determine what information a client needs to know about a new product idea, a price increase, or other types of information. Typically done by outside interviewing services, either over the phone or in person (for example, at shopping malls). Other data collection methods include mail.

4. *Tabulation:* Results from data collection stage are tabulated according to variables laid out during study design stage.

5. *Analysis:* Study results are analyzed for their relevance to client—should client develop the new product? Why or why not? What are the real implications of the study results?

At its inception, CRI did almost exclusively data collection and tabulation. The process went as follows: first, a research analyst from a client firm would request a

EXHIBIT 1
Council of American Survey Research Organizations— Quarterly Bookings Report—Firms May 26, 1987

Size of Firm	(N)	1Q87	% Change	% Change vs. Year Ago
		115,139	*+2*	*—*
10mm and over	16	119,436	+6	+4
4mm to 10mm	21	33,892	+6	−4
		11,524	*−13*	*−1*
2mm to 4mm	16	10,955	−17	−6
		2,897	*−5*	*−22*
1mm to 2mm	9	2,697	−10	−28
		2,445	*−19*	*−32*
Under 1mm	14	3,035	—	−15
		165,897	*+1*	*−2*
TOTAL	76	170,015	+4	—

Italics — Represent analysis adjusted for outliers.

Comparison of Two- or Three-Year Outlook on Primary Research Spending

Percentage that said custom research spending by their organization in the next two or three years would:

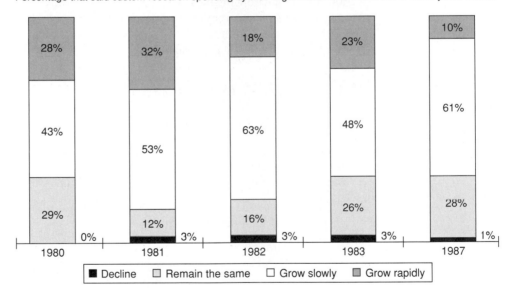

| ■ Decline | ☐ Remain the same | ☐ Grow slowly | ■ Grow rapidly |

study to test a new product idea with a certain number of consumers (e.g., the design stage was already completed by the client). CRI would receive the request and would, according to the size and scope of the study, develop a proposal with a cost and timing estimate for data collection and tabulation. At the beginning, clients would typically do the first step—study design—and the last step—analysis of the results—themselves. Later, in the early 1980s, as their client companies began to downsize, CRI began to perform the design and analysis functions as well. (See Exhibit 2 for a typical study request, results, and analysis.)

EXHIBIT 2

Mr. Joe Leim
Great Foods Company
2 White Pine Road
Jonesville, WV

Dear Joe:

Well, it's time for another wave of Pancake Mix Price Increase Awareness Study. This is the *second* of four waves. The following is our understanding of the study specifications for this study. Also included are the associated study costs and timing. Joe, please note that the costs did go up for this wave (and for each subsequent wave).

Background and Study Purpose

Due to current low supplies of the ingredients for pancake mix worldwide, the wheat futures market is extraordinarily volatile. The purpose of this study is to help you understand consumer awareness of pancake mix pricing increases and how these increases affect consumers' usage habits. You will conduct a series of four telephone surveys at six-week intervals. This study is the first of the four waves.

Specifications

Methodology

Telephone study conducted on weeknights, and weekends, using standard random digit dialing sampling procedures.

Locations

National (total U.S., excluding Alaska and Hawaii)

Quota

150 Head of Household (female/male if no female) who have bought any type of pancake mix in the past three months for use in their homes.

Each wave will consist of 150 interviews for a total of 600 interviews after completing all four waves.

Sample

RDD sample will be provided by SSI.

Incidence

When the study was costed, incidence was estimated at 70 percent. However, during the Wave 1 study, incidence was falling out at 60 percent.

Questionnaire and Interview Length

Interview length is estimated at six minutes.

Coding

There is one open-end question.

Data Tables

We will provide data tables and a top line report upon completion of the study.

(continued)

EXHIBIT 2 *(continued)*

Schedule and Budget

Schedule

We are operating under this timetable for Wave 2:

Sample at CRI	February 6
Final q'aire approved	n/a (same as Wave 1)
Data collection start	February 9
Data collection finish	February 16
Data tables and top line report to you	February 23

Budget

Joe, due to the lower than estimated incidence, the cost of each additional wave has increased from our earlier estimate. If the incidence should go up, we will adjust the costs accordingly. But, as of now, our projected costs for this wave of research (and each additional wave) will be within 10 percent of the following:

Data collection start	$6,400
Sample	$300
Data processing	$700
Total	*$7,400*

Did I get everything, Joe? If not, please let me know and I'll make the necessary modifications.

Best regards,

Norma Brennan
Sr. Research Associate

(continued)

EXHIBIT 2 *(continued)*

Pancake Price Increase Awareness Study—Wave 2

Introduction (Base = All)

Good (morning/afternoon/evening). I'm (NAME) calling
long distance from Custom Research Inc.

Today I'm collecting information for a marketing
study about products used in the home.

(Are you/may I please speak with) the female head of the household
(/lady of the house)?

IF THERE IS NO FEMALE HEAD OF HOUSEHOLD ASK:

(Are you/may I please speak with) the male head of the
household (/man of the house)?

Q1. Gender (Base = All)

RECORD GENDER.
          'Female'/
          'Male'

Q2. Pancake Mix Bought Past Three Months (Base = All)

In the past three months, has pancake mix of any type been bought for use in your
home?
          'Yes'/
          'No'

REFER TO Q2. IF "NO," DISCONTINUE.
ALL OTHER CONTINUE WITH Q3.

Q3. Usual Brand—Household Usage (Base = All)

In the past three months, what *one* brand of
pancake mix was used most of the time in your home?

IF TWO OR MORE BRANDS: Was one of these brands used more often than
the other(s), or were they both (all) used about equally?

IF TWO EQUALLY, ENTER BOTH.   IF THREE+, RECORD "NO USUAL."

RECORD ON BRAND LIST.

(continued)

EXHIBIT 2 *(continued)*

Q4. Next Brand—Household Usage (Base = All)

Thinking of the next time you buy pancake mix,
as best as you can say, what *one* brand are you most
likely to buy the next time you buy pancake mix?

IF RESPONDENT SAYS: "I buy what's on Sale/Coupon," RECORD
"(50) Whatever on Sale/Coupon."

TWO OR MORE BRANDS: Would you be more likely to buy one of
these brands than the other(s), or would you buy both (all)
equally?

IF TWO EQUALLY, ENTER BOTH.   IF THREE +, RECORD "NO USUAL."

RECORD ON BRAND LIST.

Q5. How Often Will You Buy Pancake Mix (Base = All)

In the next three months, are you likely to buy pancake mix
more often, about as often, or less often than you have in
the past three months?

> "More often"/
> "About as often"/
> "Less often"/
> "NK/Ref" /

Q6. How Much Will Buy Pancake Mix (Base = All)

Now thinking of the next time you buy pancake mix, are you
likely to buy more, about the same number of, or fewer boxes of
pancake mix than the number you usually buy?

> "More"/
> "About the same number"/
> "Fewer"/
> "NK/Ref"/

Q7. What Size Will Buy (Base = All)

The next time you buy pancake mix, are you likely to buy a
larger size, the same size, or a smaller size of pancake mix
than the size you usually buy?

> "Larger"/
> "Same size"/
> "Smaller"/
> "NK/Ref"/

(continued)

EXHIBIT 2 *(continued)*

Q8. Price of Pancake Mix Last Bought (Base = All)

Now thinking about the last time you bought pancake mix,
was the price of the pancake mix higher than, about the same, or
lower than the previous time you had bought the same brand
and type of pancake mix?

> "Higher"/
> "About the same price"/
> "Lower"/
> "NK/Ref"/

Q9. Price of Pancake Mix Increasing (Base = All)

Some people we've talked with recently mentioned
hearing about an increase in the price of pancake mix.
Have you seen or heard anything recently about pancake mix
prices increasing, or not?

> "Yes"/
> "No"/

REFER TO Q9.   IF "YES," CONTINUE WITH Q10.   IF "NO," SKIP TO DEMOS.

Q10 Cause of Increase in Pancake Mix Prices (Base = All)

What do you think is causing the increase in pancake mix prices?
  PROBE AND CLARIFY FULLY.

DEMOGRAPHICS (Demos)   (Base = All)

My last few questions are for demographic purposes only.

Number in Household (Base = All)

In total, how many people live in your household,
including children and yourself?

DO NOT READ LIST.

> Resp sp "One"/
> "Two"/
> "Three"/
> "Four"/
> "Five"/
> "Six"/
> "Seven or more"/
> "Refuse"/

(continued)

EXHIBIT 2 *(continued)*

Household Income (Base = 18+ Years Old)

Is the total yearly household income over or under
$50,000?

UNDER: Is it over or under $25,000?

OVER: Is it over or under $70,000?

"Under $25,000"/
"$25,000–$49,999"/
"$50,000–$69,999"/
"$70,000 and over"/
"Refuse"/

Education (Base = All)

What was the last grade of school that you,
yourself, completed?

IF NECESSARY, READ LIST.

"Grade School or Less"/
"Some High School"/
"High School Graduate"/
"Some College"/
"College Graduate"/
"Post Graduate"/
"Refuse (DO NOT READ)"/

Those are all of the questions I have for
you today. Thank you for participating in this
study. We value your opinion.

(continued)

EXHIBIT 2 (*continued*)

Pancake Mix Price Increase Awareness: Waves 1 & 2
Market Research Department Report

Research Purpose: To track: (1) consumer awareness of pricing changes in the pancake mix category, (2) consumer perceptions for the reasons for the price increase, and (3) expected claimed habit changes due to pancake mix pricing volatility.

Success Criteria/Expected Results: Will be used with other data to aid brand management in decisions about product, promotion, pricing, and public relations responses to the pricing increases.

Initiated By: Brand management.

Locations of Data Collection: Continental United States.

Market Research Contact: Joe L.

Background: The wheat futures market is extraordinarily volatile with the spring futures increasing by over 50 percent, the second highest level ever. Unlike the most recent 1996 run-up, which was weather-related, this market is being driven by fundamental supply and demand issues as worldwide stocks of higher quality wheat are at critically low levels and estimates for this year's crop are 10 percent lower than last year. We expect continued volatility over the next three months. In an effort to understand consumer awareness of pancake mix pricing increase and how the price increase affects consumers' usage habits, we will conduct a series of four telephone surveys at six-week intervals.

Method/Test Description: Interviews were conducted via telephone. In order to track awareness of the price increases, perceptions of the causes and changes in claimed/expected behaviors over time, four waves of this study will be conducted at six-week intervals. A total of 600 heads of households (150/wave for four waves) who have bought any type of pancake mix in the past three months for use in their home will be interviewed.

Key Dates: Wave 1 fieldwork—2/9/98 through 2/16/98. Wave 2 fieldwork—3/30/98 through 4/6/98.

Market Research Department Report

(continued)

EXHIBIT 2 *(concluded)*

Summary
Pancake Mix Increase Awareness: Waves 1 & 2

Research Purpose: To track: (1) consumer awareness of pricing changes in the pancake mix category, (2) consumer perceptions for the reasons for the price increase, and (3) expected claimed habit changes due to pancake mix pricing volatility.

The request states that the results will be used: with other data to aid brand management in decisions about product, promotion, pricing, and public relations responses to the pricing increases.

Respondents are: Heads of Household, age 18+.

Key data for Waves 1 & 2 are shown below.

	Heads of Household Who Purchased Pancake Mix in Past Three Months	
	Wave 1 2/98	Wave 2 4/98
Base = Total Interviews	150	152
	%	%
Predicts change in habits (undup.)	**30**	**24**
Amount planned to buy in next three months		
More often	4	5
About as often	77	85
Less often	18	11
Number of packages plans to buy next time		
More	4	3
About the same number	87	87
Fewer	8	9
Size of packages plans to buy next time		
Larger size	8	9
Same size	88	89
Smaller size	3	1
Noticed pancake mix price increase (aided)	**66**	**56**
Price compared to last bought pancake mix		
Compared to previous time		
Higher	41	43
About the same price	39	37
Lower	6	9
Reasons for price increase		
(Base = Noticed price increase)	(99)	(85)
Freeze/Frost/Bad weather	25	29
Manufacturer greed/Taking advantage of customer	10	11
Brand usage		
Most often past three months brand	42	43
Next brand will purchase	39	39

Market Research Department Report

ORGANIZATIONAL STRUCTURE

Once the proposal was accepted by a client, the CRI project manager would deploy staff to implement the study. Project managers were organized by industry into two main divisions. The first division included Business to Business (companies that sold products to other companies; i.e., auto parts suppliers, corporate service firms, etc.) and Medical (pharmaceutical, hospital supplies, etc.). This division accounted for only 25 percent of CRI's total revenues. Clients such as Johnson & Johnson were among CRI's first clients in the medical marketing research business.

The second division, representing the other 75 percent of CRI's business, was Consumer Research. Clients included Quaker Oats, Land O'Lakes, and Johnson Wax. A third division, Corporate Services, provided support services to the research function, such as data tabulation, copying, shipping, etc.

CRI's project managers also served as salespeople—the company had not established an independent sales department. One reason for this structure was the nature of the business. As Judy Corson explained, "At CRI, salespeople must first be researchers—you must understand the methodology and the technology or you will not be taken seriously by the client. It normally takes five years to learn the business and there is no substitute for actually doing the studies."

EXPANDING BUSINESS, DECLINING PROFITS

From 1974 to 1990, CRI's customer base expanded steadily. With a number of large corporate clients, CRI had developed a reputation as one of the premier market research firms in the United States. However, during these years, a somewhat disturbing trend had developed. The results of an extensive profitability analysis completed in 1990 showed that while new bookings, closed sales, and overall operating profit were all on the rise, the crucial measure of profit as a percentage of sales was slowly declining. (See Exhibit 3 for analysis.)

From its formation, CRI had used a detailed activity-based costing system to assign costs to each marketing research study or project. Each employee or associate recorded time spent on each job using one of more than 30 different charge rates depending on the work done. Time spent on selling projects was charged first to a "zero" account and charged back later to jobs accepted. Using this system, CRI had a record of profitability for each research study or project.

EXHIBIT 3
Fiscal 1990 Review—
Custom Research
Inc.—Confidential
(Company Total—
Fiscal 1990 Review[a])

	Actual	Plan	$ Difference	% Difference
Bookings[b]	$10,899.3M	$11,547.0M	$–647.7M	–6%
Closings[b]	10,297.0M	10,792.0M	–495.9M	–5%
Gross margins	1,677.6M	1,871.5M	–193.9M	–10%
General and administrative	729.8M	708.2M	–21.6M	–3%
Operating profit	$947.8M	$1,163.3M	$–215.5M	–19%
	9%	11%		–2%

(continued)

[a]All data and numbers in Exhibit 3 are disguised.

[b]"Bookings" refers to work under contract which in turn becomes work in progress. "Closings" is the revenue figure recorded once all costs are allocated. Typically, closings lag bookings by 5 to 10 percent as this small percentage of booked business closes in the following fiscal year.

EXHIBIT 3
(*continued*)

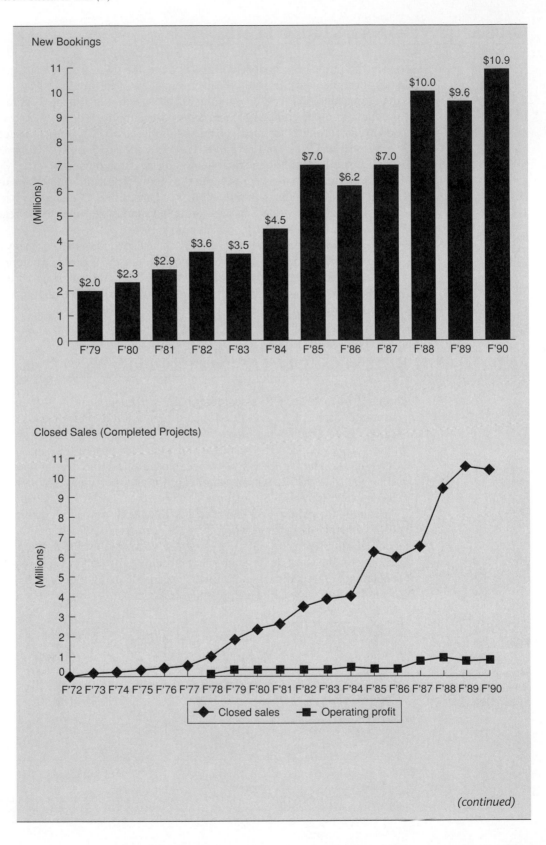

New Bookings

Closed Sales (Completed Projects)

◆ Closed sales ■ Operating profit

(continued)

EXHIBIT 3
(*continued*)

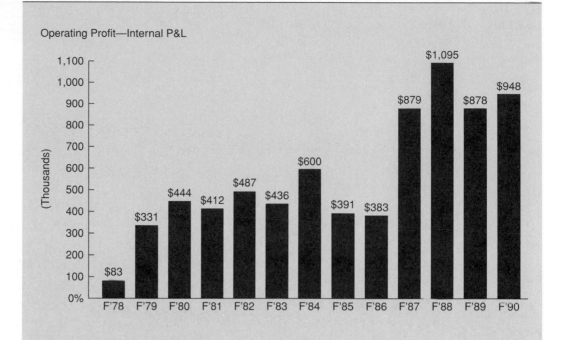

Operating Profit—Internal P&L

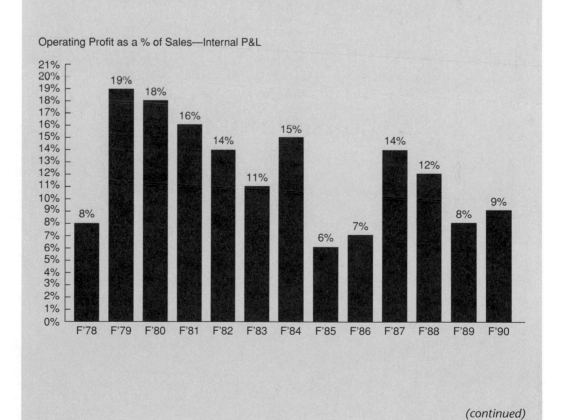

Operating Profit as a % of Sales—Internal P&L

(*continued*)

EXHIBIT 3
(*continued*)

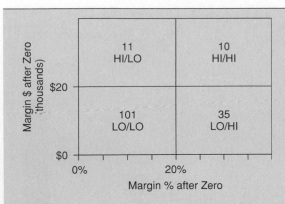

Number of Clients	$ Volume	$ Margin[a] after Zero	% Margin[a] after Zero	% of Total CRI Margin
10 HI-HI	$ 3,001K	$ 744K	25%	44%
11 HI-LO	2,919K	411K	14	25
35 LO-HI	1,094K	310K	28	18
101 LO-LO	3,283K	213K	6	13
157 Total	$10,297K	$1,678K	16%	100%

[a] "$ margin after zero" refers to the profit margin after all direct project costs (salaries, data collection and tabulation, copying, shipping, etc.), as well as sales costs (e.g., all costs involved in selling the project) have been deducted. "Margin" refers to profit margin before sales costs have been deducted.

I.D. Number	$ Volume	% Margin	% Margin after Zero	$ Margin after Zero
F-90 Closed Projects—HI/HI (over $20K/under 20% Margin)				
30	$989,387	28%	26%	253,184
29	505,426	29	26	129,440
39	410,098	24	21	86,244
15	184,700	35	30	54,560
44	266,650	23	20	54,343
45	231,300	21	20	45,450
31	156,000	27	25	39,718
12	99,815	34	30	30,234
7	81,102	36	36	29,294
18	76,600	33	29	22,000
Total 10	$3,001,077			$744,466

(continued)

EXHIBIT 3
(*continued*)

I.D. Number	$ Volume	% Margin	% Margin after Zero	$ Margin after Zero
F-90 Closed Projects—HI/LO (over $20K/over 20% Margin)				
46	$460,311	26%	19%	$88,518
60	206,125	19	16	49,531
61	281,962	22	16	45,255
54	252,269	22	18	44,904
71	276,608	15	12	32,640
78	293,600	10	10	28,685
73	232,300	20	12	26,877
68	189,358	23	14	26,529
79	258,535	22	9	24,406
76	223,681	13	10	22,592
67	144,500	15	15	21,155
Total 11	$2,919,249			$411,090
F-90 Closed projects—LO/HI (under $20K/over 20% Margin)				
13	$61,250	32%	30%	$18,449
2	32,500	57	54	17,596
8	51,940	36	34	17,576
28	65,980	31	26	17,221
27	57,300	32	27	15,282
4	39,500	46	38	15,121
23	52,200	28	28	14,376
36	62,835	26	23	14,320
19	48,521	31	28	13,785
43	56,700	22	20	11,555
17	38,150	32	29	11,144
16	36,985	32	29	10,837
41	48,151	22	21	10,054
9	30,750	35	32	9,963
24	34,900	41	27	9,580
14	31,730	35	30	9,532
34	38,000	29	23	8,900
32	35,236	25	25	8,675
42	38,660	24	21	8,022
40	37,300	24	21	7,844
20	26,922	31	28	7,552
10	23,000	34	32	7,349
22	21,300	32	28	5,924
6	15,985	38	36	5,820
26	20,300	27	27	5,475
35	21,350	26	23	4,893
3	10,600	50	46	4,862
1	4,700	100	100	4,677
25	16,500	27	27	4,455
37	16,055	38	22	3,550
11	9,250	33	31	2,831
5	3,400	43	37	1,264
21	3,650	28	28	1,018
33	1,389	100	24	332
38	800	26	21	172
Total 35	$1,093,788			$310,003

(*continued*)

EXHIBIT 3
(*continued*)

I.D. Number	$ Volume	% Margin	% Margin after Zero	$ Margin after Zero
F-90 Closed Projects—LO/LO (under $20K/under 20% Margin)				
72	$153,650	16%	12%	$18,438
66	113,780	19	15	17,067
83	186,680	17	9	16,801
59	102,501	21	16	16,400
84	203,320	14	7	14,232
47	57,900	24	19	11,001
55	59,789	22	18	10,762
82	115,925	16	9	10,433
64	57,165	24	15	8,575
49	42,100	24	19	7,999
70	62,800	22	12	7,536
63	45,850	24	16	7,336
80	74,547	11	9	6,709
58	40,650	21	16	6,504
52	35,600	23	18	6,408
56	36,660	28	17	6,232
87	110,885	7	5	5,544
69	38,494	16	14	5,389
57	31,284	23	17	5,318
53	29,000	26	18	5,220
65	29,300	20	15	4,395
75	27,500	22	11	3,025
50	15,600	27	19	2,964
62	18,000	20	16	2,880
92	91,900	12	3	2,757
81	30,600	21	9	2,754
85	36,500	13	7	2,555
96	47,250	10	5	2,363
134	38,600	30	6	2,316
123	45,000	20	5	2,250
77	19,100	22	10	1,910
48	9,685	29	19	1,840
157	31,950	6	5	1,598
125	30,150	17	5	1,508
91	36,675	17	4	1,467
155	35,800	16	4	1,432
120	22,994	26	6	1,380
74	12,350	15	11	1,359
51	7,600	26	17	1,292
94	125,055	3	1	1,251
115	23,775	22	5	1,189
114	23,500	18	5	1,175
86	18,510	15	6	1,111
128	20,700	15	5	1,035
89	18,500	17	5	925
88	16,030	5	5	802
150	15,895	5	5	795
98	15,650	20	5	783
93	36,300	3	2	726
129	11,900	25	6	714
130	35,475	5	2	710

(*continued*)

EXHIBIT 3
(*concluded*)

I.D. Number	$ Volume	% Margin	% Margin after Zero	$ Margin after Zero
F-90 Closed Projects—LO/LO (under $20K/under 20% Margin)				
95	11,500	9	6	690
141	8,900	15	7	623
127	11,100	11	5	555
153	10,990	12	5	550
90	6,100	16	9	549
144	9,100	33	6	546
142	10,400	21	5	520
119	6,750	56	7	473
131	8,350	17	5	418
156	6,100	32	6	366
160	12,100	9	3	363
97	11,739	6	3	352
100	8,700	9	4	348
136	6,900	34	5	345
148	6,300	12	5	315
132	7,800	12	4	312
113	14,922	6	2	298
122	5,500	51	5	275
121	4,800	60	5	240
106	5,000	31	4	200
126	3,900	28	4	156
118	3,100	22	5	155
110	3,800	25	3	114
117	1,778	40	6	107
149	2,080	38	5	104
158	2,500	26	4	100
101	2,000	43	4	80
151	1,700	28	4	68
152	1,225	44	5	61
104	1,200	18	5	60
116	1,200	58	5	60
112	1,000	12	5	50
109	500	31	5	25
140	210	76	5	11
135	13,000	5	0	0
124	1,200	−1	−6	−72
139	7,800	4	−1	−78
111	2,000	−4	−9	−180
108	3,100	−4	−10	−310
147	3,900	−27	−32	−1,248
133	10,900	−5	−13	−1,417
159	9,800	−17	−19	−1,862
143	28,000	0	−7	−1,960
103	19,981	−3	−10	−1,998
138	12,100	−17	−22	−2,662
154	68,470	−2	−5	−3,424
102	43,180	−4	−9	−3,886
107	113,600	−1	−4	−4,544
99	54,450	−11	−12	−6,534
105	145,800	−5	−9	−13,122
Total 101	$3,282,949			$213,353

As Executive Vice President Diane Kokal explained, profit as a percentage of sales was the main way that CRI measured its success:

> Working for a client that doesn't actually clear a profit is no fun. Obviously what you want is the highest possible profit margin, particularly in our business where the game is definitely not market share. The research business is a very fragmented one so market share is not such a meaningful measure. We knew we had to grow consistently but we also knew we must grow more profitably.

Jeff Pope further organized these data into a quadrant analysis that provided even more insight into the problem. Two-thirds of all clients were in the "Low/Low" quadrant, meaning that they contributed less than $20,000 in margin contribution and less than a 20 percent profit margin (as a percentage of sales). Thus, these were either small clients or small projects or both.

DIRECTION

The Steering Committee, made up of the two partners and the two executive vice presidents—Diane Kokal and Jan Elsesser—decided it was time to hire an outsider to facilitate the process of establishing the right direction for the future. They hired Sam Marcus, formerly of the Delta Group in New York, and the four members of the Steering Committee went off-site over a year for a series of one-day strategy meetings.

Questions were many. If a large percentage of clients contributed little or nothing to overall profit, should CRI neglect them? What would be the repercussions of such a strategy? What if the remaining clients experienced an economic downturn and cut back on their research budgets? Could CRI grow under this strategy? Jeff Pope thought CRI could focus on and grow the business of the larger, more profitable clients.

What choices must be made if the Steering Committee were to terminate relations with some predetermined group of their existing clients? What criteria should they use to decide whom to keep and whom to drop? Should they in fact maintain all profitable clients and drop all unprofitable clients? Perhaps the choice was not that simple.

Furthermore, how exactly would they explain all this to their clients? Was it their responsibility to refer those smaller clients to someone else for service? What else did the Steering Committee need to address before making this very important decision about the company's future?

And finally, what about CRI's organizational structure? While it seemed to make sense that "doers" were also sellers, the research function was quite different, and in some respects, required very different skills, than did the sales function. Furthermore, while the project managers were out selling projects, they were unable to implement others and while directing research, they were unable to sell. This seemed rather inefficient. However, everyone agreed that it was crucial that CRI's salespeople all understand (and have experience in implementing) research projects.

Case 3

NORTHWEST AIRLINES AND THE DETROIT SNOWSTORM (A)

PART I

On January 8, 1999, an article[1] appeared in *The Wall Street Journal, Interactive Edition*, an abridged version of which is reprinted below:

> Northwest Airlines faced new ire from travelers and airport officials over its response to a snowstorm this week at its largest hub, Detroit.
>
> In the midst of a major storm that prompted other carriers to curtail or discontinue service to airports all throughout the Midwest, Northwest made the decision to let 30 planes land in Detroit on Sunday. The outcome, on top of 14 inches of snow, was a mess.
>
> After landing, the planes had to sit on the tarmac for as long as eight hours because other Northwest jets were tying up the gates. Some pilots tried to calm agitated passengers by showing movies. But one captain used his cockpit phone to call John Dasburg, Northwest's chief executive, at home and declare the situation desperate.
>
> Thursday, one group of passengers filed a lawsuit in Wayne County, Mich., Circuit Court against the county, the Detroit airport and Northwest, alleging that thousands of passengers were "imprisoned" on the carrier's planes during the storm and not allowed to disembark for hours. The plaintiffs, a family traveling from the Caribbean, reported there was no food or water available, that toilets were full and that people were forced to urinate into cups. A Northwest spokesman apologized to all passengers inconvenienced by the storm, but said the lawsuit is without merit.

In the aftermath of the storm, Northwest said it couldn't get the planes out of the gates because the airport wasn't being plowed fast enough. Airline officials charged that airport plowing crews didn't work fast enough or in the right sequence, and inadvertently created giant snow walls that trapped planes in the gates.

That assertion outraged David Katz, director of Detroit Metropolitan Airport. "It was such a cheap shot," he said. Northwest employees "weren't moving any planes," he added. "They didn't have crews. Machinery wasn't working. Planes were frozen."

As for his maintenance crews, Mr. Katz said that at the height of the storm, the airport had 37 of Northwest's 70 gates fully plowed and available. "We kept the taxiways and runways open during the duration of the blizzard."

Northwest officials later conceded they made a mistake in bringing the 30 flights into Detroit, instead of holding them on the ground or diverting them to airports outside the snow belt. They also conceded that a big part of the problem was that an insufficient number of the airline's own workers showed up to help move planes away from gates. Indeed, Northwest said only half its Detroit workers made it in on Sunday because of the snow.

Big snowstorms are always difficult for airlines. They all cancel flights. Reservations lines get backed up. Agents don't always have up-to-the-minute information. It can take days to reunite travelers with their luggage.

But last weekend's big snowstorm caused worse disruptions for travelers in Detroit than in Chicago, even though Chicago's O'Hare International Airport handles far more air traffic and was hit with many more inches of snow.

In Chicago, where *AMR* Corp.'s American Airlines and *UAL* Corp.'s United Airlines operate enormous hubs, there were many fewer complaints about airplanes spending hours on runways. Both American and United canceled most of their Chicago flights on Saturday and Sunday. . . .

Operations were restored to normal by Wednesday [according to Northwest's chief spokesperson]. He added that about 5,000 suitcases still are separated from their owners and piled up at airports around the country.

On January 15, January 20, and February 24, 1999, additional articles on Northwest Airlines and the January snowstorm appeared in *The Wall Street Journal.* On April 28, *The Journal* published another article[2] which is abridged below:

The 757's toilets overflowed. A hysterical passenger vowed to blow an emergency door and jump into the freezing darkness. A grown man wept and begged to be freed. The air stank. Babies screamed. Adults screamed, too.

Anyone who flies regularly has an airline horror story. But short of a crash or a hijacking, few trips are likely to compare to the one taken by the 198 passengers and crew of Northwest Airlines Flight 1829 over the first weekend of the year. It arrived about 22 hours late, and was trapped on the tarmac at its destination for nearly seven hours more. *The Wall Street Journal* has pieced together what it was like aboard that plane, minute by minute.

Fasten your seatbelts. It's a bumpy ride.

* * * * *

On Saturday, Jan. 2, 153 vacationers . . . arrived at the Princess Juliana International Airport on the Caribbean island of St. Martin for the early afternoon departure of Flight 1829. The holidays were over.

The flight was scheduled for five hours, a straight shot back into Detroit, Northwest's largest hub. Most of the passengers were from Michigan, and most were professionals: money managers, bankers, physicians, business owners, educators. Many own villas or time-shares on the island. Some passengers had their children with them, and there were kids traveling with nannies.

[2] Susan Carey, "Seven Hours of Sitting and Waiting Leaves Northwest Passengers Near Breaking Point," *The Wall Street Journal, Interactive Edition,* 28 April 1999.

From the start, there were glitches. The airport's check-in computers broke down, fouling up seat assignments. . . .

Some passengers worried about the weather up north. The blizzard, in fact, was dumping inch after inch of snow in Michigan. But in balmy St. Martin, Capt. Peter Stabler received instructions to proceed to Detroit.

Capt. Stabler, 41 years old and a 15-year Northwest veteran, saw nothing unusual in that; there are almost always ways to beat bad weather. . . . Flight 1829 took off three hours late. It was over southern Georgia, more than halfway home, when a message flashed on the cockpit computer: "Detroit is closed." The plane was eventually rerouted to Tampa, Fla., and landed at 8:03 P.M. local time.

To some passengers, the Tampa layover alone was enough to make Flight 1829 the worst of their lives. As they got off the plane, a Northwest ground agent told them the plane would leave for Detroit the next morning at 6:15. Passengers got vouchers for a St. Petersburg hotel, but at that late hour, check-in took ages. Northwest gave out dinner vouchers, but a hastily prepared buffet was swamped by more than 200 passengers from Flight 1829 and other sidetracked flights, and many went away hungry.

Doug Post, 29, a developer in Kalamazoo, Mich., was one of them. Mr. Post had been in St. Martin on his honeymoon with bride Dawn Chamberlain. They were already feeling put out; their St. Martin hotel room had been infested with cockroaches.

They crashed around midnight. When their wake-up call came at 4:30 A.M. Sunday, they hurried to the airport—and eventually learned that Flight 1829's crew wouldn't be legal to fly until midday. Union and Federal Aviation Administration rules require a set amount of rest after a certain amount of time in the air; crew members were back at the hotel snoozing.

The flight crew had tried to alert passengers to the change Saturday night, but didn't get word to many. Mr. Post milled around with about 40 Flight 1829 passengers at the airport before dawn. They fumed as they couldn't get a straight answer about when the flight would leave. Finally, Mr. Post lay down on the airport floor and slept for four hours.

The crew threaded through some of those seething passengers when it arrived at the airport shortly after 11 A.M. The crew had been joined by Chuck Miller, an off-duty Northwest 757 captain who lives in St. Petersburg and wanted to hitch a ride in the cockpit jumpseat. Capt. Miller was toting his cell phone.

They expected an uneventful flight. Capt. Stabler thought the storm had blown through, and he assumed Detroit was open since he had been given the go-ahead to take off. In fact, Northwest's operations center in St. Paul, Minn., the airline's headquarters, already had let a few planes land in Detroit that morning.

Passengers began boarding. . . . Additional travelers had joined the flight, and now every one of the plane's 190 seats was taken. Some infants rode on laps. Northwest catering personnel, figuring Flight 1829 needed only enough food, drinks and ice for the two-hour hop from Tampa to Detroit, ordered two extra beverage carts and big bags of peanut packets removed from the plane.

The flight departed at 12:27 P.M. Passengers were served. In coach it was hot sandwiches—steak with onions and green peppers or turkey pastrami and cheese. In the cockpit, a computer message flashed on screen an hour into the flight: "Due to weather in Detroit, you can expect extensive ground delays."

Capt. Stabler wondered aloud about slowing down to give the airport more time to get ready. "Go like hell," urged Capt. Patchett, the co-pilot. "Get there in front of everybody else." They barreled on, and landed in Detroit at 2:45 Sunday afternoon. Nearly 24 hours had passed since the plane left St. Martin.

Some passengers applauded.

Michigan's Wayne County owns Detroit Metro Airport and is responsible for snow plowing. Eleven inches had fallen at the airport since Saturday, but now the sun was shining. Wind and jet exhaust whipped veils of snow across the tarmac, but all in all, Capt. Stabler thought, "I've seen worse."

So what happened next seemed odd. The air-traffic controllers told him to exit off the

EXHIBIT 1

Source: Northwest Internal Report.

SITTING ON THE TARMAC

Northwest flights that sat on the ground for more than 2½ hours on Jan. 3, 1999, shown in order of arrival:

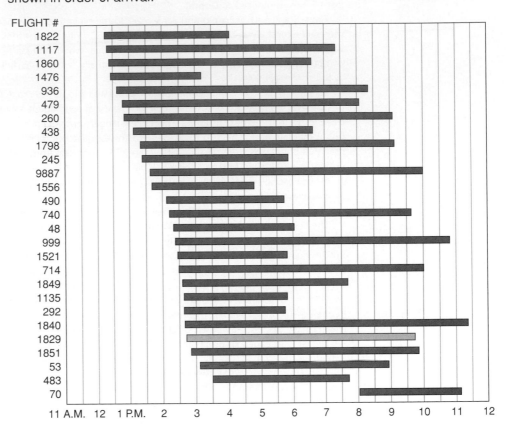

runway onto a rarely used taxiway on the far-western edge of the airport, away from the terminal. The taxiway is called Zulu. There was a conga line of other planes already there. At various times that day, that line and others around the airport would include nearly 30 Northwest flights.

From the right side of the plane, the passengers and crew could plainly see the nearest gates, along the C concourse, no more than 400 yards away. Many were occupied; some weren't. Another gate, F-5, was also visible about 900 yards away. It was vacant. A Northwest maintenance hanger was only 250 yards away, visible from the left side of the plane. Capt. Stabler tuned the cockpit radio to Northwest's "gate control," the people who organize the parking of planes. Their message for Flight 1829: "Get in line and expect at least a two-hour wait."

A groan rippled through the cabin as the captain announced the news. "Oh jeez, come on!" passenger Michelle Duran, a 34-year-old computer technician and private pilot from New Baltimore, Mich., said to herself. Flight attendant Ms. Miller overheard a 12-year-old boy tell his brother, "There's no way I'm spending two hours on this airplane."

A 757 cabin is hardly a commodious waiting room. It has a single, narrow aisle that runs 115 feet from the cockpit door to the rear galley. Along the aisle are 35 rows of seats, most of them in the cramped three-and-three layout of economy. The economy seats were 17 inches wide, as narrow as they get on U.S. commercial jet flights. The interior of the aluminum tube—navy-blue carpet and seats, red, gray and dark camel accents and off-white walls and bins—is 7 feet at its highest point, and 11½ feet at its widest. Holding tanks for the plane's four lavatories have a total capacity of 55.5 gallons.

Capt. Stabler shut down the 757's two engines, using auxiliary power to keep the jet heated and well-lighted. He opened the cockpit door and invited passengers to drop in for a tour. Many did. The crew let it be known, discreetly, that passengers could use their cell phones. Normally, airlines prohibit cell phones for fear they will interfere with navigation equipment.

Still, there were early signs of rawness. A half hour into the wait, flight attendant Forbes made an announcement: "Does anyone have any videos in your carry-on luggage?" The 757 has an audio-video system, but, to save money, Northwest no longer shows films on most North American flights. Three tapes were produced: an old *Star Trek* TV episode, *Citizen Kane*, and *The Princess Bride*.

Star Trek went on. It was the one where an enemy device freezes people in time, imprisoning them in an alien dimension. But with no headsets, the audio had to be piped through the plane's public-address system, one volume fits all. A passenger in economy griped loudly to flight attendants that the sound was interfering with her reading. So the tape was yanked, causing a general outcry.

Capt. Miller, the hitchhiking pilot, was off duty but wearing his uniform. Alerted by flight attendants, the 49-year-old pilot, a 15-year Northwest veteran, marched back and demanded to know who didn't want the video shown. No one spoke up. "OK, put the movies back on— as long as they're G-rated," he told the attendants. There were kids back there, Capt. Miller reasoned.

Following *Star Trek* came *Citizen Kane*. It belonged to Jamie Hodari, a 17-year-old Bloomfield Hills high-school junior traveling with his younger sister and two babysitters, and he loved the classic. But after 10 minutes, several passengers started booing, "Who put this goofy movie on?" one demanded. "Who would want to watch a black-and-white movie?" yelled another. *Citizen Kane* got the hook. Jamie marveled to his sister about the spectacle of middle-aged adults "acting like obnoxious kids."

The Princess Bride fared better.

As the two-hour wait slipped into two-and-a-half, the flight attendants had wheeled out the already-depleted beverage carts. They didn't have any pretzels or peanuts to hand out— all the extras had gone off the plane in Tampa. Most passengers remained fairly good-tempered. . . . A 13-year Northwest veteran watched a dentist organize a betting pool: How long would it take to get to the gate? She laughingly declined an invitation to wager. Nearby, a man with a bag of Doritos joked that they were for sale—"$1 each."

Conversations were struck up. Mrs. Ruskin, the guidance counselor, was sitting in Row 5 next to Sonya Friedman, a psychologist, author and television commentator from Bloomfield Hills. Eight other members of the Friedman family were on the flight; Dr. Friedman and Mrs. Ruskin chatted a lot about Mrs. Ruskin's fear of flying. Four 20-something passengers started a stand-up euchre game in front of one of the lavatories. Christina Wade, a 32-year-old real-estate agent from Ann Arbor, Mich., played Scrabble with her husband.

Elsewhere, however, scattered small rebellions were brewing. Initially, the crew refused to serve alcohol. Some people provided their own from bags of duty-free booze from St. Martin. Mr. Forbes, the flight attendant, warned them that it was prohibited. But as time slipped by, Mr. Forbes, 41 and a 19-year veteran, decided to let them drink.

The cabin crew eventually relented and served cocktails to those who wandered into the galleys to ask. But in the economy cabin, they still charged. At around 5 P.M., Dr. Goldstein, the ophthalmologist whose blustering over seats had caused such a stir in St. Martin, headed back for a gin-and-tonic for himself and a beer for his brother-in-law. Mr. Forbes asked for $7.

"I can't believe you're charging for this," Dr. Goldstein spluttered. He paid, but steamed. Eugene Pettis had a similar reaction after being hit up for $3 for a beer. "Come on!" the 67-year-old director of a Detroit mental-health center groused to his seatmates. "The least they could do is give us free drinks."

Exactly, thought his traveling buddy, Leslie McCoy. He went to the galley and asked for a rum and Coke. "I'm not going to pay," he declared. Mr. McCoy, a 33-year-old artist for the Detroit Police Department, got his drink on the house, and another rule went by the wayside.

Time ticked by. Capt. Stabler played the outside man, making announcements and chatting with passengers. He often praised them: "You're being wonderful. You're so calm. We're all stuck in this together," he said over the loudspeaker. Positive reinforcement and a little all-for-one, he thought. Can't hurt.

Capt. Patchett mostly stayed in the cockpit listening to gate radio. The 40-year-old, a 12-year Northwest veteran, helped pass the time by tuning a second radio to the day's pro-football games. Monitoring other pilots talking to—and arguing with—the hapless radio operator for Northwest in Detroit, the flight-deck crew on 1829 could tell things weren't improving. The 757 that was first up for a gate—757s can fit only into certain jetways—hadn't budged for an hour and a half. Flight 1829 was 30th in line.

Suddenly, there was motion. At about 5:30, controllers ordered pilots on the Zulu taxiway to fire up their engines. Some passengers cheered again as the plane shook to life. It taxied north, with a line of other planes. The jet had been moving for five minutes when it bumped to a halt. In Row 8, Scott Friedman, Sonya's son, peered out the window. A collective groan was rising from other passengers. It took a moment for Scott to realize that the plane's little journey had resulted in it ending up almost exactly where it had started.

"What the heck's happening now?" he demanded.

Capt. Miller was asking the question himself up in the cockpit. The maneuver, it turned out, had been meant to let one plane—one plane!—out of the conga line. Capt. Miller, anger rising, broke out his cell phone and dialed Northwest's chief Detroit pilot at the time, Gary Skinner. "It's a nightmare out here," Capt. Miller barked. He handed the phone to Capt. Stabler. "Something has to be done," Capt. Stabler pleaded. But the chief pilot was unable to offer much help. Capt. Stabler phoned Northwest's ground-service duty manager. "We have minimum people working," the manager reported. "Gates are blocked and broken. I'm working with headquarters."

Capt. Miller was thunderstruck. "We have this phenomenal weather department that can forecast turbulence all over the world," he snorted to the other pilots. "Why didn't they see this storm coming?" An idea formed: "Why don't we just turn around and get out of here?"

By now, more than three hours into the wait, many passengers were having similar thoughts. Stephen London, a Toronto software engineer, kept looking at the terminal, tauntingly close, and the Northwest hangar even closer. "Bring the stairs," he said to himself. "Bring the bus. Dump the people."

The trapped pilots, in fact, were suggesting various avenues of escape. One was to concentrate what ground workers there were on just a few gates, pull the planes in, let the people off, and back the planes out again, with crew and luggage still aboard. They thought of using the nearby hangars, and of using other airlines' gates. "Forget protocol," Capt. Stabler urged over gate radio.

But ground control would not authorize any of the moves. (Northwest says it considered these options and others. It says they were too dangerous—it had stopped snowing but the cold, wind and ice were fierce—or [the equipment] were otherwise unworkable.) Time after time, Capt. Stabler heard the radio operator reply, "We're working on it. Copy that." After Flight 1829 had been stalled for about four hours, Capt. Patchett heard the pilot of another plane announce that a passenger was headed for diabetic shock in an hour. The response: "Roger that."

Tempers were flaring on some of the tarmac-bound planes. A pilot of a Northwest Airbus burst on to the radio, hollering, "I'm about to lose control of the passengers!" In the cabin of Flight 1829, the mood also was souring. The movies were long over. The beverages were almost gone. There was no more airline food. It had gotten dark. The windchill factor outside was more than 20 below.

Rumors began washing over the now-dim cabin. A baby had been born on one plane; a man had died of a heart attack on another; on another, passengers had gone berserk and were tearing each other and the crew apart. Arielle Hodari, Jamie's 15-year-old sister, felt a surge of dread when she heard the rumors. "I'm scared," Arielle told her babysitter, sitting across the aisle in Row 15. "Is it true?" Her babysitter shrugged; she didn't know.

Hunger and thirst intensified, presenting many dilemmas. Mr. Post, the newlywed, knew his wife had some M&Ms, but she was reluctant to open them while other people around her had nothing. Go ahead, eat them, he urged quietly: "You can't share them with everybody."

Arielle unearthed a small box of Frosted Flakes in her backpack and jubilantly announced the find to her babysitter. "I'd eat them in the bathroom if I were you," her babysitter said softly. Arielle was scared again. She scooted to the lavatory and ate the cereal.

Nicotine cravings weren't helping matters, and some people sneaked into the lavatories for a smoke. Mr. Forbes, the flight attendant, didn't bother trying to stop them. Passengers could smell cigarettes, and the smoke alarms were beeping intermittently. Nobody complained.

The wait stretched on. The cabin seemed to shrink. Mr. Pettis, the clinic director, was trying to read Toni Morrison's *Beloved* but couldn't concentrate. Babies were crying. The children behind him kept kicking his seat, and when he asked their mother to make them stop, she flared up. "If you move your seat up, it will stop," she snapped.

It was past 7 P.M. now, and even the flight attendants' reserves of cool were ebbing. Ms. Ward, on top of everything else, worried about her own 17-year-old daughter, home alone in the blizzard. Ms. Ward, a 28-year veteran, was tiring of the cascading passenger complaints.

"There are worse scenarios, folks," she told several complainers. "We didn't land in the Andes. No one has to eat each other."

It didn't seem to soothe anybody. By 7:45, five hours into the wait, Capt. Stabler phoned the Northwest duty manager he had called a couple of hours before—and even the captain's studied control showed cracks. "People are starting to lose their composure here," he yelled at the manager. "People are really irate. I'm afraid somebody will make a panic evacuation."

The manager was unmoved. "You should see what it's like in the terminal," he said. "There are thousands of people in here. There are fistfights. The airport police are arresting people." (Airport officials say there were no arrests that weekend.)

The unraveling of Flight 1829 was picking up pace. Capt. Stabler could feel the situation shifting into what he told himself was a "psychological and emotional dance." People were out of baby formula, out of diapers. Things were happening all at once. A man in first class began hyperventilating. A young woman in coach whimpered that she was having a heart attack. Scott Friedman, a physician, treated the woman—by pointing out that her arm had fallen asleep, which explained the tingling. "Just shake your arm," he prescribed.

At about the same time in the rear of the plane, Mr. Forbes, the attendant, was informed that the left lavatory in coach, behind row 26 near door 3A, appeared to be clogged. He could see blue fluid lapping up into the bowl. Mr. Forbes wrapped a garbage bag around his arm and used a rolled-up plastic safety placard to plunge the toilet. He determined that its waste-holding tank was full, but didn't block off the door because the toilet itself seemed to continue receiving waste.

Just as he emerged from the lavatory, a man in his 50s assailed him. "If I were in charge of the situation, I would have us at the gate!" the man yelled, jutting his face close to Mr. Forbes. The stress, the man continued, wasn't helping his heart condition; he needed to see the pilot. Mr. Forbes walked him toward the cockpit. "Heads up," Ms. Ward warned Capt. Stabler from her position in the first-class galley. "Here he comes."

Capt. Stabler intercepted the man in the galley. "I'm a stent patient," the man bellowed. "What if I start having trouble?" He began to cry. "What would it take to get us off this airplane?"

Capt. Stabler took the man's hand. "I understand why you feel provoked," he said.

"If we had a medical emergency, that may move us to the head of the line," the man sobbed.

"It really has to be an authentic problem for us to declare that," the captain said.

"I'll do it if it will get us off the airplane," said the sobbing man.

Ms. Ward, standing beside the captain, observed that feigning a medical emergency "will be a federal offense. There are stiff penalties."

EXHIBIT 2

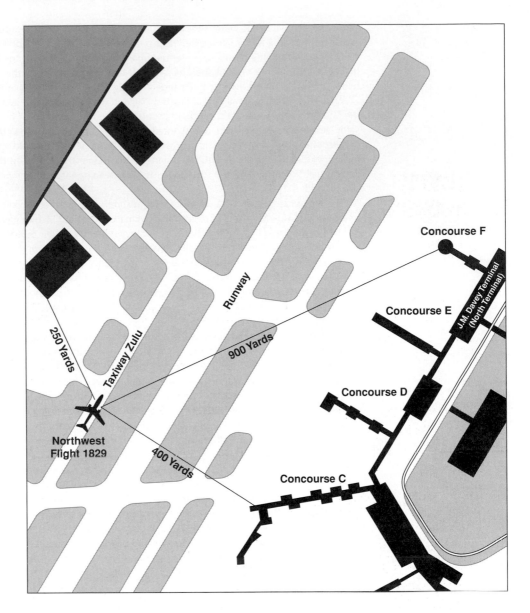

The man sniffled, and slunk to his seat.

He had hardly settled in when Sharon Friedman, Sonya Friedman's daughter, had her own crisis. A flight attendant had mentioned that the scene inside the terminal was like "a refugee camp." Something about that image got to Sharon, a 41-year-old psychologist and lawyer. She walked forward into first class, leaned her head into the cabin wall and cried. Her husband approached with their five-year-old son, Gordon, but she shooed them away.

It was about 8:15. Flight 1829 had been on the ground for 5½ hours.

The 60 gallons of potable water on the plane had almost run out, including the water to the lavatory sinks. The plane had long since begun to smell: a mix of used diapers, dirty clothes and sweat. Mrs. Ruskin, the guidance counselor, thought of it as "the odor of being confined."

There was another odor. The lavatory holding tanks had reached their 55.5 gallon capacity. Mr. Pettis, the clinic director, in seat 32C near the back of the plane, had gone into the right rear lavatory about an hour earlier—and immediately turned around, repulsed:

There were empty beer cans in the sink, the bowl was backed up, the trash bins were stuffed with diapers. Now, he detected a thin stream of sewage oozing from under the door of that lavatory.

"Now we have a health hazard," he blurted to flight attendant Ms. March. She agreed: "These toilets are disgusting." From then on, every time someone emerged from any of the three rear lavatories, a chorus rang out from nearby passengers:

"Close the door! It stinks!"

The five or six lawyers on board were fast becoming the most popular passengers, as others quizzed them about the possibility of a lawsuit. Mr. London, the passenger from Toronto, found one attorney who figured there might be a case against the airline for "false imprisonment." Seizing the moment, Mr. London, 32, circulated a notebook through the cabin. Gathering that it was from a lawyer enlisting clients, more than 50 passengers signed up on behalf of themselves and their families.

In 32D, Mr. McCoy, the police artist, was starting to lose his grip. "I've wasted almost two days of my vacation on an airplane with a bunch of crying-ass kids and big fat people I don't know," he thought to himself. A woman sitting behind him began carping about how much she wanted off. Mr. McCoy exploded.

"I'm sick of sitting on this goddamn plane!" he shouted. "I watched the sun go down and I'm still sitting in this little chair."

Two rows forward, a man swiveled and ordered Mr. McCoy to watch his language. "Don't tell me what to do!" the police artist roared. "I'm a grown man. I'm going to cuss as much as I goddamn please. If you don't like it, get me off this f—— plane."

As the two men argued, Ms. Ward, the lead attendant, hurried all the way back from first class. "I don't appreciate this," she told Mr. McCoy. He backed off.

More passengers were complaining about hunger. Ms. Ward gave away her own instant oatmeal, and used the last of the hot water to mix it. She gave it to a mother with a wailing baby. Another mom, sitting in the back of economy, demanded to see Ms. Ward.

"What are you going to do about feeding my children?" she huffed. "Get some food from the terminal!"

"We can't," Ms. Ward replied. "Besides, there's no food in the terminal." Galled, she marched to the cockpit and related the conversation to the pilots. They eyed their own leftovers from lunch. "We haven't touched these sandwiches, but they're ice cold," Capt. Stabler said. Ms. Ward bagged them up and returned to the passenger.

"Ma'am, this is what we're doing about feeding your children," she said, thrusting the sack at the woman. (Later, Ms. Ward would notice that the bag had never been opened.)

Sharon Friedman had settled down since her tears, but she faced a new quandary. Her five-year-old boy was thirsty. But she was holding back the one remaining bottle of water she had in case she ran out of formula for her three-month-old daughter, Shayna. It hurt to deprive one child over the other. But Ms. Friedman now feared that they would have to spend the night on the plane.

Her sister-in-law, Amy Friedman, Scott's wife, also had an infant, seven-month-old Madison. She had enough formula for one more bottle and she had two diapers. When another mom asked her for a diaper, Amy turned her down. The guilt stung.

By now, flight attendants were about as fed up as anyone, and they took an unauthorized emergency step: They started encouraging passengers to send letters of complaint to John Dasburg, Northwest's chief executive. "Do it for your peace of mind," Ms. Ward told some passengers. One attendant held up the in-flight magazine, open to page 4, pointing to Mr. Dasburg's picture and his letter to customers. It touted Northwest's "wide range of new benefits" and closed, "Have a Happy New Year." Another attendant urged Ms. Duran, the private pilot, "Write and tell him what a chicken-s—— operation we're running."

Dr. Goldstein, the ophthalmologist, wasn't impressed. "I don't think Dasburg knows or cares what's going on in Detroit," he told his wife, Diane. "I want to talk to him."

The Goldsteins figured Mr. Dasburg must live in one of the nicer suburbs of Minneapolis. Mrs. Goldstein's uncle lives in one of those suburbs, Edina, Minn. They called Edina directory assistance on their cell phone. To their amazement, they found a listing.

The doctor dialed at once and got Mary Lou Dasburg, the CEO's wife, who said her husband wasn't at home. "I'm currently on one of your husband's planes in Detroit," Dr. Goldstein, 35, said. "There are 30 planes on the ground here. He needs to know." As the two talked, passengers in nearby rows leaned in to listen. According to Dr. Goldstein, Mrs. Dasburg promised to call flight operations herself to find out what was going on. (Mrs. Dasburg confirms the call.)

In Row 9, Seat D, Christina Wade, the real-estate agent, had been growing increasingly anxious. She was obsessing on the obvious fact that few planes were moving. She'd had a couple of Bacardi and orange juices. She snapped.

"I've had enough of this!" she screamed. "I have to get off this plane. I'm going to open this door!" Crying hysterically, she put on a cashmere pants-and-sweater set over her shorts and T-shirt and gathered a credit card, her cigarettes, and her cell phone. She prepared to pull the emergency-exit lever next to her seat and leap into the night.

"No, don't do it!" her husband, John, urged. "No! No!" some passengers pleaded. Others made plans to follow her out the door.

Flight attendants positioned themselves in front of the exits, and warned that bailing out would be hazardous and illegal. "An FBI holding cell would be nicer than this plane," Ms. Wade snapped.

"How about a Valium?" Ms. Ward said. She knew that some of the physicians on the plane had some of the tranquilizers. "I can get you a Valium."

"I don't want a Valium!" Ms. Wade roared. "Get me off this f—— plane! I'm jumping!"

Capt. Stabler heard the uproar and raced back from the cockpit. He knelt in front of Ms. Wade, touching her shoulder. "Really, we don't want to open any doors," he said.

Ms. Wade curled up in a ball on the floor next to the emergency exit and wept.

John Wade, 31, tried to lift his wife back into her seat. "Honey, please get out of that corner," he implored. "It's making you claustrophobic."

She went on, but finally was coaxed back into her seat. Capt. Stabler returned to the cockpit. But Ms. Wade, terror rising again, quickly resolved anew to bail out. She knew pulling the emergency lever would deploy the emergency slide; she figured she could handle the 20-foot drop to the tarmac.

Ms. Wade's sister was also on the plane. Christina walked back to her and simply announced, "I'm going to jump." Christina went back to her seat—and began loudly setting deadlines: "If we're not moving in 15 minutes, I'm gonna open the door!" By now, her husband was blocking the exit nearest her, while flight attendant O'Keefe guarded the one across the aisle.

Only Scott Friedman seemed to get through to her. Sitting a row ahead of Ms. Wade, the 37-year-old dermatologist pleaded, "I've got a baby. It's 23 degrees below zero. Once the cabin temperature equalizes, what am I going to do with my baby?" . . .

It went on, and it made for macabre theater. . . . Meanwhile, word of Dr. Goldstein's call to Minnesota had spread. Ms. Ward heard about it and headed straight to the cockpit.

"Somebody back there just talked to Mrs. Dasburg," she told Capt. Stabler.

His eyes widened. "How? I want to talk to him."

Dr. Goldstein was summoned to the cockpit. His stomach tightened. There was probably some rule against calling the chief executive's wife. Capt. Stabler asked what he had done. "I called Dasburg's house," he confessed. "His wife said he wasn't home."

"Fantastic," the captain exclaimed. "Give us that number."

Capt. Stabler dialed quickly on Capt. Miller's cell phone. It was past 9 P.M. and the plane had been pinned for more than six hours. Mr. Dasburg himself answered.

"We're out of food, out of water," Capt. Stabler informed his boss. The captain's voice was steely, commanding. "Lavatories aren't functioning. We've got a passenger threatening to pop the chute. It's minus-30 windchill. There are active taxiways. It would make a very bad news story for Northwest. You've got to do something."

Capt. Stabler got the impression that, despite the many planes' hours-long ordeal in Detroit, Mr. Dasburg did not know how critical things were. The captain elaborated. He felt that if a door opened, there would be 50 people out on the frozen runway. According to

Capt. Stabler, Mr. Dasburg replied, "This should never have happened to you guys. We'll get you out of it right now."

Mr. Dasburg, 56, and Northwest decline to comment on any phone conversations. Northwest says "senior executives" were well aware of the crisis.

Capt. Stabler quickly got on the gate radio and told the other stranded pilots, "I have just talked to John Dasburg and something is going to get done." He also told his passengers, "We've called the top dog," he said. "Hopefully, something will get done."

Few in the cabin seemed to believe it. But 20 minutes later, at 9:25, gate radio cracked. "1829? Do you have direct access to Fox 5?" That would be F-5, the gate that had been empty for hours. Capt. Stabler had asked several times if he could dock there, but had been told by ground control that the jetway was malfunctioning. (Northwest says it was never broken, but that the path to it had been blocked by another plane, a contention disputed by Flight 1829's pilots.)

The captain cranked up the engines and eased the plane into motion. Suddenly, gate radio exploded with complaints from other pilots: "Why does he get that gate? We've been waiting longer!" . . .

The jet was towed into the angled parking spot, and ground workers dug out snow from the jetway wheels and stairs. After a few false starts, Flight 1829 docked. The door opened. Capt. Stabler made his final announcement: "I sincerely apologize. There were decisions that weren't made, and improper decisions. We have a great group of passengers."

The passengers, numb and exhausted, moved slowly. Many stopped by the cockpit to thank the pilots and shake their hands. But First Officer Patchett thought a few flashed "the look of death."

It was 9:42. They had been on the tarmac for 6 hours and 57 minutes. . . .

In the crowded, trash-strewn terminal, Ms. Wade told Scott and Amy Friedman that she hadn't blown the door because of their baby. Mr. McCoy apologized to the man he had cursed. Mr. London ran back onto the plane to retrieve his wife's purse, and decided to snap a few photos of a trashed lavatory. Others vowed lawsuits, and indeed, one of the Flight 1829 passengers who signed Mr. London's list, Tim Koczara, a builder from Grosse Pointe Woods, Mich., later became the first named plaintiff in a suit filed by Detroit law firm Charfoos & Christensen against Northwest and other defendants.

Capt. Stabler walked purposefully to the Northwest gate-control office to try to talk to the manager he had yelled at hours before. But there were 20 people buzzing around; the crisis was still on. The captain went home.

It was 10 P.M. Out on the tarmac, five other planes still waited.

PART II

U.S. Congressman John D. Dingell heard about the problems in Detroit that Sunday and asked the Department of Transportation, which has regulatory oversight of U.S. airlines, to prepare a report. Portions of that report[3] are reproduced below.

Introduction

This Report can be summarized as follows:

- Saturday's ground delays were largely a result of the decision by Northwest's operations planners . . . to continue limited operations at Detroit well after other airlines had canceled their flights for the day because of the snowstorm. As the snow worsened, flight departures were increasingly delayed because of rapid snow accumulation, drifting snow, and de-icing difficulties. When Northwest finally shut down its Detroit operations, a dozen

---

[3] "Report on the January 1999 Detroit Snowstorm," submitted to the Honorable John D. Dingell, United States House of Representatives, by The Secretary of the Department of Transportation, June 1999.

of its aircraft were still waiting to take off and, at the height of the storm, were forced to make their way back to a terminal with limited gate availability.

- On Sunday, a lack of clear and coordinated communications between Northwest's operations planners in Minneapolis and Northwest's management in Detroit prevented the operations planners from realizing that Northwest's Detroit terminal could not accommodate even the limited number of arrivals scheduled for Sunday. . . .
- While Northwest's Detroit employees worked very hard in attempting to prepare the airport for Sunday operations, they were so preoccupied with "putting out fires" that they failed to recognize and communicate the overall severity and implications of the problems they faced throughout the day. Had Northwest had a snow emergency plan for Detroit . . . then the planners would have received a more accurate assessment of that progress and would likely have implemented a more conservative Sunday arrival schedule.
- Both Northwest and the Wayne County Department of Airports could have improved snow removal and aircraft positioning efforts, and thus helped mitigate ground delays, through formal communications channels. . . .
- Northwest failed to anticipate the severity of the flight crew shortage at Detroit on Sunday. The shortage was caused by a number of factors, including difficulties in getting to the airport terminal and the overloading of the airline's various automated crew communication and scheduling systems. Without sufficient crews, Northwest could not launch enough aircraft from Detroit to free sufficient gates to deplane passengers on incoming flights in a timely manner.
- Northwest's efforts to deplane stranded passengers were hindered by the lack of a contingency plan for the storm's effects on gates and taxiways. Attempts to secure unused gates of other airlines were not well coordinated: although one airline, Continental, provided an unused gate for Northwest's use, other airlines indicated that Northwest either did not ask them for use of their gates or, when it did ask, that their gates were occupied or about to be occupied. The lack of such a plan also contributed to Northwest's inability to deplane passengers with mobile or integrated aircraft stairs or to provide stranded aircraft with remote lavatory and catering services.

The Federal Aviation Administration has determined that neither the airport nor any air carrier serving Detroit violated Federal Aviation Regulations in their handling of the January 2–3 Detroit snowstorm. It is also important to note that even some of the angriest complaint letters received by the Department from passengers who experienced ground delays complimented the fine performance of Northwest's flight crews. However, notwithstanding the often exceptional efforts of those crews, conditions on many of the aircraft stranded on the airport's taxiways were severe enough to have jeopardized passengers' well-being. These conditions included a shortage or complete lack of food, beverages, and water, and nonfunctioning lavatories. Conditions were particularly difficult for persons traveling with infants in need of formula or for persons with certain medical conditions. At least two individuals required emergency treatment [for diabetic shock and cardiac arrest symptoms] by paramedics brought to the aircraft, and others were assisted by doctors already on board the aircraft. While these cases represented only a small percentage of the total number of passengers stranded by ground delays, they were serious and indicate important implications for passenger safety. Moreover, even if the well-being of passengers had not been an issue, the review team believes that the stranding of passengers on aircraft queued on taxiways for up to 8½ hours invites more serious problems and is simply unacceptable. *None of the other airlines serving Detroit experienced ground delays approaching the magnitude of Northwest's delays.* [Emphasis added.]

In understanding the events detailed in this Report, it is important to recognize the various roles and responsibilities [of the different parties involved]. . . . The airport is responsible for the operating condition of the airport, including snow removal, and determines when a runway or taxiway must be closed. The Federal Aviation Administration . . . is responsible for the safe and efficient management of air traffic while air-craft are en route. . . . [I]ndividual airlines are responsible for managing disruptions to their schedules at particular airports. The airlines decide what flights to operate and have exclusive responsibility for canceling specific flights. . . .

Wayne County Detroit Metropolitan Airport and NWA

DTW is operated by the Wayne County Department of Airports and is the largest of NWA's three major air travel hubs. NWA's flight operations at DTW are typical of any major airline's at one of its hub airports. Several times each day, large numbers, or "banks," of NWA aircraft flying domestic and international routes arrive within a short period of time and deplane their passengers, many of whom board NWA connecting flights for their ultimate destinations. After one bank of aircraft has arrived and departed, the new bank soon follows. These banks of aircraft have use of 60 NWA gates at DTW, although not all of these gates can accommodate all seven aircraft types flown by NWA. (NWA operates all seven types through DTW.) . . . In 1998, NWA's flights accounted for approximately 57% of DTW's total scheduled passenger operations.

An aspect of DTW that is important to a discussion of the impact of the snowstorm is its gate configuration. . . . [D]omestic gates are grouped in seven piers that extend out from the main terminal buildings. The areas between the piers housing NWA's gates . . . known as "alleys," are among the narrowest at any U.S. airport. Even in good weather conditions, aircraft congestion in these alleys can cause arrival and departure delays for NWA. These narrow alleys are particularly ill-suited for operations during and after a snowstorm.

NWA's Operations Planning

NWA's daily operations are planned and controlled by the groups that comprise Systems Operations Control ("SOC"). An SOC Director ensures that the SOC groups act as a coordinated team. . . . During a snowstorm, the SOC Operations Planners . . . receive data from each of these departments and from the airports served by NWA, and are responsible for monitoring and coordinating NWA's response to schedule problems and any other potential problems.

Friday, January 1

A description of the January 2 snowstorm, its impact on the airport and NWA's operations, and NWA's response to it must begin with NWA's planning for the storm on January 1. At noon on that day, NWA's meteorologists predicted that light snow would begin falling at DTW on Saturday morning, with accumulations of one to three inches possible. Accumulations of 8 to 10 inches were predicted by midnight, followed by additional precipitation in the form of snow and sleet from 4:00 A.M. to 8:00 A.M. Sunday, changing to freezing rain or rain after that. This weather forecast prompted a decision at a 2:00 P.M. conference call to reduce the number of arrival/departure combinations at DTW on Saturday afternoon by 50 flights. NWA's meteorologists issued a less severe weather forecast for DTW on Friday night, but NWA did not change its flight-thinning plan.

Saturday, January 2

. . . NWA experienced no major operational problems that morning. At 12:15 P.M., NWA's meteorologists predicted a snowfall rate that afternoon of up to two inches per hour. Every other airline had already canceled their afternoon and evening flights in and out of DTW. In many cases they had done so the day before. NWA, however, did not cancel its flights.

At 1:00 P.M. on Saturday, the NWA SOC Director, located at NWA headquarters in Minneapolis, was asked by the NWA Control Center Manager at DTW to further trim afternoon arrivals in light of deteriorating weather conditions in Detroit. One half-hour later, NWA's Chief Dispatcher, also located at NWA headquarters in Minneapolis, suggested that . . . the conditions were bad enough to justify a shutdown of NWA's operations. . . . Given that conditions were still above legal minimums, however, the SOC Director decided that NWA's operations at Detroit should continue, although he did reduce the number of arrivals from 39 to 25 per bank.

By 2:00 P.M. on Saturday, the snowfall and the winds had intensified. . . . At 3:30 P.M., the NWA Control Center Manager at DTW advised the SOC Director that more arrival thinning was required because they only had sufficient gate availability for 13 more flights. When the SOC Director determined that this count included aircraft still queued for departure at the remote de-icing pad, he ordered a "ground stop" that halted all remaining flights bound for DTW that were still on the ground. In addition, he began diverting flights that were already on their way. The last NWA arrival of the day landed at 4:46 P.M., nearly five hours after all other airlines had canceled their DTW flights.

. . . Shortly before 6:00 P.M., the ground stop halting all NWA flights bound for DTW was extended to 8:00 P.M., but NWA hoped that departures would continue, freeing gates currently in use. At 6:40 P.M., however, the NWA Control Center Manager at DTW asked the SOC Director to shut down NWA's DTW operations until at least noon on Sunday. At 7:00 P.M., a dozen NWA aircraft were still queued for pre-takeoff remote de-icing when de-icing crews working one of those aircraft found that ice was reforming before they could complete de-icing the aircraft. The de-icing crews gave up, and the 12 aircraft headed back to the terminal to deplane passengers as gates became available. All NWA flights to and from DTW were canceled for the rest of the night. In addition, virtually all of Sunday morning's flights and approximately 90% of all Sunday's flights were ultimately canceled. Dry blowing snow drifting up to two feet covered open taxiways. At the gates, frozen jet bridges started going out of service. Passengers on the last of the 12 aircraft that had been queued for de-icing and departure in the storm were not unloaded until early Sunday morning. Estimates of the number of people who were forced to sleep in the airport terminal overnight ranged between 1,000 and 3,500.

After passengers were deplaned, NWA had to move many of its aircraft to clear gates for additional aircraft. It moved 15 of those aircraft to the center of three of its terminal alleys because weather conditions made it unsafe to taxi or tow the aircraft to a hanger or other remote parking area. NWA would normally store its baggage carts overnight at empty gates, but because on Saturday night virtually every gate was occupied by aircraft, NWA moved many of its baggage carts to the alley between piers C and D.

Overall, on Saturday there were 444 total operations at DTW, of which 249 were arrivals and 195 were departures. As the storm increased in intensity, 28 NWA flights scheduled to depart from DTW experienced ground delays because of snow accumulation at the remote de-icing facility and the inability to de-ice. As noted above, some of these flights were ultimately canceled and forced to return to the terminal, thus adding to NWA's ground delays. These NWA departure delays are summarized as follows:

NWA *Departure* Ground Delays on Saturday, January 2, 1999

Hours of Delay	No. of Flights	Estimated No. of Passengers
9+	3	240
8–9	4	320
7–8	2	160
6–7	0	0
5–6	1	80
4–5	1	80
3–4	5	400
2–3	1	80
1–2	4	320
<1	7	560
TOTAL	28	2,240

On Saturday, there were 116 NWA arrivals. The arrival delays for these NWA flights are summarized as follows:

NWA *Arrival* Ground Delays on Saturday, January 2, 1999

Hours of Delay	No. of Flights	Estimated No. of Passengers
4+	1	80
3–4	1	80
2–3	3	240
1–2	16	1,280
<1	66	5,280
On time	29	2,320
TOTAL	116	9,280

Sunday, January 3

. . . Wayne County Department of Airports snow removal crews worked through the night plowing runways and taxiways. Alley entrances had been plowed, as had alleys used by other airlines serving DTW, but several NWA alleys could not be plowed because they were clogged with parked aircraft and baggage carts. . . . NWA Maintenance ("Maintenance") which was nearly 100% staffed, committed to tow the aircraft from the alleys by 10:00 A.M. Despite a number of assurances that this could be done, at 8:55 A.M. Maintenance informed the NWA Control Center Manager that they would "do what we can" about moving the aircraft parked in the alleys. At 11:15 A.M., they reported that the aircraft could not be moved because alleys needed plowing. (It should be noted that the SOC Director did not recall a conversation with NWA DTW personnel at 10:40 A.M. in which he was supposedly told to "shut it down, nothing's moving.")

At approximately noon on Sunday, when the first NWA departures from DTW were to have resumed, the SOC Director became concerned that no aircraft were leaving the gates. Over the next hour, he was first told by NWA's Detroit control center that the effort to launch departures "is going, but really slow" and then, 20 minutes later, told that the "Aircraft aren't going anywhere." By 1:00 P.M., the SOC Director learned that ramps and alleys around the terminal piers were not plowed, that far fewer flight crews than had been estimated were available to operate departing flights, and that ground personnel staffing levels (other than Maintenance personnel) were at less than 50%. At 1:00 P.M., the SOC Director advised the Chief Dispatcher to cancel any departing flights that would arrive at DTW before 3:30 P.M., although flights that were already en route, including those that had already taxied away from their gates at their originating airports, could continue to DTW.

. . . At 1:45 P.M., the SOC Director advised the Chief Dispatcher to hold all flights scheduled to depart for DTW until further notice because gates would not be available for at least another hour.

By 2:00 P.M. on Sunday, NWA's various automated crew communication and scheduling systems were becoming overloaded by the high volume of calls from delayed or stranded flight crew members, creating additional impediments to getting proper crews to flights waiting to depart DTW. Meanwhile, some arriving NWA aircraft were having difficulties negotiating taxiways. During the afternoon, a 747's engine hit three snowbanks and a number of aircraft skidded on ice, in some cases blocking alleys until they could be towed. High winds continued throughout the day, causing drifts and below-zero wind chills. Several jet bridges went out of service.

At 3:40 P.M. on Sunday, the SOC Director requested a national ground stop of flights scheduled to depart for DTW until at least 5:30 P.M. because of the continued shortage of gates. This ground stop was subsequently extended until 6:10 P.M., and again until 1:00 A.M. on Monday . . .

Passengers reported that the conditions on the aircraft stranded for longer periods were dreadful. Few aircraft had any food on board and those that did had only peanuts and pretzels. Beverages, or at least water, were available on most, but not all, flights, and some eventually ran out. Some aircraft lavatory tanks filled up and, in some cases, overflowed, leaving passengers without functioning lavatories for up to four hours and creating foul odors in the affected aircraft cabins. NWA was able to arrange remote lavatory servicing for three aircraft. Flight crews were generally polite throughout the ordeal and passed on what information they could to passengers, although this information was sometimes incomplete or incorrect. The latter reportedly included statements that FAA regulations precluded beverage service or remote deplaning, or that the FAA's air traffic control tower was denying planes access to gates. . . .

At 7:15 P.M. on Sunday, NWA canceled all flights to DTW for the rest of the evening with the exception of the three DTW-bound flights that had been diverted to Minneapolis.

In summary, there were 398 total operations at DTW on Sunday, of which 223 were arrivals and 175 were departures. Of the arrivals, only 39 were NWA flights. The following charts summarize the ground delays experienced by those NWA flights:

NWA *Arrival* Ground Delays Experienced on Sunday, January 3, 1999

Hours of Delay	No. of Flights	Estimated No. of Passengers
8+	4	320
7–8	5	400
6–7	4	320
5–6	3	240
4–5	2	160
3–4	8	640
2–3	4	320
1–2	5	400
<1	4	320
TOTAL	39	3,120

There were 122 NWA departure delays or cancellations after gate departure on Sunday. They are summarized as follows:

NWA *Departure* Ground Delays Experienced on Sunday, January 3, 1999

Hours of Delay	No. of Flights	Estimated No. of Passengers
8+	4	320
7–8	0	0
6–7	6	480
5–6	3	240
4–5	6	480
3–4	9	720
2–3	11	880
1–2	17	1,360
<1	66	5,280
TOTAL	122	9,760

Sunday Ground and Flight Crew Staffing Levels, and NWA's Treatment of Passengers

- Although it had stopped snowing at approximately 6:00 A.M. Sunday, partially plowed and unplowed streets and highways, bitter cold temperatures, high winds, and drifting snow made travel to the airport difficult. Heavy traffic and partially unplowed roads and parking lots hampered entry to the airport itself.

- NWA's overall Sunday staffing at DTW was less than 50% in the morning, increasing to about 66% through the afternoon. NWA's Maintenance Department, the group assigned NWA's snow removal responsibilities, was almost fully staffed on Sunday due to the fact that the midnight maintenance shift was held over Sunday morning and that many maintenance employees drive four-wheel vehicles and thus did not have as difficult a time driving to work on Sunday. NWA management in Detroit indicated that it had sufficient ground personnel to handle the number of departures or movements of empty aircraft from gates that would have been necessary to allow the timely deplaning of passengers on arriving aircraft.

- Wayne County Department of Airports had 98% staffing on Sunday. . . . Many Wayne County Department of Airports employees reported to work even though it was their day off. Lack of staff did not hinder Wayne County Department of Airports's Sunday operations. Wayne County Department of Airports booked hotel space for employees so they would not need to make difficult trips to and from the airport.

- Most other airlines serving DTW had close to 100% staffing once they restarted their operations on Sunday. . . . Most of these airlines booked hotel space for employees so they would not need to make difficult trips to and from the airport, but none of these airlines indicated that the availability of these hotel rooms was critical to maintaining adequate staffing levels that weekend.

- Approximately 70% of the NWA flight crew members who are based in Detroit do not live there and therefore must commute to Detroit from other cities, usually on NWA flights. Some of these crews were unable to get to Detroit as planned on Saturday. Others were stranded on Sunday arrivals that sat for hours on taxiways waiting for gates to clear. In one case, a flight carrying a number of flight crews from Minneapolis was assigned a gate only after a member of one of those crews used his cellphone to call a dispatcher in Minneapolis and advise him of the situation. Because of poor road conditions, many hotels in the area were not running their airport shuttles, thus stranding crews staying at those hotels. Crews that were able to make it to the airport were not necessarily qualified on the types of aircraft that were scheduled to depart.

- NWA's various automated crew communication and scheduling systems were overloaded and in many cases rendered ineffective. Crew Schedulers and Crew Coordinators were so overwhelmed by the flight crew call volume that they were unable to pass crew availability information on to Operations Planners. Many crew members could not get through to Coordinators and Schedulers to report their status, and they eventually stopped trying. Operations Planners were unable to work with Crew Coordinators because they were taking calls directly form crews. Scheduling and coordination problems created by these circumstances exacerbated crew shortages.

- . . . [M]any passengers interviewed by DOT stated that when they finally deplaned and sought out their baggage on Sunday night, there were few, if any, NWA personnel to be found in a terminal environment that was characterized as "a zoo," lacking any organization whatsoever. Some passengers who were assisted by NWA personnel thought they were doing the best they could under the circumstances, while others stated that NWA personnel were "clueless" and "couldn't have cared less." The latter type of observation was also made by passengers who were returned to the terminal on Saturday night.

- Many NWA managers interviewed by the review team unequivocally agreed that ground delays of the length experienced on the first weekend of January are unacceptable from a customer service standpoint. . . . It should also be noted, however, that some NWA executives interviewed minimized the impact of the long ground delays. One NWA executive suggested that experiencing these delays, which resulted in passengers spending up to 8½ hours in a confined space at times without food, lavatories, and, in some cases, water, was no worse than being diverted to another airport and being forced to sleep in a terminal. Another observed that many NWA customers pay considerable sums to sit in their aircraft for as many as 13 hours on nonstop flights from the United States to Asia, implying that passengers' experiences at DTW were somehow comparable. Some also stated that the remedial measures that NWA has implemented or is contemplating are to correct "errors on the margin" and would not necessarily prevent a recurrence of lengthy passenger strandings.

- One airline, Continental, provided an unused gate for NWA's use at NWA's request. NWA deplaned passengers from three flights at this gate. Other airlines indicated that NWA either did not ask them for use of their gates or that when NWA did ask, their gates were not available because they were occupied or about to be occupied by their own aircraft. All of the airlines that NWA did not ask for gates stated that they would have made unused gates available had NWA asked. Only one airline, US Airways, declined to offer an available gate when asked for fear that NWA would not be able to move its aircraft from the gate once passengers had deplaned. The other airlines were not aware of NWA's stranded passenger situation until NWA contacted them about the use of their gates. . . .

- NWA considered and rejected twice using the integrated stairs on some of its aircraft to deplane passengers away from the gates into waiting car rental company buses that had been requisitioned by Wayne County Department of Airports per Wayne County Department of Airports's contract with those companies. It was NWA's ultimate judgment, including that of a veteran NWA de-icing manager, that it was too cold, windy, and icy on Sunday to safely deplane passengers in this manner.

Representatives from every other airline interviewed stated that they would have found a way to safely accomplish remote deplaning to avoid stranding passengers on their aircraft for up to 8½ hours. Moreover, NWA's own irregular operations plan for its Minneapolis hub includes stair deplaning procedures. And at DTW that Sunday, Spirit Airlines did in fact safely deplane passengers using the integrated stairs on one of its DC-9 aircraft, which are similar to the DC-9s flown by NWA. That deplaning occurred in Spirit's hangar, with passengers being taken into waiting rental car company buses and then to the terminal. . . .

With respect to its aircraft lacking integrated stairs, NWA understandably rejected the use of relatively unstable maintenance stairs, the only type of mobile stairs they owned, but apparently did not consider borrowing the appropriate mobile passenger stairs from another airline. . . .

Case **4**

ERNST & YOUNG LLP— THE EVOLUTION OF A REVOLUTIONARY IDEA ERNIE®: ERNST & YOUNG'S ONLINE CONSULTING SERVICE

This Best Practice Case Study explores the development of Ernie, Ernst & Young's innovative online consulting service. In examining this unique service, this case study details the complete product development process, as well as the ongoing marketing strategies that have contributed to the success and growth of this service offering.

ITSMA has selected Ernie and Ernst & Young LLP as a Best Practice Case Study for several reasons: First, Ernie is the first example of a professional services firm launching an Internet-based service offering. The uniqueness of this example makes it worthy of close examination. Second, the unique product development methodology utilized by Ernst & Young to design, launch, and introduce Ernie ensured that it could flourish both outside of its traditional development channels and within the unique business conditions of the Internet. Third, as ITSMA continues to explore the new product development processes of IT services firms, this case study provides many interesting lessons.

BACKGROUND

Ernst & Young LLP is a leading professional services firm with worldwide revenues of $9.1 billion that employs more than 80,000 people in 130 countries. In the United States, revenues exceed $4.4 billion, and it is the fastest growing of the Big Five firms in the United States (growing at just over 23 percent per annum from 1996 to 1997). The firm provides a range of assurance, tax, and consulting services to the information, communications, entertainment, insurance, health care, financial services, real estate, energy, transportation, and consumer products industries. Ernst & Young provides services for more *Fortune* 500 businesses than any other professional services firm.

Ernst & Young's Consulting Practice has grown to become a cornerstone of the firm's business. The firm's expertise spans highly strategic advisory services, outsourcing, organizational design, business change implementation, communications, Year 2000 services, and technology enablement across a range of industries. Consulting revenues in 1996 were $2.1 billion, growing at 30 percent to 40 percent each year. The Consulting Practice employs more than 13,000 client-serving consultants worldwide.

Even with the success Ernst & Young has been experiencing and the strength of its market position, the firm is not standing still, as this case study demonstrates. Rather, Ernst & Young is aggressively pursuing business expansion opportunities that are likely to secure future growth and profitability. Furthermore, within an industry that is not known for risk taking or imaginative offerings and marketing initiatives, Ernie stands out. The unique nature of this service offering and its marketing reflect its rogue development process and the freedom it gained by being just "off the radar screen."

WHAT IS ERNIE?

Ernie is the first-ever online consulting service. Launched in May of 1996, Ernie provides emerging growth companies with business solutions, self-service tools, market and competitive data on a near-real-time basis, drawing on Ernst & Young's 29,000 professionals throughout the United States. Ernie marries the Internet with Ernst & Young's corporate Intranet and its global deployment of Lotus Notes. It was designed to play an integral role in the decision-making process of senior executives by helping them make better-informed decisions faster and more efficiently.

How Does Ernie Work?

Users submit questions via the Ernie website. Once a question is submitted, it is routed to a Focal Knowledge Provider in each area of expertise. These Focal Knowledge Providers are Ernst & Young consultants who can either answer the question or route it to the most appropriate resource. Consultants answering a specific question may be located anywhere and have available to them Ernst & Young proprietary databases providing them with best practices, competitive intelligence, market trends, implementation issues and strategies, and more. Customized answers are routed back to the subscriber within two business days. Users may also search the database of previously asked questions.

The Dialogue with Ernie (the standard query and answer service) addresses questions in the following categories: general management, human resources, information

EXHIBIT 1   How Ernie Works

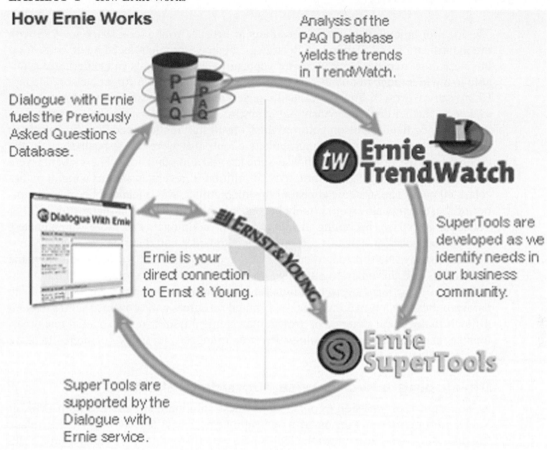

How Ernie Works

Analysis of the PAQ Database yields the trends in TrendWatch.

Dialogue with Ernie fuels the Previously Asked Questions Database.

Ernie is your direct connection to Ernst & Young.

SuperTools are developed as we identify needs in our business community.

SuperTools are supported by the Dialogue with Ernie service.

Source: Ernst & Young.

technology, corporate finance, sales and marketing, real estate, tax, accounting, operations, and business strategy. The types of questions that Ernie has addressed include

- How can I make my accounts payable processes faster and more accurate?

- Can you provide recommendations of pursuing cost savings on electricity pending deregulation?

- What is the proper internal methodology for valuing our stocks?

- Can you establish a peer-to-peer network using Windows 95 or do you have to use WindowsNT?

- In evaluating the net worth of a business to buy, what are the top 10 key measures to make this assessment?

Users of the Ernie service include CEOs, COOs, CFOs, IT, and HR managers.

Since its launch, Ernst & Young has added a number of other features to Ernie including Ernie SuperTools, MediaWatch, and TrendWatch, which are described in Exhibit 1.

GENERATING A NEW IDEA

The idea for an online or virtual consultant at Ernst & Young took shape in 1995 with the identification and definition of a strategic business problem faced by its consulting business: how to make Ernst & Young's consulting professionals and experience available to a wider range of clients. This was the strategic issue that Roger Nelson, Deputy Chairman of Ernst & Young's Consulting Services Practice, worked to address as he looked to further grow the consulting business.

More specifically, Nelson believed the Consulting Practice needed to find a means for tapping into 14,000 emerging markets clients that were doing business with the other side of the Ernst & Young house—the tax and audit divisions. These clients were companies generating $20 million to $250 million in revenues and growing at an accelerated pace. The strategic appeal of this marketplace was enhanced because a number of these companies would likely become significant players in the Fortune 500 or 1000 market space, becoming prime targets for additional, and more sophisticated, professional services. For this reason, these companies could not be ignored.

Additionally, Nelson identified a market requirement that further compelled the firm to tap into this emerging and fast-growing marketplace: entrepreneurial companies are faced with an "overwhelming glut of unfiltered business information" that can paralyze the decision-making process. Limited resources and/or infrastructure make it difficult to deal with strategic or growth management issues such as human resources, finance, and information technology. Ernst & Young was uniquely positioned to solve this challenge.

Developing a New Service "Outside of the Box"

Nelson's gut-level decision to pursue a business solution that benefited both Ernst & Young (through the expansion of its consulting business) and its target marketplace (by providing previously unavailable business expertise) ultimately resulted in the development and deployment of Ernie. As Deputy Chairman of the Consulting Practice, Nelson was in a unique position to bring the resources required for success of this new project. He had both access to the resources required to pursue and answer this business challenge, as well as the respect and clout required to act quickly and bring this timely concept to fruition. (Nelson is credited with having transformed the consulting unit into a highly profitable business in four years.)

While a new service development process exists at Ernst & Young, Nelson decided not to adhere to this formal and procedural process, realizing that it is better suited for traditional products and services. By contrast, this new business concept would be highly unique, with no other product or service quite like it. Because applicable metrics and models would be unavailable, it was necessary to make many of the decisions about this project on instinct.

IDENTIFYING A DELIVERY CHANNEL

Once the business and market requirements were established for the emerging entrepreneurial market, Nelson set clear strategic priorities that further helped to define the future of the new service. It would

- Provide as close to real-time consulting as Ernst & Young could deliver.

- Respond to the anywhere/anytime needs of business organizations today.

- Be highly accessible.

- Address the unique business problems faced by this emerging market segment.

- Leverage Ernst & Young's vast reservoir of experience and global presence.

Although the formula for Ernie had been established, the means for delivering the service was an entirely different matter. The traditional face-to-face consulting model involved long-term projects with price tags that reflected the in-depth, customized, and strategic nature of the work involved. Already, Ernst & Young's Entrepreneurial Services organization had launched a face-to-face consulting practice for the smaller high-growth company market. It was quickly realized that this distribution model was inconsistent with the needs of this market from both a time and cost perspective. What was required for the entrepreneurial market, Nelson believed, was a transactions-based model that delivered the real-time support required by executives of these smaller but fast-growth companies.

The decision of what delivery channel to pursue was further complicated by the reality that there was no road map to follow or business model to leverage. Accordingly, Ernie's developers explored a number of different models and channels through which it could reach its target market and through which the market could reach Ernie. An early alternative to the traditional consulting delivery channel was a call center structure. The center would be manned by a team of people available to answer subscribers' questions. However, further study revealed that while this approach would be cost-effective compared with traditional face-to-face consulting, users would have been limited to the expertise of those people answering the telephones.

What about the Internet?

Coincidence or not, the idea for Ernie coincided with the period during which the Internet was just making its presence known in the business world. This emerging technology was quickly identified as the channel of delivery that could take advantage of the market and the resources available at Ernst & Young. As the potential for the Internet became evident, Ernst & Young developers identified it as the ideal way to leverage both the existing technology infrastructure with Ernst & Young, as well as its vast network of business professionals.

Ernst & Young also had several important technological advantages that were critical to the deployment of Ernie via this online technology. First, the technology infrastructure and data warehouse were already in place. Ernie leverages an extensive Lotus Notes deployment that is available to all consultants to access a "knowledge web" of best practices and other relevant information. Ernst & Young's Center for Business Knowledge is responsible for refining and improving the knowledge web, thus ensuring its effectiveness and usefulness for all Ernst & Young employees. Additionally, as information technology consultants and systems integrators, Ernst & Young had considerable experience in the development and use of Intranets.

THE EARLY PILOT: JUSTIFYING THE CONCEPT

Nelson assembled a team to conduct a 30-day skunk works development project. In September of 1995, an initial pilot was conducted over a three-to-four-month period with 88 existing Ernst & Young clients. Users posted questions on topics ranging from new product launches and pending business legislation, to human resource issues and cost accounting methods. The results were "overwhelmingly" positive on factors such as ease of use, perceived value, and relevance to the changing needs of businesses. The results of this early pilot program validated both the market need and the efficiency of the online delivery channel.

A COMPLETE DEVELOPMENT PROCESS

Once the pilot was completed late in 1995, Ernst & Young's next step was to build a comprehensive team within the Entrepreneurial Services practice to develop the new service. An aggressive launch date was established for March 1996, just three months later.

The development plan reflected an important finding of the early pilot program: while an online consulting service was appropriate for the marketplace, it was an entirely different offering and business model both for the firm and for the professional services industry as a whole. Accordingly, the development process first focused on building a unique team that combined outside professionals with Ernst & Young resources who offered professional and consulting expertise. Because this team would be working on a new concept for Ernst & Young, it was critical to balance the perspectives of internal and external resources. Resources were added as required.

A critical hire was made in January 1996 with the addition of Brian Baum, Director of Market Development for Online Consulting. What was most significant about the hiring of Baum was that he was brought in from the outside, where his most recent experience was at Bell Atlantic. The reason was quite simple: Ernst & Young is a highly experienced consulting organization, working closely with leading organizations on many strategic issues. At the time, however, the firm itself did not have the right mix of dedicated, experienced resources needed to launch a new business of its own. Additionally, the firm recognized that it required strong marketing skills to launch Ernie—marketplace analysis, packaging, and messaging. Baum was brought in because he possessed a proven track record and strong leadership in high-technology marketing.

At its peak, the development team included approximately 25 people. Their areas of responsibility included

- Operations: maintain the subscriber base.

- Help Desk: monitor reactively and proactively how subscribers use the service; assist users on how to use the service more effectively.

- Marketing: develop a high profile in the marketplace for the new concept.

- Sales: conduct face-to-face sales to communicate the concept and value for this new service concept.

- Development: develop software using internal resources and outside consultants.

- Knowledge network: manage the team of online consultants that provide answers to subscribers of the service; set consistent standards for communications with subscribers.

Testing the Concept: A Milestone

As the project progressed, the core question and answer function began to expand and change. Its next iteration was a "cityscape" online environment with a bookstore, library, information kiosks, and other elements of a city. The idea was to allow users to perform a number of information-related functions, such as asking questions, conducting research, purchasing a variety of items, and so on. However, a focus group conducted in late January proved that this concept was too confusing. Users could not find the right place to get the information they sought.

The key finding from this group was that the service should concentrate on what the firm does best—consulting services. The other services were extraneous and confusing. As a result, the team threw out all but the core Q&A offering, known today as Dialogue with Ernie, and the freedom to search the database of previously asked questions. This watershed event allowed the team to streamline and focus on the simplicity of the online offering and, in many ways, shaped the success of Ernie for the future.

THE MARKETING OF ERNIE

The Strategy

The marketing strategy for Ernie was formulated to address a number of highly unique challenges:

- Define and connect with what the "world" will be like once it has embraced the new service.

- Gain the attention of a marketplace that does not know it needs the service.

- Identify and leverage early adopters.

- Continue to penetrate the marketplace until the new service model has been institutionalized.

Market Research

During the development of Ernie, marketing activities centered on focus groups and telephone surveys. Several focus groups were conducted, including the one discussed above, that were highly effective in helping to streamline the product and identify the difficulties that would arise in launching a tool that had broad problem-solving capabilities.

Additional research was conducted via telephone surveys specifically with the people who participated in the early pilot because they already had familiarity with the concept. These surveys were used to get an idea of pricing and usage. The results of this research showed that simplicity in pricing arrangements was key both to attract users and because it was so difficult to project usage of the service.

However, the research also revealed an important void. The team was unable to project how customers would use the service and therefore what behavior to expect. This issue—and the real impact of the online consulting service—would remain unclear until shortly before the launch and would continue to reveal itself during the months following the launch.

Creating the "Ernie" Brand

A key goal for the early marketing development of the new online service was the creation and establishment of a brand. Ernst & Young employed a naming consultant to begin this process. The result of this early work was a list of 800 naming possibilities, many of which had a strong "Internet feel" or were very strategic.

As the team began to tackle this expansive list, it was obvious that more information

EXHIBIT 2
Sample of Ernie
Graphics

Source: Ernst & Young.

needed to be conveyed to the consultants regarding the vision for the brand. Baum communicated that the final brand name must break the stereotypes often associated with the professional services business: high end, high cost, senior level, and highly strategic. Instead, this brand should communicate a more informal, accessible, connected, and responsive image.

The name "Ernie" was part of the original naming options offered by the consultants; however, it was not seriously considered by some in the early stages. As careful consideration was given to the many naming options, the team began to appreciate the way "Ernie" conveyed personality, people, and informality. Ultimately, it was decided that "Ernie" packaged the elements of what they were trying to communicate.

Initially, the marketing plans included the name only; however, at the last minute, the Ernie figure was added to drive home the idea that there are people behind the service (Exhibit 2). Today, Ernie has become analogous with Ernst & Young and the online service. Future plans call for phasing out the Ernie character and replacing it with head shots of the people who are involved in delivering the Ernie service, further emphasizing the people and expertise behind the scenes.

Initial Pricing Strategy

The initial pricing strategy was designed to be simple. Ernie was launched with a highly appealing price tag: $6,000 for one annual subscription with an unlimited number of users and queries. The goal of this approach was to begin to create a new market space in which it was impossible to predict usage. It also gave the early users immediate access to Ernst & Young's expertise, making Ernie a tangible service and establishing its value. In return, the firm hoped for testimonials and support that would enable Ernie to gain further exposure.

The Ernie Launch

The launch of Ernie also marked a significant departure from the way Ernst & Young traditionally conducts its marketing. The initial plan was to launch Ernie to existing Ernst & Young clients of the Entrepreneurial Services Group in March of 1996, with a broader market rollout to follow several months later in the fall. In a typical service launch, the firm would have notified consultants of a new service via e-mail; clients likely would not have been part of the formula. However, because the Entrepreneurial Services practice was a high-growth area of the firm, but not the mainstream business of Ernst & Young, it did not receive the scrutiny that other, more lucrative practices might get. Consequently, Baum and his team were able to create and implement a launch that diverged significantly from the traditional product launches the firm had pursued.

However, the early launch plan was suddenly revamped based on the early feedback from industry analysts. The preliminary meetings revealed that analysts viewed Ernie as truly innovative and without precedent. The practical, high-payoff use of the Internet for knowledge transfer on an unlimited scale was a highly appealing—and a first of its kind—message. For the first time, Ernst & Young began to recognize and understand the broad-reaching impact that Ernie might have on the way companies conduct business.

As a result, the full rollout of Ernie to clients and the marketplace was moved up from fall of 1996 to May 1996. It was a kickoff designed to rival the performances of consumer-oriented IT companies such as Microsoft and Intel. The marketing plan included a number of components to

- Leverage the Ernst & Young brand to gain credentials and legitimacy.

- Capitalize on the interest that had been sparked via early introductions with the pilot participants and the analyst community.

- Leverage the high level of interest in the Internet.

- Connect with the press and analysts who were considered market observers and influencers and most likely to grasp the concept quickly.

- Leverage press and analysts as allies or resources in the broader market introduction and education.

This launch program included

Direct mail teaser campaign: Three mailings were sent to target media, analysts, and existing Ernst & Young clients at one-week intervals. The first card carried the message: "Ernie Is Coming." The second asked, "Who Is Ernie?" The final card invited recipients to "Meet Ernie." Additionally, a separate mailing to the media and analysts included a "magic 8-ball" that carried a message about Ernie as a business resource. This group also received a faxed invitation to the press event officially unveiling the new service.

Analyst briefings: Advance meetings with industry analysts were held to both provide a comprehensive briefing on Ernie and to solicit feedback and comments on the service. For this program, the launch team leveraged Ernst & Young's corporate marketing resources that had established relationships with the analyst community.

Advertising campaign: Direct marketing and press relations were backed up by two high-profile advertisements in *The Wall Street Journal.* The first, a half-page ad placed on the day prior to the launch, announced "Ernie Is Coming." A three-quarter page "Meet Ernie" ad was placed on the day of the launch. While a relatively small portion of the overall launch program, the advertising campaign was designed to reinforce the strategic initiative being undertaken by Ernst & Young with Ernie. Accordingly, the ad campaign leveraged both the specific media channel and the brand recognition of the firm.

Launch: Ernie's official debut took place at the Hudson Theater in New York City. A high-tech multimedia environment using still and video images, music, sound effects, and computer animation prepared the audience to meet Ernie. The Ernie online service was demonstrated, and was followed by a Q&A session with the audience. The presentation also included a live satellite link with Ernst & Young's chairman.

THE RESULTS: ERNIE IS A SUCCESS!

The success of Ernie was evident from the start. As a result of the media activities surrounding the launch, Ernst & Young estimates that hundreds of articles about the Ernie service were printed. Baum, Director of Market Development, believes that potentially millions of readers were exposed to the coverage that contributed substantially to the early success of the service.

Within four months of the launch, Ernie had successfully answered 1,000 queries and reached the $1 million revenue mark. (Ernst & Young has not released any revenue or profit figures for Ernie since this point.) During the same time period, Ernie attracted 250 customers, of which nearly one-third were new to Ernst & Young. This spectacular early growth has not subsided and has led to new features, more sophisticated pricing plans, and the expansion of target markets.

The Ernie business is run as a stand-alone profit center. In its second year, Ernie subscriptions more than doubled on a month by month basis. The distribution of Ernie subscribers finds 70 percent of subscribers are existing Ernst & Young customers and 30 percent are new to the firm.

ONGOING MARKETING STRATEGY

Since the prelaunch activities, Ernst & Young has developed a strong appreciation for the full impact that Ernie can have on the way companies conduct business. Ernie is more than an Internet system—it represents a major change of behavior that was initially underestimated. For the companies that have allowed this change to penetrate the organization, the response to Ernie has been overwhelming.

Accordingly, the ongoing marketing strategy for Ernie has three primary goals. The first is to communicate the degree to which Ernie represents a change initiative for subscribing organizations. The second goal is to create and expand the general market awareness of Ernie. The third goal is to encourage the use of the Ernie service and further penetrate existing client organizations. The ongoing marketing programs reflect this three-pronged strategy.

Strategy 1: Marketing a Strategic Change Initiative

Ernst & Young is using several tactics to communicate this true sense of change that Ernie represents for businesses. New pricing arrangements that encourage usage and enhance value are being introduced (and are described below). Packaging and pricing are increasingly aimed at engaging users more consistently, with a focus on project-level requirements. Additionally, the framework for the Ernie website is being changed to demonstrate how online resources can change the way a company manages its business. For example, the Q&A capabilities have evolved to a "dialogue" with Ernie, emphasizing the interactive exchange between the client and Ernst & Young consultants. The query capability has been further refined to identify the way in which the responses will be used—executive summary, opposing/supporting viewpoint, etc.—to enhance the respondent's ability to tailor the most appropriate answer. Future enhancements will focus on framing Ernie for users requiring a project management perspective.

Strategic Research with Duke University

Another approach is a unique research project cosponsored with Duke University's Fuqua School of Business to document the implications and dynamics of online consulting within corporate organizations. The "Wired for Growth" project focused on two mid-sized businesses. Students were assigned to work with each company to analyze the adoption, use, and impact of Ernie in managing their business issues. Over a five-month period, the two companies used Ernie in their daily work activities while students observed and recorded the use of the service.

The study identified four key findings required to establish successful use of online consulting:

- Buy-in and commitment from the executive team.

- Ability to rapidly deploy new technology throughout an organization.

- Ability to accelerate organizational change relative to workplace innovations.

- Ability to communicate value at the outset to all levels in an organization.

Strategy 2: Creating Awareness

The second component of the Ernie marketing strategy is sustaining broad market interest and awareness. To achieve this, Ernst & Young is utilizing a number of different approaches:

- Continuous contact with analysts and media.

- Ernie website.

- Refinement of sales and distribution strategy.

The focus of this portion of the marketing strategy is high-profile initiatives, events, and product launches that will sustain a high level of interest among press, analysts, and target users.

Ernie MediaWatch

The firm has launched Ernie MediaWatch as a means of creating even greater awareness for Ernie. This initiative combines the strengths of Ernie with industry-leading journalists. Each month, editors of the journals participating in the MediaWatch service write articles on the most critical trends identified by TrendWatch, an Ernie analysis tool that identifies trends and macro issues based on input into the Dialogue with Ernie. The initial participants include *HRfocus, Real Estate Forum,* and *Management Review* magazines. Future topics to be covered include accounting, corporate finance, finance, information technology, and sales and marketing.

This type of exposure provides Ernst & Young with strong marketing value on several fronts. First, by working with these leading publications, the firm is able to gain further legitimacy for its thought leadership and strategic initiatives. Second, Ernst & Young gains exposure to additional prospective clients via the high-level readership of these magazines. Third, the MediaWatch program generates additional content and feedback, further shaping the insights the firm is able to share with its clients.

Strategy 3: Incenting Use and Penetrating Client Accounts

Interestingly, Ernst & Young has found that 90 percent of Ernie subscribers who have dropped the service never used it. This creates a marketing challenge of how to encourage activity within an Ernie account. The firm has a four-pronged strategy to encouraging the continued use of Ernie: subscription, penetration, utilization, and retention (SPUR):

• Subscription: Drive sales and new subscribers.

• Penetration: Penetrate subscribing accounts at a rate of five users per account.

• Utilization: Stimulate the utilization and purchase of additional services.

• Retention: Create a community environment that encourages renewal of subscriptions.

SPUR focuses on subscriber development: the activities that kick in once a sale has been finalized and a company has joined the Ernie community. It is a methodology that was designed to ensure the long-term success of the account and of the Ernie service. SPUR's goal is to enable subscribers to understand and experience the Ernie value proposition through quick utilization of the initial subscription, to gain additional sales penetration based on client usage and need, and to achieve long-term retention of the client base.

A focus of SPUR is guiding clients on the usage of Ernie. Once a client is signed on, an enablement process tracks the first month of the subscription. Interaction with clients via the desktop welcomes them into the community and encourages them to initiate an inquiry. If the client has not used the service within the first week, a call is made to the main contact. If the client cannot be reached, the Ernst & Young sales contact is notified. In the fourth week of nonusage, the partner managing the account is notified. Usage is monitored over time, and additional contact will be made with the account if utilization thresholds are not met.

Additionally, Ernie itself will become a valuable tool in enabling the firm to create even tighter bonds with its users and further penetrating accounts. As the technology management capabilities of the service continue to develop, the goal is to learn and predict the needs of a user within a specific service area. Rather than passively reacting to a client's needs, Ernie will proactively deliver information to users' desktops. For example, as a new user pursues a multi-inquiry dialogue with Ernie, a pattern of established Q&A can be established based on previous subscribers' inquiries. Ernie can proactively provide insight into what the user needs to think about or address as the issue is explored.

Internal Marketing

Perhaps an additional component of the Ernie marketing strategy is the internal marketing efforts aimed at gaining acceptance and credibility for the service across the firm. The current internal acceptance of Ernie reflects another important addition to the Ernie team. In April 1997, Bob Center was brought on to lead the Connected Consulting Services practice and largely to act as the internal champion for Ernie. Center is a true "insider" with 20 years of experience at Ernst & Young, having most recently served as a Vice Chairman.

Prior to Center's arrival, the focus of the Ernie activities was largely on gaining external credentials and testing the potential market success of the online service. With his in-depth knowledge of the firm and its senior leaders, Center was brought in to rally these senior-level resources required to commit the firm to Ernie for the long term. The result of his work, combined with others on his team, is most accurately reflected in the strategic commitment the firm has made to the Ernie model.

HOW HAS ERNIE EVOLVED?

Even upon its launch, Ernie was intentionally characterized as a work in progress. Ernst & Young has recognized that Ernie must continuously change and evolve both to meet the requirements of the users and to adjust to the business issues that are of greatest interest to subscribers. Ernie continues to receive further validation of concept and is gaining the interest of larger organizations. Accordingly, the responsibility for Ernie has been moved into another consulting practice, Middle Market Consulting Group, to accommodate these larger companies, with up to $1 billion in revenue. Ernst & Young is also considering expanding into the Fortune 500 and 1000 markets. However, even with the modifications in its target market, Ernie's core offering, Dialogue with Ernie, has not changed and will not.

Ernie leverages its own TrendWatch functionality to help developers identify new issues that are of primary concern to the marketplace. Since its launch, Ernie has been upgraded and expanded to include the following:

October 1996—Ernie Business Analysis: As a follow-up to initial dialogue with users, Ernie Business Analysis allows subscribers to commission tailored analysis of specific business issues (e.g. market assessment, competitive analysis, and competitive profiles). A typical Ernie Business Analysis runs 15 to 30 pages.

May 1997—Ernie TrendWatch: Analysis of the most commonly described issues and concerns of Ernie subscribers. Users can use TrendWatch to identify issues by several categories: analyzed concerns of all Ernie users; concerns by industry; concerns by occupation; and concerns by company size.

June 1997—Ernie SuperTools: A series of sophisticated "self-service" consulting tools that provide the online implementation of Ernst & Young's methodologies in software selection, supply chain diagnostics, and customer satisfaction. By making these tools available via the Internet, organizations benefit from the immediate availability and implementation of these methodologies. SuperTools launched on this date included Ernie Business Analysis and Ernie Software Selection Advisor.

July 1997—Ernst & Young Technologies Web StoreFront: A virtual computer store that makes software, hardware, and other IT solutions available to Ernie subscribers at below retail costs.

August 1997—Gartner Learning's Technology Training Programs: More than 90 online educational programs from Gartner Learning were made available to Ernie subscribers. Ernie subscribers can purchase multimedia-based software training at a discount below Gartner Learning retail price. Topics include Networking, Database Management, Operating Systems, Desktop Applications, Client/Server, and Systems Development Tools.

April 1998—Ernie Supply Chain Diagnostix: An Ernie SuperTool that assesses supply chain performance. It provides tools and databases to benchmark a company's processes and strategies against other companies, identifies problem areas, and offers solutions in these areas: Demand and Supply Planning, Sourcing and Supplier Management, Manufacturing and Operations, Transportation and Distribution, and Customer and Order Management.

EXHIBIT 3
Pricing: Ernie
Options Portfolio

Source: Ernst & Young.

	Member	Nonmember
Ernie Software Selection Advisor*	$4,000	$5,000
Ernie Supply Chain Diagnostic Tool*	$3,000	$4,000
Ernie Business Analysis	Pricing varies based on the nature and the requirements of the analysis or research. Prices range from $1,500 to $15,000.	
Gartner Learning Center	Courses range from $79 to $159.	

*Options include a one-time usage license for up to one year and three customized answers from the Dialogue with Ernie.

May 1998—Ernie MediaWatch: An innovative link between Ernie and leading industry trade publications. MediaWatch provides readers of these leading journals with an impartial editorial perspective on key business trends identified by Ernie.

June 1998—Customer Feedback Report (CFR): Through a strategic relationship with WalkerInformation, a measurement firm specializing in customer feedback, Ernie offers customer feedback and satisfaction analysis. The information provided in the CFR includes company's overall performance index, key improvements and opportunities for leverage, loyalty indicators reflecting customers' intentions, action priorities, and customer comments and suggestions.

Pricing

Along with the content, the pricing for Ernie began to evolve in 1997. Ernst & Young began to experiment with pricing that was different from the initial flat-rate plan. The first step was the introduction of pricing based on usage: $2,750 for 10 queries and an unlimited number of users. Beyond this, subscribers could purchase additional packages of 20 queries for $4,000.

In 1998, another pricing strategy was released that was a hybrid of the earlier models but also reflected the usage and the value of Ernie. Two pricing options are available and vary by member versus nonmember status. (Ernie members are companies that purchase any service over the course of a one-year period or are current Ernst & Young clients.) The Connected Project option targets companies with a discrete project and project team. For a fee of $3,500 ($2,500 for members), the subscribing company can assign up to five seats and is allotted 10 queries focusing on one information area. Additional inquiries can be purchased in increments of 20 at $4,000.

The Connected Business Plan also allows for five users with an unlimited number of inquiries at a cost of $18,000 ($15,000 for members). Companies selecting this plan typically assign users across different functional areas. At any time during the subscription period, additional users can join the Connected Business plan for an additional $2,800 per user.

In addition, Ernie offers optional services that are available both with memberships and separately (Exhibit 3).

WHAT'S NEXT FOR ERNIE

New Service: IPOs

A new layer of expertise will be added to the Dialogue with Ernie, Ernie TrendWatch, and Ernie Business Analysis. For companies with a goal of transforming from private ownership to public, Ernie will provide guidance to senior executives on mission-critical problems and challenges faced throughout the IPO process, from planning to execution to realization.

International Growth

Another aspect of Ernie's growth involves its expansion to markets outside the United States. During its development and its introduction to the market, international issues and markets were not a primary focus. Rather, the firm chose to focus on the consulting resources it had available in the United States. The specific time frame for expanding Ernie outside the United States has not been established.

A STRATEGIC CORNERSTONE OF THE ERNST & YOUNG BUSINESS MODEL

With its remarkable evolution and market acceptance, Ernie has also evolved to become a cornerstone of Ernst & Young's strategy for delivering online services. With the support of the media, customers, and analysts, the firm has learned that Ernie is not only a landmark of how to deliver services, but also serves as a model of how to pursue services delivery for the future. This model is driven by several market realities: increased need for services at the desktop, need to leverage knowledge, speed of change in the business place, and resource shortages.

Ernie has also had an impact on the overall market perception of Ernst & Young. Ongoing brand awareness research indicates that Ernie has led to the company being perceived as more responsive, accessible, and technologically innovative. These results are a clear reflection of Ernie's marketing strategy and implementation, which emphasized all of these characteristics.

Additionally, in its current form, Ernie is considered a "near perfect" model for both users and the firm. Based on the technology used, interactions with subscribers benefit both the user and Ernst & Young. Subscribers have round-the-clock access to a dynamic tool for accessing information. At the same time, via TrendWatch, the system actually learns from itself as user information is aggregated, allowing Ernst & Young to stay ahead of the curve by identifying critical business trends. From here, new service requirements can be identified and a means for delivering the service can be explored. Ernst & Young also believes that the Ernie model enables the firm to connect at a much broader level to target organizations and deepen relationships already established with clients of its tax and audit divisions.

THE QUALITY IMPROVEMENT CUSTOMERS DIDN'T WANT

Jack Zadow, the consultant, was persuasive. Wrapping up the hour-long presentation, he still seemed as energized as he had in the first five minutes. "Your biggest competitor, HealthCare One, has already begun using a computerized reception system in 14 of its 22 facilities," he said, pointing to the overhead projection illuminating the darkened conference room. The image was a regional map with red stars on every HealthCare One facility and yellow circles around the ones using the new system. "When their members come in the door, they go right to a computer and slide their identification card through. Then the computer leads them through a set of questions about their current medical condition, the reason for the visit, and so on. Everything is done electronically: The computer pulls the member's record, processes the new information, and then routes the member to the appropriate staff person for consultation."

He slipped the next image over the map. It showed Quality Care's own facilities in dull brown. "HealthCare One will have all its facilities up and running on the new system by June. The number two player, MediCenters, is planning to install a similar system by January 1997. I think you should consider it seriously—it's really the wave of the future."

The last overhead. A model of a "new and improved" Quality Care reception area. No more crowded waiting room. Patients talking with nurses in the privacy of small, partitioned cubicles. Other patients checking in, paying bills, even having their blood pressure taken at attractive computer stations.

"I think this one speaks for itself." Jack let the image sink in for a moment. "But I'll comment anyway. With this system, you take a giant step forward in the quality of your service. Your staff will be able to devote more energy to making sure that each patient receives prompt, unhurried, personal attention." He switched off the projector and stepped back to flip on the lights.

Blinking, Allan Moulter accepted the report summary Jack handed him. He had been the CEO at Quality Care for nine years—how many meetings did that mean he had attended? He looked at Pat Penstone, the company's CIO. She seemed enraptured. He rubbed his forehead. "Thanks, that was informative," he said. "You've given us a good overview of an intriguing trend in service delivery in the industry—at a regional level and at a national level. But can you tell us a little more about the specifics of installing a system like that? How is HealthCare One handling the transition? How has it measured the improvements in service quality? How much has the company invested in training? Computer consultants? Troubleshooters? HealthCare One is a staff-model HMO like us, so I know we can look at them for comparison, but I have to say that I'm a little concerned. You seem to be telling us that our image as a quality health care provider will suffer if we don't make this move, but we're talking about an important change in a lot of daily routines. We have just under 3,000 employees and 200,000 members. Think of the procedural changes. The timing changes. And with more automation, wouldn't we want to think about cutting the administrative staff by what, by two at each facility? Four? Six?"

"You could cut several positions from each location," Jack said. "But HealthCare One isn't cutting staff—this is strictly a quality improvement, and it's paying for itself in increased customer retention over the long term. What's more, the transition isn't difficult. In the pilot location, they're already testing the next generation of the system: artificial intelligence diagnostic programs. They're incorporating scales and the blood pressure machines you saw in the last overhead. That saves a step or two for the nurse practitioner, so it simplifies service operations. They're also going to upgrade so that the computer will be able to produce records that can be standardized for insurance companies. Within a few months, the nurses and physicians will be experimenting with a prototype for their own notes on patients, which will streamline follow-up care as well."

"If they're not cutting staff, and they're investing in new generations of the system, where's the real advantage? There is a cost-control element to consider as well, isn't there?" Allan looked around the room, then back at Jack. "The system itself is a big investment—it would run the company more than $350,000 when you include development, installation, training, consulting, and so forth. What's more, the network would have to operate across all of our locations. And if we wanted to do it right, we would probably tackle a whole host of ancillary projects at the same time, things like rethinking the design of our reception areas and our workstations.

"I'm not sure it's worth it. Our customer retention rates are good. They've been steady for the past two years. And our customers are satisfied with the service—on a scale of one to five, 86 percent of our customers are either a four—that's satisfied—or a five—that's completely satisfied. We survey them constantly.

"Frankly, I'm not convinced that investing in a new system will improve the quality of our care. As I said, you're talking about a major shift in how our people get their work done—all the way up the line. That's disruptive. Would the gains be worth it?"

"Ultimately," Jack said patiently, "if your staff is less stressed and your care is more personalized, your quality improves. And—this is almost more important, although it's going to sound strange—the *image* of your quality also improves. Remember, the top two HMOs in this region are installing this system. Quality Care is the number three player—you can't afford to look as though you're behind the times."

Pat could not contain herself.

"I'd hate to see the industry moving toward this technology while we sit on our hands doing nothing," she said, straight to Allan. "I mean, okay, it's just the reception function, but what if a patient assumes that because we're not high tech with our sign-in procedures, we're also not up to speed on our medical procedures? The reception area, taken alone, isn't a big deal. But as a part of our whole offering, it's critical. It's the first thing our customers see. It tells them what we are and how we work."

She nodded at Jack and continued. "Not to mention that we'll have to install a system like this at some point anyway, as soon as the government or the insurance companies decide that it's the way to go. Once a method is standardized, we don't want to be playing catch-up."

"Right. Well." Allan looked at his watch, an impassive expression on his face. "I can see this warrants some further discussion, but we'll have to leave it for the time being." He stood up, ending the meeting. "Jack, thanks," he said again. "We'll go over the reports and I'll see you later this week."

Back in his office, Allan swallowed two aspirins with the one gulp of coffee he had left in his mug. Then he reached for the box of crackers he kept in his top drawer. He knew he should get some lunch, but he wanted to think about this issue some more without distraction. The afternoon was booked solid; then he wanted to catch at least part of his son's ice hockey game at 5:30, and he had to be back in town to participate in a panel discussion on health care for the elderly at 8:00. Munching, he thought about Quality Care's position in the market and the kinds of things that had made the company successful to date.

Quality Care had never been the region's largest or most profitable HMO. But it was doing well. This past year, its total revenues were $450 million, with profits of $8.1 million after expenses. And it did have a good track record when it came to customer retention. Businesses kept the contract because their employees were satisfied with Quality Care, and Allan liked to think that he had played an important role in creating that loyalty.

Allan had begun his career with a large manufacturer of electronics equipment, where talking with customers had been his passion. He had brought that passion to Quality Care. During his tenure, the HMO had instituted regular customer satisfaction surveys. Patients were asked how they felt about the service they received: Were they waiting too long to see a doctor? Were they satisfied with the location and upkeep of the facilities? Did they want more information on health clubs or wellness programs? One survey had revealed the need for increased communication with pregnant members. Now expectant mothers received regular newsletters geared to provide timely advice and support during their pregnancies. The company had also provided a dedicated toll-free number so that pregnant customers would have easy access to advice and information. Allan was proud of the program.

And the surveys weren't the only way the company solicited information from its customers. Each facility also had a "feedback box" in the waiting area—paper and pens were provided, and patients were encouraged to offer anonymous comments on any aspect of their experience with the company. In addition, Quality Care frequently and systematically surveyed other constituents: its corporate members, affiliated hospitals and health clubs, even its own employees.

His peers often complained about how hard it was to increase customer satisfaction these days. Allan knew why it was so hard—keeping all the constituents happy was an insane balancing act. Still, Allan figured it was the open communication and the feedback that kept the company effective and competitive.

That's why he was more than a little concerned about Jack's presentation. Quality Care's own marketing staff hadn't turned up any dissatisfaction with the current reception procedures. And yet Allan was drawn to the possibilities presented by the new system. He picked up his phone and punched in Ginger Rooney's extension. Ginger was the vice president of marketing for Quality Care. She was part of the team that was scoping out locations for expansion and possible new alliances. She had flown in from Pittsburgh that morning—too late to attend Jack's presentation.

"Do you have a minute right now to hear about that meeting?" Allan asked. She was in his office moments later, folder in hand.

"Cracker?" he offered, holding out the box. She declined. He took another one and plunged into the topic.

"I'm not entirely convinced we need this system," Allan said. "But I'll tell you, I was playing devil's advocate in there, and I was having a hard time. I don't want us to fall behind the curve."

"We're ahead of the curve, if anything," said Ginger, holding a familiar survey report out for his inspection. "Why you and Pat are so gung ho about this computerized reception area, I'll never know. If you'll remember, we were approached by a sales rep from the Technomedic Software Company 18 months ago. We looked into a similar system then and dismissed the idea. We took the concept to our members in a special survey and they said they'd hate it."

"But then why would HealthCare One go forward with it? They're the one to beat. I know they must have done their homework on this—maybe better than we did. Don't take this the wrong way, but they've got a more sophisticated organization. I'm sure they've weighed the risks against the benefits. Our study might have been inaccurate. Is it possible that the results are out of date already?"

Ginger didn't take offense. "I doubt it," she said mildly. "Think about why the customers said they wouldn't like it. Human contact versus machine. Health care is a personal field—one on one attention is what makes a satisfied customer. They just didn't like the idea of a computer, at least for this part of their interaction with the HMO. They come into one of our facilities for some health-related exam. Often it's just routine, but sometimes they're a little nervous and they appreciate all the human contact they can get. It's reassuring. The idea of having the first 'person' they meet when they come in the door turn out to be a machine was quite disconcerting to many of the people we surveyed. Especially the seniors." She fell silent, but spoke again as she saw Allan framing a response. "We spent a lot of time and money on that special study—why are you so willing to disregard it?"

"Look at ATMs," Allan said. "Older people got used to them."

"I'm not sure that's true. And even so, does that mean that we'll try to encourage all our members to use the computer but that we'll need human receptionists anyway for older members? Isn't that making the operation more complicated, not less? That doesn't sound like cost savings or quality improvement to me."

"We've invested a good deal in Zadow's research as well," Allan said. "HealthCare One hasn't reduced staff, but we could. And what happens when all the other organizations have signed on and the government or the insurance companies start requiring standardized reports? Pat brought that up in the meeting. It's a valid concern."

"There's more than one way to create a standard report." Ginger began to look frustrated. "I'll bet half the time, the patients enter information incorrectly anyway. Someone would have to double-check the files on a daily basis."

She returned to his earlier point. "If HealthCare One hasn't cut staff, how can you be sure that we would be able to? And keep in mind whom we should really be talking about—the customers. Their perception is what's important. Remember, our *employees* were the only ones who really liked the idea. The administrative staff thought that a computerized reception area would make their jobs easier. And the nurse practitioners have so many routine procedures to do that they're just racing patients by on a conveyor belt. They thought the system would give them time for the human touch."

"Now you sound like you're arguing for the system, Ginger. You can't disregard employee input. Our employee turnover rate is average for this industry, but it has increased over the last two years. That's a reason to reconsider the system in light of Jack's report," Allan said. "It's important to keep our employees happy—we want to keep good people. In fact, as I recall, it took a lot of tap dancing to explain to them why we weren't proceeding with the computer system last time."

"But the point still remains that the members didn't like the idea," Ginger said. "They thought that it was just another sign of big corporate America depersonalizing something that in this case happens to be one of the most personal services there is. You mentioned us retaining our 'leading edge' image. But a computer sends an impersonal image as well. I just don't think that a computer at the front desk will make or break us. You know that my department's reports consistently show favorable customer satisfaction results. They already think we're doing a good job by them. If I can be blunt, I think that you've been romanced by a consultant's very savvy presentation. And I think that we've spent so much money on the consultant that you feel we wouldn't get our money's worth if we didn't follow his recommendations. I seem to be the only one thinking about what's right for the company."

"Ginger, what happens in a year or so when everyone but us has this system installed?" Allan threw up his hands. "Don't you find it strange that we're trying to choose between installing a system that we think might enhance our quality as a provider and not installing a system because we want to please our members?"

Ginger spotted Pat in line at the cafeteria on the first floor of the building that housed Quality Care's administrative offices. She caught up with her just as Pat was paying for lunch. "Not to ruin your digestion, but I have a problem I'd like to talk about with you for a few minutes. Do you mind?"

"Not at all," Pat smiled. Ginger knew the smile was strained. The two had just never really gotten along. For people whose departments were usually in agreement about new initiatives and plans for the company, Pat and Ginger had often found themselves holding opposing views, or at least misunderstanding each other's motives.

"I'll get right to the point, and I won't take much of your time. I know that you support the idea of a computerized reception area, but I'd like to know more about why. You know that the customers are not in favor of it."

"No, I don't really know that." Pat looked uncomfortable for a moment and then seemed to gain resolve. "I may as well say this. I know that Allan has a personal interest in how the company communicates with customers, but I have some serious doubts about the way all of those customer satisfaction surveys are carried out. You don't personally oversee the surveys, do you? That's Mike Farrow's bailiwick, isn't it?"

"Yes, it is," Ginger said. "But we use the same sorts of surveys as most companies do. Frankly, I do agree with you about some of that. I don't put much stake in some of the information we get from the complaint boxes, for example. Those comments reflect the views of only one person. 'Change the night you're open late from Monday to Thursday.' 'Change the color scheme in the examining rooms.' Those comments aren't significant. But we asked a significant number of our members straight out, in a special study, how they would feel about a computerized system. They said they wouldn't like it."

"I just don't have a sense that any of that information is to be trusted. People need to be told what they want—and people will recognize quality care when they see it. That's why I think we need this system."

"I'm thinking about the bottom line," Ginger said. She wished she had waited until later in the afternoon to approach Pat. In fact, she wished she had written her a memo and sent it over by e-mail. "Why go through all the trauma if we already know how the customers will receive the change?"

Pat hadn't yet touched her lunch. She picked up a packet of salad dressing and pulled it open. "You say you're thinking of the bottom line, but which one?" she asked. "Today's or tomorrow's?"

Case **6**

GENERAL ELECTRIC MEDICAL SYSTEMS— ESTABLISHING AN ONGOING DIALOGUE WITH CUSTOMERS

GE Medical Systems (GEMS), a $4 billion division of General Electric Company (GE), is at the forefront of GE's transition from a manufacturing company to a services company. This case study examines how GEMS has used its customer education services to establish an ongoing dialogue with customers that has resulted in dramatic improvements in customer satisfaction and has contributed to market gains. GEMS took its "number-one *dissatisfier*," applications training, and turned it into its "number-one *satisfier*." GEMS is incorporating customer feedback and other information gained during the delivery of customer education services to fuel marketing programs that better address customer needs. A culture of innovation and a commitment to serving the customer has enabled the GEMS customer education organization to cross internal boundaries to work with the GEMS sales organization, services delivery, services marketing, and even NBC, to develop new, creative marketing and customer training programs.

INTRODUCTION

The medical systems market, especially in the United States, has been characterized by slow growth and intense competition. To get ahead, market participants need to develop deeper customer relationships that engender loyalty. Through the creative use of technology, GEMS has dramatically increased the number of times it "touches" each of its customers with virtually no increase in costs. The company has invested in new product and service offerings development, despite the industry downturn, to position itself for growth. In fact, GEMS innovations such as comprehensive multivendor services solutions, sophisticated software applications, and customer satellite TV training are fueling a rejuvenation of the market. The company's strong 1996 operating results will provide the momentum needed to support continued growth.

This case study describes a number of original programs implemented by the GE Medical Systems' customer training organization. The customer satellite training network, in particular, is highlighted. All of the programs described in this Best Practice Case Study have something in common: They provide a means for GE to communicate with its customer base and use the knowledge it gains to improve its relationship with customers. The ensuing dialogue builds a foundation for trust and loyalty—an undeniable competitive advantage.

CASE BACKGROUND

GE Medical Systems designs, manufactures, sells, and services a wide range of diagnostic medical imaging systems, radiation therapy systems, and diagnostic information management systems. Products include magnetic resonance (MR) and computed tomography (CT) scanners, positron emission tomography (PET), X-ray, nuclear imaging, ultrasound, and other diagnostic imaging equipment. Global revenue in 1996 was approximately $4 billion. About half of GE Medical Systems global revenue is derived from services.

Services revenue is growing faster than total revenue. Total revenue growth in the last few years has been modest due to weakening of the U.S. and European markets. Market growth in the United States has slowed because of economic pressures impacting the health care industry and relative maturity and saturation of the market. Consequently, the company has placed a greater emphasis on growing its non-U.S. business. In 1996, slightly more than half of total revenue came from nondomestic markets, including Europe and Asia/Pacific. Furthermore, the company has implemented initiatives to rejuvenate its growth. The 1995 annual report states: ". . . three-quarters of 1996's orders and sales will be generated from offerings introduced in just the past two years." In addition to new medical products, GE has introduced a number of major new service initiatives, setting the company apart as a leader: multivendor diagnostic imaging services and biomedical services. The company also continues to innovate within its existing service product lines.

Medical Systems: A Software- and Services-Driven Business

Historically, the medical equipment industry has not been considered a computer or software business. Today, however, medical systems are driven by CPUs and software. Similar to the mainstream computer industry, the medical equipment hardware technology is fast becoming a commodity. It is the software and services that will

differentiate the players. Consequently, vendors of diagnostic imaging systems are learning how to develop and deploy sophisticated applications. These applications are often networked with the main hospital information systems, allowing access to centralized databases and digitized medical records.

The Medical Systems Customer

GEMS' customers range from doctors' offices and clinics to large multihospital systems. Some major trends impacting these customers have had a double effect on GEMS, resulting in a slowdown in its revenue growth while also creating some new and exciting opportunities:

- There is an enormous amount of pressure to reduce health care costs. Health care institutions are looking for ways to increase efficiency, but at a lower cost. Return on capital investments is of great concern. Assets need to be productive from day one. Many customers are putting off purchases of new equipment to eke out another year or two of use from existing assets.

- More health care is being provided beyond the walls of the hospital. This is creating a need for networks to link satellite clinics, doctors' offices, HMOs, etc.

- Hospitals and other major health care institutions are consolidating at a breakneck pace to eliminate redundant costs and take advantage of economies of scale. Consequently the number of potential customers is shrinking.

- Larger, more powerful health care institutions are looking for strategic suppliers.

Medical Equipment Services: At a Turning Point

As the medical equipment systems market shifts from a hardware-driven business to a software- and services-driven business, the strategic importance of services is intensifying.

- Until 1996, growth in the medical systems equipment market had been flat to negative. The market is essentially a replacement market for hardware with growth coming primarily from software upgrades and services.

- Customers are increasingly looking for one-stop shopping in the form of multivendor services.

- Customer–vendor interactions are evolving from a series of transactions to long-term relationships. Outsourcing relationships are becoming more commonplace.

- Traditional maintenance services are expanding to include more value-added enhancement services, such as asset management and equipment utilization management.

- There is a burgeoning need for software and network support as the software and networking content of the equipment expands. Systems are becoming significantly more sophisticated.

- Health care institutions are implementing comprehensive computerized medical records, including diagnostic imaging. Integration of the medical imaging equipment with centralized databases is increasingly demanded.

- In an environment that prizes system uptime and reduced costs, remote system diagnostics and repair are becoming essential.

- With intense margin pressure on the hardware, medical products companies can no longer afford to include services with the equipment purchase. Services are transitioning from "free" to "fee."

GEMS TRAINING IN PARTNERSHIP (TIP™)

GEMS recognized early on that a well-trained customer is a happy customer. Furthermore, there is an inverse relationship between the amount of training customers receive and the cost to support them (Exhibit 1). For example, statistical analysis led GEMS management to conclude that 10 percent of service calls resulted from operator error. Improved training would eliminate those service calls. With multiyear, fixed rate contracts, any reduction in the number and costs of service calls goes straight to the bottom line.

GEMS customers have some unique training needs that directly impact their satisfaction with GE equipment and, ultimately, their tendency to repeat purchase. GE faces many challenges in its quest to train its customers:

- The buyers and users (technologists and doctors) of medical diagnostic equipment are relatively computer illiterate. GEMS is incorporating computer hardware and software technology in its products at a rapid pace. One of the more recently developed GEMS educational programs is designed to teach elementary computer skills, such as how to use a mouse.

- Computer users of office productivity software can usually get away with learning just enough about their software to "get the job done." Medical users, on the other hand, can continuously improve patient care, job satisfaction, and productivity if they take the time and have the opportunity to learn new applications and system features.

- GEMS business is global. The skill level of users varies greatly from country to country. This makes staffing and managing the resources of a global customer training organization very complex.

In 1990, Jack Albertson, Applications Program Manager, was hired by GEMS to develop a new, formal customer education program to address the changing needs of the customer base. He began this task by surveying GEMS customers to determine their wants and needs and current impressions of GE Medical Systems' customer education services. The surveys uncovered a number of problems:

EXHIBIT 1
Well-Trained Customers Can Be Supported At Lower Costs

Source: ITSMA, 1997.

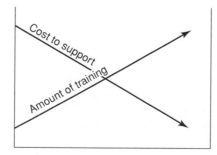

One Benefit of High-Performance Customers

- Customers did not perceive that the training they received was sufficient. They wanted more training to increase their comfort levels with using the new, sophisticated equipment and applications.

- Education and training services were one of the top dissatisfiers with GEMS.

- Customers wanted more contact with GEMS to learn about new products, upgrades, and applications.

- Despite the desire for more training, many customers lacked a commitment to education, making it difficult to free up equipment and staff for training sessions. Customer education budgets were insufficient to cover the costs of training.

At the time, training was being provided almost exclusively at the customers' sites. Training, included in the purchase price of the medical systems, was delivered in a one-week, intensive dose with little or no follow-up. GE could not afford to include additional on-site training with the equipment purchase. Furthermore, staff resources to provide the on-site training were limited. GE needed to find a way to reach its customers more economically, without the requirement of dramatically increasing staffing levels. Thus, the GE Training in Partnership (TiP™) program was born.

The TiP™ program is more than training classes and multimedia materials. The company takes a very broad view of customer education. Its education services incorporate help desk services and user documentation, which together with training classes, seminars, and multimedia materials influence the customers' ultimate success in using GEMS products (Exhibits 2 and 3). GE's philosophy is to extend classroom learning into the job—to provide support before, during, and after the traditional on-site training. GEMS provides educational support throughout the life cycle of the product. The ultimate goal is to provide "just-in-time" training—training at the precise moment it is needed.

For instance, user documentation, formerly written exclusively by the engineers, is now much more "user friendly." User manuals are now written in both computer-based tutorial and quick reference formats by application specialists who have an extensive background in training customers on system operations and applications. The new documentation essentially integrates all knowledge of the global TiP™ applications team. In addition, the user documentation can be integrated into product training and

EXHIBIT 2
GEMS' Broad View of Customer Education

Source: ITSMA, 1997.

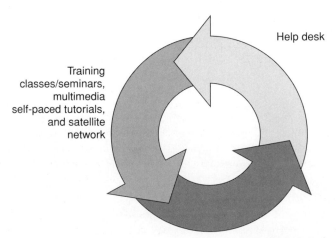

Help desk

Training classes/seminars, multimedia self-paced tutorials, and satellite network

User documentation

EXHIBIT 3
GEMS' TiP™
Customer Education
Product Offerings

Source: GEMS, 1997.

- On-site training: Product-specific, competency-based training for complete system and clinical applications.
- Education center classroom training: Hands-on and didactic training in modality-specific theory and product use.
- Computer tutorials: Individual, self-paced product training through interactive computer-based tutorials on product consoles.
- Videotapes: Product-specific videotapes.
- Online services: Nonemergency phone assistance for questions regarding system operation.
- Telephone conference training: Customized telephone training to fit specific customer training needs.
- Local and national seminars: Guest presenters and GE experts provide current information on clinical procedures and software updates.
- Consultant services: Customized applications training services to assist in departmental analysis and productivity.
- User documentation: Manuals provide applications training, reference materials, and "quick look-up" sections.
- TV satellite training: Interactive training broadcasts ranging from general to advance topics transmitted directly to health care facility. Broadcasts can be custom tailored for large multihospital systems customers.

continuing education, as well as used by the applications support specialists staffing the customer support lines. User documentation in the form of TiP™ Applications Operator Information becomes the foundation, or core, for all other TiP™ customer education products.

Moreover, GE recognizes that its education programs are crucial for developing a closer relationship with the customer. GE uses its education services to identify ways to add value to the customer–vendor relationship and seed future business. As a result, GEMS customer education programs are a strong contributor to customer satisfaction.

HIGH-PERFORMANCE CUSTOMERS

Organizations that treat their customers as only end-user consumers of their services will lose the service game to organizations that involve their customers in a variety of other roles that deepen the customer–service provider relationship. . . . Although it is obvious that these firms highly value their customers as consumers, they have gone beyond that to create other opportunities for collaboration and partnership. . . . Managers would benefit from thinking of customers as possible "partial employees" of the firm or as "co-producers" of services . . . the payoff then comes from having the best customers in the business. We propose that having the most competent customer base can be a source of sustainable competitive advantage just like having the most skilled employee base. (Schneider and Bowen, *Winning the Service Game,* Harvard Business School Press, 1995)

High-performance customers are customers that have the ability and motivation to actively contribute to their relationships with their vendors. High-performance customers are not just satisfied; they are committed and loyal. GEMS' customer education programs aim to create high-performance customers.

CUSTOMERS AS "COPRODUCERS"

GEMS has certain expectations of its customers as contributors to the service process and as owners and users of GE medical systems. As such, customers act as "coproducers" of the services they receive. GE provides the enabling knowledge and resources to ensure their success. Even the name of GE's customer education organization denotes this philosophy: "TiP™: Training in Partnership." For example, prior to delivery, TiP™ on-site education customers are responsible for readying the installation site. GE provides information, checklists, manuals, and guidance. Furthermore, the GEMS Customer Education Center classes use the "train the trainer" format. GE trains the "master trainer" from the customer site. The master trainer is then responsible for training the remainder of the staff. This results in transferring a good deal of the training responsibility to the customer.

After the initial equipment installation and training, GE expects customers to continue training to further their skills and maximize their use of the sophisticated equipment. This training is not mandatory; however, GE has provided the necessary motivation (through improved job performance and continuing education accreditation by professional associations) and convenience, to keep its customers in the training loop.

GE even encourages its customers to take an active role in the marketing of its TiP-TV™ satellite customer education network. At each customer site, a coordinator is assigned to take on the marketing role. The coordinator is responsible for posting announcements and scheduling training sessions.

GEMS conducts an ongoing appraisal of its customers' performance through its TiP™ OnLine phone support. Questions and problems are logged and categorized in a comprehensive database that is used to remedy problems and provide input to TiP™

EXHIBIT 4   GEMS Service Organization Chart

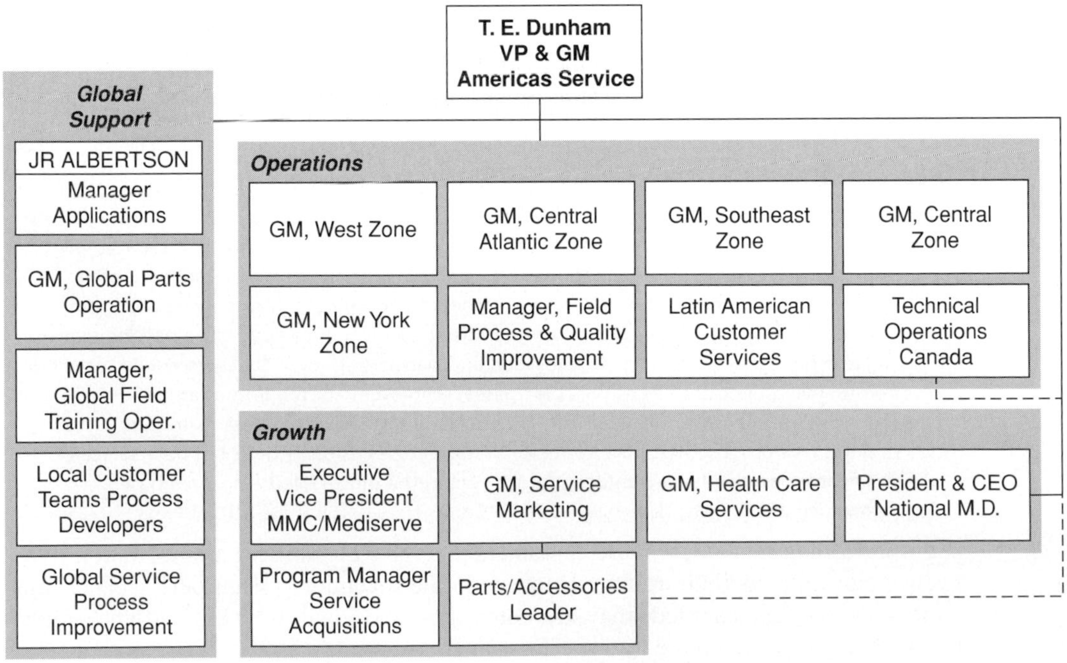

Source: GEMS, 1997.

curriculum development. GEMS takes corrective action when performance problems are unearthed through a variety of programs, some of which are described in this case study. Left untouched, low-performing customers become frustrated and dissatisfied. Customers that are "touched" become advocates.

TIP™ ORGANIZATION

The GEMS customer education organization, TiP™, is structured as a cost center. Its mission is to cost-effectively create educational opportunities to improve customers' growth and productivity. A primary goal of customer education is customer satisfaction. The key measurements of success are customer satisfaction survey results and the number of times the customer is "touched" by GE.

The TiP™ organization itself is part of the GEMS services organization, reporting directly to the Vice President of Service (Exhibit 4). At this time, the TiP™ program is developing two types of products: training products that come as entitlements with the purchase of hardware and software; and training products that are fee for service.

Exhibit 5 summarizes the vision and mission statements for GEMS and its primary service organizations.

ENTREPRENEURIAL SPIRIT AND INTERNAL PARTNERING

GE's top corporate management aims to create "a new kind of company—one that has, and uses, all the strengths of a big company while moving with the speed, hunger and urgency of a small company" (1995 Annual Report). The result is an entrepreneurial environment that is conducive to risk taking. Thomas Dunham, the Vice President and General Manager of GEMS Service, allows his managers to operate with a great deal of autonomy. If someone has a good idea, GEMS finds a way to make it happen. Seed

EXHIBIT 5
Vision and Mission Statements for GEMS Total Business and GEMS Services

Source: GEMS, 1997.

GEMS Vision: To grow as the global leader in quality, productivity, information, and technology solutions to the health care industry, providing superior customer and patient satisfaction delivered by energized employees who meet commitments.

GEMS Services Mission Statement: To be the recognized global leader in the health care equipment services industry, achieving sustained profitable growth by maximizing customer satisfaction and providing the highest quality and value-added services for the customer.

GEMS Services Marketing Mission Statement: Lead the development and implementation of customer-focused integrated marketing strategies and offerings that sustain profitable growth and position GEMS as the recognized leader in the health care equipment service industry.

GEMS TiP™ Vision: To be the worldwide leader in marketing applications education products that support the delivery of quality health care/imaging solutions for productivity and growth of GEMS and our customers.

GEMS TiP™ Mission Statement: To develop and market global, quality, state-of-the-art education products for GEMS and our customers:
* that promote solutions for productivity and growth;
* which improve health care delivery;
* in a cost effective manner.

EXHIBIT 6
TiP-TV™ Facts and Figures

Source: GEMS, 1997.

Number of TV shows aired	125 annually
Number of subscribers	1,635
Subscribers with multiyear educational service commitments	95%
Renewal rate	90%
Viewers claiming continuing education credits	83%

money is available pending approval of a review board. GE funds new programs that will do one or more of the following:

• Provide profitable growth.

• Improve productivity/reduce costs.

• Increase customer satisfaction.

• Drive quality.

Within these guidelines, GEMS has introduced a number of new services and marketing programs. What sets these programs apart from the ordinary is the fruitful collaboration of multiple GEMS organizations and other organizations within the GE family of businesses. The goals of increased customer satisfaction, revenue growth, and improved productivity appear to supersede individual departments' objectives.

ITSMA has identified the partnerships between marketing, sales, customer education services delivery, and ultimately the customer as best practices contributing to extraordinary results. GEMS has cost-effectively increased the number of times it "touches" its customers, improved customer satisfaction, and increased revenue growth and market share. The information obtained during customer interactions easily crosses organizational boundaries. The ensuing dialogue builds a foundation for trust and loyalty—an undeniable competitive advantage.

TIP-TV™: UTILIZING TECHNOLOGY TO COST-EFFECTIVELY INCREASE CUSTOMER "TOUCHES"

Prior to 1992, GEMS had already used its internal TV network acumen (GE is the parent company of NBC) to produce and transmit training programs for GE-employed field engineers. This system had an abundance of excess capacity. An incremental $4 million investment, on top of a $25 million lease investment for a new GEMS education center, launched TiP-TV™. Fourteen pilot programs were produced, and the program was tested at hospitals already equipped for satellite transmission. The pilot program was an overwhelming success (Exhibit 6). GEMS had uncovered a customer need and a way to fulfill it. TiP-TV™ was introduced for general availability in 1993. After the first six months, GE had signed up six paying customers. It now has nearly 1,700 (Exhibit 7).

What Is TiP-TV™?

TiP-TV™ is a paid hospital subscription satellite training network. It offers live, interactive training programs on both GEMS-specific equipment and applications, and more general health care and management topics. Courses range from basic to advanced. TiP-TV™ is sold on a flat rate, annual basis for a specified number of live program broadcasts. Discounts are offered for multiyear subscriptions. Alternatively, TiP-TV™ can be purchased through a GEMS services contract with programming specific

EXHIBIT 7
TiP-TV™ Subscriber Growth

Source: GEMS, 1997.

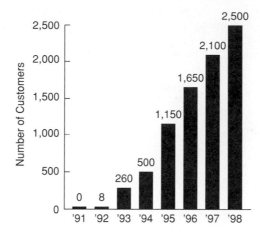

to the equipment type on the contract. Approximately 80 percent of subscribers purchase TiP-TV™ through their service contracts.

TiP-TV™ is accredited by all of the major professional organizations for continuing education credits. GEMS provides its subscribers with all of the required paperwork and submits the paperwork to the appropriate organizations.

Fees range from $3,000 for a one-year subscription including 10 customer-selected broadcasts to $22,800 for a five-year, 30 program per year package.

TiP-TV™ Growth and Expansion Plans

There are approximately 5,700 American Hospital Association (AHA) short-term hospitals in the United States. GE has sold its medical systems to 3,700, or nearly two-thirds, of these hospitals. Just under half (1,700) of GE's medical systems customer base subscribes to TiP-TV™. In other words, GE has a 50 percent penetration of its original target market. In 1997, GE expects to have 2,100 subscribers.

TiP-TV™ currently generates approximately $4 million in revenue. In comparison, TiP-TV™ on-site training sold after the initial equipment installation generates $700,000. (The bulk of the on-site equipment installation, or turnover, training performed by GEMS is included with the equipment purchase and is not contained in the customer education revenue numbers.) Although the revenue numbers for TiP-TV™ seem small in relation to GEMS' overall revenue, TiP-TV™, in a few short years, now accounts for just over 80 percent of GEMS' total customer education revenue (Exhibit 8).

While there is clearly more room for growth for TiP-TV™ within the GEMS installed base, GEMS managers are in the beginning stages of broadening TiP-TV™'s scope and target market. Future revenue growth will come from two sources:

• Signing up additional—especially global—hospital subscribers.

• Selling TiP-TV™ network access to other content providers that want to address the same health care audience in the network.

GEMS has already forged an agreement with several health care companies that have produced original programs to be aired on the TiP-TV™ network. In many cases, the programs will be offered to subscribing hospitals free of charge. GEMS will charge the health care companies a fee to use its TiP-TV™ network access. The intent is to address more needs within the hospital beyond radiology, and at the same time defray TiP-TV™ radiology programming production costs.

EXHIBIT 8
1996 TiP-TV™
Revenue Sources

Source: GEMS, 1997.

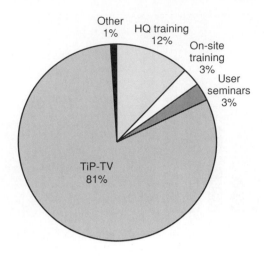

TiP-TV™ Customer Benefits

TiP-TV™ is designed to be a customer-driven service product. GEMS customers regularly contribute to program production in partnership with GE. Through TiP-TV™, GEMS is able to demonstrate a total commitment to customer support through the entire product life cycle. The specific benefits to customers include these:

• Cost-effective training: The average hospital has 14 diagnostic imaging technologists. The average cost of sending one of these technologists to a GEMS training class program at the GEMS Education Center is $1,900. A more economical solution is on-site training, which costs, on average, $1,100 per day. On-site trainers will train up to four technologists for this price. The primary drawback is that the hospital's equipment must be taken out of production to be used for training. An average subscription to TiP-TV™ is $3,000 per year. For this price, all 14 technologists can receive the benefits of training either live or through videotaped programs.

• Point of need training: GE encourages TiP-TV™ subscribers to videotape the initial, interactive program broadcasts. Subscribers can build their own library of programs to be used when needed, such as for new hires and refresher courses.

• CEU credits (continuing education units): Coincident with the full-scale launch of TiP-TV™, the ARRT (American Registry of Radiologic Technologists) passed a mandatory requirement for continuing education credits. In addition, the Society of Nuclear Medicine and the Society of Diagnostic Medical Sonographers also require continuing education. TiP-TV™ is approved by all of the major professional organizations and state licensing bodies for continuing education credits.

• Improved quality of patient care through more knowledgeable technologists and fewer retakes.

• Higher hospital employee satisfaction—with TiP-TV™, hospitals are more willing to invest in continuing education (Exhibit 9).

Sales and Marketing for TiP-TV™

GEMS services are sold either by the product salesforce or the dedicated service salesforce. Telesales are also involved. The dedicated service salesforce, which reports to

EXHIBIT 9
An Actual Letter from the Field

Source: GEMS, 1997.

February 3, 1997

Dear Jack,

I am the service manager covering Tennessee. Not too long ago I was visiting with Sherry Brown,* Radiology Manager for one of my major medical center customers. During our visit, Sherry brought up the subject of TiP-TV™. At the time, the medical center did not have a
TiP-TV™ subscription. Sherry told me she was prompted to ask me about TiP-TV™ after interviewing a person for a technologist position in the radiology department. She said the person being interviewed asked if the medical center had TiP-TV™. The interviewee also stated she ultimately wanted to work at a place which offered continuing education opportunities, specifically TiP-TV™!

Sherry immediately realized the value of TiP-TV™ not only as continuing education for her staff but also as a "recruiting" tool. Well, not too long after our conversation, I had customized a nice TiP-TV™ subscription for Sherry. They are now on-line and I have received VERY positive feedback from Sherry on the broadcasts which have been viewed so far!

From a service manager's perspective, TiP-TV™ rates right up there with InSite™ when it comes to demonstrating value to our customers! Keep up the good work!

Ron

*fictional name

the service delivery organization, sells most of the subscriptions. TiP-TV™ was built into a service contract offering package for GEMS equipment service customers. The majority (80 percent) of subscribers purchase TiP-TV™ in conjunction with their equipment service contracts. The other 20 percent of subscribers purchase TiP-TV™ services a la carte.

TiP™ coordinates its marketing efforts with those of GEMS' Services Marketing Department. The marketing strategy is based on leveraging multiple channels to accelerate market penetration. Typical marketing communications and promotional activities include

- Trade journal ads.

- Trade show exhibits.

- Videos.

- Course catalogs.

- Customer testimonials.

- Descriptive brochures.

- Direct mail.

- Customer tours of the GEMS education center.

- Internet/intranet.

A Marketing Strategy to Move from Free to Fee

GE has historically provided "free" application training. GEMS is challenged to shift to a direct fee-for-service model in its education offerings. Diagnostic medical systems are large, complex, and expensive. It is not possible for technologists to use the equipment without thorough training. Consequently customers believe that the training should be "free." At the same time, the customer wants to start running patients through its new $1.5 million systems as soon as possible to start generating revenue. Customers are not willing to invest time, money, and resources into training.

ITSMA has often noted that when a company moves its services from "free" to "fee," it is often the salespeople, not the customer, who are most resistant to the change. GEMS recognized that it needed to convince the sales representatives of the benefits of TiP-TV™ to their customers. The marketing strategy included providing sales representatives with a laptop software program that does a cost–benefit analysis for TiP-TV™. The program demonstrates how the customer will save money because of reduced pilot error and image retakes, better equipment utilization, and improved diagnostic quality.

TiP-TV™ Competition

Competition for TiP-TV™ comes from two sources:

- Television networks, such as HSTN Network/Wescott Communications, Lambert (now defunct), Voluntary Hospitals of America (VHA): In comparison to these competitors, GEMS TiP-TV™ has a larger subscriber base and provides a greater breadth of coverage and, GE believes, better quality programming.

- Imaging and medical systems companies, such as Philips, Picker, Siemens, and Toshiba: These companies are not currently offering customer satellite training. Therefore, the competition is in the form of traditional on-site training classes and seminars.

No other medical systems company has a customer satellite TV training program. Even four years after the launch of TiP-TV™, no other manufacturers have entered the market. Consequently, TiP-TV™ continues to be a key differentiator for GEMS in a market where much of the core technology has reached competitive parity.

Results

The initial goals of the TiP-TV™ program were to

- Increase the number of times GEMS "touches" the customer.

- Increase customer satisfaction and loyalty.

- Improve the skill level of the customer.

In light of the large up-front capital investment, TiP-TV™ was not expected to be profitable. It was expected to be virtually self-funding by reallocating the TiP™ applications organization's resources. At this time, TiP-TV™ breaks even. The program has the potential to turn profitable in 1997 or 1998.

GEMS has achieved its initial goals for TiP-TV™. The number of times GEMS "touches" the customer has increased dramatically since the inception of the program. There are three ways that TiP-TV™ has positively impacted GE's contact with customers. TiP-TV™ has increased the number of

- Times one customer site can be touched.

- People per customer site "touched."

- Sites that can be touched with a single effort.

Four years ago the average number of customer training "touches" per customer was nine days per year. Today, GEMS estimates the average number of "touches" per year to be 21 days.

Customer training satisfaction, the primary measurement, is at an all-time high. GEMS surveys its customer base on a regular basis. Applications education was the number one dissatisfier five years ago. Today, applications education is the number one *satisfier.* Over half of the customers surveyed rate education a "five" on a one-to-five scale (Exhibit 10).

The increases in customer satisfaction and times customers are "touched" are even more impressive when one considers that the costs of serving the customers have remained virtually flat. By substituting technology for on-site visits, GEMS has succeeded in solidifying its customer relationships without incremental cost (Exhibit 11).

EXHIBIT 10
GEMS' Customer Satisfaction Survey Results

Source: GEMS, 1997.

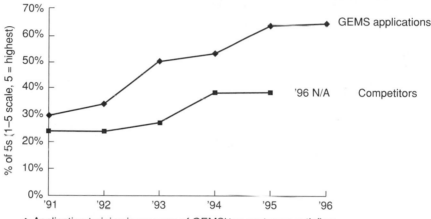

◆ Application training is now one of GEMS' top customer satisfiers.
■ GEMS is widening its competitive advantage.

EXHIBIT 11
Technology-Based Training (TBT) Plays a Key Role in TiP™ Educational Offerings

Source: GEMS, 1997.

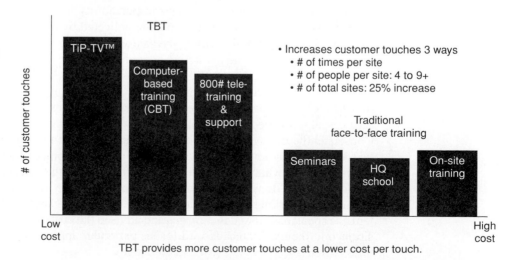

TBT provides more customer touches at a lower cost per touch.

A secondary benefit of TiP-TV™ is slowing the erosion of service-contract average sale price (ASP) in a very competitive market. Furthermore, better-trained, high-performance customers are less likely to commit pilot error and need support center assistance.

Through a combination of excellent product support and new product technology, GEMS has succeeded in gaining market share. Every avenue to sustain or grow market share is significant in a low growth market. In the last few years, GEMS estimates that it has gained approximately four to five points of market share in the United States.

TiP-TV™ is not the only best practice program coming from GEMS' customer education organization. There are other TiP™ programs that demonstrate how partnerships between multiple functional departments to create learning relationships with customers can lead to superior business performance and customer satisfaction.

TWO TELEPHONE HELP LINES, ONE SUPPORT CENTER

GEMS' OnLine Center houses two distinct customer support answer lines:

- OnLine Center Engineers.

- TiP™ Applications OnLine.

The OnLine Center Engineers telephone support organization is staffed with 180 engineers who are prepared to resolve any *emergency* repair or equipment maintenance issues. They use the specialized, proprietary technology called InSite™ to perform remote maintenance on customer imaging systems. GEMS remote diagnostic system, InSite™, is a cornerstone in GEMS' maintenance services strategy. InSite™ technology also plays a major role in training customers, as will be discussed in the paragraphs that follow.

The GEMS customer education organization runs a toll-free help line called TiP™ Applications OnLine. This is a *nonemergency* information source. Applications support specialists are available to answer questions regarding the everyday operation of the equipment, as well as the support services available from GEMS. TiP™ Applications OnLine functions as the centerpiece of GEMS' TiP™ educational programs. Its applications experts have the primary responsibility for building and maintaining the dialogue with customers. The information collected by the Applications OnLine staff is collected and analyzed, forming the basis of the ongoing *learning* relationships that help GEMS customize its marketing and educational services.

Although the OnLine Center Engineers and TiP™ Applications OnLine support lines perform two very different functions and report to two distinct organizations, they are colocated at a centralized support center. In fact, TiP™ Applications OnLine services support specialists sit in the same work areas with OnLine Center Engineers. Consequently, they work together to solve applications and repair problems in a way that is transparent to the customer. For example, a customer called the OnLine Center Engineers with what appeared to be a malfunction of the equipment; the images did not look right. GE avoided a time-consuming and costly troubleshooting process due to the close working relationship with the applications specialists. The Applications OnLine specialist viewed the images and advised the customer that the patient was positioned in the machine backward for the particular application!

CUSTOMER EDUCATION AND INSITE™: TELETRAINING

GEMS has developed a remote customer training program, TiP™ Telephone Conference Training. The TiP™ training team uses the GEMS InSite™ technology as the foundation of these cost-effective training sessions. With the remote diagnosis tools, the GE trainers can dial directly into some customers' equipment consoles to demonstrate the use of product features and capabilities. Teletraining is offered to customers free of charge. It is a cost-effective way to spend concentrated time with customers, responding to their individual training needs. GE conducts approximately 2,200 to 2,500 training teleconferences each year. Still, the full potential of this training modality has yet to be tapped. There is a great opportunity to use this powerful teaching tool globally.

The applications support specialists that staff the TiP™ Applications OnLine help desk identify training deficiencies in the installed customer base. They track the questions they receive and suggest TiP™ programs the customers may take advantage of for further training. GE uses the information it receives from the service relationship to deliver customized training to correct knowledge or usage problems. GE is identifying and satisfying a customer need that the customer may not even be aware of. This is yet another way for GE to "touch" the customer, gain intelligence, and ensure satisfaction with GE products and services.

"TRY IT, YOU'LL LIKE IT" PROGRAM

People do not often think of education and training services as a channel of distribution. Nevertheless, some at GE have realized that education services provide an ideal access point to the equipment installed base. By modifying an existing program and taking advantage of already developed technology, GE has created a very successful sales and marketing "try it, you'll like it" program called Flex-Trial.

One of the TiP™ educational offerings, described above, is teletraining—a formal training session conducted by telephone. GEMS uses the InSite™ technology to communicate interactively with the equipment at the customer's site, making this a very effective medium. The teletraining program has recently been expanded to support the Flex-Trial program.

GEMS has developed approximately 20 different software applications that are "add-ons" to the basic applications that come with its equipment. The economics of the direct GEMS salesforce do not allow them sufficient time for selling the new software. Consequently, GEMS has established a telemarketing team to aid in the sale of its more advanced applications software. Telemarketing representatives identify appropriate customers that are interested in learning more about the new applications software programs. They are sent a copy of the software that is good for 60 days after installation. Once the software is installed, a 1.5 hour "TiP™ Teledemo" is scheduled with the prospect to introduce the features of the software. After the telephone conference training session, the telemarketing team follows up with the customer to get feedback, and hopefully, close the sale.

The Flex-Trial program has been operational for approximately eight months. By all accounts it has been very successful. In addition to selling the software applications, GEMS has increased the number of customer "touches." In the process, GE has gleaned some very important feedback from the customers about its products and services, and any other issues important to the customers. Customer satisfaction improves as customers have more opportunity to learn about the capabilities of their GE equipment.

The Flex-Trial program is a wonderful example of a partnership between marketing, sales, and a services delivery organization. The program itself is structured as a marketing/sales program. The customer education organization receives no revenue for its services, but does get some help from marketing to offset costs. Beyond the cost recovery, GEMS customer education believes that the value of the information it obtains from the additional customer interactions and the impact on customer satisfaction are well worth its time and resources.

THE TiP™ GUARANTEE

TiP™ offers its on-site applications training customers an unconditional, easy to understand, and easy to invoke training services guarantee:

> Should you feel that any fully participating attendees in a guaranteed TiP™ on-site training program are not competent in performing at least 95% of the tasks required for the basic operation of the system, we'll return for up to two days to revisit the areas in which they need additional work. There will be no charge, provided you notify us of deficiencies within two months of course completion.

Despite the unpredictability inherent in providing services, GEMS has chosen to guarantee its customer education services. No other medical imaging vendor has an explicit customer education guarantee. The message conveyed is that GEMS has confidence in its ability to deliver customer satisfaction. The guarantee supports the notion of a committed partnership between GEMS and the costumer.

Approximately 5 percent of GEMS on-site training customers invoke the TiP™ training guarantee. In many of these cases, GEMS can use its carefully documented training logs to trace the nonperformance issues back to failure of the customer's technologists to "fully participate" in training. Still, GEMS honors these guarantees as part of its mission to maximize customer satisfaction.

To reduce the number of times customers invoke the training guarantee without justification, GEMS is challenged to better set customers' expectations. There are a number of avenues to influence customer expectations that span marketing, sales, and services delivery. TiP™ collateral and trainers carefully describe the need for full participation. Working closely with the GEMS sales organization, TiP™ aims to educate its customers about the importance of training and the need for "full participation." However, initiatives for getting the salesforce to focus on this issue have been only partially effective to date.

Case **7**

NORTH PITTSBURGH TELEPHONE COMPANY

INTRODUCTION

In late fall 1992, Mr. Greg Sloan, Marketing Supervisor of the North Pittsburgh Telephone Company (NPT), was wondering what position to take at the next management committee meeting regarding the possible introduction of usage-sensitive pricing for NPT's new CLASS services. Greg was responsible for marketing all NPT's network services. NPT was introducing CLASS services January 1, 1993, on a subscription pricing basis, but there was some management support for offering usage-sensitive pricing for CLASS features as well. The next meeting would be critical in determining whether to offer usage-sensitive pricing and if so, how.

Greg pondered:

> This is a big decision. We've had a lot of success with other services. We've always found revenue potential in our central-office-based services and of course we try to maximize it as new opportunities come along. We always offer a full range of customer options. These central offices are a gold mine to us. That's where we make our money—toll and our network features. There has to be a big potential for revenue gains. Even so, Marketing will be held accountable for our revenue projections with or without usage-sensitive pricing.

NORTH PITTSBURGH TELEPHONE COMPANY

As of 1992, North Pittsburgh Telephone Company and Penn Telecom, Inc., were wholly owned subsidiaries of North Pittsburgh Systems, Inc. Founded in 1906, North Pittsburgh Telephone Company was an independent operating company, a regulated public utility, with approximately 250 employees servicing approximately 49,000 subscribers in a predominantly rural area about 15–20 miles north of Pittsburgh, Pennsylvania. NPT was ranked the 31st largest telephone company in the United States in 1992, based on access lines. NPT's area comprised eight exchanges in a 285 square mile (738 square km) territory. Toll-free dialing within the NPT area was available to all subscribers. Greg thought of NPT as follows:

> We're sandwiched between Bell Atlantic to the south and Sprint/United to the north. Our location relative to Bell, with Bell being so big, is always a factor in anything that we do. They are intending to go into CLASS services and they have access to all the Pittsburgh radio and TV stations. When they start flooding the market with their advertising, they can be a driver of demand in our area.

The main office of NPT is in Gibsonia, PA, a rural community about a 45-minute drive north from the Pittsburgh airport. Three host digital switches (Northern Telecom DMS-100) were linked to the other six remote switches, providing NPT with state-of-the-art digital switching capability. With SS7 signaling capability, fiber optics between switches, and a history of early adoption of new telecommunications technology, NPT management regarded themselves as leading edge in the industry.

Penn Telecom was formed in 1979 as a nonregulated provider of telecommunications products and services in partnership with NPT. This organization focused on PBX, key systems, fax, and the like.

As of December 1992, NPT had 36,453 residence lines and 12,671 business lines (including pay phones and foreign exchanges). The average residential customer paid $15 per month for local access and optional network services such as Custom Calling Features (Call Waiting, Call Forwarding, and Three-Way Calling). Custom Calling Features (CCF) were available only on a monthly subscription basis. The monthly rates are shown in Exhibit 1. As of December 1992, NPT had penetration rates for Custom Calling Features approaching 25 percent, as shown in Exhibit 2.

Access lines and network features such as Custom Calling features were traditionally provided to customers on a monthly subscription basis. A customer would order a service from NPT by telephone (to the Business Office in Gibsonia) or in person (by visiting their Talk Shoppe at NPT in Gibsonia). Telephone terminals were also sold, but not leased, to NPT customers at the Talk Shoppe. NPT would commence the service and then bill the customer monthly at a flat rate regardless of usage until the customer said to stop. There was no disconnection charge for terminating a service.

Such an arrangement provided the telco with a relatively steady stream of income,

EXHIBIT 1
North Pittsburgh
Telephone Company
Pricing Information

Custom Calling Features—Monthly Subscription Rates		
	Residence	Business
Call waiting	$2.00	$3.35
Call forwarding	2.00	3.35
Three-way calling	2.00	3.35
Speed calling	2.00	3.35
IdentaRing	2.00	3.35

EXHIBIT 2
North Pittsburgh
Telephone Company
Access Line/Custom
Calling Information

	12/92 Residence	12/92 Business	12/92 Total
Service lines	36,453	12,671	49,124
Centrex	0	1,151	1,151
PBX trk	0	762	762
Call wait	9,311	625	9,936
Call forward	344	742	1,086
Three way	170	31	201
Package	456	58	514
Speed call	46	5	51
IdentaRing	172	11	183
Rmt call for	3	228	231
Totals	10,502	1,700	12,202

Residence Custom Calling penetration '92—28.8%
Business Custom Calling penetration '92—13.4%
Residence/business Custom Calling penetration '92—24.8%

particularly as experience indicated what normal rate of churn (connects and disconnects) could be expected over time. Usage-sensitive pricing would be quite different. This approach meant establishing a flat or variable rate for each use of a service, then determining the amount to bill the customer at the end of each month.

Greg added,

Another important thing always to think about is, of course, the local exchange competition. It's coming, it's slow in coming, but it will be here. We see it happening more and more. We've always wanted to offer our customers everything we can at the best prices with the best service. We think if we get into new services and people use them, then people will depend on them and use us. Then when our competition comes in, we'll have the competitive advantage.

THE INTRODUCTION OF CLASS

CLASS services referred to a new generation of network features which offered the telephone user greater control over incoming calls. NPT called these services Advanced Custom Calling Features (ACC). These features were possible because of the Northern Telecom digital DMS-100 switch. NPT had the choice of making ACC features available on demand to individual subscribers for a monthly fee, or making them universally available to everyone and then charging for each use of the feature by any individual customer. As NPT management prepared to launch these services, they felt they had little information from other phone companies about customer acceptance of ACC.

The ACC features NPT was about to introduce included the services listed below (as described in the words of their forthcoming promotional materials). Rates were to be identical for residential and business customers.

Return Call. Return Call redials your last caller and, if busy, keeps trying for up to 30 minutes. To activate this, press *69. Cost $3.75 per month.

Select Forward. This feature lets you transfer select calls to any location. Select Forward will hold up to 12 numbers and only those calls will be forwarded to the number you choose. Press *63 and follow instructions. Cost $3.50 per month.

Select Accept. With this feature you can program a list of up to 12 numbers from which you wish to receive a call. Numbers not on your list will be blocked and routed to a message stating that you don't wish to take the call. Press *64 and follow instructions. Cost $3.50 per month.

Call Block. Call Block allows you to reject calls from a list of up to 12 numbers. You can add or delete numbers from your list, including the last call you received without even knowing the number. To program Call Block, press *60. Cost $5.00 per month.

Priority Call. This feature allows you to identify up to 12 numbers by providing a distinctive ring on those incoming numbers you have programmed in. Press *61. Cost $2.75 per month.

Repeat Call. This feature automatically redials the last number you called and keeps trying for up to 30 minutes. Repeat call keeps dialing for you, while allowing you to make or receive other calls. Cost $2.75 per month.

Call Trace. This feature lets you trace harassing or threatening calls. After such a call comes in, just hang up the phone, pick up the handset again and when you hear the normal dial tone, press *57. Call Trace will record the number of that call and send it directly to the phone company. Further instructions will be provided as you use the service. Trace information is provided to the local authorities.

Voice Mailbox Service (VMS) was also being introduced in January 1993. This service would provide continuous automatic telephone answering to subscribers, even when the line is busy. Customers will be able to customize their mailbox, using a personalized greeting, for example. The subscriber will be able to retrieve messages from home or remotely.

While all CLASS features would be available as of 1993, NPT decided to begin by actively promoting only three of them: Return Call, Repeat Call, and Call Block. Promotion had begun with a North Pittsburgh Telephone News bill insert in November. In the December statement, there would be a free installation offer in the bill insert. A news release was planned for the local newspapers. Meanwhile, NPT customer contact employees (Business Office, Talk Shoppe, Installation & Repair, and Telemarketing) were being trained and supported through production of customer handouts such as user guides for all ACC features. (As a regulated utility, the local PUC requirements specified how NPT was to handle customers; for example, they were required to give customers a full menu of everything available.)

Greg reflected on communicating the launch of ACC:

Marketing communications have always been difficult for us. There is no newspaper that goes out to all our customers. There are local papers, but each part of our area relies on different papers. They all have different cable companies. So, while we have no local media to speak of, the Pittsburgh media reach a lot of people we don't serve. We get ads from Bell Atlantic here that create expectations amongst our customers for what we should be doing. We try, therefore, to stay a step ahead of them in terms of what we offer and to use direct media to reach our customer base.

We do have the regular monthly bill. We feel we are aggressive because we do things in addition to that. I don't think leaving it with just the monthly bills would give us the success we are looking for. For example, we have done a lot of technology seminars where we reach out to the business community, at least annually. We have a speaker program. It is extremely successful. We have a fellow who is a retired admiral from the U.S. Navy who does speaking for us. He knows magic so he goes out and books about two appointments a week with the Rotary, the Elks, etc. He talks about a product and does a trick that relates to the product. He leaves information and premiums for them. We get a lot of response from this. He books just about year-round. He's been with us for about four years.

NPT planned to offer subscribers monthly subscription discounts for taking more than one of any of the network features (CCF and ACC): 15 percent off for two features, 20 percent off for three, 25 percent off for four, and 30 percent off for five or more features.

NPT did not undertake regular market surveys of its customers other than those required by the PUC regulators. Those questions were along the lines of, "Did your service go in at a reasonable time?" and shed little light on likely acceptance of new network features. Greg recalled asking Northern Telecom for any available information about CLASS acceptance rates, but learned NPT was too early in the market process to benefit much from the experience of others. The key piece of industry wisdom was that those customers already subscribing to CCF and already "technologically advanced" in their home electronics equipment would likely be the earlier adopters of ACC.

Expectations were running high, particularly for the upscale exchanges in the western part of the territory where NPT business had been growing at 7 to 9 percent per year. Greg described the NPT territory:

We have a fairly affluent population moving into our territory and many of these people are from the Pittsburgh area. The western portion of our territory is growing extremely fast. It is the fastest growing community in the state of Pennsylvania. The reason it is growing so quickly is that there are great access routes going into it. People can live out here and be in Pittsburgh in half an hour.

Previous introductions of new services had always resulted in above-average response rates for all of NPT's areas, particularly the west. Greg was trying to forecast what might happen. He expected NPT's lines to grow 13.75 percent over the five-year period, maintaining the current residential/business split. He also had some estimates from Northern Telecom regarding the expected impact of usage-sensitive pricing (Exhibit 3). He was not sure of the applicability of these estimates for NPT.

EXHIBIT 3
Forecasts by
Northern Telecom

Projected percentage of lines using CLASS on a usage-sensitive basis:
Year 1   —   18%
Year 2   —   22%
Year 3   —   26%
Year 4   —   30%
Year 5   —   30%
Projected number of (usage-sensitive) activations per month per line:
Year 1   —   8
Year 2   —   10
Year 3   —   12
Year 4   —   12
Year 5   —   12
Projected number of lines subscribing to CLASS on a flat-rate basis:
Year 1   —   4%
Year 2   —   6%
Year 3   —   7%
Year 4   —   8%
Year 5   —   10%

USAGE-SENSITIVE PRICING

The NPT committee considering usage-sensitive pricing included representatives from Marketing, Network Operations, and Finance. The planning engineer, Al Weigand, was the chair of the committee. This committee had to recommend whether to offer usage-sensitive pricing for ACC, and if so, how.

Greg knew that a decision to offer usage-sensitive pricing would involve deciding such questions as whether to offer both subscriptions and usage-sensitive options, what rates to charge, whether to cap the usage-sensitive fee each month at a maximum level and if so at what level, whether to price each service at the same rate, when to proceed, and how to launch the whole idea.

No capital investment would be required because all the necessary hardware had already been purchased and the approximate $1 million in additional software costs (largely for billing) would be regarded as a period expense. There would be additional expenses for training and service representatives' time in handling this new option. The remaining major foreseeable incremental costs would be in advertising and promotion. Greg expected that with some rearrangement of his budget, plus some additional money, he could expect additional costs of $35,000 to $50,000 over five years for training and promotion of usage-sensitive pricing for ACC, should they decide to launch it during 1993.

The committee knew senior management would not support any proposal to proceed that did not offer strong possibilities to at least recover all costs over a five-year period.

There was no clear consensus on what rates to charge should they proceed with usage-sensitive pricing or even whether to offer this option for all ACC features. The range of rates being considered was $0.25 to $1.00 per use. There was some agreement that $0.25 increments were best.

Another hurdle was the PUC. Greg knew the company had to be mindful about the tariffs Bell Atlantic would file. The PUC would not allow much discrepancy for the same offerings across the different utilities.

Greg was also wondering about how to communicate about usage-sensitive pricing to customers and employees. Would bill inserts and other typical approaches be appropriate?

Greg knew other telcos were exploring usage-sensitive pricing for CLASS. For example, Nynex had recently introduced a trial of their PHONESMART service in the Long Island, New York, serving area with usage-sensitive pricing and flat-rate pricing. The features introduced were Call Return, Repeat Dialing, Caller ID, and Call Trace, but only Call Return and Repeat Dialing were available on a per use basis. A two-month free trial was being offered to encourage use. Heavy promotion was under way using direct mail, radio, print, radio, and television. After the free trial period, per use charges were being capped at twice the monthly rate. Unfortunately, at this stage, Greg did not have any results from Nynex upon which to base his decisions. Greg viewed NPT's situation as follows:

> In previous meetings, we've talked about the capabilities and the investments, the uncertainties about getting involved in this usage-sensitive idea. We were looking for some data to help support our decision and there wasn't a lot out there about usage-sensitive. When you are one of the first into a business, there is not a lot of history. We really don't know what to expect.

The next committee meeting was due shortly. Greg knew he had to have his position clear by then.

Case 8

GIORDANO

We are committed to provide our customers with value-for-money merchandise, professional customer service, and a comfortable shopping experience at convenient locations.

Giordano's corporate mission

Giordano is a retailer of casual clothes in East Asia, South-East Asia, and the Middle East. In 1999, it operated outlets in China, Dubai, Hong Kong, Macao, Philippines, Saudi Arabia, Singapore, South Korea, and Taiwan. Giordano's sales grew from HK$712 million in 1989 to HK$3,092 million in 1999 (see Exhibit 1). This case study describes the success factors that allowed Giordano to grow rapidly in some Asian countries. It looks at three imminent issues that Giordano faced in maintaining its success in existing markets and in its plan to enter new markets in Asia and beyond. The first concerns Giordano's positioning. In what ways, if at all, should Giordano change its current positioning? The second concerns the critical factors that have contributed to Giordano's success. Would these factors remain critical over the coming years? Finally, as Giordano seeks to enter new markets, the third issue, whether its competitive strengths can be transferred to other markets, needs to be examined.

This case was prepared by Jochen Wirtz as the basis for class discussion rather than to illustrate effective or ineffective handling of an administrative situation. Jochen Wirtz is Associate Professor of Marketing with the NUS Business School, Faculty of Business Administration, National University of Singapore, 17 Law Link, Singapore 117591, Tel: +65-8743656, Fax: +65-7795941, E-mail: fbawirtz@nus.edu.sg. Http://www.nus.edu.sg. Not to be reproduced or used without written permission.

The author acknowledges the generous support in terms of time, information, and feedback on earlier drafts of this case provided by Charles Fung, Chief Operating Officer and Executive Director of Giordano (Southeast Asia), and by Jill Klein, Associate Professor at INSEAD. Furthermore, the author gratefully acknowledges the input by Ang Swee Hoon, who co-authored earlier versions of this case published in the Asian Case Research Journal (2000), Volume 4, Issue 2, pp. 145–67, and in *Principles of Marketing: An Asian Casebook* (2000), Ang et al., Prentice Hall, pp. 80–87. Finally, the author also thanks Jerome S. W. Kho and Jaisey L. Y. Yip for their excellent research assistance in gathering much of the data and assisting with the write-up.

The exchange rates at the time the case was written (February 2001) were US$1 = HK$7.80 and S$1 = HK$4.49.

EXHIBIT 1 Financial Highlights (in Millions of HK$)

(Consolidated)	2000*	1999	1998	1997	1996	1995	1994
Turnover	1,661.4	3,092.2	2,609.2	3,014.4	3,522.0	3,482.0	2,863.7
Turnover increase (percentage)	16.2%	18.5%	(13.4%)	(14.4%)	1.2%	21.6%	22.7%
Profit after tax and minority interests	173.3	360.0	76.1	68.0	261.2	250.2	195.3
Profit after tax and minority interests increase (percentage)	31.1%	375.0%	11.9%	(74.0%)	4.4%	28.1%	41.9%
Shareholders' fund	NA	1,250.8	1,111.1	1,068.9	1,138.3	911.7	544.5
Working capital	701.1	762.3	700.6	654.2	670.3	496.0	362.0
Total debt to equity ratio	NA	0.5	0.3	0.3	0.4	0.7	0.9
Bank borrowings to equity ratio	NA	0	0	0	0	0	0.1
Inventory turnover on sales (days)	28	28	44	48	58	55	53
Return on total assets (percentage)	NA	18.8%	5.3%	4.8%	16.5%	16.4%	18.8%
Return on average equity (percentage)	NA	30.5%	7.0%	6.2%	25.5%	34.4%	39.1%
Return on sales	NA	11.6	2.9	2.3	7.4	7.2	6.8
Earning per share (cents)	24.5	51.3	10.8	9.6	36.9	38.8	30.9
Cash dividend per share (cents)	8.5	34.5	4.5	5.0	16.0	13.5	11.0

Note: "NA" indicates data were not available at time of print; *2000 figures are for the first six months of Giordano's 2000 financial year, ended 30 June 2000. Percentages for 2000 were calculated over the figures for same period in the previous year.

COMPANY BACKGROUND

Giordano was founded by Jimmy Lai in 1980. To give his venture a more sophisticated image, Lai picked an Italian name for his retail chain. In 1981, Giordano started in Hong Kong selling casual clothes manufactured predominantly for the United States market by a Hong Kong–based manufacturer, the Comitex Group. Initially, it focused on wholesale trade of high-margin merchandise under the Giordano brand in Hong Kong. In 1983, it scaled back on its wholesale operation and started to set up its own retail shops in Hong Kong. It also began to expand its market by distributing Giordano merchandise in Taiwan through a joint venture. In 1985, it opened its first retail outlet in Singapore.

However, in 1987, sales were low and the business became unprofitable. Lai realized that the pricy retail chain concept was unprofitable. Under a new management team, Giordano changed its strategy. Until 1987, it sold exclusively men's casual apparel. When it realized that an increasing number of women customers were attracted to its stores, Giordano changed its positioning and started selling unisex casual apparel. It repositioned itself as a retailer of discounted casual unisex apparel with the goal of maximizing unit sales instead of margins, and sold value-for-money merchandise. Its shift in strategy was successful. Its sales almost quadrupled, from HK$712 million in 1989 to HK$3,092 million in 1999 (see Exhibit 1). A typical Giordano store is shown in Exhibit 2.

EXHIBIT 2
Typical Giordano Storefront

Source: Courtesy of Giordano.

MANAGEMENT VALUES AND STYLE

Being Entrepreneurial and Accepting Mistakes as Learning Opportunities

The willingness to try new ways of doing things and learning from past errors was an integral part of Lai's management philosophy. The occasional failure represented a current limitation and indirectly pointed management to the right decision in the future. To demonstrate his commitment to this philosophy, Lai took the lead by being a role model for his employees ". . . Like in a meeting, I say, look, I have made this mistake. I'm sorry for that. I hope everybody learns from this. If I can make mistakes, who the hell do you think you are that you can't make mistakes?" He also believed strongly in empowerment—if everyone is allowed to contribute and participate, mistakes can be minimized.

Treating Employees as an Asset

Besides the willingness to accept employees' mistakes, another factor that contributed to the success of Giordano was that it had a dedicated, trained, ever-smiling sales force. It considered front-line workers to be its customer service heroes. Charles Fung, Giordano's Chief Operations Officer and Executive Director (South-East Asia), said, "Even the most sophisticated training program won't guarantee the best customer service. People are the key. They make exceptional service possible. Training is merely a skeleton of a customer service program. It's the people who deliver that give it form and meaning."

Giordano had stringent selection procedures to make sure that only those candidates who matched the profile of what it looked for in its employees were selected. Selection continued into its training workshops. Fung called the workshops "attitude training." The service orientation and character of a new employee were tested in these workshops. These situations, he added, were an appropriate screening tool for "weeding out those made of grit and mettle."

Giordano's philosophy of quality service could be observed in its overseas outlets as well. Its Singapore operations, for example, achieved ISO 9002 certification. Its obsession with providing excellent customer service was best described by Fung. "The only way to keep abreast with stiff competition in the retail market is to know the customers' needs and serve them well. Customers pay our paychecks; they are our bosses . . . Giordano considers service to be a very important element [in trying to draw customers] . . . service is in the blood of every member of our staff."

According to Fung, everyone who joined Giordano, even office employees, worked in a store for at least one week as part of his or her training. "They must understand and appreciate every detail of the operations. How can they offer proper customer assistance—internal and external—if they don't know what goes on in operations?"

In Singapore, for instance, Giordano invested heavily in training its employees. In 1998, it spent 3.9 percent of its overall payroll on training, with each employee receiving an average of 224 hours of training per year. It had a training room complete with one-way mirrors, video cameras, and other electronic paraphernalia. A training consultant and seven full-time trainers conducted training sessions for every new sales staff member, and existing staff were required to take refresher courses. Its commitment to training and developing its staff was recognized when it was awarded the People Developer Award in 1998.

However, providing training programs was not as important as ensuring the transfer of learning from the workshops and seminars to the store. As Fung explained, "Training is important. Every organization is providing its employees training. However, what is more important is the transfer of learning to the store. When there is a transfer of learning, each dollar invested in training yields a high return. We try to encourage this [transfer of learning] by cultivating a culture and by providing positive reinforcement, rewarding those who practice what they learned."

For Giordano, investment in service meant investment in people. It paid high wages to attract and keep its staff. Giordano offered what Fung claimed was "one of the most attractive packages in an industry where employee turnover is high. We generally pay more than what the market pays." With higher wages, there was a lower staff turnover rate. The higher wages and Giordano's emphasis on training resulted in a corps of eager-to-please sales force.

Managing its vital human resources (HR) became a challenge to Giordano when it decided to expand into global markets. To replicate its high service—quality positioning, Giordano needed to consider the HR issues involved in setting up retail outlets on unfamiliar ground. For example, the recruitment, selection, and training of local employees could require modifications to its formula for success in its current markets owing to differences in the culture, education, and technology of the new countries. Labor regulations could also affect HR policies such as compensation and providing welfare. Finally, expatriate policies for staff seconded to help run Giordano outside their home country and management practices needed to be considered.

Focusing Giordano's Organizational Structure on Simplicity and Speed

Giordano maintained a flat organizational structure. Fung believed that "this gives us the intensity to react to market changes on a day-to-day basis." It followed a relaxed management style, where management worked closely with line staff. There were no separate offices for higher and top management; rather their desks were located next to their staff's, separated only by shoulder-high panels. This closeness allowed easy communication, efficient project management, and speedy decision-making, which are all critical ingredients to success amidst fast-changing consumer tastes and fashion trends. Speed allowed Giordano to keep its product development cycle short. Similar demands in quickness were also expected of its suppliers.

KEY COMPETITIVE STRENGTHS

Giordano's home base, Hong Kong, was flooded with retailers, both big and small. To beat the dog-eat-dog competition prevalent in Asia, especially Hong Kong, Lai felt that Giordano must have a distinctive competitive advantage. Although many retail outlets in Hong Kong competed almost exclusively on price, Lai felt differently about Giordano. Noting successful Western retailers, Lai astutely observed that there were other key factors for success. He started to benchmark Giordano against best practice organizations in four key areas: (1) computerization (from The Limited), (2) a tightly controlled menu (from McDonald's), (3) frugality (from Wal-Mart), and (4) value pricing (from Marks & Spencer) (Ang 1996).

The emphasis on service and the value-for-money concept had proven to be successful. Lai was convinced that the product was only half of what Giordano sells.

Service was the other half, and Lai believed that service was the best way to make customers return to Giordano again and again. Lai said, "We are not just a shirt retailer, we are not just an apparel retailer. We are also a service retailer because we sell feeling. Let's make the guy feel good about coming into here [our stores]" (Ang 1996).

Service

Giordano's commitment to excellent service was reflected in the list of service-related awards it had received. It was ranked number one by the *Far Eastern Economic Review*, for being innovative in responding to customers' needs, for three consecutive years—1994, 1995, and 1996. And when it came to winning service awards, Giordano's name kept cropping up. In Singapore, it won numerous service awards over the years. It was given the Excellent Service Award for three consecutive years: 1996, 1997, and 1998. It also received three tourism awards: "Store of the Year" in 1991, "Retailer of the Month" in 1993, and "Best Shopping Experience—Retailer Outlet" in 1996. These were just some of the awards won by Giordano (see Exhibit 3).

How did Giordano achieve such recognition for its commitment to customer service? It began with the Customer Service Campaign in 1989. In that campaign, yellow badges bearing the words "Giordano Means Service" were worn by every Giordano employee. This philosophy had three tenets: We welcome unlimited try-ons; we exchange—no questions asked; and we serve with a smile. The yellow badges reminded employees that they were there to deliver excellent customer service.

Since its inception, several creative, customer-focused campaigns and promotions had been launched to extend its service orientation. For instance, in Singapore, Giordano asked its customers what they thought would be the fairest price to charge for a pair of jeans and charged each customer the price that they were willing to pay. This one-month campaign was immensely successful, with some 3,000 pairs of jeans sold every day during the promotion. In another service-related campaign, customers were

EXHIBIT 3   Recent Giordano Company Awards

Award	Awarding Organization	Category	Year(s)
Excellent Service Award*	Singapore Productivity and Standards Board	—	1996, 1997, 1998
American Service Excellence Award	American Express	Fashion/Apparel	1995
ISO 9002**	SISIR	—	1994
People Developer Award	Singapore Productivity and Standards Board	—	1998
Ear Award	Radio Corporation of Singapore	Listeners' Choice (English Commercial)	1996
Ear Award	Radio Corporation of Singapore	Creative Merits (English Jingles)	1996
1999 HKRMA Customer Service Award	Hong Kong Retail Management Association	—	1999
The Fourth Hong Kong Awards for Services	Hong Kong Trade Development Council	Export Marketing & Customer Service	2000

Note: Awards given to the Giordano Originals Singapore.

*ISO 9002 refers to the guidelines from the Geneva-based International Organization for Standardization for companies that produce and install products.

**To be nominated for the Excellent Service Award, a company must have had, among other things, significant training and other programs that ensured quality service. These include systems for recognizing employees and for customer feedback.

given a free T-shirt for criticizing Giordano's service. Over 10,000 T-shirts were given away. Far from only being another brand-building campaign, Giordano responded seriously to the feedback collected. For example, the Giordano logo was removed from some of its merchandise, as some customers liked the quality but not the "value-for-money" image of the Giordano brand.

Against advice that it would be abused, Lai also introduced a no-questions-asked and no-time-limit exchange policy, which made it one of the few retailers in Asia outside Japan with such a generous exchange policy. Giordano claimed that returns were less then 0.1 percent of sales.

To ensure that every store and individual employee provided excellent customer service, performance evaluations were conducted frequently at the store level, as well as for individual employees. The service standard of each store was evaluated twice every month, while individual employees were evaluated once every two months. Internal competitions were designed to motivate employees and store teams to do their best in serving customers. Every month, Giordano awarded the "Service Star" to individual employees, based on nominations provided by shoppers. In addition, every Giordano store was evaluated every month by mystery shoppers. Based on the combined results of these evaluations, the "Best Service Shop" award was given to the top store.

Value for Money

Lai explained the rationale for Giordano's "value for money" policy: Consumers are learning a lot better about what value is. Out of ignorance, people chose the brand. But the label does not matter, so the business has become value driven, because when people recognize value, that is the only game in town. So we always ask ourselves how can we sell it cheaper, make it more convenient for the consumer to buy, and deliver faster today than yesterday. That is all value, because convenience is value for the consumer. Time is value for the customer.

Giordano was able to consistently sell value-for-money merchandise through careful selection of suppliers, strict cost control, and resisting the temptation to increase retail prices unnecessarily. For instance, to provide greater shopping convenience to customers, Giordano in Singapore located its operations in densely populated housing estates in addition to its outlets in the traditional downtown retail areas.

Inventory Control

In markets with expensive retail space, retailers would try to maximize every square foot of the store for sales opportunities. Giordano was no different. Its strategy involved not having a back storeroom in each store. Instead, a central distribution center replaced the function of a back storeroom. With information technology, Giordano was able to skillfully manage its inventory and forecast demand. When an item was sold, the barcode information, identifying size, color, style, and price, was recorded by the point-of-sale cash register and transmitted to the company's main computer. At the end of each day, the information was compiled at the store level and sent to the sales department and the distribution center. The compiled sales information became the store's order for the following day. Orders were filled during the night and were ready for delivery by early morning, ensuring that before a Giordano store opened for business, new inventory was already on the shelves.

Another advantage of its IT system was that information was disseminated to production facilities in real time. Such information allowed customers' purchase patterns to be understood, and this provided valuable input to its manufacturing operations, resulting in fewer problems and costs related to slow-moving inventory. "If there is a slow-selling item, we will decide immediately how to sell it as quickly as possible. When the sales of an item hit a minimum momentum, we pull it out, instead of thinking of how to revitalize its [slow-selling] sales." Giordano stores were therefore well stocked with fast-moving items, and customers were happy as they were seldom out of stock of anything.

The use of technology also afforded more efficient inventory holding. Giordano's inventory turnover on sales was reduced from 58 days in 1996 to 28 days in 1999, allowing it to thrive on lower gross margins. Savings were passed to customers, thus reinforcing its value-for-money philosophy. All in all, despite the lower margins, Giordano was still able to post healthy profits. Such efficiency became a crucial factor when periodic price wars were encountered. Giordano was able to carve out ever-greater slices of the market, because it was easy money competing against companies that were used to relying on high gross margins to make up for slow inventory turnover.

Besides the use of IT and real-time information generated from the information system, Giordano's successful inventory control was achieved through close integration of the purchasing and selling functions. As Fung elaborated, "There are two very common scenarios that many retailers encounter: slow-selling items stuck in the warehouse and fast-selling popular items that are out of stock. Giordano tries to minimize the probability of the occurrence of these two scenarios, which requires close integration between the purchasing and selling departments."

But more than technology and inventory control, Giordano had another competitive edge over its competitors. As Fung explained, "In the 1980s and early 1990s, when few retailers would use IT to manage their inventory, the use of IT gave Giordano a leading edge. However, today, when many retailers are using such technology, it is no longer our real distinctive competitive strength. In a time when there is information overload, it is the organizational culture in Giordano to intelligently use the information that sets us apart from the rest." And this was further explained by Lai: "None of this is novel. Marks and Spencer in Britain, The Gap and Wal-Mart in America, and Seven-Eleven in Japan have used similar systems for years. Nowadays, information flows so fast that anybody can acquire or imitate ideas. What matters is how well the ideas are executed." Indeed, with rapid development in Internet and intranet technologies, packaged solutions (e.g., MS Office, point of sale [POS] and enterprise resource planning [ERP] software), and supporting telecommunications services (e.g., broadband Internet access), acquiring integrated IT and logistics technology has become easier and more cost-effective than ever before. Hence, a competitive advantage based on technology and its implementation is likely to become smaller and more difficult to maintain in the medium- to long-term future.

Product Positioning

When a business becomes successful, there would always be a temptation to expand into more products and services to meet customer needs. However, Giordano recognized the importance of limiting its expansion and focusing on one specific area. Fung said, "Focus makes the business more manageable: positioning in the market, keeping the store simple, better inventory management. And we can get the best out of limited resources." Simplicity and focus were reflected in the way Giordano merchandised its goods. "You'll see no more than 100 items in a Giordano store. We have 17 core items; other retailers have 200 to 300 items. Merchandising a wide range of products causes retailers to take a longer time to react to market changes."

Giordano's willingness to experiment with new ideas and its perseverance despite past failures could also be seen in its introduction of new product lines. Its venture into mid-priced women's fashion, Giordano Ladies', clearly illustrated this. With its line of smart blouses, dress pants, and short skirts, the company was hoping to attract young, stylish women and benefit from the fatter profit margins enjoyed in more upscale niches of women's clothing—about 50 to 60 percent compared with 40 percent for casual wear. Giordano, however, wandered into a market crowded with seasoned players. While there were no complaints about the look or quality of the line, it had to compete with more than a dozen established brands already on the racks, including Theme and Esprit. It also failed initially to differentiate its new clothing line from its mainstream product line, and even tried to sell both through the same outlets. Nevertheless, it persisted in its efforts and Giordano Ladies' made a successful comeback. In 1999, it took advantage of the financial troubles facing rivals such as Theme, as well as the post–Asian currency crisis boom in many parts of Asia, to aggressively relaunch its Giordano Ladies' line, which met with great success. As of June 30, 2000, the reinforced Giordano Ladies' focused on a select segment, with 14 stores worldwide offering personalized service (e.g., staff are trained to memorize names of regular customers and recall past purchases). It also had plans to expand its five more Giordano Ladies' outlets in Hong Kong, Taiwan, and the Middle East.

Giordano recently began to reposition its brand by emphasizing sensible but more stylish clothes and broadening its appeal by overhauling the stores and apparel. For instance, a large portion of its capital expenditure (totaling HK$56.9 million in the first six months of year 2000) went to renovating of its stores to enhance shop ambience. This indicated its intention to reinforce its image and to position it in line with its globalization strategy and changing consumer needs. A typical store layout is shown in Exhibits 4 and 5. Giordano's relatively mid-priced positioning worked well—inexpensive, yet contemporary looking outfits appealed to Asia's frugal customers, especially during the Asian economic crisis. However, over time, this positioning became inconsistent with the brand image that Giordano tried hard to build over the years. Says one of Giordano's top executives, "The feeling went from 'this is nice and good value' to 'this is cheap.' When you try to live off selling 100-Hong Kong-dollar shirts, it catches up with you." (*AsiaWeek,* 15 October 1999)

EXHIBIT 4
A Typical Store Layout

Source: Courtesy of Giordano.

EXHIBIT 5
A Typical Store
Layout

Source: Courtesy of Giordano.

Nevertheless, while it gradually remarketed its core brand as a trendier label, Giordano continued to cater to the needs of customers who favored its value-for-money positioning. In 1999 it launched a new product line, Bluestar Exchange, to cater to the needs of its budget-conscious customers, after successful prototyping in Hong Kong and Taiwan. The good market responses to this new line, which targeted mainly families (similar to Gap's Blue Navy), triggered plans to expand from the 14 Bluestar stores in Hong Kong and 3 in Taiwan, to 20 in Hong Kong, 15 in Taiwan, 2 in Singapore, and up to 100 in mainland China (including franchised stores).

Aggressive Advertising and Promotion

Fung said, "Giordano spends a large proportion of its turnover on advertising and promotions. No retailer of our size spends as much as us." For the past five years, Giordano in Singapore had been spending about S$1.5 million to S$2 million annually on its advertising and promotional activities. It won the Top Advertiser Award from 1991 to 1994 (see Exhibit 3). Up to June 30, 2000, total advertising and promotional expenditure for the group amounted to HK$41.5 million, or 3 percent of the group's retail turnover. In addition to its big budget, Giordano's advertising and promotional campaigns were creative and appealing. One such campaign was the "Round the Clock Madness Shopping" with the Singapore radio station FM93.3 on 1 May 1994. Different clothing items were discounted from 10 to 60 percent at various times beginning at midnight. For example, jeans were offered at a 20 percent discount from 12 A.M. to 1 A.M., whereas polo shirts and T-shirts were given a 30 percent discount from 1 A.M. to 2 A.M. and then shorts at a 40 percent discount from 2 A.M. to 3 A.M. To keep listeners awake and excited, the product categories that were on sale at each time slot were released only at the specified hour, so that nobody knew the next items that would be on this special sale. Listeners to the radio station were cajoled into coming to Giordano stores throughout the night (Ang 1996). In 1996, Giordano won the Singapore Ear Award. Its English radio commercial was voted by listeners to be one of the best, with the most creative English jingle.

Another success was its "Simply Khakis" promotion, launched in April 1999, which emphasized basic, street-culture style that "mixed and matched" and thus fitted all occasions. In Singapore, within days of its launch, the new line sold out and had to be relaunched two weeks later. By October 1999, over a million pairs of khaki trousers and shorts had been sold. This success could be attributed partly to its clearly defined communications objectives. As Garrett Bennett, Giordano's Executive Director in charge of merchandising and operations, said, "We want to be the key provider of the basics: khakis, jeans, and the white shirt." Elsewhere in the region, sales were booming for Giordano, despite only moderate recovery experienced in the retail industry. Its strength in executing innovative and effective promotional strategies helped the retailer to reduce the impact of the Asian crisis on its sales and take advantage of the slight recovery seen in early 1999. Aggressive advertising and promotions also played a significant role in the successful remarketing of its core brand and relaunch or introduction of sister brands, Giordano Ladies', Giordano Junior, and Bluestar Exchange.

THE ASIAN APPAREL RETAIL INDUSTRY

Hit severely by the Asian crisis from 1997 to 1999, the Asian retail industry went through dramatic restructuring and consolidation. Many retailers reduced the number of shops in their chains, or closed down completely. Almost everyone in the industry implemented cost-cutting measures while at the same time cajoling reluctant customers with promotional strategies. Yet, there was a silver lining, as the more competitive firms were able to take advantage of lower rentals and the departure of weaker companies. Some firms, including Giordano, worked toward strengthening their positioning and brand image to compete better in the long run. Some retailers also explored opportunities, or accelerated their presence in markets that were less affected by the Asian crisis—mostly in markets outside Asia.

During the crisis and for the immediate future until a full recovery set in, industry analysts predicted that opportunities would continue to be driven by value. Thus, Giordano's value proposition appeared appropriate during these times. It was not surprising, then, that in spite of its problems, Giordano was ranked the 14th most competitive company overall in Asia by a regional business magazine (*Asia Inc.,* 6 June 1997). It even won a place on *Forbes Global*'s 1999 list of the World's 300 Best Small Companies, indicative of world-class performance, together with eight other Hong Kong companies. Giordano's performance was accredited to its management's swift cost-control strategies in the areas of rents, outsourcing, inventory control, cash management, and overseas travel. The economic downturn had indeed revealed the management's flexibility and responsiveness in making decisive moves.

The retailing environment was becoming more dynamic, a change that was perhaps led by growing sophistication of tastes and rapid advancements in the media, communications, and logistics environment. Giordano's response to these trends would be the key to its ability to compete in the future, especially as these trends seem to "commoditize" its current competitive edge in IT, stock control, and logistics.

GIORDANO'S COMPETITION

Until recently, Giordano's main competitors for low-priced apparel were Hang Ten, Bossini, and Baleno. However, its shift in positioning, and the squeeze of the retailing sector caused by the crisis, pushed formerly more upmarket firms such as Esprit and Theme to compete for Giordano's value-for-money segment. Exhibit 6 provides a list of their websites for more information regarding their product lines and operations.

EXHIBIT 6
Websites of Giordano and Its Closest Competitors

Firm	Website Address
Baleno	www.baleno.com.hk
Esprit	www.esprit-intl.com
The Gap	www.gap.com
Giordano	www.giordano.com.hk
Hang Ten	www.hangten.com
Theme	www.theme.com.hk

EXHIBIT 7
Competitive Positioning

Firms	Positioning	Target Market
Giordano and The Gap	Value for money Mid-priced but trendy fashion	Unisex casual wear for all ages (under different brands)
Hang Ten	Value for money Sporty lifestyle	Casual wear and sports wear, teens and young adults
Bossini	Low price (comparable to Giordano)	Unisex apparel, both young and old (above 30s)
Baleno	Value for money Trendy, young age casual wear	Unisex appeal, young adults
Esprit	More upmarket than Giordano Stylish, trendy	Ladies' casual, but also other specialized lines for children
Theme	Upmarket, stylish	Ladies' smart fashion, ladies' business wear

EXHIBIT 8 Competitive Financial Data for 1999: Giordano, Esprit, The Gap, Theme and Bossini (Amounts Expressed in Millions of HK$)

	Giordano	Esprit	The Gap	Theme	Bossini
Turnover	3,092	5,994	90,756	319	1,109
Profit after tax and minority interests	360	430	8,791	(218)	18
Working capital	762	478	3,470	(243.0)	182
Return on total assets (percentage)	18.8%	NA	24.6%	NA	NA
Return on average equity (percentage)	30.5%	33.1%	59.2%	NA	6.5%
Return on sales (percentage)	11.6%	7.2%	9.7%	(68.3%)	1.6%
Price/sales ratio	2.07	1.33	1.97	.82	0.23
Sales growth	18.5%	17.8%	28.5%	(69.8%)	(22.4%)
No. of employees	6,237	4,471	NA	NA	869
Sales per employee	495,779	1,340,599	NA	NA	1,276,254

Note: Esprit reports its earnings in Euro and The Gap in US$. All reported figures have been converted into HK$ at the following exchange rate (as of Feb. 2001): US$1 = Euro$1.09 = HK$7.8. Sources: *Annual Report 1999*, Giordano International; *Financial Highlights 1999*, Esprit International; *Annual Report 1999*, The Gap Financial Report 1999, Bossini International Holdings Limited.

Exhibit 7 shows the relative positioning of Giordano and its competitors: The Gap, Bossini, Hang Ten, Baleno, Esprit, and Theme. Financial data for Giordano, Esprit, and The Gap are shown in Exhibit 8. The geographical areas these firms operate in are shown in Exhibit 9.

United States–based Hang Ten and Italy-based Bossini were generally positioned as low-price retailers offering reasonable quality and service. The clothes emphasized

EXHIBIT 9   **Geographical Presence of Giordano and Current Competitors**

Country	Giordano	Hang Ten	Bossini	Baleno	Esprit	Theme
Asia						
HK/Macao	X	X	X	X	X	X
Singapore	X	X	X	—	X	X
South Korea	X	X	—	—	X	X
Taiwan	X	X	X	X	X	X
China	X	X	X	X	X	X
Malaysia	X	X	—	—	X	X
Indonesia	X	X	—	—	X	X
Philippines	X	X	—	—	X	X
Thailand	X	X	—	—	X	X
World						
US and Canada	—	X	X	—	X	X
Europe	—	X	X	—	X	X
Japan	X	X	—	—	X	X
Australia	X	X	—	—	X	X
Total	**750**	**NA**	**173**	**125**	**8,470**	**200**

Note: Data are as of February 2001; X indicates presence in the country/region; — indicates no presence; NA indicates data not available at time of print.

versatility and simplicity. But while Hang Ten and Baleno were more popular among teenagers and young adults, Bossini had a more general appeal. Their distribution strategies were somewhat similar, but they focused on different markets. For instance, according to Fung, while Hang Ten was only strong in Taiwan, Baleno was increasingly strong in China and Taiwan. On the other hand, Bossini was very strong in Hong Kong and relatively strong in Singapore but had little presence in Taiwan and China.

Esprit is an international fashion lifestyle brand, engaged principally in the image and product design, sourcing, manufacturing, and retail and wholesale distribution of a wide range of women's, men's, and children's apparel, footwear, accessories, and other products under the Esprit brand name. The Esprit name was promoted as a "lifestyle" image, and products were strategically positioned as good quality and value for money—a position that Giordano was occupying. As of 1999, Esprit had a distribution network of over 8,000 stores and outlets in 40 countries in Europe, Asia, Canada, and Australia. The main markets were in Europe, which accounted for approximately 65 percent of sales; and in Asia, which accounted for approximately 34 percent of 2000 sales. The Esprit brand products were principally sold via directly managed retail outlets, by wholesale customers (Including department stores, specialty stores, and franchisees), and by licensees for products manufactured under license, principally through the licensees' own distribution networks.

Theme International Holdings Limited was founded in Hong Kong in 1986 by Chairman and Chief Executive Officer Kenneth Lai. He identified a niche in the local market for high-quality, fashionable ladies' business wear, although it subsequently expanded into casual wear. The Theme label and chain were in direct competition with Giordano Ladies'. From the first store in 1986 to a chain comprising over 200 outlets in Hong Kong, China, Korea, Macao, Taiwan, Singapore, Malaysia, Indonesia, the Philippines, Japan, Thailand, Canada, and Holland, the phenomenal growth of Theme was built on a vertically integrated corporate structure and advanced management system. However, its ambitious expansion proved to be costly in view of the crisis, with interest soaring on high levels of debt. In 1999, the company announced a HK$106.1 million net loss for the six months up to 30 September 1998, and it closed 23 retail outlets in Hong Kong, which traded under its subsidiary The Clothing Shop. Theme International had since been acquired by High Fashion International, a Hong Kong–based fashion retailer specializing in upmarket, trendy apparel.

In general, although these firms had slightly different positioning strategies and targeted dissimilar but overlapping segments, they all competed in a number of similar areas. For example, all firms heavily emphasized advertising and sales promotion—selling fashionable clothes at attractive prices. Almost all stores were also located primarily in good ground-floor areas, drawing high-volume traffic and facilitating shopping, browsing, and impulse buying. However, Giordano clearly distinguished itself from its competitors with its high-quality service and cost leadership that together provided great customer value that none of its competitors had been able to match.

In a study by *Interbrand* on top Asian marquees, Giordano was Asia's highest-ranking general apparel retailer. It was ranked number 20. The clothing names next in line were Australia's Quicksilver at number 45 and Country Road at number 47. However, Giordano as a world label was still far off. As a spokesman on consumer insights for advertising agency McCann-Erickson said, "It is a good brand, but not a great one. Compared to other international brands, it doesn't shape opinion."

A threat from US–based The Gap was also looming. Giordano was aware that the American retailer was invading Asia. The Gap was already in Japan. After 2005, when garment quotas are likely to be abolished, imports into the region should become more cost-effective. Hence, Giordano had to examine whether its intention to shift toward a higher position from its current value-for-money position was viable.

GIORDANO'S GROWTH STRATEGY

As early as the 1980s, Giordano realized that it was difficult to achieve substantial growth and economies of scale if it operated only in Hong Kong. The key was in regional expansion. By 1999, Giordano had opened 740 stores in 23 markets, out of which Giordano directly managed 317 stores (see Exhibit 10). Until 2000, four markets

EXHIBIT 10 **Operational Highlights for Retail and Distribution Division (Figures as at Year-End Unless Specified)**

	1999	1998	1997	1996	1995	1994	1993
Number of retail outlets							
• Directly managed by the Group	317	308	324	294	280	283	257
• Franchised	423	370	316	221	171	77	481
Total number of retail outlets	740	678	640	515	451	360	738
Retail floor area directly managed by the Group (sq. ft.)	301,100	358,500	313,800	295,500	286,200	282,700	209,500
Sales per square foot (HK$)	8,400	6,800	8,000	9,900	10,500	10,600	12,600
Number of employees	6,237	6,319	8,175	10,004	10,348	6,863	2,330
Comparable store sales Increase/(decrease) (percentage)	21%	(13)%	(11)%	(6)%	8%	(9)%	15%
Number of sales associates	2,026	1,681	1,929	1,958	2,069	1,928	1,502

EXHIBIT 11   **Regional Highlights**

	Taiwan 1999	Hong Kong 1999	China 1999	Singapore 1999	Malaysia 1999
Net sales (HK$ millions)	953.1	681.7	543.7	349.2	66.6
Sales per sq. ft (HK$)	6,000	9,400	22,500	13,800	3,600
Comparable store sales increase (percentage)*	31%	8%	4%	48%	69%
Retail floor area (sq. ft.)	165,700	100,000	24,700	24,400	20,400
Number of sales associates	827	441	350	228	115
Number of outlets					
• Directly managed	178	61	10	27	23
• Franchised	0	0	243	0	11

*Note: Figures as compared to previous financial year.

dominated its retail and distribution operations—Hong Kong, Taiwan, China, and Singapore (see Exhibit 11). By 2000, Giordano had 895 Giordano stores in 25 markets.

Giordano cast its sights on markets beyond Asia, driven partially by its desire for growth and partially to reduce its dependence on Asia in the wake of the 1998 economic meltdown. In Giordano's first full year of operation in Australia, sales turnover reached HK$29 million (US$3.72 million) in December 2000. The number of retail outlets increased from 4 in 1999 to 14 in 2000. With the opening up of its first retail outlet in Sydney in September 2000, Giordano outlets could now be found in both Melbourne and Sydney. As part of Giordano's globalization process, it planned to open up its first shops in Germany and Japan during the first half of 2001. Currently, Giordano planned to focus its globalization efforts on new markets like Germany, Japan, Australia, Indonesia, and Kuwait.

When the crisis made Giordano rethink its regional strategy, it was still determined to enter and further penetrate new Asian markets. This determination led to the successful expansion of Giordano in Mainland China, which saw the retail outlets grow from 253 stores in 1999 to 357 stores in 2000. Due to the expanded retail network in Mainland China and improvements made to the product line, sales turnover increased by 30.9 percent to HK$712 million (US$91.3 million) in 2000. Faced with the imminent accession of Mainland China to the World Trade Organization, Giordano's management foresees both challenges and opportunities ahead. In Indonesia, Giordano opened up 7 more stores in 2000, bringing the total number of retail stores to 10. These stores covered areas in Jakarta, Surabaya, and Bali. However, with the political and social instability in Indonesia, coupled with the downward pressure on the Rupiah, Giordano was cautiously optimistic about further expansion and planned to proceed with caution. In Malaysia, Giordano planned to refurnish its Malaysian outlets and intensify its local promotional campaigns to consolidate its leadership position in the Malaysia market.

Giordano's success in these markets would depend on its understanding of them, and consumer tastes and preferences for fabrics, colors, and advertising. In the past, Giordano relied on a consistent strategy across different countries, and elements of this successful strategy included its positioning and service strategies, information systems and logistics, and human resource policies. However, tactical implementation (e.g., promotional campaigns) was left mostly to local managers in their respective countries. A country's performance (e.g., sales, contribution, service levels, and customer feedback) was monitored by regional headquarters (e.g., Singapore for South-East Asia) and the head office in Hong Kong. Weekly performance reports were made accessible to all managers. In recent years, it appeared that as the organization expanded beyond Asia, different strategies had to be developed for different regions or countries.

THE FUTURE

Giordano was confronted with some important issues as it prepared itself for the new millennium. Although it had been extremely successful, as its revenue, profits, and the many awards that it received clearly show, the question was how it could maintain this success in the new millennium. First, how, if at all, should Giordano reposition itself against its competitors in its existing and new markets? Would it be necessary to follow different positioning strategies for different markets (e.g., Hong Kong versus South-East Asia)?

The second issue was the sustainability of Giordano's key success factors. It clearly understood its core competencies and the pillars of its success, but it had to carefully explore how they were likely to develop over the coming years. Which of its competitive advantages would be sustainable and which ones were likely to be eroded?

A third issue was Giordano's growth strategy in Asia as well as across continents. Would Giordano's competitive strengths be transferable to other markets? Would strategic adaptations to IT strategy and marketing mix be required, or would tactical moves suffice?

STUDY QUESTIONS

1. Describe and evaluate Giordano's product, business, and corporate strategies.

2. Describe and evaluate Giordano's current positioning strategy. Should Giordano reposition itself against its competitors in its current and new markets, and should it have different positioning strategies for different geographic markets?

3. What are Giordano's key success factors (KSF) and sources of competitive advantage? Are its competitive advantages sustainable, and how would they develop in the future?

4. Could Giordano transfer its key success factors to new markets as it expanded both in Asia and the other parts of the world?

5. How do you think Giordano had/would have to adapt its marketing and operations strategies and tactics when entering and penetrating your country?

6. What general lessons can be learned from Giordano for other major clothing retailers in your country?

REFERENCES

"Aiming High: Asia's 50 Most Competitive Companies," *Asia Inc.,* 6 June 1997, pp. 34–7.

Ang, Swee Hoon (1996), "Giordano Holdings Limited," *Cases in Marketing Management and Strategy: An Asian–Pacific Perspective.* Quelch, John A., Leong,

Siew Meng, Ang, Swee Hoon, and Tan, Chin Tiong (eds.): Prentice Hall, pp. 182–190.

"An All-New Dress for Success," *AsiaWeek,* 15 Oct. 1999, volume 25, no. 41.

"And the Winning Store Is, Again . . ." *The Straits Times (Singapore),* 2 Dec 1995.

"Asia: Giordano Plans Expansion," *Sing Tao Daily,* 29 June 1999.

"Asian IPO Focus: Analysts See Little to Like in HK's Veeko," *Dow Jones International News,* 12 April 1999.

Austria, Cecille (1994), "The Bottom Line," *World Executive's Digest,* 19 Dec, pp. 17–20.

"Casual-Wear Chain Prospers on Cost-Cutting Regime," *South China Morning Post,* 15 Oct 1999.

"China: HK Companies Commended by *Forbes* for Best Practices," *China Business Information Network,* 12 Nov 1999.

Clifford, Mark (1993), "Extra Large," *Far Eastern Economic Review,* 2 Dec 1993, pp. 72–76.

"Company Looks Outside Asia," *Dow Jones International News,* 12 Aug 1998.

"Creditors Push Struggling Theme Fashion Outlet into Liquidation," *South China Morning Post,* 11 March 1999.

Esprit International, *Financial Highlights 1999.*

"Fashion Free-Fall," *The Asian Wall Street Journal,* 9 Nov 1998.

"Giordano 12-Month Target Price Raised to 16.00 HKD," *AFX (AP),* 16 May 2000.

"Giordano's After-Tax Earnings Soared in First Half," *The Asian Wall Street Journal,* 27 July 1999.

"Giordano Comes Out of the Cold," *Business Week,* 31 May 1999.

"Giordano Details $700 Million Expansion," *South China Morning Post,* 4 Dec 1999.

"Giordano Dreams Up Sale for Insomniacs," *Business Times (Singapore),* 6 May 1994.

"Giordano Expects to Set Up Ops in Europe October," *AFX (AP),* 19 June 2000.

Giordano Holdings LImited, *Annual Report 1993.*

Giordano Holdings Limited, *Annual Report 1997.*

Giordano International Limited, *Announcement of Results,* 31 Dec 2000.

Giordano International Limited, *Annual Report 1998.*

Giordano International Limited, *Annual Report 1999.*

Giordano International Limited, *Interim Results 2000.*

"Giordano Intl 1998 Net Profit," *AFX (AP),* 25 March 1999 (from Dow Jones Interactive).

"Giordano Out of the Running to Buy Theme: High Fashion International Emerges as Favorite in Race for Control," *South China Morning Post,* 25 Nov 1999.

"Giordano Predicts Further Growth as Net Profit Reaches $46.3 Million," *Asian Wall Street Journal,* 3 March 2000.

"Giordano Scores with Smart Moves," *The Straits Times (Singapore),* 11 Sept 1993.

"Giordano Seeks to Acquire Chain Stores in Australia," *AFX (AP),* 8 February 2000.

"Giordano Spreads Its WIngs," *The Straits Times (Singapore),* 13 March 1994.

"Good Service Has Brought Giordano Soaring Sales," *Business Times (Singapore),* 6 Aug 1993.

"High-End Training to Get More Funding," *The Straits Times,* 1 Oct 1998.

"HK Bossini International Fiscal Year Net Profit HK$17.6 Million vs. HK$45.5 Million Loss," *Dow Jones Business News,* 16 July 1999.

"HK Giordano Gets Green Light to Reopen in Shanghai," *Dow Jones International News,* 9 June 1999.

"Hong Kong: High Fashion to Take Over Theme," *Sing Tao Daily,* 26 Nov 1999.

"Hong Kong Retailer Raced to New Markets, Spurring Everbright Loan," *The Asian Wall Street Journal,* 7 April 1998.

"Hubris Catches Up to Theme," *The Globe and Mail,* 7 April 1998.

"In HK: Retail Shares Win Praise Amid Companies' Losses," *The Asian Wall Street Journal,* 25 June 1999.

"Interview," by Frances Huang, *AFX (AP),* 16 Sept. 1998 (from Dow Jones Interactive).

Mills, D. Quinn, and Richard C. Wei (1993), "Giordano Holdings Ltd.," *Harvard Business School,* N9-495-002.

"Old Loss Masks Giordano Growth," *South China Morning Post,* 5 March 1999.

"Service Means Training," *The Straits Times,* 7 Oct 1998.

"Simple Winning Formula," *Business Times,* 6 Aug 1993.

The Gap, *Annual Report 1999.*

"The Outlook for Asian Retailing," *Discount Merchandiser,* May 1999.

"Theme International Unit to Close 23 Stores," *The Asian Wall Street Journal,* 4 Aug 1998.

"US News Brief: Benetton Group," *The Wall Street Journal Europe,* 17 Dec 1998.

"What Is the People Developer," *The Straits Times,* 30 Sept 1998.

INDEX